A Handbook of Modernism Studies

Wiley-Blackwell Critical Theory Handbooks
Each volume in the *Critical Theory Handbooks* series features a collection of newly-commissioned essays exploring the use of contemporary critical theory in the study of a given period, and the ways in which the period serves as a site for interrogating and reframing the practices of modern scholars and theorists. The volumes are organized around a set of key terms that demonstrate the engagement by literary scholars with current critical trends, and aim to increase the visibility of theoretically-oriented and -informed work in literary studies, both within the discipline and to students and scholars in other areas.

Published:
A Handbook of Romanticism Studies
Edited by Joel Faflak and Julia M. Wright

A Handbook of Anglo-Saxon Studies
Edited by Jacqueline Stodnick and Renée R. Trilling

A Handbook of Middle English Studies
Edited by Marion Turner

A Handbook of Modernism Studies
Edited by Jean-Michel Rabaté

A Handbook of
Modernism Studies

Edited by
Jean-Michel Rabaté

A John Wiley & Sons, Ltd., Publication

This edition first published 2013
© 2013 John Wiley & Sons Limited

Wiley-Blackwell is an imprint of John Wiley & Sons, formed by the merger of Wiley's global Scientific, Technical and Medical business with Blackwell Publishing.

Registered Office
John Wiley & Sons Ltd, The Atrium, Southern Gate, Chichester, West Sussex, PO19 8SQ, UK

Editorial Offices
350 Main Street, Malden, MA 02148-5020, USA
9600 Garsington Road, Oxford, OX4 2DQ, UK
The Atrium, Southern Gate, Chichester, West Sussex, PO19 8SQ, UK

For details of our global editorial offices, for customer services, and for information about how to apply for permission to reuse the copyright material in this book please see our website at www.wiley.com/wiley-blackwell.

The right of Jean-Michel Rabaté to be identified as the author of the editorial material in this work has been asserted in accordance with the UK Copyright, Designs and Patents Act 1988.

Library of Congress Cataloging-in-Publication Data
A handbook of modernism studies / edited by Jean-Michel Rabaté
      pages cm
  Includes bibliographical references and index.
  ISBN 978-0-470-65873-4 (cloth)
  1. Modernism (Literature) – Handbooks, manuals, etc. 2. Literature, Modern – History and criticism – Handbooks, manuals, etc. I. Rabaté, Jean-Michel, 1949– editor of compilation.
  PN56.M54H35 2013
  809'.9112 – dc23

                                                                    2012046874

A catalogue record for this book is available from the British Library.

Cover image: Top: Joseph Kosuth, *A Phenomenon of the Library*, 2006. Courtesy of the artist and Joseph Kosuth Studio, London. Below: Ludmila Popova, *Composition*, 1920. Krasnodar Museum of Fine Arts. Photo akg-images / Erich Lessing.
Cover design by: Nicki Averill Design

Set in 10.5/13pt Minion by Laserwords Private Limited, Chennai, India
Printed and bound in Singapore by Markono Print Media Pte Ltd

1   2013

Contents

Notes on Contributors

Jeremy Braddock is Associate Professor of English at Cornell University. He is the author of *Collecting as Modernist Practice* (2013) and co-editor of two collections, *Paris, Capital of the Black Atlantic* (2012) and *Directed by Allen Smithee* (2001). He is completing a book-length project titled *The Archive of the Twentieth Century*.

Bill Brown is the Karla Scherer Distinguished Service Professor in American Culture at the University of Chicago. His publications include *A Sense of Things: The Object Matter of American Literature* (2003), *Things*, a special issue of *Critical Inquiry* (2001), *Reading the West: An Anthology of Dime Novels* (1997), and *The Material Unconscious: American Amusement, Stephen Crane, and the Economies of Play* (1996). Currently, he is completing a book entitled *Other Things*.

Judith Brown is Associate Professor of English at Indiana University, Bloomington. She is the author of *Glamour in Six Dimensions: Modernism and the Radiance of Form* (2009), and is currently at work on a book called *Passive States: Modernism and the Unproductive Life*.

Eric Bulson, Associate Professor of English at Claremont Graduate University, is the author of *The Cambridge Introduction to James Joyce* (2006) and *Novels, Maps, Modernity: The Spatial Imagination, 1850–2000* (2007). He is the recipient of the 2012 Charles A. Ryskamp Research Fellowships for his project on *Little Magazine, World Form*.

Christopher Bush is Associate Professor of French and Program Director of Comparative Literary Studies at Northwestern University. He is the author of *Ideographic Modernism: China, Writing, Media* (2012). His next book project, forthcoming, is entitled *The Floating World: Japoniste Aesthetics and Global Modernity*.

Robert L. Caserio, Professor of English at The Pennsylvania State University, University Park, is co-editor, with Clement Hawes, of *The Cambridge History of* the *English Novel* (2012) and editor of *The Cambridge Companion to the Twentieth-Century English Novel* (2009).

Sara Crangle, Senior Lecturer in English at the University of Sussex, is the author of *Prosaic Desires: Modernist Knowledge, Boredom, Laughter, and Anticipation* (2010) and the editor of *Stories and Essays of Mina Loy* (2011). She has co-edited *On Bathos: Literature, Art, Music* (2010) with Peter Nicholls.

Marian Eide, Associate Professor of English and Women's and Gender Studies at Texas A&M University, is the author of *Ethical Joyce* (2002). She is completing a book on the aesthetic of violence in twentieth-century culture. She has edited the issue of the *South Central Review* "On Forgiveness" (2010).

Maud Ellmann is the Randy L. & Melvin R. Berlin Professor in English at the University of Chicago. She is the author of *The Poetics of Impersonality: T.S. Eliot and Ezra Pound* (1987), *The Hunger Artists: Starving, Writing, and Imprisonment* (1993), *Elizabeth Bowen: The Shadow Across the Page* (2003), and *The Nets of Modernism* (2010). She has edited *Psychoanalytic Literary Criticism* (1994) and has published widely on Joyce, psychoanalysis, and Irish studies.

James F. English, the John Welsh Centennial Professor of English at the University of Pennsylvania and Director of the Penn Humanities Forum, is the author of *Comic Transactions, Literature, Humor, and the Politics of Community in Twentieth-Century Britain* (1994), *The Economy of Prestige Prizes, Awards, and the Circulation of Cultural Value* (2008), and more recently *The Global Future of English Studies* (2012).

Shanyn Fiske is Assistant Professor of English at Rutgers-Camden University, where she directs the writing program and the Classical Studies minor. She is the author of *Heretical Hellenism: Women Writers, Ancient Greece, and the Victorian Popular Imagination* (2008) as well as numerous articles on nineteenth-century literature and classical reception studies. She is completing a book about Greek tragedy and trauma literature.

Catherine Flynn is Assistant Professor of English at U.C. Berkeley. She has published several articles on Joyce, Kafka, Surrealism, Walter Benjamin, Brecht, and the theories of the Avant-Garde. Her two book projects are *James Joyce, Walter Benjamin and the Matter of Modernity* and *Flann O'Brien and the Second World War: The Cruiskeen Lawn, 1940–1945*.

Matt Hart is Assistant Professor of English and Comparative Literature at Columbia University. He is the author of *Nations of Nothing But Poetry: Modernism, Transnationalism, and Synthetic Vernacular Writing* (2010) and has co-edited "Contemporary Literature and the State," a special issue of *Contemporary Literature* (2008). He is completing a book on extraterritoriality in contemporary art, fiction, and political theory.

Benjamin Kahan, an Assistant Professor of English and Women's and Gender Studies at Louisiana State University, has held postdoctoral fellowships at Washington University in St. Louis, Emory University, and The University of Pittsburgh. His book *Celibacies: American Modernism and Sexual Life* is forthcoming from Duke University Press.

Vivian Liska is Professor of German Literature and Director of the Institute of Jewish Studies at the University of Antwerp. She is the co-editor of *Modernism* (2 vols, 2007). Other books include: *Giorgio Agambens leerer Messianismus* (2008), *When Kafka says We: Uncommon Communities in German-Jewish Literature* (2009), and *Fremde Gemeinschaft: Deutsch-jüdische Literatur der Moderne* (2011).

Jonathan Loesberg, chair of the Department of Literature at the American University, is the author of *Fictions of Consciousness: Mill, Newman and the Reading of Victorian Prose* (1986), *Aestheticism and Deconstruction: Pater, Derrida, and De Man* (1991), and *A Return to Aesthetics: Autonomy, Indifference, and Postmodernism* (2005) He has published numerous articles on Victorian literature, the novel, literary theory, and the connections between literature and philosophy.

Vicki Mahaffey is the Clayton and Thelma Kirkpatrick Professor of English and Gender and Women's Studies at the University of Illinois at Urbana-Champaign. She is the author of *Reauthorizing Joyce* (1995), *States of Desire: Wilde, Yeats, Joyce, and the Irish Experiment* (1998), and *Literary Modernism: Challenging Fictions* (2007). She has edited *Dubliners, Collaborative Dubliners: Joyce in Dialogue* (2012) and is completing a monograph on *The Joyce of Everyday Life*.

Laura Marcus, Goldsmith's Professor of English Literature at New College, Oxford, is the author of *Auto/biographical Discourses: Theory, Criticism, Practice* (1994), *Virginia Woolf: Writers and their Work* (1997), and *The Tenth Muse: Writing about Cinema in the Modernist Period* (2007). She has co-edited *The Cambridge History of Twentieth-Century English Literature* (2004). Her research projects include a book on British literature 1910–1920, and a study of the concept of rhythm in the late nineteenth and early twentieth centuries.

John Marx is Associate Professor of English at UC Davis. He has published two books, *The Modernist Novel and the Decline of Empire (2006)* and *Geopolitics and the Anglophone Novel, 1890–2011* (2012). He is completing a third book entitled *After the Urban Revolution*. Marx is an editor of the *Journal Contemporary Literature* and the author of numerous articles on globalization, cities, the work of Georg Lukács, modernism, and postcolonialism.

Peter Nicholls, Professor of English at NYU, is the author of *Modernisms: A Literary Guide* (2nd edn 2009), *George Oppen and the Fate of Modernism* (2007), and *Politics, Economics and Writing: A Study of Ezra Pound's Cantos* (1984). He has co-edited *The Cambridge History of Twentieth-Century English Literature* (2004), *Ruskin and Modernism* (2001), *On Bathos: Literature, Art, Music* (2010) (with Sara Crangle), and *Regarding the Popular: Modernism, the Avant-Garde, and High and Low Culture* (2012).

Molly Anne Rothenberg is a Professor of English at Tulane University and a practicing psychoanalyst. Her books include *Rethinking Blake's Textuality* (1993) and *The Excessive Subject: A New Theory of Social Change* (2010). She has co-edited *Perversion and the Social Relation* (2003) and *Žižek Now* (forthcoming).

Joseph Valente, Professor of English and Disability Studies at SUNY-Buffalo, is the author of *James Joyce and the Problem of Justice: Negotiating Sexual and Colonial Difference, Dracula's Crypt: Bram Stoker, Irishness and the Question of Blood*, and *The Myth of Manliness in Irish National Culture, 1880–1922*. He has edited *Quare Joyce*, co-edited *Disciplinarity at the Fin de Siecle* and the forthcoming *Yeats and Afterwords*. He is completing a book on *Autism and Moral Authority in Modernist Literature* and co-writing *Ireland's War on Children: A Literary Perspective*.

Dirk Van Hulle is Professor of English Literature at the University of Antwerp, where he directs the Centre for Manuscript Genetics. He is the author of *Textual Awareness* (2004), *Manuscript Genetics, Joyce's Know-How, Beckett's Nohow* (2008), and *Samuel Beckett's Library* with Mark Nixon (forthcoming). He is currently working on a genetic edition of Beckett's *The Unnamable* for the Beckett Digital Manuscript Project.

Steven G. Yao, Professor of English at Hamilton College, is the author of *Translation and the Languages of Modernism* (2002) and of *Foreign Accents: Chinese American Verse from Exclusion to Postethnicity* (2010). He is the co-editor of *Sinographies: Writing China* (2008), *Pacific Rim Modernisms* (2009), and *Ezra Pound and Education* (2012).

Ewa Plonowska Ziarek is Julian Park Professor of Comparative Literature at the University of Buffalo. She is the author of *Feminist Aesthetics and the Politics of Modernism* (2012), *An Ethics of Dissensus: Feminism, Postmodernity, and the Politics of Radical Democracy* (2001), *The Rhetoric of Failure: Deconstruction of Skepticism, Reinvention of Modernism* (1995), the co-editor of *Revolt, Affect, Collectivity: The Unstable Boundaries of Kristeva's Polis* (2005), *Time for the Humanities* (2008) and *Intermedialities: Philosophy, Art, Politics* (2010).

Introduction

Jean-Michel Rabaté

One often hears the complaint that Theory has had a negative impact on students interested in English and American literature: the lure of Theory with a capital T tempts them to read philosophers they are ill-equipped to understand, and they neglect the patient close reading of literary texts that once defined competence in the field of literary studies. True or not, the reproach has never been valid for students who have decided to focus on modernism, since from the very constitution of modernism as a literary field – say, since the end of WWII – the interpenetration of theory and texts has been its dominant feature. Today, with the rapid growth of modernist studies, the field has been inflected by historical or historicist studies; at the same time, the interconnection between literature and theory has not lost its appeal, urgency, and productivity.

The canonization of modernism by poets such as Ezra Pound and T. S. Eliot, by literary critics such as Hugh Kenner and Marjorie Perloff, art critics like Clement Greenberg, and philosophers like Adorno, has always implied concepts and criteria that correspond with the main tenets of what is now recognized as Theory. As a precise example, I will discuss Greenberg's dependence on Kant's philosophy for his imposition of an American modernism as a new and dogmatic rationale for the aesthetics of the new. The emergence of high modernism in literature, architecture, film, and the other visual arts could not have happened without significant borrowing from philosophers' theories: Yeats's version of Irish modernism would have been unthinkable without Nietzsche; Eliot's anti-Romantic and neoclassical bias obscure his reliance on the neo-Hegelian Bradley as well as his readings of Husserl and Bertrand Russell; Beckett discovered in Descartes and then Geulincx philosophical sensibilities akin to his; T. E. Hulme and Wyndham Lewis meditated on Bergson's philosophy before criticizing it; Virginia Woolf and the whole Bloomsbury group

A Handbook of Modernism Studies, First Edition. Edited by Jean-Michel Rabaté.
© 2013 John Wiley & Sons, Ltd. Published 2013 by John Wiley & Sons, Ltd.

paid attention to the redefinition of philosophy as logical theory brought about by Moore and Bertrand Russell. Even before the New Critics in America and F. R. Leavis in England put authors like Eliot, Joyce, and Lawrence on the map of academic curricula, most modernist authors knew that their success would depend on their ability to create their own audiences, to explain what they were doing, and to durably transform the taste of the common reader. This they did by introducing the terms in which they wanted to be read. If notions such as "epiphany," "mood," or "objective correlative" have now lost much of their relevance and turned into academic clichés, we should not forget that they were effective in shaping certain habits of reading and promoting intellectual discernment. Joyce, for instance, always struck his friends by the passion with which he followed the dissemination of his texts via critics who could provide new concepts for further discussion ("plane of meaning," "new mythos," and "language of the night" were not canonized but proved effective in that endeavor).

In a similar manner, the aim of this collection is to help students who want a better grasp on major modernist texts to make sense of the conceptual, philosophical, and theoretical terms that underpin the efforts of writers like Virginia Woolf, T. S. Eliot, Hilda Doolittle (H. D.), Franz Kafka, Dorothy Richardson, James Joyce, Wyndham Lewis, Gertrude Stein, Wallace Stevens, to name but some of the most obvious suspects. All the contributors to the collection have distinguished themselves in the two aspects of modernist scholarship I have outlined: they have written monographs or detailed analyses of individual texts and also provided broader syntheses. Each has engaged with concepts, theories, and theoreticians while discussing the writings of major modernist authors.

The affinity of visible theoreticians for modernist texts is well known; one can think of Adorno and Beckett, Derrida and Joyce, Foucault and Borges, Jameson and Wyndham Lewis, Cixous and Lispector, Deleuze and Proust, Žižek and Kafka, de Man and Yeats, to mention just essays or books written on individual authors. There are also many hidden or latent links, as when one parallels Derrida's work on "difference" with Beckett's interrogations of the voice and writing,[1] or refer Deleuze's and Guattari's critique of psychoanalysis back to D. H. Lawrence's essays and novels. And even if Virginia Woolf stated that she was not a feminist, one wonders what feminist theory would be today without her groundbreaking texts.

The excellent conversations about the links between modernism and theory gathered by Stephen Ross in *Modernism and Theory: A Critical Debate* in 2009 have highlighted numerous aesthetic and methodological parallels. The discussions have assessed the role of theory in contemporary interpretations of modernism, providing numerous examples of intersections between modernist authors and theoretical problematics. In a similar fashion, this collection of newly commissioned essays will explore the use of contemporary critical theory in the study of modernism. It will probe the ways in which the modernist period (its peak being in the second and third decades of the twentieth century) can serve as a site for interrogating and reframing the practices of scholars and theorists. In our current conversation about modernism, no one has done more to promote the interaction between theory and the cultural historiography of the "modern moment" than Walter Benjamin. It is no coincidence that his essays and books have been cornerstones of definitions of modernism.

Indeed, Benjamin's main effort, his unfinished compendium called *The Arcades Project* for want of a final title, keeps delineating the fault-lines between modernity and modernism. Benjamin was not duped by the shrill claims of recent authors to be "absolutely modern" (a task that Rimbaud had argued would loom larger at the end of the nineteenth century[2]). He notes wryly that each epoch believes itself to be at the vanguard of the modern: "Each age unavoidably seems to itself a new age. The 'modern' (*das 'Moderne'*) however, is as varied in its meaning as the different aspects of one and the same kaleidoscope."[3] Benjamin is less asserting a reshuffling of moving elements caught up in a machine to imply that variety merely veils sameness, than quoting obliquely Baudelaire's famous phrase comparing the new subject of modernity to a "kaleidoscope gifted with consciousness." This phrase would provide a good description of what this collection would aim to be: an accretive and dialogic immersion in a domain that will be explored through multiple angles and points of view. This is also how Baudelaire defined the rapture of the subject of modernity, a new "man of the crowd," as Poe saw him, who is also a "lover of universal life" joyfully entering the mass of urban passersby in order to tap this "immense reservoir of electrical energy."[4] Benjamin meditates at length on Baudelaire's concept of modernity, and brings it into close connection with the two important philosophies of history of the nineteenth century, those of Hegel and Marx. In the same chapter, he quotes Roger Caillois in French about Paris, this "modern myth." Caillois states that "modernity" (*modernité*) implies the "elevation of urban life to the level of myth" (AP, 555, PW, 689), a feature that we would tend to associate with Joyce, Eliot, and Pound, but was surely present in Baudelaire. Is this a sign that *modernité* has insensibly led us to *modernism*? We could believe this when we reach this isolated sentence, a simple question: "How does modernism become Jugendstil?" (AP. 561, PW, 697).

Here, one should pay attention to a subtle shift in gender: what the translators have correctly translated as "modernism" is not in the neutral as before (*das Moderne*) but in the singular feminine, *die Moderne*. Benjamin also uses the term *Neuheit* (translated as "Novelty"), or the "New," but not yet the masculine term of *Modernismus*. Beyond arbitrary grammatical rules (in French, for instance, we have the masculine *modernité* and the feminine *modernisme*, yet their mythical qualities, the hardness of the masculine and the softness of femininity, have been exchanged), one may ask more pointedly what is the "gender of modernism."[5] This is a question that several contributors will tackle in this collection, since there was a sense that the "high modernism" had to be masculine, hence "hard," aggressive, ferocious even, against an effeminate culture of decadence, or even worse, the production of mass culture for a dominantly feminine audience, allegedly the consumers of popular novels. Yet, within the field of modernist theory, a number of authors like Peter Bürger (who will be discussed in these pages) argued that modernism had kept elements of the "soft" aestheticizing touch, whereas the real revolution in the arts and everyday life was to be found only in the "historical" avant-gardes. This is a debate that will be surveyed here. We can also remember that, not so long ago, such an influential critic as Hugh Kenner refused to grant the epithet of "modernist" to Virginia Woolf, who was deemed too "soft" and not experimental enough, reserving the term to the group animated by Ezra Pound, a group including, it is true, Hilda Doolittle alias H. D.[6] And Gertrude Stein could state that all geniuses were men – which included her as well! In all these discussions, gender and politics are inextricably mixed.

As for Benjamin, his use of a feminine term (*die Moderne*) may be linked with what he criticized in the "*Jugendstil*" moment, a movement which is often rendered in English as "art nouveau." It is the post-symbolist generation of 1890–1910, the lineage linking Baudelaire to Mallarmé, Laforgue, Wilde, Jarry, the younger Gide and Yeats. Odilon Redon and Beardsley would be its main artists. Needless to say, Benjamin, who embraced the material, technological, and ideological acceleration of modernity, cannot but reject the legacy of the *Jugendstil*, a movement that he always associated with the decadent poetry of Stefan George, with whom he had fought at the beginning of his career. Sexual perversion and fake mysticism are the ways in which *Jugendstil* would attempt to bring back a lost aura: "Jugendstil forces the auratic" (AP, 557, PW, 692). In other words, we see here that Benjamin points to possible links between modernism and regressive aestheticism, which leads to stillborn productions or bad art, simply put, to Kitsch. This will provide an exactly identical point of departure for Clement Greenberg.

What remains of Clement Greenberg's impact today is that he succeeded in promoting modernism in the visual arts after 1945, and justified his preference by establishing a solid theory of modernism.[7] For this he had to invent a specific blend of philosophy, cultural critique, and aesthetics that corresponds rather well with what we understand by "Theory." Like Benjamin, Greenberg was struck by the cultural scandal constituted by the coexistence of "Kitsch," or debased popular art in all its commercial dilutions, with high art. Avant-garde or modern art and Kitsch not only rubbed shoulders in the marketplace, but reinforced each another. Thus only clear and precise sets of criteria will allow one to make necessary distinctions. In his inaugural essay on "Avant-garde and Kitsch," Greenberg asserts that " . . . with the entrance of the avant-garde, a second new cultural phenomenon appeared in the industrial West: that thing to which the Germans give the wonderful name of *Kitsch*: popular, commercial art and literature with their chromeotypes, magazine covers, illustrations, ads, slick and pulp fiction, comics, Tin Pan Alley music, tap dancing, Hollywood movies, etc., etc."[8] Two "etceteras" call up the bad infinity of Kitsch, the endless tide of debased objects that threatens to engulf the authenticity of modern art. In order to ward off this threat, often identified with the market or capitalism, it is vital to define strictly the conditions of possibility of true artistic judgments. One will have to distinguish between a priori conditions of any artistic experience and the value judgments that underpin it so as to build foundations for an accurate appreciation of taste.

Quite naturally, this position led Greenberg back to Kant, a philosopher whose concepts proved invaluable if one searched for a secure foundation in aesthetics.

Greenberg was a hero of theoretical modernism, but he had a darker side, above all the fact that he appeared as a theoretical bully. He did not hesitate to knock out an aged Max Ernst who had poured on the critic's bald head an ashtray full of cigarette butts; Ernst's silly joke meant to allude to a consecration as King of Critics. Greenberg's answer was to punch him in the face, to Ernst's infinite amazement. Modernism would only accept titles granted by itself; one would have to fight to uphold the "autonomy" of judgment. Indeed, Greenberg insisted that criticism is based on judgments, which led him to place modernism durably in the context of neo-Kantianism. Thierry de Duve points out some equivocations in the appropriation of Kant in *Clement Greenberg Between the Lines*,[9] but on the whole attests to the seriousness of his critical discourse. For de Duve, Greenberg appeared first as a doctrinaire and a militant, a committed ideologist who managed, almost single-handedly, to change American taste in contemporary art; evolving from a Trostkyite avant-garde entrenched in little New York magazines, in a decade he reached the envied position of Pope of Abstract Expressionism. A second aspect defines the daily practice of an art reviewer whose journalistic forays into galleries responded to the solicitations of the art scene; there he displays an extraordinary virtuosity in reviews in which he would "discover" artists such as Pollock and Still while attacking the French like Rouault or the Surrealists; he was an "eye," a witness whose curiosity was always on the alert. The third aspect of Greenberg may interest us here: the theoretician who elaborated a comprehensive doctrine of modernism, and who can be called an "author," or, as Michel Foucault has it, an "inventor of discursivity." Still today, "Greenberg" as a name stands for theoretical modernism and thus condenses a whole set of values, analyses, and appreciations.

Greenberg's problematic of modernism started, as we have seen, from the fruitful opposition between Kitsch and the avant-garde, and it ended up promoting the New York school of abstraction in the 1950s because this school embodied what his aesthetics promoted. The reference to Kant in connection with the promotion of Abstract Expressionism corresponded to a strategy that was meant to debunk two rival theories: a parochial praise of American values, in which he recognized the language of exceptionalism and jingoism, and the blurred messianic promise of an avant-gardist internationalism. Greenberg used Kant selectively: for instance, he never invoked the theory of the Sublime in his aesthetics (to which several contributors will allude). He does not seem to pay attention to the passage of the *Third Critique* when Kant praises the Jewish religion's prohibition of human representation, although this could point to non-representational painting. In fact, Greenberg heeds takes the axiom that "The Deduction of aesthetic judgments upon objects of nature must not be directed to what we call sublime in nature, but only to the beautiful."[10] The main concepts used to promote modernism are the idea of a Critique, of the Beautiful, and of Taste as a common discourse on art.

In 1946, when the New York school was emerging, Greenberg used Kant's philosophy in order to debunk American provincialism, as he did in a review of McMahon's *Preface to an American Philosophy of Art* (1945). McMahon thought that he could "demolish" the German school of aesthetics by seizing on a contradiction between Kant's idea that "Nature is beautiful because it looks like art," an idea that would suggest that art must imitate nature, and the idea that Beauty has nothing to do with Truth (CE II, 66). Greenberg has no difficulty in demonstrating that Kant never posits the imitation of nature as an ideal. Kant states only that art's finality has to be like that of Nature: its forms must be free of constraints, devoid of arbitrary rules. As Greenberg points out, Kant's "revolutionary insights" were trivialized by McMahon who reduced them to a self-canceling plea for mimesis (CE II, 66). Such a forcible critique testifies to the seriousness of his reading of Kant. At the same time, Greenberg similarly reproached Claude-Edmonde Magny for not having understood Kant. Her 1945 book *Les Sandales d'Empédocle* refuses the "fiction" of a universal point of view and questions the possibility of proffering general aesthetic judgments. Greenberg sees her contradiction: hasn't she made a judgment herself when she debated about the limits of literature? (CE II, 68). This implies that we are all Kantian, even without knowing it: as soon as we talk about art, we cannot help making a judgment. Finally, Ernst Cassirer emerges as a model of intelligent Kantianism open both to *Geisteswissenschaften* and to the analysis of language and symbols (CE II, 27). Greenberg's concept of modernism goes back to the program of the Enlightenment. Here is how "Modernist Painting" (1960) begins:

> Modernism includes more than art and literature. By now it covers almost the whole of what is truly alive in our culture. It happens, however, to be very much of a historical novelty. Western civilization is not the first civilization to turn around and question its own foundations, but it is the one that has gone furthest in doing so. I identify Modernism with the intensification, almost the exacerbation, of this self-critical tendency that began with the philosopher Kant. Because he was the first to criticize the means itself of criticism, I conceive of Kant as the first real Modernist. // The essence of Modernism lies, as I see it, in the use of characteristic methods of a discipline to criticize the discipline itself, not in order to subvert it but in order to entrench it more firmly in its area of competence. (CE IV, 85)

Modernism inherits from the Enlightenment the wish to found each discipline by criticizing it, in a critique that does not come from outside but from inside: "The limitations that constitute the medium of painting – the flat surface, the shape of the support, the properties of the pigment – were treated by the Old Masters as negative factors that could be acknowledged only implicitly or indirectly. Under Modernism these same limitations came to be regarded as positive factors, and were acknowledged openly" (CE IV, 86). Consequently, modernism discloses a doctrine of the "purity" of art. Purity based upon "self-definition" depends upon a rigorous deployment of the formal properties of the medium. Cézanne's revolution came from the exploration of the "limits" of his art, and modernism already began at the end of the nineteenth century.

Kant gives philosophical weight to an insight attributed to Aristotle in "Avant-garde and Kitsch." If the coexistence of Eliot's poems and Tin Pan Alley songs created a scandal for Greenberg, he saw in the avant-garde a paradoxical defense of absolute values in art, even if the avant-garde's origins are historically linked to the industrial revolution. Yet artists who invoke the absolute prefer certain values to others: "The very values in the name of which he invokes the absolute are relative values, the values of aesthetics. And so he turns out to be imitating, not God – and here I use 'imitate' in its Aristotelian sense – but the discipline and processes of art and literature themselves. This is the genesis of the 'abstract.' In turning his attention away from subject matter of common experience, the poet or artist turns it upon the medium of his own craft" (CE I, 8–9). Greenberg reminds us that, for Aristotle, music is the most "imitative" of all arts, which confirms a link between Aristotle and Kant. Both focus on how the arts imitate the workings of nature (*e techne mimeitai ten physin*), which does not mean that art should imitate or reproduce natural objects. Joyce had already noted in 1903[11] that Aristotle asserts that the "artistic process is like the natural process," yet does not lead to a doctrine of realist representation. The arts "imitate" by following the "natural" drift of their own process of "imitation": "Picasso, Braque, Mondrian, Miro, Kandinsky, Brancusi, even Klee, Matisse and Cézanne derive their chief inspiration from the medium they work in. The excitement of their art seems to lie most of all in its pure preoccupation with the invention and arrangement of spaces, surface, shapes, colors, etc., to the exclusion of whatever is not necessarily implicated in these factors" (CE I, 9). A roll call of modernist poets, Rimbaud, Mallarmé, Valéry, Eluard, Ezra Pound, Crane, Stevens, Rilke, and Yeats, comes to confirm that the same process obtains in literature.

This Aristotelian-Kantian theory will be applied to modernist works, and even re-title some of these as modernist, as we see in Greenberg's changing opinion on Monet. After having been dismissed, Monet was reassessed more positively by Greenberg later. In "The Later Monet" (1957), Greenberg admits that he was wrong to downplay Monet, even if the painter was mistaken in his understanding of art. For Monet, what mattered above all was to be faithful to Nature, to reproduce as accurately as possible the colored world out there. His genius was to radicalize this wish, and this led him to refuse the Old Masters as models (even Cézanne kept them as models). "In the end he found what he was looking for, which was not so much a new principle as a more comprehensive one: and it lay not in Nature, but in the essence of art itself, in its 'abstractness.' That he himself could not consciously recognize or accept 'abstractness' – the qualities of the medium alone – as a principle of consistency makes no difference: it is there, plain to see in the paintings of his old age" (CE IV, 8). True to the end to his visual sensations, Monet gave all his attention to problems of equivalences without dominances. He created a superior unity when the colored surfaces turn into flat, unmodulated monochromes. Pissarro could quip that Monet was a "decorator without being decorative." The truth is that Monet's later paintings anticipated the wallpaper effect given by the all-over paintings produced by Pollock and other American abstract expressionists.

Thus modernist abstraction insists on the idea of equivalence in difference, an effect produced by the feeling that each brushstroke is autonomous. Every part of the painting embodies the whole (think of the more experimental work of Gertrude Stein). This experimental modernism abolishes hierarchies between high and low, top and bottom, horizontal and vertical, hung or flat, centered or non-centered.

Modernist abstraction is the logical consequence of a process that is the culmination of a historical progress, but it also answers to a theoretical need. The exploration began with Kandinsky, Malevitch, and Mondrian, but the perfect realization of the autonomous medium was left to American artists of the 1950s like Pollock, Rothko, Still, and Newman. Here, Greenberg's logic is "plokeic," in the sense that it follows the trope of emphatic repetition. He keeps urging: "Let painting be painting!" This would be true of modernist music and of literature; they too can only progress by exploring the properties of their own mediums.

Greenberg assumes that there has been a historical evolution leading to his sense that the best artists of the 1950s were abstract painters, but he has more difficulties in explaining why in 1953 the New York school (Gorky, Gottlieb, Hofmann, Kline, de Kooning, Motherwell, Newman, Pollock, Rothko) is better than the Parisian school (Fautrier, Dubuffet, Hartung, Tal Coat) who are also abstract. The judgment falls, without equivocation: "Do I mean that the new American abstract painting is superior on the whole to the French? I do" (CE III, 156). French painters have neglected Klee and Miró; they have not learned enough from Matisse; they have little regard for a precursor like Masson. More precisely, the concept of taste intervenes. Thus the Kantian theory of modernism will rely on value judgments based on artistic competence. Greenberg managed to achieve what for Remy de Gourmont was the aim of criticism: to transform one's personal impressions into universal maxims. Greenberg's experience, nourished as much by Corot and Velasquez as by Mondrian and Pollock, tells him that in the 1950s the best painters are American abstract painters.

Similarly, Greenberg's analysis of the failure of the first abstract school of New York is instructive; since it cannot claim to be linked with Kantian concepts, it has to be ideological: "It was this misconception of non-naturalistic art as a vehicle for an esoteric message that encouraged Miss O'Keefe, along with Arthur Dove, Marsden Hartley and others, to proceed to abstract art so immediately upon her first acquaintance with the 'modern'" (CE II, 86). As with Benjamin's rejection of the *Jugendstil*, the innate mysticism of the New York avant-garde of the twenties prevented artists from being radical or systematic. In fact, they lacked a theory for their practice. Unlike Eliot or Pound, avant-gardists did not create a critical discourse to make sense of their efforts. They were blind as to their involvement in a "tradition of the new." This is why they rapidly abandoned abstraction and devoted themselves to a pseudo-modernism, and it soon degenerated in high-end Kitsch. Typically, popular success crowned the post-abstract or post-experimental efforts of artists and writers; Greenberg mentions O'Keefe in painting, but one can think of the later Gertrude Stein or of E. E. Cummings in poetry.

Nevertheless, in 1964, Greenberg had to acknowledge that there had been a second "crisis of abstract art" (CE IV, 176). By then, the admission was less damaging. The battle had been won, New York had triumphed against Paris. Greenberg's modernist criteria had lain down the law for the art market; his judgments were shared by the network of galleries, American modern art museums, and collectors. If they were at the peak of an evolution in aesthetics, how could it be that Pollock, Rothko, and their friends were reinventing an abstract art that had been launched thirty years earlier? This paradox of a "modernizing" evolution has been well analyzed by Bourdieu in *The Rules of Art*. Bourdieu quotes Marcel Duchamp, who was opposed to the spirit of the 1950s, and rejected the modernist abstraction promoted by Greenberg. "The characteristic of the century that is ending is to be like a double-barrelled gun: Kandinsky and Kupka invented abstraction. Then abstraction died. One wouldn't talk about it any more. It came back thirty-five years later with the American abstract expressionists. You could say that Cubism reappeared in an impoverished form with the postwar Paris school. Dada has similarly reappeared. Second shot, second wind. It is a phenomenon particular to this century."[12] Bourdieu comments on this by adding that "each artistic act which leaves its mark by introducing a new position in the field 'displaces' the entire series of previous artistic acts" (RA, 160), a view consistent with Eliot's concept of "tradition" in "Tradition and the Individual Talent." Bourdieu defines this constant reshuffling of values as a "struggle" but the fundamental view is the same: "Contemporaneity as presence in the same present only exists in practice *in the struggle* that *synchronizes* discordant times or, rather, agents and institutions separated by time and in relation to time" (RA, 158). We return to Bourdieu's views on modernism in these pages.

Greenberg's theory agrees with this, especially in "Avant-Garde and Kitsch," a text blending Marxism and high modernism à la Eliot. One of his most ambitious essays from the 1950s is a review of Eliot's *Notes Toward the Definition of Culture* (CE III, 122–152). In an interview conducted in 1994, the year of his death, Greenberg confessed that even if he had to admit to an influence, he resented Eliot's tone of smug superiority, while confessing that he was most in agreement with Adorno.[13] In spite of his likes and dislikes, Greenberg had incarnated the synthesis of modernism and theory that the Zeitgeist requested when he transformed an elitist Eliotian Trotskyism with an American slant into a consistent definition of modernism in the arts. Greenberg provided his solution to Eliot's postulation of an "ideal order" of culture destined to be changed each time a new masterpiece arrived. Do new artists coexist peacefully with the previous ones or do they murder each other? Greenberg would suggest that evolution comes from struggle, often to the death: one has to destroy other reputations if one's criteria are to shape dominant taste. This begs the issue of power, money, and politics, a social game that Eliot had learned to play as well.

Why then did Greenberg's theory avoid Kant's concept of the Sublime? This would bring him too close to his enemy Marcel Duchamp and the then nascent conceptual art. When in 1952 Greenberg praised Barnett Newman whose titles often referenced the Sublime, he did not mention this term once (CE III, 103–104). The Kantian Sublime risks introducing too much negativity. For Greenberg, the act of looking at an abstract painting does not offer the experience of "nothing" but of something: the painting's bi-dimensionality, its shape and color, its boundaries on a canvas. Kant's theory of the sublime simultaneously blends fear and pleasure: the imagination experiences its own limits, understanding that it is overwhelmed and cannot comprehend the sight, whether natural or artistic. Greenberg's modernist aesthetic is not one of powerlessness or impotence, as the later Beckett's aesthetic turned out to be. Unlike Adorno, Greenberg shies away from any experience of negativity. He wants to remain in control, reach a common "truth" underpinned by categories of taste and universalism, whereas Duchamp insisted on complex calculations and subjective freedom deriving from indifference to artistic values. Greenberg starts from a phenomenology of sensation; sensory impressions will be filtered, discussed, classified, and rationalized. Art is based upon "reflective judgments,"[14] which start from singular objects and the subject's feelings facing them. Only then do they go back to categories that give coherence, finality, and a *raison d'être* to the object. This Kantian principle could be generalized to the use of theory to discuss modernist texts: there should be an experience of the text; theory is not meant to replace it or denigrate it, let alone stand higher than the personal interaction with a given object.

Thus we can learn from Greenberg's experiential model underpinned by theory. His theory faithfully enacts Kant's "finality without end," this *Zweckmässigkeit ohne Zweck*, a notion that defines the essence of art that imitates the functioning of nature. What it asserts, most fundamentally, is that if nature is not absurd, then neither is art as social production begging the existence of a common taste. Greenberg ends up defending modernism with formal judgments buttressed by a concept of history that demands the notion of progress. Both Adorno and Greenberg believed that there were "discoveries" in the arts: one could not continue to write harmonic music pieces after Schönberg without being reactionary, or paint realistically after Mondrian without regressing. Neither Adorno nor Greenberg wanted to imagine a cyclical return of genres, techniques, and schools, parodic "revolutions" in a saturated field homogenized by the "end of history" deduced by Kojève from Hegel. Abstraction defines an aesthetic of taste and will not consider the end of a social consensus about the idea of art or about history. Those who destroy the consensus, like Duchamp, stick to nominalist aesthetics; their central claim becomes: "I call this art because this is what I do." Greenberg has reintroduced the issue of value; he prefers saying: "Here is what I like, and we can all agree that it is good art." He was indeed the last American critic who could reign over the world of museums and gallery owners, collectors and rich buyers; only he could reconcile the influence of money with the taste of sophisticated connoisseurs. Kantian theory as invoked by Greenberg to promote modernism led the New York school to the pinnacles of the art market. Was it only a tool in a struggle for prestige and power? Did that formalist theory of modernism mask and justify a geographical reshuffling from Paris to New York, did it merely serve the interests of international capital?

The history of art theory succeeding Greenberg has shown that, as Hegel himself had to confess, there is no "end of history." Which also means that there is no end of theory, even if theories moved on, if taste changed, if Abstract Expressionism is only one among many schools. Even the concepts that have been offered as an antidote to Kant's formalism, such as Bataille's notion of the "formless,"[15] require definitions and other theoretical deployments of concepts. Thus, quite logically, this volume is organized around concepts such as race, gender, class, the body, nation, politics, ideology, history, aesthetics, material objects, visual culture, etc. All these terms demonstrate an engagement with current critical trends. The collection first surveys the main terms underpinning a critical consensus about modernism before pointing to emergent domains for which new methodologies are needed. Issues of class and race will be debated in the context of the Harlem Renaissance and of Marxist approaches to modernism. The politics of modernism show that its practitioners were as often reactionaries tempted by fascism as left-wing writers committed to internationalist activities. The old couples of the Hard and the Soft, of the High and Low, have operated in dichotomies that have structured the field. It has also been marked by technical discoveries such as "interior monologue" or the "stream of consciousness" technique, which lead to considerations about what is specific to modernism as a style.

There is also the question of periodization, which will not be tackled directly, since what matters most for the critics gathered in this volume is less the question of when modernism began exactly or when it ended (but has it really ended?), than pragmatic considerations of how and why important authors like Joyce, Woolf, Beckett, or Kafka have forced us to expand and broaden the term of modernism. It seems today that modernism has absorbed most of the twentieth century, that it goes back deep into the nineteenth century and that it has moreover swallowed postmodernism. This notion, which emerged in the 1980s, has surprisingly lost all of its purchase, in a sudden disaffection that some have found disappointing. This may be due to the new capaciousness discovered in modernism, since it had always included myth, rituals, and the archaic, as well as several varieties of Orientalism, but now is seen to move on to translation studies, to textual studies focusing on the archives, manuscripts, and history of the book. More recently, it has solicited the approaches of film studies, of phenomenology, of ethical theory, of queer studies, of the sociology of culture, of disability studies, of political studies, and even of fashion theory. All these critical discourses are represented in these pages. Finally, the discussion had to return to the question of aesthetics with which I have begun. The juxtaposition of the parody of the sublime (in a feminine mode) and the aesthetics of a new formalism provides a last but not final reconfiguration of modernism in our ever-revolving kaleidoscope.

*

I want to thank Jennifer Mondal who helped me edit the collection.

Notes

1 See Derrida's interview by Derek Attridge in *Acts of Literature*, 1992, 60–62.
2 I have pointed to the deep ambivalence of Rimbaud's famous statement "One has to be absolutely modern" in *The Ghosts of Modernity*, 194–195.
3 Walter Benjamin, *The Arcades Project*, 1999, 545. For the German original, see Walter Benjamin, *Das Passagen-Werk*, ed. Rolf Tiedemann, Frankfurt, Suhrkamp, 1983, vol. 2, 677. All other references to *The Arcades Project* will be abbreviated as AP and page number.
4 Charles Baudelaire, "The Painter of Modern Life," in Leitch, 2nd edn, 2010, 683.

5   By this, I want to pay homage to the groundbreaking anthology *The Gender of Modernism: A Critical Anthology*, ed. Bonnie Kime Scott. In 1990, it redefined the field in an important way by highlighting many forgotten female authors. This was followed by two anthologies that also shaped the modernist canon: *Modernism, An Anthology of Sources and Documents*, ed. Vassiliki Kolocotroni, Jane Goldman, and Olga Taxidou, 1998, blended theory and literature in a powerful synthesis, whereas *Modernism, An Anthology*, ed. Lawrence Rainey, 2005, less theoretical, introduced New Critical essays. The latter, at 1181 pages, betrays a significant expansion of the modernist canon.

6   Virginia Woolf was not part of "international Modernism," for she was above all "an English novelist of manners," writes Hugh Kenner in "The Making of the Modernist Canon," 1989, 37. Kenner excludes Wallace Stevens as well, but for different reasons (40). Needless to say, this view is not shared by many today.

7   The pages that follow revise and condense an analysis of the opposition between Greenberg and Duchamp that was part of a chapter in Rabaté, Jean-Michel, *Given: 1) Art, 2) Crime, Modernity, Murder and Mass Culture*, 2007, 172–189.

8   Clement Greenberg, "Avant-Garde and Kitsch," in *The Collected Essays and Criticism*, I, *Perceptions and Judgments, 1939–1944*, 11. I will use the four volumes of these essays. Clement Greenberg, *The Collected Essays and Criticism*, ed. John O'Brian, vol. 1, *Perceptions and Judgments, 1939–1944* (1986), vol. 2, *Arrogant Purpose* (1986), vol. 3, *Affirmations and refusals, 1950–1956* (1993), vol. 4, *Modernism with a Vengeance, 1957–1969* (1993), University of Chicago Press, abbreviated as CE I, CE II, CE III and CE IV, and followed by the page number.

9   Thierry de Duve, *Clement Greenberg Between the Lines: Including a Debate with Clement Greenberg*, 2010.

10 Immanuel Kant, *Critique of Judgment*, 1952, 133.

11 Joyce, "Paris Notebook," *Critical Writings*, 145.

12 Quoted by Pierre Bourdieu, *The Rules of Art: Genesis and Structure of the Literary Field*, 1995, 160. Hereafter, RA and page number. See the discussion by James English later in the volume.

13 See "The Last Interview," in Clement Greenberg, *Late Writings*, 2003, 236.

14 Immanuel Kant, *Critique of Judgment*, 1952, 26 and sq.

15 See the excellent catalogue by Yve-Alain Bois and Rosalind Krauss, *Formless: A User's Guide*, 1997.

References

Benjamin, Walter. (1999). *The Arcades Project*, trans. Howard Eiland and Kevin McLaughlin. Cambridge, MA: Harvard University Press.

Bois, Yve-Alain, and Rosalind Krauss. (1997). *Formless: A User's Guide*. New York: Zone Books.

Bourdieu, Pierre. (1995). *The Rules of Art: Genesis and Structure of the Literary Field*, trans. Susan Emanuel. Stanford: Stanford University Press.

De Duve, Thierry. (2010). *Clement Greenberg Between the Lines: Including a Debate with Clement Greenberg*. Chicago: Chicago University Press.

Derrida, Jacques. (1992). *Acts of Literature*. New York: Routledge.

Greenberg, Clement. (1986–1993). *The Collected Essays and Criticism*, ed. John O'Brian, vol. 1, *Perceptions and Judgments, 1939–1944* (1986), vol. 2, *Arrogant Purpose* (1986), vol. 3,

Affirmations and refusals, 1950–1956
(1993), vol. 4, *Modernism with a
Vengeance, 1957–1969* (1993). Chicago:
University of Chicago Press.

Greenberg, Clement. (2003). *Late Writings*,
ed. Robert C. Morgan. Minneapolis:
University of Minnesota Press.

Joyce, James. (1959). *Critical Writings*, New
York, Viking.

Kant, Immanuel. (1952). *Critique of Judgment*, trans. James Creed Meredith.
Oxford: Oxford University Press.

Kenner, Hugh. (1989). *Mazes*. San Francisco:
North Point Press.

Kolocotroni, Vassiliki. (1998). *Modernism,
An Anthology of Sources and Documents*,
ed. Jane Goldman and Olga Taxidou.
Chicago: Chicago University Press.

Leitch, Vincent, ed. (2010). *The Norton
Anthology of Theory and Criticism*, 2nd
edn. New York: Norton.

Rabaté, Jean-Michel. (1996). *The Ghosts of
Modernity*. Gainesville: University Press
of Florida.

Rabaté, Jean-Michel. (2007). *Given: 1) Art,
2) Crime, Modernity, Murder and Mass
Culture*. Brighton, Sussex: Academic
Press.

Rainey, Lawrence, ed. (2005). *Modernism:
An Anthology*. Oxford: Blackwell.

Ross, Stephen, ed. (2009). *Modernism and
Theory: A Critical Debate*. New York:
Routledge.

Scott, Bonnie Kime, ed. (1990). *The Gender of Modernism: A Critical Anthology*.
Bloomington: Indiana University Press.

1

Hard and Soft Modernism
Politics as "Theory"

Peter Nicholls

In an age of "Theory," can we still think of literary modernism in terms of exclusionary dualisms? One invitation to do so is the fact that modernism was itself deeply rooted in dualistic and oppositional modes of thinking – the "figure of a defiant speech in excess of the norm is salient in modernism," declares one critic (Al-Kassim 2010, 12). Yet even Ezra Pound (1968a), originator of many of the pithy antitheses that continue to be ritually invoked in accounts of modernist writing, broached his distinction between "hard" and "soft" forms of writing with uncharacteristic hesitation: "I apologize for using the semetaphorical [sic] terms 'hard' and 'soft' in this essay, but after puzzling over the matter for some time I can see no other way of setting about it" (285). Then follows the elaboration of the terminology that would be so influential in subsequent readings of modernism ("the word 'hard,'" notes Hugh Kenner (1988), "was coming into vogue" [131]):

> By "hardness" [writes Pound] I mean a quality which is in poetry nearly always a virtue – I can think of no case where it is not. By softness I mean an opposite quality which is not always a fault. Anyone who dislikes these textural terms may lay the blame on Théophile Gautier, who certainly suggests them in *Emaux et Camées*; it is his hardness that I had first in mind. He exhorts us to cut in hard substance, the shell and the Parian. (Ezra Pound 1968a, 285)

As in the earlier manifesto statements for Imagism, Pound associates "hardness" with a constellation of "textural" features that favor "definiteness" of presentation over "abstraction," and the external "shell" over the "muzziness" of unfettered intro- spection (Pound 1968a, 3–14). Although "softness" is "not always a fault" – Pound notes that it is "tolerable" in "the good Chaucerian" style – it tends to produce a "swash" of rhetoric that is at odds with the "clear hard" quality that he regards as a

A Handbook of Modernism Studies, First Edition. Edited by Jean-Michel Rabaté.
© 2013 John Wiley & Sons, Ltd. Published 2013 by John Wiley & Sons, Ltd.

defining quality of the strong lyric tendency in French verse (Gautier versus "Hugo, De Musset & Co") (286). This "hardness" will constitute the trademark style of the new modernism: the writing of "the next decade or so," Pound insists, "will be harder and saner . . . . It will be as much like granite as it can be . . . " (12).

It is worth noting the conjunction here of "clarity" and "hardness" since, paradoxically perhaps, it affirms "a hardness which is not of necessity 'rugged'; as in 'Past ruin'd Ilion Helen lives'" (286). The line Pound quotes from Walter Savage Landor is, indeed, far from "rugged" or granite-like, exemplifying in its sinuous weaving of /i/ and /l/ sounds a musicality grounded in clearly marked syllabic differentiation rather than in a "muzzy" melisma. This emphasis on differentiation underpins his related arguments for aesthetic autonomy: the "clean," "hard," inorganic values of Imagism and Vorticism are the only ones which seem adequately to represent an intelligence which avoids surplus and works by reduction, denying itself the immediate pleasures of the "caressable" and the mimetic ("The caressable," says Pound, "is always a substitute" [1960, 97]). "Hardness," by this account, is a stylistic and ethical feature of verse that represents a challenge to poetic convention: "Gautier is intent on being 'hard': is intent on conveying a certain verity of feeling, and he ends by being truly poetic. Heredia wants to be poetic *and* hard; the hardness appears to him as a virtue in the poetic" (285). Pound's own distinction could be clearer here, but he seems to suggest that the particular "hardness" of Heredia's work is governed by preexisting poetic models – Gautier, chiefly – rather than by a "verity of feeling" that properly precedes the discovery of the "truly poetic." As a result, Heredia's poems tend somewhat toward the "frigid," their "hardness" ultimately a product of stylistic mannerism, while Gautier's verse, in contrast, cleaves to the supple contour of an original emotion.

At this point in his career, Pound's influential advocacy of "hardness" over "softness" is expressed in predominantly stylistic terms, and so it would be grasped by subsequent generations of poets who would see the emphasis on precision and economy as a *sine qua non* of any theory of modernist writing.[1] It was hardly surprising, though, that in composing his essay on French poetry Pound had found the use of these terms ineluctable ("I can see no other way of setting about it") because their transparently gendered inflections already implied political preferences yet to be clearly announced. Indeed, for Pound, the favored "hardness" would soon come to be equated with the political as such, characterizing the emotional tonality and rigor appropriate to the "verities" to be expressed. In the political realm, this "hardness" would connote a directness and a lack of ambiguity easily distinguishable from allegedly decadent forms of "softness"; in Pound's later writing, as in that of Yeats, Wyndham Lewis, and (perhaps less obviously) Eliot, it would often be colored by a kind of bravado through which certain rhetorical postures – Lewis as "the Enemy," for example – were adopted in support of claims for artistic authority.[2] When it came to poetic style, however, the clear separation of qualities was somewhat harder to sustain and this perhaps explains Pound's caveat that "softness . . . is not always a fault." In the case of *The Cantos*, passages of sustained lyricism were intended to achieve a sculptural "hardness" through visual clarity and syllabic patterning ("Rhythm is a form cut into TIME, as a design is determined SPACE," Pound emphasized (1968b, 198) but, as Lewis remarked of a visionary episode in Canto XVII, the verse was to some extent still dependent on "swinburnian stage-properties", a sure sign of a lingering "softness" ("it is composed upon a series of histrionic pauses, intended to be thrilling and probably beautiful," Lewis cuttingly concluded [1993, 71]).

Lewis's own art would always be more uncompromisingly "hard" than Pound's, in part because his commitment to what he called a "philosophy of the Eye" (1987, 97) – "This is another condition of art; *to have no inside*, nothing you cannot *see*" (1990, 300) – was closely bound up with his conception of satire, a mode that requires a "petrification" of the human into the thing-like, an ensemble of grotesque surfaces rather than "classical proportion" ("art," he writes, "consists . . . in a *mechanising* of the natural" [1987, 129; his emphasis]). Lewis's repudiation of the natural in favor of the "deadness" of the artwork accordingly values the "hippopotamus' armored hide" above the "naked pulsing and moving of the soft inside of life." The satirical attitude, as he defines it, entails an absolute embrace of "hardness," asserting the artistic necessity of distance and objectivity. Yet it is exactly the seductive appeal of the "soft inside" of life that he detects everywhere in the arts of democratic modernity where "*otherness*, like *opposition*, is reactionary. We are all One Fellow" (1984, 73). Lewis sees the works of his modernist colleagues as variously capitulating to this failure of "opposition," as trading the "otherness" that should properly define the aesthetic for the "soft" consolations of primitivism, childish innocence, and the self-regarding rituals of democratic identification.

There are, we might note, some significant limits to Lewis's critique of his fellow modernists, and what he condemns as invertebrate empathy is at times more critical and "external" than he acknowledges: even Gertrude Stein (1946 [1971]), arch-exemplar, for Lewis, of "the child-cult," believed that "Nobody can enter into anybody else's mind; so why try? One can only enter into it in a superficial way" (993). Lewis's critique of Pound's work, however, strikes a more direct hit, mainly because he traces the lingering "softness" there to a persistently romantic attitude toward history:

> *By himself* he would seem to have neither any convictions nor eyes in his head. There is nothing that he intuits well, certainly never originally. Yet when he can get into the skin of somebody else, of power and renown, a Propertius or an Arnaut Daniel, he becomes a lion or a lynx on the spot. This sort of parasitism is with him phenomenal. (1993, 68; his emphases)

Readers weighing this passage might assent to Lewis's description of Pound's habitual use of *personae* and textual ventriloquism but would probably also object that these are the very devices that underlay the poet's innovative handling of translation and textual collage. Generally less noticed is Lewis's criticism of his friend's lack of intuition and originality and this goes deep, suggesting a fundamental division that Lewis sees as crucially damaging to Pound's whole project.[3] The comment in fact tacitly transposes the "hard"/"soft" distinction to one between what we might call the theoretical and the aesthetic. In this respect, Lewis's thinking has something in common with that of Mikhail Bakhtin whose unfinished text now translated as *Toward a Philosophy of the Act* was composed several years before *Time and Western Man* (1927).[4] Bakhtin (1993) there describes what he calls "the theoretical world" as one which is "obtained through an essential and fundamental abstraction from the fact of my unique being" and in its place he proposes a "participative" thinking that is "unindifferent" and "engaged": "Every thought of mine, along with its content, is an act or deed that I perform – my own individually answerable act or deed [*postupok*]" (9,3). The truth of thought lies in the uniqueness and situatedness of the moment of its performance; hence "It is an unfortunate misunderstanding (a legacy of rationalism) to think that truth [*Pravda*] can only be the truth [*istina*] that is composed of universal moments; that the truth of a situation is precisely that which is repeatable or constant in it" (37).[5] The aesthetic world might seem to offer an attractive alternative to theory's pull toward abstraction, but it, too, proves ultimately inadequate:

> ... aesthetic being is closer to the actual unity of Being-as-life than the theoretical world is. That is why the temptation of aestheticism is so persuasive. One can live in aesthetic being, and there are those who do so, but they are *other* human beings and not I myself.... But I shall not find *myself* in that life; I shall find only a double of myself, only someone pretending to be me. All I can do in it is play a role, i.e., assume, like a mask, the flesh of another – of someone deceased. (18; his emphases)

Like Lewis, Bahktin regards aestheticism as evading the whole question of the thinker's "answerability" which "remains in actual life, for the playing of a role as a whole is an answerable deed performed by *the one playing*, and not the one represented, i.e., the hero" (18; his emphases). This is the import of Lewis's emphatic "*By himself*" which suggests that the abstraction of "theory" is registered in Pound's work by the poet's effective absence from his own thought (for it is never, according to Lewis, truly his own, originating instead in the dead "flesh" of someone else).[6] Through his habitual ventriloquism, Pound "becomes a lion or a lynx on the spot," and this "parasitically" acquired power substitutes for the authority that should properly accrue from "answerable" thinking.

In this confrontation of Lewis's thought with Pound's we see how unstable "hard" and "soft" can be as descriptive and evaluative terms. For Lewis, a "hard," "non-human outlook" is necessary "to correct our soft conceit" while for Pound the human is, ideally, at one with nature and its rhythms – a "soft" metaphysics, in Lewis's view, and one that means that the "hard" side of the equation comes to express itself in Pound's work only through abstractions imported from sources external to it (1987, 99). In this sense, we might say that *The Cantos* would turn out to be (as Lewis's comment partly predicts) determined by a constellation of "theories" on whose iterable truths – economic, political, philosophical – the poem would increasingly come to depend. Against the pressure of rhetorical and didactic insistence that accompanied this dependence, the "soft" dimensions of the poem – its imagistic riches, its intoxicating musicality – would, for many readers, prove a saving grace, though whether these were in turn merely evidence of a lingering aestheticism presented for others another pressing question. Pound was himself, it seems, intermittently aware that his practice of juxtaposition might finally reveal mere incommensurability rather than the cross-weave of connection he sought, but his solution to that problem was the traditional one of hierarchical order. This would be the source of a fundamental paradox in *The Cantos*: for while the long poem was structured around lyric "bust thru"'s from the demotic turmoil of "history," in that sense privileging the "soft" moments of lyric epiphany, these were increasingly to be found earning their place through association with the "harder" ideological truths that drove the poem forward (Pound 1971, 210). We may again recall Bakhtin's notion of "participative" thinking:

> Everything that is actually experienced is experienced as something given and as something-yet-to-be-determined, is intonated, has an emotional-volitional tone, and enters into an effective relationship to me within the unity of the ongoing event encompassing us. An emotional-volitional tone is an inalienable moment of the actually performed act, even of the most abstract thought, insofar as I am actually thinking it, i.e., insofar as it is really actualized in Being, becomes a participant in the ongoing event. (1993, 33)

Bakhtin's way of linking "intonation" to the present tense of a thought taking shape thus opposes any view of thinking that understands its objects as merely "representative of a certain large whole" (1993, 53).

The Cantos – and particularly its late sequences, *Rock-Drill* and *Thrones* – exemplifies both modes: extended incantatory passages present the vision "Taking form now, / the rilievi, / the curled stone at the marge / Faunus, sirene, the stone taking form in the air . . . ," the language dominated by participles and deictics and by an allusive echoing of items from earlier Cantos; complementing this mode are "harder," more expository passages where Pound is working up his source material, often moving passages from his notebooks directly into the text (1996, 627–628). We have already noted the instability of the "hard"/"soft" dichotomy, but in the case of *The Cantos* this antithetical pairing undergoes a fundamental reversal: as the political framing of the poem comes more sharply into focus, so "hardness" begins to attach itself to apparently incontestable ideological "verities," while "softness" connotes a mythic, pre-political world where "musical" values hold sway. Take, for example, the difference between two passages, the first from Canto CVII where Pound is drawing on the *Institutes* of the English jurist Edward Coke:

> Each wench to a pillar
> "as do the Serjeants at lawe"
> To use grain for food only;
> build no more houses in London
> de heretico comburendo

> Bacon for, Coke opposing.
> In a white sheet in the Savoy
>   500 marks, be imprisoned
>   Sir Henry (1628) Martin gave sentence. (1996, 781)

The lines nod to the prostitutes plying their trade in the Inns of Court ("Each wench to a pillar"), noting Coke's opposition to the burning of heretics ("de heretico comburendo"), and so on. But the writing is increasingly turning in on itself, and almost literally so, as Pound habitually inverts the propositional logic of his broken phrases. Note the lines beginning "In a white sheet in the Savoy . . . ": this is classic late Pound, unsettling the reader by beginning at the end of the story, folding back bit by bit, but never quite getting to the heart of the matter. Here, for example, we can see – but not until two lines later – that Sir Henry Martin sentenced someone to wear a white sheet in the Savoy, but for some reason Pound won't tell us that this is Frances, Coke's legendarily beautiful daughter, who, as punishment for adultery, was ordered to walk barefoot in a white sheet from Paul's Cross to the Savoy church in the Strand (Bowen 1957, 457–458). Compare now the lines that close the same Canto:

> So that Dante's view is quite natural;
>   this light
>   as a river
>   in Kung; in Ocellus, Coke, Agassiz
>   ῥεῖ, the flowing
>   this persistent awareness
> Three Ninas from Gaudier
>   Their mania is a lusting for farness
>   Blind to the olive leaf,
>   not seeing the oak's veins
>   Wheat was in bread in the old days
>   (1.46 after mid-night)
>   Alan Upward's seal showed Sitalkas.
>   Coin was in Ambracia;
> The caelator's son, named Pythagora. (1996, 782–783)

Here Pound evokes again the Dantescan clarity celebrated at the opening of Canto CVII and this is now associated not with the narcotic movements of the earlier "underwave" sequence (781) but with a more purposive "flowing." Coke is placed alongside Kung, the mystic Ocellus, and the scientist Louis Agassiz, and here the "persistent awareness" opposes any "lusting for farness" or transcendence, directing attention to natural detail, to the quality of bread and the god of wheat, Sitalkas, and finally to an ancient coinage apparently touched by the mystical, the Pythagorean (783). These last lines render the sought-after "awareness" as a core wisdom of *The Cantos* in its disclosure of the spiritual in the quotidian. Elliptical this passage may be, but it clearly reaffirms a commitment to accurate perception that Pound finds equally active in Coke's exposition of the common law and in the clarity of vision that remains attentive to the veins in the oak leaf.

More could be said about these closing lines, mainly, I think, because we are dealing here with a poetics of allusion and not simply with direct reference to a source, as in most of Pound's dealings with the text of the *Institutes*. What complicates matters at this late stage in the poem is that he seems to have become increasingly conflicted about that referential move, on the one hand wanting the reader to follow his trail back to Coke's text, while on the other investing in a dream of his own poem's self-sufficiency, in its capacity to serve as indeed "a portable substitute for the British Museum" (1968a, 16).[7] Does this explain why the pull of Pound's text toward a prior one is increasingly fraught with contradiction, as he at once belabors his readers to go back to the source and at the same time deliberately obstructs their passage to it? Envisaged as a "substitute," *The Cantos* exemplifies a logic of supplementarity according to which the source text is at once valued as origin *and* seen as somehow lacking, as requiring the Poundian text aesthetically to complete it.[8] That may explain the way in which quotation and citation seem to honor their original even as, arguably, they *dis*honor it by their deformation and decontextualization of its constituent elements. That doubleness seems to haunt the movement of reference here, the backward turn demanded of the reader finding almost parodic expression in the fondness for inversion already noticed in the "white sheet in the Savoy" lines. At the same time, though, as we can see from the final lines of Canto CVII, when Pound's lines allude rather than simply refer, the poem acquires a forward-moving, propulsive energy that can connect and extend thoughts and images previously established in the poem. As William Irwin (2001) notes in one of the rare technical discussions of allusion, the device "is reference that is indirect in requiring more than the mere substitution of a referent" (288). This "more" that takes us beyond the backward movement of reference, with its locked binary of text and source, is, I would suggest, prosodic, a rhythm of allusive thinking which gathers up its materials into new and independent wholes. This, perhaps, is the authentic "supplement" to Pound's various sources, something that, by the nature of the case, they themselves generally lack; and it is precisely what struck William Carlos Williams (1969), whose fine grasp of Pound's early prosody reminds us poignantly of what struggles to survive in Canto CVII:

. . . the material is so molded that it is changed in *kind* from other statement. It is a *sort* beyond measure.

The measure is an inevitability, an unavoidable accessory after the fact. If one move, if one run, if one seizes up a material – it cannot avoid having a measure, it cannot avoid a movement which clings to it – as the movement of a horse becomes a part of the rider also –

That is the way Pound's verse impresses me and why he can include pieces of prose and have them still part of a *poem*. It is incorporated in a movement of the intelligence which is special, beyond usual thought and action –[9] (108; his emphases)

Williams emphasizes here the way in which a certain "measure" of thinking allows a whole range of disparate materials ("pieces of prose") to be caught up into the rhythmic articulation of the poem. What is "theoretical," in Bakhtin's sense – the product of "a fundamental abstraction from the fact of my unique being" (1993, 9) – is transformed into poetry by what Pound (1968a) had much earlier described as an "absolute rhythm": "A man's rhythm must be interpretative, it will be, therefore, in the end, his own, uncounterfeiting, uncounterfeitable" (9). Perhaps, then, poetry in its confrontation with politics must of necessity prove "soft" and allusive in the sense outlined above; at least its constituent elements must be more than just metonymic references to what Bakhtin calls dismissively "a certain large whole," offering instead an alternative language to that of the "hard" discourse of pedagogical and political power. Pound, it appears, both saw and did not see this, finding himself in the late reaches of his long poem caught in an oscillation between a "soft" hermetic language protective of the essential "mysteries" and an ostentatiously "hard" and self-consciously non-poetic one that tended to reproduce the violence and coerciveness of the social injustices he meant to attack ("that slobbering bugger Jim First / bitched our heritage," "In 33 years Noll cut down Charlie," etc. [1996, 777]).

The problem posed by *The Cantos* and by Pound's career generally would leave its mark on the work of younger modernist poets. As if by direct reaction, it would become almost an article of faith for them that the thought articulated in a poem should have no antecedent occasion. George Oppen (1990): "there must be no possible impression of a statement having been *put* into verse" (104; his emphasis); Robert Duncan (Duncan and Levertov 2004): "the material of a poem is not brought into it but native to it. Any material gives rise to a poem when you start 'making' in the material, seeking its inherent creative form" (545); Louis Zukofsky (1931): "Writing occurs which is the detail, not mirage, of seeing, of thinking with the things as they exist, and of directing them along a line of melody" (273). Each of these declarations comes with a slightly different inflection, but each in its way seeks to distinguish poetry from what we might call the moment of "theory," associating this last with "disembodied" thinking and with, in a word, the political.

The tension that has gathered in the later phase of modernism around the political entailments of poetry or its necessary freedom from them can be focused in a vivid exchange of letters between Robert Duncan and Denise Levertov. Beginning in the mid-50s, it is a voluminous and largely affectionate correspondence, each poet discovering in the other a generous and like-minded interlocutor. With the intensification of the Vietnam War, however, the two writers found their work compelled in very different directions. Both, of course, were objectors to the war, but while, in Duncan's view, the "hardness" of Levertov's response issued in mere stridency of tone and empty moralizing, Duncan himself, in the words of one critic, "treats historical actualities as the evolution of myth . . . on the other, he writes the historical as an *incarnation* of eternal forms" (Nichols 2010, 120; see also Perloff 1998). For Duncan, Levertov's work gives up on "poetry's potential to create new meaning by insisting on the urgency of the historical here and now" (135).

Potentiality is placed over against actuality:[10] once again, the argument is not about a particular stance toward the war but rather (as Duncan sets the terms of debate) about a conception of poetry; so he writes to her in March 1972:

> . . . I was attempting to define your not believing in the primary meaning of the art of the poem itself, but more and more thinking of the poem as communication of meanings whose primacy was posited outside the art, in "Life" or social realities, causes that had clear and urgent priorities. (701)

Through the twists and turns of this increasingly troubled exchange, Duncan insists on his distinction between "the idea of the poem as revelation, as primary knowledge of the truth of things – and of the poem as a vehicle for personal, social, political or religious convictions" (687). As with Pound's "hard"/"soft" distinction, there is a sexual politics behind this argument: rather absurdly casting Levertov as the savage goddess Kali "whirling her necklace of skulls" in a 1971 poem called "Santa Cruz Propositions" (in Duncan 1984), Duncan began to read works like her "Life at War" and "Tenebrae" not as primarily responses to the conflict in Vietnam "but in relation to the deep underlying consciousness of the woman as a victim in war with the Man" (Duncan and Levertov 667). Already offended by this high-handed "psychoanalytic" reading of her work, Levertov was even more shocked by Duncan's remarks in an interview published three years later (Mersmann 1974, 94) describing her attitude to the war as governed by "her own sadism, and masochism" ("the poem is not a protest though she thinks she's protesting"). Levertov concluded that "our friendship [is] twice broken, deeply betrayed" (711).

As the two poets' relationship unravels through these letters we begin to see with increasing clarity that two very different conceptions of poetry and poetic language are at issue. Levertov (1992) dissociates herself from the "field" poetics of Duncan, Creeley, and Olson – "Form is never more than the REVELATION (not extension) of content, " she argues (Duncan and Levertov, 680) – and imagines instead that as "the poet stands open-mouthed in the temple of life, contemplating his experience, there come to him the first words of the poem: the words which are to be his way in to the poem, if there is to be a poem" (Levertov 1992, 68–9).[11] This moment of contemplative mediation is absent from Duncan's sense of the poem's origin: "we do not say something by means of the poem but the poem itself is the immediacy of the saying" (668), and while he frequently returns to Pound's dictum that "Great literature is simply language charged with meaning to the utmost possible degree" (1968b, 36), this "charge" involves something quite different from the semantic "condensation" Pound had sought, signaling for Duncan the possibility of "rhythmic and tonal seizure": "In that charge there are meanings we are not prepared for. Language so charged is not simple, it is multiphasic. And there is a sinister, a duplicit, possibility in the charge" (Duncan 1985, 126; see also Mackey 2005, 131). Duncan may follow Pound in reading H. D.'s work as "hard" – "Her art, and her sense of the passionate, demanded figures of feeling, exactness, that was not soft and compliant but hard and resistant" (Duncan 2011, 51) – but what also especially impressed him was something Pound did not or chose not to see: in Mackey's words, "her openness to and her giving in to feelings that might be criticized as uncalled for, inappropriate, excessive" (2005, 10). H. D.'s work, then, might not be stylistically "soft," but its particular "hardness" expresses an emotional release that was quite at odds with the restraint Pound valued; in Duncan's words, "Language suddenly runs loose, out of bounds, and so does knowledge" (Duncan 1985, 128).

In contrast, Levertov's war poetry is seen by Duncan as shackled to the very language it should displace: there is, he says, "something wrong to my sense of life in urging the conscience to take up arms against the war" (608) and his letters repeatedly argue against any tendency to make "war against war" (661). This was the cause of his later dissatisfaction with his own long poem "Essay At War" – "Give over trying to win thru the poem," he admonished himself (565) – though parts of that work did indeed argue for a deliberate taking of distance from a "war-like" language:

> The war is a mineral perfection, clear,
> unambiguous evil   within which
> our delite, our life,   is the flaw,
> the contradiction? (Duncan 1968, 23)

Like fine marble, war is "perfect," as is the language deployed in its name, a language that operates to settle all contradictions "unambiguously" (elsewhere Duncan quotes from Levertov's "Staying Alive" a statement by an American general that "In order to save the village it was necessary to destroy it" [Duncan and Levertov 2004, 664]). The false "perfection" Duncan considers in the poem may recall Roland Barthes's account of the tautological closure that is the temptation of all political speech:

> In the Stalinist world, in which *definition*, that is to say the separation between Good and Evil, becomes the sole content of all language, there are no more words without values attached to them, so that finally the function of writing is to cut out one stage of a process: there is no more lapse of time between naming and judging, and the closed character of language is perfected, since in the last analysis it is a value which is given as explanation of another value. (Barthes 1968, 24; his emphasis)

This language has no place for what Duncan's poem calls "our life," and it is, of course, precisely that life and the "delite" we may take in it that threaten to produce a fundamental "flaw" or fissure in the otherwise "unambiguous" logic of war.[12] Here as elsewhere Duncan's anachronistic spelling registers the pathos of historical distance, but as the poem's declarative mode shifts abruptly into an interrogative one, so the tone of the lines rises unexpectedly from elegy to defiance.

For all this, Duncan's posture may strike us, perhaps, as damagingly abstract and aloof, and as Michael Davidson has recently put it, the poet's "tendency to mythologize the war seems, by current standards, inadequate" (2011, 175).[13] On the other hand, that maneuver is deliberate and underwritten by a conviction that "The poet's role is not to oppose evil, but to imagine it" (Duncan and Levertov 2004, 669). It is in the language of such imagining that Duncan sees the way beyond both the circularity of the state's war-speak and the "political stance" of Levertov's war poems ("These, Denny, are empty and vain slogans because those who use them are destitute of any imagination of or feeling of what such greed, racism or imperialism is like" [Duncan and Levertov 669]). Duncan's charge of mere sloganizing hardly represents the whole truth about Levertov's sometimes moving and galvanizing war poetry, but once again it gestures toward what he regards as a damaging division between "theory" and the purpose of poetry.

That criticism can be heard again in George Oppen's letters to Levertov where he takes particular exception to a poem in *The Jacob's Ladder* (1961), "During the Eichmann Trial," which includes the lines "we are members // One of another." Oppen remarks: "I think too that we are members of each other: – I believe that;...or would like to...but what a poem it would be in which one saw and tasted that!" (1990, 81). Like Duncan, Oppen regrets the loss of the sensory immediacy that characterized much of Levertov's earlier work. He has particular praise for her poem "Matins" in his 1962 essay "The Mind's Own Place" (2003, 176), but it is there that he also castigates what he sees as her new way of making the poem a vehicle for political statement: "the poet's business," he declares, "is not to use verse as an advanced form of rhetoric, nor to give to political statements the aura of eternal truth" (2003, 182). The criticism is similar to Duncan's; indeed, when Levertov showed him Oppen's letter, Duncan commented: "I'm as leery of approved social, political, religious sentiments as ever Oppen might be" (Duncan and Levertov 2004, 404). Yet while they share a wariness of poetry as a vehicle for political belief, Duncan and Oppen disagree as to how the poet should then react to the problematic divergence between poetry and social commitment. Duncan cleaves to a "mystical pacifism" (1985, 115) that resists the closure of a damaged political language by according the poet a bardic "power" far in excess of mere moralism; Oppen, interestingly, takes a quite opposite path, seeking, as he puts it in "Song, the Winds of Downhill," a poetry "impoverished // of tone of pose that common / wealth of parlance" (2008, 220). This is a poetry "which may be sung / may well be sung," but its expression of what he calls in another poem "The lyric valuables" (2008, 50) is won by a kind of literary asceticism. Indeed, the stripped-down style of Oppen's late work, with its eschewal of punctuation and visual imagery, constitutes, perhaps, a kind of "poor" poetry (by analogy with Jerzy Grotowski's "Poor Theatre") where all signs of a conventional literariness must be expunged. Oppen is not, of course, the only artist to take the path of deliberate verbal "impoverishment": we think, for example, of Paul Celan, or of Samuel Beckett who reserved special praise for the painter Bram van Velde as "the first whose painting is bereft, rid if you prefer, of *occasion* in every shape and form, ideal as well as material, and the first whose hands have not been tied by the certitude that expression is an impossible act" (2006, 561; his emphasis). Beckett's "occasion" is Oppen's "pose": in each case we are dealing with what Leo Bersani and Ulysse Dutoit have defined in their account of *The Arts of Impoverishment* as "an art at war with culture," a pithy phrase that has several possible meanings – it might imply that art exists in opposition to the ensemble of social practices that provides its generative context, but it also suggests that art is at war with art, a proposition that expresses the dissatisfaction the avant-garde has consistently felt with the pretensions of something we may call, by way of distinction, the "merely" aesthetic (1993, 2).

That "merely" points up the problem, of course, namely that the capacity of the arts to effect social change appears thoroughly incommensurable with the entrenched powers of what Oppen calls "an enemy world" (1990, 409 n.25). This is why he insists in "The Mind's Own Place" that "There are situations which cannot honorably be met by art, and surely no one need fiddle precisely at the moment that the house next door is burning" (2003, 181). It is not just incommensurability that is the issue here, but the fact that to carry on "fiddling" (or making art) while the fire rages is to act *dishonorably* by invoking aesthetic values in a situation in which properly they have no place. At the same time, he continues, "It is possible that a world without art is simply and flatly uninhabitable, and the poet's business is not to use verse as an advanced form of rhetoric, nor to give to political statements the aura of eternal truth" (182). What Oppen seems to mean is that we cannot do without art and for that reason we must not damage its capacity to make the world habitable by reducing it to a vehicle for "political statements." "The poet," Oppen concludes, "speaking as a poet, declares his political non-availability," a declaration that, in contrast to Duncan's handling of this question, discovers in a necessary "impoverishment" the means by which to evade a writing caught up in the toils of both the "merely" aesthetic *and* the "merely" political. As is well known, while Oppen was involved in the practical politics of the Left he stopped writing poetry altogether, refusing, as he put it, to write "Marxist poetry" (1990, 277). That decision seemed to him a necessary one because in the radical climate of the period, politics and art were increasingly being drawn into a reciprocal and instrumental relation, art becoming political, of course, but politics in its turn becoming, in a peculiar sense, a kind of "art." Mary Oppen recalled that "even the vocabulary within the Party was a different vocabulary than I had known" [1978, 153]), and in a poem called "Eclogue," Oppen alludes to the endless committee meetings in which that particular "vocabulary" was forged – "The men talking / Near the room's center . . . Pinpointing in the uproar / Of the living room // An assault on the quiet continent" (2008, 39). This "talking" – Heidegger's *Gerede* or "babble," which Oppen would frequently invoke – is the "uproar" of what Bakhtin calls "theory." "There are words that mean nothing," Oppen declares in the poem called "The Building of the Skyscraper" (2008, 149), and there are also ways of talking and writing that amount to little more than the empty self-legitimation of which Barthes speaks in *Writing Degree Zero*.

That sense of tautological "closure" would become oppressively evident to Oppen in the war-speak of the Vietnam period, a "ferocious mumbling, in public / Of rootless speech" (2008, 173). With "Insanity in high places," it is not only that political discourse withdraws into seamless circularity, but that the very possibility of the political disappears, in "A plume of smoke, visible at a distance / In which people burn" (173). As Oppen puts it in "Of Being Numerous," "They await // War, and the news / Is war // As always"; this perpetual war, sealed into its own self-justifying *mythos*, is the consequence of an ethical impoverishment so colossal that it compels the poet to discover a completely different vocabulary of critique and protest (174). As Duncan concludes:

> If our manner of speech has come, as it has, to be so much a cover that for the sake of freedom men are drafted against their will; for the sake of peace, armed men and tanks fight in our streets; and for the sake of the good life, the resources of our land are ruthlessly wasted, and waterways and air polluted, then we need a new manner of speaking. (1985, 119)

For Duncan, this new speech will scrupulously dissociate itself from the language of power and domination, not by some simple swerve into a compensatory aestheticism – though this is an ever-present risk, given the extreme hermeticism of much of his work – but by the revealing of a mythic power in speech itself. Hence this argument against Levertov's concept of "organic form":

> Where "organic" poetry refers to personal emotions and impressions – the concourse between organism and his world; the linguistic follows emotions and images that appear in the language itself as a third "world"; true to what is happening in the syntax as another man might be true to what he sees or feels. (Duncan and Levertov 2004, 408)

As Albert Gelpi (2006) has noted, Duncan's "linguistic gnosticism" – "language as the source and means, the substance and end of the poet's special knowing" – predicts in some ways the emergence of Language Poetry in the 1980s (186). Poets associated with that tendency have had little time, of course, for the mystical theories that attach to Duncan's particular "search for a poetry that has not come to a conclusion," though it might be argued that the new experimental poetry is itself in varying degrees dependent on an absent theoretical ground of which it is, tacitly, the designedly opaque verbal figure or instance (1985, 114).

The direction taken by Oppen in his later work is significantly different and points to a way in which poetry might transform the political into something resistant to the abstracting pull of "theory." The deliberately "impoverished" manner of Oppen's later poems is "hard," perhaps, in its refusal of ornamentation and fluent musicality, but this particular "hardness" expresses a fundamental resistance to what Oppen calls "a ruined ethic // Bursting with ourselves" (2008, 98). Pound's distinction between "hard" and "soft" becomes a kind of irrelevance here, with poetry grasped instead as a means of eliding thinking and being: "Prosody: the pulse of thought, of consciousness, therefore, in Heidegger's word, of human *Dasein*, human 'being there'" (Oppen, unpublished note, quoted in Nicholls 2007, 72); as he puts it in "World, World –," "We want to be here. // The act of being, the act of being / More than oneself" (159). The ontological desire "to be here" – here in the world and in the world of the poem – is underwritten throughout by Oppen's near-death experience in the Battle of the Bulge, an experience that places enormous pressure on any idea of "the lyric valuables":

> And war.
>
> More than we felt or saw.
> There is a simple ego in a lyric,
> A strange one in war.
> To a body anything can happen,
> Like a brick. Too obvious to say.
> But all horror came from it. (53)

This reduction of self to body and ultimately to mere thing, a brick, underlies the degradation of the political in Oppen's thinking. In the "half life" of war, he writes in another poem, "We crawled everywhere on the ground without seeing the earth again" (81). This image of debasement strikingly brings to mind Giorgio Agamben's account of "the radical transformation of politics into the realm of bare life" (1998, 120) and it registers, too, Oppen's countervailing attempt to translate the prescriptive categories of the political into the qualitative ones of social being.[14] Agamben puts it like this: "There is in effect something that humans are and have to be, but this something is not an essence nor properly a thing: *It is the simple fact of one's own existence as possibility or potentiality*" (1993, 43; his emphases). Being-political, then, gestures not to some kind of transcendental relation but to one of immanence that is expressed not in terms of subject and object, of essence and thing, but rather as life and potentiality. "Life" as conceived here exceeds the individual life and compels the poet toward a lyric register that rigorously rejects any unearned sublimity.[15] If this is a "hard" modernism, it is one that is hard on itself, discovering "possibility or potentiality" in the condition of its own formal "impoverishment."

Oppen's ambitious attempt to transform the political by poetic means and thereby to rescue it from the condition of "theory" can be seen in the first section of his late serial work "The Book of Job and A Draft of a Poem to Praise the Paths of the Living" (2008, 240–246).[16] The poem is dedicated to Mickey Schwerner, one of three Civil Rights workers murdered by Klan members in Philadelphia, Mississippi in 1964. Schwerner, James Chaney, and Andrew Goodman suffer the fate of Job in their subjection to a meaningless and vindictive force; their murderers, like God in the biblical story, reveal the law in all its arbitrariness and violence. This "force" is at the poem's enigmatic center and in his late writings Oppen constantly associates it with Blake's "burning" Tyger, a principle of both creation and wrathful destruction. Force opposes force: the strength of "the half-lit jailwinds" at the beginning of the poem is met by the "morning's force" that names the three young men, this collision producing a sequence of apocalyptic images punctuated by "hard" caesural breaks. The tone is one of anger, though Oppen scrupulously forgoes the consolations of a rhetorical identification with the victims ("not we / who were beaten"), proposing instead that the sincerity of their actions unleashes a "force" that somehow illuminates reality and gives purpose to "the paths of the living." It is the same "force" that in the biblical story finally compels God to answer Job:

> there builds there is written
> a vividness   there is   rawness
> like a new sun the flames
> tremendous the sun
> itself ourselves ourselves
> go with us *disorder*
>
> *so great the tumult wave*
>
> *upon wave* this traverse
>
> this desert   extravagant
> *island of light*   (2008, 241)

The poem as a whole is, as Oppen noted in a letter, "startling in view of the number of quotes," though these are "Quotes from memory" and he is offhand about sources ("I'd made myself a list of the references, but seem to have lost it") because his fragmentary borrowings have been fully assimilated or interiorized into the texture of the poem (1990, 264). [17] In his late works, Oppen indicates partial quotation by using italic, though this signaling is not necessarily meant to encourage us to trace their source. If we do detect an echo of another text, Oppen has usually rewritten it or presented it in a teasingly elliptical form.[18] So the lines above seem to recall Kafka's gnomic parable "The Savages" ("Die Wilden"):

> Those savages of whom it is recounted that they have no other longing than to die, or rather, they no longer have even that longing, but death has a longing for them, and they abandon themselves to it, or rather, they do not even abandon themselves, but fall into the sand on the shore and never get up again. Those savages I much resemble, and indeed I have fellow clansmen round about, but *the confusion in these territories is so great, the tumult is like waves rising and falling by day and by night, and the brothers let themselves be borne upon it.* (Kafka 1958, 121; my emphases)

Oppen's attention may have been drawn to this passage by the translation of Kafka's "Stammesbrüder" as "clansmen," and certainly the image of self-abandonment to the deathly "tumult" speaks grimly, if obliquely, to the racism of the Southern "lynch gangs" and the self-hatred it conceals (Kafka's parable ends with the exclamation: "How people do always carry their own enemy, however powerless he is, within themselves").[19] And while the "savages" desire only death, "life in all its might would go on just the same." It is difficult to determine the value attaching to life, "this barrel organ," in Kafka's text,[20] but the rising of "a new sun" in Oppen's lines signals less equivocally that something in the very frame of things – in life itself – will ensure that the poor and the weak exert some equivalent "force" against their oppressors: "the ant / hath her anger and the emmet / his choler."[21] It is this anger which blazes out as a "general Vengeance" in this first section of the poem and which is reaffirmed in the final line "*island of light*," probably an allusion to Hölderlin's celebration of the island of Patmos where John, author of *Revelation*, was exiled.[22] Apocalyptic revelation haunts these lines, though that which stands ready to be revealed is implicitly nothing more nor less than being itself. What is remarkable about the whole passage is, finally, its avoidance of conventional ways of confronting the political violence that is its subject: it is not, in any simple way, elegiac, nor is it straightforwardly a poem of protest or even complaint. Nor, again, does it express a facile acceptance, that these are just "*the world's deeds*" (2008, 240).[23] Neither "hard" nor "soft," in Pound's sense, the passage offers contradiction in place of antithesis, finding in the "rawness" of political tragedy a "vividness" that transforms a desert into an "*island of light*." As Oppen put it in a richly enigmatic note, this is, indeed, to discover a poetics of being at "the edge of despair, the edge of the void, a paean of praise to the world" (quoted Nicholls 2007, 192).

Notes

1   See, for example, Oppen 2003, 175.

2   See Nicholls 2012.

3   Eliot, of course, famously considered Pound's unoriginality one of his principal strengths – see Eliot 1928, 10–11.

4   It is thought that Bakhtin worked on this text between 1920 and 1924 (Bakhtin 1993, xxiii). The work was not published until 1986. For a brief but helpful account, see Rabaté 2002.

5   For a general objection to this conception of the performative, see Derrida 1978, 18: "Could a performative utterance succeed if its formulation did not repeat a 'coded' or iterable utterance . . . ?"

6   Cf. Lewis 1986, 30: "the life of the crowd, of the common or garden man, is exterior. He can live only through others, outside himself."

7   Pound similarly described his plan for Guide to Kulchur in an unpublished letter (1937) to Faber and Faber's Frank Morley: "Wot Ez knows, or a substitute (portable) for the British Museum" (quoted in Paul 2005, 65).

8   See Derrida, 1978, 212: "The supplement, which seems to be added as a plenitude to a plenitude, is equally that which compensates for a lack (*qui supplée*)." As Paul 2005, 73 notes, by the late 1930s "Pound rejects his older method of letting quoted text speak for itself." What then matters increasingly is "Not the document but the significance of the document" (Pound 1966, 220–221).

9   Cf. Duncan and Levertov 2004, 163: "he [Pound] does not need poetic 'touches,' when the lyric and melodic occurs it is inherent in the statement."

10   Cf. Duncan 1985, 117 on Dante's concept of the "potential intellect."

11   See also Levertov 1992, 213–214 where she disputes Duncan's reading of her essay "Notes on Organic Form": "I mean 'discoverable' quite precisely – not 'that which comes into being only in the work' but that which, though present in a dim unrecognized or

ungrasped way, is only experienced in any degree of fullness in art's concreteness" (emphases in original). See also Gelpi 2006, 188 noting that Levertov "resolutely maintained Emerson's distinction (in his essay on 'The Poet') between the creative process and the resulting poem: 'the thought and the form are equal in order of time, but in the order of genesis the thought is prior to the form.'"

12   See Duncan and Levertov 2004, 661: "men at war against war are hypocrites if they argue that there can be no peaceful ways in a time of war. THERE HAS BEEN NO TIME IN HUMAN HISTORY THAT WAS NOT A TIME OF WAR. And any peaceful ways and deeds of peace have had to be created in the face of the need for war – for war against oppression, for war against injustice, etc."

13   Davidson concludes, however: "I find myself in agreement with Duncan on the limits of Levertov's war poetry. Levertov's work of the late 1960s is pious and doctrinaire, often relying on a rhetoric of indignation and anger to deal with impossible contradictions."

14   Oren Izenberg has noted this distinction, though his general argument moves in a rather different direction from mine: "A radical poetics . . . is not radical for its political commitments but for its pre-political or ontological commitments" (35).

15   See Agamben 1999, 224 on Gilles Deleuze's conception of life as "not belonging to a subject."

16   For an extended reading of this important work, see Nicholls 2007, 162–179.

17   In some cases, Oppen's unpublished notes provide a revealing context for particular passages. In this case, the references to "rawness," "vividness," and the sun recall an account of reading Heidegger – see Nicholls 2007, 66.

18   Compare poet Michael Palmer's account of his own practice: "Occasionally I'll appropriate a source verbatim, but often it will be slightly or radically altered. It becomes altered by the impetus of the poem itself, the demands of the rhythm, the surrounding material, whatever. And so it's not a quotation, exactly. It's a form of citation, but it's layered, covered over" (Palmer 1999, 286).

19   The translators ignore the incomplete sentence with which the original concludes: "On this account, on account of this powerless enemy, they are . . . ."

20   See Anidjar 2003, 155: "No doubt 'The Savages' is a parable in which absolute loss lets nothing, no eternity or law, maintain its transcendence. The impossibility of distinguishing whether eternity is a figure for the player of life or whether it is stowed away in a crowded attic among unused flags and abandoned instruments – or both – indicates that what remains is life itself, 'life in all its might,' which is the only life we have."

21   The allusion is, unexpectedly, to a letter from Sir Francis Drake to Queen Elizabeth I: "There is a general Vengeance," Drake says, "which secretly pursueth the doers of wrong and suffereth them not to prosper. . . . For as ESOP teacheth, even the fly hath her spleen, and the emmet is not without her choler; and both together many times find means whereby, though the eagle lays her eggs in JUPITER's lap, yet by one way or other, she escapeth not requital of her wrong done [to] the emmet. (Eliot 1910, 133; my emphases)

22   See Hölderlin 1994, 501: "O island of light!"

23   The phrase may also echo the earlier version of "Patmos" (Hölderlin, 1994, 495): "lightning is explained by / The deeds of the world until now . . . ."

References

Agamben, Giorgio. (1993). *The Coming Community*, trans. Michael Hardt. Minneapolis: University of Minnesota Press.

Agamben, Giorgio. (1998). *Homo Sacer: Sovereign Power and Bare Life*, trans. Daniel Heller-Roazen. Stanford: Stanford University Press.

Agamben, Giorgio. (1999). *Potentialities: Collected Essays in Philosophy*, ed. and trans. Daniel Heller-Roazen. Stanford: Stanford University Press.

Al-Kassim, Dina. (2010). *On Pain of Speech*. Los Angeles: University of California Press.

Anidjar, Gil. (2003). *The Jew, The Arab: A History of the Enemy*. Stanford: Stanford University Press.

Bakhtin, M. M. (1993). *Toward a Philosophy of the Act*, ed. Michael Holquist and Vadim Laipunov, trans. Vadim Laipunov. Austin: University of Texas Press.

Barthes, Roland. (1968). *Writing Degree Zero*, trans. Annette Lavers and Colin Smith. Hill and Wang.New York:

Beckett, Samuel. (2006). *Samuel Beckett: The Grove Centenary Edition*, 4 vols, ed. Paul Auster. Vol. IV: *Poems, Short Fiction, Criticism*. New York: Grove Press.

Bersani, Leo and Ulysse Dutoit. (1993). *The Arts of Impoverishment: Beckett, Rothko, Resnais*. Cambridge, MA: Harvard University Press.

Bowen, Catherine Drinker. (1957). *The Lion and the Throne: The Life and Times of Sir Edward Coke 1552–1634*. London: Hamish Hamilton.

Davidson, Michael. (2011). *On the Outskirts of Form: Practicing Cultural Poetics*. Middletown, CT: Wesleyan University Press.

Derrida, Jacques. (1978). *Writing and Difference.*, trans Alan Bass.London: Routledge & Kegan Paul.

Derrida, Jacques. (1988). "Signature, Event, Context." In *Limited Inc.*, ed. Gerald Graff, trans. Samuel Weber and Jeffrey Mehlman. Evanston, IL: Northwestern University Press.

Duncan, Robert. (1968). *Derivations: Selected Poems 1950–1956*. London: Fulcrum Press.

Duncan, Robert. (1984). *Ground Work: Before the War*. New York: New Directions.

Duncan, Robert. (1985). *Fictive Certainties: Essays*. New York: New Directions.

Duncan, Robert. (2011). *The H. D. Book*, ed. and intro. Michael Boughn and Victor Coleman. Berkeley: University of California Press.

Duncan, Robert and Denise Levertov. (2004). *The Letters of Robert Duncan and Denise Levertov, ed.* Robert J. Bertholf and Albert Gelpi. Stanford: Stanford University Press.

Eliot, Charles W., ed. (1910). *Voyages and Travels, Ancient and Modern*. New York: Collier & Son.

Eliot, T. S. (1928). "Introduction: 1928." In Ezra Pound, *Selected Poems* (pp. 7–21). London: Faber and Gwyer.

Gelpi, Albert. (2006). "Poetic Language and Language Poetry." In Albert Gelpi and Robert J. Bertholf, eds, *Robert Duncan and Denise Levertov: The Poetry of Politics and the Politics of Poetry* (pp. 180–198). Stanford: Stanford University Press.

Hölderlin, Friedrich. (1994). *Poems and Fragments*, trans. Michael Hamburger. London: Anvil Press Poetry Ltd.

Irwin, William. (2001). "What Is an Allusion?" *Journal of Aesthetics and Art Criticism*, 59.3: 287–297.

Izenberg, Oren. (2011). *Being Numerous: Poetry and the Ground of Social Life*. Princeton, NJ: Princeton University Press.

Kafka, Franz. (1958). *Parables and Paradoxes*. New York: Schocken Books.

Kenner, Hugh. (1988). *A Sinking Island: The Modern English Writers*. London: Barrie & Jenkins.

Levertov, Denise. (1992). *New & Selected Essays*. New York: New Directions.

Lewis, Wyndham. (1984). *Rude Assignment*, ed. Toby Foshay. Santa Barbara, CA: Black Sparrow Press.

Lewis, Wyndham. (1987). *Men Without Art*, ed. Seamus Cooney. Santa Rosa, CA: Black Sparrow Press.

Lewis, Wyndham. (1990). *Tarr: The 1918 Version*, ed. Paul O'Keefe. Santa Rosa, CA: Black Sparrow Press.

Lewis, Wyndham. (1993). *Time and Western Man*, ed. Paul Edwards. Santa Rosa, CA: Black Sparrow Press.

Mackey, Nathaniel. (2005). *Paracritical Hinge: Essays, Talks, Notes, Interviews*. Madison: University of Wisconsin Press.

Mersmann, James. (1974). *Out of the Vietnam Vortex: A Study of Poets and Poetry against the War*. Lawrence: University Press of Kansas.

Nichols, Miriam. (2010). *Radical Affections: Essays on the Poetics of Outside*. Tuscaloosa: University of Alabama Press.

Nicholls, Peter. (2007). *George Oppen and the Fate of Modernism*. Oxford: Oxford University Press.

Nicholls, Peter. (forthcoming, 2013). "Bravura or Bravado? Reading Pound's *Cantos*." In *Modernism and Masculinity*, ed. Natalya Lusty and Julian Murphet. Cambridge: Cambridge University Press.

Oppen, George. (1990). *The Selected Letters of George Oppen*, ed. Rachel Blau DuPlessis. Durham, NC: Duke University Press.

Oppen, George. (2003). *Selected Poems*, ed. and intro. Robert Creeley. New York: New Directions.

Oppen, George. (2008). *New Collected Poems, ed.* Michael Davidson. New York: New Directions.

Oppen, Mary. (1978). *Meaning a Life: An Autobiography*. Santa Barbara, CA: Black Sparrow Press.

Palmer, Michael. (1999). "Interview." In *Regions of Strangeness*, ed. Thomas Gardner. Lincoln: University of Nebraska Press.

Paul, Catherine. (2005). "Italian Fascist Exhibitions and Ezra Pound's Move to the Imperial." *Twentieth-Century Literature*, 51.1: 64–99.

Perloff, Marjorie. (1998). "Poetry in time of War: The Duncan–Levertov Controversy." In *Poetry On & Off the Page: Essays for Emergent Occasions*. Evanston, IL: Northwestern University Press.

Pound, Ezra. (1960). *Gaudier-Brzeska: A Memoir*. Hessle, UK: Marvell Press.

Pound, Ezra. (1966). *Guide to Kulchur*. London: Peter Owen.

Pound, Ezra. (1968a). *Literary Essays, ed.* T. S. Eliot. London: Faber and Faber.

Pound, Ezra. (1968b. *ABC of Reading*. London: Faber and Faber.

Pound, Ezra. (1971). *Selected Letters 1907–1941, ed.* D. D. Paige. London: Faber and Faber.

Pound, Ezra. (1996). *The Cantos of Ezra Pound*. New York: New Directions.

Rabaté, Jean-Michel. (2002). *The Future of Theory*. Oxford: Blackwell.

Stein, Gertrude. (1971). "A Transatlantic Interview." In *A Primer for the Gradual Understanding of Gertrude Stein*, ed. Robert Bartlett Haas. Los Angeles: Black Sparrow Press.

Williams, William Carlos. (1969). *Selected Essays*. New York: New Directions.

Zukofsky, Louis. (1931). "Sincerity and Objectification." *Poetry*, 37.5: 272–285.

2

Streams Beyond Consciousness
Stylistic Immediacy in the Modernist Novel

Vicki Mahaffey

In Rose Macaulay's 1926 novel *Crewe Train*, Arnold writes and publishes a novel that he is particularly eager for his wife, Denham, to like, because he identifies her with the female protagonist in his novel. Denham, however, objects to the way the protagonist thinks, especially in the following passage:

> A woodpecker, that's a woodpecker, because the woodpecker would peck her, why did the lobster blush, because it saw the salad dressing, no, because the table had cedar legs: can't remember the questions, only the answers. Answers, Tit-bits, Pink'un, John Bull, other island, Shaw, getting married, why get married, ring, wedding dress, Mendelssohn, bridesmaids, babies, *is* marriage worth while, does one survive death? My religion, all the novelists, is marriage worth while? Love, dove, shove, glove, oh my love I love you so much it hurts, yes, marriage is worth while, oh yes, oh yes: oyez all round the town.[1]

The effect produced by this representation of a character's thoughts becomes the subject of marital disagreement: Denham thinks the character must have been "a little queer in the head," whereas Arnold, rather vexed, insists, "it's the way we all think." Denham remains unconvinced and insists that she does not associate via rhyme ("I don't think glove when I've thought shove, just because it rhymes. I don't see why anyone should"). Arnold holds his ground, asserting, "if one tries to follow the mazes of one's thoughts, one finds they're astonishingly incoherent" Denham "obstinately" maintains her own position, declaring, "But not like that" (143).

What is at stake in the disagreement between husband and wife in *Crewe Train* is the psychological realism of a particular style of writing, one that has been called both the "stream of consciousness" technique and "interior monologue." By 1926, when Macaulay's novel was published, something extraordinary had happened in

A Handbook of Modernism Studies, First Edition. Edited by Jean-Michel Rabaté.
© 2013 John Wiley & Sons, Ltd. Published 2013 by John Wiley & Sons, Ltd.

the modern novel; as Jean Giraudoux wrote in his 1924 novel *Juliette au pays des hommes*, the city of Paris was currently intrigued not by "death, but interior monologue."[2]

The novel underwent a remarkable stylistic change or shift of focus shortly before the start of the twentieth century, a change that seems to have happened a little earlier in France than in England, Ireland, and America: it turned sharply inward, its locus not so much the world as the individual mind (or "soul"). The innovator of this new technique in France was Édouard Dujardin, who employed it in his novel *Les lauriers sont coupés* in 1887; in England, the pioneer was Dorothy Richardson, who used a technique that many regarded as similar in her sequence of *Pilgrimage* novels, the first of which, *Pointed Roofs*, was published in 1915. But the person who brought the technique to the attention of the world by using it to speak of private thoughts more explicitly than anyone else was an Irishman, James Joyce, who used it most scandalously in Molly Bloom's soliloquy at the end of *Ulysses* (1922).

The first problem to confront when discussing this tremendous stylistic shift is the slipperiness of the terminology that has variously been used to designate it. The terms "stream of consciousness" and "interior monologue" are often used interchangeably, and the problem is confounded by the fact that the French typically prefer the term *monologue intérieur* (according to Melvin Friedman, "there is no direct equivalent of the expression stream of consciousness in French"[3]), whereas English-speakers tend to favor "stream of consciousness." Robert Humphrey, another early critic who wrote a book on *Stream of Consciousness in the Modern Novel* in the 1950s,[4] argues that stream of consciousness should be considered a genre, whereas interior monologue is a technique, but this distinction has been difficult to maintain, partly because interior monologue seems to be structured as a metaphorical "stream" of consciousness, if by consciousness we mean all levels of awareness. The phrase itself was first used by William James in his *Principles of Psychology*, which was originally published as a series of articles that appeared between 1874 and 1890 (the first volume of the book appeared in 1890). The phenomenon James is referring to (which writers attempt to capture in language through the technique of interior monologue) – our experience of the external world in relation to our memories and desires – is not limited to *conscious* awareness, however; it includes sensory perceptions that "color" our thoughts with the experience of the body, as well as experiences in the penumbra of consciousness, evoked by unconscious associations. Moreover, some of the novels that attempt to capture individual subjective consciousness in all its idiosyncratic intensity depict characters in the act of unconsciously *denying* or defending themselves against certain kinds of awareness, and the role of the author is to dramatize that denial without editorializing about it. May Sinclair's novels often do this, as do the stories and novels of James Joyce. A succinct example may be found in Dujardin's *Les lauriers sonts coupés*, when the protagonist, Daniel Prince, passing Place Clichy, remembers an encounter with a prostitute that must have been his own, but from what must be some combination of shame and disgust, he identifies the man kneeling in her bed only as "the beast": "hurry up; long, dismal walls, without a break; deeper shadow on the roadway; street girls now, three street girls talking; they don't notice me; one very young and frail, with shameless eyes, and what lips! in a room, bare, indistinct, high-ceilinged, bare and grey, in the smoky candle light, in the somnolence of the tumult of the swarming street; yes, a narrow, high-ceilinged room, and the mean bed, the table, the chair, the grey walls, and the beast kneeling in the bed, and the lascivious lips, swelling and swelling again while the beast groans and pants for breath."[5] Stream of consciousness, then, as a term fails to emphasize the wholeness and intensity of the subjective experience being referred to; it is too easy for those who first encounter the phrase to assume that consciousness designates only fully formed thoughts, or the process of rational cognition. The metaphor of awareness as an ever-changing stream, however, works well in that it draws attention to the technique's attempt to capture the relentless movement of the always-evanescent present moment, laden as it is with echoes of the past as well as anticipations of the future.

The imprecision licensed by the term "stream of consciousness," coined by a psychologist and evoking cognition, is the impression that the literary method we are describing focuses on the *mind* of an individual. That notion is too limited, and it is worth noting that both Dujardin and Joyce claimed to be interested not in the minds but in the *souls* of their characters. Dujardin dedicated his novel to Racine, "supreme novelist of souls" (*suprême romancier d'âmes*), and Louis Gillet, in the *Revue des Deux Mondes*, quoted Joyce as having said that "the soul, in a sense, is all that exists."[6] Later readers shied away from the idea of the soul, perhaps because of its religious overtones, but the soul or psyche is a more capacious idea than the mind, because it designates not only thoughts occurring on different levels of awareness that are constantly overlaying images of past and future onto the present, but also emotions and perceptions. According to this view, the novel gradually changed its aim by forgoing traditional narrative, a sequential chronicle of the lives of characters in specific, usually realistic social settings; it attempted, instead, to give readers a much more varied and intense experience of a character's "soul" in the flow of the present moment. This attempt resulted in a transformation of the style of the novel that brought it closer to drama, poetry, and music.

The increasingly close kinship between the novel and drama is acknowledged through the monologue portion of the continental term "interior monologue," which some literary historians associate with dramatic monologue in both poetic drama (especially Shakespearean soliloquy) and poetry, such as the dramatic monologues of Robert Browning.[7] As Friedman explains, "when interior monologue has been employed with any consistency, the mind of the character is revealed as dramatized. This fulfills all the requirements for the 'cinema intérieur' Bergson outlined so elaborately" (1955, 5). Of course, as the omniscient narrator disappears, the novel begins to "stage" experience instead of narrating it.

In addition to being linked with drama, interior monologue is also often described as "poetic." The connection with poetry is apt, in that interior monologue's closer focus on the internal experience of one or more individuals produces a lyrical quality. The lyricism of private first-person utterance is unexpectedly enhanced by the disjunctive nature of the connections being made in a character's mind, which loosely resemble the line breaks and unexpected metonymic juxtapositions found in lyric poetry. Interior monologue is also often linked with (unheard) music, but in order to explain how that operates, we must first construct a history of the technique.[8]

In the mid-to-late nineteenth century, the German composer Richard Wagner changed the way opera was performed by extinguishing all lights in the theater except for those that illumined the stage, so that his audience watched and listened in darkness; their focus was trained on the opera instead of being split between the operatic performance and the social spectacle. This change of emphasis enhanced Wagner's more radical change: what people did and sang on stage represented aspects of experience that the characters performed for (and with) others, and the orchestral music expressed their private experience, an emotionally intense, often subconscious set of experiential undercurrents. His operas were long, and the length was probably an important feature because it gave the audience time to acclimate to what felt like a full – vicariously interactive *and* private – immersion in another world. Most importantly from a technical point of view, Wagner used musical patterns of ever-changing but recognizable short phrases, later given the name of leitmotifs, to create an emotional coherence in the orchestral score and to intensify the audience's experience of the work as it progressed. The leitmotifs served as musical "memories." The operas were long enough to create a musical "past" for themselves. What triggered the audience's emotion-charged memory as the opera developed was not a Proustian madeleine, but a complex pattern of interwoven, familiar yet always slightly different leitmotifs.

Jump to Paris in 1885. Édouard Dujardin publishes the first issue of the *Revue Wagnérienne* on February 8 (he is joined by Teodor de Wyzewa[9]). Two years later, in *La Revue Indépendante*, he publishes *Les lauriers sont coupés*, a novel made up entirely of interior monologue. Many years later, in May of 1930, when presenting a series of lectures in Marburg, Berlin, and Leipzig on Interior Monologue, he announces that he is "going to divulge a secret":

> *Les lauriers sont coupés* was undertaken with the wild ambition of transposing into the literary field Wagnerian procedures which I defined for myself as follows: the life of the soul expressed through the incessant eruption of musical motifs, coming up to speak, one after the other, undefined and in succession, the 'states' of thought, feeling, impressions, brought into existence, or tentatively brought into existence, in an undefined succession of short phrases, each rendering one of these states of thought, in no logical order, in the form of bursts of thought rising from the depths of the self, from what we today would call the unconscious or the subconscious.[10]

In 1903, James Joyce reads a copy of Édouard Dujardin's *Les lauriers sont coupés* in Paris. After the publication of *Ulysses* in Paris in 1922, when Joyce is hailed as the inventor of the stream-of-consciousness technique, he demurs, identifying Dujardin as the innovator in *Les lauriers sont coupés* and himself as "*le larron impénitent*" (the unrepentant thief).[11]

Les lauriers sont coupés

Since Dujardin's short novel is still not widely known, it might be useful to characterize it briefly for the English-speaking reader. Its title is taken from a French children's "circle game" song, *Nous n'irons plus au bois* (We'll go to the woods no more), the lyrics of which date from the eighteenth century. The lighthearted song traces a movement from the withering of the laurels to their regrowth, and the chorus is an invitation to dance, jump, and kiss whomever you want. Dujardin's novel is written very much in the spirit of the song. It attempts to capture the moment-by-moment experience of a young, dandified law student over the course of six hours on an April evening in Paris. Edmond Jaloux summarized it in 1929 as follows:

> In *Les lauriers sont coupés*, almost nothing happens: a young man is in love with a pretty girl, gives her some money, goes out with her and finally obtains nothing. He leaves, stating that he will not see her again, but it is not absolutely certain that he will keep his word. (Suter 1991, 87)[12]

In a 1924 preface, Valery Larbaud quoted Joyce as having said "the reader was, in *Les lauriers sont coupés*, placed inside the thought processes of the main character, and it is the uninterrupted unfolding of this thought process which, completely replacing conventional narrative form, informed the reader of what this character is doing and what happens to him" (88). Dujardin also quotes several responses to his novel from Stéphane Mallarmé and George Moore, such as a letter dated April 8, 1888 in which Mallarmé writes that the novel's method serves "to express, without misapplication of the sublime means involved, everyday experience which is so difficult to grasp" (88). Similarly, George Moore stressed the novel's innovative style, writing on May 17, 1887 that in Dujardin's "story," "the daily life of the soul [is] unveiled for the first time; a kind of symphony in full stops and commas" (90). Moore later told Dujardin that he "had found the most original literary form of our time." According to Edmond Jaloux, the technique of the novel "gives to reality the intensity of a hallucination" (104), and Jean Giraudoux described interior monologue in 1924 as a way of undressing the soul, a "soulquake": it was "a movement of such frankness that the coverings which had been forced on the soul from the time of Aristotle till that of the Symbolists had been shaken off."[13] Perhaps the most poetic description of Dujardin's technique is that of Pierre d'Exideuil, who compared it to

> a diving-bell which suddenly plunges us into marine depths. Amidst a magic or unreal vegetation suspended in the mass of water, grows a profuse fauna, fauna composed of strange animals and fish with their bodies made transparent by the conical glare of the spotlights. We can see them in movement at the same time as we can study the contractions of their bodies, their comings and goings, their habits, their reflexes. If they catch something to eat, we can then follow the food through their insides right to the cloaca.[14]

As Dujardin points out, d'Exideuil's description anticipates Louis Gillet's description of Joyce's technique in *Ulysses*, which resembles a "searching X-ray photograph of fleeting life in its perpetual becoming" (106). But it is also interesting to see how Dujardin himself describes the method employed in *Les lauriers sont coupés* as follows: "The character in *Les lauriers sont coupés* reveals not what is happening around him, but what he sees happening; not the movement he makes, but those [sic] he is conscious of making; not the words spoken to him, but the ones he hears; all that, as he incorporates it in his own and only reality" (106).

Dujardin's novella makes for delightful reading despite the frothiness of its subject matter. The "princely" protagonist comes across as youthfully indolent and idealistic, a sybaritic, privileged, and French anticipation of Stephen Dedalus. The flow of Prince's thoughts, however, read more like Bloom's than Stephen's. In chapter three, for example, Prince elaborates a daydream of what he would do if he became rich that resembles Bloom's fantasy of purchasing a two-storey cottage of southerly aspect named Flowerville (although Bloom's fantasy is not presented through interior monologue, but is instead elaborately detailed by the punctilious narrator of the "Ithaca" episode of *Ulysses*, U 17.1497–1753). Prince "plays at dreaming" while he walks toward home shortly after half past seven in the evening:

> I have no wish to live extravagantly at home; I'd have a bachelor flat and set Léa up in a town house; I'd willingly keep on my fourth-floor place in Rue du Général Foy: something of the kind, but better; live at home in the style of a man with thirty odd thousand francs private income and spend one's million a year on one's mistress; I'd like to have a little ground-floor flat for myself in a house in the Parc Monceau area, it goes without saying; five or six rooms; a carriage-entrance; then two steps; the door; a hallway; in the front part a small drawing-room; a dining-room, a smoking-room; at the back, the kitchen, the privies, a big dressing-room and the bedroom; the bedroom opening onto a courtyard garden. (1981, 22)[15]

In *Les lauriers sont coupés*, as in *Ulysses*, the narrative focus on the present activity of daydreaming shows how the present can be invaded by the (imagined) future, even as it is sometimes haunted by a half-remembered past.

Some of the other moments in the novel that have close ties to *Ulysses* include the time in chapter seven when Daniel Prince falls asleep, an experiential change that Dujardin portrays from Prince's point of view as an increasing fragmentation of language, much as Joyce will do when Bloom begins to doze at the end of the "Nausicaa" episode of *Ulysses*. Prince thinks, "she sleeps; I feel sleep coming over me; I half close my eyes . . . there . . . her body; her breast swells and swells; and the sweet scent mingled . . . fine April night . . . in a while we'll go for a ride . . . the cool air . . . we're going to leave . . . in a while . . . the two candles . . . there . . . along the boulevards . . . 'love y' more than m'sheep' . . . love y' more . . . that girl, slender, with the brazen look, red lips . . . the bedroom, the tall mantelpiece . . . the room my father . . . all three sitting, my father, my mother . . . myself . . . " (55).[16] Joyce uses a very similar technique when trying to filter Bloom's short nap through thoughts that progressively lose coherence, freed from the rational and conventional constraints of grammar. Bloom thinks, "Short snooze now if I had," and then after he closes his eyes a moment his thoughts jumble together into memories that Freud might describe as "day residue," and that a Wagnerian might see as a cluster of leitmotifs in the form of phrases encountered earlier in the book: "O sweety all your little girlwhite up I saw dirty bracegirdle made me do love sticky we two naughty Grace darling she him half past the bed met him pike hoses frillies for Raoul de perfume your wife black hair heave under embon *señorita* young eyes Mulvey plump bubs me breadvan Winkle red slippers she rusty sleep wander years of dreams return tail end Agendath swoony lovey showed me her next year in drawers return next in her next her next" (*U* 13.1274, 1279–1285).

The almost cinematic, poetic quality that the style invites into the narration is particularly apparent when Prince takes a drive in a carriage with Léa and watches her face as it moves through light and then shadow:

> how pretty, there, half-reclining in the carriage! alternately her face is in the light and shade, alternately in the dim shadow and in the pallor of the lights while the carriage moves along; near the gas-lamps there is indeed bright light, then, after the lamps, a darkening; again; the gaslight to the right is burning more brightly; her lovely white face, mat white, ivory white, white of snow in darkness, in the black that enfolds her, more luminous under the lights, becoming subdued in the shadows, then flaring out again; while over the even wood roadway our carriage goes on its way.[17]

But the technique is not merely lyrical and aesthetically pleasing; it is flexible enough to dramatize the aspects of Léa to which Prince is blind, especially her hardscrabble pragmatism, her determination to use his adoration to her own pecuniary advantage. This technique, which introduces an irony into the novel to which Prince remains oblivious, is used in chapter five, when Dujardin introduces Léa's voice into Prince's mind not through their dialogue (the usual method), but by having him reread her letters and his own diary entries over the last four months, the period of their acquaintance. Here the interior monologue approaches a "drama" of jostling narrative voices. We hear of Léa's tantalizingly seductive gestures, as when they dance and her skirts come undone, and we also hear her importunate demands for money, often in her own words. We also hear Daniel's determination to interpret all her imperious mood-changes as evidence that he needs to be increasingly patient and undemanding in his self-sacrifices for her so that she will one day "love him." Only once, near the end, does he wonder about the purity of his own motives, anticipating Gabriel's epiphany about Gretta in Joyce's "The Dead," when Prince thinks, "perhaps she is right, and that it's rare for a man to love, and that she has never been loved; could it be that I don't love her either then? I'm sorry I love her so little, so little, when I try so hard to love!" (77).[18]

One of the main differences between *Les lauriers sont coupés* and Joyce's *Ulysses*, as many commentators point out, is that Joyce's stylistic techniques are more numerous, varied, and flexible than the interior monologue that Dujardin sustains throughout.[19] This brings me to the second part of the essay, in which I argue that instead of speaking of "stream of consciousness" fiction, we should perhaps consider a more expansive category, something like fiction that stages the animated, moment-to-moment experience of one or more characters against the backdrop of a larger frame of reference. Such fiction could include novels that use interior monologue, much as a landscape might include a stream, but it would also encompass different varieties of the free indirect discourse that had been so masterfully anticipated by Gustave Flaubert. This larger category would draw attention not only to the lyrical flow of a character's thoughts, but also to the dramatic technique whereby an author, after seducing the Gustave reader to see through a character's eyes, prompts the reader to see him or her from the outside as well. Novels that depict a character both from the inside and the outside, using a narrative technique that seduces readers to share in that character's perceptions, emotions, and memories, yet also to note his or her shortcomings and self-delusions, short-circuit any unconscious assumptions of superiority on the part of the reader. The reader is implicated in a character's experience while at the same time exposed as incomplete by the limitations of that character's vision, sex, nationality, age, and presuppositions. It is for this reason that the modernist novel was revolutionary: it found a new stylistic repertory for making the reader not only see but also experience a character's most intense and private reality while differentiating that vivid stream of experience from larger, more powerful social, historical, and literary countercurrents. From the longer point of view of that ongoing world, individual experience is exposed as incomplete and distorted, but it is not invalidated. Such fiction changes the nature of the psychological novel, offering readers the means of experiencing themselves (through vicarious identification with a character) as simultaneously great and small.

In order to appreciate how this works, we should now turn to the alternate genealogy for the stream-of-consciousness technique: specifically, to its genesis in England, by a writer who was also a woman, Dorothy Richardson. Richardson, as she recounts in her foreword to *Pilgrimage*, discovered her signature style through an attempt "to produce a female equivalent of the current masculine realism."[20] I see no reason to choose between these two "inventors" of interior monologue, since both are important in different ways. The stream of consciousness appeared in France before it emerged in England, and the most famous uses of the technique – by the Irish James Joyce in his notorious banned book of 1922 – were influenced by the French rather than the English. But the emergence of the technique in England, pioneered by women, is important in a different way, and this history sheds light on the different motivations for and methods of staging individual, private experience through new uses of prose.

Stylistic Treatments of Individual Subjectivity by Women Writers

By now, it should be clear that the term "stream of consciousness" needs to be supplemented, for clarity, with the other phrases that William James used to identify the same idea, such as "stream of subjective life," which more clearly includes the subconscious currents of experience.[21] One advantage of using the metaphor of a stream is that it contains currents, and the word "current" conveniently has an appropriate double meaning referring not only to the flow of a stream, but also to anything connected to the present, ever-changing moment. Why might a woman have been more likely to feel the need for a novel centered in the present, one that incorporated interior perceptions, thoughts, and feelings as well as objective reporting of events? The first volume of Richardson's pioneering novel, *Pilgrimage: Pointed Roofs*, appeared in 1915, only three years before the first (limited) women's suffrage act was passed (The 1918 Representation of the People Act granted the vote to women of property over age thirty; women twenty-one and over weren't enfranchised until 1928). Was Richardson's experiment partly a response to the cloistered position of women in society, a cloistering that may well have put intelligent and sensitive women more sharply in touch with the intensity of what Bergson described as an "inward self" with different levels of consciousness?[22]

It was May Sinclair who first described Dorothy Richardson's *Pilgrimage* as a "stream of consciousness" in a 1918 review of the first three volumes, although Richardson objected to the description.[23] Sinclair described Richardson's "art and method and form" in these novels as "carried to punctilious perfection." She concedes that "nothing happens" in them, that "It is just life going on and on. It is Miriam Henderson's stream of consciousness going on and on," but she nonetheless claims that Richardson gets "closer to reality than any of our novelists who are trying so desperately to get close."[24] Richardson, for her part, characterized the term "stream of consciousness" as a "perfect imbecility," and noted that although the continental equivalent "interior monologue" was also inadequate, it at least carried a meaning. Like Dujardin's *Les lauriers sont coupés*, Richardson's novels (she called them "chapters") did not sell well and often inspired those who did read them to complain about their "formlessness" and apparent triviality of subject. But Richardson seems to have fully grasped the importance of finding a new language and style for expressing subjective experience, of throwing off limiting expectations born of habit, not only when writing, but when reading as well. This is nowhere more apparent than in her appreciative review of Joyce's *Finnegans Wake* in 1939, where she proposes that readers do what the author is asking, and "Really release consciousness from literary preoccupations and prejudices, from the self-imposed task of searching for superficial sequences in stretches of statement regarded horizontally, . . . and plunge, provisionally, here and there; *enter* the text and look innocently about."[25] Basically, Richardson is proposing to view the novel as what Henry James once referred to as a "chamber of experience," which includes raw apprehensions triggered by sensual perceptions of phenomena – some completely new – as well as incompletely recognized memories.[26]

In *Pointed Roofs* (1915), Richardson beautifully captures the unexpected sensual shocks of new experience when Miriam is having her hair washed with raw egg, her "outraged head" hanging over a steaming basin:

> Then her amazed ears caught the sharp bump-crack of an eggshell against the rim of the basin, followed by a further brisk crackling just above her. She shuddered from head to foot as the egg descended with a cold slither upon her incredulous skull. Tears came to her eyes as she gave beneath the onslaught of two hugely enveloping, vigorously drubbing hands – "sh-ham-poo" gasped her mind.[27]

Miriam revels not only in what she calls "her present bliss" (114), but also in music, since she is a pianist capable of being transported by the beauty of sound to be found in Beethoven's Sonata Pathétique, for example. Unlike Dujardin, who tried to compose his novella as Wagner might compose an opera, Richardson "plays" language as one might play a piano to evoke the emotions and sensations of experience. Miriam at one point even personifies music, thinking of Grieg's "Solveig's Song" as "going on, walking along, thinking to itself" (133). Her perceptions and ideas are almost all conscious ones, however; Miriam's experience seems to lack depth because the novel fails to intimate anything to the reader about layers of experience that lie beyond Miriam's awareness. Unlike Dujardin, who stages the incongruity between Daniel Prince's awareness and the complex reality that exceeds it by dramatizing Daniel's blindness to the way Léa uses his romantic idealism to her own advantage, Miriam seems oddly congruent with the circumstances in which she finds herself in Germany, and there is almost no irony in the book at all. If we compare Richardson's *Pointed Roofs* to Joyce's roughly contemporary *A Portrait of the Artist as a Young Man*, we could describe it as having the stylistic innovation of *Portrait* without the troublingly problematic staging of the protagonist's shortcomings alongside his strengths. Had Joyce changed the style of *Stephen Hero* while keeping Stephen "heroic" (or at least consistently sympathetic), the result might have resembled *Pointed Roofs*.

When Richardson portrays Miriam's mind in a feverish state, she makes her thoughts more staccato and fragmentary, and the resulting "stream" might seem to resemble, at least superficially, the depictions of Prince and Bloom falling asleep in *Les lauriers sont coupés* and *Ulysses*, respectively. But the phrases and images that rush through Miriam's mind are not leitmotifs; instead, they more closely resemble the random pastiche of the portrayal of Jane's thoughts in Arnold's novel in Macaulay's *Crewe Train*. Miriam's thoughts are highly visual, almost cinematic, but they do not reveal anything of which she is not fully conscious, and they aren't linked to anything that has happened elsewhere in the novel; they do not form part of a complex underlying pattern that intensifies the reader's feeling of intimacy (and even complicity) with a character.

> She conjured up a vision of the backs of the books in the bookcase in the dining-room at home . . . Iliad and Odyssey . . . people going over the sea in boats and someone doing embroidery . . . that little picture of Hector and Andromache in the corner of a page . . . he in armour . . . she, in a trailing dress, holding up her baby. Both, silly . . . She wished she had read more carefully. She could not remember anything in Lecky or Darwin that would tell her what to do . . . Hudibras . . . The Atomic Theory . . . Ballads and Poems, D. G. Rossetti . . . Kinglake's Crimea . . . Palgrave's Arabia . . . Crimea . . . The Crimea . . . Florence Nightingale; a picture somewhere; a refined face, with cap and strings . . . She must have smiled. (161)

Here, Miriam's fevered stream of consciousness seems believable, but the books and images that rush through her mind have no additional significance other than the fact that she once saw or read them. It is not revelatory, partly because Richardson deploys no subtle symbolism to make her character's thoughts be anything more than mental snapshots of things she once looked at growing up. What is lacking is any "clause where the cry of the subconscious gushes up," to quote Dujardin, a cry that would enable the reader to see *through* the character's consciousness to something usually hidden, a revelation that interior monologue facilitates in the novel and that Wagner achieved through his orchestra (100–101).[28] Virginia Woolf made a similar criticism of Richardson in an anonymous review of the fourth volume of Richardson's *Pilgrimage, The Tunnel* (1919), that was published in the *Times Literary Supplement* in 1919. "That Miss Richardson gets so far as to achieve a sense of reality far greater than that produced by the ordinary means is undoubted. But, then, which reality is it, the superficial or the profound?" And she writes of Miriam, "Her senses of touch, sight and hearing are all excessively acute. But sensations, impressions, ideas and emotions glance off her, unrelated and unquestioned, without shedding as much light as we had hoped into the hidden depths."[29]

In May Sinclair's earlier review of Richardson, she presents the sensuality of Miriam's consciousness as what helps to make the narration so vibrant: "You look at the outer world through Miriam's senses, and it is as if you had never seen it so vividly before" (444). But in a later interview on "The Future of the Novel," Sinclair is more careful to stress the limitations of a method in which "the author never [adopts] the attitude of God Almighty as he used to do in the ordinary traditional novel."[30] She calls the method of "proceeding from one consciousness, and seeing and feeling everything through that consciousness" as "one of the most interesting developments of the psychological novel," but she also says that the challenge for those who use such a method is to "present things so that they appear both as they really are and as they appear to the consciousness of his one subject." This, arguably, is what Richardson does not do: things as they are seem identical with things as they appear to Miriam. Miriam simply sees a smaller slice of the real than the old omniscient narrator. Sinclair herself, however, who remains largely overlooked, succeeds in preserving that distinction, creating an ironic tension between the perceiving character and the larger reality that the reader glimpses through that character's consciousness. I would argue that Sinclair's novels should be classed with those of Woolf and Joyce as attempting to stage the immediacy of subjective experience by focalizing the novel through the consciousness of a character, although Sinclair is less ambitious in that she limits her focus to the experience of a single character and favors free indirect discourse over interior monologue. She clearly understands the importance of "direct presentment of the subject," however, emphasizing that "The modern novelist should not dissect; he should not probe; he should not write about the emotions and thoughts of his characters. The words he uses must be the thoughts – be the emotions."[31]

Sinclair's novels, such as *Life and Death of Harriett Frean* (1922) and *A Cure of Souls* (1924), illustrate exactly why most definitions of stream-of-consciousness fiction or interior monologue are too narrow. The best of these too-limited definitions is that of Dujardin, who characterizes interior monologue as "a speech by a character, the object of which is to introduce us directly into the interior life of that character, without the author intervening with explanations or commentaries, and which, like any monologue, is unheard and unspoken" (111). But Dujardin still focuses on "speech *by* a character," however unheard or unspoken it may be. By his own admission, Joyce's *A Portrait of the Artist as a Young Man* would not qualify as an example of the new novelistic style, because it contains only a few lines of interior monologue that Joyce told Dujardin he had written more or less unconsciously (85). But the revolution in the novel that took place near the beginning of the twentieth century was not limited to novels that used interior monologue; it included, more broadly, novels that use a range of different techniques to dramatize immediate subjective experience as it unfolds in the present, with all the intensity and potential blind spots of such experience. The supplementation or broadening of the revolutionary category is important, because otherwise it is not readily apparent how closely related to interior monologue are those works of fiction in which characters refuse or evade consciousness, which includes the aforementioned novels of May Sinclair, the stories of Joyce's *Dubliners* and all of *A Portrait of the Artist as a Young Man*. In order to show how characters evade consciousness, an author must often resort to free indirect discourse unless he or she has chosen to deploy what T. S. Eliot famously called "the mythical method," in which an author relies upon a well-known mythical narrative to "frame" or implicitly contexualize the scene unfolding in the present.[32] Simply by expanding the category of stylistic innovation in the twentieth-century novel from "stream of consciousness" to "stream of immediate subjective experience," we can see the relation between interior monologue and novels in free indirect discourse that similarly stage individual experience against a larger backdrop, whether that backdrop is cultural, mythic, or literary (furnished by Homer's *Odyssey*, Ovid's *Metamorphoses*, or Dante's *Inferno*), or whether it is simply social reality itself, in all its dynamic complexity.

Think of the moment in Joyce's story "Clay" in which Maria puts on a blindfold to play a divination game on All Hallow's Eve. In a third-person voice that imitates Maria's own credulous, obedient, almost childlike idiom, the narrator tells us:

They led her up to the table amid laughing and joking and she put her hand out in the air as she was told to do. She moved her hand about here and there in the air and descended on one of the saucers. She felt a soft wet substance with her fingers and was surprised that nobody spoke or took off her bandage. There as a pause for a few seconds; and then a great deal of scuffling and whispering. Somebody said something about the garden, and at last Mrs Donnelly said something very cross to one of the next-door girls and told her to throw it out at once: that was no play. Maria understood that it was wrong that time and so she had to do it over again: and this time she got the prayer-book.[33]

Here, the only context we need is the title of the story and the fact that it takes place on Halloween. We are kept within Maria's consciousness as it evades an awareness that her fate is death, according to the fortune-telling game she has just played, a death represented by the "clay" from the garden that the next-door girls put on the table as a joke. The story also tells us, indirectly, that she was hoping to get the "ring," not the clay; she longs to get married, as we see when she is flustered by the politeness of an attractive older gentleman on the tram and later, when she sings "I Dreamt I Dwellt in Marble Halls," when she omits the verse about dreaming of being besieged by suitors. The narrator keeps the reader in the present moment, shut in the chamber of Maria's unfolding experience, but at the same time opens windows into the disturbing realities and hopes that Maria will not allow herself to recognize.

Joyce's *A Portrait of the Artist as a Young Man* exhibits a comparable stylistic complexity. As in *Dubliners*, Joyce fuses the lyric and the dramatic to produce a different kind of narrative. Specifically, when he restricts the narrative perspective to Stephen Dedalus' experience in the present moment using free indirect discourse, he is able to produce "lyrical" intensity associated with individual experience. He creates surprising dramatic effects by "staging" (without authorial commentary) the self-importance and defensive anguish of this impecunious young man against the grand ambitiousness of his dreams to create ingenious art that will redeem the whole disenfranchised Irish "race." It is still difficult for many first-time readers to navigate the lyrical and dramatic extremes of Joyce's method, to balance an appreciation for Stephen's imagination with a humorous recognition of his youth and inexperience. Because Stephen is based on Joyce himself when he was younger, readers find it hard to believe that he is being set up as a figure to be laughed at as well as admired.

May Sinclair's *Life and Death of Harriett Frean* is a crucial companion-novel to Joyce's *A Portrait of the Artist as a Young Man* that is seldom read, much less taught. Like Joyce's novel, Sinclair's is a novel of development, but it focuses on a young woman instead of a young man. Like Joyce's Stephen, Harriett Frean grows older, developing certain kinds of awareness, but she also fails to develop in other crucial ways. If Stephen loses the capacity to feel for others (especially women), Harriett never gains autonomy. The reasons for her failure are rooted in what it means to be female at the end of the Victorian period, and the result is dramatized as crippling. This is a failed *bildungsroman*, but it could never be a *künstlerroman*, because Harriett could not become an artist any more than she could gain independence from her parents, especially her mother. Written for the most part in the third person, with occasional first-person inserts, the novel dramatizes Harriett Frean's experience of the world from childhood to death, which is represented (from Harriett's point of view) as an "ecstatic" recovery of a childhood that she lost only in the literal sense of aging. Like Joyce's Maria in "Clay," Harriett never really grows up. The novel enlists the reader to empathize with Harriett by allowing him or her to see the world through her eyes, but it simultaneously dramatizes how her affections for her family turn into a fatal limitation that, in a developmental sense, keeps her psychologically in the nursery (her association with the nursery is dramatized by a nursery rhyme with which the novel begins: "Pussycat, pussycat, where have you been?"). We see Harriett learn to be beautiful and obedient in all things, and to identify herself so completely with her mother that she can never taste autonomy without risking the shame of ugliness: "Ugly. Being naughty was just that. Doing ugly things. Being good was being beautiful like Mamma. She wanted to be like her mother. Sitting up there and being good felt delicious."[34] The novel dramatizes Harriett's mastery of a chilling social lesson: that to be a beautiful woman is to remain a child emotionally while embracing the self-sacrificial ethos of the "good" mother.

Sinclair uses the same technique in *A Cure of Souls* to draw the reader into the mind, thoughts, and sensations of a lazy, selfish cleric, Canon Clement Chamberlain.[35] Again, Sinclair allows readers to experience with immediacy the pleasure with which the rector tastes the peaches from his back garden, and the delicious freedom he feels when he sits in his armchair to read the scandalous *Madame Bovary*. Sinclair's technique draws the reader into the character's experience, his breathing in of the scent of lavender and warm roses from an open window, the feeling of the stiff bristles of his hairbrush as they scrape his scalp. Only gradually does the reader become aware that despite the feeling of intimacy with Chamberlain that the novel offers by re-creating his luxurious idleness with such sensuous immediacy, the character slowly reveals disturbing flaws through the "drama" of his interactions with other characters, and we see him evade recognizing those shortcomings in a chillingly believable way. The method of the novel is to make the reader imaginatively complicit with a selfish, lazy, and unwittingly hurtful man who occupies a position of spiritual and social influence in his community. Sinclair's strategy, then, is to invite empathetic identification with the main character only to fissure that identification with an uncomfortable awareness of the insensitivity and lack of self-awareness that the character alternately fights and embraces. Sinclair offers insight into the complexity of her artistic aim at the end of the novel, when the rector is confronted by the sister of a woman to whom he had given principled but uncaring advice about an episode in which she had been unfaithful to her long-absent husband (although Chamberlain wished to help the woman, he was distracted by the smell of his dinner being ruined). He defends himself to the sister by saying he simply advised the woman to tell her husband the "truth," but her sister objects, "It seems to me that it takes two people to make truth. One to speak it and one to understand it. If I tell you a thing that's true in a way that makes you not understand it, I'm not telling the truth. I haven't allowed for your understanding" (318). This is what Sinclair's method (like Joyce's in *Dubliners* and *Portrait*) is designed to facilitate: it enacts the truth of the teller while dramatizing its insufficiency in the context of a larger social world. And it does so by immersing the reader in a character's experience of the flowing, present moments that are ironically "framed" by reminders of other truths, and other times. The insufficiency of one individual's truth does not invalidate its beauty or diminish its uniqueness, but it serves to remind readers of the necessity for tempering receptivity and sensual aliveness with imaginative empathy and self-awareness. And all this is accomplished not through traditional narrative methods, which are retrospective, but dramatically, by inviting the reader to look through the eyes of another character, then look at the character from the outside, and to continue to alternate between these opposed, equally vital perspectives.

The question we are left with is this: when, in 1888, Mallarmé told Dujardin that in *Les lauriers sont coupés* "the moment [had been] gripped by the throat" (89), and when he described Dujardin's method as an attempt to "express, without misapplication of the sublime means involved, everyday experience which is so difficult to grasp" (88), what aspects of everyday experience were being captured? Is the innovation in the novel that took root in French Symbolism and German opera as one-sidedly subjective as it may seem? Or, in the most rewarding novels of the early twentieth century, does subjective experience in the present moment offer the reader a mask (or series of masks) through which to observe and simultaneously participate in the increasingly complex drama of moment-by-moment existence on a larger social and natural stage?

I have tried to suggest that although the new styles of the modernist novel seem highly subjective in their various ways of directly presenting individual experience in all of its sensual and psychological complexity, such novels also, in their emphasis on the limits of individual experience, afford readers a freshly objective view as well. In *The Waves*, Virginia Woolf attempted to stage the collaborative or collective aspects of individual development, set against the backdrop of a single landscape under the changing light of a passing day. In *Ulysses*, Joyce not only characterized the thoughts of his main characters through highly distinctive idioms, but he also changed styles on the hour. Style, for him, needed to reflect not only the colors and layers of inner experience rendered through interior monologue, but to change in distinctive relation to the place and time of day, as well.

And this brings us, at the end, to Samuel Beckett. One of the advantages of broadening the stylistic revolution undergone in the modernist novel so that it encompasses not only interior monologue but also dramatic irony, and specifically the dramatic irony that "frames" a character's limitations without denigrating the uniqueness of his or her individual perspective, is that it allows us to appreciate the antecedents of Beckett's dark comedy, and to understand the logic of his turn to drama in the last half of the twentieth century. Earlier in the century, most experimental novels (with the possible exception of those by May Sinclair) put more emphasis on the vivid subjective experience of the characters as it changed moment by moment, and less on the dramatic irony that exposed these perspectives as partial and finite (as well as vibrant and rich). Beckett, while making extensive use of interior monologue, especially in several of his stories and his prose trilogy, put more emphasis on his characters' limitations, which are the limitations of all individuals: their disabilities, the fact of their mortality, the circumscription of their perspective that comes from being restricted to one place and one time at any given moment, and the restrictive legacies of the past. That effort to dramatize those forces that handicap individual movement and consciousness eventually propelled Beckett to abandon the novel altogether as too rooted in subjective experience. His move to the stage brought him back to the place where interior monologue began, but with a difference: Beckett used drama to visualize the constraints on individual movement and development for his audience: his characters were buried up to their necks in sand (*Happy Days*), potted in rubbish bins (*Endgame*), or speaking from urns (*Play*). Alternatively, they compulsively repeated the same patterns with minor variations with the same group of people (*Quad*), or they returned day after day to the same deserted spot, passively hoping to be "saved" (*Waiting for Godot*). Beckett staged the other side of stream of consciousness, what we might call the fly caught in amber. The lyricism of individual utterance is still audible, but audiences have to strain to hear it. The "Not I" has almost displaced the "I."

Notes

1   Rose Macaulay (1926), 142. I am grateful to Tania Lown-Hecht, Elaine Wood, and Cecily Garber for their help with the research for this article.
2   Cited by Édouard Dujardin in *Interior Monologue* (Suter, trans.), 87.
3   Friedman (1955), 2–3.
4   Humphrey (1954), 4.
5   "sans cesse, de longs murs tristes; sur l'asphalte une ombre plus épaisse; à présent des filles, trois filles qui parlent entre elles; elles ne me remarquent pas; une très jeune, frêle, aux yeux éhontés, et quelles lèvres! en une chambre nue, vague, haute, nue et grise, sous un jour fumeux de chandelle, dans l'assoupissement des tumultes de la rue grouillante; oui, une haute chambre étroite, et le grabat, la chaise, la table, les murs gris, et l'agenouillement de la bête parmi le lit, et les lèvres luxurieuses, montantes et remontantes tandis que geint la créature et qu'elle halète . . ." *Les lauriers sont coupés*, Préface de Valery Larbaud (1925; Le chemin vert, 1981), 53.
6   Cited in Suter's translation of *The Bays Are Sere* and *Interior Monologue*, 136.
7   See Dujardin, *Interior Monologue* (Suter trans.), 126–129, for his answer to critics who trace interior monologue to Browning, and 118–119 for his account of how interior monologue differs from other monologues. Dujardin credits Valery Larbaud for coining the term interior monologue, 99. Friedman alludes to comparisons between interior monologue and the "intimate monologue of Balzac and Stendhal, the dramatic monologue of Browning and Tennyson, and the recapitulative monologue of Proust," 1.
8   This history gets told in various ways, but certain key influences are mentioned frequently, including French Symbolism, Wagner, and the theories of Henri Bergson. Most commentators see Freud as a product of the same forces that produced the shift in technique more than as an instigator.

9   Wyzewa, perhaps influenced by Dujardin's novel, predicted that Wagner's changes would influence the novel of the future (an echo of Wagner's rallying call for an "artwork of the future") when he wrote in *Nos maîtres: études et portraits littéraires* (Paris, Perrin, 1895), 52: "The novelist of the future will erect a single consciousness, which he will imbue with life; through it, images will be perceived, themes will be resolved, emotions will be felt. The reader, in the same way as the author, will see everything – inanimate as well as animate – through this unique consciousness, whose life he will experience." Cited in Friedman, 8, n.8.

10 *Interior Monologue*, trans. Suter, 135. Interestingly, Dujardin begins (as did Wagner) with Schopenhauer, especially Schopenhauer's insistence on "the fundamental opposition between the world of 'Representation' and the world of 'Life Force.'" Schopenhauer identified music as the art form that had the power to express the Life Force, because it was free of anything conceptual. Dujardin argues that life consciousness became "the subject of poetry, the musical conception – namely the de-intellectualization of poetry," and eventually this de-intellectualized conception of poetry made a "shattering" entry into prose and especially the novel as one of the fundamental principles of interior monologue, 133–134.

11 Dujardin relates that Joyce, by proclaiming him inventor of interior monologue, brought Dujardin's book out of the tomb, positioning Joyce as Jesus and Dujardin's almost-forgotten book as the dead Lazarus (*Interior Monologue*, 91). For Dujardin's account of Joyce's interest in his novel over thirty-five years, see *Interior Monologue*, 91–97. Suter tells the story of how Joyce encouraged (and helped) Stuart Gilbert to translate *Les lauriers*, and how Joyce tried (and failed) to get Dujardin's old friend George Moore to write a preface for the English translation, xxxiii–xxxiv. Joyce recounts in a letter to Harriet Shaw Weaver of November 22, 1929 that he inscribed Dujardin's copy of Ulysses to "E.D. Annonciateur de la parole intérieure," and signs it "le larron impénitent, J.J." Cited in Suter, xxxiii.

12 *Revue Nouvelle*, July–August 1929, cited by Dujardin in "Interior Monologue," Suter trans., 87.

13 In *Juliette au pays des hommes*, cited by Dujardin in "Interior Monologue," 104.

14 *Les Marges*, February 1929, cited by Dujardin, "Interior Monologue," 105. It is interesting to compare d'Exideuil's metaphor with that employed by Jean-Dominique Bauby in his memoir, which Julian Schnabel made into the 2007 stream-of-consciousness film, *The Diving-Bell and the Butterfly*.

15 "Je ne souhaite pas le grand train de maison; j'aurais un appartement de garçon et installerais dans un hôtel Léa; volontiers je garderais mon quatrième de la rue du Général Foy: quelque chose dans ce genre, mais mieux; avoir le train chez soi d'un garçon de trentaine de mille francs de rentes et chez sa maîtresse dépenser son million annuel; je me voudrais un petit rez-de-chaussée; dans une maison quartier Monceau nécessairement; cinq ou six chambres; entrée par une porte cochère; puis deux marches; la porte; un vestibule; sur le devant, un petit salon, une salle à manger; un fumoir; derrière, la cuisine, les privés, un grand cabinet de toilette et la chambre à coucher; la chamber à coucher ouvrant sur une cour-jardin." *Les lauriers sont coupés*, Préface de Valery Larbaud (1925; Paris: Le Chemin vert, 1981), 22. Compare Bloom: "the premises to be held under feefarm grant, lease 999 years, the messuage to consist of 1 drawingroom with baywindow (2 lances), thermometer affixed, 1 sittingroom, 4 bedrooms, 2 servants' rooms, tiled kitchen with close range and scullery, lounge hall

fitted with linen wallpresses, fumed oak sectional bookcase containing the Encyclopaedia Britannica and New Century Dictionary," etc. (*U* 17.1518–1524).

16 "moi je sens que je m'endors; j'entreferme mes yeux . . . voilà son corps; sa poitrine qui monte et monte; et le très doux parfum mêlé . . . la belle nuit d'avril . . . tout à l'heure nous nous promènerons . . . l'air frais . . . nous allons partir . . . tout à l'heure . . . les deux bougies . . . là . . . au cours des boulevards . . . "j'taim' mieux qu'mes moutons" . . . j't'aim' mieux . . . cette fille, yeux éhontés, frêle, aux lèvres rouges . . . la chambre, la cheminée haute . . . la salle . . . mon père, ma mère . . . tous trois assis, mon père, ma mère . . . moi-même . . . " *Les lauriers sont coupés*, 61.

17 "combien jolie, là, mi-renversée, dans la voiture! Tour à tour son visage est éclairé puis obscurci, tour à tour dans l'ombre indécise et dans le blanc des lumières, tandis que s'avance la voiture; près des becs de gaz, en effet, est une grande clarté, puis, après les becs, un obscurcissement; encore; le gaz de droite brille davantage; oh! Sa belle blanche face, blanche mat, blanche d'ivoire, blanche de neige obscure, dans le noir qui l'enserre, et tour à tour plus blanche, plus lumineuse dans les lumières, et dans l'ombre s'atténuant, et puis resurgissant; cependant sur le bois uni du pavé roule la voiture où nous sommes," *Les lauriers sont coupés*, 67–68.

18 "peut-être qu'elle avait raison, et qu'il est rare, l'homme qui aime, et que jamais elle ne fut aimée; moi non plus ne l'aimerai-je donc pas? Hélas! Que je l'aime peu, que peu je l'aime, moi que m'efforce à l'amour!" *Les lauriers son coupés*, 86. Compare Gabriel's thought in Joyce's "The Dead" after hearing the story of Michael Furey's love for Gretta: "He had never felt like that himself towards any woman but he knew that such a feeling must be love," *Dubliners*, 224.

19 See, for example, Ben Hutchinson's *Modernism and Style*, 143: "Although *Ulysses* undertakes the familiar modernist move of foregrounding its own style, it does so in a way that differs from its stylistic predecessor *Les lauriers sont coupés*. Where Dujardin's novel is characterized by a single homogenous style (which one might define as the Wagnerian-Schopenhauerian idiom typical of symbolism), *Ulysses* revels in an exuberance of heterogeneous *styles*."

20 Dorothy Richardson, *Pilgrimage*, vol. I, 10. The first volume of the *Pilgrimage* series, *Pointed Roofs*, appeared in 1915. The whole series consists of fifteen novels or what Richardson called "chapters," twelve of which are complete. For an excellent analysis of the consciousness-centered style of the series, see Shirley Rose, pp. 366–382.

21 William James, vol. I, 239: "Consciousness . . . does not appear to itself chopped up in bits . . . It is nothing jointed; it flows. A 'river' or a 'stream' are the metaphors by which it is most naturally described. In talking of it hereafter, let us call it the stream of thought, of consciousness, *or of subjective life*" (my emphasis).

22 For Richardson's interest in issues concerning women and feminism, see the articles collected in *The Gender of Modernism: A Critical Anthology*, ed. Bonnie Kime Scott, on such topics as "The Reality of Feminism," "Women in the Arts," and "Women and the Future," 401–425.

23 May Sinclair, "The Novels of Dorothy Richardson," *The Egoist*, V (April 1918), 57–59. It was originally written for *The Little Review*, which published it the same month (pp. 3–11). It has been reprinted in *The Gender of Modernism: A Critical Anthology*, ed. Bonnie Kime Scott, 442–448. In addition to *Pointed Roofs*, Sinclair was responding to *Backwater* (1916) and *Honeycomb* (1917).

24 "Dorothy M. Richardson," in *Authors Today and Yesterday*, ed. Stanley Kunitz (New York: H. W. Wilson, 1933), 562.

25　Richardson, "Adventure for Readers," *Life and Letters* 22 (July 1939): 45–52; reprinted in *The Gender of Modernism*, 428.

26　Henry James, p. 388.

27　Dorothy Richardson, *Pilgrimage: Pointed Roofs*, 48.

28　Melvin Friedman explains the problem as follows (although not in relation to Dorothy Richardson): "The apparent unselectiveness of the 'silent' or unspoken monologue makes some pattern all the more essential. When the inner voice unfolds, there are presumably no logical or syntactical restraints. The movement is controlled completely on the levels of reason and language by the capricious emotions of the monologueur. If not carefully controlled, the dangerous facility of this method may cause a complete disregard of literary values. The uninterrupted flow of thought must be relieved by some contrivance, delicately interwoven in the pattern of the monologue, subtle enough to indicate direction without jarring the sensibility of the reader. The leitmotiv when effectively applied does exactly this . . . Its contextual position even in music is decided on emotional rather than logical lines." *Stream of Consciousness*, 15.

29　Cited by Deborah Parsons, p. 60.

30　This interview, published in *The Future of the Novel: Famous Authors and Their Methods: A Series of Interviews with Renowned Authors*, ed. Meredith Starr (Boston: Small, Maynard, 1921), 87–89, has been reprinted in *The Gender of Modernism*, 476–478.

31　" 'The Future of the Novel': An Interview," *The Gender of Modernism*, 477–478. Compare Sinclair's proclamation with that of Samuel Beckett on James Joyce's *Finnegans Wake* in *Finnegans Wake: A Symposium: Our Examination Round His Factification for Incamination of Work in Progress*. He argues that Joyce's "writing *is not about something; it is that something itself*," 14.

32　T. S. Eliot's November 1923 review of Joyce's *Ulysses*, "Ulysses, Order and Myth," in *The Dial*.

33　James Joyce, *Dubliners*, 101.

34　May Sinclair, *Life and Death of Harriet Frean*, 15.

35　May Sinclair, *The Cure of Souls*, 1.

References

Banfield, Ann. (1982). *Unspeakable Sentences: Narration and Representation in the Language of Fiction*. New York: Routledge.

Cohn, Dorritt. (1984). *Transparent Minds: Narrative Modes for Presenting Consciousness in Fiction*. Princeton, NJ: Princeton University Press.

Dujardin, Édouard. (1991). *The Bays Are Sere and Interior Monologue*, trans. Anthony Suter. London: Libris.

Friedman, Melvin. (1955). *Stream of Consciousness: A Study in Literary Method*. New Haven, CT: Yale University Press.

Humphrey, Robert. (1954). *Stream of Consciousness in the Modern Novel*. Berkeley: University of California Press.

Hutchinson, Ben. (2011). *Modernism and Style*. Basingstoke: Palgrave.

James, Henry. (1905). "*The Art of Fiction*." In *Partial Portraits*. London: Macmillan.

James, William. (1950). *The Principles of Psychology*. New York: Dover.

Joyce, James. (1967). *Dubliners, Dubliners*, intro. and notes by Terence Brown. New York: Penguin.

Macaulay, Rose. (1998 [1926]) . *Crewe Train*. London: Little, Brown-Virago.

Parsons, Deborah. (2007). *Theorists of the Modernist Novel: James Joyce, Dorothy Richardson, Virginia Woolf*. London: Routledge.

Richardson, Dorothy. (1938). *Pilgrimage*, 4 vols. New York: Alfred A. Knopf.

Richardson, Dorothy. (2010 [1915]). *Pilgrimage: Pointed Roofs*. London: Dodo Press.

Rose, Shirley. (1969). "The Unmoving Center: Consciousness in Dorothy Richardson's *Pilgrimage*." *Contemporary Literature*, 10.3 (Summer).

Sinclair, May. (1924). *The Cure of Souls*. New York: Macmillan.

Sinclair, May. (1980 [1922]) *Life and Death of Harriet Frean*. London: Virago Press.

Wyzewa, Teodor de. (1895). *Nos maîtres: études et portraits littéraires*. Paris: Perrin.

Scott, Bonnie Kime, ed. (1990). *The Gender of Modernism: A Critical Anthology*. Bloomington: Indiana University Press.

3

Modernisms High and Low

Eric Bulson

Ich bin schon da[1]

Announcing the death of the avant-garde is nothing new. Sure, some articulations lasted longer than others, but ephemerality, obsolescence, and dissolution were always built in from the beginning, since the very idea of "making it new," as the slogan goes, always came with an expiration date. Any hope of being avant-garde in the nineteenth and twentieth centuries has, by necessity, required the embrace, however ambivalent, of modernity's march forward, and the avant-gardists, the ones with any modicum of dignity, never let themselves end up like so many aging rock stars of today staging comebacks at out-of-the-way amusement parks when they once played sold-out stadiums. Even the German Expressionists made concessions when, as Theodor Adorno observed, "they became older and had to earn a living," and the Dadaists, aging like everyone else, were next in line with so many of them converting to Catholicism or joining the Communist Party (1997, 30). Beginning with the Utopianists of Saint-Simon and the Symbolists of Mallarmé in the nineteenth century and followed by the Futurists, Expressionists, Dadaists, Surrealists, Constructivists, Abstract Expressionists, and Situationists in the twentieth, it's clear that the avant-garde didn't just arrive by fiat and disappear from the cultural landscape; it died over and over again, each incarnation picking up the torch and lighting up the world, before burning to the ground and leaving someone else to scatter the ashes.

Whatever one may think about this or that "ism," the truth is that the European avant-gardes, even when they failed (which they always did), radically influenced how we continue to theorize the production and consumption of art in the twentieth century and after. The tactics for each movement varied widely, but in every case, there was an idea that traditional forms of art were not capable of representing

A Handbook of Modernism Studies, First Edition. Edited by Jean-Michel Rabaté.
© 2013 John Wiley & Sons, Ltd. Published 2013 by John Wiley & Sons, Ltd.

experience in the modern world, and the modern artist, the one experimenting with techniques of representation and the materiality of the media, was capable of resisting manipulation by the political and cultural forces controlling the production and distribution of artworks. For Adorno, the "rise of high capitalism" in the mid-nineteenth century fed this frenzy for newness in literature, music, and the visual arts. "Since that moment," he writes, "no artwork has succeeded that rebuffed the ever fluctuating concept of the modern" (1997, 19). Modern artists were not the first ones to worry about originality, of course, but from Baudelaire on, they were part of an emerging capitalist system that was changing how art could be made, seen, circulated, and experienced by an increasingly dominant bourgeois class. This relentless search for the "new" in the arts, then, was intimately linked with the formation of a cultural apparatus undergirded by capitalist interests and an ideology of progress. The work of art in the age of high capitalism was a commodity like any other: production was motivated by profit and consumption was calculated from above.

And that's where the avant-garde comes in. For its artists, the search for newness was not simply about staying modern for its own sake. Rather, the creation of new art-forms enabled them to reflect critically on what being modern meant in the first place, and, in doing so, they attempted to resist, if only temporarily, becoming part of the commercial and cultural machine so eager to appropriate and/or denounce them. It was this desire for resistance from within, in fact, that brought the avant-garde into such close contact with mass culture at the beginning of the twentieth century. By adapting the techniques and technologies of mass media – film, radio, print – avant-gardists could expose the appropriation of art for ideological ends. For Walter Benjamin, it was the Dadaists who provided one of the most successful campaigns. They responded to the commodification process by deliberately creating works that emphasized their own uselessness. "Their poems," Benjamin elaborates, "are a 'word salad' containing obscenities, and every imaginable waste product of language. The same is true of their paintings, on which they mounted buttons and tickets. What they intended and achieved was a relentless destruction of the aura of their creation which they branded as reproductions with the very means of production" (2003, 266). The Dada work of art, if you can even call it that, was not a unique, sacred object intended for solitary consumption in a museum by the bourgeois. Instead, it was a reproducible object from the very moment of its creation intended to circulate among the masses and be forgotten like any lost button or bus ticket.

With the formation of the avant-garde, the very institution of art was under attack. The Italian Futurists were vowing to burn down the museums (which they never did), Dadaists were submitting mass-produced objects to art exhibitions, and the Surrealists were experimenting with automatic writing. But it is too often forgotten that not long after these artistic revolutions were afoot, a series of heated debates were also underway among some of the leading Marxist philosophers and writers of the time – Georg Lukács, Ernst Bloch, Bertolt Brecht, Adorno, and Benjamin – all of them keen to assess the triumphs and failures of modernism and its relationship to mass culture. The contribution of the avant-garde to art theory and aesthetics began with these figures; under their influence, later critics like Peter Bürger and

Andreas Huyssen would assess the "historical avant-garde" and its neo-avant-garde legacy in the second half of the twentieth century when, to borrow the hedgehog's fateful words to the hare, it all seemed as if we've been there before.

Why, the fellow writes for money

It may seem like a contradiction to treat the avant-garde as a unified subject for critical analysis. Each movement wanted revolution in art and life, not institutionalization by museums or academic departments. And yet, looking back from the other end of the twentieth century, it's clear enough that they never really had a chance. Already by the late 1950s, advertisers in the culture industry appropriated the shock effects first developed by the Surrealists and Dadaists, academia enshrined high modernism, and neo-avant-garde movements, particularly within the United States, rallied around their avant-garde ancestors for the sake of cultural legitimacy. But even if the memory of these avant-gardes was alive and well when they were long gone, no one had yet fully assessed what they left behind and why the avant-garde spirit continued to circulate, albeit problematically, in the cultural sphere.

Peter Bürger's *Theory of the Avant-Garde* marked a significant intervention. Published in German in 1974, in the wake of the failed student protests of the 1960s, it was the first full-scale attempt to see the avant-garde less as a series of isolated responses to art vis-à-vis art and more as a collective response to the rise of capitalism and the commodification of art from the end of the eighteenth century to the middle of the twentieth. This theory, then, treats the avant-garde as a subject in its own right and distinguishes the formation of an "historical avant-garde" that failed in its objectives (which I'll say more about shortly) from the post-WWII neo-avant-garde that "institutionalize[d] the *avant-garde as art* and thus negated genuinely avant-gardiste intentions" (1984, 58). Bürger's book, then, is a product of its time and place, positing a theory of art and aesthetics that turns, somewhat despondently, against the May '68 hopes for a resurgence of an original avant-gardist ethos in art and society.

The historical avant-garde did not emerge fully formed like Athena from the head of Zeus. It was a stage in a much longer historical process intimately bound up with the institutionalization of art in bourgeois society. The technologies of mass production and distribution, which were making art more accessible to the masses, simultaneously generated a different response from a bourgeois audience eager to protect culture from contamination. The effect, then, was twofold, giving rise to a "low" culture for the masses and a "high" culture for the elite, both caught up in a capitalist system that traded art works like commodities while treating them as autonomous objects allegedly separate from the world of money and politics.

Autonomy, Bürger explains, was the goal of the bourgeoisie; it was based on the belief that art could be stripped of any social function, marginalizing the artist in the process. And the more asocial art and the artist became, justifying *l'art pour l'art* of Gautier and the hermetic aestheticism of the symbolists, the more detached they were from everyday life itself. It was this separation of art and life that would become particularly problematic. For one thing, it was built on the false assumption that works of art were either socially engaged or asocial and worthless. For another, it emphasized the false opposition between the form and content of works of art: they either presented a political or socially directed message or retreated into formalism for its own sake. What happened to art at the end of the nineteenth century is more complicated than either of these facile formulations might lead us to believe. The autonomy that comes with the institutionalization of art coincides with the emptying out of social content, and, as Bürger explains, "the apartness from the praxis of life that had always constituted the institutional status of art in bourgeois society now becomes the content of works" (1984, 27). Put another way, the more disengaged art became from the social world, the more it came to represent nothing but its own "apartness."

The autonomy of art in the nineteenth-century art for art's sake movement paved the way for the rise of the historical avant-garde at the beginning of the twentieth century. Instead of simply accepting the artificial divide between art and life, high and low, autonomous and engaged art, the movement actively sought to collapse it. To do so, the avant-garde did not worry itself with specific movements, styles, or traditions; it attacked the institution of art itself, focusing its energy on the distribution apparatus responsible for the circulation and reception of art (1984, 22). There are a variety of different approaches – often depending on the particular programs of each movement – but in general, the movement involved producing works of art self-conscious about their own status as commodities within an exchange-based economy. The avant-garde artwork, then, was as much a product of technologies of mass production and reproduction as it was an item with a price tag waiting to be bought and sold. Ironically enough, worthlessness was the goal. It is no wonder that Bürger's theory fell on fertile ground in the United States in the 1980s (translated into English only in 1984), just when the critique of art institutions and of art as institution had been revived in a postmodern context.

However noble the intention to merge art and life, the historical avant-garde ultimately failed. The autonomy of art could not be sublated in life through the tactics and techniques developed by Dada or the Surrealists, and the bourgeois institution of art it supported remained very much intact while they fell apart. Looking at the neo-avant-gardes of his own time, Bürger wondered "whether the distance between art and the praxis of life is not requisite for that free space within which alternatives to what exists become conceivable" (1984, 54). His theory is grounded in that tension between the rise of autonomy in the nineteenth century and the reaction-formation of the avant-garde. It was an autonomy established by aesthetes, enabled by capitalism, and guarded by an elite that could not be defeated. And yet, Bürger's speculation about "alternatives" leads us back to that other theorist of advanced art, Theodor W. Adorno. He argued consistently in his writings between the 1930s and the 1960s that autonomy was the only way that art could negate the alienating effects of a capitalist-supported culture industry. The avant-garde may have produced one failed response to the concrete historical conditions of modernity, but Adorno's work maps out another trajectory that follows the faultline of high modernism from Beethoven to Beckett.

For Adorno, Beethoven was one of the earliest examples of the artist-composer whose compositions bear traces of the ongoing conflict between "the market and independence in bourgeois art" (1976) Beethoven's career, which can be divided into early, middle, late, exemplifies the ongoing struggle of the modern artist to unify the subjective experience of reality with objective historical conditions. If Beethoven managed, however tenuously, to synthesize the two in his second period, his so-called "late style" demonstrates a definitive break between subject and object, the work of art and the world represented, as manifested by the fragmentary form of the music itself. For Adorno, this fragmentation within the formal structure of harmonic music signifies the negation of an alienating social reality, and points to one of Beethoven's triumphs: giving form, however fractured, to a subjective experience that points to a loss of subjectivity without ever overcoming it. That is more than can be said for his contemporary, Sir Walter Scott. Throwing one of Scott's novels across the room while on his deathbed, an enraged Beethoven exclaimed in frustration: "Why, the fellow writes for money" (Adorno, 1976). He was right.

King Ludwig II amusing himself in the cave of the Venusberg

The death of the avant-garde was not some abstract event for Adorno. He lived through it all in the 1920s and 30s during the Nazi takeover, which drove him and so many other intellectuals into exile. He also followed the 1930s Marxist debates about the legacy of Expressionism, Dada, and Surrealism. Lukács was later one of Adorno's main antagonists, and the two of them, though of a shared Marxist philosophical tradition, could not be farther apart in their assessment about modernism and the avant-gardes that had risen and fallen across Europe. Lukács championed socialist realism because he believed that it could accurately reflect contemporary reality and deemed all forms of modernist and avant-garde art decadent because they reproduced the fragmentation of modern subjectivity without providing an antidote. Adorno argued that Lukács had fundamentally misunderstood the production and reception of art under capitalism. For Adorno, the value of art was not to be found in its explicit social or political content, but in its highly mediated forms. The battle between the two in the 1950s can stand in for the Cold War conflict between Soviet socialist realism and the free art of the West.

In the Unites States, Adorno still has the reputation of being an elitist, someone interested only in a production of high modernism with an all male, all white, all Euro cast. And yet, his opposition to Lukács was, in the end, very much informed by the belief that experimental forms of art in any medium – literature, film, music, radio, painting – could play an oppositional role in society. "Experimental," as he defined it in a late essay, "Difficulties" (1964), "means nothing other than art's self-conscious power of resistance against what is conventionally forced upon it from the outside, by consensus" (2002, 651). To experiment is to resist consensus.

Sure, experiments do not always work out, but they are still necessary in breaking from the habits, routines, pressures, and ideologies from "outside," the ones that quash originality instead of encouraging it. And what is true for the artist is true for the audience who must find ways to absorb, process, and react to what is being seen or heard – not so easy in the age of mass reproduction where a medium like music is already so standardized. Instead of getting what they really want (or think they really want), listeners get what the culture industry wants them to want: the same old thing over and over again. The unconscious responses to this or that song on the radio, for instance, are programmed from the start, making it possible for "the tired businessman," as Adorno so memorably puts it, to "clap arranged classics on the shoulder and fondle the progeny of their muse" (2002, 299). This clapping and fondling is symptomatic of an inability to hear anything at all. Listeners are alienated consumers, who think they are exercising free choice when they turn the dial and recognize a song they "like." Truth is, this desire for the comfort of the status quo makes individual taste difficult, if not impossible, to cultivate.

Adorno spent his entire career thinking about the ways that mass culture was appropriated by powerful political and cultural forces urging consensus over all else and applauding forms of art that dumbed down the audience instead of raising it up. And it is this celebration of the status quo that makes dissenting voices, then and now, as urgent as ever. Adorno found other successful examples in literary figures like Kafka, Proust, and Beckett, but during his exile in Los Angeles, he also befriended the Surrealist sculptor and painter Max Ernst. Lecturing on Wagner in 1963, Adorno recalled an idea Ernst once advanced with delight: King Ludwig II amusing himself in the cave of the Venusberg (2002, 600). For Adorno, this image of a king alone in a cave amusing himself was deliberately off-putting: the two just do not belong together. And the same was true, he believed, for the contemporary productions of Wagner that wanted to follow the composer's "precise instructions." History, however, had intervened in the meantime with the Nazi Wagner cult making this totalizing version of the world as problematic as ever. That, in the end, was one reason that "experimental solutions" were necessary for contemporary reproductions of Wagner's operas: they had the power to force "what is false, flawed, and antinomical out into the open," and in doing so make Wagner relevant to another time and place (Adorno 2002, 600).

What after all is left to do but scream

Adorno did not devote more than a few brief essays to the subject of the historical avant-garde as Bürger defined it. And yet, his essays on Wagner, Schönberg, Mahler, Kafka, Benjamin, Beckett, Proust, Jazz, Radio, and Film as well as his books – *The Dialectic of Enlightenment*, *Negative Dialectics*, and *Aesthetic Theory* – were both an historical example of modern art's failure under high capitalism and a testing ground for the techniques co-opted by artists searching for autonomy and a culture industry vying for total control. In both cases, the avant-garde circulates throughout Adorno's early and late writing with unusual frequency, sometimes there to provide an offhand example, other times as the counterpoint within a much larger argument. It is this constant presence that inspired Bürger's claim that Adorno brought out the significance of the avant-garde "for aesthetic theory in our time" (1984, 87).

How can this be? How is it possible that a series of failed avant-garde movements could become so central to Adorno's aesthetic theory in the twentieth century? In order to begin answering this question, a few clarifications are in order. The historical avant-garde, as mentioned, was dissatisfied with this separation between life and art in bourgeois society, and in an attempt to reintegrate the two, it tried to re-socialize art by doing away with its autonomy – a goal with which Adorno never agreed. But here's the problem: while the avant-garde was attacking the commodification of art, as Adorno would, totalitarian governments in Germany and Russia were assuming complete control of artistic production and distribution for ideological ends. The fusion of art and life, then, happened in the 1920s and 30s, but it was a success reserved for Stalin and the Nazis, not Dada and the Surrealists.

Though he was always more pessimistic than Benjamin about the avant-garde's revolutionary potential, Adorno did acknowledge that the production of a "shock" effect through the individual work of art was one of the avant-garde's more important discoveries. In "Why is the New Art so Hard to Understand?" he explains that shock is the ultimate expression of the "new" in modernity; it is an effect produced by the work of art on the listener, viewer, or reader, who is roused into a state of self-consciousness and made to reflect on the production of the work of art. This effect is intimately connected with the work's difficulty, deriving, as it does, from a formal complexity within itself that cannot be immediately digested or understood. This is a familiar motif in Adorno's aesthetic theory: under capitalism, art is made for easy consumption, a way to generate a culture for the masses that they can understand. In his mind, however, the dumbing down of music, literature, and art for mass consumption is another form of ideological control from above, since it is produced by an industry that pretends to celebrate individuality and freedom when it simply wants acquiescence. That is why the shock of the avant-garde was so significant: it foregrounded the separation between "production and consumption," and, in doing so, it showed that "art no longer ha[d] the task of representing a reality that preexisted for everyone in common, but rather of revealing, in its isolation, the very cracks that reality would like to cover over in order to exist in safety; and that, in so doing, it repel[led] reality" (2002, 131).

Administering shocks to the minds of a docile public was a common tactic of the avant-garde. More than a publicity stunt or a way to garner attention, shock was one way to try to change the function of art in society. Experimental forms of production, they set out to demonstrate, had the power to inspire new modes of consumption. The shock was itself a way to break through habitual modes of perception that were increasingly in the grip of institutions and governments eager to suppress individuality, sensuality, desire, and taste. To choose one common example, the Cubists and Surrealists preferred montage and collage: juxtaposing images stripped from their original context and forced into unexpected relationships that resisted any easy interpretation. Composed entirely of fragments, montage and collage do not reflect an external, objective reality. Rather, they are a subjective representation of a broken reality referring back only to itself, with the potential to, as Bürger puts it, "change one's conduct in life" by breaking through aesthetic immanence and ushering in "a change in the recipient's life praxis" (1984, 80).

That was the goal at least: to rouse individual consciousness by generating shock effects with techniques like montage. What happened instead should have been predicted from the start: the newness of these shocks eventually wore off. This loss of the new was not reserved only for montage. Modern artistic production in different media under capitalism was eager to make it new but unable to keep it new. "From photographs and movies," Adorno writes, "one knows the effect produced by the modern grown old, an effect originally used by the surrealists to shock and subsequently degraded to the cheap amusement of those whose fetishism fastens on the abstract present" (2002, 311). This fetishism, he explains elsewhere, was visible in the popular practice of modernizing opera sets to produce a "surrealist tease" before the deadening effect of institutionalization begins (2002, 384).

The "modern grown old" is a common refrain in Adorno. It is connected to the idea that the more commodified art becomes within society, the more difficult it is to provide alternative possibilities for resistance. The avant-garde ultimately gave Adorno a negative example of hope for modern art under capitalism. Its formal experiments tried, but ultimately failed, to counteract the rationalization of cultural production and reception in the twentieth century. In itself, weakening of the shock was not what brought the historical avant-garde down for good, nor was it Hitler and Stalin, though their repressive cultural policies both accelerated the process. Rather, it was, in a more general sense, their inability to move art beyond the expression of an "absolute subjectivity," one that would allow the individual to see himself as an other, to see the object of art as an other, and in doing so, to come face to face with the fractured image of an alienated self that finds meaning in a meaningless existence. Faced with this powerlessness, then, Adorno, evoking the image of Edvard Munch's famous painting, asks the question on everyone's mind: "what after all is left to do but scream" (1997, 30).

The devil speaks Adorno's mind

The term modernism should not be conflated with avant-garde and vice versa. For Adorno, they represent different critical responses to the commodification of art at the same historical moment: the former opting for autonomy as a strategy of resistance, the latter striving to conflate art and life, thereby rendering autonomy unnecessary. And if the avant-garde engaged directly with the media and message of mass culture, modernists (in Adorno's version at least) took refuge in high culture, producing works characterized by their difficulty and intended for the fit and few.

Autonomy was one way for art to avoid the corrupting influence of the culture industry, and novelists like Proust, Kafka, and Beckett and composers like Schönberg, Berg, and Webern clung to it like the rapidly disappearing mast of a sinking ship.

They were not, however, the first ones who longed for freedom. Valéry and Mallarmé fought for it a generation earlier, believing that art could exist in the rarefied space of the parlor detached from the goings-on of culture, and duped into thinking that capitalism, and "the bloated pleasure apparatus" it supported, could be kept at bay simply by closing the shutters. After World War I, however, with the avant-garde in position and the culture industry tightening its grip on high and low culture alike, the struggle for autonomy was fierce. The standardization of cultural products made it even more difficult for artists to express themselves freely and for consumers to decide for themselves what to read, listen to, or watch. In Adorno's analysis of high/low, producer/consumer, culture was not something that circulated upward from the masses. It was a top-down procedure supported by an industry that "intentionally integrates its consumers from above" (1975, 12). The masses, though consumers necessary for the culture industry's survival, do not have much say in the matter: culture is produced for them and even though they have their likes and dislikes, the truth is that none of it matters anyway: even the most unlikeable cultural products have a place in a system that quells opposition by embracing it.

Worst of all, for Adorno, the culture industry collapses the spheres of high and low together, and, in doing so, denies the seriousness of both. "The seriousness of high art," he explains in "Culture Industry Reconsidered," "is destroyed in speculation about its efficacy; the seriousness of the lower perishes with the civilizational constraints imposed on the rebellious resistance inherent within it as long as social control was not yet total" (1975, 3). Put another way, the value of high art gets determined by the price it can bring within a market economy or the immediate social function it can serve, while low art, historically a place where resistance against institutions of power was exerted, becomes one more place where the master, pretending to be the benevolent uncle, can exert control. When seriousness disappears, the bar gets lower and lower; instead of producing cultural forms that offer more complex, intelligent, sophisticated options to the public, it gives the masses what they want them to want. Hollywood, then, can go on producing what it calls "serious" movies that eleven-year-olds can understand and enjoy, and, in doing so, makes the adults in the audience more, not less, like them.

In collapsing high with low, the culture industry kills autonomy. Of course, individual examples of autonomous art can be found in Ancient Greece, the Middle Ages, and the Renaissance, but, as Adorno was always quick to point out, autonomy never existed in an entirely pure form. The very need for autonomous art presupposes the presence of an outside force – be it political or social – so that the two are related dialectically. In the twentieth century, with a culture industry firmly entrenched, the degree of this external pressure was markedly different, and serious art – and the truth it had the potential to deliver – was only possible if it was kept separate from having to serve any claims of a didactic or social function. To be autonomous, then, art had to serve only itself, and it could only do so, as Huyssen contends, by negating "the negativity of reality." That at least is one of the ideas Thomas Mann borrowed from Adorno when he was writing *Doctor Faustus*. And

Huyssen was not alone in realizing that it was "the devil" and not the composer who "speaks Adorno's mind" (1986, 144).

To explain what this "negation of negativity" means, it is worth looking briefly at what Adorno had to say about Wagner, Schönberg, Kafka, and Beckett. These pairs of artists – two composers, two writers – circulate consistently throughout his writing. Each of them represents a particular response to the alienation of modern life and the role of the artist and the work of art in society. Though at root subjective in their experience, they still managed to create works that capture something objectively true about the fragmentation of identity under capitalism.

Wagner the spider

Wagner, the nineteenth-century composer, lived through the explosive transition from a premodern to a modern world and witnessed the birth of the culture industry. Returning to the subject of Wagner repeatedly throughout his life, Adorno sought to demystify the process by which works of high art bind to more abstract social processes responsible for the production of mass culture. His 1938 essay on Wagner, in particular, attempts to excavate the social and cultural roots of German fascism in the nineteenth century, which in its totalitarian ambitions and rationalized administration prefigured the culture industry, and to account for the impact of commodification on the internal structure of musical compositions and their reception. "Everything in Wagner has its historical core," he contends: "Like a spider, his spirit sits in the gigantic web of nineteenth century exchange relations" (2002, 599). Indeed, Wagner may have tried to resist the market's demand for "easy listening" (a term that Adorno keeps in English) by composing works that made serious demands on the attention span and intelligence of listeners. What he didn't realize, according to Adorno, was his own entanglement in the very web on which he sat: the more Wagner attempted to free himself from commercial pressures, the more commodified his compositions became. Wagner therefore represents the artist who, in resisting the system, ends up unknowingly acquiescing. His works reflect the compromise between the desire to create wholly from within the subject and the pressures that made such autonomous creation impossible.

Taking this web apart strand by strand, Adorno argues that commodification infiltrated every aspect of Wagner's *Gesamtkunstwerk*, from the conductor on stage beating the bewildered audience into submission to the leitmotiv running steadily throughout the melody for the forgetful listener unable to keep track. This analysis of the total work of art reveals, as Huyssen points out, the impact of commodification inside the structural organization of the work (its melody and fragmentation) and outside in its production and reception. Most frightening of all is the suggestion that the total work of art, which Wagner perfected, prefigured the formation of a totalitarian government not far off on the horizon. No one in Wagner's time could have fully understood the extreme violence and fragmentation hidden underneath the music, but Adorno, writing in an age of a Fascist Wagner cult, tried to show how his music concealed where the battle for autonomy was being fought. In doing so, he was able to analyze the emergence of the culture industry in Wagner before he ever got to Hollywood.

Schönberg the builder

Adorno's avant-garde hero, if there ever was one, misunderstood by the public, denigrated by critics, and betrayed by musicians unable to perform his works or tricked into believing in a Schönberg formula. He was the composer from the second Viennese school who proclaimed the "end of conformity," rejecting fin-de-siècle aestheticism and the chromaticism of Wagner (1983, 150). But he did so immanently, working within the musical structures themselves and bringing them to their objective conclusions. The result was the invention of the twelve-tone technique that revolutionized modern music. Going this far with his experiments, Schönberg was not unlike Beethoven in his second and third phases, who "reproduced the meaning of tonality out of subjective freedom." But being the product of another *hic et nunc*, namely Vienna after World War I, there was a dramatic difference, and it was most notable in his late style, defined by an atonality that "virtually extinguished the subject" (1973, 89). This association between the near-death of the subject and the birth of the twelve-tone technique comes from the idea that the tone row in classical compositions, which was once free from static recurrence, develops into a more rigid, hierarchical formula that dominates the structure, reflecting, as Eugene Lunn observes, the "repressively rationalized social whole" (1982, 263–264). By employing the twelve-tone technique, Schönberg produced music that was both "explosively anti-conventional" and "cohesively constructed" (640).

Atonality is the closest that Schönberg comes to achieving autonomy in his music, but it is never entirely independent and his achievement, though noble, fails to liberate the subject. Still, it provided a negative possibility for freedom conceived against, and in response to, a more repressive traditional structure. In one of his many attempts to define twelve-tone technique, Adorno explains:

> it follows that the origin of the new harmony must be sought in the realm of the emphatically expressionless, as much as in the realm of expression, as much in hostility to language as in language – even though this hostile element, which is alien to the continuum of the idiom, repeatedly served to realize something that was linguistic in a higher degree, namely the articulation of the whole. (Adorno 2002, 119)

The twelve-tone technique gives form to an expressionless expression. There is no false reconciliation between the notes. Rather, dissonance itself becomes a way to resist it. Schönberg managed to create compositions that embodied the struggle of a fettered subjectivity still trying to make itself heard. In doing so, the dissonance from this subjective expression captures what is so often inexpressible by words or notes.

Like the avant-garde movements with which he is often compared, Schönberg also managed to shock his audience "by not making any concessions" (1983, 154). The hostile reactions and genuine frustration of listeners were symptomatic of regressive listening habits reinforced by commercialized music. With the arrival of Schönberg, the truth about alienated art was all before them, but the audience either could not make any sense of what he was trying to say or, as Adorno suspects, they knew all too well and didn't want to face it. Unfamiliar, dissonant, and uncomfortable, his compositions demanded active listening and were just the kind of thing Adorno imagined would act as an antidote against the total manipulation of the culture industry, which is why, I suspect, the essay which contains his most sustained critique of reified listening ends with such a triumphant crescendo:

> The terror which Schönberg and Webern spread, today as in the past, comes not from their incomprehensibility but from the fact that they are all too correctly understood. Their music gives form to that anxiety, that terror, that insight into the catastrophic situation which others merely evade by regressing. They are called individualists, and yet their work is nothing but a single dialogue with the powers which destroy individuality – powers whose 'formless shadows' fall colossally on their music. (2002, 315)

Difficulty is itself an expression of this alienation and its potential antidote, a way in which the modern artist creates something new by forcing the audience to face its own reified subjectivity.

Kafka the run of the mill insurance company employee

Along with Beckett, Kafka was responsible for creating the "dark works of modernism" by which Adorno means to say those works devoted to the absurdity of modern life that were unafraid to confront and then laugh at all that is untrue about truth (1997, 318). Like Schönberg, Kafka struggled to find a form of writing that would enable him to resist from within as he wove together stories, parables really, about rationalized life told in the plainest language possible by narrators as guarded and mysterious as the desperate characters they are always sending for and then avoiding. In *Aesthetic Theory* (1991), Adorno proudly points out that even Lukács, when imprisoned in Romania, had to admit that Kafka was a realist, but of course, a far cry from the likes of Dickens and Tolstoy, writing "negative epics" instead of novels (35). His is a realism for the twentieth century that reflects the liquidation of individuality instead of creating an illusory social totality. But in this regard, Kafka is also an expressionist, someone who manages to harness this experience of reified subjectivity into an objectively realized form. "The more the I of Expressionism is thrown back upon itself," Adorno writes in his "Notes on Kafka," "the more like the excluded world of things it becomes.... Pure subjectivity, being of necessity estranged from itself as well as having become a thing, assumes the dimensions of objectivity which expresses itself through its own estrangement."

Kafka and Schönberg have a lot in common then: both found ways to make art reflect the experience of an estranged subject seeing itself as an object staring back. That, in effect, is the only hope for modernist art, not the illusion of an artificial reconciliation imposed from without, but the act of recording that gap – insurmountable, and yet, still worth the effort of jumping. Elsewhere in that same essay on Kafka, Adorno explains that so many of the decisive parts in his novels and stories "read as though they had been written in imitation of expressionist paintings that should have been painted but never were." There is no better definition for the negation of negativity than the work of art as denial, as resistance, as emptiness, and as silence which, in its fragmented form, actually captures the authentic ineffability of an alienated human existence.

He over whom Kafka's wheels have passed

Adorno is referring to Beckett. In his work, Beckett is the one against whom all high modernist art gets measured. In fact, you find references to him everywhere, in the most unlikely places. He is to Adorno what Baudelaire was to Benjamin: a literary companion, someone he counted on to define the possibility for authentic art in an alienated age. In the *Aesthetic Theory*, the posthumously published book he intended to dedicate to Beckett, there is a stunning passage summarizing all I've discussed so far, that begins with references to Dada, Expressionism, Surrealism, Picasso, and Schönberg, and ends with a sustained reflection on Beckett's novels:

> The narratives are marked as much by an objectively motivated loss of the object as by its correlative, the impoverishment of the subject. Beckett draws this lesson from montage and documentation, from all the attempts to free oneself from the illusion of a subjectivity that bestows meaning. Even where reality finds entry into the narrative, precisely at those points at which reality threatens to suppress what the literary subject once performed, it is evident that there is something uncanny about this reality. Its disproportion to the powerless subject, which makes it incommensurable with experience, renders reality unreal with a vengeance. The surplus of reality amounts to its collapse; by striking the subject dead, reality itself becomes deathly; this transition is the artfulness of all antiart, and in Beckett it is pushed to the point of the manifest annihilation of reality. (1997, 30–31)

Beckett's novels and plays do not provide a reflection of reality. They are the absence of a reflection, that "annihilation of reality," seen from the perspective of a subject who is already too alienated to know the difference. That, in the end, is the best possible outcome for modern art, a way to articulate the entire experience of finding meaning in a meaningless universe. His works, and the characters who inhabit them, are damaged goods through and through, and they make even the very act of interpretation useless, since, as Adorno concedes, "Beckett shrugs his shoulders at the possibility of philosophy today, at the very possibility of theory" (244). Still, as Adorno's appropriately titled essay "On Trying to Understand *Endgame*" proves, it is worth trying, if only to finally discover that there is nothing to be found except the knowledge that there are others like you still sitting on the top of the trash heap joking as Hamm and Clov do: "Mean something! You and I, mean something! (Brief laugh.) Ah that's a good one!"

Lukács of the Postmodern . . .

Huyssen ends his 1983 essay on Adorno with a question: "Who, after all, would want to be the Lukács of the postmodern . . ." (1986, 43). It is a question without a question mark. Instead, Huyssen inserts an ellipsis that makes his statement seem more like an open-ended possibility than a rhetorical backhand at poor Lukács's expense. When he wrote this line during the heady days of postmodernism, Huyssen made it clear that Lukács's ideas about the avant-garde and mass culture, opposed as they were to the virtues of socialist realism, just did not translate well in the second half of the century; wearing his mantle to navigate the postmodern landscape, then, would be a lot like sporting a hairshirt to the pool. Adorno, with his love of Proust, Kafka, Joyce, and Beckett, his disdain of socialist realism, and his ambivalence about the avant-garde's legacy especially as it related to "shock" as a technique, was more malleable. And if Bürger saw Adorno as a "theorist of the avant-garde," for Huyssen he was something else: a "theorist par excellence of the Great Divide" (1986, ix).

There's an important difference here, and it comes from these critics' understanding of the historical avant-garde's legacy and its relation to the emergence of postmodernism in the 1960s and 70s. For Bürger, as I said before, institutionalizing the historical avant-garde by resuscitating its message contradicted everything it once stood for, making the avant-garde one more cog in the culture industry's massive machine (film, advertising, etc.). For Huyssen, who began writing his essays on postmodernism at the same time in the United States, the institutionalization of modernism in the academy and the museum and the commodification of the avant-garde by the culture industry were a reality, but there was a lot more to it. The historical avant-garde may have failed in Western, Central, and Eastern Europe during the 1930s, but it paved the way for postmodern experiments in the United States, a country largely devoid of an indigenous avant-garde tradition. The so-called Great Divide, then, identifies this separation between postmodernism, with its love for mixing high and low cultural forms, and a high modernism, so carefully fashioned during the Cold War and distinguished from an explicitly political avant-garde. Instead of opposing modernism and mass culture, high and low, Huyssen used the postmodern to foreground how much they were already intertwined in the 1920s and 30s. Postmodernism seemed less a radical break from modernism and the avant-garde and more a new departure.

Huyssen's "Mapping the Postmodern," an essay that functioned for academics in the 1980s and 90s the way that Baedeker's guidebooks did for tourists a century earlier, fundamentally changed the direction of the conversation by demonstrating that postmodern art, literature, architecture, and music was itself a reaction-formation against this canonization of high modernism in the United States, the separation between high and low by artists, working in a variety of different media, who appropriated tactics and techniques invented by the avant-garde to produce serious works of art. Postmodernism was not as much a break from either high modernism or the avant-garde as it was another historically contingent stage in the development of modern art and aesthetics that elaborated on, and, at times, upended, experiments that first began on the other side of the divide. From this perspective, postmodernism was necessary to the avant-garde's legacy, and high art, once separated from the contamination of mass culture during the Cold War's canonization of modernism as unpolitical, was becoming its proponents' most welcome ally. For Huyssen, this blurring of high and low, which occurred in both directions (low to high and in reverse), represented a unique "opportunity" rather than a "loss of quality and failure of nerve" (1986, ix). Once cultural hierarchies began to fall apart, it became possible for artists excluded from the institutions controlling the circulation of art, to participate, creating works that could only have happened with this high/low, low/high collapse. As so often happens, the artists caught on quickly, but it was the critics who were lagging behind: they still used the same rigid binaries to discuss a version of modernism that had changed once postmodern was in progress.

Huyssen, then, picks up where Adorno and Bürger left off but not without acknowledging the crucial differences between them. Bürger, he points out, is never specific enough about how the avant-garde tried to overcome this dichotomy between art and life or adapt technology to the rise of mass culture. In addition, Adorno is also vague about the avant-garde's political options within their respective cultural contexts and how the way they affected artistic production, consumption, and distribution could be transformed into a new social reality. In Adorno's work, the culture industry under fascism was not any worse than under New Deal capitalism, but in his bleak view of the total commercialization and manipulation of culture, Adorno is unwilling to provide any antidote other than an autonomy of negativity. Indeed, following Kafka, Adorno might also have said that there's "plenty of hope, an infinite amount of hope – but not for us." But with Huyssen's more affirmative diagnosis of a postmodernism that resurrected the spirit of the avant-garde and responded critically to the elitism of high modernism and the lowness of low culture, it turns out that there just might be some hope after all.

In an introduction to a translation of Adorno's "Culture Industry Reconsidered" (1975), Huyssen identifies Adorno's key insights into modernism that are the points of departure for his own work on postmodernism: "the shrinking of the sphere of circulation of the era of liberalism, the standardization and administration of culture, the reification and commodity nature of aesthetic products, the predominance of exchange value and its impact on culture, the denial and suppression of human sensuality and spontaneity" (8). In an interesting twist, though, Huyssen, while recognizing the need for continued critical reflection on these processes of standardization, reification, and commodification in the age of postmodernism, is also attuned to the fact that there are neoconservative critics using them either to announce the end of art or to dismiss postmodernism *tout court* in order to protect a high modernist heritage. But that, in effect, is one more reason why postmodernism proved to be such a site for debate over the future of culture, and it was Huyssen who helped explain just what was at stake for those who wanted the divide up or down.

The divide is "great," it turns out, for those who either control the institution of art from above or huddle underneath its umbrella. For the rest, it functions more like a deep chasm that keeps the undesirables out. The avant-garde's attacks in the 1920s and 30s ultimately failed, but in the 1960s and 70s the situation changed, with new groups of undesirables – women, minorities – lining up to continue an old war with new strategies. The conditions on the ground, of course, were different. American mass culture in the 1950s and after was not under the control of a totalitarian government as it was in Russia and Germany in the 1920s and 30s, but the culture industry had infiltrated all spheres of everyday life. And as was true in Europe at an earlier stage in the history of modernity, the institutionalization of art in America (happening simultaneously) was generating a lively avant-garde reaction: Pop Art, happenings, psychedelic art, acid rock, alternative and street theater were the places where new "creative relationships" between high art and mass culture were being formed. The result, then, was a critical reappraisal of art itself and the role that it should, or could, play in society.

And the results were mixed. Pop Art, for instance, appropriated mass consumerism as a subject and advertising as a style, but its political bite in the 1960s was more evident in Germany than in the United States. This difference in reception had a lot to do with where these works were produced and shown. American critics were content in seeing an affirmation of consumer culture in Warhol's soup cans, while their German counterparts – trained in *Kulturkritik* – identified a more radical denunciation of the institution of art criticism and a closing of the gap between high and low. Pop Art never produced the revolution some of its practitioners wanted, but, Huyssen explains, it revealed the esoteric and elitist nature of avant-gardism by exposing, more than any other movement before it, "the commodity character of all contemporary art production." By so blatantly unmasking the commodity character of all works of art, Pop artists were questioning whether there is anything more to it than the buying and selling of goods. Huyssen, for one, believes that art does not have to be defined only by its exchange value. Autonomy and uselessness are still effective modes for resistance within the marketplace, and consumption, though manipulated to a degree by the culture industry, can still fulfill a basic human need and encourage an authentic aesthetic experience.

Postmodernism, for Huyssen, was the endgame of "international avant-gardism" (1986, 195). And in the United States this enabled some necessary reflection on what being avant-garde meant in the first place and how it could be remobilized within a different political, social, and cultural constellation, especially after the heyday of poststructuralism, which heavily critiqued Western Enlightenment ideology of which the avant-garde, even in its opposition, was a part. If it was started by groups of rebellious European males raging against the bourgeois institution of art, it ended up taken over by minorities and women historically excluded from its bases of operation. And that, in effect, is one of the historical avant-garde's greatest achievements: it created the conditions for resistance from below in the second half of the twentieth century by showing how mass cultural forms could be adapted. And they would, by women and minority artists interested in recuperating "buried and mutilated traditions," producing works that emphasized "gender- and race-based subjectivity," and refusing the "standard canonizations" that proved to be so limiting. The effect of this American avant-garde was enormous, precisely because it "added a whole new dimension to the critique of high modernism and to the emergence of alternative forms of culture." Postmodernism was not a mindless free-for-all for the dispossessed (1986, 198). Rather, it was a battleground over the very idea of art, aesthetics, and politics after World War II that revealed how strategies for resistance could still be adapted, even if they were provisional, before getting sucked into the culture industry's fulcrum and defanged. But even as this cycle of resistance, appropriation, resistance within the culture industry continues, the point is not to forget that art is always about the individual and collective struggle over expression, a site where resistance is possible no matter how powerful these economic, political, and social forces can be.

Kafka's axe

With postmodernism come and gone, Huyssen has redrafted the map once again, though this time around he is acutely aware that a global perspective on modernism, postmodernism, and after is more urgent than ever. Postmodernism, he admits, for all of its interest in "otherness," was largely an American phenomenon, and this same restricted view of cultural production, with roots firmly planted in the modernist soil of Western Europe and the United States, is no longer viable today. Through postcolonialism especially, which effectively rewrote the narrative on high modernism through the lens of imperialism and decolonization, and with even more recent advances in media, transport, and communications technologies, the world is getting smaller and the circuits of cultural production and consumption more tangled than ever. According to Huyssen, modernism therefore needs to be analyzed within a transnational context that involves "dynamic processes of cultural mingling and migration" (2007, 205). The trick, of course, is figuring out how to do this comparative work within a field so clearly divided along national lines, and with not only multiple modernisms but also alternative modernities that cannot be adequately understood by uncritically applying preexisting Western-based distinctions about art, culture, aesthetics, and politics.

In "Geographies of Modernism," Huyssen's manifesto for modernist studies in the twenty-first century, the high/low divide that was "prematurely put to rest by postmodernism" remains a useful category for comparative cultural analysis, but it needs to be reconceived less as a rigid binary and more as a "complex set of relations involving palimpsests of times and spaces" (2007, 197). Here, Huyssen recommends a more relativistic, culturally specific, comparative approach to the study of modernism that can accommodate forms of cultural production in "peripheral," postcolonial, and postcommunist societies that do not follow Western hierarchies. "High" and "low," in other words, are not universal categories. They have different histories in Asia, Latin America, and Africa very much tied up with global processes of modernization, sometimes following the periodization of Western modernism and other times not. "Then and now," Huyssen points out, "modernity is never one" (2007, 191). But as the conditions of modern life have proliferated globally, and modernity has assumed many local inflections, then it is only by mapping out these alternative configurations, with their points of intersection and avoidance, that modernism can be sufficiently de-Westernized, making it more of a subject for the global study of literature and art in the twenty-first century and less of an Ameuropean relic left behind in the twentieth.

This renewed emphasis on the relationship between high/low in a global context can furthermore mark the productive return to questions regarding aesthetics and form, which have dropped out of the discussion, in part, due to an anti-aesthetic habitus of "U.S. style cultural studies" so prominent in the 1980s and 90s. The debates between members of the Frankfurt School about form and content, modernism and mass culture are as relevant now after 2010 as they were almost a century ago, but only if conceptual modifications are made to account for the social, political, and religious differences that are part of a global world order quite different from the one they lived in, with modes of cultural production and consumption that "cross the imaginary spatial borders between high and low rather easily" (2007, 206).

Kafka once referred to the book as an axe for the frozen sea within us. Huyssen, adapting the quotation, believes that it can help us think about modernism's legacy and the potential of globalization. Sure, our perspective on modernism differs now from the 1980s and 90s (or the 1940s and 50s for that matter). Yet that, in effect, is a reminder of how it can continue to function critically as we disentangle the complex relationships between aesthetics and politics on a global scale where the oppositions between Western and non-Western, center and periphery, high and low, elite and mass culture are not so clearly marked. Along the way, the axe of the historical avant-garde should not be abandoned. After all, it was the explosive energy of the Expressionists, Dadaists, and Surrealists at the beginning of the twentieth century that made the contradictions of artistic production and reception under capitalism impossible to ignore. Even if they were appropriated by the institution of art and their techniques included in the repertoire of totalitarian governments and the culture industry alike, they left behind the poignant example of what Huyssen calls "a utopian social imagination," a critical faculty that made them unafraid to imagine a better world even if they were realistic enough to know it wouldn't last and unrealistic enough to believe it still might.

Note

1   In "In Search for Tradition: Avant-garde and postmodernism in the 1970s," Andreas Huyssen discusses the presence of a literary father or artistic predecessor who is "always already there." He takes the example of Duchamp who could tell the American avant-garde: "Ich bin schon da," as the hedgehog would say to the hare. In *New German Critique*, number 22, Winter 1981, 32.

References

Adorno, Theodor. (1973). *Philosophy of Modern Music*. New York: Seabury Press.

Adorno, Theodor. (1975). "Culture Industry Reconsidered," trans. Anson Rabinbach. *New German Critique* 6: 12–19.

Adorno, Theodor. (1976). *Dialectic of Enlightenment*, trans. John Cumming. New York: Continuum Books.

Adorno, Theodor. (1981). *In Search of Wagner*, trans. Rodney Livingstone. New York: Verso.

Adorno, Theodor. (1983). *Prisms*, trans. Shierry and Samuel Weber. Cambridge, MA: MIT Press.

Adorno, Theodor. (1991). *Notes to Literature*, vol. 1, trans. Shierry Weber Nicholsen. New York: Columbia University Press.

Adorno, Theodor. (1997). *Aesthetic Theory*, trans. Robert Hullot-Kentor. Minneapolis: University of Minnesota Press.

Adorno, Theodor. (2002). *Essays on Music*, trans. Susan Gillespie. Berkeley: University of California Press.

Benjamin, Walter. (2003). *Selected Writings, Volume 4: 1938–40*, ed. Howard Eiland, Martin Jennings et al., trans. Rodney Livingstone. Cambridge, MA: Harvard University Press.

Bürger, Peter. (1984). *Theory of Avant-Garde*, trans. Michael Shaw. Minneapolis, University of Minnesota Press.

Huyssen, Andreas. (1975). "Introduction to Adorno." *New German Critique*, 6: 3–11.

Huyssen, Andreas. (1986). *After the Great Divide: Modernism, Mass Culture, Postmodernism*. Bloomington: Indiana University Press.

Huyssen, Andreas. (1999). "After the High/Low Debate."

Huyssen, Andreas. (2007). "Geographies of Modernism in a Globalizing World." *New German Critique*, 34: 189–207.

Lunn, Eugene. (1982). *Marxism & Modernism: An Historical Study of Lukács, Brecht, Benjamin, and Adorno*. Berkeley: University of California Press.

4

Kafka, Modernism, and Literary Theory

Vivian Liska

"But this is only theoretically so . . . "

Franz Kafka, "He"

Worrying about Modernism

In Franz Kafka's "Die Sorge des Hausvaters," literally "The Worry of the House-father," a mysterious and mobile creature named Odradek roams around in the garrets and hallways of a house owned by a *pater familias*. The master of the house, who turns out to be the narrator of the story, unsuccessfully tries to get a hold on the creature and becomes increasingly irritated by its elusiveness. The story consists of five paragraphs, the first four describing various fruitless attempts to pin down Odradek and put an end to its rambling disturbances. The first attempt to "capture" Odradek consists of a vain endeavor to elucidate its name, the second in a detailed description of its puzzling appearance, the third in an inquiry into its uncertain genealogy, the fourth in an effort to locate its abode. In the course of these ineffective investigations Odradek becomes more and more alive, and its presence transforms first from a mere denomination to an oddly shaped thing, then to a formed figure, and finally to a speaking being capable of responding, and even of refusing to respond, to the one who examines him. Above all, the relation between Odradek and the housefather changes. The register of the investigation shifts from termino-logical to phenomenological, to spatiotemporal, and finally to existential concerns when, in the fifth and final paragraph, the housefather wonders about the creature's future and the implications of its prospects for his own existence. The inquiry about Odradek starts out as a thwarted questioning of *meaning* and ends in an awareness of the impact of Odradek's continuing presence, of the ways in which it *matters* to the

A Handbook of Modernism Studies, First Edition. Edited by Jean-Michel Rabaté.
© 2013 John Wiley & Sons, Ltd. Published 2013 by John Wiley & Sons, Ltd.

housefather's life itself. The story, barely a page, ends on the unsettled housefather's worry that Odradek could outlive him and forever elude his grip.

With the intangible figure of Odradek, Kafka could be said to sketch in miniature his view of the effect of his own work and of the ways in which it operates in a world bent on order and control. "The Worry of the Housefather" is a quintessentially modernist text reflecting on its own mode of being and performing the disturbance of certainties and claims to mastery that it relates. Beyond such modernist self-mirroring, the story can be read as a foreshadowing of critical endeavors to capture and grasp modernism itself. Although it can arguably be understood as a general reflection on the futility of attempts to gain definitive knowledge of *any* concept, it applies to modernism in more specific and diverse ways because of its simultaneously metonymical and metaphorical relation to modernism. The story's enactment of Odradek's impact on the housefather is part and parcel of a modernist poetics. Simultaneously, the story prefigures various attempts to come to terms with modernism itself. Like the housefather, consecutive generations of scholars have tried in vain to capture and "fix" modernism in successive efforts to bring it into their grip. And like the housefather, they experienced not only the creature's elusive nature and its flight from their grasp, but also its resilience. Modernism indeed escaped and time and again survived them and their clutches. It could, and – as I will argue, possibly should – evade and eventually outlive our own.

"Some say that the word Odradek is of Slavic origin, and try to account for the formation of the word on that basis. Others again believe it to be of German origin, only influenced by Slavic. The uncertainty of both interpretations allows one to assume with justice that neither is accurate, especially as neither of them provides a meaning of the word" (Kafka 1976, 427–428). This first attempt to capture Odradek, the etymological and onomastic search for the constitution of its name, brings to mind numerous opening paragraphs of books and articles on modernism. Predominant between the mid-1960s and the later 1970s, definitional efforts accompanied, pulled together, and tried to come to terms with the multiple close readings produced by New Critical interpretations of individual modernist works. A case in point is Malcolm Bradbury and James McFarlane who, in their introduction to *Modernism. A Guide to European Literature 1890–1930* published in 1976, write that "matters have now reached the point where we wish to fix and stabilize the modern" (22). What seemed to them the culmination of a development towards an increasing semantic instability was, however, really only the beginning of critical controversies and activities that would question established approaches to literary modernism in order to reshape its canon, concept, and characterization. Thirty years later, after innumerable anthologies and studies of modernism, this endeavor seems to have become outdated. The opening sentences of *The Future of Modernism*, an anthology of critical essays published in 1997, still state that "modernism is a word often used but rarely defined" and worry about its "extreme semantic confusion" and the absence of an "international agreement" about the term.[1] However, it becomes obvious in this book and in most recent studies of modernism that this concern has paled. Questions of terminology have remained unresolved, but where they persisted they became linked to larger, mainly comparative explorations of the various international migrations and subsequent transformations of the term and its correlatives. Recently, *modernism, moderne, modernité, modernismo* and similar names are rarely discussed in terms of etymology and "meaning." Instead, terminology and related issues are explored in conjunction with the interrelationships, influences, and relocations of modernist innovation and have become, or were revealed to be, one of the stakes in the manifold cultural and ideological re-evaluations of modernism.

A similar development can be observed for other attempts to fix the meaning of modernism. Along with New Critical theory and praxis, encyclopedic studies of modernism flourishing in the years before the "Cultural Turn" significantly contributed to establishing modernism studies as a respected and even primary area of academic research through rigorous efforts at describing the constitutive textual aspects and characteristics of the literature to which the term referred. Beyond often fruitless and, as for Odradek, contradictory terminological clarifications, they drew the shaggy contours of modernism with great detail and precision, depicting its appearance and characteristics somewhat like the scholars in Kafka's story and in terms that often resemble Kafka's creature: "At first glance it looks like a flat star-shaped spool for thread, and indeed it does seem to have thread wound upon it; to be sure, they are only old, broken-off bits of thread, knotted and tangled together, of the most varied sorts and colours" (Kafka 1976, 428). The portrayal of the creature's outer appearance corresponds to features attributed to modernist works and their fragmentary, complex, and collaged texture. But Odradek, we learn, is not only a spool of entangled threads: there is also a small wooden crossbar sticking out at a right angle from the middle of the star: "By means of this latter rod on one side and one of the points of the star on the other, the whole thing can stand upright as if on two legs" (428). The appearance of Kafka's composite and hybrid creature resembles common descriptions of modernism: its post-realist emphasis on the visibility of the threads and textures of literary works, its heterogeneous nature and its construction out of rests and pieces of older traditions "knotted and tangled together". Odradek's simultaneous footing on a point of a star and a wooden leg recalls McFarlane's diagnosis of the "Janus face"[2] of modernism: its lofty visions and its concurrent grounding in concrete reality, its juxtaposition of "logic and fantasy, the banal and the sublime"(Bradbury and McFarlane 1976, 49; 86). In accordance with the New Critical catchwords "ambiguity" and "paradox," the duality emphasized in these characterizations of modernism, notably in queries about its primary emphasis on either metaphysical abstraction or material reality, paradoxically participated in attempts to categorically describe modernist art and literature. However, as for Odradek, these simultaneously contradictory and unifying descriptions of modernism did not put an end to efforts at defining it. The specific, yet puzzling description of Odradek's ambivalent foothold still invites parallels with newer accounts of modernism. Recent controversies about modernism's penchant for idealist notions of freedom, agency, and the subject on the one hand, and material concerns of everyday life on the other, are proof that these questions are far from settled and that the stakes in these debates increasingly point beyond mere description and meaning to concerns about the significance and relevance of modernism for our own times.

The story's third paragraph describes the next attempt to grasp Odradek, this time in terms of its genealogy: "One is tempted to believe that the creature once had some sort of intelligible shape and is now only a broken down remnant. Yet, this doesn't seem to be the case; at least there is no sign of it. Nowhere are there any visible beginnings or breaks to suggest anything of the kind. The whole thing looks senseless enough, but in its way perfectly finished" (Kafka 1976, 428). Odradek's temporal being is full of contradictions: seemingly the product of historical developments, it nevertheless shows no traces of a beginning or an ending. Seemingly fragmentary and open-ended, it nonetheless looks flawlessly rounded off and completed. Is it the waste product of earlier times, the result of a fall from a significant existence, or has it always already been there? Is it still in the process of becoming or has its evolution come to a halt? Beyond these speculations about its past and future, the suggestion arises that it could be altogether timeless, an autonomous creature grounded in itself alone, whose meaning cannot be elucidated in terms of temporal modes altogether. Again, these contradictory speculations about Odradek's history, its origin and development, display analogies with discussions about the beginnings and endings of modernism, its subsequent evolution, its potential closure, and the possibility of its timelessness altogether. Early constructions of the meaning of modernism were bent on drawing out its intrinsic novelty through a clearly delineated distinction from earlier and later literary modes and epochs. Simultaneously, this research on modernism often explored "old threads" contained in it, such as the role of myth as ordering principle or remnants of modernism's precursors, particularly romanticism and naturalism in modernist works. For all the critical awareness of modernism's intent to "make it new," the demarcation from previous traditions and literary periods as well as questions about the possible end of modernism and its relationship to its successor, postmodernism, have fueled numerous controversies. More recent reflections go as far as challenging the very idea of an origin or an end of modernism altogether and suggest that it is either entirely made up of recycled shards and ruins of past traditions or a large intertextual web extending across time. Both the demise of an a-historical view of modernism constructed by the New Critics and the blurring of modernism's temporal boundaries backwards and forwards have lately been reconsidered in terms of the significance of these issues for today. That this effacing of clear "time-lines" increases the difficulty of settling modernism corresponds to the insight of Kafka's narrator that Odradek's mobile nature impedes more exacting delimitations. The paragraph concludes on the insight that "closer scrutiny is impossible since Odradek" – and for that matter modernism – " is extraordinarily nimble and can never be laid hold of"(428).

Following the vain efforts to situate Odradek in time, the fourth and most elaborate attempt to locate and fix it occurs in space. Odradek, it is said, "lurks by turns in the attic, the stairway, the lobbies, the entrance hall. Often for months on end he is not to be seen; then he has presumably moved into other houses; but he always comes faithfully back to our house again" (428). Clearly, Odradek shuns the main quarters of the house, living instead in its dark and hidden corners and its *lieux de passage*, places where others merely pass through. One encounters it "when one goes out of the door" and is inclined to address it as it stands "at the bottom of the staircase" (428). Odradek lives at the threshold between horizontal and vertical spaces. Not surprisingly, it replies to those who, irritated about this unwieldy lack of a proper room and determined to re-establish a controllable order, inquire about its location with an unaccommodating answer: "And where do you live?" "No fixed abode." Odradek's dwelling in the margins and passageways of the house coincides with recent relocations of modernism. These inquiries about the emplacements of modernism have yielded the most innovative explorations in recent years. While earlier studies notoriously restricted the places where modernism "happened" to very limited and strictly defined geographical areas – in its now most contested version, the Anglo-American sphere – the location of modernism increasingly expanded and multiplied. This broadening of the terrain became a crucial element in the internationalization and globalization of modernism studies. Its move toward the margins and borders, thus to less visible and prominent places, participated in the dismantling of the hegemony and dominance of the "West" over the "Rest" and in making modernism matter for a contemporary multicultural and postcolonial sensibility. A more metaphorical reading of Odradek's mode of dwelling in space points in the direction of recent explorations of modernism influenced by poststructuralist celebrations of the perpetually itinerant or liminal signifier. Odradek's refusal to be located in any single place prefigures the entire register of the nomadic, errant, exiled, and diasporic mobility so prominent in current discourse about modernism.

The parallels drawn here between the housefather's attempts to come to terms with Odradek and the endeavors to "settle" modernism all indicate that in both cases the creature may in the end indeed have escaped the patriarchal grasp and that concerns with the meaning of modernism have become replaced by preoccupations with the way it can matter for reconfigurations of the present. The last paragraph of Kafka's story exposes the difference between these two approaches and suggests what is at stake in ensuring that Odradek continues to matter.

The housefather's story captures one of the central experiences of becoming modern: his claim to epistemological mastery fails and ends on his existential consternation about losing control of his house. In the final paragraph, the housefather, thoroughly unsettled, worries about what primarily concerns us here, the creature's future. "I ask myself, to no avail, what is likely to happen to him? Can he possibly die?" Or will he "always be rolling down the stairs, with ends of thread trailing after him, right before the feet of my children, and my children's children?" (428). Odradek has, by now, changed from a thing to a living creature, a "he." More importantly, and only in the very last lines, where the narrator wonders about Odradek's mortality, the questioning subject is no longer presented in the impersonal form "man" (one), as in the previous passages: "Man wäre versucht zu glauben," "fragt man ihn" (one is tempted to think, one asks him), but in the first person singular, thereby introducing the housefather's own subjectivity and perspective. At this point, not only the housefather's existence is seen in light of his relationship to Odradek, but also Odradek's existence – and survival – is no longer to be conceived independently of its effect on the housefather. The mode of the story's ending indicates that the significance of the creature's survival is concurrent with its continuing potential to disturb the housefather, his children, and his children's children.

If Kafka's housefather can historically be imagined as a late nineteenth-, early twentieth-century bourgeois *pater familias*, we are, a century later, these "children's children" evoked in his worry and therefore the ones addressed in the housefather's final questions about Odradek: "I often wonder, to no avail, what is likely to happen to him? Can he possibly die?" What, we now wonder, "*has* happened to Odradek?" Is he still "rolling down the stairs, with ends of thread trailing after him, right before our feet"? Is it, is he, that unsettling obstacle still? What, we ask ourselves, has happened to modernism? Could it possibly have died?

Broadening Modernism

With the rise of postmodernism in the early 1980s the possibility arose that modernism, or rather its relevance for us, had indeed come to an end. There are certainly those who do not hesitate to affirm this possibility, pointing out that the central modernist literary works have become "modern classics," that modernism had moved into the family room of the *Bildungsbürger* and now belonged to tradition. However, today this seems to have been but a brief moment in the history of modernism scholarship. This history is by now a well-known story that goes somewhat like this: New Criticism fixed, tamed, and stabilized modernism, turning it into the dutiful child of a powerful housefather. The next generation of critics, often subsumed under the adjective "postmodernist," paradoxically took over the New Critical definition of the modernist canon and its poetics, and assumed it "to be synonymous with authority, hierarchy, patriarchy, phallogocentrism, elitism, fascism, racism, formalism and universalism" (Witemeyer 1997, 2). Constructing their own postmodernist paradigm as a negative image of this New Critical modernism, they performed what Antonio Ribeiro (1994) has called the "euphoric awakening from the modernist hibernation strategy" (Ribeiro, 154). For some scholars, such as Andreas Huyssen, the many analogous concerns between modernist literature and poststructuralist theory, notably its deconstructive performance and its assumption of a ubiquitous textuality, further encouraged this view of a conservative modernism in the eyes of critics skeptical of the supposedly formalist, elitist, and a-historical attitude of both. It is only with the "ethical turn" taken by deconstruction in its interaction with cultural studies that poststructuralist strategies of reading, which project their own premises onto modernist texts, would be taken into the service of detecting and rescuing the subversive thrust of such texts. This turn coincided with the next move in this story, a large-scale defense of modernism against postmodernists' accusations of its ethical and ideological emptiness and irresponsibility. This response is still largely with us today. The values that postmodernist or cultural critics had found lacking in modernism – openness, mobility, social awareness, opposition to the established order, proximity to popular culture, and participation in a multicultural decentering of a hegemonic West, to name only a few of the features deemed to distinguish postmodernism from its predecessor – were read back into modernism. This critical move was executed in several ways: an expansion of the existing canon toward authors and areas previously considered silenced or marginal, a rereading of the canonical modernist authors against the New Critical grain, and a more generalized reconceptualization of the modernist enterprise in accordance with postmodernist criteria and expectations. The apparent purpose of this critical move was to substantiate what Sanford Schwartz, in *The Future of Modernism*, calls "The Postmodernity of Modernism" (9). Underlying these critical activities was the belief that the time of pondering over the "meaning of modernism," itself considered a stabilizing and conservative attitude, was over, and that new explorations searched for ways of making it matter for present concerns. As a result, modernist scholars assume that the view of modernism as a subversive force arose from its slumber, resulting from the New Critical and the postmodernists' attempts to lay it to rest in the housefather's own master bedroom. From the perspective of Cultural Theory today, Odradek seems alive and well, and the worries firmly on the housefather's side.

"Modernism Resartus" is the title of the introduction to *The Future of Modernism* published in 1997, a volume consisting primarily of a rereading of canonical modernist works. Equally, if not more significant for this reassertion of modernism's vitality than these reassessments of Joyce, Pound, Eliot, Woolf, and others, were the critical gestures leading to the broadening of modernism in various directions. This expansion occurred primarily through the inclusion of other players, cultures, and locations into the modernist pantheon on the one hand, and the undoing of borders with different registers, poetics, and literary periods and movements on the other.

The expansion of modernism toward other participating agents resulted largely from explorations driven by various theoretical endeavors such as feminist, black, queer, and postcolonialist studies and opened up inquiries about modernist phenomena in a great many places and languages all over the world. A paradigmatic example for the first broadening, the inclusion of other participating agents, is the role of women in modernism. Given the nature and gender of the housefather, it may not be surprising that feminist theory became one of the fields on which the controversies about modernism in the 1980s and 90s were most vehemently and fruitfully played out. As I have shown elsewhere,[3] these reconsiderations started with a fierce attack on New Critical modernism and ended up rehabilitating modernism as a subversive and ethically as well as politically effective paradigm. Feminist revisions of modernism, like many of its companions and correlatives from postcolonial and cultural theories, lead from a critique of modernism as a monolithic enemy of the people – of women and other marginalized groups in particular – to the embrace of a polyphonic modernism *sur mesure* for our own times. Although these reappraisals of modernism from the perspective of the housefather's united adversaries undoubtedly contribute to the renewed vitality of modernism studies in recent years, the menace lurking today is that these perspectives themselves turn into a new self-serving dogma. Not only do these very selective readings often tend to efface modernism's disturbing contradictions, but their emphasis on those aspects of modernism that fit today's theoretical expectations risks turning them into a new conformism. Proving that Joyce, Pound, and Eliot were really good feminists or postcolonials *avant la lettre* or demonstrating that whatever is worthwhile about modernism was really and primarily feminine, Caribbean, or sentimental is barely the point. Furthermore, the broadening of the modernist canon and concept toward what Bonnie Kime Scott approvingly calls a "wide appeal" risks neglecting the aesthetic substance and literariness of modernist texts and therefore the difficult and defiant texture that would ensure Odradek's escape from the housefather's control.

The most frequently practiced version of a second form of broadening modernism, the expansion of its borders through a blurring of the dividing lines between other modes and registers than those considered to be "classical modernism," resulted from Cultural Theory's concern with the gap between high and popular art. In response to New Critical configurations, modernism has often been accused of being elitist and ignoring popular interests. It is now increasingly being reassessed in "postmodern" terms that emphasize its closeness to "low art," and for a good reason, since many canonical works of modernism indeed turn out to be riddled with interests in the popular and the quotidian. The facets of modernism revealed in these explorations seem a far cry from the detached, autonomous, and immobile works of art that have so often been variously celebrated or censured as the central outputs of modernism. Modernist works, when "culturally" observed, indeed often reach for the margins, for "subcultural" experiences, in a broad sense of these terms and sometimes in the same movement, attend to the less noticed aspects of everyday life. In some cases, the alleged fortress of hermetic art may, at a closer look, indeed turn out to be a laboratory of the quotidian, the "daily bread" of artistic creativity and aesthetic rituals. However, there are risks involved in such reassessments of modernism as popular art: Odradek may be nothing but a spool, a household object turned into a children's toy and belonging to the most banal register, but Kafka's story is not. It is, instead, a highly complex, if not hermetic text: a difficult "read." In some recent attacks on highbrow modernism, difficulty itself became the scapegoat to be sacrificed on the altar of a new, topical modernism. An example of this rereading is Leonard Diepeveen's 2003 study, *The Difficulties of Modernism*. This rebuttal of the modernist creed that art *must* be difficult goes beyond earlier critiques blaming difficulty for excluding specific groups of artists or particular registers of aesthetic expression. The mystique of difficulty, Diepeveen believes, alienated all but the most professional public, narrowed the scope of aesthetic experience, imposed a canon on the basis of "in-crowd" criteria, and, often via implausibly "difficult readings," forced even seemingly "simple" art into a modernist mold. As a result, the modernist aesthetics of difficulty became a dogma to such a degree that it paradoxically turned its own transgressions, disruptions, and inconsistencies into the most conventional and expected artistic and critical approaches of the twentieth century. However, this perspective dismisses modernist difficulty too lightly. In warding off a critical aesthetics for its bleakness while simultaneously worrying about its loss of appeal among a wider public, this call for a "modernism light" abides by prevailing moods, tastes, and ideas. Not surprisingly, the introduction to

The Future of Modernism announces its rereadings of canonical modernist works in terms of laughter, nonsense, irony, and humor. Paradoxically, the critical enterprise that set out to make modernism matter for a wider audience risks getting caught in its own logic. Where "user-friendliness" and "wide appeal" are taken as main criteria to measure the contemporary relevance of art, Odradek is defeated.

As can be inferred from these two examples illustrating the theory-induced expansion of modernism toward other players and other registers, modernism survived those New Critical and postmodernist critics who tried to cast it into a narrow, conservative mold. This process resulted in a remarkable body of scholarly work that considerably broadened the scope of modernism. It took place in the name of renewing its political and ethical appeal and demonstrated its concordance with contemporary concerns for our own times. The ICLA modernism volume is an illustration of these achievements. However, after having been neutralized by New Criticism and declared dead by postmodernism, modernist literature risks being recuperated by the good theoretical – cultural, social, political – intentions of today. We possibly have reached the point where this drive to de-limit modernism in order to make it fit the expectations of Cultural Theory must in turn be put into question and where the ongoing critical enterprise of revising modernism must reflect anew on its own premises and goals.

Readings of modernist literature can validate the actuality of these works only if they avoid turning them either into "classics" or into politically, culturally correct supports of our most recent academic creeds. To avoid misplacing the impact of modernist literature, we may have to focus less on ways it obediently conforms to our theoretical frameworks and more on its power to both fuel and resist them. It is only when we grant literature a life of its own, in close proximity but distinguishable from theory, that it can remain relevant, not least for theoretical thinking itself.

Coda: Literature in Theory

A "return to literature" is often invoked in queries about what is to follow "after theory" (Butler et al. 2000, x). What would it mean to return to modernist literature "after theory"? Obviously, theory "happened" and left an indelible mark on the way we read this literature. Much has been gained by the broadening of its canon and status; what may have been lost is this literature's strangeness to our contemporary perspective. While in many ways still contiguous with our own late modernity, modernist literature is in some ways also remote to us. Partly due to theoretically informed readings that have aligned it to our own times, the specificity of its literary vocabulary conveying the unsettling experiences of becoming modern has, by now, become indistinct from our own experience. The theoretical emphasis on playfulness, on gendered and cultural identity, on popular appeal is often incompatible with the literary memory of these unsettling early responses to modernity. However, making modernism matter for today could imply precisely the exposure and recovery of this beginning of our times. It could result in a beneficial and concomitant estrangement from a modern world that has, by now, become all too familiar to us. Today's post-theoretical modernism, broadened, expanded, enlivened, and lightened, may obstruct our view of these threshold experiences. Furthermore, new social, gendered, ethnic players and new geographical, linguistic, and cultural places have rejuvenated the modernist scene. It may be time to confront these new perspectives with the oldest intuitions about this literature: that it helps us think about what it means to become modern. Juxtaposing the different ways in which these participating agents and spaces have enacted modernism's "primal scenes" can intensify our vision of the transitions taking place in modernity as such. Rather than asserting collective identities competing for their place under the modernist sun, rather than seeking alignment with existing critical expectations, these studies could participate in a joint "archaeology of modernity" and, uncovering new nuances and layers, open up new views on how literature participated in our theoretical constructions of modernity in the first place. Theory has been diligently applied to modernist literature in ways that cannot and should not be undone, but maybe it is time for a reversal of focus.

In a recent book entitled *The Literary in Theory* Jonathan Culler suggests a return to literature in terms that go beyond a mere revival of traditional philology or New Critical formalism. Rather than continuing to apply theory to literature, he argues, critics should explore the ways in which what he calls "the literary" has shaped theory itself. What he defines as "the literary" – the performative dimension revealing the constructedness of our presuppositions, the self-reflective insight into the "incompleteness and instability of all knowledge claims," the "appeal to vividness of realization as the substitute for claims to mastery" – carries the unmistakable traits of modernist literature (2007, 289). Culler, quoting David Simpson, pertinently observes that literature's "awareness of its own fictionality and performative efficacy" has, in recent years, triumphed in other fields of the humanities – psychology, history, anthropology, and political theory. Culler concludes that literature may have lost its prestige and attractiveness to other media or more directly political discourses, but that "the literary" – the modes of relating to reality associated with literature – and perhaps particularly in modernist literature – have triumphed in other domains of the humanities. With Culler I believe that it is now "time to reground the literary in literature, to go back to the actual literary works to see whether the postmodern condition is indeed what should be inferred from the operations of literature."[4] Calling theory "an exfoliation . . . of the literary," he points to the necessity of exposing the biased and reductive readings of literary text in theoretical writings (286). Culler's model is Judith Butler's (2007) critique of the selective readings of Sophocles' *Antigone* by theorists from Hegel to Luce Irigaray. Studies such as these, which investigate the ways in which literature is invoked and processed in theoretical writings, are indeed a challenging enterprise, but they must reach further than a mere dismantling and setting right of theory's misreadings. To explore the impact of literature on theory, I recently initiated a project concerned with the study of Kafka in theoretical writings from Benjamin and Blanchot to Butler and beyond. In the past year I have written several articles about the ways in which literary texts feature in the recent theoretical writings by one of the current cult-thinkers, Giorgio Agamben. I am embarking on these endeavors in the belief that theory is far from over, that it constitutes a important mode of thinking about modernity, and that it is one of the sites where the impact of literature as a mode of thinking became and becomes manifest.

Something significant about the specific knowledge conveyed by literature can be revealed in such investigations. A great deal, for example, can be learned by distinguishing between the various modes of using literature in theory – as example, model, illustration, pre-text, and the like – or by asking which authors are invoked in theoretical writings and why. Comparing Adorno's Beckett to Badiou's or Benjamin's Kafka to Agamben's, or, for that matter, the latter's interpretation of Kafka's "Before the Law" to Derrida's reading of the same story also reveals something about the changing modes of knowledge assigned to literature. While I do indeed find delight in showing that literature "knows more" than the theories using it, my point is not to discredit theory at the expense of literature or to criticize the use of literature for theoretical purposes. I side neither with those who sacralize the irrecuperable nature of the literary word nor with those who promote literature as a convenient tool to teach justice or civilize our gentlemen. Rather, I want to know more about what it is that literature knows, and it is rather mischievously that I have so unashamedly – and playfully – put Kafka's Odradek "to use" in my introductory paragraphs: Obviously, I don't think that Odradek "is" modernism or that Kafka's story cannot feature in countless different accounts. Instead, something in its structure allowed me to get a grasp on modernism in ways I might otherwise not have had. Inversely, the analysis of Agamben's use of Kafka's texts revealed to me the strategies of selection and emphasis that were necessary to bend these texts to Agamben's theoretical purposes but also how Kafka "works" in these theoretical writings, in terms of their import as well as their resistance to this task. I therefore concur with Culler's call for a return to literature starting from the insight that literature is indeed "good to think with." Investigating the use of literary texts in theoretical writings is obviously only one way of exploring this dimension of literature. Recent titles such as Stathis Gourgouris's "Does Literature Think?", Michael Woods's "Literature and the Taste of Knowledge," or Hillis Miller's "On Literature. Thinking in Action" point in a similar direction. Culler's final statement is as suggestive as it is ominous when he speaks of the possibility "that a return to ground the literary in literature might have a critical edge, since one of the things we know about literary works is that they have the ability to resist or to outplay what they are supposed to be saying." Just as individual literary texts resist being simply absorbed by the theoretical texts that invoke them, so literature as a whole – and modernist literature in particularly significant ways – refuses to be dissolved or diluted into theory. This resistance to appropriation by any single theory or point of view is what makes thinking *with* literature possible.

Odradek's survival means not so much his victory, but the vitality of the difference his presence makes in the housefather's awareness. His name and nature may remain impossible to pin down, but the story leaves little doubt as to why and how Odradek matters. Kafka's story reminds us of one of the basic premises of modernist art: "Anything that dies," the housefather muses, "has had some kind of purpose in life, some kind of activity, which wore it out; but that does not apply to Odradek" (Kafka 1976, 429). It is true that it is only without an explicit, predetermined purpose and activity that Odradek can outlive the housefather. Rather than assigning more and ever broader definitions, descriptions, genealogies, and locations to Odradek, one must ensure that it continues to matter. If it is to survive the potential housefathers – or, let's say, theorists – of today and tomorrow it must live on as an independent co-inhabitant that both inspires and unsettles those who want to lay it to rest. Taking literature in theory literally, we may indeed discover not only how Odradek, this odd elusive creature, always escapes the housefather's grasp but also how it makes him think about the nature of language, about the shape of the other, or about his own mortality – in short, how it inspires his deepest thoughts.

Notes

1 Hugh Witemeyer, *The Future of Modernism*, 1. Witemeyer quotes Julian Symons, Malcolm Bradbury and James McFarlane, and Monique Chefidor.
2 Malcolm Bradbury and James McFarlane, *Modernism: A Guide to European Literature 1890–1930*, 49.
3 Vivian Liska, "From Topos to Trope. Feminist Revisions of Modernism," 1994.
4 The perspective of regrounding "the literary" in modernist literature invites following up on Andreas Huyssen's challenging insight made twenty years earlier that theory, more particularly poststructuralist theory, is an "archeology of modernism" that derives its main assumptions from modernist literary texts.

References

Bradbury, Malcolm and James McFarlane. (1989). *Modernism: A Guide to European Literature 1890–1930*, rev. edn (p. 49). Penguin Literary Criticism. Harmondsworth: Penguin.

Butler, Judith. (2007). *Antigone's Claim*. New York: Columbia University Press.

Butler, Judith, et al. (2000). *What's Left of Theory? New Work on the Politics of Literary Theory*. London: Routledge.

Culler, Jonathan D. (2007). *The Literary in Theory*. Stanford: Stanford University Press.

Diepeveen, Leonard. (2003). *The Difficulty of Modernism*. New York: Routledge.

Kafka, Franz. (1976). *The Complete Stories*, ed. Nahum Glatzer. New York: Schocken Books.

Liska, Vivian. (1994). "From Topos to Trope. Feminist Revisions of Modernism." In *The Turn of the Century. Modernism and Modernity in Literature and the Arts* [Le tournant du siècle. Le modernisme et la modernité dans la littérature et les arts], ed. Christian Berg, Frank Durieux, and Geert Lernout (pp. 66–77). Berlin: De Gruyter.

Ribeiro, Antonio. (1994). "Karl Kraus and Modernism: A Reassessment." In *The Turn of the Century: Modernism and Modernity in Literature and the Arts*, ed. Frank Durieux, Christian Berg and Geert Lernout (pp. 143–154). Berlin: De Gruyter.

Witemeyer, Hugh. (1997). "Modernism Resartus." In *The Future of Modernism* (pp. 1–8). Ann Arbor: University of Michigan Press.

5

Race

Tradition and Archive in the Harlem Renaissance

Jeremy Braddock

Writing in *Modernism and Theory*, Susan Stanford Friedman (2009) reminds the reader that "[t]he hegemony of French 'high theory' in the United States *follows*, not precedes, the radical critique of prevailing notions of the literary and the canon, and of the methodologies and institutions of literary studies" (239). Demurring from the volume's introduction, Friedman's point is to stress the multiple determinants that informed the "new modernist studies" of the mid-1990s, emphasizing in particular the identitarian movements that authored the radical critique – feminism, queer studies, and race studies – and preceded high theory's institutional dominance in the 1980s. Friedman's genealogy is a helpful and salutary complication of the new modernist studies' origins. But if we were to take African American studies as the primary field of inquiry among three terms – modernism, theory, and race studies – the genealogy would become intriguingly, and tellingly, more involuted.

Although African American studies began to achieve institutional recognition somewhat before the period of high theory's influence, the field was substantially developed and transformed during the time of theory's hegemony, and meaningfully shaped by it. One of the period's key documents is Henry Louis Gates, Jr.'s "*Race*," *Writing, and Difference* from 1986 (an edited collection recently revisited in the pages of *PMLA* by Valerie Smith, Farah Jasmine Griffin, and Eric Lott).[1] In his introduction, Gates asserted that "[r]ace is the ultimate trope of difference because it is so very arbitrary in its application" (5). These are words few would disagree with today, but they are also notable for the way they placed race theory intellectually in the context of the transition from structuralism to poststructuralism, even as the dual nature of the word *arbitrary* emphasizes, in a more material dimension, the enduring legal and explanatory force of the fiction of racial difference. It will be instructive, too, to see a partial list of contributors to Gates's collection: Anthony

A Handbook of Modernism Studies, First Edition. Edited by Jean-Michel Rabaté.
© 2013 John Wiley & Sons, Ltd. Published 2013 by John Wiley & Sons, Ltd.

Appiah, Edward Said, Mary Louise Pratt, Homi K. Bhabha, Gayatri Chakravorty Spivak, Hazel V. Carby, Barbara Johnson, Jacques Derrida, Tzvetan Todorov, and Houston A. Baker, Jr. Though not all of them poststructuralists, brought together they confirmed the central association of race studies and theory in the most prestigious US literature departments.

It is significant that this influential encounter between high theory and race studies should have occurred, as Friedman says, *before* the period of modernist studies' revisionism because black literary study developed to some degree in reaction to the prestige and presumptions of institutionalized "high" modernism. In the mid-1980s, no field better exemplified Friedman's "prevailing notions of the literary and the canon" than literary modernism. This was true because of its canon's profound exclusivity, and for the related fact that many of its authors had had a strong hand in securing the terms of their later academic prestige. Foremost among those authors was T. S. Eliot, author of *Sweeney Agonistes* and the King Bolo poems, who had famously written that the mature writer must write "with the feeling that the whole of the literature of Europe from Homer and within it the whole of the literature of his own country has a simultaneous existence and composes a simultaneous order" (1932, 14). Though the argument is more subtle taken in context, I use it here to emphasize its effective legacy as an *institutional* – rather than a more figuratively ethical or creative – prescription. It was that legacy, as honored and substantiated by the Southern Agrarians and the New Critics, that justified Gates's declaration that "[t]he citizens of the republic of literature [. . .] were all white, and mostly male. Difference, if difference obtained at all, was a difference obliterated by the simultaneity of Eliot's tradition" (4).

In one line of critique, the racial exclusivity of the modernist canon was revealed to be symptomatic of a broader repression, or "covering," of modernity's essential constitution by black culture. Looking back to the dawn of that modernity, James A. Snead's 1984 essay "Repetition as a Figure of Black Culture" argued that "Hegel was almost entirely correct in his reading of black culture, but what he could not have guessed was that in his very criticism of it he had almost perfectly described the 'there' to which European culture was 'headed' [. . .]. Only after Freud, Nietzsche, comparative and structural anthropology, and the study of comparative religion could the frantic but ultimately futile coverings of repetition by European culture be seen as dispensable, albeit in limited instances of 'uncovering'" (64).[2] Snead revealed a modernism that had taken more from Africa than a series of aesthetic forms it could appropriate and exploit, but rather owed it the entire ground of its critique of Enlightenment epistemology. "Repetition as a Figure of Black Culture" pointed the way toward a more comprehensive analysis of modernity as such.

The best-known theoretical work of the 1980s, by contrast, was instead largely concerned to comprehend the internal logic of black cultural production, while affirming in a slightly different key Snead's emphasis upon repetition. Baker and Gates explicitly worked to establish an indigenous African American literary *and critical* tradition engaging tropes that were simultaneously derived from within a wider-ranging conception of "the tradition," tropes that were at the same time shown to be totally amenable to the procedures of poststructuralist theory and deconstruction.[3] Thus, Gates's famous theorization of African American vernacular practice, "Signifyin(g)" – or "repetition with a signal difference," is elaborated as a form of Derridean *différance*: "Black people vacated this signifier [i.e. 'signifying'], then – incredibly – substituted as its concept a signifier that stands for the system of rhetorical strategies peculiar to their own vernacular tradition" (1988, 45–47).

The concern to define a theory of the tradition, and to decide upon its most characteristic texts, undoubtedly had practical aims (Gates himself is a legendary institution-builder). Yet they have implications extending beyond the context of the culture wars, and these implications may also cast a new light on Gates's negative citation of Eliot. The latter's 1919 essay "Tradition and the Individual Talent," which we have already seen Gates engage, was a frequent and in truth ambiguous touchstone for Gates and for Baker. In *Modernism and the Harlem Renaissance*, for instance, Baker characterized Amiri Baraka's rhetorical figure "the changing same" as describing "the interplay between tradition and the individual talent in Afro-American music" (15). And in *The Signifying Monkey*, Gates (1988) remarked on the extraordinary "self-reflexivity" of the black tradition, "a tradition exceptionally conscious of its history and of the *simultaneity of its canonical texts*" (my emphasis), and then went on to explain that "because of the experience of diaspora, the fragments that contain the traces of a coherent system of order must be reassembled," thus extending the reference from Eliot's essay into the text and technique of *The Waste Land* in the service of claims epistemological as well as institutional (xxiv).

Freighted as they are, Gates's and Baker's citations were undoubtedly meant to signify on the Eurocentrism and prestige of Eliot's essay. Yet it will be possible to indicate a deeper relationship among their conceptualizations of tradition, one we will find already articulated in a foundational text of the Harlem Renaissance. This can be done, I want to suggest, without uncritically celebrating Eliot as the theory's originator. Proceeding, rather, in the spirit of Snead's still-important essay, we may suggest that these theorists are in different registers and literary situations responding to and representing a common problematic, one that has had more violent material and epistemological historical consequences for black people, and therefore is in Stuart Hall's phrase "structured in dominance."[4] For Eliot, as for Gates, the tradition is a foundational concept because it names the collective as well as the subjective determination of historical memory. But both figures' conception of tradition – literally "handing over" or "handing down" – depends upon an elision of categories whose distinctions are otherwise of crucial importance to them: the literary text on one hand and on the other the cultural practices that precede, surround, or evade the text and are valued for their extra- or pre-literary dimensions. It is no accident that the first open acknowledgment of this problematic for the field of black letters should have occurred in the preface of a field-defining literary anthology. As I will argue in the final section, this culturally productive problematic can be read anew in the context of, but can also itself actively contribute to, contemporary theories of the *archive*.

With its broadly expanded canon and its gravitation toward cultural theory, the revisionist new modernist studies no longer very much resembles the field that was so profitably attacked by Gates, Baker, and others in the 1980s.[5] But this does not mean that the relationship of modernism to the Harlem Renaissance – two terms devised largely retrospectively – has been decisively or unproblematically determined. Indeed, because these parallel and sometimes overlapping fields have been in many ways sublated within a newly inclusive modernist studies, the terms of a meaningful logic of relationship or comparison have not been thoroughly schematized.[6] If there has not recently been a need to *justify* the Harlem Renaissance as "modernist," this might in fact mask the overdue task of considering both the surprising depth as well as the critical limitations of such an enterprise.

A brief outline of broad factors structuring African American modernity must begin by acknowledging the continuing legacy of the slave trade (Cugo, or Cudjoe, Lewis, considered the last former slave to have been born in Africa, lived until 1935 and was the source of two folk tales in Alain Locke's *New Negro* anthology of 1925) as preface to a more immediate history in which the promises of emancipation and reconstruction had given way, by the second decade of the twentieth century, to a state of strenuous retrenchment. The 1896 Supreme Court decision *Plessy v. Ferguson* affirmed the legality of segregation laws and inscribed the parameters of a legal, and legally enforceable, definition of racial identity, thus forming a direct referent for Gates's argument ninety years later concerning the arbitrariness of race. During the first two decades of the twentieth century, the social effects of *Plessy v. Ferguson* became more palpable, as American society became increasingly separated along racial lines. During this same time, cities to the north of the United States experienced an enormous influx (perhaps more than 300,000 laborers and domestics) of African Americans who left the South between 1910 and 1920, most in the last three years of the decade. These years witnessed a resurgence in lynching deaths, which reached an apogee in 1919, the "red summer" that saw major race riots (and anti-labor riots) in cities across the United States.[7]

These events formed the background for the first generation of African American writers to come of age post-slavery and must be kept in mind while viewing the proximate or parallel relationships – rhetorical, spatial, institutional – that structured African American cultural production in relation to modernist culture. The very name "New Negro Renaissance" – the more historically accurate term for the movement – asks to be read in relationship to Ezra Pound's slogan "Make It New!" for both its consonances and dissonances. It is consonant insofar as both mandates for the new envision a modernity ambiguously promising a radical break with the past, which is at the same time premised on the renovation of an object from that past. Over against the point that these phrases invoke multiple and differential pasts, the New Negro concept is also dissonant from the high modernist imperative in the way it explicitly associated aesthetic form with social identity. In his introduction to *The New Negro* anthology, Alain Locke (1992) suggested that the new black art was both representative of, as well as actively engineering, a new mode of being: "a stock figure perpetuated as an historical fiction, [. . .] the Old Negro had long become more of a myth than a man"; "vibrant with a new psychology [. . .] the New Negro is keenly responsive as an augury of a new democracy in American culture" (3, 9). In this figuration Old and New Negroes appear as both literary fictions and living social actors. As Locke acknowledged, it was the specific concentration and mixing of black peoples in the northern cities (not all of them from the United States) that was achieving from this heterogeneity a "great race-welding" (7). Locke's attention to the function of the metropolis can be read in relation to Raymond Williams's late work in *The Politics of Modernism* (1989), which emphasizes the importance of the "new kind of open, complex and mobile society" epitomized in European cities after World War I, where "small groups in any form of divergence or dissent could find some kind of foothold, in ways that would not have been possible if the artists and thinkers composing them had been scattered in more traditional, closed societies" (45). Attending to the critical qualification that segregation imposed upon the black experience of this cosmopolitan openness and mobility, much of the most important theoretical work concerning the black urban experience in the 1920s (particularly that of Hazel V. Carby) has similarly been Marxist in character.[8]

A systematic comparative study could continue by considering the relationship of each field across discrete literary genres. Thus *The Waste Land* (1922) can be read alongside Countee Cullen's "Heritage" (1925), each of them conceived as major poems meditating on historical ruins and cultural memory. Joyce's *A Portrait of the Artist as a Young Man* (1916) is anticipated by James Weldon Johnson's *The Autobiography of an Ex-Colored Man* (1912), each text a *Künstlerroman* in which the protagonist's aesthetic achievement is ironized and qualified by conditions of political domination that differently structure the world of each text. Jean Toomer (as well as Sterling Brown and Zora Neale Hurston) can be read together with Yeats for their shared interest in capturing for their own aesthetics the dying accomplishment of folk cultures, ravaged by modernity, each releasing its truth in extinction. Turning to the valences and vagaries of collective interaction, the proliferation of British modernist *romans à clef* recently studied by Sean Latham can be put in relief by the perhaps even more self-reflexive Harlem Renaissance novels that either are, or contain elements of, that subgenre.[9] A list of these works would include not only Wallace Thurman's *Infants of the Spring*, Richard Bruce Nugent's *Gentleman Jigger*, Countee Cullen's *One Way to Heaven*, George Schuyler's *Black No More*, and Nella Larsen's *Passing*, but also extend to *Mumbo Jumbo*, Ishmael Reed's great Harlem Renaissance novel of 1972. Would one go so far as to read *The Great Gatsby* as a novel of racial passing? As Michael North's *The Dialect of Modernism* has shown, the power relations inevitably structuring such relationships are abundantly evident in the formal example of dialect writing, which white modernists appropriated as a sign of their modernity at the very moment it had become, in James Weldon Johnson's words, a medium "not capable of giving expression to the varied conditions of Negro life in America, and much less [. . .] capable of giving the fullest interpretation of Negro character and psychology" (1922, xli).

It is very telling that North's book begins with a study of a paradigmatic cultural institution, the *Oxford English Dictionary*, for the movements' connections at the level of *genre* can be extended to, and to some extent explained by, the occasionally identical but more typically parallel and unequal institutions that structure them. An incomplete list of these institutions, both formal and informal, would include patronage, small publishing houses, little magazines, literary anthologies, prizes, coteries, salons, even the very idea of the movement as such.[10] The story of the Locke/Du Bois agon, for instance, which centered on the question of the political orientation of art, is also the story of two organizations (the Urban League and the National Association for the Advancement of Colored People (NAACP)) and two journals (*Opportunity* and *The Crisis*). These cultural institutions were at times designed to foster forms of social and aesthetic integration, as George Hutchinson has argued, but they were also structured in dominance as can be immediately appreciated by comparing the $2000 *Dial* prize won by Eliot for *The Waste Land* in 1922 with the 1925 *Opportunity* prize which awarded $40 to Langston Hughes for "The Weary Blues."[11] All were concerned with staking positions within fields both cooperative and antagonistic, as they set about the work of both reaching and delimiting their audiences. The well-documented polemicism attending modernist aesthetics is no less a feature of New Negro literary culture, where aesthetics and theory interpenetrated in the unusual form of such texts as *The New Negro* anthology or Du Bois's *The Souls of Black Folk*, both of which have in recent years been commonly read as objects of modernist art.

To emphasize the relation of aesthetic forms to cultural institutions is to suggest the value of sociological theory for Harlem Renaissance studies, which would oblige the reader to understand writing as "an indissolubly formal and material search," in Pierre Bourdieu's words, "in which the work comes to contain those structures that the writer, like any social agent, carries within him in a practical way [...] and through which is achieved the anamnesis of all that ordinarily remains buried, in an implicit or unconscious state" (108–109). In the classic study *The Rules of Art* (1996), Bourdieu painstakingly revealed the way Baudelaire and (especially) Flaubert represented such social structures within the work in order to exercise "a more complete use of the freedoms concealed by the constraints" of the literary field as it was then constructed, and ultimately "to produce himself as creator, that is, as the *subject* of his own creation" – thus effecting a transition in the cultural field in which aesthetic autonomy is itself devised as a new social structure, arrogating certain cultural privileges to the artist (104).

This dynamic would not be reproduced in the New Negro literary field (Bourdieu himself acknowledged that late nineteenth-century France represents a very strong degree of autonomization: stronger, implicitly, than that of Anglo-American modernism). Yet its example can nevertheless be understood as *naming the desire* of a significant subfield of New Negro artists and intellectuals. Thurman's *Infants of the Spring* and Nugent's *Gentleman Jigger*, for instance, can be quite specifically read as novels about the failure – more accurately, the impossibility – of Harlem bohemia's attempt to compose itself as an autonomous avant-garde, its position within multiple fields of power preventing the accrual of sufficient symbolic capital to ensure its artists' "durable consecration."[12] Both novels represent Harlem bohemians' awareness of the culturally legitimating economies of modernist consecration, such as the scandal of obscenity (both books refer to the American suppression of Joyce's *Ulysses*). In *Infants of the Spring* the desire to participate in these economies is answered in a horrifying negative image when the talentless singer Pelham Gaylord is imprisoned and convicted on false rape charges, an event that hastens the dissolution of the bohemian community.

The Harlem bohemian group these books documented, organized around Thurman's short-lived dissident journal *Fire!!*, aimed to make a break from the bourgeois literature of uplift and protest associated with *Opportunity* and especially *The Crisis*. In some of the foundational scholarship on the Harlem Renaissance, that dominant literary culture was characterized as one in which "[a]mbiguity in language [...] garnered hostility and suspicion," with "disastrous" results for a growing black literature (Gates 1987, 29). Today it is easier to see how even the most conventional New Negro writing is often animated by a carefully crafted ambiguity in which multiple readings exist in parallel. This is true not only of Nella Larsen's *Passing* (1929) and its famous lesbian subtext, or Langston Hughes's poems of the 1920s (with their speakers' multiply uncertain identities, as in "The New Cabaret Girl" or "The Weary Blues"), but of much more apparently conservative verse such as that of Countee Cullen (whose sonnets and ballads generate both "universal" and queer readings) and Georgia Douglas Johnson (1928), whose "I Want to Die While You Love Me" reads at first glance as a moderately accomplished love lyric but is in fact also a rich meditation upon the specifically gendered perils of racial passing in relationship to sexuality and pregnancy:

> I want to die while you love me,
>   While yet you hold me fair,
> While laughter lies upon my lips
>   And lights are in my hair.
>
> I want to die while you love me,
>   And bear to that still bed,
> Your kisses turbulent, unspent
>   To warm me when I'm dead. (42)

These works exhibit, and exploit, an intense awareness of the different constituencies, and interpretive conventions, of their multiple audiences, and thus about their relationship to the institutions of literary reception, dissemination, and production in which they operated.

Because of the force of segregation, these works were not the means through which writers transcendently "created themselves as creators" (a phrase Bourdieu uses semi-ironically to name the process of autonomization, which he insists is often attended by privileged social origin and large symbolic capital). But taken together with the proliferation of African American *romans à clef*, their very acute awareness of their own aesthetic and material situation shows them as corresponding to C. D. Blanton's characterization of modernism, albeit offered in a different context, as "[t]he moment art begins to formulate the components of its own production [. . .] and take those components or media as its own material [. . .]" (2009, 143). As opposed to Bourdieu's minute attention to a carefully defined field, Blanton's concern – like Friedman he too is writing in the *Modernism and Theory* collection – is to invoke a global perspective from which modernism is conceived as a "ruptural unity." What is important here is not simply that modernism exhibits an unprecedented engagement with its own conditions of production. It also "emerges in the interval between planetary economy in concept and in practice" with the implication that modernist art must itself be read as an act of theorization that refracts these multiple instantiations of a global economy, acknowledging and representing "the rough striations that history would smooth" (2009, 148–149). This planetary economic view has also recently been invoked by Phillip Brian Harper (2012), as he insisted upon a necessary racial dimension of modernism's vocation: "No less a concomitant of modernity than the globalization of the market – and no less consequential for those whom it implicates – blackness rightfully demands the investigative accounting that only modernism can provide" (372). To adopt this broad economic view is not only to acknowledge how the globalization of market enabled, as Brent Hayes Edwards has shown, a transnational circulation of black intellectual culture beginning in the modernist period.[13] It is also to insist upon a more broadly historical view that comprehends the centrality of the slave trade as one of the earliest impetuses in the market's globalization. This returns us to the Africanist source that James Snead has proposed for the modernist critique of the Enlightenment, and in a related key recalls Paul Gilroy's resonant phrase from *The Black Atlantic* (1993): "modernity frames the complicity of rationality with the practice of white supremacist terror" (117–118).

This long historical perspective, in turn, brings us to another of Henry Louis Gates, Jr.'s striking early achievements, which was to explain how the centrality of writing to Western culture, framed as its "*visible* sign of reason," both facilitated the "urge toward the systematization of all human knowledge (by which we characterize the Enlightenment)" and "led directly to the relegation of black people to a lower place in the great chain of being," because of their averred lack of a written tradition or Western rationality (8). One year before *The Signifying Monkey* pursued its virtuosic exegesis of black texts' internal structures, Gates's *Figures in Black* (1987) opened with an extensive critique of this culture, where literacy obtained for African Americans the status of both a "technology and a commodity" (11). The acquisition of literacy became a prerequisite for the demonstration of a common humanity, and its ultimate iteration would be in the creation of writing that could be authenticated as literature. "Any serious theory of the nature and function of writing in the Western tradition," Gates insisted, "must [. . .] take the critical reception of this unique genre into full account" (1987, 14).

To provide this specific historicity to the political authority of writing in the West, and of a special project provided for it in the form of literature, is to have a more temporally and materially bounded sense of the literary than we have seen Eliot or Gates associate with the concept of the *tradition*, a point to which we will return.

Such a delimiting also recalls the work of Jacques Derrida and the way the concept of the *archive* is a recurring preoccupation within it. When speaking of archivization, a process that involves any form of inscription and preservation but most especially writing, Derrida like Gates identifies two "synchronous formations": "on the one hand, we have the principle of reason [. . .] and on the other hand we have the project of literature in the strict sense, the project which cannot be shown to antedate the seventeenth and eighteenth centuries" (1984, 27). And like Gates again, he is more interested in the latter formation, literature, which Derrida contends "has not been possible without a project of stockpiling, of building up an objective archive over and above any traditional oral base" (26). The archive serves the purpose of providing a referent for all subsequent literary production.

Derrida is thinking here of the dominant culture of the West, and his words have a somewhat different resonance when applied to the field of African American letters, where the work of "building up an objective archive over and above [a] traditional oral base" could be seen to refer to two distinct but related projects: to the project of producing writing recognized and authenticated by the West (literature as "technology and commodity"), and to the practice of preserving archivally the traces of non- or pre-literary cultural practices, which had been subjected to erasure or violent suppression beginning with the middle passage. These two senses of archive each contributed to the drive toward the institutionalization, during the modernist period, of the great archival collections at Howard and Yale Universities, and at the 135th Street branch of the New York Public Library. It is not accidental that the theme of Derrida's essay is nuclear annihilation, which he takes to have been a premonitory referent of the project of literature since the Enlightenment. As he will later more epigrammatically express it, "there is no archive fever without the threat of [the] death drive" (1996, 19). The context of an African American literature that develops in the shadow of these formations may also be seen to have been determined by a premonition of disappearance or extinction.

These three subjects just surveyed – the relationship of cultural institutions to literary production, the planetary dimensions of the color line, and the role of the archive – were all matters meditated upon by the sociologist, activist, author, and institution-builder W. E. B. Du Bois. No early twentieth-century writer had a more comprehensive view of the global ramifications of race, or by the 1920s of race's imbrication with capitalism, than Du Bois. Even the most famous passage from the epochal *Souls of Black Folk* (1903), though it purports to describe African *American* psychology, frames the problematic as one of global modernity:

> After the Egyptian and Indian, the Greek and Roman, the Teuton and Mongolian, the Negro is a sort of seventh son, born with a veil, and gifted with second-sight in this American world, – a world which yields him no true self-consciousness, but only lets him see himself through the revelation of the other world. It is a peculiar sensation, this double-consciousness [. . .]. One ever feels his two-ness, – an American, a Negro; two souls, two thoughts, two unreconciled strivings; two warring ideals in one dark body, whose dogged strength alone keeps it from being torn asunder. (1986, 364)

Written just three years after *The Interpretation of Dreams* (though Du Bois would not himself read Freud until several years later), these lines on "double-consciousness" have served as touchstone for an enormous range of scholarship, including but not limited to the scholarship of race and psychoanalysis.[14] "A model of the psyche," in Vilashini Cooppan's words, "deeply embedded in the most material questions," Du Bois's thesis appears at the most immediate level to be describing the psychological effects of segregation in the United States (2005, 307).

Yet as Cooppan and others have recognized, Du Bois's Negro is not a specifically national category but is rather a way of naming the diaspora, indicating a "folk," in Eric Sundquist's words, "whose double consciousness is grounded in the soil of slavery but may ultimately be traced to an African home" (1993, 488). In the formulation of double-consciousness, Du Bois pointedly revised Hegel's classification of the six world civilizations, which had excluded Africa on the grounds of its "historylessness" (*Geschichtslosigkeit*), predicated upon the absence of a tradition of writing. In Du Bois's revision the diasporic Negro is figured as a seventh world-historical people. Over the next two decades, Du Bois would make more expressly political claims about the international dimensions and economic implications of race. In 1915 he located the causes of World War I in the European contest for the domination of Africa and attendant expansion of the global market; in Du Bois's analysis, the democratization of labor in the West proceeded dialectically with increased domination in the colonies: "the most rapid advance of democracy [goes] hand in hand in its very centres with increased aristocracy and hatred toward darker races, and [. . .] excuses and defends an inhumanity that does not shrink from the public burning of human beings" (1982, 98).

These prescient auguries of globalization can be traced to *The Souls of Black Folks'* claim that "the problem of the twentieth century is the problem of the color-line" (1986, 359). But *Souls* is also a work with more specifically literary ambitions, which are themselves directly linked to the questions of tradition and archive. Here the relevant section is the book's final chapter on the African American spirituals, or "sorrow songs," which Du Bois characterized as the "articulate message of the slave to the world" (538). In addition to presenting passages from the songs in transcription, the chapter provided Du Bois's readings of the songs, exegeses that required an especially sensitive hermeneutics because, as he noted, "the circumstances of the gathering [i.e. the occasion of each discrete musical performance], the rhythm of the songs, and the limitations of allowable thought, confined the poetry for the most part to single or double lines," and these lines themselves often contained "eloquent omissions and silences" whose meaning was not obvious from outside (543, 542). In Gilroy's words, Du Bois's readings demonstrated how "[i]t was in religious practices that the buried social memory of that original terror [the middle passage and slavery] had been preserved" (129).

At the same time, these acts of interpretation, as well as the operations of transcription upon which they depended, served another set of purposes linked to the promotion of black vernacular expression to the status of literature, in the historically bound yet temporally powerful sense of the word. It is this strategic accomplishment that Sundquist suggests is Du Bois's "most compelling modulation in the trope of double consciousness": "While writing his own book and placing it within the canonical tradition of Western individual authorship – making himself first among the 'co-workers in the kingdom of culture' – he at the same time wove into its most essential structure [not only in the book's conclusion but in the headnote to each of its chapters] the communal creation of African America, the cultural work not of 'unknown bards' alone but of a whole people whose words and song continued to be recorded and transformed in the constant evolution of the spirituals" (1993, 539). Du Bois is here understood both to have defined a tradition, and to have made an incursion into the Western literary canon. Yet if Sundquist's gloss is apt, we can see how the "double-consciousness" that defines Du Boisean authorship may also be understood as a version of the problematic, *avant la lettre*, of tradition (as embodied in music and religious practices) and the individual talent (as manifested by the critical-creative tradition self-consciously instantiated by Du Bois). Whereas Eliot's essay is concerned to attack the Romantic idea of authorship by pointing to the determining force of tradition – in which the dead, precisely, "are that which we know" – Du Bois strives to obtain the privileges of authorship, an authorship enabled by, while also justifying, a vernacular tradition and helping commit it to the archive (1932, 16).

This and many other implications of Du Bois's foundational work were expressly crystalized and extended in one of the Harlem Renaissance's foundational texts, James Weldon Johnson's preface to *The Book of American Negro Poetry* (1922). This work, as is obvious, was explicitly concerned with the question of defining a Negro literature, choosing its texts, whereas *Souls of Black Folk* more precisely indicated the originary conditions of its being. The stated purpose of the anthology was to advance the causes of American Negroes through the example of their literary accomplishment, since "[t]he final measure of the greatness of all peoples is the amount and standard of literature and art they have produced" (vii). It was Johnson's positing of a relationship between racial progress and art, and the desire to produce a literature (Derrida's "objective archive") toward this end, that Gates would ruefully name "the apocalyptic notion of the Negro arts," using it as the target of his earliest critical researches which culminated in the critique of writing in *Figures in Black* (23). Gates's critique extended across all of the New Negro movement and to Du Bois, who at the apex of the Harlem Renaissance had insisted that "all Art is propaganda and ever must be" (1986, 1000).

Yet gambling upon the political capital of a literary archive was not the only way in which Johnson had indebted his project to Du Bois. In the preface, Johnson does not in fact follow his opening remark with a celebration and justification of Negro literature, but instead engages in a lengthy digression on the cultural accomplishment of African American vernacular practices (ragtime, cakewalk, spirituals, folktales), cultural productions indicating a tradition of expressivity that neither belonged to the Western literary canon nor were even exclusively linguistic. In this sense Johnson pursued the implications of Du Bois's exegeses of the sorrow songs – whose importance resided in music, and in silence, as well as in language – while also suggesting that such collective practices were not only vestigial survivals but continued to thrive and evolve in the modern vernacular forms of ragtime and the cakewalk.

In order to understand the theoretical consequences of this strategy, and perhaps to suggest why it goes unremarked in Gates's discussion, it will be helpful to refer to another theorization of the archive, one that has helped shape the contemporary discipline of performance studies. Diana Taylor's *The Archive and the Repertoire* (2003), in its study of Latina/o American performance practices, aims to "challenge the preponderance of writing in Western epistemologies," a challenge that clearly has affinities with the motivations of Gates and, as she acknowledges, Derrida (16). But Taylor is also critical of the Derridean position for its failure to consider seriously systems of "learning, storing, and transmitting knowledge" that are neither archival nor belong to language in any primary sense – systems presumably indicated by Derrida's "traditional oral base." Against the authority of archival knowledge, Taylor emphasizes vernacular practices such as "spoken language, dance, sports, [and] ritual," practices resembling the ones named in Johnson's preface (19). Taylor's focus on "embodied knowledge" has indeed informed recent Harlem Renaissance studies such as Shane Vogel's *The Scene of Harlem Cabaret* (2009), which takes as its subject multiple instantiations of Harlem's "everynight life." Vogel's attention to Harlem's underground performers, and to their audiences, reveals an alternative version of the Harlem Renaissance whose most salient cultural productions were frequently not literary, not directly recorded nor meant to be, and often devised in opposition to the dominant cultural authority of the literary renaissance.

Stressing the opposition between embodied and archival systems of knowledge transmission, Taylor also means to engage the terms proposed in the French historian Pierre Nora's widely influential 1989 essay, "Between Memory and History: On *Les Lieux de Mémoire*." Here Nora had proposed a general transition from premodernity to modernity in which "real memory – social [or collective] and unviolated, exemplified in but also retained as the secret of so-called primitive or archaic societies" has been supplanted by "history" which is not "true memory" but rather a deritualized "modern memory" that is "above all, archival" (285, 290). Although his theory implies an epochal shift, whose totalizing character Taylor disparages, Nora's true interest is in describing a contemporary interaction between archive and ritual practice that he discovers in what he calls *les lieux de mémoire*. In the absence of an organic environment of communal memory, and in the face of the "tyranny of historicized memory," Nora's *lieux*, or "sites of memory," are occasions for a kind of collectively performed remembering that often uses the objects of official memory for the purposes of counterhistory. "[A]n invisible thread link[s] apparently unconnected objects [. . .], an undifferentiated network to which all of these separate identities belong, an unconscious organization of collective memory that is our responsibility to bring to consciousness" (299).

Nora's *lieux de mémoire* thesis has become one of the most frequently cited in African American literary study, beginning with *History and Memory in African-American Culture*, a book of essays edited by Geneviève Fabre and Robert O'Meally in 1994 that was specifically organized around a discussion of Nora's essay. In their introduction, Fabre and O'Meally averred that their concern was to follow Nora's example in resisting "the conventional wisdom of viewing orality and literacy as opposite cultural modalities; rather, we have seen them as parts of a tightly interwoven matrix of expression for a people who have nurtured a rich oral tradition and who at the same time have set literacy as a persistently sought ideal" (9). In this way they muted the critique of writing and archive implicit in the original theory. Although most of the essays use literature as their basis, they belong solidly to the cultural turn in literary study, some of them extending into embodied practices such as choreography, burial practice, and the inhabiting of city space.

Such, arguably, was the longer legacy of James Weldon Johnson's abrupt digression in the preface to *The American Book of Negro Poetry*, hailing the spirituals, ragtime, the cakewalk, and the Uncle Remus stories as the "only things artistic that have yet sprung from the American soil" (viii). But Johnson's concern was not to situate, as contemporary scholars have often done, literature as one among many cultural discourses operative within black modernity, nor did he follow Taylor in issuing a critique of the archive as such, though the jarring disjuncture between vernacular and archival forms may have implied a critique of the historical instrumentality of writing as a mode of domination over African Americans. Johnson's project, rather, was to call for a new specifically literary form that drew out of the vernacular tradition, to proceed, that is, from tradition to archive. This strategy involved an oblique but significant engagement with the procedures and rhetoric of literary modernism (an engagement echoed in the way the ostensibly historical anthology stretched no further back than the poetry of Paul Laurence Dunbar, who had died in 1906).

Such engagement is represented in an oft-quoted passage where Johnson summoned the agencies of the Celtic Revival: "What the colored poet in the United States needs to do is something like what Synge did for the Irish [. . .] to find a form that will express the racial spirit by symbols from within" (xl–xli). Yet the most compelling intimation of Johnson's programmatic theory obtained in a more hermetic reference:

> The earliest Ragtime songs, like Topsy, "jes' grew." [. . .] Later there came along a number of colored men who were able to transcribe the old songs and write original ones. [. . .] [My brother and I] appropriated about the last one of the old "jes' grew" songs." It was a song which had been sung for years through the South. The words were unprintable, but the tune was irresistible, and belonged to nobody. We took it, rewrote the verses [. . .], left the chorus as it was, and published the song. (xi)

Johnson presents here, *in reductio*, a theory of artistic production in which the procedures of appropriation, archivization, and assignation of conventional authorship are always preceded by the cultural object's collective production within the community (borrowing Topsy's words from *Uncle Tom's Cabin*, they "jes' grew"). He goes on to insist that this system is paradigmatic of all music and, because it prepares the example of Synge, all artistic production as such: "The fact is, nothing great or enduring in music has ever sprung full-fledged from the brain of any master; the best he gives the world he gathers from the hearts of the people, and runs it through the *alembic of his genius*" (my emphasis) (xiv).

It is not assuming too much to suggest that Johnson's idiosyncratic citation of the alembic (a vessel once used for distilling) means to allude to another programmatic essay from three years earlier, Eliot's "Tradition and the Individual Talent." What appears to interest Johnson are the fraught metaphors Eliot uses to bolster his attack upon the "substantial unity of the soul," and in its place represent the poet's mind not as a personality, but as a *medium*. Eliot's first analogy is, like Johnson's, scientistic: the poet's mind is a filament of platinum in whose presence two discrete gases combine to form sulfurous acid, while the shred of platinum remains unchanged. When Eliot unexpectedly refigures his metaphor, it is in a way that still corresponds with Johnson's alembic: "The poet's mind is in fact a receptacle for seizing and storing up numberless feelings, phrases, images, which remain there until all the particles which can unite to form a new compound are present together" (1932, 18–19). Johnson's metaphor in a sense unites Eliot's contradictory figures: the alembic is a receptacle, a figure for the way the poet's mind receives and contains tradition, yet it also possesses the agency to create a new work out of the given material through distillation, or by alchemy (another traditional use for the alembic).

Johnson's curiously antique metaphor encourages us to read Eliot's programmatic essay not for its quasi-scientific presentism (its "modernism"), but rather for its own deeply archaic sensibilities. It sees Eliot, in other words, reaching beyond literature as archive to the embodied practices that were the subject of the anthropological writings he was then avidly reading, such as the volumes on Adonis, Attis, and Osiris in J. G. Frazer's *The Golden Bough*.[15] According to the terms we have been using, Eliot's thesis reveals his nostalgia for Nora's ritual, communal, or "real" memory, in which the tradition is experienced not only intellectually but *affectively*. This is why the young man who aspires to be a great poet must write with a feeling of his own generation, and of the past, "in his bones," and why the essay must be stopped "at the frontier of [. . .] mysticism."(15, 21). It is by a similar logic that we can read past Johnson's opportunistic tale of appropriating and popularizing the last "jes' grew" song, and perceive Johnson the poet-theorist, author of *God's Trombones*, who perceives a form of collective practice that precedes and determines the work of art, but also extends beyond the archive and the protocols of individual authorship. The most striking diversion between these surprisingly correspondent theories is Eliot's admission that tradition can no longer be inherited and can only be obtained by great labor.

The issues of tradition and archive, embodiment and inscription, can also guide a brief final reading of *Mumbo Jumbo* (1972), Ishmael Reed's great parodic *roman-à-clef* about the Harlem Renaissance. The story involves the epidemic outbreak of "Jes Grew," a disease whose symptoms are manifested in spontaneous and uncontrolled performances of black embodied practices: dancing, ragtime, the blues. The contagion of Jes Grew is an allegory of the 1920s vogue for the Negro, and represents as well the threat of its commodification. At the same time, the book's expressions of desire (and fear) for Jes Grew "catching on" across the country represent the desire for the political potential of black art. At the heart of the novel is a highly symbolic confusion of a book and a body. As we learn, Jes Grew has an impetus of its own: it has come to New York in search of its sacred text, "an anthology, the archives of an ancient people," which the reader learns is the ancient Egyptian Book of Thoth (1972, 131). The sacred book, however, has been divided into fourteen pieces, with a specific reference to Set's dismemberment of Osiris, and sent circulating around New York in the manner of a chain letter. One of its recipients manages to assemble and translate the anthology, but later burns it. Jes Grew recedes as the novel's central figure, private eye and HooDoo impresario Papa LaBas, opens the box he believes contains the book and finds it empty.

Gates has read this final revelation as a demystification of an essential blackness, and the novel as a whole as "a brief for the permanence of the written text" over against (quoting Reed) "the so-called oral tradition" (1988, 223). But it is possible to read an *anarchival*, or more strictly embodied, principle in the book as well: "We were dumped here on our own without the Book to tell us who the [. . .] spirits were," a young friend tells Papa LaBas. "We made up our own. [. . .] I think we've done all right. The Blues, Ragtime, The Work that we do is just as good. [. . .] Doing the Work is not like taking inventory"; upon hearing this, LaBas admits that he has been too rigid (1972, 130). Figured as an epidemic, Jes Grew's search for its text may resemble nothing so much as Derrida's concept of archive fever, a "painful desire for a return to the authentic and singular origin," and a passionate need to create archives which are themselves predicated on the possibility of their own destruction (1996, 85). In this sense the archive is constructed as a form of prosthetic memory. But in all its Dionysian permutations, Jes Grew epitomizes the principle of the tradition outside the archive as well, resisting its own inscription and expressive of multiple forms of embodied knowledge.

Notes

1 The critical retrospectives by Griffin, Lott, and Smith appear in " '*Race,' Writing, and Difference*: A Meditation" (2008).
2 "The outstanding fact of late twentieth-century European culture is its ongoing reconciliation with black culture. The mystery may be that it took so long to discern the

elements of black culture already there in latent form, and to realize that the separation between the cultures was perhaps all along not one of nature, but one of force"
(75).

3   The key works here are Baker's *Blues, Ideology, and Afro-American Literature* (1984)
and *Modernism and the Harlem Renaissance* (1987); and Gates's *Figures in Black* (1987)
and *The Signifying Monkey* (1988). The subject of a vexed exchange in the pages of *New
Literary History* in 1987, a more useful critique of Gates's and Baker's 1980s work can be
found in Sandra Adell's excellent *Double-Consciousness/Double Bind: Theoretical Issues
in Twentieth-Century Black Literature* (1994), 118–138.

4   Stuart Hall, 305–345. Hall borrows the term from Louis Althusser, but uses it as a
means of instigating a Marxian investigation into the nature of "racially-structured
social formations" (305).

5   On the supplanting of poststructuralist with cultural theory in the new modernist
studies, see Friedman (2009), 241–242.

6   Some notable exceptions to this claim include Michael North's *The Dialect of Modernism:
Race, Language, and Twentieth-Century Literature* (1994), Laura Doyle and Laura
Winkiel's *Geomodernisms: Race, Modernism, Modernity* (2005) (though this collection
casts its eye globally rather than focusing on black American literature and culture), and
the work of Aldon Lynn Nielsen, in particular *Reading Race: White American Poets and
the Racial Discourse in the Twentieth Century* (1988) and *Writing between the Lines: Race
and Intertextuality* (1994).

7   David Levering Lewis, 17–22.

8   Hazel V. Carby, "The Politics of Fiction, Anthropology and the Folk: Zora Neale
Hurston," 71–93; Carby, "Policing the Black Woman's Body in an Urban Context";
Carby, *Reconstructing Womanhood: The Emergence of the Afro-American Woman Novelist*,
163–175. See also Farah Jasmine Griffin, *"Who Set You Flowin'?": The African-American
Migration Narrative* (1995).

9   Sean Latham, *The Art of Scandal: Modernism, Libel Law, and the Roman à Clef* (2009).

10 A selective list of scholarship on these black institutions includes Abby Arthur Johnson
and Ronald Mayberry Johnson, *Propaganda and Aesthetics: The Literary Politics of
Afro-American Magazines in the Twentieth Century* (1979); George B. Hutchinson,
The Harlem Renaissance in Black and White (1997); Janet Lyon, "Josephine Baker's
Hothouse" (2001), 29–47; Carolyn Goeser, *Picturing the New Negro: Harlem Renaissance
Print Culture and Modern Black Identity* (2007); James C. Davis, *Commerce in Color:
Race, Consumer Culture, and American Literature 1893–1933* (2007); Jeremy Braddock,
Collecting as Modernist Practice (2012), 156–208.

11 "Contest Awards" (1925): 142–143. On the *Dial* prize, see Lawrence Rainey, 77–106.

12 Bourdieu (1996), 215–223. Scott Herring traces this failure to the institutions of
publicity that surrounded and commodified the New Negro movement.

13 Brent Hayes Edwards, *The Practice of Diaspora: Literature, Translation, and the Rise of
Black Internationalism* (2003).

14 On race and psychoanalysis in the United States context, see Hortense J. Spillers, "All
the Things You Could Be By Now if Sigmund Freud's Wife Was Your Mother: Race and
Psychoanalysis" (2003), 376–427; Claudia Tate, *Black Novels and Psychoanalysis: Desire
and the Protocols of Race* (1998); Anne Anlin Cheng, *The Melancholy of Race* (2001). The
most consequential international theorist of psychoanalysis and race is Frantz Fanon;
see his *Black Skin, White Masks* (1967).

15 T. S. Eliot, *The Waste Land* (2001) 21.

References

Adell, Sandra. (1994). *Double-Consciousness/ Double Bind: Theoretical Issues in Twentieth-Century Black Literature.* Urbana: University of Illinois Press.

Baker, Houston A., Jr. (1984). *Blues, Ideology, and Afro-American Literature.* Chicago: University of Chicago Press.

Baker, Houston A., Jr. (1987). *Modernism and the Harlem Renaissance.* Chicago: University of Chicago Press.

Blanton, C. D. (2009). "Invisible Times: Modernism as Ruptural Unity." In *Modernism & Theory: A Critical Debate,* ed. Stephen Ross (pp. 137–152). New York: Routledge.

Bourdieu, Pierre. (1996). *The Rules of Art: Genesis and Structure of the Literary Field,* trans. Susan Emanuel. Palo Alto: Stanford University Press.

Braddock, Jeremy. (2012). *Collecting as Modernist Practice.* Baltimore: The Johns Hopkins University Press.

Carby, Hazel V. (1987). *Reconstructing Womanhood: The Emergence of the Afro-American Woman Novelist.* New York: Oxford University Press.

Carby, Hazel V. (1990). "The Politics of Fiction, Anthropology and the Folk: Zora Neale Hurston," *New Essays on Their Eyes Were Watching God,* ed. Michael Awkward (pp. 71–93). Cambridge: Cambridge University Press.

Carby, Hazel V. (1992). "Policing the Black Woman's Body in an Urban Context," *Critical Inquiry* 18.4: 738–755.

Cheng, Anne Anlin. (2001). *The Melancholy of Race.* New York: Oxford University Press, "Contest Awards." (1925). *Opportunity* 3.29 (May): 142–143.

Cooppan, Vilashini. (2005) "The Double Politics of Double Consciousness: Nationalism and Globalism in *The Souls of Black Folk.*" *Public Culture* 17.2: 299–318.

Davis, James C. (2007). *Commerce in Color: Race, Consumer Culture, and American Literature 1893–1933.* Ann Arbor: University of Michigan Press.

Derrida, Jacques. (1984). "No Apocalypse, Not Now (Full Speed Ahead, Seven Missiles, Seven Missives)," trans. Catherine Porter and Philip Lewis. *Diacritics* 14.2: 20–31.

Derrida, Jacques. (1996). *Archive Fever: A Freudian Impression,* trans. Eric Prenowitz. Chicago: The University of Chicago Press.

Doyle, Laura and Laura Winkiel, eds. (2005). *Geomodernisms: Race, Modernism, Modernity.* Bloomington: Indiana University Press.

Du Bois, W. E. B. (1982). "The African Roots of the War." *Writings in Periodical Literature. Vol. 2 1910–1934,* ed. Herbert Aptheker (pp. 96–104). Millwood, NY: Kraus-Thomson.

Du Bois, W. E. B. (1986). *Writings,* ed. Nathan Huggins. New York: Library of America.

Edwards, Brent Hayes. (2003). *The Practice of Diaspora: Literature, Translation, and the Rise of Black Internationalism.* Cambridge, MA: Harvard University Press.

Eliot, T. S. (1932). "Tradition and the Individual Talent." In *Selected Essays* (pp. 13–22). London: Faber and Faber.

Eliot, T. S. (2001). *The Waste Land,* ed. Michael North. New York: W. W. Norton.

Fabre, Geneviève and Robert O'Meally, eds. (1994). *History and Memory in African-American Culture.* New York: Oxford University Press.

Fanon, Frantz. (1967). *Black Skin, White Masks.* New York: Grove.

Friedman, Susan Stanford. (2009). "Theory." In *Modernism & Theory: A Critical Debate,* ed. Stephen Ross (pp. 237–245). New York: Routledge.

Gates, Henry Louis, Jr., ed. (1986). *"Race," Writing, and Difference*. Chicago: The University of Chicago Press.

Gates, Henry Louis, Jr. (1987). *Figures in Black: Words, Signs, and the "Racial" Self*. New York: Oxford University Press.

Gates, Henry Louis, Jr. (1988). *The Signifying Monkey: A Theory of African-American Literary Criticism*. New York: Oxford University Press.

Gilroy, Paul. (1993). *The Black Atlantic: Modernity and Double Consciousness*. Cambridge, MA: Harvard University Press.

Goeser, Carolyn. (2007). *Picturing the New Negro: Harlem Renaissance Print Culture and Modern Black Identity*. Lawrence: University Press of Kansas.

Griffin, Farah Jasmine. (1995). *"Who Set You Flowin'?": The African-American Migration Narrative*. New York: Oxford University Press.

Hall, Stuart. (1980). "Race, Articulation and Societies 'Structured in Dominance.'" In *Sociological Theories: Race and Colonialism* (pp. 305–345). Paris: UNESCO.

Harper, Phillip Brian. (2012). "Black Modernism's Unfinished Business." *American Literary History* 24.2: 356–373.

Herring, Terrell Scott. (2001). "The Negro Artist and the Racial Manor: *Infants of the Spring* and the Conundrum of Publicity." *African American Review* 35.4: 581–597.

Hutchinson, George B. (1997). *The Harlem Renaissance in Black and White*. Cambridge, MA: The Belknap Press of Harvard University Press.

Johnson, Abby Arthur and Ronald Mayberry Johnson. (1979). *Propaganda and Aesthetics: The Literary Politics of Afro-American Magazines in the Twentieth Century*. Amherst: University of Massachusetts Press.

Johnson, Georgia Douglas. (1928). "I Want to Die While You Love Me." In *An Autumn Love Cycle*. New York: Harold Vinal.

Johnson, James Weldon, ed. (1922). *The Book of American Negro Poetry*. New York: Harcourt Brace.

Latham, Sean. (2009). *The Art of Scandal: Modernism, Libel Law, and the Roman à Clef*. New York: Oxford University Press.

Lewis, David Levering. (1981). *When Harlem Was in Vogue*. New York: Oxford University Press.

Locke, Alain, ed. (1992). *The New Negro: An Interpretation*. New York: Atheneum.

Lyon, Janet. (2001). "Josephine Baker's Hothouse." In *Modernism, Inc.: Body, Memory, Capital* (pp. 29–47), ed. Jani Scandura and Michael Thurston. New York: New York University Press.

Nielsen, Aldon Lynn. (1988). *Reading Race: White American Poets and the Racial Discourse in the Twentieth Century*. Athens: University of Georgia Press.

Nielsen, Aldon Lynn. (1994). *Writing between the Lines: Race and Intertextuality*. Athens: University of Georgia Press.

North, Michael. (1994). *The Dialect of Modernism: Race, Language, and Twentieth-Century Literature*. New York: Oxford University Press.

Rainey, Lawrence. (1998). *Institutions of Modernism: Literary Elites and Public Culture*. New Haven, CT: Yale University Press.

Reed, Ishmael. (1972). *Mumbo Jumbo*. New York: Scribner.

Smith, Valerie, Farah Jasmine Griffin, Eric Lott, and Henry Louis Gates, Jr,. (2008). "'Race,' Writing, and Difference: A Meditation." *PMLA* 123.5: 1516–1539.

Snead, James A. (1990). "Repetition as a Figure of Black Culture." *In Black Literature and Literary Theory*, ed. Henry Louis Gates, Jr,. (pp. 59–80). New York: Routledge.

Spillers, Hortense J. (2003). "All the Things You Could Be By Now if Sigmund Freud's Wife Was Your Mother: Race and Psychoanalysis." *Black, White, and in Color: Essays on American Literature and Culture* (pp. 376–427). Chicago: The University of Chicago Press.

Sundquist, Eric J. (1993). *To Wake the Nations: Race in the Making of American Literature*. Cambridge, MA: The Belknap Press of Harvard University Press.

Tate, Claudia. (1998). *Black Novels and Psychoanalysis: Desire and the Protocols of Race*. New York: Oxford University Press.

Taylor, Diana. (2003). *The Archive and the Repertoire: Performing Cultural Memory in the Americas*. Durham, NC: Duke University Press.

Vogel, Shane. (2009). *The Scene of Harlem Cabaret: Race, Sexuality, Performance*. Chicago: The University of Chicago Press.

Williams, Raymond. (1989). *The Politics of Modernism: Against the New Conformists*. London: Verso.

6

Empire, Imperialism, and Modernism

John Marx

Early twentieth-century novelists replaced the Victorian notion of imperial core and colonial periphery with the alternate formulation of a global network. In the pages of modernist novels, that network appeared to be composed of locales and populations that could be administered by English-speaking (if not always British) experts. I will attempt to explain how modernists linked up with scholars and commentators from across the disciplines to generate a revised geopolitical model, one in which English language and literature appeared part and parcel of a differential system that spanned the globe.[1] I note that wide-reaching associations among modernist readers and writers formed even as British policy makers began to emphasize financial investment and interconnection over and above the conquering and holding of territory. Fiction secured its status in this recalibration, in part, by promoting itself as a curator of discrete and various vernacular languages and cultures worldwide.

Literary Experts, Imperial Networks

Joseph Conrad, James Joyce, and Virginia Woolf refuted the notion that there should be, or in fact could be, any singular standard English unmarked by demographic or disciplinary distinction. Instead of promoting populations and individuals willing to mimic the Queen's speech, modernist fiction proliferated parallel forms of English each bearing the accent of time and place. These multifarious versions of English appeared in novels by writers living and working within the British Isles as well as in the larger empire. While Woolf, Joyce, and others elaborated the varieties of English found in England and the Celtic Fringe, novels by the likes of

A Handbook of Modernism Studies, First Edition. Edited by Jean-Michel Rabaté.
© 2013 John Wiley & Sons, Ltd. Published 2013 by John Wiley & Sons, Ltd.

J. E. Casely-Hayford, C. L. R. James, R. K. Narayan, and Krupabai Satthianadhan indigenized the English-language novel farther afield.

In addition to featuring vernaculars that were localized geographically, fiction also detailed idioms specific to institutions and disciplines. While Woolf's *Mrs. Dalloway* (1925) generates literary means for representing Westminster's "beating...stirring...tapping," Lawrence's *Women in Love* (1920) captures the jargon of artists and aesthetes (7). While James's *Minty Alley* (1936) records colloquialisms on a "small island" in the West Indies, Conrad's tales offer primers in the vocabularies of ship captains, colonial adjutants, and myriad other sorts of imperial expert (23). Casely-Hayford's *Ethiopia Unbound* (1911) links geographic particularity to disciplinary specificity by planning a Pan-African university capable of educating an "unspoilt son of the tropics, nursed in a tropical atmosphere, favourable to the growth of national life" (173). Narayan and Satthianadhan also link education to local culture. Satthianadhan's *Kamala* (1894) describes a woman whose bookish learning turns her into an activist, while Narayan's *The Bachelor of Arts* (1937) is an archetype of the colonial campus novel. For its part, Joyce's *Ulysses* (1986) disassembles English into heterogeneous components before reassembling what amounts to a global tongue. His "Oxen of the Sun" chapter moves from Latin dialect to pidgin English, collating myriad Englishes (ancient and modern, written and spoken) into an array of almost, but not quite English sentences. Collectively, these novels show how English language and culture have been so tainted by an imperial history of lexical cross-pollination that they can no longer be considered national categories.

Because it is necessary to actually read *Ulysses* to make sense of the fragmented linguistic and cultural history the novel reconfigures, Joyce's tome suggests how much fiction began to appear a medium wherein English could receive new formal coherence even as it was in the process of breaking down. Such a specialized purpose was not unique to *Ulysses*, but rather linked that volume to a whole range of literary efforts to remake the English language and through that project revise what was thought of as English-language fiction.

Such literary efforts should be understood as contributing to an early-twentieth-century social and cultural transformation of expertise. Fredric Jameson (2002) identifies disciplinary specialization as a defining feature of modernity – "the gradual separation of areas of social life from each other, their disentanglement from some seemingly global and mythic...overall dynamic, and their reconstitution as distinct fields with distinct laws and dynamics" (90). He also sees this process as modernism's condition of possibility, since differentiation encourages an unprecedented sense of aesthetic autonomy (2002, 146). Niklas Luhmann (1995) argues that processes of differentiation went so far as to beg the "question of whether the self-description of the world society is possible" (430). Since "there is no longer a 'good society'," a standard against which all else can be measured, the broad terms of culture as civilization proffered by the Victorians must necessarily give way, Luhmann teaches us, to more "regional delimitations" (1995, 430, xii). Expert specialization and regional delimitation went together: fiction demonstrated its difference from other forms of writing in part by arguing that that its pages could preserve local and regional cultures, in part by propagating those hallmarks of difficulty and obscurity that generations of readers have learned to equate with modernism.

Such form and content helped to distinguish modernist prose in an increasingly global and increasingly crowded marketplace for fiction. Thomas Strychacz (1993) treats Henry James's conception of a market "subdivided as a chess-board" as emblematic: on that board, "each little square" represented a niche "confessing only to its own kind of accessibility" (21). Jennifer Wicke (2001) argues that *Ulysses* models discriminating consumer behavior in the "bookstall placed within its chapters, so that as readers hold the book in their hands they are inevitably repeating the distracted colportage encountered in the text" (399). Readers all around the world proved capable of such discrimination. Conrad identified the emergence of a far-flung audience for his brand of idiosyncratic fiction. He claimed in a letter to the publisher Blackwood's that his writing appealed "to such widely different personalities as W.H. Henley and Bernard Shaw – H.G. Wells and professor Yrgö Hirn of the Finland University – to Maurice Greiffenhagen a painter and to the skipper of a Persian Gulf steamer who wrote to the papers of my 'Typhoon' – to the Ed. of PMM to a charming old lady in Winchester" (Karl and Davies 1983–2002, 2: 416). With its Finnish reader and Polish writer, Persian Gulf skipper and "charming old lady" from Winchester, Conrad's readership broke the rule stipulating a necessary correlation between English fiction and British nation. Instead of composing a national audience, Conrad's readers confirmed the international appeal of the challenging sort of English-language prose he wrote.

Scholars agree that to understand how English went global means grappling with tendencies in communication technology, global economy, and geopolitics that made possible far-flung audiences of the sort Conrad imagined. In the first decades of the twentieth century, Stephen Kern (1983) explains, barriers broke down "horizontally across the face of the land and vertically across social strata," as innovations in transportation accelerated movement across continents and new communication devices rapidly transmitted information to multitudes (316). Connectivity means something different to Rudolf Hilferding (1981) in his classic account *Finance Capital: A Study of the Latest Phase of Capitalist Development*: for him, technological invention spurred a "revolution" in the activities of financial speculation, which Britain's banking sector proved very well equipped to exploit (315, 323). "The export of capital was . . . an English monopoly," Hilferding observed, "and it secured for England the domination of the world market" (323). By the early decades of the twentieth century, the British service sector was outpacing manufacturing, and with increased market share came increased clout. P. J. Cain and A. G. Hopkins (1993) contend that "management of the economy [left] the hands of party politicians and transferred . . . to the Treasury and the Bank of England," which in turn took advice from the City and from economists of Oxford and Cambridge (1: 148–149). City professionals developed a thoroughly cosmopolitan commercial program orchestrated by monetary experts well versed in the specialized language of global speculation.

These specialists behaved as if the best way to expand Britain's worldwide influence was to forge new and deeper ties with foreign powers. To this end, they welcomed overseas investors to park money in London's banks, encouraged town and village bankers to invest accounts abroad, urged politicians to negotiate treaties allowing them to fund development in territories not controlled by Britain, and thus created a "marriage of English capital with foreign demand" (1993, 1: 182, 1: 384–385; Davis and Huttenback 1987, 212). "In this way, the City and sterling acquired a world role," Cain and Hopkins write, "and London became the center of a system of global payments that continued to expand right down to the outbreak of war in 1914" (1993, 1: 468). Even after the war, and through the period of mid-century decolonization in fact, Britain extended its influence by solidifying financial ties rather than conquering new territories. Britain might not govern the countries where its banks did business, but its banks lent the money that kept myriad colonial and postcolonial states afloat.

To envision a globe crisscrossed by economic and technological pulses meant heightening interest in location. This should not be surprising, argues David Harvey (1989), for the "flow of capital across the globe...places strong emphasis upon the particular qualities of the spaces to which capital might be attracted" (271). Likewise, the "shrinkage of space that brings diverse communities across the globe into competition with each other implies...a heightened sense of awareness of what makes a place special" (271). Kern (1983) argues along similar lines, observing that technological innovation affirmed the "plurality of time and spaces" rather than flattening social, cultural, and geographic distinction (8).

Imperial administration sought to manage this plurality: the name for an approach that delegated territorial ownership while consolidating command and control was Indirect Rule. First practiced in India's "princely states" in the nineteenth century, reproduced across the empire in the twentieth century, Indirect Rule meant establishing local proxies to facilitate the administration of empire on the cheap. A whole hierarchy of more or less specialized mediators grew to staff networks linking London, colonial capitals, and so-called "native states." District Officers controlled access to inner regions, ethnographers studied local culture, and missionaries taught English to potential adjutants. For an ethnographer like Bronislaw Malinowski (1930), competition among such varied experts created an opportunity to test his skills against those of the administrator who, "however much he may sympathize with the natives, is bound to have more sympathy with his wife and children, with his dream of success and constructive enterprise" (422).

Administrators and anthropologists reserved their most pointed barbs for the English-speaking, -reading, and -writing populations from which they drew their valued subordinates. Malinowski (1936) warned that "the educated African may be useful as a laborer, clerk or assistant, [but] he also grows into a dangerous competitor" (484). Colonial administrators were only too aware of this threat. In Nigeria, Frederick Lugard outlined a program to counteract a century of missionary and charter company contact. He charged District Officers with playing the role of the sympathetic expert in the bush, the better to usurp and undermine the influence of African intellectuals such as Edward Wilmot Blyden, John Payne Jackson, and Mojola Agbebi. In his widely circulated manifesto, *The Dual Mandate in British Tropical Africa*, Lugard (1922) promoted government residents as particularly "in touch with native thought and feeling" (194). He described local populations "naturally industrious" in farming but reliant on European intermediaries to plug them into regional and international networks of exchange (1922, 401). As the political scientist Mahmood Mamdani (1996) puts it, "the African was containerized, not as a native, but as a tribesman" (22). The historian Sara Berry (1992) observes that this campaign gave local culture a malleable quality: "Colonial 'inventions' of African tradition served not so much to define the shape of the colonial social order as to provoke a series of debates over the meaning and application of tradition which in turn shaped struggles over authority and access to resources" (328). Administrators and ethnographers thereby contributed to what Arjun Appadurai calls "the production of locality." "Much that has been considered local knowledge," he explains, "is actually knowledge of how to produce and reproduce locality under conditions of anxiety and entropy, social wear and flux, ecological uncertainty and cosmic volatility, and the always present quirkiness of kinsmen, enemies, spirits, and quarks of all sorts" (Appadurai 1996, 181). Administrators and anthropologists did not discover these mitigating historical and political terms but invested them with new importance by making them the concern of specialists.

Fiction contributed to this effort. The colonial governmental field of operations is the setting for Conrad's *Lord Jim* (1899), which describes a network of managers who share a language if not a nation, and who labor to administer a dazzling array of local places. On Patusan, Jim finds himself called upon to mediate among multiple factions and shifting alliances. When he "leaps . . . into the life of Patusan, into the trust, the love, the confidence of the people," Jim achieves a level of authority that would be the envy of any colonial administrator (1899, 284). "He had regulated so many things in Patusan!" Marlow exclaims. "Things that would have appeared as much beyond his control as the motions of the moon and the stars" (164). Sympathy is the hallmark of expertise in this novel, just as it was in Malinowski's anthropology or Lugard's Indirect Rule. Sentimental bonds among men of the sea, extended to Dain Wairis, and heightened by romance with Jewel, appear to give Jim an almost supernatural capacity to reshape the colonial environment. Jim clearly relishes his newfound authority, but seems to recognize that in order to retain it he must not be seen as a threat to the local leaders in whose name he acts. He must remain a stranger, one who lives with the locals and who understands them better for his outsider status. In truth, Conrad's hero faces what would become the fundamental challenge of early-twentieth-century imperial governance: how to administer territory he does not profess to own but learns to know.

Lord Jim was not alone in considering how imperial organization altered local culture. Works from E. M. Forster's *A Passage to India* (1924) to Sarath Kumar Ghosh's *Prince of Destiny* (1909), Sol T. Plaatje's *Muhdi* (1930) to Joyce Cary's *Mister Johnson* (1939), offered narrative case studies of changing relations among colonial administrators and their subjects. That fiction might be capable of capturing shifting power dynamics surely came as no surprise to readers used to literature weighing in on politics and culture. Fiction relied upon its historical strength of describing geopolitical change from the standpoint of interpersonal relations. From the love triangle in Ghosh's novel of revolt in a princely state to the ties that bind Forster's Fielding and Dr. Aziz, modernist fiction behaved as if the way to understand local features of imperial power was to zero in on the most personal of interactions. Thus did fiction compete with the sympathy of an ethnographer like Malinowski or an administrator like Lugard, or for that matter his successor in Nigeria, Sir Hugh Clifford (1922), who described the ideal district officer as a man who "never offends" the "sensibilities" of his charges, who "can feel as they feel, rejoicing in their jobs, sorrowing in their pains" (180). Imperial interconnection, personal and political, was a matter of concern for novelists as much as it was for governors and social scientists. All of these specialists, moreover, understood global connectivity as vital for the way it impacted the definition of region, locality, and place.

Imperial Places, Novelistic Settings

In the eighteenth century, Linda Colley (1992) contends, Britons "came to define themselves as a single people not because of any political or cultural consensus at home, but rather in reaction to the Other beyond their shores" (6). Although nineteenth-century writers may well have found it equally important to preserve a British identity opposed to the foreign cultures of Europe and the larger world, increasing imperial traffic made this difficult to sustain. In the early twentieth century, as administrators, fiction writers, and anthropologists detailed the connections political, economic, and interpersonal that bound together the various places of the British Empire, those places in India, sub-Saharan Africa, and elsewhere could only have appeared less foreign than ever before. England, meanwhile, must certainly have appeared more alien than ever before.

Some turn-of-the-century novelists staged last-ditch efforts to stave off the inevitable transformation. General William Booth's *In Darkest England* (1890) and William Reeves's *In Darkest London* (1891) were among the tracts to sound the alarm about foreign infiltrators. They detailed migrants rapidly transforming London into an "urban jungle" and described international commerce as inherently dangerous (McLaughlin 2000, 4–5). In popular fiction such as the detective stories of Arthur Conan Doyle, foreign bodies and foreign things represented an influence every bit as pernicious as the opium slowly killing Holmes. Paradoxically, by locating the foreign in every pore of the English body, such writing undermined the very opposition of core and periphery it hoped to sustain. Jed Esty (2004) describes the quiet desperation of 1930s modernists who tried in vain to distill an English essence from ever more polluted soil. The "redemptive discourse of Anglocentrism," as Esty calls it, was the project of "English intellectuals who were inclined to believe that an insular culture, but not a baggy multinational civilization, could unify its fragments" (2004, 10).

A remarkable range of modernist writers were willing, even eager, to give up on purity and embrace the cultural and linguistic mixtures threatening Anglo-authenticity. Novelists from Sarah Grand to D. H. Lawrence developed a literary language of primitivism that competed with, even as it borrowed from, anthropological and evolutionary writing. The heroine of Grand's celebrated *The Heavenly Twins* (1893) experiences a sort of primitive desire that appears to alter her very physiognomy: "Evadne's face recalled somewhat the type of old Egypt," the narrator reports (32). In "Mornings in Mexico," meanwhile, Lawrence (1927) describes a market where "only that which is utterly intangible, matters. The contact, the spark of exchange" (52). Europeans could experience this spark through the exotic goods they imported, as suggested by *Women in Love* (1920), wherein sculptures from the tropics appear to be Rupert's "soul's intimates" (253). With "thousands of years of purely sensual, purely unspiritual knowledge" behind them, they "knew what he himself did not know" (253). Lawrence's very negation affirmed the future of English language, literature, and culture, even as he made it easier to believe that the invasion of England meant the end of its centrality within a larger Britain. Though a genealogy of writers leading straight to Enoch Powell persisted in attempting to reinscribe "an old insular culture from within the bloated, multicultural empire," Lawrence and others fell in love with the alien stuff they discovered from Manchester to Liverpool, Dover to Edinburgh (Esty 2000, 9). They expressed their affection for foreign matter by mixing domestic romance with the romance of adventure, thus muddying distinctions between the genres that had once separated home from abroad. They acquired an assortment of strange and wonderful commodities with which they proceeded to redecorate the English home. They deposited lust for foreign travel in the heads of the very sorts of fictional heroines who for more than a century had dreamed only of marriage and motherhood.

Even as tropes of British imperial decline persisted in many circles, they were accompanied by countervailing excitement at how intoxicating exoticism could be. The larger world not only threatened but also offered a new source of energy, the means to reinvent English in all of its incipient diversity. Early-twentieth-century novelists routinely juggled what seemed twin imperatives to demonstrate, first, that global forces were altering the fabric of life within the British Isles and, second, that local culture could accommodate such influence. This is certainly apparent in the urban fictions *Ulysses* and *Mrs. Dalloway*, which challenged readers to absorb the notion that cosmopolitanism was a boon to local culture. Each novel describes a native population that is not less particular for being multifarious. Readers of *Mrs. Dalloway* confronted a thoroughly exoticized corner of London populated largely with eccentric characters: Peter Walsh just "back from India," Doris Kilman the German sympathizer, Septimus Smith the shell-shocked soldier with the Italian wife Rezia, the anonymous "Colonial" who insults the House of Windsor, even Richard Dalloway the "pillar of the metropolitan establishment" who craves nothing but to get away (1925, 5, 21). Westminster is awash in foreign goods and foreign consumers: diamonds "tempt Americans"; bookstore window displays proffer *Soapy*

Sponge alongside *Big Game Shooting in Nigeria*; glowing arrangements of blooms capture Clarissa's eye (1925, 7, 12, 15–16). Woolf fills the minds of her characters with complaints about those "nincompoop" Anglo-Indian women, memories "of the dead; of the flag; of Empire," longings to reside in "foreign parts" (10, 21, 32). When Clarissa "plunges" into the streets she finds the noise and hum to be "absolutely absorbing," "loving it as she did with an absurd and faithful passion, being part of it" (11, 7). Such is the local culture of London.

Joyce's Dublin is just as busy and just as absorbing, although the difference between it and London remains evident. What counts as the Dublin average is no more uniform than the Westminster norm. People walk Dublin's streets fresh from Italy, from soldiering in India, and planning emigration to the United States – "America . . . . What is it? The sweepings of every country including our own" (1986, 10: 734–735). The languages invoked within *Ulysses* include French, Latin, Gaelic, and Italian, not to mention Joyce's idiosyncratic English (10: 182, 197, 1006, 344). Wildly various commerce takes place here too, in the lapidary shop with its "lozenges of cinnabar . . . rubies, leprous and winedark stones," at the Empire Theatre where the English comedienne and singer Marie Kendall performs, and in the stall where Bloom flips through *Aristotle's Masterpiece* and von Sacher-Masoch, as well as the book he purchases, *Sweets of Sin* (10: 800, 495, 585). The social fabric of *Ulysses* is "radically pluralistic," Michael Tratner (1995) observes, and "constantly shifting" (184). Such a fluid situation composes, rather than undermines, Dublin's sense of place. Joyce's "Wandering Rocks" chapter in particular refuses to stabilize the scene by authorizing any one vantage point, any singularly defining perspective on Dublin. No one is simply an observer in this chapter, nor is anyone simply observed. Instead, Father Conmee provides the first link in a chain to which each character contributes: he spies the "gentleman with glasses" on the tram, speculates on what exactly that man might have been telling the woman next to him, and is subjected to a grimace from Mr. Eugene Stratton (10: 120–141). A Viceregal cavalcade brings the chapter to a close by providing an impetus to public display – Tom Kernan's vain greeting, Simon Dedalus's effort to cover his open fly, and John Wyse Nolan's "unseen coldness" (10: 1176–1282). Idiosyncratic local response to unmistakably British authority gives us a sense of the place: Dublin is part of a colony that nevertheless reveals the variety within categories like "Irish" or "colonial."

As much as urban prose demonstrated that imperial interconnection was altering place, prose about the rural regions of England equally attended to the traffic that promised to revamp both country and city. Highway projects and electrification forged new ties among parts of the British Isles that had long relied on slower and less reliable commercial and communication networks. Those networks extended far beyond the shores of Britain, moreover, and linked towns small and large into a grid that seemed to stretch around the world. Modernism brought provincialism to the metropole – in the form of dialect and regional idiom punctuating prose and poetry – and reciprocated by bringing the city to the country – via the cosmopolitanism that framed modernist literature as a whole and shaped the outlook of characters no matter where they found themselves.

Fiction developed a meta-commentary on the expert observation necessary to analyze how imperial networks altered a sense of place. Evelyn Waugh's *Brideshead Revisited* (1945), Mary Webb's *Precious Bane* (1924), and other novels modeled strategies for observing how rural regions were changing. Waugh went so far as to show how an outsider might end up going native, as his protagonist does in one of England's more curious county seats. Most tellingly, perhaps, the technique that various commentators developed was comparable to the analytic approach employed to evaluate cultural alteration overseas. James Buzard (2003) traces the term "auto-ethnography" to 1938, to debate surrounding the publication of Jomo Kenyatta's *Facing Mount Kenya: The Traditional Life of the Gikuyu* and to "Mass-Observation, a social research movement devoted to the anthropological study of British culture by ordinary Britons" (66). "Rather amazingly," Buzard explains, "this amateurish populist enterprise gained the qualified imprimatur of Malinowski himself, who declared the 'Home-Coming of Anthropology' to be the 'inevitable consequence' of his own path-breaking researches among tribal peoples half a world away" (66). By importing imperial techniques, modernist observers swept aside the chiasmatic relation of inside and outside that had enabled earlier distinctions between English and British, not to mention British and foreign.

Global Culture, Global Experts

Recent scholarship has detailed the many heteroglot places that modernist fiction made intelligible to English-language readers. In their introduction to the edited collection *Geomodernisms*, Laura Doyle and Laura Winkiel (2005) explain they want "more global and longer histories for modernism" (14). The contributors to this and other recent collections such as *Pacific Rim Modernisms* (2009), scholars such as Christopher Bush (forthcoming), Simon Gikandi (2001), and Eric Hayot (2009), as well as many more pursuing the transcultural influences of modernism have identified myriad connections among various writings and writers worldwide, growing the very category of "modernist fiction" even as they testify to the role literature played in redefining imperial places and populations.

Modernist traffic was institutional as well as intercultural. As Gikandi explains, moreover, "the discipline of English literature at the colonial university was an important precursor to the theories of globalization" (2001, 651). To the extent that modernist fiction exploited imperial networks by forging idiosyncratic connection among readers of difficult novels, it anticipated utopian accounts of how globalization could foster alternative forms of intellectual exchange. Modernism's increasing role in university curricula also anticipated the planetary spread of professional hierarchy, however. Edward Said (1983) observes that "the intellectual hegemony of Eliot, Leavis, Richards, and the New Critics coincides not only with the work of masters like Joyce, Eliot himself, Stevens, and Lawrence, but also with the serious and autonomous development of literary studies in the university" (164). To the extent that modernist writers helped codify highly specialized aesthetic vernaculars, they helped lay the conceptual foundation for degree-generating programs in which the demonstration of literary expertise appeared very much akin to knowledge work in the sciences or social sciences. Over the course of the twentieth century, English programs born of empire contributed to the production of accredited experts who collectively merited the name global professional managerial class.

To understand modernist literature as part of a century-long proliferation of authoritative specialized languages is to understand it as an active participant in what Harold Perkin (1989) refers to as the "triumph" of professionalism. Professionalism represented a dream to do away with the inequality of class society by shedding the "binary model [of] a small ruling class exploiting a large underclass," but, as Perkin maintains, professionalism also replaced that binary with new "inequalities and rivalries of hierarchy" (9). Disciplinary-specific studies of anthropology, economics, and imperial administration by the likes of Gaurav Desai (2001) and Timothy Mitchell (2002) show professionalism and imperialism operating in tandem as experts spread out across the empire, often acquiring new recruits from the very subject populations Britain sought to control. Such scholarly accounts logically require us to triangulate modernism, professionalism, and imperialism, the better to perceive all three as components in a new whole.

In the nineteenth century, officers in India complained that "the greatest difficulty" in ruling "springs from . . . ignorance of the spirit, principles and system of the British Government" (Pennycook 1998, 72). Part of the solution to this problem emerged as "the content of English literary education [was adapted] to the administrative and political imperatives of British rule" (Viswanathan 1989, 3). Though English study in the colonies was intended as a tool for discipline, as Salman Rushdie (1990) observes, "those people who were . . . colonized by the language [were also] rapidly remaking it, domesticating it" (64). By spreading literary study throughout the colonies, British administrators facilitated the proliferation of local English dialects. They also suggested that literary expertise might represent a truly valuable form of capital, one capable of legitimating the construction of a whole new class to organize the not entirely un-English cultures being generated worldwide. This endeavor "focused attention on the high literati," the historian Sumit Sarkar (1997) observes, pushing them to the center of colonial historiography as well as anti-colonial politics (189).

Underwriting the growth of imperial higher education in the humanities was the "implicit claim," as Gikandi puts it, "that even students in colonial universities, such as Makerere and Ibadan in Africa, could be trained to read culture and morality in literary texts the same way that these tropes were read at University College, London, the 'mother' institution" (2001, 349). When professors at these and other schools taught students to understand fiction and poetry for its insight into local culture, their instruction facilitated the emergence of literate minorities along the lines promoted by F. R. Leavis in his English School. Imperialism authorized such readers and writers to speak for Indians and Africans in general even as it distinguished them from "the people." Distinguishing literary experts in the colonies, further, primed them to compete and to collaborate with European counterparts.

Perhaps the most famous setting for such competition and collaboration was Bloomsbury. Raymond Williams (1989) famously argues that mass immigration to urban centers like London generated "productive kinds of strangeness and distance" and, in turn, artistic and intellectual communities "of the medium" (45–46). The web site for the interdisciplinary "Making Britain" research project at The Open University captures such community with a map that notes the proximity of, for example, the office of *Poetry London* edited by M. J. Tambimuttu roughly two blocks from the Tavistock Square location of The Hogarth Press, just a little farther from the Indian Students' Union and Hostel, and a not too strenuous walk from the Penguin office where Krishna Menon launched the Pelican imprint (2012). Of course, not everybody who migrated to a metropolis joined a salon or artists' collective, a memoir club or a midnight society. Not everyone who experienced the volatility of Bloomsbury the neighborhood ended up joining Bloomsbury the group. Urban migration brought artists and intellectuals into geographical proximity, but if we are to understand what bound communities "of the medium," as Williams calls them, "the city" is hardly a sufficient answer. Instead, as a glance at the map of Bloomsbury suggests, it is vital to recall that the neighborhood's presses and societies, writers' associations and poetry journals thrived in adjacency to universities.

As with Bloomsbury the neighborhood, so Bloomsbury the group is hardly thinkable absent the institutions of higher education and the ideas that intellectuals had about them. "They met in the casual way students at colleges meet," Leon Edel (1979) reports; Woolf and Strachey, Bell and Thoby Stephen argued like "young intellectual 'outsiders,'" "playing with ideas" (40). "From such discussions Vanessa and I got probably much the same pleasure that undergraduates get when they meet friends of their own for the first time," Virginia Woolf recalls (Rosenbaum 1995, 49). Cambridge and Gordon Square engendered cliquish relationships that did not so much ignore racial typology and gendered distinctions as transform them into aspects of intellectual idiosyncrasy, which in turn made them grist for gossip and group discussion. To treat Cambridge (and Cambridge-style) debate as facilitating and helping to reproduce friendships that bridge divides of gender, ethnicity, sexuality is to recast an institution equally responsible for the reproduction of aristocratic class and a strict sexual division of labor. The collective willingness of those intellectuals in the orbit of Bloomsbury to revolt made them, Williams asserts, "a fraction" whose attacks on "the ideas and institutions of their class as a whole" anticipated and even facilitated change (1980, 162). "At the same time," he contends, by performing this "service for its class," Bloomsbury helped ensure that professional class ideas and institutions would persist "because these adaptations have been made and continue to be made" (1980, 163).

Mulk Raj Anand's 1984 autobiographical novel *The Bubble* provides a retroactive gloss on Bloomsbury's reach. Among other episodes, the book portrays its author's alter-ego Krishnan Chander Azad dreaming of the possibility that Virginia Woolf might see him as a writer. He sends her "the beginning of my confession called Seven Summers," and yearns to express their shared writerly interest in "this inbetween. Things beyond big words" (1984, 416). Krishnan imagines that when he joins the

Bloomsbury cohort he will become "the natural man I was and yet be taken for granted" (1984, 417). The novel does not disabuse him of this dream, but it does suggest that Bloomsbury is not the only prototype for such a welcoming clique.

After his time in London, Krishnan travels to Ireland and India, where he finds himself in equally cosmopolitan territory. In Dublin, Maud Gonne brings up D. H. Lawrence, who she says "has ripped the veil off all those fake feelings"; Francis Stuart complains that Tagore's poetry is "all sing song!"; and W. B. Yeats steers conversation around to the problem of renovating the university: "Our academy will be different," he declares (1984, 490–493). Once Krishnan hears that Bertrand Russell has approved his thesis, he moves on to India. "I am anxious to revise [my] novel under the advice of Mahatma Gandhi," Krishnan reports to his father (1984, 585).

Anand's relationship with E. M. Forster helped him find a British publisher for his first book, but *The Bubble* makes clear that Bloomsbury is not the only group capable of nurturing a young writer and encouraging his career. Instead, Bloomsbury appears as a group in competition with a global array of such cliques, each of which has a distinct if related approach to inclusiveness, collaboration, and professional development. Inclusiveness was perhaps the most critical distinction between professional meritocracy and previous social models associated with the aristocrat and entrepreneur. "Whereas their ideal citizen had been a limited concept," Perkin contends, "the professional ideal could in principle be extended to everyone. Every landlord and industrialist could be transformed into a professional manager, every worker into a salaried employee" (1989, 8). Every aspiring writer, Anand might add, could be transformed into a novelist. That ideal was altered in its realization, however. Professionalism did not create an egalitarian society during the age of empire or in its aftermath. "To paraphrase George Orwell," Perkin writes, "all professionals are equal but some are more equal than others" (1989, 9). Modernism's version of this contradiction entailed soliciting readers from all walks of life and from every region of the planet but arranging that audience hierarchically. Further distinguishing among qualified readers and writers capable of fulfilling the discrete functions of a modernist author confirmed a commitment to both expertise and hierarchy.

Modernism's vision of heterogenous local cultures networked together by literary experts endured after the fall of empire. It did so because the tactic of treating English as a medium for international exchange between specialized readers and writers proved eminently appropriable by non-European novelists. "English" in the wake of modernism does not name a series of homogeneous ethno-linguistic entities, each of which reproduces the nation-form of the others, but rather identifies a way to compare English vernaculars through a logic of parallelism. A global field of competing English literatures may seem like a pipe dream in the context of empire, one as patently fantastic as Stephen Dedalus's desire to "fly by those nets" of church, nation, and family (Joyce 1976, 203). It remains the case, however, that modernists of various nationalities reproduced something very much like Stephen's dream in generating a plurality of variously transnational English-language novels. Modernist fiction informed its readers that Victorian empire was dead, assured those readers that something new was on the horizon, and affirmed that thing would be, if not traditionally English, insistently Anglophone.

Note

1 I make this argument at greater length in my book, *The Modernist Novel and the Decline of Empire*.

References

Anand, Mulk Raj. (1984). *The Bubble*. New Delhi: Arnold Heinemann.

Appadurai, Arjun. (1996). *Modernity at Large: Cultural Dimensions of Globalization*. Minneapolis: University of Minnesota Press.

Berry, Sara. (1992). "Hegemony on a Shoestring: Indirect Rule and Access to Agricultural Land." *Africa* 62.3: 327–355.

Bush, Christopher. (forthcoming). *The Floating World*. New York: Columbia University Press.

Buzard, James. (2003). "On Auto-Ethnographic Authority." *Yale Journal of Criticism* 16.1: 61–91.

Cain, P. J. and A. G. Hopkins. (1993). *British Imperialism*, 2 vols. New York: Longman.

Cary, Joyce. (1939 [2009]). Mister Johnson. London: Faber.

Casely-Hayford, J. E. (1911 [1969]). *Ethiopia Unbound*. London: Frank Cass and Co.

Clifford, Hugh. (1965). "The Clifford Minute." In *The Principles of Native Administration in Nigeria: Selected Documents 1900–47*, ed. A. H. M. Kirk-Greene (pp. 174–186). London: Oxford University Press.

Colley, Linda. (1992). *Britons: Forging the Nation, 1707–1837*. New Haven, CT: Yale University Press.

Conrad, Joseph. (1899 [1963]). *Lord Jim*. New York: Doubleday.

Davis, Lance E. and Robert A. Huttenback. (1987). *Mammon and the Pursuit of Empire: The Political Economy of British Imperialism, 1860–1912*. Cambridge: Cambridge University Press.

Desai, Gaurav. (2001). *Subject to Colonialism*. Durham, NC: Duke University Press.

Doyle, Laura and Laura A. Winkiel. (2005). *Geomodernisms: Race, Modernism, Modernity*. Bloomington: Indiana University Press.

Edel, Leon. (1979). *Bloomsbury: A House of Lions*. Philadelphia: Lippincott.

Esty, Joshua. (2000). "National Objects: Keynesian Economics and Modernist Culture in England." *Modernism/Modernity* 7.1: 1–24.

Esty, Joshua. (2004). *A Shrinking Island*. Princeton, NJ: Princeton University Press.

Forster, E. M. (1924 [1952]). *A Passage to India*. New York: Harcourt.

Ghosh, Sarath Kumar. (1909). *Prince of Destiny*. London: Rebman Ltd.

Gikandi, Simon. (2001). "Globalization and the Claims of Postcoloniality." *South Atlantic Quarterly* 100.3: 627–658.

Gillies, Mary Ann, Helen Sword, and Steven G. Yao. (2009). *Pacific Rim Modernisms*. Toronto: University of Toronto Press.

Grand, Sarah. (1893 [1992]). *The Heavenly Twins*. Ann Arbor: University of Michigan Press.

Harvey, David. (1989). *Condition of Postmodernity*. Oxford: Blackwell.

Hayot, Eric. (2009). *The Hypothetical Mandarin*. New York: Oxford University Press.

120   *John Marx*

Hilferding, Rudolf. (1981). *Finance Capital*.
London: Routledge.

James, C. L. R. (1936). *Minty Alley*. London:
New Beacon.

Jameson, Fredric. (2002). *A Singular Modernity*. London: Verso.

Joyce, James. (1976). *A Portrait of the Artist as a Young Man*. New York: Penguin.

Joyce, James. (1986). *Ulysses*. New York:
Vintage.

Karl, Frederick R. and Laurence Davies, eds.
(1983–2002). *The Collected Letters of Joseph Conrad*, vols. 1–6. Cambridge:
Cambridge University Press.

Kern, Stephen. (1983). *The Culture of Time and Space: 1880–1918*. Cambridge, MA:
Harvard University Press.

Lawrence, D. H. (1920 [1987]). *Women in Love*, ed. David Farmer, Lindeth Vasey,
and John Worthen. Cambridge: Cambridge University Press.

Lawrence, D. H. (1927 [1981]). Mornings in Mexico, Etruscan Places. New York:
Penguin.

Lugard, Sir F. D. (1922). *The Dual Mandate in British Tropical Africa*. Edinburgh:
Blackwood.

Luhmann, Niklas. (1995). *Social Systems*,
trans. John Bednarz, Jr. Stanford: Stanford University Press.

Malinowski, Bronislaw. (1930). "The Rationalization of Anthropology and Administration." *Africa* 3.4: 405–429.

Malinowski, Bronislaw. (1936). "Native Education and Culture Context."
International Review of Missions, 25:
480–515.

Mamdani, Mahmood. (1996). *Citizen and Subject: Contemporary Africa and the Legacy of Late Colonialism*. Princeton,
NJ: Princeton University Press.

Marx, John. (2005, 2009). *The Modernist Novel and the Decline of Empire*. New York: Cambridge University Press.

McLaughlin, Joseph. (2000). *Writing the Urban Jungle*. Charlottesville: University of Virginia Press.

Mitchell, Timothy. (2002). *Rule of Experts*.
Berkeley: University of California Press.

Narayan, R. K. (1937 [1980]). *The Bachelor of Arts*. Chicago: University of Chicago Press.

Pennycook, Alastair. (1998). *English and the Discourses of Colonialism*. London:
Routledge.

Perkin, Harold. (1989). *The Rise of Professional Society: England Since 1880*. New York: Routledge.

Plaatje, Sol T. (1930 [2005]). *Mhudi*. London:
Penguin.

Rosenbaum, S. P., ed. (1995). *The Bloomsbury Group: A Collection of Memoirs and Commentary*. Toronto: University of Toronto Press.

Rushdie, Salman. (1990). *Imaginary Homelands*. London: Granta.

Said, Edward. (1983). *The World, the Text, and the Critic*. Cambridge, MA: Harvard University Press.

Sarkar, Sumit. (1997). *Writing Social History*.
New Delhi: Oxford University Press.

Satthianadhan, Krupabai. (1894 [1998]).
Kamala: The Story of a Hindu Child-Wife. New Delhi: Oxford University Press.

Strychacz, Thomas. (1993). *Modernism, Mass Culture, and Professionalism*. Cambridge: Cambridge University Press.

The Open University. (2012). "Making Britain: Locations Map." At http://
www8.open.ac.uk/researchprojects
/makingbritain/location/makingbritain (accessed November 30, 2012).

Tratner, Michael. (1995). *Modernism and Mass Politics*. Stanford: Stanford University Press.

Viswanathan, Gauri. (1989). *Masks of Conquest: Literary Study and British Rule in India*. New York: Columbia University Press.

Waugh, Evelyn. (1945). *Brideshead Revisited*.
Boston, MA: Little.

Webb, Mary. (1924 [1980]). *Precious Bane*.
Notre Dame, IN: Notre Dame University Press.

Wicke, Jennifer. "Appreciation, Depreciation: Modernism's Speculative Bubble." *Modernism/Modernity* 8.3 (2001): 389–402.

Williams, Raymond. (1980). "The Bloomsbury Fraction." In *Problems in Materialism and Culture* (pp. 148–169). New York: Verso.

Williams, Raymond. (1989). *The Politics of Modernism*. New York: Verso.

Woolf, Virginia. (1925). *Mrs. Dalloway*. New York: Harcourt.

Further Reading

Arrighi, Giovanni. (1994). *The Long Twentieth Century*. New York: Verso.

Baucom, Ian. (1999). *Out of Place: Englishness, Empire, and the Locations of Identity*. Princeton, NJ: Princeton University Press.

Cheah, Pheng and Bruce Robbins, eds. (1998). *Cosmopolitics: Thinking and Feeling Beyond the Nation*. Minneapolis: University of Minnesota Press.

Daly, Nicholas. (1999). *Modernism, Romance, and the fin de siècle*. Cambridge: Cambridge University Press.

Gandhi, Leela. (2006). *Affective Communities: Anti-Colonial Thought, Fin-de-siècle Radicalism, and the Politics of Friendship*. Durham, NC: Duke University Press.

Gilroy, Paul. (2005). *Postcolonial Melancholia*. New York: Columbia University Press.

GoGwilt, Christopher. (2000). *The Fiction of Geopolitics*. Stanford: Stanford University Press.

Krishnan, Sanjay. (2007). *Reading the Global: Troubling Perspectives on Britain's Empire in Asia*. New York: Columbia University Press.

Menand, Louis. (1987). *Discovering Modernism*. New York: Oxford University Press.

Said, Edward. (1993). *Culture and Imperialism*. New York: Knopf.

Walkowitz, Rebecca. (2006). *Cosmopolitan Style: Modernism Beyond the Nation*. New York: Columbia University Press.

7

Marxist Modernisms
From Jameson to Benjamin

Catherine Flynn

A common objection to Marxist literary criticism is that it sees literature as determined by its economic and material context. Even the agile Jonathan Culler (1997) falls prey to a "crude Marxism" in his swift summary: "For Marxism, texts belong to a superstructure determined by the economic base (the 'real relations of production'). To interpret cultural products is to relate them back to the base" (129). This approach would reduce literature to a mere reflex of its economic context, undoing the possibility of artistic agency or creativity. Furthermore, this vision of culture suggests that society as a whole is subject to the iron laws of economic development. We might look to the scientific encyclopedism of Georgi Plekanov for an example of a didactic, positivist, and even fatalistic vision of culture in lockstep with the forces of production.

In contrast, this essay deals with cultural and literary critics who identify a productive heterogeneity in texts, discovering and analyzing the representation and figuration of different temporalities and possibilities even while they also note how these texts mark the failures of society to realize its potential. I consider here critics who understand the individual moment or text as something that is not defined and quantifiable but rather an elastic opportunity in which defeat, loss, and waste are mingled with promise, energy, and hope. These critics take up Marx's sense of the multidimensional and asynchronous nature of any moment in social history. In the Preface to *A Contribution to the Critique of Political Economy*, Marx writes that any time new "material, productive forces" emerge they come in conflict with the existing relations of production:

> In considering such transformations a distinction should always be made between the material transformation of the economic conditions of production, which can be determined with the precision of natural science, and the legal, political, religious, aesthetic or philosophic – in short, ideological forms in which men become conscious of this conflict and fight it out. (Eagleton and Milne 1996, 31)

A Handbook of Modernism Studies, First Edition. Edited by Jean-Michel Rabaté.

Marx repeatedly stresses both the embeddedness of consciousness in the "material life-process" and also the importance of consciousness in the transformation of the world. In *The German Ideology*, he writes: "Men are the producers of their conceptions, ideas, etc., that is, real, active men, as they are conditioned by a definite development of their productive forces and of the intercourse corresponding to these . . . [M]en, developing their material production and their material intercourse, alter, along with this their actual world, also their thinking and the products of their thinking" (Marx 1996, 42). In this active struggle, language and literature are not passive byproducts. Marx opposes the boundary between "art" and "life" as an artificial one, conceiving of words as worked matter, "agitated layers of air" (49).

Marx emphasizes the creativity and even virtuosity required to grasp the ultimate significance of a particular moment: "The critic can start from any form of theoretical or practical consciousness and develop out of the actual forms of existing reality the true reality as what it ought to be, that which is its aim" (Marx 1975, 142). In this teleological, dialectical thinking, the truth of a particular cultural artifact is seen as its intimation of a future. This truth is not conceived of as an element in a linear continuum but rather as a final goal.

In exploring "Marxist modernisms," I consider the relation of two discursive practices that are concerned with the transformation of traditional society. If common to both is the sense of the historical moment as possessed of multiple potentialities, they also share an interest in constructing the future through a reworked past. Marx seems to render faint Ezra Pound's slogan "Make It New" with his policy of "ruthless criticism of all that exists," yet Marx too intends "to find a new world through criticism of the old one" (Marx 1975, 142). This interrogation of the past involves imagination as much as critique. Marx writes in the same text: "the world has long dreamed of possessing something of which it only has to become conscious in order to possess it in reality" (144). Society's deliberations on its ideal form thus takes place in indirect, unconscious, and self-divided ways. I explore here critical approaches to modernism that respond directly or indirectly to this idea and that deal with intimations of utopia that are irrational, imagined, and even negated.

We might say that if any moment in history is heterogeneous, modernity is a period more heterogeneous than any time before, as the burgeoning of productive forces of different kinds coincides with a dismantling of traditional practices and social forms. Susan Buck-Morss (1989) observes the consequent freedom of language in the period of modernity: "the rupture of tradition now frees symbolic powers from conservative restraints for the task of social transformation, that is, for a rupture of those social conditions of domination that, consistently, have been the source of tradition" (279). The experimentation of modernism takes place within a societal and cultural context in which unified discourse no longer holds, as a plurality of ways of speaking and making sense emerge along with the development and proliferation of forms of industrial production.

As I focus on critics' elaboration of heterogeneity and asynchronicity in modernist texts as a means of uncovering the "dream of the thing," I explore a Marxist criticism that is very different from that of Georg Lukács. Famously, Lukács considered modernism a failure because it represents fragmentation rather than achieving a synthesis. Lukács insists on the representation of totality: "What matters is that the slice of life depicted by the artist and re-experienced by the reader should reveal the relations between appearance and essence without the need for external commentary" (2010, 33–34). Modernist texts, unlike realist ones, "remain frozen in their own immediacy; they fail to pierce the surface to discover the underlying essence, i.e. the real factors that relate their experiences to the hidden social forces that produce them" (36–37). If modernism achieves a synthesis, in Lukács' view, it does so only artificially through the imposition of symbolic meaning. The critics I will examine here do see the modernist texts they examine as offering revelations about society as a whole yet they focus on the "opaque, fragmentary, chaotic and uncomprehended" (39). In this, these Marxist critics themselves carry out their own modernist practices. Their sense of multiplicity and heterogeneity rather than distillation allows the question of the relation of modernism to modernization to be opened up in ways that are fruitful and relevant today.

In his recent work, *A Singular Modernity*, Fredric Jameson (2002) rejects not only the usefulness of the term modernism but also of periodization entirely, as "intolerable and unacceptable in its very nature, for it attempts to take a point of view on individual events which is well beyond the observational capacities of any individual and to unify, both horizontally and vertically, hosts of realities whose interrelationships must remain inaccessible and unverifiable, to say the least" (28). Jameson goes on to argue that modernity is not a period but a narrative category, "the positing of a beginning" (31), a trope which offers a "powerful displacement of previous paradigms" (35) and a "unique kind of intellectual excitement" (34). In its anticipation of the future, the trope of modernity has something of a utopian energy about it, yet this narrative can be applied to any historical transition, from the advent of double-bookkeeping to the beginnings of Western rationalism in the medieval monastic orders. If the narrative trope of modernity is a trace of a "real historical event and trauma," namely "the overcoming of feudalism by capitalism, and of the aristocratic social order of castes and blood by the new bourgeois order which at least promised social and juridical equality and political democracy," Jameson argues that it is now merely an effect and one that is often hijacked to depict the most inhumane accommodations to the exigencies of the free market as instances of progress (39, 9).

Within this context, Jameson rejects any theory of modernism "capacious enough to include Joyce along with Yeats or Proust, let alone alongside Vallejo, Biely, Gide or Bruno Schulz, [as] bound to be so vague and vacuous as to be intellectually inconsequential" (104). Yet no text can be read in a purely empirical way; Jameson even suggests that "each text comes before us both as itself and as an allegory of the modern as such" (113). Jameson links this doubling to the way in which Marxism itself is both a "master code" and an "arbitrary narrative" (118). Having presented these complex and provocative qualifications, Jameson then presents a series of conjectures about modernism. If modernism fetishizes the new, Jameson links this dynamic of perpetual innovation and originality to the capitalist market and the commodity form. Yet, modernists nonetheless carve out a space of resistance within the language of the contemporary world: the high modernists devised unique, autonomous, subtle, untheorized artistic languages within the "daily hegemonic koiné of the master" (100–108).

Jameson associates these innovations with a sense of the "Utopian and revolutionary transmutation of the world of actuality itself": the innovative forms of modernism "as symbolic acts, testify to immense gestures of liberation and new construction which we can only glimpse retrospectively, by historical reconstruction" (136). Here, Jameson adapts Perry Anderson's argument that the mood of modernism is inspired by the socialist revolutions of the time and the overthrow of the *ancien regime.* Yet he develops this idea to see modernism as presenting alternative subjectivities that he associates with a world transfigured by technology and social ferment. In contrast with the depiction of the individual in earlier texts, modernist subjectivity is "allegorical of the transformation of the world itself, and therefore of what is called revolution" (136). It is not then that modernism represents what has not hitherto been represented but rather that it gestures towards what has not yet been realized. This sense of a transformed world is not only inspired by politics but is also dependent upon a reality of technological advance: "Only the secular modernity of industrial capitalism vouchsafed a glimpse of the new collective and historical praxis such a mutation of the self was capable of promising" (137).

If Jameson emphasizes in *A Singular Modernity* the anticipatory quality of high modernism, an earlier essay, "Modernism and Imperialism" from *The Modernist Papers* (2007) presents specific examples of modernist texts that are marked by a disrupted perception of the present. Jameson presents imperialism in this essay as experienced according to the dynamic of capitalism rather than of violent conquest. The imperialism of modernism, Jameson emphasizes, is that of the rivalry of metropolitan nation-states, rather than our more contemporary sense of the exploitation and subordination of the colonial. Modernist representation responds to the absence of the segment of the economic system that is outside of the experience of the metropolis. As an example, Jameson presents the description in E. M. Forster's *Howards End* of the Great North Road as seen from the train; this cinematographic perception is neither personal and private, nor objective and empirical. Commonsense perception is disrupted by the emergence of the sense of a "non-perceptual, spatial totality" (160). The description of the Road is a new account of space, where the road is both a vehicle for an impossible meaning and also a banal physical thing. The road is the "marker and the substitute of the unrepresentable totality" (163). This "hesitation" between symbol and meaning is the key accomplishment of modernist representation, a paradoxical "enlargement of our sensorium" (163).

Jameson presents another account of modernism in his earlier work, *The Political Unconscious*: "vertical repression and layering or sedimentation is the dominant structure of the classical modernist text" (1981, 214) Jameson posits three successive phases of interpretation, or three "concentric" frameworks for the "semantic enrichment and enlargement of the inert givens and materials of a text" (75). The first stage considers the text as a symbolic act: the resolution of a political contradiction. To this end, it involves the reconstruction by the critic of a political or social subtext that is perhaps not initially apparent. The next phase of interpretation considers the place of the text in the struggle between social classes. In this framework, the text is an "*ideologeme*, that is the smallest intelligible unit of the essentially antagonistic collective discourses of the social classes" (76). While canonical texts may perpetuate the voice of the dominant or hegemonic class, there may also be traces of forms of expression of subordinated groups. The third phase considers the text as an "*ideology of form* . . . the conjuncture of coexisting modes of production at a given historical moment" (99).

In the case of *Lord Jim*, Jameson estranges Conrad's overt theme, the ethical or existential exploration of courage, cowardice, and morality, in order to examine the implications of his impressionistic style, his strategy of rewriting "the world and its own data in terms of perception as a semi-autonomous activity" (230). Jameson argues that modernism "is itself an ideological expression of capitalism, and in particular, of the latter's reification of daily life . . . Yet modernism can at one and the same time be read as a Utopian compensation for everything reification brings with it" (236). While the term "reification" is never fully explicated in *The Political Unconscious*, it can be taken to refer to the dissolution of relations between people, and between people and things, and the reconstruction of these relations according to the logic of production and profit. Sensory perception, Jameson argues, has little exchange value in a money economy dominated by "considerations of calculation, measurement, profit and the like" (229). Conrad's aestheticization of the visual, or his "declaration of the independence of the image as such" (232), is thus both determined by and subversive of the novel's economic context, both accustoming the individual to the fragmentation of life in capitalism and providing aesthetic relief. Conrad's writing offers "Utopian compensation for everything lost in the process of the development of capitalism" (236): amidst processes of quantification, abstraction, and desacralization, it offers experiences of quality, of the archaic, of color, and of intense feeling.

Jameson also sees Conrad's style as presenting alternative politics. A submerged political reality emerges in the following passage from *Lord Jim*:

> and short metallic clangs bursting out suddenly in the depths of the ship, the harsh scrape of the shovel, the violent slam of the furnace door, exploded brutally, as if the men handling the mysterious things below had their breasts full of fierce anger. (214)

This description of the sounds of labor operates *almost* as a metaphor, "as if" the noises expressed a barely contained force of political upheaval. Jameson also reads Conrad's "sensory abstraction" as presenting intimations of a utopia: Conrad's stylistic practice "projects a unique sensorium of its own, a libidinal resistance" (237). Conrad's prose thus acts not only as an index of the deformations of subjectivity and society by the economic context of monopoly capitalism but also as an indicator of an alternative existence, as a generator of utopian energies. As critic, Jameson himself enacts a creative operation on Conrad's prose, invested as he is in what he calls the "semantic enrichment and enlargement of the inert givens and materials of a text" (75).

In *A Singular Modernity*, such creative elaboration is absent on principle. Modernism, Jameson argues, is time-bound. In its true, active sense, it responds to a state of incomplete modernization; with the comprehensive colonization of the life-world by industrial agriculture, mass culture, and a globalized, standardized free market, no trace of alterity remains to prompt meaningful formal innovation. Jameson goes on to distinguish between the allegorical innovations of high modernism and the self-reflexivity of the late modernism of postwar consumer culture; once technology becomes focused on the production of commodities, modernism performs an entirely self-reflexive engagement with form and language, which is erroneously celebrated as the "autonomy of the aesthetic" (208). While Jameson gives up on the utopian capacities of late modernism, he nonetheless detects such potential in more recent fictional works. His 2005 work *Archaeologies of the Future* examines both the programmatic and allegorical explorations of utopia in science fiction. In the foreword, Jameson points to Ernst Bloch as a source for a theory of the utopian impulse "governing everything future-oriented in life and culture" (2).

If modernism is for Jameson an untimely source for utopian energies, we might begin to consider Bloch and other Marxist critics for whom modernism is a question of the present moment. In his 1935 essay, "Marxism and Poetry," Bloch's theory of reality is itself modernist in its logic:

> the process of reality as such, traced by Marxism, is still open therefore objectively fragmentary. It is only because of the really possible that the world is not made into a sophisticated book, but into a process dialectically mediated, therefore dialectically open. And realism, too, reveals itself poetically time and again as created in a rough and extended way. One might even say that wherever realism appears as a complete portrayal of reality without interruption and openness, then it is not realism but rather the remains of the old idealist structure of beauty as such. (161)

Bloch thus associates the notion of a fixed homogenous present with an earlier, even neoclassical yearning after an organic whole; it is a totality that resists and denies the moments of possibility that permeate reality. A unified world is in fact a reified world, which lacks the dynamic nature of reality. The world is not a "sophisticated book," recalling the medieval notion of "the Book of the World" written by God; it displays instead the qualities of a modernist text. Bloch's realism approaches the realism of modernism, as described by Eagleton in his essay "The Contradictions of Modernism": modernism rejects traditional nineteenth-century realism with its integrity, truth, reality, coherence, unity, in the aspiration toward a higher form of realism which captures the fragmentary and unpredictable disorder of the experiential world (2000, 35). Reality exists not as an objective thing but awaits the actions of individuals in a dialectical process of realization. This is indeed Bloch's poetics of hope:

> Marxism's sole theme is that of forming-transforming, and it scares away the dreamers but not the precise imagination. It is this imagination, which is dialectically trained and mediated with tendency and latency of existence, with those time-spaces of real possibility. (159)

Here, Bloch states dramatically the key focus of Marxist cultural criticism: in contrast to a sense of change as the expression of iron laws of inexorable development, Bloch emphasizes an endless process of making and remaking. The fluidity of reality then is not to do with arbitrary, whimsical, or relativistic perceptions but rather with an actual set of conditions and possibilities that await perception and actualization. The imagination required to see reality is thus a "precise" one that grasps the "not-yet-lived possibility." Furthermore, this understanding of reality grants an important role to literature; Bloch cites Aristotle's weighing of the poet and the historian:

> The historiographer and the poet do not distinguish themselves from one another through the use of verse or prose. Their difference consists in the fact that one expresses what really happened; the other one, what might well happen. Therefore, poetry is more philosophical than historiography because it shows the universal more. (160)

The "poet" here might just as well be the fiction writer: it is not the genre but the attitude that distinguishes him from the historian purveyor of (mere) facts. What Aristotle calls the "universal" is perhaps understood in Bloch's context in the sense not of what is common to all individuals but rather of what awaits us all, what we might indeed realize. Bloch adds: "In such a manner meaningful poetry makes the world become aware of an accelerated flow of action, an elucidated waking dream of the essential." Poetry here recalls its original sense of the Greek *poesis*, making.

In many ways, Jameson's closing words in *A Singular Modernity* recall Bloch, as he presents the challenge of describing what there is and what there might be:

> What we really need is a wholesale displacement of the thematics of modernity by the desire called Utopia. We need to combine a Poundian mission to identify Utopian tendencies with a Benjaminian geography of their sources and a gauging of their pressure at what are now multiple sea-levels. Ontologies of the present demand archeologies of the future, not forecasts of the past. (2002, 215)

Jameson's figures of archeology and meteorology point to alternative conditions in evocative yet elusive ways. The paradoxical temporalities of these two alternatives lend new dynamism to Marx's "dream of the thing": here, attention is directed to the human rather than the natural world (to built forms rather than the weather); the activity of discovering and analyzing is preferred to that of prediction.

The contradictory quality of a present that contains the ruined vestiges of the future renders more urgent the realization of thwarted potential.

Jameson's "ontology of the present," driven by the "desire for Utopia" is marked by the absence of coherence, or rather is enlivened by a productive incoherence. His heterogeneous conjunction of Pound and Benjamin is itself a modernist gesture. This disjunctive collocation also extends to Jameson's views of the progressive and transformational within Pound's work, as he subsumes under the title "sociability" radically different political perspectives ranging from the poetry of medieval Italy to founding fathers of the American Republic and from the American twentieth-century avant-garde to European fascism. Jameson nonetheless uses the same term as Bloch, precision, to describe both Pound's poetics and his "measurements" of modernist energies, "new thoughts," and "intensities promising a whole new culture" (213).

But what of the other element in this recipe for an ontology of the present: Benjamin's "geography" of the sources of utopian tendencies? Jameson cites the beginning of Benjamin's essay on Surrealism:

> Intellectual currents can generate a sufficient head of water for the critic to install his power station on them. The necessary gradient, in the case of Surrealism, is produced by the difference in intellectual level between France and Germany. What sprang up in 1919 in France in a small circle of literati may have been a meager stream, fed on the damp boredom of postwar Europe and the last trickle of French decadence. The German observer is not standing at the source of the stream. This is his opportunity. He is in the valley. He can gauge the energies of the moment. (1996, 207)

This sense of an external view provides an answer to a problem that Jameson raises early in *A Singular Modernity*: the different understandings and instantiations of modernism, modernity, and indeed modernization in the Anglo-American, French, and German contexts. Benjamin's speculation forms a solution to this problem by harnessing this difference, achieving comprehension through triangulation described here in geographical terms.

If Jameson's model for utopian exploration conjoins two past writers, Benjamin speaks of a contemporary conjunction. Writing in 1929, Benjamin describes an art movement that is still in motion. If Bloch's precise imagination is to do with the not-yet-lived possibility, the Surrealist imagination that Benjamin is concerned with here bursts forth from the realm of art: "the sphere of poetry was here exploded from within by a closely knit circle of people pushing the 'poetic life' to the utmost limits of possibility" (208). Art here attempts to enter into everyday existence. Benjamin calls the Surrealists' aim to "win the energies of intoxication for the revolution" a "poetic politics" (216). They fail, in his opinion, as they remain within the sphere of intoxication and do not translate the dream energy into political action. Benjamin himself harnesses this energy, adopting the dream world of writers like Aragon to devise a politically radical reading of the modern urban world.

Benjamin's choice of a technological metaphor – of intellectual activity as hydropower, the marriage of technological innovation and the natural world – indicates his modernist aesthetic. If Bloch's reference to childhood, fairy tales, rebellious dream images, and cheap and popular literature as repositories of untapped potential recalls Benjamin's writings (for example, his essay on Goethe's novella *Elective Affinities*), Benjamin's most powerful example of untapped potential comes from the "new nature" of modern technology. In his introductions to *The Arcades Project*, the Exposés of 1935 and 1939, Benjamin provides an account of his intentions and of the ideas that guide the project:

> Corresponding to the form of the new means of production, which in the beginning is still ruled by the form of the old (Marx), are images in the collective consciousness in which the new is permeated with the old. These images are wish images; in them the collective seeks both to overcome and to transfigure the immaturity of the social product and the inadequacies in the social organization of production. At the same time, what emerges in these wish images is the resolute effort to distance oneself from all that is antiquated – which includes, however, the recent past. These tendencies deflect the imagination (which is given impetus by the new) back upon the primal past. In the dream in which each epoch entertains images of its successor, the latter appears wedded to elements of primal history – that is, to elements of a classless society. And the experiences of such a society – as stored in the unconscious of the collective – engender, through interpenetration with what is new, the utopia that has left its trace in a thousand configurations of life, from enduring edifices to passing fashions. (1999, 4)

This modernist aesthetic is a superimposition of different temporalities. Benjamin provides a guide to understanding these dense, temporally layered images by introducing the passage with a quotation from Michelet: "Each epoch dreams the one to follow" (4). This dream of the future performs a temporally complex negotiation: inspired by the newest technological innovations, these images gesture toward an ideal future, repulsed by the failures of the recent past and bearing the repressed memory of an ancient Arcadia. Benjamin's modernist aesthetic relies upon the notion of a "primal" past that is egalitarian and abundant – a "classless" "utopia," a "land of milk and honey" (5). Perhaps within the realm of Marxist theory this notion of an ideal primitive age is unusual; yet, this overlay of the most recent innovation with an Arcadian mythical past is a move that is familiar to literary modernism. One wonders what Benjamin would have written about James Joyce, Ezra Pound, and T. S. Eliot.

If Benjamin describes a collective unconscious memory of an original Arcadia, he also emphasizes the power of the industrial revolution to transform society in radical ways. This massive transformative potential is thwarted by the relations of production in capitalist commodity culture, in which technology is directed toward profit rather than benefit. Also, as Rolf Tiedemann (1999) writes: "Benjamin discovered the signature of the early modern in the ever more rapid obsolescence of the inventions and innovations generated by a developing capitalism's productive forces" (932). The unprecedented powers brought about by the industrial revolution have been directed from creative construction to mere novelty.

Benjamin's explicit focus in *The Arcades Project* is on nineteenth-century Paris. He devotes sections to Fourier's phalansteries and the early World Expositions as offering new kinds of social organization. Yet he also touches briefly but significantly on modernist works such as Le Corbusier's architectural designs as presenting a classless society. Having presented a nineteenth-century account of a British Embassy ball at which the interpenetration of interior and garden resembles the dream spaces of Surrealist literature, he declares swiftly, "Today the watchword is not entanglement but transparency. (Le Corbusier!)" (419). This sense of openness is underlined in a later excerpt from Sigfried Giedion:

> "Le Corbusier's houses depend on neither spatial nor plastic articulation: the air passes through them! Air becomes a constitutive factor! What matters, therefore, is neither spatiality per se nor plasticity per se but only relation and interfusion. There is but one indivisible space. The integuments separating inside from outside fall away." (1999, 423)

If Benjamin withholds explicit or explanatory statements, Susan Buck-Morss (1989) presents his aims very clearly: Benjamin "affirmed the new, modernist aesthetics for the transparency of its 'social content' as well as social function . . . Benjamin seems to have seen the change in cultural forms as anticipatory, illuminating the tremendous social(ist) potential of the new nature" (303). In a rare and lucid statement of his aims, Benjamin (1999) remarks: "To encompass both Breton and Le Corbusier – that would mean drawing the spirit of contemporary France like a bow, with which knowledge shoots the moment in the heart" (459). Once again, we see the harnessing of disparate artistic phenomena to create a dynamic critical engagement. Benjamin's metaphor of deadly precision suggests an awakening from the dream by the advent of reason.

If here Benjamin addresses literature and architecture, elsewhere in *The Arcades Project* he identifies a new expressive potential and semantic complexity in objects that were long considered to be outside the modernist canon: furniture, clothes, household appliances, and machinery. In ascribing this complex overlay of temporalities, energies, and aspirations to modernism, we might understand Benjamin as offering a way out of the cul-de-sac in which Peter Bürger sees modernism. For Bürger, modernism is merely a style that fetishizes novelty in the rejection of tradition while nonetheless remaining true to the principles of bourgeois art: individual creativity and reception, and the coherent and autonomous work of art (1984, 55). Bürger contrasts this conservatism with the avant-garde's radical aim of dismantling the institutions of art in order to merge art with the praxis of life. Marcel Duchamp's exhibition of a urinal under the title of *Fountain by R. Mutt*, for example, subverts the notion of the artwork as aesthetically valuable or pleasing, as the product of individual creativity, and as belonging to the rarified world of art. Bürger celebrates avant-garde collages as inserting everyday reality into the artwork and commends their inclusion of the haphazard, the unpredictable, and the marvelous as resisting the tyranny of means–end rationality. Benjamin, meanwhile, sees creative symbolic practice as occurring spontaneously, folded into "life," overlaid upon or embedded in the innovations of industrial production. According to Benjamin, the wish images that overlay technical innovations come from a shared unconscious – they are thus no longer merely the act of individuals but rather expressions of the collective imagination. Rather than the avant-garde's attempt to subvert the institutions of art – the museum, the artwork itself – these elements contain a powerful if unarticulated urge to restructure society as a whole. For Benjamin, it is the task of the critic to understand this content, to recognize the "alternatives to what exist" that are presented unconsciously in the wish images of modern production (Bürger 54).

Theodor Adorno (2010) raises some serious objections to these ideas. He criticizes the notion that "Each epoch dreams its successor" for its "direct – I would almost say: developmental – relatedness to the future as Utopia" (111). Adorno was happier, if that is the word, with Benjamin's characterization in earlier sketches of *The Arcades Project* of modernity as hell, which provided a purely negative image of utopia. He objects to Benjamin's shift to archaic wish images from the "dialectical images [that are] generated by the commodity character... in alienated bourgeois individuals" (113). The notion of a dreaming collective is problematic for Adorno: "in a dreaming collective no differences remain between classes" (113). Social existence has been atomized by the inhuman calculations of commercial exchange and instrumentalization. The principle of profit enters into and distorts all: "as Horkheimer puts it, a mass ego exists only in earthquakes and catastrophes, while otherwise objective surplus value prevails precisely through individual subjects and against them" (113). In an essay entitled "What is meant by working through the past," Adorno sees memory as an increasingly threatened category in modern society:

> All of bourgeois society stands under the law of exchange, of the "like for like," of calculations which leave no remainder. By its very nature, exchange is something atemporal, like the *ratio* itself... But this means no less than that memory, time and recollection are liquidated as a kind of irrational remnant. (qtd Bürger 1984, 59)

It is thus impossible that a collective unconscious, a store of primal images, would survive the annihilating rationality of modern structures of exchange. Benjamin meanwhile provides multiple, conflicting, and even non-rational accounts of this utopian energy. For example, his explanation of the complex relation of superstructure to base offers another source of utopian energy. Wish images are here explained as contemporary byproducts of the gorged wealth of industrial production:

> The economic conditions under which society exists are expressed in the superstructure – precisely as, with the sleeper, an overfull stomach finds not its reflection but its expression in the contents of dreams, which, from a causal point of view, it may be said to 'condition.' The collective, from the first, expresses the conditions of its life. These find their expression in the dream and their interpretation in the awakening. (1999, 392)

With this idea, Benjamin perhaps responds to Adorno's objection to the notion of a dreaming collective that is society-wide; the overfed "collective" to which

Benjamin refers is surely the privileged sector of society. The editors of *Aesthetics and Politics*, Rodney Livingstone, Perry Anderson, and Francis Mulhern, put it beautifully, although with critical intent: "it is clear that Adorno was not mistaken in detecting a deeper aversion in Benjamin to systematic theoretical exposition as such, an innate reluctance to decant the mysterious elixir of the world into any translucent vessel or ordered discourse" (2012, 104). Where Benjamin's vision is multifarious and ambivalent, Adorno's vision is total, rigorous, and pessimistic. If Benjamin's modernist aesthetics is invested with a temporal complexity and multiple modalities of thought, aspiration, frenzy, and revulsion, Adorno's scenarios of alienation and reification, which he depicts with rigor and austere beauty, allow no egress.

For Adorno, art and mass culture, or in his term the culture industry, are radically opposed. The work of art resists the commodity form: in refusing communication it refuses the twin evils of consumption and instrumentalization. In opposition to Lukács' sense of the individual artist's responsibility for an integrated vision of society, for Adorno the recovery and the authentic representation of a positive community is impossible until the radical political and economic restructuring of the social world. In an essay on Schoenberg, Adorno (1981) writes: "the whole as a positive entity, cannot be antithetically extracted from an estranged and splintered reality by means of the will and power of the individual; if it is not to degenerate into deception and ideology, it must assume the form of negation" (164). Authentic modern art critiques the administered and antagonistic society it is in, through making "an uncompromising reprint" of that society (1997, 28). Modern art responds to modern society through its embodiment of dissonance and fragmentation. Adorno's essay "Trying to Understand Endgame," for example, presents Beckett's play as exemplary in staging the last, fragmentary utterances of a subjectivity that has already passed.

In deliberately resisting mass culture by taking the form of difficult works produced for small coteries, Adorno's modernist art takes on a character that resembles the more conventional perceptions of modernism. Yet, despite deliberately resisting consumption and easy enjoyment, the successful work of art also prompts a dialectical vision like the commodity itself: it "expresses the idea of harmony negatively by embodying the contradictions [of the existent], pure and uncompromised, in its innermost structure" (1981, 32). It is in this sense of the dialectic that the dead-end of modernity, as understood by Adorno, can be seen to be invested with another, positive dimension; the artwork's critical negation creates a utopian content out of the present moment.

Benjamin offers a discussion of the productive relationship of the work of art to the commodity. In "Central Park," the fragmentary 1939 essay garnered from one of the longest sections of *The Arcades Project*, Benjamin writes of Baudelaire's use of the allegory to intervene in the illusion of contemporary capitalist consumer society, "to interrupt the course of the world" (170). To examine how Baudelaire achieved this with his poetry, some explanation of Benjamin's understanding of the term allegory is necessary. In *The Origins of German Tragic Drama*, Benjamin contrasts the figurative mode of the symbol with that of the allegory: while the meaning of a symbol is instantaneous, timeless, and organic, and often even divinely sanctioned, an allegory presents a meaning that is conventional, contingent, and even arbitrary. In *The Origins of German Tragic Drama*, Benjamin argues that the allegorical mode responds to the profound upheaval and destruction of the seventeenth century; following the collapse of rule, authority, and the sense of providence after the ravages of the Thirty Years War, allegory points to a hopeless plurality of cosmologies. The allegory presents sundry elements that have been wrenched from different temporal and spatial contexts: "That which the allegorical intention has fixed upon is sundered from the customary contexts of life: it is at once shattered and preserved. Allegory holds fast to the ruins. It offers the image of petrified unrest" (169).

Benjamin sees Baudelaire as using the disruptive mode of allegory to rupture the pleasing image of progress in nineteenth-century Paris. The deathly meaninglessness which the allegory makes visible can also depict commodity culture: "The devaluation of the world of things in allegory is surpassed within the world of things itself by the commodity" (1996, 164). Allegory thus enacts in the space of literature the destruction of organic contexts associated with the production, distribution, and consumption of the commodity: "The wrenching of things from their familiar contexts – the normal state for goods on display – is a procedure highly characteristic of Baudelaire. It is linked to the destruction of organic contexts in the allegorical intention" (173). Benjamin points to the poems "*Une Martyre*" and "*Madrigal triste*" as examples. For Benjamin, Baudelaire's poetry is filled with spleen, a destructive impulse, that responds "to catastrophe in permanence" (164), the perception that social and political development has stalled. "The Baudelairean allegory – unlike the Baroque allegory – bears traces of the rage needed to break into this world, to lay waste its harmonious structures" (174). The fragmentary nature of the poems is constituted by the use of classical forms, such as the alexandrine, that are interrupted with caesurae and ruptures, and filled images of disjunction and dismemberment.

Baudelaire's modernity, as Benjamin sees it, is possessed of a contradictory temporality: the revelation of the ancient within the modern, the ruin within the new. Baudelaire himself offers a famous definition of modernity: "Modernity is the transitory, the fugitive, the contingent; it is one half of art, the other half being the eternal and immutable" (1999, 239). Yet, Benjamin's understanding of the modernity of Baudelaire's art includes this very sense of the eternal and the immutable. If modernity seems to be the opposite of antiquity, and Benjamin writes: "Modernity stands opposed to antiquity; the new, to what is always the same" (1996, 183), there is nevertheless a relationship between the two: antiquity is contained within modernity because the constant failure of novelty in modernity to fulfill its endless and unchanging promise renders modernity itself into a ruin. It is in poems such as "*Le Cygne*" which show "modernity in its interpenetration with classical antiquity" (2003, 50) that Baudelaire captures this sense of the ancient within the modern. In "*Le Cygne*":

> the ever-changing city grows rigid . . . The condition of Paris is fragile; it is surrounded by symbols of fragility – living creatures (the black woman and the swan) and historical figures (Andromache, "widow of Hector and wife of Helenus"). What they share are mourning for what was and lack of hope for what was to come. In the final analysis, this decrepitude constitutes the closest link between modernity and antiquity. (50)

If Baudelaire presents modernity in a tragic mode, his shattering of the surface appearance of progress and his melancholic staging of ruined hope lead to the possibility of authentic political experience and action.

In writing about Baudelaire, and indeed about the nineteenth century in general, Benjamin hopes to address the political and aesthetic issues of the twentieth century. Benjamin's early work, *The Origin of German Tragic Drama*, engages with the aesthetic features of the seventeenth century as an indirect way of dealing with the modernist aesthetics of a post-World-War-I Europe. Asja Lacis reports that Benjamin told her *The Origin* "had a direct connection to very actual problems of contemporary literature. He expressly emphasized that in his work he described Baroque plays in search of linguistic form as a phenomenon analogous to Expressionism" (Buck-Morss 1989, 15).

If *The Origin of German Tragic Drama* deploys six hundred quotations in its exploration of the cultural forms of the seventeenth century, *The Arcades Project* is composed using overtly modernist techniques and practices of collage and montage. Published after Benjamin's death, the unfinished *Arcades Project* is a quintessential modernist work with fragmentary quotations, commentaries, and speculative scenarios. Benjamin's suspicion of expository prose and his use of fragmentary, allusive forms to place a past moment in dialogue with a darkening twentieth century ask to be compared to the formal experiments of the literary modernists who were his contemporaries. If some critics see *The Arcades Project* as merely a repository of notes, we must look to Benjamin's celebration of Bertolt Brecht's use of modernist techniques of interruption and montage. Brecht's epic theater becomes an important example for Benjamin of the use of disjunctive forms to stimulate a new mode of production of the work of art, in the collaboration of audience and artist.

In his essay "The Work of Art in the Age of Its Technological Reproducibility," Benjamin cites film as the model and even the instance of transformative action. Whereas film fails as an artistic medium for Adorno because of its mass distribution and consumption, for Benjamin it presents a new, empowering vision of things which were formerly inaccessible. As opposed to the singularity and permanence of the older work of art, the modern artwork is transitory and repeatable, yet the reproduced media of film and photography are characterized by a new power over the moment, an ability to disrupt time. The material world takes on a new closeness, prompting a new sense of power over things as film allows a journey into the heart of the moment, through the close-up, the slow-down, and the exploration of what is otherwise the "optical unconscious." Film's accessibility and the accessibility which film affords to the world are seen by Benjamin in Marxist terms: "the desire of the present-day masses to 'get closer' to things spatially and humanly, and their equally passionate concern for overcoming each thing's uniqueness by assimilating it as a reproduction" (1996, 255). The new tasks of perception which film allows are thus linked to a proletarian consciousness in which the material world is available for manipulation and transformation. In this, Benjamin presents, in a different way, Lukács' ideal of an art that allows the comprehension of the world.

Benjamin extends the imperative to take hold of the world to the critic. In his essay, "Edward Fuchs, Collector and Historian," Benjamin cites Engels' criticism of the notion of "the closed unity of the disciplines and their products" (1996, 261). Benjamin goes on to reject "the convention in the history of ideas which represents a new dogma as a 'development' of an earlier one, a new poetic school as a 'reaction' to one preceding, a new style as the 'overcoming' of an earlier one" (261). He adds: "The historical object . . . does not offer vague analogies to actuality, but constitutes itself in the precise dialectical problem which actuality is obliged to resolve" (269). Here, we return to Jameson's questioning of periodization. The very notion of modernism as a disciplinary object of study then comes into question, as a symptom of a scholarly occupation that seeks to reify the past rather than to engage actively with its as yet unrealized potential. This potential, it must be emphasized, becomes apparent only from the context of the critic. Indeed, the engagement of the critic in this moment is crucial to his or her ability to recognize the past. As Benjamin writes: "It is an irretrievable image of the past which threatens to disappear in any present that does not recognize itself as intimated in that image" (262). Marxist modernism thus becomes truly modern as it recognizes and articulates the repressed potential of the past in an awareness of the necessities and possibilities of the present.

References

Adorno, Theodor. (1981). *Prisms*, 1st MIT Press edn. Cambridge, MA: MIT Press.

Adorno, Theodor. (1997). *Aesthetic Theory*. Minneapolis: University of Minnesota Press.

Adorno, Theodor, Walter Benjamin, Ernst Bloch, Bertolt Brecht, and Georg Lukács. (2010). *Aesthetics and Politics*. London: Verso.

Benjamin, Walter. (1996, 1999, 2002, 2003). *Selected Writings*, ed. Howard Eiland and Michael Jennings, trans. Edmund Jephcott, vols. 2, 3 and 4. Cambridge, McLaughlin: The Belknap Press of Harvard University Press.

Bloch, Ernst. (1988). *The Utopian Function of Art and Literature: Selected Essays*. Cambridge, MA: MIT Press.

Buck-Morss, Susan. (1989). *The Dialectics of Seeing: Walter Benjamin and The Arcades Project*. Cambridge, MA: MIT Press.

Bürger, Peter. (1984). *Theory of the Avant-Garde*. Minneapolis: University of Minnesota Press.

Culler, Jonathan D. (1997). *Literary Theory*. Oxford: Oxford University Press.

Eagleton, Terry. (2000). "Contradictions of Modernism." In *Modernity, Modernism, Postmodernism*, ed. Manuel Barbeito (pp. 35–44). Santiago de

Compostela: Universidade de Santiago de Compostela.

Eagleton, Terry and Drew Milne. (1996). *Marxist Literary Theory: A Reader.* Oxford: Blackwell.

Jameson, Fredric. (1981). *The Political Unconscious: Narrative as a Socially Symbolic Act.* Ithaca, NY: Cornell University Press.

Jameson, Fredric. (2002). *A Singular Modernity: Essay on the Ontology of the Present.* London: Verso.

Jameson, Fredric. (2005). *Archaeologies of the Future: The Desire Called Utopia and Other Science Fictions.* London: Verso.

Jameson, Fredric. (2007). *The Modernist Papers.* London: Verso.

Lukács, Georg. (1971). *History and Class Consciousness: Studies in Marxist Dialectics.* Cambridge, MA: MIT Press.

Further Reading

Adorno, Theodor W. and Rolf Tiedemann (1991). *Notes to Literature.* New York: Columbia University Press.

Anderson, Perry. (1988). "Modernism and Revolution." In *Marxism and the Interpretation of Culture,* ed. Cary Nelson and Lawrence Grossberg (pp. 317–333). Urbana: University of Illinois Press.

Eagleton, Terry. (1976). *Marxism and Literary Criticism.* Berkeley: University of California Press.

Jameson, Fredric. (2007). *Jameson on Jameson: Conversations on Cultural Marxism,* ed. Ian Buchanan. Durham, NC: Duke University Press.

Lukács, Georg (1971). *The Theory of the Novel: A Historico-Philosophical Essay on the Forms of Great Epic Literature,* 1st MIT Press edn. Cambridge, MA: MIT Press.

Lunn, Eugene. (1982). *Marxism and Modernism: An Historical Study of Lukács, Brecht, Benjamin, and Adorno.* Berkeley: University of California Press.

Marx, Karl, Friedrich Engels, Ernest Mandel, Ben Fowkes and David Fernbach. (1990). *Capital: A Critique of Political Economy.* London: Penguin Books in association with New Left Review.

Williams, Raymond. (1977). *Marxism and Literature.* Oxford: Oxford University Press.

Williams, Raymond and Tony Pinkney. (1989). *The Politics of Modernism: Against the New Conformists.* London: Verso.

8

Reactionary Modernism

Robert L. Caserio

If we think of prominent modernists who involve politics with their literary art, W. B. Yeats, Ezra Pound, and Virginia Woolf come to mind; so do George Bernard Shaw and H. G. Wells, who merit inclusion in surveys of modernism. To be sure, each figure exemplifies a different political stance. Shaw and Wells propagandized for a socialist world order; Pound proselytized for Mussolini's Italian fascism; Yeats positioned himself as an Irish nationalist to the left of British imperialists; Woolf undermined patriarchy in all its economic and political manifestations.

But the differences among the writers are not always as stark as capsule descriptions suggest. Woolf has no truck with fascism, which her *Three Guineas* (1938) identifies as reactionary masculinism. Nevertheless, Woolf writes *Three Guineas* in reaction – a reactionary modernist! – against feminism, a label that she thinks should be retired because its aims – women's rooms of their own – have been achieved. She calls for an "Outsiders' Society": a post-masculinist, post-feminist alliance of persons who will not serve under the labels of any already formed social, economic, or political order, and who thereby will subvert the global aggressions into which patriarchy has been sublated. Woolf is a writer who belongs to an advance guard of progressive politics, and who at the same time negates politics, in a search for something beyond it. She exemplifies a provocative, characteristically modernist perplexing and eluding of political labels.

Gertrude Stein is an unsettling example of the provocation. Stein told *The New York Times* in 1934 that Hitler was promoting peace by "driving out the Jews and the democratic and Left elements" (Warren 1934). Not surprisingly, then, Stein, living in France under the puppet government installed by Nazi occupiers in 1941, translated into English the speeches of the puppet president, and sought their publication in New York. Those speeches endorsed the barring of Jews from positions of power.

A Handbook of Modernism Studies, First Edition. Edited by Jean-Michel Rabaté.
© 2013 John Wiley & Sons, Ltd. Published 2013 by John Wiley & Sons, Ltd.

From the perspective of "democracy" Stein's prejudice is reactionary. But when Stein says what characterizes one side of the political spectrum, she is simultaneously taking an opposite side. In the interview she upholds the American color line, but she criticizes "stringent immigration laws in America today" that discriminate against cultural aliens. When France was liberated by Allied forces, she wrote *Yes Is for a Very Young Man*, a play celebrating the French guerillas who resisted the Nazi occupiers. Does this mean that Stein was a protofascist in the 1930s; that she was a committed fascist during the war; and that she covered her tracks when the Allies won? Or was she, Jewish-born, camouflaging herself – during the war years – as pro-fascist, in order to escape a concentration camp? Answers to those questions remain unresolved, perhaps because of Stein's indifference to political labels. "Government does not matter," she says in her interview; "any form of government may be good, and any form of government may be bad."

Shaw (1928) called the ideological labels meaningless: "mere electioneering vituperation.... A confusion of names prevents us from finishing the social edifice" (1931, 498–499). Among leading modernists, only Pound can be definitely assigned one "governmental" rubric – fascism – because of his activist commitment in Italy to Mussolini. But even Pound overturns the apple cart of political terminology: he saw fascism in Italy as a revival of Jeffersonian ideas, and also as a unique political experiment. After the political disillusionment produced by World War I, writers whose metier was experimentation with literary forms invested in what they took to be experimental political forms. Fascism was one of them, for worse rather than for better.

For worse certainly, given the mass murders and concentration camps of the losing side of World War II. The evaluation overlooks, however, what might count as barbarisms on the winning side: the fire-bombing of Dresden, the nuclear holocausts of Hiroshima and Nagasaki. Partly as a consequence of what is overlooked, in the conflict's succeeding years a hard and fast division of the political labels and values at issue in the war emerged. A vague "democracy" became opposed to everything else. The division remains in play (there are Americans who, in the name of "democracy," equate Barack Obama with Hitler and with "socialism"), even as the political referents of "socialist," "leftist," "progressive," "liberal," "conservative," "reactionary," and "fascist" have been eroded and distorted. Given the threadbare condition of the referents in current praxis, it is surprising that the name-tags have become all the more prominent in literary criticism and theory. It is as if the political factions of nearly a century ago must be replayed by literary analysts and also be simplified, as a substitute for history's evacuation of what once had vital complexity. Little room is left for tolerating ambiguities. It has become conventional to tie the interpretation of prominent modernists to something like a show trial of their politics.

The study of Yeats is an example. In the 1920s and 30s Yeats sympathized with the Irish Blue Shirts, a fascist organization; he also at times condoned Mussolini, and Hitler's Germany. The most recent fallout of this fact for literary history begins with Edward Said's 1988 theorizing of Yeats as a postcolonialist writer.

Said mixes advocacy of Yeats's status as a political liberator with an assertion of Yeats's "indigestible reactionary politics – his outright fascism" (81). Continuing the charge of "outright fascism," David Lloyd claims that "one should not underestimate either the depth or the endurance of Yeats' fascist sympathies" (2010, 191). Yet the case of Yeats also receives an opposite judgment. R. F. Foster (2010), Yeats's most authoritative biographer, finds an extenuation for each of Yeats's inclinings to fascism.

Foster is attempting to allow for the poet's experimental groping with governmental forms. That is not to say that Yeats's ideological veerings do not produce shocks. Shocking indeed – to post-World War II simplified political alignments – is one of Yeats's last publications: the initial number of a journal called *On the Boiler* (1938–1939). A collage of prose, lyric, and drama entirely by Yeats, it includes statements that can be called "reactionary" because the label has become a marker for elitism and racism (and, by historical association, for "fascism"). According to *On the Boiler, the* social problem of the 30s is "eugenic and ethnic," because, Yeats believes, democracy and mass education have destroyed Irish intellect, and "the better stocks" of the Irish population (19, 18). The worse stocks, Yeats asserts, should not be allowed to propagate. After all, the poet declares, "The caste system has saved Indian intellect" (19); and the caste system would be better than "the growing frenzy, everybody thinking like everybody else" (18) of new Irish national cohesiveness. "The mere multitude is everywhere, with its empty photographic eyes" (25). As for "democracy," Yeats presents his six years in the Irish Senate as evidence for the claim that "Our representative system has given Ireland to the incompetent," and for advising "those that should rule here: If ever Ireland again seems molten wax, reverse the process of revolution. Do not try to pour Ireland into any political system.... Republics, Kingdoms, Soviets, Corporate State, Parliaments, are trash" (11, 13). So are "the Fascist countries," because their populism, insufficiently eugenic, "accelerate[s] degeneration" (19).

Yeats's assertions indicate an historical impasse. Resistance to "any political system" shapes Yeats's perspective; in contrast, a demand for conformity to *some* already recognizable political system – "democracy," above all – shapes Yeats's trial by current literary historians and critics. Hence readings of the one-act play, *Purgatory*, which concludes *On the Boiler*, estimate it, in the context of Yeats's adjuration to "reverse the...revolution," as reactionary. The critic Charles Ferrall adduces *Purgatory* as Yeats's identification with Ireland's English oppressors. To arrive at his reading Ferrall (2001) interprets the play as a parable, in terms of the maternal figure whom the play's protagonist, the mother's son (now an Old Man), asserts is in Purgatory, where souls must "[r]e-live their transgressions," so that they "know at last" the consequences of their sins (Yeats 1953, 431). The mother's transgression, according to the Old Man, is that, despite her superior class standing, she married a stable groom. The groom, the Old Man's father, a drunkard and waster, accidentally set the maternal great house on fire; during the blaze, his son vengefully murdered him. But the son is also a wastrel. Grown into an aged peddler traveling with a bastard whom he has sired on the road, the Old Man returns to the scene of his patricide. He now stabs his son to death, as a way, he says, of preventing "pass[ing] pollution on" and of "finishing all [the] consequence" of his mother's impulsive marriage (435). As Ferrall construes the mother, she is Anglo-Irish Ireland, before the liberation of Ireland from England; and the murdered son, who is at sixteen the same age as independent Ireland in 1938, is the postcolonial state that was forged by revolution. The Old Man thus can be understood as enacting a rage against the revolutionary generations – his father, himself, and his offspring. He illustrates Yeats's command to "reverse the revolution." His mother will be trapped in Purgatory, obliged to witness the everlastingness of her error. In Ferrall's reading the error will be England's consent to the vulgarity of Irish independence.

Even without critical recourse to parabolizing, Yeats's text can support Ferrall's reading. The Old Man's violence complements *On the Boiler*'s declaration that Yeats's readers must "love war, because of its horror, [so] that belief" – in "trash" – "may be changed" (1939, 19–20). The Old Man also appears to claim Yeats's respect because he will stop at nothing. No matter the price – patricide and filicide – he is a man of action. After all, Yeats says in *On the Boiler* that "thought is not more important than action" (33). And if we are to believe Yeats's "Introduction for My Plays," Yeats deliberately rid his drama of everything but "action always in end and theme" (1937, 24). The Old Man, then, in whom reaction is apparently for Yeats the one tolerable form of "revolution," is legible as an heroically ruthless activist.

Yet it is hard to imagine an audience not feeling horror at the deeds of this "hero." It is equally hard to imagine Yeats taking a sane pleasure in him. The parabolizing approach negates the immediacy of the Old Man's violence; and it thus negates a meaning of it uttered by the Old Man almost at once: "Twice a murderer, and all for nothing" (1953, 436). In other words, the action, or the activism, that is reaction is useless; it is no more efficacious than what it reacts against. Such a meaning rhymes with Yeats's declaration that all political forms are "trash." If the critical interpreter refuses to contemplate the possibility that the forms, whether revolutionary or imperialist-reactionary, are indeed used up, then the interpreter does violence of his own to the possible truth of Yeats's judgment.

Undue assurance in writer or critic or theorist is problematic. There is less assurance in *On the Boiler* than quotation so far suggests. The title, Yeats says, alludes to an old mad ship's carpenter, who regularly broadcast ravings from astride one of his ship's junked boilers. Taking on the mask of the madman, Yeats suggests that the text be read dramatically, as a performance of conflicting perspectives, sane and insane. The text's hybridity abets its aesthetic character: calling attention to itself, it unsettles one's impulse to take its discourse at face value. Something other than allegory is going on. Yeats's self-division appears in declarations such as "Opposites are everywhere face to face, dying each other's life, living each other's death" (15, 22). What Yeats says about the Renaissance – "I detest the Renaissance because it made the human mind inorganic; I adore [it] because it clarified form and created freedom" (27) – appears to be replicated in Yeats's love–hate relation to Ireland. The rants of the madman persona about degenerate elements in Ireland

(and the world) undergo contradiction. When one reads that "eugenical and psychical research" (27) constitute the only revolutionary movements that Yeats endorses, one assumes he will name fascism's usual suspects as the victims of the research. But he does not. He couples "the negro and the peasant" as vanguard figures on the eugenic–psychic frontier. They represent subterranean "precious faculties" (26) that can help repair the decadence of political forms.

Repair of political forms is also to be understood as their purgation. The Old Man says that his mother must endure *her* remorse for her marriage; but the remorse is the Old Man's projection of remorse for *his* crimes. The mother does not appear in the play; our knowledge of her is in suspense. The suspense intensifies *after* what the Old Man does, rather than, as in conventional drama, *before* a deed resolves uncertainty. With action's efficacy exemplified as horrible and meaningless, uncertainty grows about the possibility of salutary activity, ever. Yeats's "delight in active men" and his plays' dedication to "action always in end and theme" (Yeats 1937, 24) are hoist on the petard of Yeats's brilliant revision of dramatic form. The revision makes action identical with anticlimax and with false climax. In *Purgatory* the heightened suspense that follows the inefficacy of action is made identical with the place of spiritual probation. This matches the political bearing of *On the Boiler*: its suspense about what order of politics or society can follow the failure of traditional and revolutionary forms; and about what activism, if any, can yield trustworthy innovation. While the suspense lasts, Yeats falls back on the virtue of "the Irish mind": "an ancient, cold, explosive, detonating impartiality" (31). The epithets attached to "impartiality" sound terroristic, but the final emphasis of *On the Boiler* is distant from any propaganda of the deed, of whatever ideological purport. Instead, Yeats celebrates suspense of will. Will drives the man of action. His tragedy inheres, Yeats says, in the loss of his aims; but, Yeats adds, "when the [will's] limit is reached it may become a pure, aimless joy" (35).

An aimless joy, subtending old-man crankiness, is written into *On the Boiler*. It is curious that Yeats continues to be labeled as a fascist because he dramatizes the need to suspend political enactments of all kinds, as a purgatorial interim until better political forms come along. Perhaps one explanation for the critical insistence derives from commentators' impatience with, or incomprehension of, the mystical aspects of Yeats's "detonating impartiality." Foster notes that in Yeats "the transcendence of supernatural belief inevitably outweighs [his] attempt to arrive at a political philosophy" (2010, 223). Yeats, in "The Statues," a poem given a prose re-statement in *On the Boiler*, makes the lyric's speaker declare that the Irish, "Thrown upon this filthy modern tide / And by its formless spawning fury wrecked, / Climb" – for refuge – " to our proper dark" (Yeats 1960, 323). The ascent is to a native visionary obscurity. There the cold impartiality of Irish mind does its work.

It is a significant fact about "reactionary" modernists – especially the male ones – that their work constellates mystical or religious feeling with fierce criticism of "democracy" and with conflict-laden assessments of "active men." The constellation appears to open such modernists to an investment in fascism, or a tolerance of it.

The mystical dimension, I suggest, ultimately counterweights or undermines the writers' investment in fascism, but it appears to dispose most commentators, rightly or wrongly, to treat it reductively. For Yeats's latter-day critics there is in Yeats's appeals to transcendence only political mystification, an improper dark.

In the case of Ezra Pound, any resistance to reductive judgment now appears to be irrelevant. A previous generation of critics supported Pound's escape, on an insanity plea, from a trial for treason; but the surge of political vehemence in literary study means that Pound no longer obtains sanctuary. After all, the poet affixes the fascist label to himself. Although Pound argues for the suspension of commitments to available models of politics, unlike Yeats he does not suspend them altogether. And because of the ethnic and racial hatreds that became interwoven with fascism, the combination of Pound's wholehearted support of Mussolini with Pound's anti-Semitic bigotry makes Pound the consummate reactionary modernist. In the late 1980s Robert Casillo (1988) initiated the reversal of extenuations of Pound's fascism. Subsequently, with unquestionable force Casillo resisted the finely researched assessment of Tim Redman (1991), who articulates the strands of Pound's thought so that Pound can be seen to have affinities with Marxism and even with Zionism.

Casillo's forcefulness is unquestionable given his grounding assumption: that everything in Pound is an interlocked totality, and that, because Pound's fascism is inseparable from the whole, only at the cost of bad conscience can criticism value some of the totality's components, and not others. That this assumption might be a literary-critical version of totalitarianism, or that its absolutism of moral judgment amounts to a good totalitarianism in contrast with Pound's bad version, is worth pondering. What is immediately relevant is Pound's relation to the topos of the man of action, and the relation of his handling of the topos to religious or mystical phenomena.

Pound in the interwar years has no patience with the inhibition of a practical address to the world. He claims that art's function is to exemplify "inherent activity, [the] desire to MAKE something, the fun of constructing and the play of outwitting and overcoming obstruction" (1973a, 239). His celebration of artistic fabrication is in line with his definition of culture as "a direction of the will" (1973b, 320). Poetry is a crucial agent in any cultural direction of the will, Pound insists – an insistence that Pound's recent judges share, for they assume that poetry is a form of agency, and makes political things happen. I shall be pointing out that Pound's thought and poetics are not only about will; but certainly in Pound's polemics about economics and politics the direction of the will is not satisfied by suspense. "The idea is completed by the word. It is completed by its going into action" (1973b, 334). "The name of the Fascist era is *Voluntas*" (1973b, 312); i.e., will.

For Pound, Mussolini was to be the unique agent of a transformative relation between action-directed will and new thought about economics. World War I and the Treaty of Versailles drove Pound to the judgment (shared with Yeats and Wyndham Lewis) that Western democracy, in its liberal state-form, was a failure; and Pound blamed the failure on "democracy's" surrender to an unjust economics.

"Liberalism," Pound writes, "conceals its baneful economics under two pretexts: the freedom of the spoken and written word, and the freedom of the individual, protected in theory, by trial in open court" (1973c, 342). Empire and capitalism negate those freedoms. Their "baneful economics" gains profits for the wealthy on the basis of manipulative speculations, and leaves profitless, and without adequate access to their own products, the laboring masses. Money becomes part of the manipulation: kept in short supply so that the material wealth it represents is made scarce, for the sake of additional profits for the plutocrats. Here Pound follows the thought of economists of his era who argued for a system of "social credit" that would guarantee to an entire populace a just share of the products of capitalism, and of money itself. The "social credit" economy would draw on socialist and communist ideas; but it would have to make them – shades of modernism! – new. For Pound estimated that the Soviet Union's political experiment was a cul-de-sac because it was based on an economics of production rather than of consumption. As for German fascism, in 1933–35 Pound expressed contempt for its "hysterical Hitlerian yawping" (127). It seemed to Pound that Mussolini alone could unfold the aims of the social credit thinkers, and that he could do so because his fascism was, according to Pound, a purely nationalist form, precisely adapted to Italian history and problems.

Yet despite Pound's emphasis on the uniqueness of Italian fascism, its distance from "*revolution according to preconceived type*" (24), one irony of his reactionary modernism is its non-Italian inspiration. Pound becomes a fascist because he is proudly American. He argues that the Italian leader replicates, under Italian conditions, the virtues of Jefferson, John Adams, Andrew Jackson, and Martin Van Buren – the subjects of Pound's *Eleven New Cantos XXXI–XLI* (1934). The presidents lost their struggle against the banker-speculators who took the country into their hands; nevertheless, "No man in history," Pound says of Jefferson, "had ever *done* more and done it with less violence or with less needless expenditure of energy" (15). Mussolini, Pound suggests, has taken the opportunity to do as much.

The translation of ideas into action will not be without some version of violence, Pound admits. Mussolini's "doing" will likely inhibit the freedom of the press. Pound accepts the probability because, he argues, the freedom already has been debased by the irresponsibilities of journalism. Pound also accepts the prospect that Mussolini will inhibit other "theoretical" freedoms (43). He will inhibit a multi-party political system; for, Pound explains, "corrupt oligarchy...will...set up in theory a two-party system, controlling both" in order to insure the oligarchy's endurance (25). The only way for Mussolini to consummate "any great constructive activity" is "under a de facto one-party system" (125). Was Jefferson's era not practically such a system? As for Mussolini's *voluntas*, it is a will directed at order, Pound declares, not at power. Mussolini's authority comes "from right reason" (1970, 110), not from dictatorship.

Had Pound checked his compulsion to idolize what Yeats calls "active men," and to be a political actor himself, he might have been saved from fascism. Allying himself with actional violence in order to reverse once and for all the ruins of his patrimony (an American patrimony made Italian-American), Pound becomes a version of Yeats's Old Man in *Purgatory*. *The Pisan Cantos*, in one of their most famous moments, which derides "vanity," repeat Pound's fatal activist commitment: "But to have done instead of not doing / this is not vanity . . . Here error is all in the not done" (1956a, 99–100).

What Pound did, as the complement to his thoughts or his poetry, has become for literary history his greatest mistake. But does what Pound *did* close the books on his case? A totalitarian verdict on Pound's totalitarianism would argue so. But the argument overrides distinctions that are not justly attributable to the bad conscience of interpreters. Pound does not repent his loyalty to Mussolini – *The Pisan Cantos* (LXXIV–LXXXIV, 1948), which Pound wrote in an Allied forces detention camp in Italy, begin with a lament for Mussolini, and end with the poet's hailing of fascist collaborators. It does appear, however, that Pound repents his alliance with violence and war. The Pisan sequence repeatedly invokes "The Spring and Autumn," a Confucian text declaring that "there/are/no/righteous/wars"; i.e., "that is, perfectly right on one side or the other / total right on either side of the battle line" (1956a, 61, 103). A totalitarian critic might call this Pound's sour-grapes way of diminishing the victory of his opponents. But Pound's commitment to Confucius pre-dates his fascism, so Pound's inclusion of "there/are/no/righteous/wars" in *The Pisan Cantos* convicts himself of having acted against his own principles. In the Italian-language Canto LXXIII the fourteenth-century poet Guido Cavalcanti is made to ventriloquize a paean to fascist military self-sacrifice. If there are no just wars, by Canto LXXVIII Cavalcanti and Pound turn out to be in a dissonant relation to each other. A lyric about the Wars of the Roses that closes Canto LXXX, asserting that there is no more right on one side of combat than another, expresses the speaker's contrition for his faults.

The faults of "poor old Benito" – as well as of Ezra – also show themselves in *The Pisan Cantos* in the poet's thought about mistaken "emphasis": "but on the other hand emphasis / an error or excess of / emphasis / the problem after any revolution is what to do with / your gunmen" (73–74). The lines indicate that the problem was not solved by Mussolini or by Pound when they supported gunmen for a war that, by definition, could have no perfect rightness. The mistaken emphasis on war and right suggests a wrong emphasis also in "to have done instead of not doing . . . is not vanity." "Doing" does not escape the imputation of "vanity" as fully as the line at first makes it appear. By virtue of a resonance available to ordinary language-use of the phrase "to have done," the line might mean "to be finished" – to have done, to be finished, with the vanity of politics – is not vanity, not an error, in comparison with the apparent error of "not doing" something activist. The surface assertion that inaction is a vanity also turns against itself with the broken-off ending of Canto LXXXI: a comma (in earlier editions) or an ellipsis (after 1956) followed by blank space. "Here," the canto's final line says, "error is all in the not done, / all in the diffidence that faltered . . ." [sic] (100). Because the line itself is faltering and diffident, it suggests that a stronger diffidence in Pound – one that did not falter in *its* strength – would have meant a less aggressive, less vain partisanship, in him. *Un*faltering diffidence keeps Pound from asking to be forgiven for his faults. Forgiveness would abet the vanity of what he has done.

Whether or not Pound is finished with what he has done (and if distinctions among the elements of the work's totality can be allowed), the moments in which *The Pisan Cantos* evoke a suspense of will, and openness to mystical vision, are a brake on the fatality of Pound's commitment to action. That the poet frequently attests the superior value of quasi-religious contemplation over action makes it possible to continue to read the poetry – possible, at least, for readers who are not fascists and not as captivated by activist values as Pound was, or as his judges are.

It is unclear if current criticism can countenance the possibility. Lawrence S. Rainey, Pound's most formidable antagonist after Casillo, called in 1991 for a return of literary history and theory to the study of contexts that shape modernist artifacts. Rainey found that, behind Pound's celebration in Cantos VIII–XI (*A Draft of XXX Cantos* [1930]) of the cultural achievement of the Renaissance condottiere Sigismundo Malatesta, there lay a centuries-deep archive increasingly expunging the criminal violence of Malatesta's record. Collaborating in this tendency, Pound made it possible for himself to consider Mussolini as Malatesta's avatar – and to downplay the aggressions of both. Criticism followed suit, Rainey contends, in regard to Pound himself, by severing his poetry "from all . . . social and histor-ical dimensions" (221) – including, above all, the violences they harbor. Rainey argues that the severance can be cured by historical facts alone, the fruits of the archive. Facts are, Rainey reminds us, not "knowable . . . apart from the institu-tional apparatuses and historical processes that transmit them" (154). But not only disinterested reattachment to facts or history is at issue, given Rainey's declaration that fascism is "the central experience of Western culture in the twentieth cen-tury" (224). In the light of this claim, facts and history, no matter how complexly conceived, are entry points for criticism's political contentions. Those contentions return critics and readers to the very arenas of action and will that Pound's case makes problematic.

Attention to where *The Cantos* divest themselves of voluntas, and check their maker's violence, might point to the modernist innovation whereby Pound revises epic, replacing the telos-driven action of narrative with a lyric withdrawal from drive. The poet's procedure is non-directive: "according to the ideogramic [sic] method of first heaping together the necessary components of thought" (1973a, 239). In volitional terms the heaping together is like a throw of the dice. Thereafter, as the elements of cultural achievement and personal history reassemble themselves, *The Cantos* disclose a coherence that offers a new sense of the world. The authority of the revelation may be trusted because it is immanent in the heap, rather than willed or manipulated by "makers." "Outwitting and overcoming obstruction" is itself overcome. The agent of the overcoming is impersonal "light," one of Pound's terms for revelatory illumination. His other terms include "precision," "verbum perfectum" – the right signifier for an essential signified – and "sinceritas," truthfulness. The discovery of "light" is due to a "paraclete": a transcendent entity.

The paraclete, whose medium is *vita contemplativa*, appears "in the stillness outlasting all wars" (1956a, 5). "Boon companion to equity" (1956a, 109), the paraclete discloses fragments of already-achieved intellectual, erotic, and societal bliss, each of which incapsulates utopia or paradise.

The poets and the men of action must conform to sinceritas, not coerce it. The factitiously activist Cavalcanti of Canto LXXIII is scarcely the contemplative Cavalcanti of an earlier poem, Canto XXXVI (*Eleven New Cantos*, 1934). There Cavalcanti's definition of love is shown by Pound to be difficult to elucidate, because the definition is rationally articulate yet mystical. The mystical aspect derives from the way in which love in Cavalcanti, even when emotionally "moving," is not an "idea in act": Love "himself moveth not, drawing all to his stillness" (1956b, 28). In response to the revelations of the paraclete and of love, the worth of a culture is to be found not in a direction of the culture's will toward action, but in a direction of its will toward receptivity. When any person speaks truly (as, Pound insists in Canto LXXXII, his fellow modernist Ford Madox Ford always did), he speaks or acts receptively rather than aggressively. What *The Pisan Cantos* calls the "tragedy" (1956a, 3) of Mussolini and his supporters is a result of an exceeding impatience – Pound's no less than his hero's – to will utopia into existence by closing the gap between contemplation and action.

Pound's stature as leading reactionary modernist is shared by Wyndham Lewis, novelist, visual artist, polemical theorist, and founder of *Blast* (1914) and Vorticism, a journal and a movement aimed at overturning multiple conventions. The labeling of Lewis as reactionary begins with response to Lewis' *Paleface* (1929), which I shall come to, and with Lewis's sympathetic study, *Hitler* (1931); and the tradition is consolidated with Fredric Jameson's *Fables of Aggression* (1979), an account of Lewis subtitled *The Modernist as Fascist*. While the label suits Pound, it does not suit Lewis. The ironies of literary history's critical judgments show in the way the careers of Pound and Lewis culminate in a relation to the United States. Pound's Americanism helped make him a fascist; Lewis, after repudiating Hitler in *The Hitler Cult* (1939) and repudiating anti-Semitism in the same year (in *The Jews: Are They Human?*, a plea to anti-Semites not to be *in*human), emerges from the war with a celebration of the United States in *America and Cosmic Man* (1949). Lewis reads US history as the sign of a coming world culture, preeminent in "the raw human material of Socialism" (17), which will respect national and ethnic differences and yet subordinate them to a cosmopolitan and "cosmic" order, a new melting pot wherein nationalisms and ethnic identities – and "'big-shot' politics" (193) – will no longer generate global conflict.

"Cosmic order" names the experiment that Lewis hopes to see replace the old political models. "Luckily we have a Socialist government" (193) in postwar England, Lewis notes, so that the English political scene can model itself on America, which has advantageously "turned its back" on race and class. While Lewis is aware of US racial problems, he argues that American capitalism soon will see the wisdom, if only for profit's sake, of erasing bigotry. Moreover, defeating racial prejudice will be an inevitable result of America's not being "locked up . . . in that antiquated group-pen, the 'nation,' and pretend[ing] to be a 'race,' and a mighty fine one too, as did par excellence the National Socialists [i.e., Nazis]" (197). How can those views belong to an author whom literary history calls a fascist? An author who in *The Writer and the Absolute* (1952) takes André Malraux to task for attaching neo-Nazi thrills to political assassination, and who estimates George Orwell's relation to politics, in contrast to Malraux and Sartre's, as nearly ideal?

Part of the answer is that Lewis's profile repeats the elements – including the other-worldly dimension – that figure in Yeats's and Pound's problematic relations to politics and literary critics. Those elements also become the bedrock of Lewis's polemics about the character of modernist art. But whether his polemics are political or aesthetic, Lewis insists on a maverick relation to classificatory labels. That insistence is the one point on which he is not slippery. Critical distrust of him is made grave by this point as well as by the others. Often confoundingly, Lewis intermingles even his advocacies with qualifying criticisms.

For example, in *America and Cosmic Man* he celebrates a "strange and beautiful solidarity" among people of diverse global origin that typifies American freedom; yet he simultaneously argues that "political democracy" in the United States is "quite distinct" from the beautiful solidarity (1949, 218). His analysis sounds Poundian or Yeatsian: the two-party system in the United States invests in a mere fantasy of opposition; the Presidency is "Caesarism of an oddly elaborate and roundabout kind" (69); and, "however much we may believe in the ultimate possibility of full 'popular sovereignty' – ... at present to say that 'men are competent to govern themselves' ... does not agree with the facts" (156).

Criticism rarely reaches to *America and Cosmic Man*. It is bad enough, in today's view of reactionary modernists, that Lewis wrote *Hitler* in 1931. His intention then was to assess neutrally – "not as critic nor yet as advocate" (4) – the rising leader. The neutrality is hard to distinguish from sympathy (although Lewis says Hitler must be warned against anti-Semitism, a "racial red herring" [43]). In *The Hitler Cult* Lewis revokes *Hitler*. But what today would be picked out as further specimens of Lewis the "reactionary" are interwoven with the revocation. In *Hitler* and a subsequent book about the Spanish Civil War, *Count Your Dead: They Are Alive* (1937), in which Lewis indirectly (via two fictive personae he adopts as mouthpieces) berates communist manipulation of the conflict, Lewis saw nationalism as the refuge from a new empire of international loan-capital lording it over global debtors (including the Soviet Union). In 1939, however, Hitler has become "a Jingo God," and Lewis feels "unresponsive to, all 'nationalist' excitements" (1939, x, 13). Nevertheless, although Lewis despises "John Bull," he confesses a nostalgia for the British Empire. The nostalgia includes the assertion that British imperialism "was a natural ... expansion, secured at the expense of no one except dusky beings who were as different from ourselves as they inhabited another planet: great jibbering creatures with rings in their noses" (188).

Such crudeness – in the context of a repudiation of Nazi racism – seems to us worse than reactionary. There is still worse, for current sensibilities. *Paleface*, a reading of W. E. B. Du Bois, the Harlem Renaissance writers, H. L. Mencken,

D. H. Lawrence, and Sherwood Anderson, mercilessly (and often hilariously) criticizes them because Lewis feels "driven into the position of the Devil's Advocate to some extent . . . by the excesses of the anti-Whites" (20). The position of Devil's Advocate is not confined to this text. In *The Art of Being Ruled* (1926) he describes feminism and homosexual liberation movements as symptoms of what he calls "child-cult," escapes – no matter what new freedoms they represent – from personal and social responsibilities that Lewis continues to respect. Lewis can be nasty about homosexuality, even though it is prominent throughout his work: in *The Human Age* (a trilogy of novels about the afterlife [1928–1955]), the protagonist, although he is coupled posthumously with a younger man whose erotic inclinations are male-centered, resists seduction: "'I am allergic to homosexuals'" (1966, 191). Lewis seems allergic even to modernism. A writer whose prewar prose deranges the meanings of words and the structure of sentences as if he were a fellow traveler with Joyce and Stein, or with Eugene Jolas and Elliot Paul's avant-garde literary journal *transition*, opposes Joyce, Stein, and *transition*, as well as Lawrence, Hemingway, Faulkner – and Pound (in *Paleface* Lewis remarks on "This fascist or marinettian (futurist) appetite for violence . . . encouraged . . . by that perfect 'American Baby' . . . , Ezra Pound" [145]).

No wonder that the inveterately feisty Lewis only intermittently gains the attention of scholars of modernism: the judgment seems to be that, given his "reactionary" character all round, he merits marginalization. The judgment puts political values first and last – Lewis's racism or anti-feminism or homophobia are wrong because they are tied to imperialism and to anti-democratic bias; and his art is wrong consequently. But such assessment overlooks the possibility that there are values other than political ones – personal, ethical, aesthetic, or religious values – worth cultivating, especially if the political ideas already in action are bankrupt (or merely bankrolled), as Yeats, Pound, and Lewis (and T. S. Eliot and D. H. Lawrence, one might add) agree. It is non-political values, Lewis insists, that should be operative in art and philosophy. His modernism seeks the same suspense of the political that in Yeats's case heightens critical anxiety – anxiety based on thinking that political terms are ultimate. Lewis refuses that ultimacy. "There is no occasion to . . . hold any political creed to . . . practise experiment in art," Lewis writes. "I advance the strange claim . . . to act and to think non-politically in everything, in complete detachment from all the intolerant watchwords and formulas by which we are beset" (1931a, 37).

That detachment – a variant of Yeats's "detonating impartiality" – qualifies and even cancels the racism, the anti-feminism, the homophobia, and the assaults on Joyce, Stein, and the others, in most of Lewis's arguments. The arguments, depending on dialectical juxtapositions of assertions and negations, seek the radical liberty of detachment as their goal. How does this detachment affect *Paleface*? Lewis's aim in *Paleface* is, paradoxically, to clarify progress toward the global melting pot. His dialectic contends that a new reification of racial identity – and hence a newly chic racism – has occurred in the shift of white and black writers' attention to blackness. At the beginning of *Paleface* Lewis points out that race is a construct fabricated by the economic interests of those who assume "the race-prejudice or traditional superstition of some absolute or mystical 'superiority'" (17). Because he hypothesizes that the superstition is now merely changing hands, he wants to debunk it. One way is to remind readers that white culture is not inferior to whatever will supersede it. However, what should supersede it, for whites and for blacks, Lewis hopes, is cosmic cosmopolitanism, which must liberate its constituents from every group identity ("white," "black"), for those identities magnetize the labelings on which "politics" depends. *Politics* is reactionary for Lewis, because it attaches everything to its worn-out terms and praxes.

Lewis offers his opposition to feminists and homosexuals as true friendship. *The Art of Being Ruled*, an investigation of the prospects for a world order to be evolved from anarchist and communist traditions, is written as a polemic (characteristically modernist) "*against the family*" (179, italics in original), which Lewis sees as "the model of all governmental despotism" (178). Lewis sees feminists, gays, and lesbians as an anti-familial coalition, and therefore is their partisan. But, in line with his dialectical thought, Lewis argues that gender and sexual dissidents are being co-opted by a new variant of what they oppose. They do not see how their emergence as newly identifiable groups makes them available to the manipulation of powers that have relocated the old seats of authority:

> A kind of gigantically luxurious patriarchate is what democracy and monster industry together have invented... There is no king; but there are many mercantile despots, more or less benevolently patriarchal, indistinguishable... from their... 'clients.' This is how it comes [about] that the family once more occupies the foreground of our lives. With a new *familiarity* and a flesh-creeping 'homeliness' entirely of this unreal, materialist world, where all 'sentiment' is coarsely manufactured and advertised..., disguised for the sweet tooth of a monstrous baby called 'the Public,' the family as it is, broken up on all hands by the agency of feminist and economic propaganda, reconstitutes itself in the image of the state. (1989, 181, italics in original)

That homosexuals contribute to the subversion of the family and of "normal" male roles is all to the good for Lewis; but he warns that the politicizing of homosexuality develops on the basis of an unfortunate foundation: a heightening of eros as the ground of being. The problem with such heightening is that it becomes "propaganda *for* sensation" (218, italics in original). It enlists intellect to justify sensation, and compromises intellect by subordinating it to sensation. Heightening sensation as a norm of life, as Lewis sees it, has an infantilizing effect on its subjects, and is the means by which they are surrendered to the new patriarchate. The patriarchate cannot dominate detached intelligence; but it can dominate sensations, and identities that center on them.

Lewis thinks of sexuality and gender as historically constructed, as changeable and not "natural." His alliance with homosexuality, despite his criticism of it, is preeminent in his study of Shakespeare, *The Lion and the Fox* (written in 1925, published in 1927). He theorizes that one foundation of Shakespeare's greatness is his homosexual "inversion," because homosexuality enables Shakespeare to be creatively detached from what Lewis takes to be a prime evil of Shakespeare's day: the cult of the man of action, especially as he appears in Machiavelli's *The Prince*, and as he is embodied in Shakespeare's tragic heroes. Lewis identifies a political "agent-function" or "agent-principle" as the root of Renaissance government and imperialism. With its addiction to the seizure of power by ruthless male will, and with its bias for the imposition of order on any terms, the agent-principle is arguably protofascist. Pound's Malatesta (and Rainey's) exemplifies it. Shakespeare is its critic, and opposed to the violence it engenders. Although Shakespeare loves his great male heroes, Lewis claims, Shakespeare loves more to see them lose the names of action, empire, and will. Shakespeare himself, Lewis thinks, is projected especially into Falstaff, whom Lewis identifies with transvestism. Exposure to life's risks on Falstaff's irresponsible, hence (according to convention) "anti-masculine" terms, Lewis comments, "is a very radical, . . . inversely heroic, or heroically inverse, proceeding" (223).

For all Shakespeare's queerness, Lewis does not see him as a figure who subordinates intellect to sensation. Contrastively, in *Time and Western Man* (1927) Lewis estimates his fellow modernists – Joyce, Stein, and Pound – as propagandists of the senses, who thereby have lessened art's potential for stimulating creative detachment. He is wary too of Henri Bergson, Alfred North Whitehead, and Oswald Spengler. Those thinkers reinforce sensational life, not only in terms of bodily being, but also in terms of time and space. They and the literary modernists together proclaim space-time as a medium of flux. The flux is said to bring about a relativizing of all values, dissolving objectivity and truth in favor of "a sort of visceral, abdominal mind [as] . . . a new revolutionary capital, the rival and enemy of the head" (1973, 178).

Assessing the modernist emphasis on flux as a reversion to a Rousseau-ist romanticism that exalts childish intensities of feeling at the expense of rational maturity, *Lewis* finds *Pound*'s work reactionary. Pound's novelty, Lewis writes, "consisted largely in the distance it went *back*, not forward; in archaism, not in new creation" (1993, 38). Pound's attempts at evocative sensation – to purvey ideas thereby – are lifeless: *The Cantos*, Lewis thinks, "belong to the repetitive hypnotic method of Miss Stein" (70f). Despite Pound's archaisms, however, Pound insists on being in the revolutionary vanguard, which means, Lewis says, that Pound requires "*disturbance* . . . He is never happy if he is not sniffing the dust and glitter of *action* kicked up by . . . more natively 'active' men" (39, emphasis in original). The time-flux of *The Cantos* moves inevitably toward Mussolini, finding its justification, for worse rather than for better, in a neo-Renaissance condottiere.

In the context of the contradictions that beset the world's established politics, Lewis proposes a reaction against action: a state of disinterested spectatorship, an "art" of being ruled, rather than of ruling, as the best form of life. (Individuals must cultivate it, for group thinking counters detachment.) "Utopia is not necessarily an active Utopia," he writes. "To be receptive rather than active . . . is by no means a humiliating role" (1989, 160). The last chapter of *The Art of Being Ruled* further unfolds the idea:

> [I]ntelligence suffers today . . . in consequence of the attack on all authority, advantage, or privilege . . . [That] is a danger to all of us . . . The intellect is more removed from the crowd than is anything: but it is not a snobbish withdrawal, but a going aside for the purposes of work . . . More than the prophet or religious teacher, [the intellectual leader] represents at his best the great unworldly element in the world, and that is the guarantee of his usefulness. It is he and not the political ruler who supplies the contrast of something remote and different that is the very stuff of which all living (not mechanical) power is composed. (374)

The "something remote and different" that Lewis refers to is, paradoxically, "what *is*." Art and intellect furnish "unobstructed access to the true" (1952, 198). Art's "best credential," Lewis writes in *The Dithyrambic Spectator* (1931), is its ability to disclose the "backgrounds" of life, the finalities that underlie experience. Those are not "facts" or "history" or politics, but "terrible truths"; "it is as spectators that [men] survey these terrible truths, with the atmosphere of distance which art maintains, and the measure of its trance, to soften them" (1931a, 237).

Lewis is convinced that "people of considerable intelligence" have "the ability to *perceive* the true – which is under everybody's nose but not seen by everybody" (1952, 198); and he labors in book after book to vindicate his own claims to such enabling perception. Literary criticism shows its saturation in the modernist values that Lewis criticizes when it reproves Lewis for designating himself such a perceiver – a mere subjectivity, amid the relativities of an ever-indeterminate time-space flux, presuming to resurrect objectivity and disinterestedness, yet in an idealist rather than materialist mode! And obsessively commenting on politics all the while he seeks an exit from politics!

Charging Lewis with contradictions that exceed his conscious dialecticism is central to Fredric Jameson's study. The charge, despite Jameson's remarking that Lewis prefigures Samuel Beckett, Louis Althusser, Herbert Marcuse, and the Frankfurt School, derives from an un-nuanced strand of Jameson's Marxism: Lewis' ideas symptomize the uncertain, resentment-laden class status of the petty-bourgeoisie (16). That class position, Jameson claims, is rightly called "protofascist," even if it renounces fascism. Protofascism is inevitably anti-communist. Hence Lewis's "life-long implacable opposition to Marxism" (18) means that "the value of fascism as a reaction [in Lewis] is determined by communism, against which the anticapitalist posture of protofascism (which Lewis approved) must be understood" (184). *Pace* Jameson, however, Lewis is not implacably anti-Marxist or anti-communist: in 1926 he endorsed "the sovietic system" as "the best" form of socialism (1989, 320); and he remained a socialist fellow-traveler. That Lewis also criticized Communism and socialism, even as he endorsed them, cannot justly be construed, and censured, as Jameson does. Jameson's "demonstration," via a Greimasian semiotic square, that

Lewis equated "socialist Britain" with "diabolical sexuality" and "non-intelligence" (120) especially flouts the contrary evidence (for example, in *America and Cosmic Man*). Jameson's suturing of "protofascism" to Lewis's satire also is debatable. Equating satire with deadly aggression facilitates Jameson's prosecution of Lewis's politics as violent: satire is "protoHitlerian," if not Hitlerian. But the prosecution is out of touch with the criticism of the agent-principle, and *its* inevitable violence, that remains a keystone of Lewis's work.

Jameson's singly, straightforwardly focused readings of Lewis's novels *The Revenge for Love* (1937) and *Self Condemned* (1954) are acute. But Jameson's study is usually less focused. His analysis relies on a restless, even hectic, solicitation of critical, historical, and theoretical domains: Marxist, Freudian, Lacanian, structuralist-narratological, genre theory, to name a few. The reliance, despite its influence on the past thirty years of scholarship, argues a liability in methodological eclecticism. The Jamesonian net of involved theories captures Lewis, and also allows him (and critical accuracy) to escape. Criticism that is more certain than Lewis, that does not play Devil's Advocate to itself, risks aggressions of its own.

Another modernist version of Purgatory, *The Human Age* trilogy records Lewis's Devil's Advocacy, pitted against the author's hard-won certainties. The protagonist Pullman, a distinguished writer killed in the Great War, enters the afterlife, hoping for a purgatorial assignment. The immediate judge of souls is a Bailiff in charge of deciding where newcomers will be placed. He is an entertaining modernist orator, who ventriloquizes Stein or *Finnegans Wake*. Pullman's relation to him is uneasy, but once Pullman enters the purgatorial domain called Third City, where the Bailiff rules, Pullman accepts an alliance with him, and with the time-flux and sensation-bound relativisms that the Bailiff also represents. The alliance is cemented when the Bailiff transports Pullman to Dis, where Satan himself is in charge.

The site is not Hell, but it houses punishment of unpardonable sinners. It also includes a colony of angels who stay away from the devil. Satan is about to enact a revolution, however: he plans to reform the dire punishments, indeed to humanize entirely this outpost – the angels too. He will persuade them to marry choice posthumous women, and to establish suburban family households; Satan, although a misogynist, also will marry, to set an example. Pullman, abetting this scheme, becomes Satan's chief advisor. The duo's plans are Machiavellian: the new human age, whose form of government will be liberal democracy, will mask the agent-principle's cold war to the death with Heaven's distant divinity.

Pullman's support of Satan reminds a reader of a cold-blooded moment in *The Art of Being Ruled*. Having decided on "the sovietic system be[ing] the best" form of socialism, Lewis goes on to say that Mussolini's fascism, in 1926, is "the sort of socialism that this essay would indicate as the most suitable for Anglo-Saxon countries or colonies" (321). It would be most suitable, Lewis explains, because its "complete political standardization will rescue masses of energy otherwise wasted in politics" (321). Accordingly, it will get rid of all "the pretences of democracy" (322). And, as a facet of establishing this "sort of socialism," political assassination by "fascist bands" will be condoned. Does Pullman's service to Satan hark back to Lewis's prescription of thirty years earlier?

If so, the prescription is undergoing purgation. Pullman becomes sickened by his identity with the Satanic man of action, and by his alliance with the treacheries and violences of "politics." The more the human age advances, the more Pullman longs to be God's Advocate. "God *values* man," Pullman thinks. "It is this valuing that is so extraordinary. There are men who only value *power*. This is absurd, because power destroys value. Value can only exist with multiplicity. The only value for Sammael [i.e., Satan] is solipsistic. I, Pullman, am acting in a valueless vacuum called Sammael" (1966a, 181–182). On the last page of his history Pullman "knew that he should never have assisted at the humanisation of the Divine" (211).

One must not assume, of course, that Pullman, or Lewis, means to return to "liberalism" or "democracy" as the source of value. What those labels mean remains, for Lewis, terminally compromised. For him the ultimate values are service to truth via spectator-like detached intellect and art, in imitation of God's detachment (in *The Human Age* He allows Satan the freedom to rebel against him, still); and the global multiplicity that Lewis invokes in the name of cosmic man. If Lewis can be labeled a fascist on the basis of what he said, in part, in 1926 and 1931, and cannot be identified in any other way, one might wonder what values motivate the nomenclature: the *power* sought by literary historians and critics, or equitable disinterestedness.

References

Casillo, Robert. (1988). *The Genealogy of Demons*. Evanston, IL: Northwestern University Press.

Ferrall, Charles. (2001). *Modernist Writing and Reactionary Politics*. Cambridge University Press.

Foster, R. F. (2010). "Fascism." In *W. B. Yeats in Context*, ed. David Holdeman and Ben Levitas (pp. 213–223). Cambridge: Cambridge University Press.

Holdeman, David and Ben Levitas. (2010). "Introduction." In *W. B. Yeats in Context*, ed. David Holdeman and Ben Levitas (pp. 1–13). Cambridge: Cambridge University Press.

Jameson, Fredric. (1979). *Fables of Aggression*. Berkeley: The University of California Press.

Lewis, Wyndham. (1927). *The Lion and the Fox: The Role of the Hero in the Plays of Shakespeare*. New York: Harper & Brothers.

Lewis, Wyndham. (1931a). *The Diabolical Principle* and *The Dithyrambic Spectator*. London: Chatto & Windus.

Lewis, Wyndham. (1931b). *Hitler*. London: Chatto & Windus.

Lewis, Wyndham. (1939). *The Hitler Cult*. London: Dent.

Lewis, Wyndham. (1949). *America and Cosmic Man*. Garden City, NY: Doubleday.

Lewis, Wyndham. (1952). *The Writer and the Absolute*. London: Methuen.

Lewis, Wyndham. (1966a [1955]). *Malign Fiesta*. London: Calder and Boyars.

Lewis, Wyndham. (1966b [1955]). *Monstre Gai*. London: Calder and Boyars.

Lewis, Wyndham. (1973 [1929]). *Paleface*. New York: Gordon Press.

Lewis, Wyndham. (1989 [1926]). *The Art of Being Ruled*. Santa Rosa, CA: Black Sparrow Press.

Lewis, Wyndham. (1993 [1927]). *Time and Western Man*. Santa Rosa: Black Sparrow Press.

Lloyd, David. (2010). "Nationalisms and Post-Colonialism." In *W. B. Yeats in Context*, ed. David Holdeman and Ben Levitas (pp. 179–192). Cambridge: Cambridge University Press.

Pound, Ezra. (1956a [1948]). *The Pisan Cantos*. In *The Cantos (1–95)*. New York: New Directions.

Pound, Ezra. (1956b [1934]). *Eleven New Cantos*. In *The Cantos (1–95)*. New York: New Directions.

Pound, Ezra. (1970 [1935]). *Jefferson and/or Mussolini*. New York: Liveright.

Pound, Ezra. (1973a [1939]). "ABC of Economics." In *Selected Prose*, ed. William Cookson (pp. 233–264). New York: New Directions.

Pound, Ezra. (1973b [1942]). "A Visiting Card." In *Selected Prose*, ed. William Cookson (pp. 306–335). New York: New Directions.

Pound, Ezra. (1973c [1944]). "Gold and Work." In *Selected Prose*, ed. William Cookson (pp. 336–351). New York: New Directions.

Rainey, Lawrence S. (1991). *Ezra Pound and the Monument of Culture. Text, History, and the Malatesta Cantos*. Chicago: The University of Chicago Press.

Redman, Tim. (1991). *Ezra Pound and Italian Fascism*. Cambridge: Cambridge University Press.

Said, Edward W. (1990 [1988]). "Yeats and Decolonisation." In *Nationalism, Colonialism, and Literature*, ed. Terry Eagleton, Fredric Jameson, and Edward W. Said. Minneapolis: University of Minnesota Press.

Shaw, Bernard. (1931 [1928]). *The Intelligent Woman's Guide to Socialism and Capitalism*. In *The Collected Works of Bernard Shaw*, vol. XX. New York: Wm. H. Wise & Co.

Warren, Lansing. (1934). "Gertrude Stein Views Life and Politics." *The New York Times*, May 6. At http://www.nytimes.com/books/98/05/03/specials/stein-views.html (accessed November 14, 2012).

Woolf, Virginia. (1966 [1938]). *Three Guineas*. New York: Harcourt Brace Jovanovich.

Yeats, W. B. (1960). *The Collected Poems of W. B. Yeats*. New York: The Macmillan Company.

Yeats, W. B. (2001 [1937]). "Introduction for My Plays." In *The Collected Work of W. B. Yeats*, Vol. II, *The Plays*, ed. David R. Clark and Rosalind E. Clark (pp. 23–26). New York: Scribner.

Yeats, W. B. (1938–1939). *On the Boiler*. Dublin: The Cuala Press.

Yeats, W. B. (1953 [1939]). *Purgatory*. In *The Collected Plays of W. B. Yeats*, (pp. 430–436). New York: The Macmillan Company.

Further Reading

Brooke-Rose, Christine. (1971). *A ZBC of Ezra Pound*. London: Faber and Faber.

Rabaté, Jean-Michel. (1986). *Language, Sexuality and Ideology in Ezra Pound's Cantos*. Albany: State University of New York Press.

Sieburth, Richard. (2003). "Introduction." In Ezra Pound, *The Pisan Cantos* (pp. ix–xliii). New York: New Directions.

Will, Barbara. (2011). *Unlikely Collaboration: Gertrude Stein, Bernard Faÿ, and the Vichy Dilemma*. New York: Columbia University Press.

9

Transnationalism at the Departure Gate

Matthew Hart

Four years ago, two influential critics identified a distinct "transnational turn" in scholarship about modernist literature and culture. Selecting only the most illustrative examples of this tendency within the "New Modernist Studies," Douglas Mao and Rebecca L. Walkowitz[1] nevertheless listed over thirty titles, most published since the millennium, that variously focus on how modernist literary history – not to mention the construction of "modernism" as a category of thought and practice – overflows the boundaries of any one nation-state. In their assessment, this developing field includes three types of intellectual work: "widening the field" of modernist studies so as to include "alternative traditions"; studying and explaining the centrality of "transnational circulation and translation" to modernist aesthetics; and reconsidering the relation between a literary canon historically conceived as metropolitan (even, sometimes, as reactionary or racist) and the cultural legacy of anti-colonial movements and postcolonial peoples (739). Although no such survey of an academic field can be comprehensive, if I were to write a similar essay in 2012 the greatest change would come not in the terms of this analysis but in the length of my bibliography.

The figure of the "turn" is nicely flexible.[2] It implies a movement in some new direction: a collective shift toward a novel goal or trend, or away from an error. It also leaves open the possibility that, having turned, the field might turn back or turn full circle. As with the "linguistic turn" in the social sciences, transnational literary studies might become unfashionable or subject to correction. From the perspective of this volume, however, the task of measuring any sort of turn is complicated by the fact that the scholarship gathered under the sign of the transnational is reducible to no single theoretical tendency. It contains conceptually sophisticated work, sometimes overtly oriented toward the canon and idiom of critical theory – one thinks, for instance, of how Nicholas Brown's answer to the

A Handbook of Modernism Studies, First Edition. Edited by Jean-Michel Rabaté.
© 2013 John Wiley & Sons, Ltd. Published 2013 by John Wiley & Sons, Ltd.

question "what does British modernism have to do with African literature?" takes him on a journey through Marxism and poststructuralism as much as the works of Ngugi wa Thiong'o and Ford Madox Ford.[3] But for all that the scholars listed by Mao and Walkowitz are often interested in critical theory, it is impossible to read their work and then distill the outlines of some general theory of the transnational as such. It would even be difficult to identify the terms under which this heterogeneous group of scholars would disagree about the meaning and limits of that term.

Part of this is due to the often historicist nature of the work in question, in which the desire to generalize is sacrificed on the altar of particularity. But that proposition, while reasonable, nonetheless minimizes the extent to which transnational modernist studies combines an attention to historical specificity with the desire to articulate portable concepts and interpretive models that can subtend generalizations across national traditions usually studied separately. Michael Rubenstein's *Public Works* (2010),[4] for instance, widens the field of Irish modernism by arguing that "Irish modernism ought to be studied in the context of comparative postcolonial literary studies." Its greatest innovation, however, comes in the connections it draws between aesthetic modernism and infrastructural modernization. In this context, the very idea of a "public work" aspires to become a "portable heuristic" that links a canonical literary work such as Joyce's *Ulysses* to the history of state-formation and economic development in postcolonial Ireland (2). It thereby connects the aesthetic strategies European modernism to postcolonial literatures from countries that faced equivalent problems of cultural and infrastructural modernization in the years after winning independence from European empires. Similarly, Laura Winkiel's *Modernism, Race, and Manifestos* (2008) considers the popularity of the manifesto form in places as different as Florence, Paris, New York, and Port-au-Prince.[5] In so doing, it respects the specificities of artistic and political activism across several countries. Nevertheless, its primary interest is in the manifesto as a form that encodes, as a kind of traveling aesthetic and ideological engine, the unevenly developed nature of the modern world. In its "movements across the colonial divide," she writes, "[the manifesto] brings with it altered experiences and effects of modernity and registers the urgency of formulating alternative modernisms."

There is theoretical labor aplenty, then. Still, as these examples suggest, much of that work is oriented toward theorizing the nature of modernity rather than the transnational as such. Transnationalism is not an end in itself; it is more often adjectival than nominative, more method than theory. Because modernity is assumed to travel, or have multiple origins, so must the intellectual horizons of its critics and historians. If literary modernism is characterized by its peripatetic character – if the assumption that a literary work "will express a writer's nationality [. . .] is not only antimodernist but anterior to modernism"[6] – then any proper account of what's modern in Joyce or Gertrude Stein must first of all account for the way that they, their art, and their readers refuse to be contained within Ireland or America, Dublin or Baltimore. Transnationalism functions as a method, then, because it is a property of modernity at large.[7] The theoretical object under analysis, however, remains the modern and its aesthetic expressions.

There is a theoretical thin-ness, then, to transnationalism that belies its status as an "ism" – a suffix that usually suggests the presence of an ideology. No one believes in transnationalism as they might believe in socialism or Freudianism, not even as they might be influenced by a philosophical tendency such as poststructuralism. Transnationalism bespeaks an orientation to literary history – and, thus, to the history of the world in general – but it would be a mistake to assume that it represents a coherent scholarly praxis.[8]

This does not mean, however, that the term has no content. First, the figure of the transnational should be distinguished from the global. Gayatri Spivak argues that the figure of the globe implies "the imposition of the same system of exchange everywhere. In the gridwork of electronic capital, we achieve that abstract ball covered in latitudes and longitudes, cut by virtual lines."[9] Similarly, the editors of a volume of essays on "minor transnationalism" distinguish between economic globalization, "defined vis-à-vis a homogeneous and dominant set of criteria," and a transnationalism that "designates spaces and practices acted upon by border-crossing agents, be they dominant or marginal."[10] This differentiation between types of agent and system is common to transnationalism talk. Thus, at the methodological level, it is also common to distinguish between transnationalism and an older concept of internationalism, which the cultural historian Micol Seigel defines as "the interaction of nation-states as such."[11] Here, the international is a matter of state-to-state relations – the province of diplomatic and military history – and is thus largely the concern of social elites. A scholar of the black diaspora, Seigel adopts a transnational historiographic method because it is better attuned to non-elite subjects and practices "that spill over and seep through national borders, units both greater and smaller than the nation-state" (63). This language of "greater and smaller" – or, as it also appears, "above and below" – is significant for two reasons. First, it enables distinctions between the transnationalism of the privileged – the well-traveled rich, for instance, such as the globe-trotting managerial classes studied by Aiwha Ong[12] – and groups such as migrant workers or refugees whose movements between and among national communities are often a matter of exigency. Second, distinctions of scale or elevation allow one to differentiate between the experiences of individuals and small groups (cultural agents whom we might imagine operating "below" the radar of the nation-state) and the actions of supranational institutions such as, to use an example from the period between the wars, the Comintern. To translate these terms into the language of literary history, we might therefore say that we need "transnational" because no language or literature is truly global; we need alternatives to "international" because the language of state-to-state relations cannot describe, for example, the networks of acquaintance and shared belief that inspired Nancy Cunard, W. H. Auden, and Stephen Spender to collaborate on *Authors Take Sides in the Spanish Civil War* (1937); and we need the perspective "from below" because the wartime experiences of individual authors such as Auden, Orwell, or Lorca cannot be smoothly assimilated to the (far from smooth) institutional history of the Popular Front.

Empirical roots, however, can grow normative flowers; methodologies often embody moral and political values. And so it is with the transnational turn. Consider, for instance, Jahan Ramazani's unembarrassed declaration that his interest in transnational literary history is justified not only on historical and aesthetic grounds, but on the basis that it might help produce a "different disciplinary model of 'citizenship'" in which "instead of replicating the centripetal vortex of the nation-state [. . .] cross cultural writing and reading might evoke non-coercive and non-atavistic forms of [. . .] imaginative belonging."[13] In this account, a transnational methodology not only better reflects the nature of twentieth-century poetry; it also promotes the liberal and anti-racist social values in which Ramazani believes.

This news will surprise no one, nor will it upset very many. More problematically, however, this relationship also tracks the other way, with cosmopolitan aspirations coloring factual assertions about the extent to which our world has been transformed by transnational flows and institutions. Ramazani is careful to point out that the transnational character of much modernist and postcolonial poetry is perfectly consistent with the persistence of the nation-state as a political desideratum and object of identification (12–13). But not everyone shares his caution and rigor. Michael P. Smith and Luis Guarnizo[14] complain about the "totalizing emancipatory character of transnationalism" in cultural theories that, to use Homi Bhabha's phrase, emphasize the construction of "counter-narratives of the nation." Susan Koshy,[15] meanwhile, criticizes globalization theorists who prophesy the arrival of new transnational revolutionary subjects but neither substantiate their existence nor explain how they will avoid the wrongs committed by – or substitute for the services provided by – the national structures they are supposedly destined to replace.

If this is a warning worth heeding in the present, it is doubly so when we look back to period of the world wars. The first decades of the last century undoubtedly saw the rise of a new transnationalism, from relatively elite occurrences such as the interwar expatriate community in Paris to mass immigration to the United States from countries such as Poland and Italy. It must not be forgotten, however, that this same period also witnessed an unprecedented growth in the province and potency of national governments, in liberal as much as authoritarian states. (Among the long-lasting effects of this growth in state power: passports, immigration controls by national quota, and the welfare state.) Most importantly, we must remember that the nation-state and transnationalism are, in the modernist period and today, more often interdependent than antithetical. The League of Nations, for instance, might reasonably be considered the prototype of contemporary supranational institutions such as the European Union. But far from representing the overcoming of the nation-state or national sovereignty, the League's charter explicitly affirms the "territorial integrity and existing political independence of all Members."[16] In principle and in practice, the League was poised between its ideal position "above" the nation-state – a global arbiter of disputes between nations – and its existence as the product of an international system that struggled to balance local and imperial interests with the presumed normative status of the territorial nation-state.[17]

It is at this point, perhaps, that we can come closest to a definition of the transnational as something that, to borrow from Stephen Clingman's useful summation,[18] is characterized not by the fact of transcending national spaces, nor by their simple collision or collaboration, but by acts of "transition" across borders. These borders might be political: a frontier between states. But they might also be linguistic or cultural. They might even be temporal: an effect of moving between different developmental or cosmological worlds. This fact of movement between relatively autonomous zones is precisely what distinguishes the transnational from the vacuity and homogeneity of the global. It is also what makes it different from an internationalism in which the border, if it is considered at all, is often figured as a culturally null membrane between two sovereign plenitudes. As Clingman describes it, the transnational is a space (or, rather, a grammar) in its own right: "where the transitive and combinatory become possible [. . .] the space of crossing" (241). It is neither a network of bland equivalence nor the cosmic sublation of national or local particulars, floating above what W. H. Auden called the "possessed congested surface" of the world. Nor, as we shall see, is it a utopian space of migratory transgression or hybrid creativity. As Auden knew better than most, the space of transit can be cruel, vapid, and boring. To illustrate these claims, the second and final part of this chapter will turn to an Auden poem set in one significant site of the modernist transnational: an airport departure lounge. If transnationalism is, as I have suggested, theoretically thin, it is at least rich in exemplary geographies.

* * * *

Auden's relationship to literary modernism is vexed. Although early works such as *The Orators: An English Study* (1932) are at least superficially consistent with the revolutions in form and language demanded by the likes of Ezra Pound, there is much in his poetry – not to mention his life and opinions – that not only conflicts with popular understandings of modernism but is antipathetic to critical generalizations of that sort. If I illustrate an aspect of the "modernist transnational" via Auden's poetry, it is not, then, because I wish to annex him to a literary history he fits awkwardly at best. I do so because he understood the space of transition as one in which, to quote again from "In Transit" (1950), "fears intersect."[19]

Reading twentieth-century literature, one encounters a wide range of attitudes toward the transnational, often within the work of a single writer. Auden is no exception. His poems of the 1940s and 1950s, for instance, regularly express the hope that humanity might free itself from cultural or political determination by nation-states – as in "Streams" (1953), with its hopes for a "sort of world, quite other / altogether different from this one // with its envies and passports" (ll. 40–41). But Auden's poetry also laments the dystopian version of this "other" world, an anonymous and denatured zone that corrodes human autonomy and individuality just as surely as the patriotic bromides of a state at war. This is the overt subject, as we shall see, of "In Transit." Beneath both these possibilities lies the hope of a space in which life and art are defined not by the sublation or reification of local geographies but through their interrelation.

"In Transit," originally collected in *Nones* (1951) with the title "Air Port," was later selected by Auden to open the final part of his *Collected Shorter Poems 1927–1957* (1966). It occupies a similar position in Edward Mendelson's revised edition of the *Collected Poems* (1991), where it begins the 1948–1957 section of the volume. As its titles suggest, the poem meditates upon what, in 1950, was the still-novel experience of waiting in a departure lounge, having left one country but not yet properly arrived in another. For Nicholas Jenkins,[20] its position in Auden's collected volumes is emblematic of a new chapter of his poetic life: "With a beautiful symmetry of motif, 'In Transit' took poetic leave of America [for summer in Italy] in the limbo of an airport lounge, at a stop-off for fuel somewhere on the Atlantic crossing."

A new chapter – but, in Jenkins' own account, one that builds upon a poetic meditation at least a decade in the making. If Virgil's great "historical gesture," Jenkins writes, was to join "the poet's text to the national destiny, then the "de-linking of poetry from authentication by nationality [. . .] was Auden's" (46). The origins of this "gesture" date to the late 1930s and, thus, to a combination of factors that together soured Auden on the notion that, as he put it in an essay of 1932, "Whenever a society is united [. . .] it has an outburst of great and good writing."[21] Against that early judgment, one must pit Auden's later enthusiasm for the "absolutely free America" to which he emigrated in 1939. One must recall his increasing distaste, as Mendelson puts it, not only for the authoritarian "myths of inexorable destiny" manufactured by Hitler and Stalin but for all "historical theories of collective *mentalités*."[22] Above all, one must remember that, for the Auden of World War II and after, the notion of a collective national identity or manner of expression had not only come to seem unaesthetic ("works of art are created by individuals working alone," he wrote in "The Prolific and the Devourer") but unethical: "Whoso generalises, is lost."[23]

An art that resists generalization needs particularity, loves the local. But if localities are not to be fetishized as such – if one is to avoid provincialism, and not mistake character for self-sufficiency – then they must be placed in relation to other places, other peoples. The individual working alone must travel, or live in a great metropolis. Auden did both. Alongside his life in the "great Hotel" of New York,[24] Jenkins has shown just how far and how widely Auden journeyed, especially in comparison to more famously internationalist poets. (Pound wrote *Cathay* [1915] but Auden went to the Sino-Japanese war.) Jenkins also contends that, while the ordinariness of Auden's traveling life "is the point" (he wasn't a new Marco Polo, just a more interesting version of the tourist we have all become), it had a profound effect on his sense of place in the world: "In Auden's later years, there were for him [no] clear definitions of what 'at home' and 'abroad,' 'domestic' and 'foreign,' 'here' and 'there,' meant."[25] "In Transit" commemorates a moment of waiting in one of those journeys, a hinge point in Auden's annual transition between his winter home in New York and his summer's stay in Italy, and – at least seen from the perspective of the mid-1960s – something like the beginning of a new moment in his writing life, in which a longstanding and principled objection to generalizing abstractions was realized in poetry that celebrated the idiosyncrasies of human speech and bodily life.[26]

This latter theme is established from the poem's first verse, in which the speaker emerges from his plane into a landscape that is unnamed and out of reach, yet still possessed of a specific ecology and still marked by human labor and the sexual relation:

> Let out where two fears intersect, a point selected
>   Jointly by general staffs and engineers,
> In a wet land, facing rough oceans, never invaded
>   By Caesars, or a cartesian doubt, I stand,
>   Pale, half-asleep, inhaling its fresh air that smells
> So strongly of soil and grass, of toil and gender   (ll. 1–6)

What does the speaker fear? Flying, obviously. Although Auden boasted of being "the first major poet to fly the Atlantic," the early 1950s were a time when air tourism of any kind, especially between continents, was still exotic.[27] The better question might be, why *two fears*? "In Transit" was written from or about Shannon Airport in Ireland,[28] one of the westernmost points in Europe and, from 1945 until the introduction of long-range jet aircraft in the 1960s, a popular refueling point for transatlantic planes. The airport is, thus, not the speaker's destination but a way station, a "point" between two journeys. In geometry, a point has location but no dimension; it occupies no space and owns no physical values. In Auden's poem, the airport may take up room but it still exists outside of nature and human feeling: "here we are nowhere, unrelated to day or to Mother / Earth in love or in hate" (ll. 33–34). The airport has volume but no content: it is a "mere enclosure" (l. 36). Thus, while the airport might be located between the anxious moments of landing and take-off, it also represents a third fear: the nullity of a world stripped of meaningful human action and sensuous particularity.

As the poem moves between the first and second stanzas, we journey inside, from the ambivalent space of the "wet land" to an even more worrying zone characterized by a voice of anodyne professionalism and ersatz paternalism: "a professional friend is at hand / Who smiling leads us indoors; we follow in file, // Obeying that fond peremptory tone reserved for those / Nervously sick and children one cannot trust" (ll. 7–10). From "places where we have really been" (l. 13) we enter what Marc Augé calls the "non-place" of transit,[29] a space we can *go* but never exactly *are*. Among the few things we learn about the physical properties of the airport is that it is glazed with "modern panes," a glass bubble in which the passengers are "exposed" but which remains otherwise blank (ll. 12, 36). Through these modern windows, the speaker can see a limestone hill – the beloved vista that "In Praise of Limestone" (1948) limns as "the one landscape that we, the inconstant ones, / Are consistently homesick for" (ll. 1–2). But the airport makes no allowances for nostalgia. Stuck in his non-place, the speaker has "no permission to climb" to the horizon (l. 13). From the perspective of an imagined Irish lad – "Dreaming of elsewhere" – the speaker's status as a world-traveler endows him with "godlike freedom" (ll. 15–16). But despite his privilege and power, the laws of international travel mean that he is stuck inside and "Told to wait" (l. 39).

This is the nightmare version of Auden's poetry of a world beyond borders. Mendelson shows that "most of the poems Auden wrote in the early 1950s [. . .] concealed arguments about personal and impersonal speech and hoped to refute the voice without a face" (362–63).[30] This concern with the personal nature of ethical and aesthetic value, given shape in the figures of the face and voice, is a significant feature of "In Transit." The third stanza thus contrasts the realm of transit with the "dear spaces / Of our deeds and faces" (ll. 17–18). Here, the fact of a place being beloved is linked, via rhyme, to the performance of consequential and intentional action and to the irreducibility of the faces that are known to us in love and friendship. In transit, by contrast, no single person is ever encountered or described. Moreover, the speaker's alternations between singular and plural personal pronouns make even his own thoughts and actions ("I stand," "I admire") seem indistinct and general, and he eventually succumbs to mere membership in "Some class of souls" (l. 40). Of course, he still owns *that* voice – that urbane diction and "Audenesque" measure, halfway between the oracular and the introspective. But at the level of syntax and self-description, Auden's speaker draws attention to his selfhood only to bleed back into the group from which he emerged.

If this is a poem without faces, so is it also one in which nothing really happens. In another significant rhyme, we learn that "our occupation / Leaves no trace on this place or each other" (ll. 34–35), the implication being that real places bear the marks of those with human faces.[31] So what *does* happen? The travelers are "let out" and led indoors; they obey orders, wait, look around, and leave as soon as their plane has refueled. When the passive voice is not actually used, the poem's verbs still emphasize the static nature of the scene, with most of the really significant action being either hypothetical or remembered. This last fact explains why the speaker follows his remarks about deeds and faces by talking of "scenes" of memory, places that remain uniquely "unchanging" precisely because "there we changed" (ll. 17–19). The airport is "nowhere," then, because it is not loved. And it is not loved because the speaker cannot imagine anything memorable happening there.

This is a scene perhaps harder to imagine now. In the years since Auden wrote "In Transit," we have become accustomed to seeing airports get represented as places where things happen that are at once personal and emblematic of society at large.[32] Among the most popular of these is Richard Curtis' film, *Love Actually* (2003), which opens to scenes of loving reunion at Heathrow Airport that are soon joined by the voiceover of Hugh Grant's character, opining: "Whenever I get gloomy with the state of the world, I think about the arrivals gate at Heathrow Airport." Less bathetically, one might think of the many narratives, such as Terence Rattigan's screenplay for *The V.I.P.'s* (1963) or Rana Dasgupta's novel *Tokyo Cancelled* (2005), in which the experience of being detained at the airport, far from registering as a null point of bare existence, creates all sorts of opportunities for social and erotic exchange. In these later works, the airport does not become a *locus amoenus*, exactly. Still, it fulfills a similar function as that classical redoubt because the travelers' forced suspension from the ordinary routines of life – corralled as they are in the semi-autonomous space-time of the airport – breaks down social taboos and, most crucially, enables the swapping of stories. For Auden, however, the airport contains no stories precisely because it is a place where people "do not / Meet" (ll. 35–36). In this exquisite enjambment, "In Transit" signifies a gulf between people in a break between lines.

There are good reasons for this difference, starting with the airport's status in the poem as a stopover bubble: a space of transit, not arrival. Auden also writes before the popularization of air travel over the second half of the twentieth century, which, though interrupted on occasion by oil crises and terrorist events, gradually created a population of travelers many times larger and more diverse than his poem's small pocket of "aggressive creatures" (ll. 37). The advent of mass air travel also altered the spatial ecology of the airport. Shannon was in fact a pioneer in duty-free retail, its managers quickly recognizing the value to be extracted from the conjunction of a spatial loophole within customs regimes and a population at once bored and confined.[33] Over the years, the opportunities to buy and sell at airports have expanded massively, such that the passenger terminals of major airports now resemble shopping malls as much as transit centers. It has become common to refer to airports as urban settlements in their own right: "Terminal City," in Colson Whitehead's characteristic phrase.[34] Shannon was at the forefront of this history, but when Auden stopped there in March 1950,[35] the airport featured only one gift shop, about which the only thing his poem tells us is that it has no name (l. 19). Auden's airport is a zone, not a place; he does not even bother to tell us where it is. Its failure to embody the spirit of locality is epitomized by its desertion by its genius loci, the protective spirit who embodies the quintessence of each place's "special case" (l. 23).

Auden's speaker is trapped between two sorts of frontier. As a person in transit, he is technically subject to Irish jurisdiction, but never officially enters the Republic. (It seems, in fact, that Auden never properly visited Ireland.) Clingman calls the transnational the space of transition. But Auden's airport simultaneously enables foreign travel and arrests all significant momentum, for movement in a void is no sort of travel at all. This state of suspension then figures as the cause of, and symbol for, the greater cultural and experiential anonymity that so debilitates the landscape of the airport and the state of mind of those who tarry within it. Thus, in the fourth stanza, when the speaker finally reaches for the word "frontier," he employs it not to describe the demarcation between countries – he hasn't actually crossed one – but as a metaphor for the divide between a person's past and future, maturity and death, or childhood and rapt adolescence: "Somewhere, too, unique for each, his frontier dividing / Past from future, reached and crossed without warning" (ll. 25–26). These are the kinds of changes that never occur in the zone of transit. If Auden's late poems articulate a liberal and cosmopolitan ideal in which travel opens us up to real experience of real people and real places that are really different from us, then the departure lounge is the place that, precisely because it appears not to be a frontier, betrays the promise of a world beyond passports.

Yet, no matter how much his speaker insists, Auden knows that the space of transit is not just a non-place. Just as one can only really experience (rather than endure) foreign travel when protected by the safety of citizenship, so is this world beyond borders also the state-owned enterprise of the young Irish republic. Likewise, while the airport may seem like a "mere enclosure," Auden nevertheless implies, even against the surface meaning of his poem, that the world of transit is never wholly separate from that which lies outside its windows. The travelers in his airport feel like they are "nowhere" but they can still be seen: they "are exposed / As objects for speculation" (ll. 35–36). Auden here draws upon the visual, mental, and financial senses of "speculation." In their glass box, the travelers are gawped at, subject to the fantasies of others, invested with libidinal value and interest. If only in a small way, this moment in the poem implies an audience, a viewer who is not the speaker. It thus supposes an elsewhere that fixes the travelers in a somewhere. In so doing, it implies a frontier between the denationalized enclave of the airport and the "toil and gender" of Ireland itself. Although the speaker bemoans the absence of a boundary between actions and deeds, classes and faces, the poem draws our attention to the border that encircles, and enables, his despised and "godlike" freedom (l. 16).

Most importantly, this is a border the speaker will cross, albeit strangely. The space of transit is not restricted to the airport at all, for it includes the last stanza's beautiful evocation of the world seen from the air. It is tempting to suggest that the last stanza's movement from terminal to plane explains Auden's decision to change the poem's title from "Air Port" to one that more fully unifies its geographies. Whatever we think of that suggestion, it is clear that, when the travelers finally board their plane, the landscape of the poem bursts back into violent life:

> down there
> Motives and natural processes are stirred by spring
>   And wrongs and graves grow greenly; slaves in quarries
> Against their wills feel the will to live renewed by the song
>   Of a loose bird, maculate cites are spared
> Through the prayers of illiterate saints, and an ancient
>   Feud re-opens with the debacle of a river.   (ll. 42–48).

This, too, is the space of transit. The view from above – aristocratic, bland, macroscopic – here zooms in to the alliterative detail of green moss on a grave, the freedom of a bird's sluttish song. A city, imperfect and stained, is miraculously saved by a blessed illiterate. The ice on a river breaks up – this is what "debacle" means to a hydrologist – and from new life comes an old feud. Being "In Transit" does not only mean being without qualities; it means living amongst them. The travelers do not touch or change this landscape, it is true: to step onto the plane is to move only a short way, from stopover land to flyover country. But this space of transition now shares a border with love, hate, and Mother Nature. The air travelers are not simply suspended in a world without character, but able to observe the juncture between one state (state of life, nation-state) and another. In transit, history might happen at a distance, but it happens.

All this has implications, I think, for the first part of this chapter. I'm not suggesting that everyone should write about airports. Nor would I propose that the transnational is perfectly exemplified by international air travel – an experience that, for all its mass appeal in wealthy countries, remains inaccessible to billions. I hope to demonstrate, rather, that we might address the theoretical thin-ness of the transnational by attending to specific representations of particular sites of human exchange. This is not a new recommendation: some of the most influential works of transnational cultural studies have focused on the border and its interzones.[36] We still have much to gain, however, from thinking about these spaces in which peoples and cultures both cross and are trapped. Wendy Brown has recently argued that we have entered a post-Westphalian moment, just not in the sense that "nation-state sovereignty is either finished or irrelevant."[37] For Brown, writing about the paradoxical proliferation of new border fences and walls in our supposedly borderless world, "the prefix 'post' signifies a [. . .] condition of afterness in which what is past is not left behind but, on the contrary, relentlessly conditions, even dominates, a present that nevertheless also breaks in some way with this past" (21). Although it dates from the mid-century, "In Transit" registers something like this same tension between old and new, nation and globe. It is a space of transition in large and small ways. As well as marking the movements of its travelers, it registers the unfinished and uncertain political shift between territorial statehood and whatever comes next. "In Transit" documents a world in which new republics carve out temporary loopholes within dearly won sovereign space. It demonstrates how the invigorating experience of travel across borders also exposes us to being bored and being trapped. It helps us remember that living without roots is easier if you own a passport. And it reminds us that the transnational is not the zone of the borderless but, rather, the space in which frontiers are dispersed a little everywhere.

Notes

1   Douglas Mao and Rebecca L. Walkowitz, "The New Modernist Studies." *PMLA* 123/3 (2008): 738.

2   Scholarly trends often start to decay as soon as they can be identified. Still, measured in crudely quantitative terms, the "turn against" doesn't yet seem to have occurred. A search on the MLA International Bibliography turns up fifty-eight sources (books, edited collections, book chapters, essays, and doctoral dissertations) that include both the keywords "modernism*/modernist*" and "transnational*/trans-national*" in their title, abstract, or subject terms. Of these, 30 (51.72%) have been published since January 1, 2008, with 20 (34.48%) published in 2010 and 2011. The earliest title using both keywords dates from 1997; the latest publication year included in the search

was 2011. This search also excludes many titles that do not identify themselves so programmatically.

3   Nicholas Brown, *Utopian Generations: The Political Horizon of Twentieth Century Literature* (Princeton: Princeton University Press, 2005), 1.

4   Michael Rubenstein, *Public Works: Infrastructure, Irish Modernism, and the Postcolonial* (South Bend: University of Notre Dame Press, 2010), 2.

5   Laura Winkiel, *Modernism, Race, and Manifestos* (New York: Cambridge University Press, 2008), 25.

6   Rebecca L. Walkowitz, *Cosmopolitan Style: Modernism Beyond the Nation* (New York: Columbia University Press, 2006), 21.

7   This paragraph obviously begs the question of whether modernity is also "out there" and, if so, what it has to do with poems and stories and plays. This question is, I regret, outside the scope of this essay.

8   For this point, see Thomas Faist, "Diaspora and Transnationalism: What Kind of Dance Partners?" in *Diaspora and Transnationalism: Concepts, Theories, and Methods*, ed. Rainer Baubock et al. (Amsterdam: University of Amsterdam Press, 2010), 11.

9   Gayatri Chakravorty Spivak, *Death of a Discipline* (New York: Columbia University Press, 2003), 72.

10 Françoise Lionnet and Shu-mei Shih, Introduction to *Minor Transnationalism*, ed. Lionnet and Shih (Durham, NC: Duke University Press, 2005), 5

11 Micol Seigel, "Beyond Compare: Comparative Method after the Transnational Turn," *Radical History Review* 91 (Winter 2005): 63.

12 Aihwa Ong, *Flexible Citizenship: The Cultural Logics of Transnationality* (Durham, NC: Duke University Press, 1999).

13 Jahan Ramazani, *A Transnational Poetics* (Chicago: University Chicago Press, 2009), 31.

14 Michael P. Smith and Luis Guarnizo, "The Locations of Transnationalism," in *Transnationalism from Below*, ed. Smith and Guarnizo (New Brunswick, NJ: Transaction Publishers, 1998), 5. They quote Homi Bhabha, "DissemiNation: Time, Narrative, and the Margins of the Modern Nation," in *Nation and Narration*, ed. Homi Bhabha (London: Routledge, 1990), 300.

15 Susan Koshy, "The Postmodern Subaltern: Globalization Theory and the Subject of Ethnic, Area, and Postcolonial Studies," in Lionnet and Shih, eds, *Minor Transnationalism*, 110. Her particular target is Michael Hardt and Antonio Negri's *Multitude: War and Democracy in the Age of Empire* (New York: Penguin, 2004).

16 Article 10, Covenant of the League of Nations. *Yale Law School: Avalon Project: Documents in Law, History, and Diplomacy*. At http://avalon.law.yale.edu/20th_century/leagcov.asp (accessed November 15, 2012).

17 For an analysis of the League of Nations in these terms, see Susan Pedersen, "Getting Out of Iraq – in 1932: The League of Nations and the Road to Normative Statehood," *American Historical Review* 115 (2010): 975–1000.

18 Stephen Clingman, *The Grammar of Identity: Transnational Fiction and the Nature of the Boundary* (Oxford: Oxford University Press, 2009), 241.

19 W. H. Auden, "In Transit," in *Collected Poems*, ed. Edward Mendelson (London: Faber, 1991), 540. Poems from this volume hereafter cited by title, then parenthetically by line numbers.

20 Nicholas Jenkins, "Auden in America," in *The Cambridge Companion to W. H. Auden*, ed. Stan Smith (Cambridge: Cambridge University Press, 2005), 52. For Jenkins's fullest account of this argument, see his "Writing 'Without Roots': Auden, Eliot, and

Post-National Poetry," in *Something We Have That They Don't: British and American Poetics Relations Since 1925*, ed. Steve Clark and Mark Ford (Iowa City: University of Iowa Press, 2004), 75–97.

21 W. H. Auden, "Writing," in *The English Auden: Poems, Essays, and Dramatic Writings*, ed. Edward Mendelson (London: Faber, 1986), 311.

22 Auden, "Commentary" to *In Time of War* (1938), in *The English Auden*, 267. Edward Mendelson, *Later Auden* (London: Faber, 1999), 361.

23 Auden, "The Prolific and the Devourer" (1939), in *The English Auden*, 405, 404.

24 The "great Hotel" line about New York comes courtesy of a story told by Benjamin Britten. Quoted in Jenkins, "Writing 'Without Roots,'" 79.

25 For all quotations and factual assertions in this paragraph, I am indebted to Nicholas Jenkins, "The Travelling Auden," *W. H. Auden Society Website* (2003) At http://www.audensociety.org/travellingauden.html (accessed November 15, 2012).

26 For this argument, I am indebted to Edward Mendelson. See his *Later Auden*, 360ff, and "The European Auden," in *The Cambridge Companion to W. H. Auden*, ed. Stan Smith (Cambridge: Cambridge University Press, 2005), 55–67.

27 W. H. Auden, Letter to Chester Kallman. Quoted in Leo Mellor, *Reading the Ruins: Modernism, Bombsites, and British Culture* (Cambridge: Cambridge University Press, 2011), 10. Auden first flew the Atlantic in 1945, en route from America to Germany in order to work for the US Strategic Bombing Survey. He also flew from Italy to New York in September 1949, so that the journey that inspired "In Transit" was his third or fourth transatlantic flight (Jenkins, "The Travelling Auden").

28 David Pascoe has no doubts about the poem's setting: see his *Airspaces* (London: Reaktion Books, 2001), 221–222. He does not substantiate this assertion. Although "In Transit" does not name its setting, the internal evidence for Shannon is strong and mostly points away from the other likely location, Gander airport in Newfoundland, also used as a transatlantic refueling stop during the period. Auden writes of "a sunset that seems / Oddly early to me" (ll. 14–15), suggesting that he has not only traveled from west to east but has come sufficiently far to be surprised by an abrupt disruption of his diurnal rhythms. He also appears to mention, albeit negatively, Shannon's famous innovations in duty-free retail (ll. 17–19). Finally, although the description of the land outside the airport could plausibly describe Ireland or Newfoundland, Auden's reference to the Roman Empire suggests a European setting – after all, it is hardly unusual for a Canadian place to have avoided being invaded by Caesars. It also seems appropriate that the poet who called Yeats's birthplace "mad Ireland" should describe Eire as having escaped the "cartesian" skepticism of European rationalism (W. H. Auden, *Collected Poems*, ed. Edward Mendelson [London: Faber, 1991]: 248).

29 Marc Augé, *Non-Places: An Introduction to Supermodernity*, trans. John Howe (London: Verso, 2008). In his prologue, Augé narrates the experience of international air travel as the quintessence of human movement through the blandly standardized and homogenized landscape of the globalized "supermodern" (1–5). I do not have space here to critique this argument, so let me just merely register my sense that only a traveler blind to vernacular detail could mistake a metropolitan transit hub for a regional airport, let alone Charles de Gaulle for JFK.

30 Mendelson, *Later Auden*, 362–363.

31 Mendelson remarks that it "has the quietly unsettling tone of the poems in which Auden tried to reimagine a world of faces while admitting the strength of everything that wipes away individual features" (*Later Auden*, 379). He also comments upon the face/place

rhyme and connects it to a similar rhyme in "Mountains," a poem in which both the poet's personality and the peculiarities of the mountain landscape are irrepressible (378).

32 See Christopher Schaberg, *The Textual Life of Airports: Reading the Culture of Flight* (New York: Continuum Books, 2012).

33 For this history, see "History of Shannon Airport." At http://www.shannonairport.com /gns/about-us/media-centre/history-of-shannon-airport.aspx (accessed November 15, 2012).

34 Colson Whitehead, *John Henry Days* (New York: Anchor Books, 2002), 9. Quoted in Schaberg, *The Textual Life of Airports*, 109.

35 Jenkins, "The Travelling Auden."

36 See, most famously, Gloria Anzaldúa, *Borderlands/La Frontera: The New Mestiza* (San Francisco: Aunt Lute Books, 1987).

37 Wendy Brown, *Walled States, Waning Sovereignty* (New York: Zone Books, 2010), 21.

References

Anzaldúa, Gloria. (1987). *Borderlands/La Frontera: The New Mestiza*. San Francisco: Aunt Lute Books.

Auden, W. H. (1986). *The English Auden: Poems, Essays, and Dramatic Writings*, ed. Edward Mendelson. London: Faber and Faber.

Auden, W. H. (1991). *Collected Poems*, ed. Edward Mendelson. London: Faber and Faber.

Augé, Marc. (2008). *Non-Places: An Introduction to Supermodernity*, trans. John Howe. London: Verso.

Bhabha, Homi. (1990). "DissemiNation: Time, Narrative, and the Margins of the Modern Nation." In *Nation and Narration*, ed. Homi Bhabha (pp. 291–322). London: Routledge.

Brown, Nicholas. (2005). *Utopian Generations: The Political Horizon of Twentieth Century Literature*. Princeton: Princeton University Press.

Brown, Wendy. (2010). *Walled States, Waning Sovereignty*. New York: Zone Books.

Clingman, Stephen. (2009). *The Grammar of Identity: Transnational Fiction and the Nature of the Boundary*. Oxford: Oxford University Press.

Faist, Thomas. (2010). "Diaspora and Transnationalism: What Kind of Dance Partners?" In *Diaspora and Transnationalism: Concepts, Theories, and Methods* (pp. 9–34), ed. Rainer Baubock et al. Amsterdam: University of Amsterdam Press.

Jenkins, Nicholas. (2003). "The Travelling Auden," *W. H. Auden Society Website*. <http://www.audensociety.org/ travellingauden.html>. Accessed 13 Aug. 2012.

Jenkins, Nicholas. (2004). "Writing 'Without Roots': Auden, Eliot, and Post-National Poetry." In *Something We Have That They Don't: British and American Poetics Relations Since 1925* (pp. 75–97), ed. Steve Clark and Mark Ford. Iowa City: University of Iowa Press.

Jenkins, Nicholas. (2005). "Auden in America." In *The Cambridge Companion to W. H. Auden* (pp. 39–54), ed. Stan Smith. Cambridge: Cambridge University Press.

Koshy, Susan. (2005). "The Postmodern Subaltern: Globalization Theory and the Subject of Ethnic, Area, and Postcolonial Studies." In *Minor Transnationalism* (pp. 109–131), ed. Françoise Lionnet and Shu-mei Shih. Durham, N.C.: Duke University Press.

Lionnet, Françoise and Shu-mei Shih. (2005). "Introduction." In *Minor Transnationalism* (pp. 1–26), ed. Françoise Lionnet and Shu-mei Shih. Durham, N.C.: Duke University Press.

Mellor, Leo. (2011). *Reading the Ruins: Modernism, Bombsites, and British Culture.* Cambridge: Cambridge University Press.

Mendelson, Edward. (1999). *Later Auden.* London: Faber and Faber.

Mendelson, Edward. (2005). "The European Auden." In *The Cambridge Companion to W. H. Auden* (pp. 55–67), ed. Stan Smith. Cambridge: Cambridge University Press.

Ong, Aihwa. (1999). *Flexible Citizenship: The Cultural Logics of Transnationality.* Durham, NC: Duke University Press.

Pascoe, David. (2001). *Airspaces.* London: Reaktion Books.

Ramazani, Jahan. (2009). *A Transnational Poetics.* Chicago: University Chicago Press.

Rubenstein, Michael. (2010). *Public Works: Infrastructure, Irish Modernism, and the Postcolonial.* South Bend, IN: University of Notre Dame Press.

Schaberg, Christopher. (2012). *The Textual Life of Airports: Reading the Culture of Flight.* New York & London: Continuum Books.

Seigel, Micol. (2005). "Beyond Compare: Comparative Method after the Transnational Turn," *Radical History Review*, 91: 62–90.

Smith, Michael P. and Luis Guarnizo. (1998). "The Locations of Transnationalism." In *Transnationalism from Below* (pp. 3–34), ed. Michael P. Smith and Luis Guarnizo. New Brunswick, NJ: Transaction Publishers.

Spivak, Gayatri Chakravorty. (2003). *Death of a Discipline.* New York: Columbia University Press.

Walkowitz, Rebecca L. (2006). *Cosmopolitan Style: Modernism Beyond the Nation.* New York: Columbia University Press.

Whitehead, Colson. (2002). *John Henry Days.* New York: Anchor Books.

Winkiel, Laura. (2008). *Modernism, Race, and Manifestos.* New York: Cambridge University Press.

10

From Ritual to the Archaic in Modernism

Frazer, Harrison, Freud, and the Persistence of Myth

Shanyn Fiske

By now – through a robustly sustained critical history – the indispensability of myth to a competent understanding of modernism is well recognized. In an oft-cited 1923 review of Joyce's *Ulysses*, T. S. Eliot heralded the inevitability of modern literature's need for myth: "It is simply a way of controlling, of ordering, of giving a shape and a significance to the immense panorama of futility and anarchy which is contemporary history" (177). The replacement of the "narrative method" with the "mythical method" – to borrow Eliot's terminology – allowed the accommodation of art within radically shifting social, political, and cultural conditions at the turn of the twentieth century. Further decades thereafter accumulated theories of modernism's hunger not only for classical mythology but for the gloomy, ineffable worlds underlying these seemingly cohesive narratives; worlds whose rituals and sometimes gruesome and irrational practices seemed to anticipate or at least offer a prehistory for the moral confusion and anarchy of the post-WWI experience. "It seems to me that the characteristic element of modern literature, or at least of the most highly developed modern literature, is the bitter line of hostility to civilization which runs through it" (*Beyond Culture* 3), wrote Lionel Trilling, who elsewhere stated that "the ultimate questions of conscious and rational thought about the nature of man and his destiny match easily in the literary mind with the dark unconscious and with the most primitive human relationships" (*Liberal Imagination* 275). The now familiar assumption that modernist writers, artists, and thinkers continually appealed to the ahistoricity of the archaic (under)world as the foundation for historical self-situation has guided fresh inquiries in fields such as performance studies (e.g., Carrie Preston's *Modernism's Mythic Pose: Gender, Genre, Solo Performance* (2011)) and revisitations of Freud's distinct Hellenism in the construction of the modern self (e.g., Rachel Bowlby's *Freudian Mythologies: Greek Tragedy and Modern Identities* (2007)). As these and other works testify, engagement

A Handbook of Modernism Studies, First Edition. Edited by Jean-Michel Rabaté.
© 2013 John Wiley & Sons, Ltd. Published 2013 by John Wiley & Sons, Ltd.

with the archaic world – with all its mythic and ritual components – not only allowed for the existence of modernist art but has enabled critics to process modernism's relevance to contemporary intellectual history.

In the expanding theoretical territory of modernist mythologies, what is frequently overlooked is that the archaic world was formulated and made available for modernist usage by the unique conditions that grafted the development of science – particularly the fields of anthropology, sociology, and psychology – onto the well-established roots of classical scholarship, which, until the last decades of the nineteenth century, was dominated by literary/linguistic and textual study. As this chapter seeks to clarify, what we might call the modernist mythopoeic imagination[1] evolves from a nineteenth-century scientific discourse in which abundant empirical uncertainty was seamlessly compensated with literary invention. As Gillian Beer notes: "Within the mid-Victorian period there was already an active interplay between anthropological writing and literature, even while anthropology was attempting to determine its own independence and its own limits" ("Speaking" 42). Thus while the science of humanity was positing previously unformulated questions about kinship, race, and cultural evolution, answers for these questions arose – in the absence of pre-established scientific frameworks – from writers whose minds were shaped by a humanistic education in the classics and whose creative problem-solving was framed by literary narratives.

The merging of the scientific with the literary imagination was encouraged by the mid-nineteenth century turn away from the solar school of comparative mythology – associated primarily with Friedrich Max Müller – to the anthropological method developed by Edward Burnett Tylor. Whereas Müller's theory that myths were byproducts of a "disease of language" placed myth – and its archaic producers – at odds with reason,[2] the ethnographic/anthropological assumption that myths evolved from and thus could be studied as entryways into a civilization's social, economic, and psychological life not only allowed for but mandated the integration of narrative and scientific inquiry as a scholarly obligation.[3] As Trilling wrote: "Once we get beyond the notion that science is, as we used to be told it was, 'organized common sense,' and have come to understand that science is organized improbability, or organized fantasy, we begin to see that the willing suspension of disbelief is an essential part of scientific thought" (*Beyond Culture* 94). Ironically, the move toward an ideal of scientific objectivity required that nineteenth-century scientists draw from their well-stocked literary minds to capture and reoccupy the mythopoeic imaginations responsible for the generation of myth and by doing so to establish a pattern – later exploited by modernist writers – for which the imagined past could serve as a guide for the putative future.[4]

These simultaneous movements forward and back – at once toward scientific certainty and toward the narrative constructs of belief – are not only visible in but definitive of the three focal figures in this discussion. Roughly contemporaneous – James George Frazer (1854–1941), Jane Ellen Harrison (1850–1928), and Sigmund Freud (1856–1939) – they exemplify what Theodor Adorno and Max Horkheimer would later posit as the dialectical relationship between mythic thought and enlightenment.

"Just as myths already entail enlightenment, with every step enlightenment entangles itself more deeply in mythology" (8). While its direct application lay elsewhere,[5] the thesis encapsulates the twilight zone in the history of science that produced Frazer, Harrison, and – less directly but with more resounding impact – Freud. Each helped to shape the archaic world into an imaginatively seductive and practically usable space for the modernist imagination. That their ideas have been so completely absorbed into so as to be nearly effaced by modernist aesthetics both validates the importance of their influence and necessitates their historical recontextualization. What this chapter aims to do, then, is first to offer the beginnings of an excavation into some key concepts adapted by modernist writers from nineteenth-century scientific discourse and second to suggest that the close alignment between literary humanism and the inquiry into the foundations of humanity is in large part the product of the passionate imaginations of individuals whose deep skepticism about established systems of belief led them to challenge – and in some cases – reformulate disciplinary boundaries. More broadly, I suggest that what on the surface of both Victorian science and modernist poetics might be seen as a contradiction between the drive toward rationalism on the one hand and a reversion to archaic thoughts and practices on the other illuminates a fundamental dialectic in the quest for self-understanding.

James George Frazer and the Reinvention of the Sacred

In 1961, Trilling wrote of *The Golden Bough* that "perhaps no book has had so decisive an effect upon modern literature as Frazer's" (*Beyond Culture* 14). Although its first publication in 1890 made little impact on either its author's career or the general readership,[6] by the first decades of the twentieth century Frazer's magnum opus had thoroughly saturated the popular consciousness, prompting T. S. Eliot to acknowledge the work as "a step toward making the modern world possible for art" (1923, 178). The urgency with which *The Golden Bough* was embraced by modernist writers – and its pervasive effect on the age as a whole – gestures to a certain restlessness in the age. Virginia Woolf attributed this restlessness, in part, to the worn-out and ineffective consolations of Christianity and found partial remedy in the unknown and unknowable language of ancient Greek.[7] Joyce sought to exercise and exorcise it in his reconstitutions (and deconstructions) of the classic heroic quest. And Eliot froze it in verse tableaux that mythologized the modern experience.[8] In the aftermath of World War I – an event that, in the words of Paul Fussell "reversed the Idea of Progress" (8) and destabilized values that had previously seemed "permanent and reliable" (21) – *The Golden Bough* expanded – both literally in size and metaphorically in influence[9] – to fill the intellectual and psychological voids left by the Great War, the decline of systematic faith, and the revaluation of nineteenth-century ideologies and ideals. Rooted as it was in Victorian ethos and humanism, the Frazerian narrative also embodied enough of the renegade spirit to offer modernist writers a way both to formulate themselves in opposition to doctrinal Christianity in particular and to validate the spiritual impulses underlying religious institutions and structures. At a historical moment when faith was most necessary and most irreclaimable,[10] *The Golden Bough* – through its celebration of the creative energy generated and molded by the invention of religious narratives and rituals – helped to restore hope for the possibility of sacredness in the absence of declared faith and despite the recognition of the barrenness of existence.

One might, in fact, detect severe doubt as the fundamental motivation behind Frazer's expansive inquiry into the nature of human faith. In his introduction to the Oxford World's Classics edition of *The Golden Bough*, Robert Fraser makes a convincing case that the book might be read as the Victorian "counter-Bible" (xxv), with its subversion of the uniqueness and superiority of the Christian faith; a subversion systematically watered down through the book's various revisions and editions in response both to outright criticism and to Frazer's own increasing aware-ness that his contemporaries were ill-prepared to receive his bolder arguments. That Frazer – by the time of his writing of *The Golden Bough* – harbored a conscious, if at times suppressed, antipathy to Christianity is well recognized: "It is to be expected that Frazer's adduction of the many pagan analogues to the Christian mythos will be thought by Christian readers to have an adverse effect on faith, it was undoubtedly Frazer's purpose that it should" (*Beyond Culture* 17), observes Trilling.[11] The unset-tling analogies between Christianity and pagan practices are sprinkled throughout Frazer's discussion, punctuated by forceful – if anxious – declarations that explicitly challenge Christianity's singularity. A passing allusion to the similarities between the Christian celebration of the Assumption of the Blessed Virgin and the pagan worship of Diana early in Book I explodes in Book II, for instance, into the suggestion that the concept of the immaculate conception might arise from a custom of sanctified harlotry long practiced by pagan cultures. "In Cyprus it appears that before marriage all women were formerly obliged by custom to prostitute themselves to strangers at the sanctuary of the goddess, whether she went by the name of Aphrodite, Astarte, or what not," Frazer observes with characteristic insouciance of this widespread custom. "Whatever its motive, the practice was clearly regarded, not as an orgy of lust, but as a solemn religious duty performed in the service of that great Mother Goddess of Western Asia whose name varied, while her type remained constant, from place to place. Thus at Babylon every woman, whether rich or poor, had once in her life to submit to the embraces of a stranger at the temple of Mylitta, that is, of Ishtar or Astarte, and to dedicate to the goddess the wages earned by this sanctified harlotry" (312). The concept of prostitution as a mandatory measure of religious devotion might have been scandalous enough to warrant Fraser's claim that *The Golden Bough* "was the sort of book to read beneath the bedsheets by the light of a torch" (ix), but the sexual allusions are not more gripping than the heavy implications for the origins of Christ's conception. These implications become nearly unavoidable in the next chapter when Frazer reveals a customary remedy for barrenness derived from practices of sacred prostitution: "Multitudes of men and women, in fact, whose mothers had resorted to holy places in order to procure offspring, would be regarded as the actual children of the god and would be named accordingly. Hence Hannah called her infant Samuel, which means 'name of God' or 'his name is God'; and probably she sincerely believed that the child was actually begotten in her womb by the deity" (329). To any attentive reader, the realms of the sacred and profane are brought provocatively close at this juncture. As sensitive as Frazer was to the power of discursive subtlety, any further claims for the immaculate conception's origins in practices of orgiastic sexuality and psychological delusion may have seemed superfluous.

By Book II – containing the three chapters frequently cited as the most influential upon modernist aesthetics ("Adonis," "Attis," and "Osiris") – Frazer's comparative methods make it nearly impossible to read his survey of religious practices except through the lens of Christian skepticism. The concept of cyclicality as crucial to humanity's understanding of the natural world and its relation to it provides the master narrative into which these seeds of Christian doubt are sown. For Frazer, all religious rituals are rooted in man's urgent need to ensure the natural operations of birth, death, and renewal that govern life, and one of the most important of these practices is that of the periodic murder of a king who is believed to carry divine properties that influence the natural cycles of seasons, weather, crops, and human generation: "All that the people know, or rather imagine, is that somehow they themselves, their cattle, and their crops are mysteriously bound up with their divine king" (679). The ritual killing of the king and the belief in the resurrection of his spirit lead Frazer to his most forceful argument for a religious history that far precedes Christianity's institutionalization. In a climactic chapter on "The Crucifixion of Christ," a lengthy account of the pervasive practice of human sacrifice – performed in actuality by more primitive societies and in dramatic mimicry by more civilized ones – concludes in what Frazer himself admits might be read as a reductive and skeptical view of Christianity:

> A man, whom the fond imagination of his worshippers invested with the attributes of a god, gave his life for the life of the world; after infusing from his own body a fresh current of vital energy into the stagnant veins of nature, he was cut off from among the living before his failing strength should initiate a universal decay, and his place was taken by another who played, like all his predecessors, the ever-recurring drama of the divine resurrection and death . . . . A chain of causes which, because we cannot follow them, might in the loose language of daily life be called an accident, determined that the part of the dying god in this annual play should be thrust upon Jesus of Nazareth . . . . In the great army of martyrs who in many ages and in many lands, not in Asia only, have died a cruel death in the character of gods, the devout Christian will doubtless discern types and forerunners of the coming Saviour . . . . The sceptic, on the other hand, with equal confidence, will reduce Jesus of Nazareth to the level of a multitude of other victims of a barbarous superstition, and will see in him no more than a moral teacher, whom the fortunate accident of his execution invested with the crown, not merely of a martyr, but of a god. (675–676)

In an earlier iteration of this idea, Frazer couples the explanation of sacrificial kingship/godhead with accounts of scapegoating, arguing that "if it occurred to people to combine these two customs, the result would be the employment of the dying god as a scapegoat. He was killed, not originally to take away sin, but to save the divine life from the degeneracy of old age; but, since he had to be killed at any rate, people may have thought that they might as well seize the opportunity to lay upon him the burden of their sufferings and sins, in order that he might bear it away with him to the unknown world beyond the grave" (589). Frazer's conclusions must appear, to modern eyes and ears, whimsical and certainly flawed scientifically. Indeed, by the early twentieth century, both the substance of his arguments and his comparative method were harshly critiqued and summarily dismissed by more rigorous academicians. As Robert Ackerman acknowledges, "immediately after the First World War [Frazer's] kind of naïve, belletristic, philosophical evolutionism began to be replaced by the more pragmatic, functional, and professional approach associated with the names of Malinowski, Radcliffe-Brown, and Boas" (*Myth and Ritual School* 47). But the very decades that ushered Frazer off the scientific stage also welcomed him into the fold of writers and artists who were openly skeptical of Christianity and eager for new forms of self-expression. For these, the deconstruction of Christian iconography into component parts of archaic ritual and myth opened a treasure trove of new symbols and ideas – the dying god, the scapegoat, ritual sacrifice, the transfer of divine energy into different material/bodily forms – that at once released the imagination from increasingly sterile Christian narratives while preserving elements of the sacred and mystical.[12] By attributing the development of religious rituals and practices to the primacy of human invention, ingenuity, and exigency, Frazer makes a compelling case that the restoration of the sacred depends not on the reaffirmation of revealed faith but on the creative capacity of the human imagination and that art and religion – as entangled products of human ingenuity – ran on identical historical trajectories.

Frazer's own expansive imagination and diffusive rhetoric might be read as a model for the literary endeavors of the modernist age. For writers like Joyce, Woolf, Dorothy Richardson, and others whose stream-of-consciousness techniques seem to follow pathways as meandering as Frazer's inquiries, the resistance to a linear trajectory and the quest for points of connectivity – between ideas, images, people – offer vital antidotes to the pervasive modern anxiety of isolation. To this end, perhaps one of the most powerful aspects of *The Golden Bough* is its critique of Christianity's insistence on its own singularity and the systematic erasures of association necessary to achieve its linear self-narration and domination over Western consciousness. Indeed, if there is one element that does set Christianity apart from other belief systems in Frazer's text, it is this concerted effort to disguise the motley nature of its own invention. In the chapter "The Hanged God," Frazer goes beyond his typically tentative hints of similarity to address Christianity's efforts at domination:

> Taken altogether, the coincidences of the Christian with the heathen festivals are too close and too numerous to be accidental. They mark the compromise which the Church in the hour of its triumph was compelled to make with its vanquished yet still

dangerous rivals. The inflexible Protestantism of the primitive missionaries, with their fiery denunciations of heathendom, had been exchanged for the supple policy, the easy tolerance, the comprehensive charity of shrewd ecclesiastics, whose clearly perceived that if Christianity was to conquer the world it could do so only by relaxing the too rigid principles of its Founder, by widening a little the narrow gate which leads to salvation. (364)

For Frazer, almost every major aspect of Christianity – including the Christian calendar; the nature of its celebrations; its account of Christ's ascension and Satan's machinations – are born of a concerted attempt to eclipse rival religions rooted in archaic rituals and beliefs.[13] Christianity's successful account of its own uniqueness testifies to the marketing genius of churchmen, who were able – through a series of negotiations and substitutions – to disguise the patchwork nature of their creation. And while such an account might deal a considerable blow to faith, Frazer's simultaneous emphasis on the human craft without which the religion could not have achieved domination also suggests – perhaps paradoxically – that the wonder of Christianity lies not in its truth as revealed faith but in its mastery of narrative technique. Like the most successful of artworks, Christianity's impact lies at once in its keen insight into human desire (e.g., the human need to understand, explain, and control the "mysterious struggle between life and death" (675)) and in its ability to disguise its own mechanisms of operation. In Frazer's rehistoricization and exposure of these techniques, Christianity is effectively transformed from a faith bound by doctrinal limitations to an exemplum of great art/artifice.

By identifying Christianity as a manifestation of universal religious impulses and exposing the interconnectedness – across time and space – of diverse rituals and belief systems, *The Golden Bough* proffers a fluid account of religious history that allows for the sustenance of faith beyond the limitations of past belief systems. In Book I – The King of the Wood – an extensive theoretical discussion of the evolutionary relationship between magic and religion (the former argued as prior to and more primitive than the latter) climaxes in a pointed comment on the indistinct boundaries separating civilization and savagery:

It is not our business here to consider what bearing the permanent existence of such a solid layer of savagery beneath the surface of society, and unaffected by the superficial changes of religion and culture, has upon the future of humanity. The dispassionate observer, whose studies have led him to plumb its depths, can hardly regard it otherwise than as a standing menace to civilisation. We seem to move on a thin crust which may at any moment be rent by the subterranean forces slumbering below. From time to time a hollow murmur underground or a sudden spirt [*sic*] of flame into the air tells of what is going on beneath our feet.... But whether the influences that make for further progress, or those that threaten to undo what has already been accomplished, will ultimately prevail; whether the impulsive energy of the minority or the dead weight of the majority of mankind will prove the stronger force to carry us up to higher heights or to sink us into lower depths, are questions rather for the sage, the moralist, and the statesman, whose eagle vision scans the future, than for the humble student of the present and the past. (54)

Despite – or perhaps because of – Frazer' self-effacing conclusion, such meditations – which reveal a rhetorical capability rivaling that of any statesman or moralist – could not have failed to capture the emotions and imaginations of a generation reeling from the cataclysm of the First World War and facing the inevitable onslaught of the Second. Certainly, the brutalities of industrialized warfare could be perceived as manifestations of subterranean savagery persisting into what a previous generation had taken for granted as a civilized society. Indeed, Frazer's numerous accounts of violent rituals – involving rape, dismemberment, murder – offered some poets of the First World War a language for expressing otherwise inarticulable experiences and answered to what Fussell identifies as an urgent need to "make some sense of the war in relation to inherited tradition" (57).[14] War could, in poetry at least, be re-envisioned as a modern-day legacy of ritual violence. The grotesque irony of a historical construction that lends an aspect of the sacred to moral outrage nevertheless precisely captures – and allows for some melioration of – the cognitive dissonance created by the Great War and its aftermath. Indeed, as Frazer argues repeatedly in his discussion of taboos, there is little distinction – at least in the primitive mind – between awe of the sacred and that of the profane. In his seemingly tangential consideration of the nature and possibility of progress, Frazer effectively anticipated and manufactured a means for expressing post-WWI doubts about the possibility of social progress (an idea to which most of his own contemporaries still clung vehemently). Perhaps more importantly, by embedding such contemplations into a larger reflection on the nature of religion and ritual, Frazer offers a history – however scientifically flawed – for events that seemed to those living through them to lack any precedent. What is permanent, Frazer suggests, beneath the ephemera of social and religious structures, is the basic human impulse toward violence and destruction – an impulse that is, at its heart, also a desire for regeneration and renewal.

Jane Ellen Harrison's "Daimonic" Imagination

The multitude of theoretical and stylistic convergencies in the works of James George Frazer and Jane Ellen Harrison might encourage the assumption that the two contemporaries were close colleagues or collaborators. Both stood at the forefront of the late Victorian expansion of classics beyond textual studies into archaeological, anthropological, and sociological fields. Both acknowledged their intellectual debt to the groundbreaking works of E. B. Tylor, Wilhelm Mannhardt, and Andrew Lang – scholars who first emphasized the importance of examining archaic and primitive societies not only to understanding more accurately the classical civilizations so admired by the Victorians but to situating humanity within a broader historical and social context. More specifically, both argued for the centrality of ritual and religion in grasping and controlling the cyclical processes that governed natural phenomena and human life. Perhaps most strikingly, both were known and later criticized for the allusive, meandering, narratively captivating but academically irresponsible nature of a comparative method that tended to draw cause–effect conclusions from relationships of similarity.

But these resonances owe less to personal correspondence than to the intellectual environment Frazer and Harrison shared; one in which the expansion and resetting of disciplinary boundaries within academia and the blurring of cultural hierarchies beyond it invited intellectual experimentation and encouraged the renegade spirit. Despite sharing this inclination to push against already shaky confines, Frazer and Harrison arrived at and led very distinct careers whose differences testify to the diverse conditions governing men's and women's education and intellectual labor. While Frazer hardly acknowledged the contributions of his female contemporary, Harrison – adept at manipulating tongue-in-cheek deference – paid tribute to Frazer's work in her memoir *Reminiscences of a Student's Life*:

> Among my own contemporaries was J.G. Frazer, who was soon to light the dark wood of savage superstition with a gleam from *The Golden Bough*. The happy title of that book – Sir James Frazer has a veritable genius for titles – made it arrest the attention of scholars. They saw in comparative anthropology a serious subject actually capable of elucidating a Greek or Latin text. Tylor had written and spoken; Robertson Smith, exiled for heresy, had seen the Star in the East; in vain; we classical deaf-adders stopped our ears and closed our eyes; but at the mere sound of the magical words 'Golden Bough' the scales fell – we heard and understood. (83)

Done in her typical hyperbolic fashion, Harrison's homage draws rather more attention to the peculiarity of Frazer's fame (versus the less well-known but equally important contributions of Tylor or Robertson Smith) than to the value of his ideas. Indeed, in a letter to her friend Lady Mary Murray, she more openly voiced her frustration at the necessity of having to kow-tow to male scholars who may or may not be deserving of their reputations: "Mrs Frazer (your double!) has been sitting on my bed for two hours, telling me 'who not to know', i.e. who has not paid Mr Frazer 'proper attention'! This is the price I pay for a few shy radiant moments under the Golden Bough – Good conservative tho' I am I am ready for any reform in the Game Laws for the Preserving of Eminent Husbands" (Steward 37).[15] Polite irony aside, Harrison's impatience with a social and academic system that demands deference from women – whether wives or colleagues – sounds the keynote of her own scholarship, life, and intellectual influence. Having to struggle to acquire the education that came by course to middle-class men like Frazer, Harrison built a career out of challenging the limitations of an academic institution to which she also devoted the majority of her life. Indeed, while Frazer is tentative and even at times apologetic for his more heretical conclusions, Harrison reveled in her unorthodoxy and sought opportunities to unsettle the foundations of a discipline (i.e., classics) that she feared would become obsolete if not continually challenged. Armed with this conviction, she transformed what might otherwise have been a defeating educational deficit into the theoretical foundations of an intellectual approach that valued experience and what she called the "sympathetic imagination" over textbook knowledge. Her skepticism toward institutional traditions and her argument that the human imagination is the key to historical continuity are perhaps Harrison's most important legacy to modernist writers who, as Woolf stated in her essay "Mr Bennett and Mrs Brown," were seeking new ways of knowing and new paths to intimacy and spiritual connection even as the possibility for these things seemed ever receding.[16]

The quest for intellectual connection and moral sympathy – and anxiety over their achievement – is a defining aspect of Harrison's early life and the motivation behind her life's work. Precocious in her love of languages and learning at an early age, Harrison was discouraged from pursuing a formal classical education both by the limited opportunities available to girls in the mid-nineteenth century and by her awareness that women could not participate in the discursive arena where classical scholarship mattered. Even after establishing her reputation as a Hellenist (i.e., in her early work as an art historian and later as a scholar of archaic Greek ritual and religion), Harrison's descriptions of her relationship with Greek resonate with longing for an unattainable dream. Reflecting on her early love of Greek in a paper first read before the London Sociological Society and the Cambridge Branch of Suffragists in 1913, she wrote:

> [T]he dear delight of learning for learning's sake a "dead" language for sheer love of the beauty of its words and the delicacy of its syntactical relations, the joy of tracking out the secret springs of the human body irrespective of patient and doctor, the rapture of reconstructing for the first time in imagination a bit of the historical past, that was, that in a few laggard minds still obscurely is, unwomanly. Why? . . . "I do not see how Greek grammar is to help little Jane to keep house when she has a home of her own." . . . [T]he child understood [her aunt]: she was a little girl, and thereby damned to eternal domesticity; she heard the gates of the temple of Learning clang as they closed. *Alpha and Omega* (117)

Images of gates and barriers resurface in many of Harrisons' writings on her scholarly career. Sometimes these doors shut in her face, and sometimes they open up a vista of opportunity before her. But always in these images, Harrison is standing at the threshold, accepting neither exile nor invitation. On the one hand, this insistent liminality indicates the lasting impact that her lack of early Greek education had on her confidence as a scholar, contributing to her sense of alienation from the academic institutions that legitimate scholarship. On the other hand, these images also resonate with the excitement of one who has learned to appreciate liminality and no longer wants to relinquish the thrill of desire for the comfort of possession. For Harrison, the very seductiveness of learning lies on this borderline between the confidence of knowing and the rapturous fantasy that comes from not knowing. The "secret springs of the human body" are alluring because they are secret and thus subject to the will of the mind. "I am moving about in worlds half unrealised,"[17] she wrote in 1901, as she began the most productive period of her career.

At the time, she was working on her first major work – the *Prolegomena to the Study of Greek Religion* (1903), which was to formalize the guiding principles of her life into a method of scientific inquiry. Marking a transition from her initial scholarly focus on Greek art to the newly developing field of archaic religion, the *Prolegomena* set out to undermine the possibility of reaching a state of perfect knowledge and suggests that the real spiritual basis of ancient Greek society lay in mystic cults antithetical to the well-known Olympian deities. The book's meanderings through what one reviewer called "fanciful," "misleading," "specious" argumentation and its "wandering thoughts" and "merry jests"[18] all aim to expand the mind's conceptual parameters beyond the boundaries of literary and artistic evidence. The arguments it makes about Greek religion derive their force and conviction not from the plethora of texts and artwork it cites but from the surprising narrative twists and conclusions unfolding from Harrison's imagination. For example, in speaking of archaic rites addressed to "those below, who are black and bad and malignant," she wrote, "We know what was done, though we have no English word fully to express that doing. This fact may well remind us that we have lost not only the word but the thought, and must be at some pains to recover it.... I do not deny that the word can be translated if we are content to vary our rendering in each various case.... No one word carries the whole field. It is this lost union of many diverse elements that has to be recovered and is nameless" (*Prolegomena* 58–59). The idea of a nameless recovery is oxymoronic, especially in a textbook, and it calls into doubt the author's didactic purposes. But for Harrison, archaic religion was valuable precisely because its unknownness allows for a variability of truths that escape linguistic capture and permit an intimacy of knowledge formed through an individualized vocabulary. Through the irrecoverability of its language, archaic religion presented Harrison with an academic field wherein the consciousness of her inadequate linguistic training could be transformed into an epistemology of loss and a rationale for imaginative recovery. She writes in the *Prolegomena*:

> [I]t is only by a somewhat severe mental effort that we realize the fact essential to our study that *there were no gods at all*, that what we have to investigate is not so many actual facts and existences but only conceptions of the human mind, shifting and changing colour with every human mind that conceived them.... There is no greater bar to that realizing of mythology which is the first condition of its being understood, than our modern habit of clear analytic thought.... The first necessity is that by an effort of the sympathetic imagination we should think back... into the haze of... primitive [conceptions]. (164)

Resisting "clear analytic thought," Harrison's version of scientific investigation into archaic religion emphasizes the investigator's ability – through the employment of his or her "sympathetic imagination" – to reinhabit the primitive mentality of the archaic Greek and to discover the truth of archaic thought through identifying it with his or her own imaginative capacities. Furthering the argument – also emphasized by Frazer – that man created gods, Harrison's rejection of godhead in favor of the mind's creative energies aims to further weaken divisions between primitive and modern mentalities. Indeed, she argues here for the necessity of mental regression for the furthering of scientific inquiry. Founded upon this heuristic, the *Prolegomena* is as much Harrison's reflection on the personal, spiritual foundation of knowledge as on what is known about the Greeks.

Harrison's second major work – *Themis* (1912) – focused on a lengthy analysis of the intensely disputed idea of the "Eniautos-Daimon" and was no less rooted in her evolving personal philosophy of knowledge. "I am well aware that no such conjunction as Eniautos-Daimon exists in Greek," she wrote in the introduction to *Themis*:

> I did not set out to invent any such word, nor did I even foresee its employment; it simply grew on my hands from sheer necessity.... A word was wanted that should include ... the whole world-process of decay, death, and renewal. I prefer "Eniautos" to "year" because to us "year" means something definitively chronological, a precise segment as it were of spatialized time; whereas *Eniautos*, as contrasted with *etos*, means a *period* in the etymological sense, a cycle of waxing and waning. This notion is, I believe, implicitly though not always explicitly, a cardinal factor in Greek religion. Beyond it, to anything like our modern notion of non-recurrent evolution, the Greek never advanced. I prefer the word *daimon* to "spirit" because ... *daimon* has connotations unknown to our English "spirit." (xvii)

As an expression of what Harrison believed to be an "implicit factor in Greek religion," the Eniautos-Daimon – Harrison's reification of the cyclical phenomena discussed by Frazer – is a doubly displaced entity with no historical existence beyond Harrison's desire to bridge a spiritual and verbal chasm between spatially and temporally remote civilizations. Emerging out of the "necessity" of her passionate desire for intimacy with an antiquity she could not access through traditional linguistic study, his formation as an "unknown" concept of collective belief expresses the creative force of an imagination that insists on its individuality by refusing to accept available beliefs and categories. As the ultimate embodiment of Harrison's creative ethos, the Eniautos-Daimon not only represents a concept of cyclical time in the archaic Greek mind but also argues for an alternative sense of historical continuity for the modern mind – one that cannot be found in the records of history and literature but rather must be imagined in the interstices of measured time and metered translation.

In her book *Ritual, Myth, and the Modernist Text* (1998), Martha Carpentier has argued that Harrison's influence on modernist writers lay mainly in her emphasis on the primacy of matriarchal religious and social structures in archaic societies: "[Harrison's] scholarship provided a new understanding of the powerful female archetypes so prevalent in primitive Greek ritual and drama, leading to a younger generation of writers whose 'sympathies' could be 'almost entirely with Clytemnestra' – mother, lover, powerful queen, and vengeful witch" (6). While it may be that Harrison's theories offered writers of the early twentieth century new possibilities for conceiving female characters, we have thankfully progressed beyond archetypal criticism such that we can now see the broader and more diffuse influence of Harrison's work. While rooted in her experiences as a woman scholar in the late nineteenth century, her work was valuable in shaping alternate forms of knowing that allowed for a sense of historical, emotional, and moral continuity so desperately lacking after World War I. "In the vast catastrophe of the European war our emotions had to be broken up for us, and put at an angle from us, before we could allow ourselves to feel them in poetry or fiction," wrote Woolf in her 1925 essay "On Not Knowing Greek." "There is a sadness to the back of life which [the Greeks] do not attempt to mitigate. Entirely aware of their own standing in the shadow, and yet alive to every tremor and gleam of existence, there they endure, and it is to the Greeks that we turn when we are sick of the vagueness, of the confusion, of the Christianity and its consolations, of our own age" (*Common Reader* 34, 38). For Woolf, the ancient Greek world, by the war's end, represented not only a body of knowledge inaccessible to women who lacked a classical education but also a directness unsustainable in a new age that rejected emotion as sentimentality and honesty as naïveté. Harrison's argument that the human imagination was – and had always been – the surest path to knowledge and her conviction that knowledge thus gained could generate and sustain a foundation of belief established a precedent for writers like Woolf, for whom the lost world of the Greeks served as an instrument for accessing a vibrancy of existence and fullness of potential beyond the confines of their own age.

Oedipus, Freud, and the Therapist as Sooth-Sayer

That Freud took considerable liberties with antique sources is a fact no longer disputed but still, at times, grudgingly noted by classicists. As Jean-Pierre Vernant and Pierre Vidal-Naquet argue in *Myth and Tragedy in Ancient Greece* (1990), Freud's various renditions of the Oedipus drama – the foundation for his most influential theories – operate by "successive simplification and reduction – of all Greek mythology to one particular legendary schema, of the whole of tragedy to one particular play, of this one play to one particular aspect of the story and of this aspect to a dream" (93). The historically unlocated ("Why was tragedy born in the Greek world at the turn of the fifth and sixth centuries?" (Vernant 90)) and overly focused ("It would . . . be mistaken to concentrate exclusively upon the psychological element" (Vernant 92)) nature of Freud's approach to classical material understandably raises the hackles of classicists who, since the early twentieth century, have been struggling against the threat of becoming obsolete and striving to maintain respect for an academically rigorous discipline in a modern world increasingly prone to question the relevance of dead languages and cultures. The anxiety over Freud's threat to this ongoing endeavor is evident in Vernant's and Vidal-Naquet's argument that Freud is not seeking in antiquity "the meaning sought by the Greek scholar or historian, the meaning present within the work, contained in its structures, a meaning that must be painstakingly reconstructed through a study at every level of the message that a legendary tale or a tragic fiction constitutes" (86). It is true that Freud was neither a textual scholar nor a classicist, but it was certainly in taking such imaginative liberties with classical material that his interpretations of Greek myth and tragedy were able to enter common parlance and the popular consciousness, extending a broader influence and sustaining a shelf life longer than the theory of any classical scholar of Freud's time. Like Harrison's and Frazer's works, Freud's ideas are not used now to further our understanding of antiquity, but – as I hope this chapter has already demonstrated – it was precisely these writers' abilities to release the classical world from tight disciplinary and cultural constraints that allowed their accounts to take hold of the literary and artistic imagination such that while the cataclysm of WWI undermined the fight to keep alive traditional classical scholarship, their ideas – however historically inaccurate – acquired significant cultural capital.[19] In Freud's case, disregard for historical parameters and contingencies was fundamental. In his presentation of the Oedipus narrative in particular, Greek myth not only articulated a prehistory of human desire that could lend narrative cohesion to the obscure regions of the subconscious but offered a framework upon which to build the aesthetics of the new science of psychoanalysis.

It is perhaps ironic that a science and practice so heavily dependent upon the patient's suspension of disbelief in the narratives proffered by the therapist should have evolved out of deep religious doubt and skepticism toward any fixed system of belief. "Every scientific investigation of religion has unbelief as its presupposition" (Gay xix), Freud wrote to Charles Singer, a noted historian of science. Indeed, Freud's "unbelief," writes his biographer Peter Gay, "was more than mere indifference; it was an active, persistent, bellicose aversion to any religious belief or ritual whatever and the precondition for his investigation" (xix). Insofar as religious skepticism lay at the heart of Freud's quest for exposing hidden truths on the level of the individual and on the level of humanity as a whole, it is revealing of Freud's self-fashioning as a psychoanalyst, of his approach to the Oedipus myth, and of the strength of his legacy to examine his self-incarnation in the figure of Teiresius who, in Sophocles's *Oedipus Rex*, acts as the supreme skeptic; the one character who refuses to credit the notion of the self as a singular, coherent entity; who believes, on the contrary, that such an illusion is merely a strategy of self-deception for the purposes of self-preservation; who admits to the ambiguity of language, to the duality of meaning, to the possibility of holding contradictions within a single lens. "How dreadful knowledge of the truth can be when there's no help in truth!" (Sophocles 16) Teiresius laments, entering the scene upon Oedipus's request. He refers, of course, both to himself, the purveyor of incredible truths, and to Oedipus, whose conceit in his self-transparency blinds him to what he must subconsciously know but vigorously denies about himself (as evidenced in the numerous double-entendres that only Teiresius (and the audience) can clearly interpret). Teiresius's insight into the deceptive qualities of language and his skepticism toward the cohesion of the ego embody what Vernant and Vidal-Naquet call the "tragic consciousness" – that awareness in the dramatic spectator (and in some cases within the drama's characters themselves) that the problems posed in the narrative – as in life – have no definitive answer despite the urgent need to seek resolution, and that this failure of finality is owed largely to the inescapable ambiguity of human language and thought:

> [T]he tragic message, when understood, is precisely that there are zones of opacity and incommunicability in the words that men exchange. Even as he sees the protagonists clinging exclusively to one meaning and, thus blinded, tearing themselves apart or destroying themselves, the spectator must understand that there are really two or more possible meanings. The language becomes transparent and the tragic message gets across to him only provided he makes the discovery that words, values, men themselves, are ambiguous, that the universe is one of conflict, only if he relinquishes his earlier convictions, accepts a problematic vision of the world and, through the dramatic spectacle, himself acquires a tragic consciousness. (43)

The indefiniteness of language and self is precisely something that Oedipus cannot accept until it is too late. Teiresius, on the other hand, in his acquiescence to a fundamental uncertainty, is able to access the truth through the strength of his unbelief and his insistence on the necessity of accepting a vision of the world and of the self as irreparably fragmented. The Teiresian vision of wholeness as created through tension and struggle rather than through repose – of the necessity of resigning oneself to internal conflict – is one shared by modernist writers and artists, who hungered after a theoretical foundation upon which to build their own, potentially devastating visions of an irrecoverably fractured world.

As Bradley Buchanan has discussed in *Oedipus Against Freud* (2010), Freud was certainly not the first to model a theory of human knowledge and/or social structure upon the Oedipus myth. Throughout the latter part of the nineteenth century, Buchanan notes, "philosophers, anthropologists, and novelists had put Oedipus at the centre of humanist discourse, and saw him both as a symbol of human self-awareness and as a symptom of the flaws and limits in the exercise of rationality" (4). For Freud, Oedipus plays, of course, a myriad of roles, evolving as Freud's theory evolves: he is Freud himself, when Freud first discovers the Oedipus connection in his self-analysis; he is everyman, who must pass through the stages of the Oedipus Complex on the way to sexual maturation; and, by *Totem and Taboo* (1913), he is representative of mankind as a whole on a socio-anthropological scale. But, interestingly, it is as much Teiresius as Oedipus who seems to enchant Freud, offering the father of psychoanalysis a model upon which to build the role of the therapist and, through him, the therapy. The famous analysis of "Little Hans" offers multiple testimonials to Freud's implicit identification with and ventriloquization of the Teiresian prophet. As Freud recounts of one conversation with his five-year-old patient: "Long before he was in the world, I went on, I had known that a little Hans would come who would be so fond of his mother that he would be bound to feel afraid of his father because of it; and I had told his father this" (*Analysis of a Phobia* 42). Readers of this case analysis might now – in the age of phobias about implanted false memories – understandably shudder at the ways that Freud manipulates his young patient's words, reading into the child's accounts of his dreams and fears a theoretically over-determined narrative. The predetermined nature of his analysis even announces itself with declarations such as: "From that time forward he [i.e. Hans] carried out a programme which I was able to announce to his father in advance" (43). The use of the word "programme" here is suggestive, for the account reads as the rough draft of a script in which Freud is trying to discover his own role in the drama he is creating vis-à-vis the patient that he dubs "the little Oedipus" (97). The story of Little Hans is recounted no fewer than three times (first as a case history, then summarized, then resummarized). With each iteration, Freud's language and his narrative further obscure the voice of his patient as he (the therapist) settles into the role of Teiresian soothsayer, guiding his patient (or in this case, the patient's father as well) into the recognition of a deeply divided self. Even Freud's language, toward the conclusion of his account, takes on a mystical quality as the conduct of therapy and the orchestration of a drama seem to become one and the same: " In an analysis . . . a thing which has not been understood inevitably reappears; like an unlaid ghost, it cannot rest until the mystery has been solved and the spell broken" (122). The *Oedipus Rex*, therefore, seems to offer Freud – at least by the recording of the Hans case in 1909 – not only a source for the theory of child and human development but a model for the therapist and, ultimately, a framework for the drama of psychoanalysis.

There is a moment in Virginia Woolf's novel *Between the Acts* (1941) when the playwright character, Miss La Trobe, reflects on the thin boundaries between reality and fiction; between the serious negotiations of life and the manipulations of performance: "She wanted to expose them, as it were, to douche them with present-time reality . . . . O to write a play without an audience – *the* play" (161). It could be argued that for scientists of the late nineteenth century and artists of the early twentieth, the divisions between reality and play, were, in fact, seductively fragile. Freud himself was conscious of and entranced by the parallels between the process of discovering the buried truths of human consciousness and the action of the Oedipus play. "The action of the play," he writes in *The Interpretation of Dreams* (1900), "is nothing other than the process of revealing, with cunning delays and ever-mounting excitement – a process that can be likened to the work of a psycho-analysis – that Oedipus himself is the murderer of Laius, but further that he is the son of the murdered man and of Jocasta" (295). In his first full articulation of the Oedipus theory, Freud's excitement about the play's aesthetic possibilities for the development of his own scientific program is obvious. And it may, indeed, have been this vision of therapy as a performative narrative of suspense that allowed for the playfulness (in the sense both of frivolity and of dramatization) in his adoption of the Sophoclean tragedy into later accounts both of individual therapies (as in the Little Hans case) and in broader theories of humanity (as in *Totem and Taboo*). It could be argued that this element of play characterized the works of all three writers discussed in this chapter. Writing at a moment when the rupture of old systems and institutions invited a spirit of experimentation and license, Frazer, Harrison, and

Freud ventured – from the depths of their own doubt – to invent new mythologies, anticipating their need in a coming age that would crave new rituals and structures of belief.

Notes

1   "Mythopoeic" literally means "myth-making." The term "mythopoeic imagination" was introduced into Victorian scientific/historical discourse by George Grote in his *History of Greece* (12 vols, London, 1846–1856), which sketched out the idea of a "mythopoeic age," of which *The Odyssey* and *The Iliad* are ideal representations. For a discussion of the mythopoeic imagination as it relates to modernist art, see Bell (1997).

2   See Steven Connor's article "The Birth of Humility."

3   Various scholars have discussed the development of these fields from and into one another. The most comprehensive is George Stocking's *Victorian Anthropology* (New York: Free Press, 1987).

4   For more on this idea of myth, see Bell's introduction (1998).

5   Namely in a more general discussion of the relationship between myth and enlightenment in Western philosophical tradition and the impact of these ideas on political reality.

6   See Hyman's *The Tangled Bank*, 198.

7   See Woolf's essay "On Not Knowing Greek" in *The Common Reader*.

8   In his notes to "The Waste Land," Eliot makes special note of his debt to Frazer: "To another work of anthropology I am indebted in general, one which has influenced our generation profoundly; I mean *The Golden Bough*; I have used especially the two volumes Adonis, Attis, Osiris" (80).

9   The 1890 edition of *The Golden Bough* consisted of two volumes. By 1936, the book had grown to twelve volumes plus a supplement.

10   See Fussell, 11.

11   See Trilling (1965) and Fraser (1990) for more on Frazer's vexed relationship with Christianity.

12   See John Vickery's article and book for a thorough discussion of how these various symbols were utilized by modernist poets like Yeats, Lawrence, and Sitwell.

13   See p. 362 in particular for references to the Christian calendar.

14   See Fussell's discussion of poets like David Jones in his chapter on "Myth, Ritual, and Romance," particularly 152ff.

15   Lady Mary Henrietta Howard was the wife of Gilbert Murray, professor of Greek at Oxford University, with whom Harrison had a close friendship and avid correspondence throughout the whole of her academic career.

16   "Mr Bennett and Mrs Brown" was first read before the Cambridge Society of Heretics in 1924. This was the society at whose founding ceremony in 1909 Jane Harrison gave the inaugural speech.

17   Jane Harrison to Gilbert G. Murray, November 24, 1901, Jane Harrison Archives, Box 1, Newnham College, Cambridge.

18   W. H. D. Rouse, "Review of Jane Harrison's Prolegomena to the Study of Greek Religion," *Classical Review* 18 (1904): 465–470.

19   The relationship between Freud and Frazer was fraught. While Freud borrowed a considerable amount from Frazer's work, Frazer was famously reluctant to read Freud's writing. Harrison, however, did read Freud, and her *Epilegomena to the Study of Greek Religion* (1921) was written in light of these readings. Hope Mirrlees, Harrison's close companion in the last part of her life, after she left Cambridge and went to live in Paris, wrote a long poem "Paris" (published as a chapbook in 1920 by Woolf's Hogarth Press) in which Freud is evoked as one of the specters in a postwar, mythological landscape resembling Eliot's Waste Land.

References

Ackerman, Robert. (1991). *The Myth and Ritual School: J.G. Frazer and the Cambridge Ritualists*. New York: Garland.

Adorno, Theodor and Max Horkheimer. (2002). *Dialectic of Enlightenment: Philosophical Fragments*. Stanford: Stanford University Press.

Beer, Gillian. (1990). "Speaking for the Others: Relativism and Authority in Victorian Anthropological Literature." In *Sir James Frazer and the Literary Imagination: Essays in Affinity and Influence*, ed. Robert Fraser (pp. 38–60). London: Macmillan.

Bell, Michael. (1997). *Literature, Modernism and Myth: Belief and Responsibility in the twentieth century*. Cambridge: Cambridge University Press.

Bowlby, Rachel. (2007). *Freudian Mythologies: Greek Tragedy and Modern Identity*. Oxford: Oxford University Press.

Buchanan, Bradley. (2010). *Oedipus Against Freud: Myth and the End(s) of Humanism in Twentieth-Century British Literature*. London: University of Toronto Press.

Carpentier, Martha. (1998). *Ritual, Myth and the Modernist Text: The Influence of Jane Ellen Harrison on Joyce, Eliot, and Woolf*. Amsterdam: Gordon and Breach.

Connor, Steven. (1990). "The Birth of Humility: Frazer and Victorian Mythography." In *Sir James Frazer and the Literary Imagination: Essays in Affinity and Influence*, ed. Robert Fraser (pp. 61–80). London: Macmillan.

Eliot, T. S. (1963). *Collected Poems 1909–1962*. Boston, MA: Faber and Faber.

Eliot, T. S. (1975). "Ulysses, Order, and Myth." In *Selected Prose of T.S. Eliot*, ed. Frank Kermode. Orlando, FL: Harcourt.

Fraser, Robert, ed. (1990). *Sir James Frazer and the Literary Imagination: Essays in Affinity and Influence*. London: Macmillan.

Freud, Sigmund. (1918). *Totem and Taboo: Resemblances Between the Psychic Lives of Savages and Neurotics*. New York: Vintage.

Freud, Sigmund. (1965). *The Interpretation of Dreams*, ed. and trans. James Strachey. New York: Avon.

Freud, Sigmund. (1976). *Analysis of a Phobia in a Five-Year-Old Boy*. In *The Standard Edition of the Complete Psychological Works of Sigmund Freud*, Vol. X, ed. James Strachey. London: Hogarth Press.

Fussell, Paul. (1975). *The Great War and Modern Memory*. New York: Oxford University Press.

Gay, Peter, ed. (1989). *The Freud Reader*. New York: W. W. Norton.

Harrison, Jane Ellen. (1915). *Alpha and Omega*. London: Sidgwick & Jackson.

Harrison, Jane Ellen. (1925). *Reminiscences of a Student's Life*. London: Hogarth Press.

Harrison, Jane Ellen. (1955). *Prolegomena to the Study of Greek Religion*. New York: Meridian.

Harrison, Jane Ellen. (1962). *Themis: A Study of the Social Origins of Greek Religion.* New York: University Books.

Hyman, Stanley Edgar. (1962). *The Tangled Bank: Darwin, Marx, Frazer and Freud as Imaginative Writers.* New York: Athenaeum.

Mirrlees, Hope. (1919). *Paris, a poem.* London, Hogarth Press.

Preston, Carrie J. (2011). *Modernism's Mythic Pose: Gender, Genre, Solo Performance.* Oxford: Oxford University Press.

Sophocles. (1949). *The Oedipus Cycle, trans.* Dudley Fitts and Robert Fitzgerald. New York: Harvest.

Trilling, Lionel. (1950). "The Meaning of a Literary Idea." In *The Liberal Imagination: Essays on Literature and Society.* New York: Charles Scribner's Sons.

Trilling, Lionel. (1965). *Beyond Culture: Essays on Literature and Learning.* New York: Viking.

Vernant, Jean-Pierre and Pierre Vidal-Naquet. (1990). *Myth and Tragedy in Ancient Greece.* New York: Zone Books.

Vickery, John B. (1957). "The Golden Bough and Modern Poetry." *Journal of Aesthetics and Art Criticism* 15.3 (March): 271–288.

Vickery, John B. (1976). *The Literary Impact of the Golden Bough.* Princeton, NJ: Princeton University Press.

Woolf, Virginia. (1992). *Between the Acts.* Oxford: Oxford University Press.

Woolf, Virginia. (1924). *Mr. Bennett and Mrs. Brown.* London: Hogarth Press.

Woolf, Virginia. (1925). "On Not Knowing Greek." In *The Common Reader,* ed. Andrew McNeillie. New York: Harcourt, Brace.

Further Reading

Ackerman, Robert. (1980). *The Cambridge Group and the Origins of Myth Criticism.* Ann Arbor: UMI.

Byatt, A. S. (1990). "'The Omnipotence of Thought': Frazer, Freud and Post-Modernist Fiction." In *Sir James Frazer and the Literary Imagination: Essays in Affinity and Influence,* ed. Robert Fraser (pp. 270–308). London: Macmillan.

Stewart, Jessie. (1959). *Jane Ellen Harrison: A Portrait in Letters.* London: Merlin Press.

11

Modernism, Orientalism, and East Asia

Christopher Bush

In a letter written from Henan province, China, in January of 1913, French poet and polymath Victor Segalen explained to Jules de Gaultier the true importance of the Chinese writings that featured so prominently in his recently published prose poem collection *Stèles*: "It is [. . .] neither the spirit nor the letter, but simply the form 'steles' that I have borrowed. I deliberately seek in China not ideas, not subjects, but forms" (*Correspondance* II, 69). Segalen here seems to present as an explicit point of pride precisely what many later critics of modernist Orientalism would hold against it, namely an exoticizing formalism that cared little and knew even less about the cultures from which it extracted its aesthetic resources. As Segalen's tone suggests, the distance between Asia and its modernist refunctionalizations testified to a deliberate program of cross-cultural *non*-interpretation of which such later East Asian-inspired *écritures* as Tel Quel Maoism and Roland Barthes's *Empire of Signs* might be seen as the theoretically self-conscious descendents.

Yet the modernist archive also gives evidence of a very different relationship between European modernism and East Asia. For example, the modernist haiku (certainly the most widespread East Asian form in Euro-American modernist literature) has never been accused of being a reliable barometer of East Asian realities. Yet if we turn to one of the texts central to the international dissemination of the form, Paul-Louis Couchoud's "Lyrical Epigrams of Japan" (originally published in French 1906), we find something perhaps unexpected. In the prefatory essay to the collection in which "Epigrams" was reprinted in expanded form, *Sages et poètes d'Asie* (1916), we find not nostalgia for Old Japan, but rather the image of a contemporary, and dramatically transformative, world-historical meeting of East and West:

To confront the two halves of humanity will be the great work of this century. We are approaching an unprecedented age [. . .] For the first time, from one end of the

---

earth to the other, man is aware of man [. . .] a common life in which all of humanity participates is beginning to appear. Between the peoples who invented the ideograms of Asia and those who adopted the vocal roots of Europe, there used to be a terrifying distance and now there is a proximity no less terrifying. Mechanical inventions have accomplished this automatically: the locomotive, the steamship, the automobile, the telegraph, the daily paper, and the cinema. Today, within twenty-four hours the same news is known, at least virtually, by all peoples. This is the great new fact that will determine our future. It escapes us precisely because of its enormity. (12)

Far from contemplating Japan as a culturally unique refuge from modernization, Couchoud sees in it precisely the harbinger of a techno-mediatically interconnected global future. Couchoud, whose work was an important source for Anglo-American Imagism and some Latin American poets as well as for the French *mouvement haïkaï* of the 'teens and 'twenties, not only demonstrates an acute awareness of Japanese modernization, he correspondingly valorizes Western modernist uses of the haiku, adding to his revised version of his essay extravagant praise for Julien Vocance's "One Hundred Visions of War" (1916), an avant-garde sequence of often shocking images of trench warfare (Hokenson).

Self-satisfied formalism or historically sensitive reference? Clearly a false choice, and yet the scholarly study of literary modernism has not always dealt with this contrast in particularly nuanced or productive ways. To be fair, much of what we might today call modernist Orientalism either explicitly disavowed any relationship to a contemporaneous, or even a real East, or did such a poor job of understanding it that it might as well have. This salient disconnect has yielded two distinct modes of perpetuating the idea that East Asia was unimportant to modernism. On the one hand, there is what might be called the conservative or traditionalist view, according to which Asia merely provided an exotic supplement, a set of forms to be reshaped by the hand of some modernist master into something transcendent of its origins. According to this view, to investigate, for example, the accuracy of Pound's knowledge of Chinese, or to think there might be interpretive or historical significance to its Asian origins, is not only small-minded but naïve, demonstrating a failure to grasp the very idea of "form."

On the other hand, there is the tradition of Orientalism critique largely sparked by Edward Said's *Orientalism* (1978) and subsequently fueled by the rise of postcolonial literary studies. By tending to reduce Western representations of Asia to a history of errors and illusions, a history for which no real Asia could possibly have been important, the critique of Orientalism has too often reproduced one of the most fundamental limitations of Orientalist discourse itself. Moreover, East Asia fits very poorly into the literary-critical categories developed by postcolonial theory, if only because East Asia was never colonized. (This is not to say that the broader history of global imperialism is not essential to understanding the history and culture of modern East Asia. One might here cite coastal "semi-colonialism" in China, the proximity of French Indochina, and Japan's own history of colonialism, to begin with the most obvious.) For example, while Western languages were used in East

Asia and did influence local languages in various ways (see, for example, Saussy, Shen, Liu, and Tsu), nothing comparable to *Francophonie* or Indian English, much less the Hispanosphere, ever emerged. Similarly, while there is no shortage of anti-Asian prejudice to be found within the modernist corpus, alongside this one finds an intense Japanophilia and Sinophilia qualitatively different from primitivism or antiquarianist Orientalism. Whereas these latter were essentially colonial projects oriented toward lost or fading glories, Sinophilia and Japonophilia often imagined futures defined by variations of a "fusion of East and West," to cite Ernest Fenollosa's famous formulation. East Asia was thus tied in essential ways to the question of modernity itself, figuring less the other of modernity than another modernity (and thus, perhaps, another modernism). To distinguish this Orientalist modernism from other treatments of cultural otherness in this way is not simply to say that Western modernists liked Asian cultures more than, say, Persian or Native American cultures, but that this liking had different meanings, encouraged different representational logics, and functioned to express or address different dimensions of the fundamental problematics of modern culture.

The ideologically opposed but often mutually reinforcing critical tendencies of traditionalism and Orientalism critique live on in contemporary scholarship. Over the past ten to twenty years, however, numerous critics have reframed the issue of Asia's importance for modernism and thus for modernist studies (see, for example, Gillies et al.). This reorientation results from the convergence of a number of different changes in the field of modernist studies and in literary studies more generally: an expansion of the corpus considered "modernist" to include a much broader range of social, ethnic, and sexual identities, including writers working outside the traditional US and Western European metropoles; a corresponding expansion of the archive of relevant historical and critical material used to study literary modernism; and not least, a broadening of the range of critical methodologies used to study the period.

And yet precisely because of its often stridently formalist stances, modernist Orientalism remains in many respects a difficult object for these generally *historicizing* trends. A full account of the relationship between East Asia and modernism must therefore acknowledge both the formal-aesthetic and the geopolitical-historical dimensions of that relationship. In this sense, the interpretive challenges posed by modernist Orientalism are closely connected to those confronted by Fredric Jameson in his work on modernism and geopolitics, namely the project of understanding "modernist 'style' [... as] the marker and the substitute [...] of the unrepresentable totality" of the modern capitalist world-system ("Modernism and Imperialism" 58). I would correspondingly argue that the role of East Asia in the history of modernist aesthetic form evinces neither a transcendence of history nor a refusal of reference, but instead a kind of cultural solution to the questions raised by possible futures in which the West and the Rest might increasingly find themselves in terrifying proximity. In other words, Orientalist modernism should be understood not primarily as a more or less flawed representation of "the Orient," but as a geopolitically specific iteration of aesthetic *modernism*'s problematic relationship to the history of *modernity*. Here "modernity" must emphatically be understood not as a primarily Euro-American event that radiates outward to various "peripheries," but rather as inherently global.

In what follows I make two distinct but related claims. First, that East Asia was widespread in Euro-American modernism and therefore its study should not be dismissed to the status of a subfield such as "East/West modernism," "modernist Orientalism," "other modernisms," or the like. We need only think of the aesthetic and/or personal importance of East Asia to the work of (in no particular order) Ezra Pound, William Butler Yeats, Virginia Woolf, Bertolt Brecht, Alfred Döblin, Hermann Hesse, André Malraux, Paul Claudel, Frank Lloyd Wright, Williams Carlos Williams, Marianne Moore . . . and this is before we get to Franz Kafka's "Chinese" parables, Bertrand Russell's visit to China, Du Bois's passionate essays on Asian politics, Sergei Eisenstein's ideographs, Martin Heidegger's decades-long fascination with East Asian philosophy, the haiku of Paul Eluard and Richard Wright in literature, or of Igor Stravinsky in music, or the passing but pointed references to Japanese militarism in the novels of Marcel Proust and James Joyce. Long before Pearl Harbor, or even Pearl Buck, then, Western artists and writers were well aware of East Asia: not just its "timeless" cultural traditions, but also its current events.

The second claim requires more than a preponderance of evidence, namely that modernist Orientalism represents a very particular form of Western self-representation. The turn to East Asia in a sense constitutes a kind of elaborate self-portrait, not because it is an act of projective narcissism (although that is certainly part of it!), but rather because East Asia provided a privileged site for witnessing the increasingly global character of a modernity of which the West was itself a part. Just as some modernists' self-professed formalism should not be taken at face value (but rather itself recognized as historical), so too modernism's overt obsession with the specificity, even uniqueness of Asian cultures should be understood less as a fact and more as a symptom or side effect of the structure of a relationship, the relationship of one site of modernity to another (and sometimes of one modernism to another). The Asia of Euro-American modernism constitutes a displaced and refracted self-portrait, then, not in the sense that it is about the West *rather than* the East, but in the sense that East and West are part of the same world, part of the same system, even. To paraphrase Immanuel Wallerstein: discussing different positions in a world-system in relation to one another is not exactly an act of comparison in the sense that one does not understand the relationship between the heart, lungs, and brain by *comparing* them.

In what follows, I will first provide an overview of the inter-arts context within which literary modernism's relationship to East Asia emerged, before returning to the conceptual consequences East Asian modernity had for the Western historical imagination. The following section then briefly describes East Asian modernisms and their significance in relation to a general study of modernism, while my conclusion proposes possible directions for future research.

Modernist Orientalisms

The importance of the visual arts for even the specifically *literary* impact of East Asia on Euro-American modernism is striking. This is surely in part due to the relative lateness of East Asian literature's broader availability in the West. Just as significant is the fact that images often *seem* to facilitate cross-cultural understanding, even functioning as pseudo-universals. From the age of Impressionism to contemporary manga, "Asian aesthetics" have been claimed to be more readily accessible through art than through literature. Thus even when there are literary influences, it is often precisely in modes that appeal to the supposed universality of the visual, the most obvious instances here being the haiku and the ideogram.

The most well-known case of an East Asian art form shaping the development of a modern Western one is no doubt late-nineteenth-century *japonisme*, which many art historians have seen as playing such an important role in Impressionist and Post-Impressionist art that its continued influence should be seen in modernist-era painting and indeed beyond (Wichman). In the *manga* (sketchbooks) and color woodblock prints of such artists as Katsushika Hokusai and Utagawa Hiroshige, Western artists discovered new styles and techniques as well as dramatic affirmations of existing tendencies we today think of as contributing to the foundations of modern painting. Among these, the most important are a flattening of the picture plane; strong graphic lines in conjunction with patterns and blocks of color, rather than chiaroscuro and modeling; greater freedom in the basic parameters of composition (horizon lines moving up and down, vertically oriented compositions, asymmetry, elements breaking the frame of the picture); and not least the easily misunderstood "simplicity" of Japanese art, which to most Western observers bordered on the decorative – a useful discovery at a time when painters were testing the waters of abstraction (at least according to common understandings of the history of modern art). Although sometimes described as a "fad" or a "wave," the association of pictorial innovation with Japan lasted for decades. Before Claude Monet's "Impression, soleil levant" (1872) led to the term "Impressionism," the painters working around Edouard Manet were sometimes referred to as *les Japonais* and Japanese influences continued to feature prominently through the work of James Abbott McNeill Whistler, most of the "Post-Impressionists" (including in Van Gogh, who famously writes that he shaved his head in imitation of a Japanese monk in 1888), the Viennese Secession, certain aspects of Expressionism (Carl Einstein published a book on Japanese woodblock prints in 1922), and so on.

The connections of this reception to literature are numerous. Earl Miner has written of literary *japonisme* in relation to a "pan-Impressionism" that extended beyond the visual arts by taking the primacy of the sensory impression as the unifying element of the arts. Woodblock prints were so widely exhibited, collected, and written about that references to them can be found throughout the lives of most of the major modernists, from such early "moderns" as Baudelaire, Zola, and Mallarmé, to Valéry, Claudel, Proust, Pound and more or less everyone associated with Imagism, as well as Wallace Stevens, among others. Although East Asian literature only became widely known in translation early in the twentieth century, the late-nineteenth-century influx of East Asian visual arts would over-determine this later reception (see Couchoud and almost any of the imagists' critical writings).

I emphasize the Impressionist origins of certain aspects of modernist Orientalism because they demonstrate how early on East Asian aesthetic influence began to be separated from Asia as a subject matter or theme. Indeed, the transfer to literature of lessons taken from Japanese art was not so much thematic as formal. Just as Impressionist painters show the depth of their relationship to Japanese art in the regular emulation of formal principles rather than in the occasional choice of Japanese subjects, similarly most poets inspired by the Japanese visual arts chose not to portray Japanese subjects but rather to emulate forms and sensibilities.

Much less work has been done – and so more work remains to be done – on the reception and influence of Chinese art. As with Japanese art, it is generally less a question of borrowed themes than of formal influences and inspirations. In the case of China, however, these are considerably harder to track, if only because the history of the Western relationship to Chinese art is longer and more multifaceted (Sullivan), further complicated by the mediations of varying conceptions of "Chinese philosophy." Several recent studies (Qian; Arrowsmith) have studied the impact of Chinese art on modernist writers who had direct access to the collections and exhibitions of the British Museum. In that context, scholars associated with the museum – above all Laurence Binyon and Arthur Waley – played an important mediating role, just as Ernest Fenollosa's writings and collections did for Americans (Chisolm). Beyond the world of Anglo-American "high modernism" or even the pages of *Blast*, one can find exhibition reviews in the work of figures more closely identified with the avant-garde, including Guillaume Apollinaire and Walter Benjamin (Bush). While scholarship on modern East Asian art history generally takes into account that art's relationship to Western artists and ideas (see, for example, Danzker et al.; Rimer; Tang *Origins*; Volk; Weisenfeld), histories of modern Western art (except those specifically focused on Asian American art) seldom explore that relationship, beyond the requisite nod to *japonisme*.

In addition to painting and prints, the full version of this story would have to acknowledge the vast range of decorative arts, crafts, and *bibelots* (fans, screens, kimonos, vases, lacquer ware) that had long formed a part of Western interiors, but took a qualitative leap in the latter half of the nineteenth century. The omnipresence of these objects constitutes a significant form of what anthropologist Arjun Appadurai has called low-frequency cultural circulation, barely perceived by those listening in only on the higher frequencies at which ideas and artworks circulate. (Pound's *Cathay* travels at a high frequency, futons at a low one.) These objects can be found throughout modernist literature, with significance ranging from that of aesthetic, even spiritual models (the Chinese vases in Mallarmé's "Las de l'amer repos" or T. S. Eliot's *Four Quartets*) to the bric-a-brac cluttering Odette's rooms in "Swann in Love." The very banality of such objects reveals the breadth and the depth of "East/West" contact.

All this art, craft, and commodity was not just a source of information about its immediate subject matter (Chinese mountains or the pleasure quarters of Yoshiwara), but was understood as embodying, in its aesthetic form, another worldview. That worldview and the world from which it was born were proving to be not so remote as once believed and were indeed becoming part of the texture of everyday life in "the West." This is important not just in terms of the range of Asian "influence" in narrowly cultural or literary senses, but also points to the undeniable contemporaneity of East Asia: Japanese wares could flood into middle-class European and American homes to such a great extent because what was sought was not a rare antiquity, but the latest style, not a singular work of art, but a commodity, often made precisely for export.

But what of literary influence in a more conventional sense, the influence of literary texts on one another? Because of the relative scarcity of non-scholarly translations from East Asian languages before then, this is a story that largely begins in the twentieth century, when both the quantity and quality of literary translations increased. (There are some notable exceptions to this, the most significant being Judith Gautier's *Le Livre de jade* (1867), which offered a selection of classical Chinese poems that not only went through numerous editions, but was (re)translated into a number of European languages, ultimately finding its way into, for example, Mahler's *Das Lied von der Erde* (1908–09)).

At least in the English-speaking world, Pound's *Cathay* (1915) was the watershed moment in poetry, establishing Pound as, in T. S. Eliot's oft-quoted phrase, "the inventor of Chinese poetry for our time." In part guided by Fenollosa's unfinished essay *On the Chinese Written Character as a Medium for Poetry*, this slim volume of creative translations including such major Tang poets as Tu Fu and Li Bai ("Rihaku") established a powerful and still operative link between East Asia and poetic modernism that has extended beyond Pound's own work or even a Poundian tradition in any strict sense (see Kern, Park, Xie, and Yao). Although specific Chinese forms are almost impossible to imitate precisely because of differences in linguistic structure, "Chinese"-style poetry became an established aesthetic defined by sparseness, directness, and concision. While "Chinese" had, in the West, previously connoted excessive ornamentation and artifice, it now connoted precisely naturalness, a dismissal of rhetorical eloquence that would extend through the Beat generation and into the present (Gary Snyder being the most-cited representative). These same values would also define the reception of "Japanese" poetry (all but synonymous with the haiku during this period). As suggested by the brief discussion of Couchoud above, Japanese poetry was at least as important to Imagism as was Chinese, and its influence on modern American poetry was arguably more widespread. In any event, the relatively adaptable form of the haiku (its basic shape and scale, if not the full range of constraints to be found in Japan) makes its influence easier to track, Wallace Stevens's "Thirteen Ways of Looking at a Blackbird" and Pound's "In a Station of the Metro" being the most canonical examples. The haiku's sphere of influence included Latin America (which had its own Orientalism from the time of *modernismo*), notable practitioners of which include Mexican poets José-Juan Tablada and Carlos Gutiérrez Cruz, the latter known for his "revolutionary haiku," including a "Hai-kai comunista" (on *modernismo* see Tinajero; on Brazilian haiku, see Goga).

In theater as in poetry, one can sometimes find specific techniques adapted from Chinese or Japanese theatrical traditions (such as the kabuki *hanamichi*, a platform extending the stage out into the audience), but equally often one finds an "Asian" aesthetic synthesized to dovetail with modernist tendencies: overt artifice in the form of masks, puppets, or the incorporation of dance, a breaking of the fourth wall, or the fragmentation of the plot's spatiotemporal unity. The Noh contributed to formal innovations in Claudel's work and inspired Yeats to write his own version of a Noh play, "At the Hawk's Well" (premier 1917), while Pound found in it a possible model for composing "a long imagist poem." Some critics have thus seen the Noh as an important key to the architecture of *The Cantos*, despite the relatively small number of references to Japan in Pound's unfinished *magnum opus* (Nicholls; Ewick). Here again, Fenollosa's unpublished manuscripts were essential for both Yeats and Pound, but so too were performers such as Michio Ito (Preston), who danced the premier of "At Hawk's Well," and Sadayakko, an actress admired by Picasso and Gide, for example, but who also attained a broader popularity. Vsevolod Emilevich Meyerhold also borrowed from the Noh and kabuki, passing this along to Eisenstein, who also spent some time studying Japanese.

The most well-known connection between China and modernist theater is certainly the work of Bertolt Brecht, who used Chinese settings and plots, but more importantly whose theorization of the "alienation effect" was in part inspired by the Moscow performances of Mei Lanfang, which he attended with Meyerhold (Tatlow). Chinese influences could also be found in more popular forms as theater, such as *Our Town* (1938), whose author, Thornton Wilder, had spent part of his childhood in China.

The influence of East Asian narrative literature seems to have been fairly limited, the most notable exception being Arthur Waley's *Tale of Genji* (1921–33), which would be reviewed by Virginia Woolf and would lead C. P. Snow to recall that "in the late 1920s most literary young people whom I knew were under [its] spell" (qtd in de Gruchy 132). Also noteworthy is *Chinese Tales: Zhuangzi: Sayings and Parables and Chinese Ghost and Love Stories*, a German-language collection edited by Martin Buber that went through many editions and was owned by Franz Kafka, among other famous contemporaries. Related to the question of East Asian narrative literature's influence on Western narrative, there is the question of the former's presence *in* the latter. East Asian references and motifs abound from the age of Naturalism, but often take center stage in what might be broadly called the science fiction of the fin de siècle, ranging from the "samurai" leaders of H. G. Wells's *A Modern Utopia* (1905) to the Yellow Peril of Jack London's dystopias. China in particular would be an important setting for influential works written in the thirties, including Pearl Buck's novels and André Malraux's, from *The Temptation of the West* (1926) to *Man's Fate* (1933). As these titles suggest, links between East Asia and formal innovation in narrative prose seem to have been less widespread than in poetry or theater, but works such as Alfred Döblin's *Three Leaps of Wang Lun* (1915–16) would later be cited by Brecht as influential.

To the basic triad of poetry, theater, and narrative prose, a more comprehensive list would have to add travel literature, journalism, cinematic representations of Asia, the lingering influence of popular writers like Lafcadio Hearn, Pierre Loti, or Max Dauthendey (see Schuster), to speak nothing of the growing range of philosophical and religious works translated during this period, the latter of which in particular remain understudied in relation to literary modernism (but see Stalling).

Modernities

Despite the admiration of a Pound or a Yeats for premodern Asian cultures, the breadth and variety of East Asian/modernist connections suggests that representations of and formal borrowings from East Asia were also bound to questions of not just aesthetic modernism but also social, economic, and political modernity. Whether in the fevered nightmares of Yellow Peril or the fervent dreams of various coming commercial and cultural fusions, "the East" was not just a past to which one might escape, but an active force shaping the future in the present. This qualitative difference of East Asia from the rest of the non-West is especially salient in the period's world-historical imaginings, which often resemble a kind of emerging development theory more than those classic Orientalist philosophies of history in which "the East" had always been understood as essentially of and in the past. Thus we find modernist-era (or even late nineteenth-century) speculations on the future of East Asia's global status that resemble contemporary ideas about comparative or alternative modernities. Couchoud, for example, claims that Europe will one day have to choose between the two great global tendencies of Americanization and Japanization and does not hesitate to encourage his countrymen "Let us choose the latter!"

While it might be tempting to dismiss both Yellow Peril and Fenollosa-style visions of cultural fusion as simply Western projections, the identification of East Asia as the harbinger of a potentially global non-Western modernity would be promoted not only by pan-Asianist thinkers in Japan, but also throughout East Asia and beyond (Aydin, Duara). To cite just a few examples: in late nineteenth- and early twentieth-century Ottoman political debates, Japan would be invoked as a model by government reformers, Arab nationalists, and Young Turks alike, the last hoping to create a "Japan of the Middle East" (Worringer). Similar claims would be made in India, where there were direct connections with Japan through various pan-Asianists (Bharucha). W. E. B. Du Bois viewed Japan's defeat of Russia as a world-historical victory of a "colored race" over a "white" one (Du Bois), while Marcus Garvey too responded to the war with call for a black–Japanese alliance (Krebs). Ethiopia's 1931 constitution would be modeled on that of the Meiji government, following the successful struggles of such reformers as Heruy Welde Sellase and Tekle Hawariat Tekle Mariyam, who were known as "Japanizers" (Krebs).

Whether imagined as a coming war (Hayot "Chineseness"), an ethnically accented technological dystopia (Yu), or a multi-racial cosmopolitanism, the Asian futures of "postmodern" and contemporary literature and film did not originate with Alexander Kojève's infamous footnote about the "end of history" as the "Japanization" of the world, nor even with the Cold War more generally, but must be traced back to the encounters and imaginings of the age of high imperialism. The work of world historians has dramatically changed our understanding of the history of "modernity" and its global distribution (Frank; Pomeranz). If we believe that modernism has any relationship to the history of its time or to theories of modernity, our understanding of modernism must change accordingly.

Asian modernisms

If one grants that Asian modernity was important to Western modernism and that this might change the way we conceive of "modernism" in general, this naturally raises the question: What was modernism in Asia? A wealth of translations, transliterations, and calques present themselves: *modanizumu, kindaishugi, modan, xiandaipai, xiandaizhuyi, modeng, hyundai, keundai*, etc. But as with, for example, Spanish *modernismo* or Portuguese *modernismo* (themselves almost opposites), the range of meanings do not always line up very well with the English word "modernism." Whatever it is called, then, the real question is whether there was in any substantive sense such a thing as modernism in East Asia. It is easy enough to answer in the affirmative if by "modernism" one means Cubist paintings, Surrealist poems, or city novels informed by Joyce. But such an answer reflects an essentially diffusionist conception of modernism, as if the definitions and standards must come only from the West and all Asian modernisms therefore be understood as more or less belated, more or less successful imitations.

How to avoid the logic of diffusionism? One way is to acknowledge the extent to which similar cultural forms and common aesthetics signal similar historical experiences. No doubt *Ulysses* pushed the Asian city novel in certain directions, but this was possible only because there were cities, cities full of writers seeking forms appropriate to the new world in which they lived. Residents of Tokyo and Shanghai wanting to learn about modern urban experience hardly needed to import knowledge from Berlin or Paris, to speak nothing of Dublin, Vienna, or St. Petersburg!

Another way to resist the logic of diffusionism is simply to reject or at least de-emphasize the logic of priority. For example, the two great Japanese modernist city novels, Yokomitsu Riichi's *Shanghai* and Yasunari Kawabata's *Scarlet Gang of Asukusa*, were published in 1928–31 and 1930, respectively, a little after *Ulysses*, to be sure, but contemporaneous with *Berlin Alexanderplatz* (1929) and beating John Dos Passos's *U.S.A.* trilogy (1930–36) to any imaginary finish line, and yet neither Dos Passos nor Döblin is categorically dismissed as belated or derivative. Even if we wish to give some value to priority, we find in East Asian modernism a good deal of near-simultaneity (the "Manifesto of Futurism" was published in Japanese in the year of its initial French publication (1909)), or even precedence: the first movie theater opened in Tokyo in 1903 (a year after the first permanent theater was built in Los Angeles, but six years before the first UK theater, the Electric Theater in Birmingham); the first articles and book published on Heidegger were written in Japanese, and so on. In cultural modernism as in socioeconomic modernity, then, it is less a matter of how or when Western models reached Japan than of a more or less simultaneous development that might even show signs of Japanese priority. (From the vast scholarship on Japanese modernization and modernism, works of particular interest to those in modernist studies include Harootunian; Karatani; Starrs, ed.; and Tyler, ed.).

The situation is of course different with China. Although one might cite New Sensationism, for example, as a literary tendency with dates and aesthetic features to make it respectably "modernist" by the standards discussed so far (see Shih), with China we must rely even less on dates and instead embrace more fully the principle of questioning priority, not converting all chronological sequences into aesthetic hierarchies. This ultimately requires being open to rethinking the range of aesthetic responses to modernity, which can entail something as simple as, for example, not always taking realism as a baseline out of which more sophisticated forms of writing develop. "Realism" is, if not modern*ism*, then at least modern (see for example Chen; Denton, ed.; Lee; and Tang). It should be less tempting to regard Chinese realism as an effort to "catch up" with the West if one recalls that it was precisely at this time that Western artists and writers were turning to haiku, Noh, and Chinese script (not to mention African masks, Javanese scales, etc.) to create their "own" modernisms.

This line of thought ultimately raises questions about the relative unity of "modernism" as a period and its chronological limits, a challenge that has long been recognized by scholars working on areas in the "periphery" but whose blowback with respect to the conventional definitions of modernism has not yet been fully appreciated. Since critics have granted the idea of modernism a post-WWII life with respect to European art cinema, why should it not be extended to, for example, the Taiwanese and Hong Kong "new waves" of the late twentieth century, or contemporary Chinese art? This temporal extension raises corresponding questions about the spatial scope of "Asian modernism." What is the relationship of "Asian American" literature to this corpus (Park; Yao)? What of other East Asian diasporic legacies (one might here think of Linda Lê in France, Yoko Tawada in Germany, numerous Brazilian haiku poets), and this does not touch on the broader range of Sinophone and Japanophone literatures, to speak nothing of the other arts (Shih, Tsai, and Bernards, eds; Workman).

Does this not risk dissolving "modernism," dilating the range of examples, periodization, and geography until the Pound Era and its values have become difficult to recognize? One can only hope so. Without having at least *risked* this, the "and" of "East Asia *and* modernism" will have served only to empty the contents of the former into the latter. If the field of modernist studies cannot recognize as *real* modernism such things as Dada and Surrealist poems, stream-of-consciousness city novels or manifestos referencing Nietzsche and Futurism – all within the conventional dates of modernism as a period, no less – then it might as well admit that it defines "modernism" in geographic and ethnic rather than aesthetic or historical terms.

Asian Futures for Modernist Studies?

Perhaps the most obvious change that needs to be made is the expansion of the canon of "modernism" to include at least some of the major non-Western works. Recent expansions of the canon have tended to focus above all on previously understudied writers from within the metropole (for example, women writers) or, to a lesser degree, those writing outside it but *in European languages* (for example, Caribbean writers). A serious inclusion of East Asian works within the field of modernism would entail more than a quantitative increase in the reading list, instead requiring understandings of modernity that are not centered around Euro-American exceptionalism and the ways in which others *responded* to it. Modernism's relationship to modernity would ultimately have to be reconceived in light of these new understandings of modernity, such that what we used to call modernism becomes less the uniquely unique cultural expression of a particularly intense moment in the internal development of the Western exception, and instead appears as a regional iteration of a modernity defined by widespread geopolitical and economic interconnectedness. This "new" modernism would, as I argue elsewhere, constitute less an invention than an act of historical recovery, something much closer to how the modernists themselves experienced and understood their world.

At the same time, we must also reread the existing canon itself in ways attuned both to their celebrated formal particularities and to the historical forces that give meaning to, for example, the once-ignored references to China in a Woolf or a Benjamin or a Proust (see Laurence, Bush, and Froula, respectively). Given the centrality of formal innovation to almost any definition of modernism, it will be important that Asia is treated not simply as a theme, a topic, an historical reality that might be referenced or represented in the work of art. Indeed, as I have been suggesting throughout, one of the reasons East Asia has a singular importance for the study of modernism is the extent to which it compels simultaneously historicist and formalist readings (Bush; Hayot *Hypothetical*; Lye).

If this seems an almost utopian project, we might take courage from the example of scholars of East Asia, or indeed of any field focused outside the Euro-American metropoles, scholars who have long been required to know not only their own fields but also modernism *tout court*, that is, the world of Anglo-American high modernism with a few French or German supplements. The study of that modernism in relation to East Asia might begin moving beyond Orientalism critique and toward a more truly comparative or transnational understanding of modernism by building on the methodological insights of these scholars who have so long worked on the steeper slopes of the field's sometime precipitous asymmetries.

I suggested at the outset that modernist Orientalism might be understood as a kind of self-representation not because – or not just because – it constitutes a narcissistic projection that only talked about others in order to talk about itself. It is also a record of the historically specific forms assumed by the necessity of talking about others in order to talk about oneself. It has long been recognized as a truth, even a truism, that modern East Asia cannot be understood without reckoning the importance of its encounter with the West, but the other dimensions of that history, and the totality that the sum of these various dimensions might imply, have only begun to be described (see especially Hill). If we do it right, it would not be the case that such a history and such a totality would define and explain modernism, but rather that we will acknowledge the extent to which modernism itself has been telling that history and projecting that totality all along, not only in its ideas and its subjects, but precisely in singular shapes of its forms.

References

Arrowsmith, Richard Ruppert. (2011). *Modernism and the Museum: Asian, African, and Pacific Art and the London Avant-Garde*. New York: Oxford University Press.

Aydin, Çemil. (2007). *The Politics of Anti-Westernism in Asia: Visions of World Order in Pan-Islamic and Pan-Asian Thought*. New York: Columbia University Press.

Barthes, Roland. (1983). *Empire of Signs*, trans. Richard Howard. New York: Hill and Wang.

Bharucha, Rustom. (2006). *Another Asia: Rabindranath Tagore and Okakura Tenshin*. New Delhi: Oxford India Press.

Binyon, Laurence. (1908). *Painting in the Far East: An Introduction to the History of Pictorial Art in Asia, Especially China and Japan*. London: Edward Arnold.

Bush, Christopher. (2010). *Ideographic Modernism*. New York: Oxford University Press.

Chen Xiaomei. (1995). *Occidentalism: A Theory of Counter-Discourse in Post-Mao China*. New York: University Press.

Chisolm, Lawrence. (1976). *The Far East and American Culture*. London: Greenwood Press.

Couchoud, Paul-Louis. (1926 [1916]). *Sages et poètes d'Asie*. Paris: Calmann-Lévy.

Danzker, Jo-Anne Birnie, et al., eds. (2005). *Shanghai Modern*. Ostfildern-Ruit: Hatje Cantz.

De Gruchy, Walter. (2011). *Orienting Arthur Waley*. Honolulu: University of Hawaii Press.

Denton, Kirk. (1996). *Modern Chinese Literary Thought: Writings on Literature, 1893–1945*. Palo Alto, CA: Stanford University Press.

Duara, Prasenjit. (2001). "The Discourse of Civilization and Pan-Asianism." *Journal of World History* 12.1 (Spring): 99–130.

Du Bois, W. E. B. (2005). *W. E. B. Du Bois on Asia*, ed. Bill V. Mullen and Cathryn Watson. Jackson: University of Mississippi Press.

Ewick, David. (n.d.). "Ezra Pound and the Invention of Japan." At http://themargins.net/bib/B/BK/00bkintro.html (accessed November 15, 2012).

Frank, Andre Gunder. (1998). *ReORIENT: Global Economy in the Asian Age*. Berkeley: University of California Press.

Froula, Christine. (2012). "Proust's China." *Modernism/modernity* 19.2 (April): 227–254.

Gillies, Mary Ann, Helen Sword and Steven Yao, eds. (2009). *Pacific Rim Modernisms*. Toronto: University of Toronto Press.

Goga, Hidezaku Masuda. (1988). *O haicai no Brasil*. São Paulo: Oriento.

Harootunian, Harry. (2000). *Overcome by Modernity*. Princeton, NJ: Princeton University Press.

Hayot, Eric. (2008). "Chineseness: A Prehistory of Its Future." In *Sinographies*, ed. Eric Hayot, Haun Saussy, and Steven Yao. Minneapolis: University of Minnesota Press.

Hokenson, Jan. (2004). *Japan, France, and East–West Aesthetics: French Literature, 1867–2000*. Madison, NJ: Fairleigh Dickinson.

Jameson, Fredric. (1990). "Modernism and Imperialism." In *Nationalism, Colonialism, and Literature*, ed. Terry Eagleton. Minneapolis: University of Minnesota Press.

Jameson, Fredric. (1995). *The Geopolitical Aesthetic: Cinema and Space in the World System*. Bloomington: Indiana University Press.

Hill, Christopher. (2009). "The Travels of Naturalism and the Challenges of a World Literary History." *Literature Compass* 6: 1198–1210.

Karatani, Kojin. (1993). *The Origins of Modern Japanese Literature*. Durham, NC: Duke University Press.

Kern, Robert. (1996). *Modernism, Orientalism, and the American Poem*. Cambridge: Cambridge University Press.

Krebs, Gerhard. (n.d.). "World War Zero? Re-Assessing the Global Impact of the Russo-Japanese War 1904–05." At http://www.japanfocus.org/-Gerhard-Krebs/3755 (accessed November 15, 2012).

Laurence, Patricia. (1997). "The China Letters: Vanessa Bell, Julian Bell and Ling Shuhua." *South Carolina Review* (Spring): 122–131.

Lee, Leo. (1999). *Shanghai Modern: The Flowering of a New Urban Culture in China, 1930–1945*. Cambridge, MA: Harvard University Press.

Liu, Lydia. (1995). *Translingual Practice: Literature, National Culture, and Translated Modernity – China, 1900–1937*. Palo Alto, CA: Stanford University Press.

Lye, Collen. (2004). *America's Asia*. Princeton, NJ: Princeton University Press.

Nicholls, Peter. (1995). "An Experiment with Time: Ezra Pound and the Example of Japanese Noh." *Modern Language Review* 90: 1–13.

Miner, Earl. (1966 [1958]). *The Japanese Tradition in British and American Literature*. Princeton, NJ: Princeton University Press.

Park, Josephine Nock-Hee. (2008). *Apparitions of Asia: Modernist Form and Asian American Poetics*. Oxford: Oxford University Press.

Pomeranz, Kenneth. (2001). *The Great Divergence*. Princeton, NJ: Princeton University Press.

Preston, Carrie. (2012). "Michio Ito's Shadow: Searching for the Transnational in Solo Dance." In *On Stage Alone: Soloists and the Formation of the Modern Dance Canon*, ed. Claudia Gitelman and Barbara Palfy. Gainesville: University Press of Florida.

Qian Zhaoming. (2003). *The Modernist Response to Chinese Art: Pound, Moore, Stevens*. Charlottesville: University of Virginia Press.

Rimer, Thomas J., ed. (2011). *Since Meiji: Perspectives on the Japanese Visual Arts, 1868–2000*. Honolulu: University of Hawaii Press.

Said, Edward. (1979). *Orientalism*. New York: Vintage.

Saussy, Haun. (Forthcoming). "Askance from Translation."

Schuster, Ingrid. (1977). *China und Japan in der deutschen Literatur 1890–1925*. Berlin: Francke.

Segalen, Victor. (2004). *Correspondance*, 3 vols, ed. Henry Bouillier. Paris: Fayard.

Segalen, Victor. (2007). *Stèles*, ed. Timothy Billings and Christopher Bush. Middletown, CT: Wesleyan University Press.

Shen Shuang. (2009). *Cosmopolitan Publics: Anglophone Print Culture in Semi-Colonial China*. New Brunswick, NY: Rutgers University Press.

Shih Shu-mei. (2001). *The Lure of the Modern: Writing Modernism in Semicolonial China, 1917–1937*. Berkeley: University of California Press.

Shih Shu-mei, Chien-hsin Tsai, and Brian Bernards, eds. (2013). *Sinophone Studies: A Critical Reader*. New York: Columbia University Press.

Stalling, Jonathan. (2011). *Poetics of Emptiness*. New York: Fordham University Press.

Starrs, Roy, ed. (2012). *Rethinking Japanese Modernism*. Boston, MA: Global Oriental.

Sullivan, Michael. (1998). *The Meeting and Eastern and Western Art*. Berkeley: University of California Press.

Tablada, José Juan. (1994). *Obras*. Mexico City: Universidad Nacional Autonóma de Mexico.

Tang Xiaobing. (2000). *China Modern*. Durham, NC: Duke University Press.

Tang Xiaobing. (2007). *The Origins of the Chinese Avant-Garde*. Berkeley: University of California Press.

Tatlow, Antony. (1977). *The Mask of Evil*. Peter Lang.

Tinajero, Araceli. (2003). *Orientalismo en el modernismo hispanoamericano*. West Lafayette, IN: Purdue University Press.

Tsu Jing. (2010). *Sound and Script in Chinese Diaspora*. Cambridge, MA: Harvard University Press.

Tyler, William J., ed. (2008). *Modanizumu: Modernist Fiction from Japan, 1913–1938*. Honolulu: University of Hawaii Press.

Volk, Alicia. (2010). *In Pursuit of Universalism: Yorozu Tetsugoro and Japanese Modern Art*. Berkeley: University of California Press.

Wichman, Siegfried. (1999). *Japonisme: The Japanese Influence on Western Art since 1858*. London: Thames and Hudson.

Weisenfeld, Gennifer. (2001). *Mavo: Japanese Artists and the Avant-Garde, 1905–1931*. Berkeley: University of California Press.

Workman, Travis. (2011). "Locating Translation: On the Question of Japanophone Literature." *PMLA* 126.3 (May): 701–708.

Worringer, René, ed. (2007). *The Islamic Middle East and Japan*. Princeton, NJ: Markus Wiener.

Xie Ming. (1998). *Ezra Pound and the Appropriation of Chinese Poetry: Cathay, Translation, and Imagism*. New York: Garland.

Yao, Steven. (2010). *Foreign Accents: Chinese American Verse from Exclusion to Postethnicity*. New York: Oxford University Press.

Yu, Timothy. (2008). "Oriental Cities, Postmodern Futures: Naked Lunch, Blade Runner, and Neuromancer." *MELUS* 33.4: 45–73.

Further Reading

Barthes, Roland. (1983). *Empire of Signs*, trans. Richard Howard. New York: Hill and Wang.

Bush, Christopher. (2010). *Ideographic Modernism*. New York: Oxford University Press.

Fenollosa, Ernest. (2008). *The Chinese Written Character as a Medium for Poetry*. New York: Fordham University Press.

Gillies, Mary Ann, Helen Sword and Steven Yao, eds. (2009). *Pacific Rim Modernisms*. Toronto: University of Toronto Press.

Hayot, Eric. (2010). *The Hypothetical Mandarin*. New York: Oxford University Press.

Hill, Christopher. (2009). "The Travels of Naturalism and the Challenges of a World Literary History." *Literature Compass* 6: 1198–1210.

Hokenson, Jan. (2004). *Japan, France, and East–West Aesthetics: French Literature, 1867–2000.* Madison, NJ: Fairleigh Dickinson.

Kern, Robert. (1996). *Modernism, Orientalism, and the American Poem.* Cambridge: Cambridge University Press.

Lye, Collen. (2004). *America's Asia.* Princeton, NJ: Princeton University Press.

Miner, Earl. (1966 [1958]). *The Japanese Tradition in British and American Literature.* Princeton, NJ: Princeton University Press.

12

Translation Studies and Modernism

Steven G. Yao

The act of translation has long been a subject of both sustained and varied reflection by a significant array of practitioners and theorists alike since at least the classical period in the West. However, it was not until the 1970s that translation studies as such finally began to take shape as a cohesive – as well as recognized – intellectual enterprise. Such belatedness in acknowledging translation as a topic worthy of study in its own right lends general credence to one of the grounding critical claims of translation studies: namely, that translation as a mode of cultural, and especially literary, production has been incorrectly considered a second-order or ancillary activity, and hence unfairly overlooked as subordinate and even inferior to "original" composition in both creative and cultural significance. This longstanding bias, scholars have noted, cuts across numerous cultural traditions. Consider, for instance, the wealth of sayings in various languages that reflect a deep suspicion about translation by equating it with such despicable acts as treason or infidelity. Needless to say, perhaps, translation studies rejects this simplistic view, together with the metaphysics of originality that underwrite it, as one of its foundational disciplinary premises. Within this still evolving field, numerous critics have gone on to explore the significance, as well as the history, of translation as an instrument of both personal and ideological expression in a range of different languages and cultural contexts, further demonstrating its fundamental imbrication with such basic conceptual categories as gender, nation, and language.

Indeed, over the comparatively brief, four-decade span since its earliest formal beginnings, this emergent field has successfully made its case for the complexity and importance of translation as a manifold cultural activity. And in doing so it has undergone a genuinely remarkable expansion, to the point that translation studies now not only boasts several scholarly journals, graduate training programs,

A Handbook of Modernism Studies, First Edition. Edited by Jean-Michel Rabaté.
© 2013 John Wiley & Sons, Ltd. Published 2013 by John Wiley & Sons, Ltd.

textbooks, and other features of official institutional sanction. This field also shows other signs of having achieved a certain disciplinary maturity, such as the growth of distinct areas or branches of investigation, each focusing on a different aspect of translation as both a communicative practice and a linguistic and cultural phenomenon. These overlapping branches span the gamut from ongoing theoretical inquiry into translation as a mode of cultural production to more practical concerns such as the protocols of simultaneous interpreting to frankly technical matters such as the development of algorithms for perfecting machine translation. And within each of these branches, furthermore, competing schools of thought vie for recognition, influence, and funding. In short, translation studies has successfully established itself as a full-fledged academic discipline.

Among the many different lines of inquiry making up contemporary translation studies, the ones most germane to the study of modernism are those addressing the theory and history of translation as a mode of cultural, and specifically literary, production. Within the broad arena of translation theory in particular, George Steiner's well-known *After Babel: Aspects of Language and Translation* (1975) stands out as an important early work that continues to exert a recognizable influence over the entire field by connecting the phenomenon of translation to fundamental questions about the origins and dynamics of language more broadly. This magisterial achievement opened the door to further reflection on the philosophical significance of translation; and subsequently, feminist scholars like Lori Chamberlain and Barbara Johnson[1] exposed the remarkable continuity in Western culture, since at least St. Jerome, of expressly gendered theorizing about translation. Together, they demonstrated a persistent association between metaphorical thought about the literary practice and figures of femininity and (hetero)sexual conquest. Following these efforts, synthetic works like Douglas Robinson's *The Translator's Turn* (1991) and André Lefevere's *Translation, Rewriting and the Manipulation of Literary Fame* (1992) made the theoretical case for translation itself as an expressly generative, rather than merely mimetic, mode of cultural production. These and a host of other scholars helped to make clear that translation involves much more than just a neutral linguistic operation. Rather, it constitutes a complex cultural and social enterprise, one fraught with ethical and political implications and historical sedimentations. Hence, they explicitly rejected previous approaches to literary translation that sought merely to endorse or censure individual renderings based upon subjective conceptions of "accuracy" as the unquestioned aim of translation. As Lefevere has written,

> An approach to translation which rests content with decreeing which translations ought to exist and which ought not is very limited indeed. Rather, it should analyze texts which refer to themselves as translations and other rewritings and try to ascertain the part they play in a culture. The sheer number of rewritings should alert writers on translation of this ilk to the fact that they may not be dealing adequately with the matter at hand, just as the repeated and regular incidence of what they refer to as "mistakes" ought to alert them to the fact that an isolated mistake is, probably, just that, whereas a recurrent series of "mistakes" most likely points to a pattern that is the expression of a strategy.[2]

Alongside these efforts, figures renowned in other areas of literary and cultural theory such as Jacques Derrida, Paul DeMan, and Gayatri Spivak, among others, weighed in on translation as part of elaborating the larger architecture of their own theoretical pursuits. For their part, DeMan and Derrida have each written on the conceptual dimensions of translation, emphasizing, perhaps not unexpectedly, its paradoxical status as a task both "necessary and impossible" (Derrida 170). Comparably, Spivak has interrogated the politics of linguistic transformation in reflecting on the power relations embedded in feats of translation within colonial and postcolonial settings. These thinkers charted intersections between translation studies and other theoretical discourses such as deconstruction and postcolonial theory respectively. And in turn, they helped give rise to studies such as Eric Cheyfitz's *The Poetics of Imperialism: Translation and Colonization from The Tempest to Tarzan* (1991) and T. Niranjana's *Siting Translation: History, Poststructuralism, and the Colonial Context* (1992) that explicitly linked translation with the exercise of colonial domination and the maintenance of its asymmetrical relations of power. In this way, translation came to be seen as a central problematic within multiple theoretical discourses, which only helped to strengthen claims about the foundational importance of translation made within translation studies itself.

Complementing and extending the work of these and other theorists of translation, another group of scholars undertook more thoroughly situated analyses of the practice within various historical and cultural contexts. Antoine Berman made an important early contribution in this vein in *The Experience of the Foreign: Culture and Translation in Romantic Germany* (1984). This study mapped in exemplary detail the manifold conceptual space occupied by translation within the work of major German writers such as Herder, Goethe, A. W. Schlegel, Novalis, Schleiermacher, von Humboldt, and Hölderlin. Here, Berman gives particularly concise expression to the historicist approach to translation:

> It is impossible to separate the history of translation from the history of languages, of cultures, and of literatures – even of religions and of nations. To be sure, this is not a question of mixing every thing up, but of showing how in each period or in each given historical setting the practice of translation *is articulated* in relation to the practice of literature, of languages, of the several intercultural and interlinguistic exchanges. (emphasis in the original)[3]

Later, Lawrence Venuti in *The Translator's Invisibility: A History of Translation* (1995) offered a broader survey of views of translation across several Western cultural traditions, ultimately advocating a "foreignizing" approach to the practice over a "domesticating" one that assimilates texts in other languages to the protocols of "fluency" in the target language and thereby rendering the translator "invisible." Building on these earlier examples, my own *Translation and the Languages of Modernism: Gender, Politics, Language* (2002) focused on the tradition of Anglo-American modernism. In particular, I showed how the practice of translation constituted an integral part of the modernist program of cultural renewal, a crucially important mode of writing distinct from, yet fundamentally interconnected with, the more traditionally esteemed modes of poetry and prose fiction. In fact, during the modernist period throughout Europe more generally, translation served as a specific compositional practice by which different writers such as Victor Segalen, Paul Claudel, Ezra Pound, H. D., William Butler Yeats, James Joyce, Walter Benjamin, and Bertolt Brecht, among numerous others, each sought solutions to the various problems and issues that have come to be understood as the central thematic concerns of modernism in its continental and transatlantic formations. These include concerns about the disappearance of any stable religious or moral values by which to ground a viable society, the staggering realities of world conflict and economic collapse, the perceived radical inability of established artistic forms and genres to confront and accurately represent the new realities of the world as it existed, and, consequently, the need to develop new representational possibilities more in tune with the demands of the expressly modern world.

Collectively, these developments within and around translation studies brought renewed attention to translation and its significance across a range of literary periods, including the modernist period. To be sure, based on the prominent role of translation in the careers of writers such as Pound and even Joyce, there had been a number of studies of individual feats of modernist translation. In this regard, J. P Sullivan's *Ezra Pound and Sextus Propertius: A Study in Creative Translation* (1964) and Wai-lim Yip's *Ezra Pound's* Cathay (1969) remain early touchstones; and this approach continues to produce useful work such as Daniel Hooley's *The Classics in Paraphrase* (1988). Yet by and large, these studies, while linguistically informed, operated with an intuitive and implicitly normative conception of translation. The more formally theorized and historicized conceptual framework of translation studies has helped to extend and broaden the local insights of these earlier efforts.

As this necessarily hasty genealogy perhaps suggests, in turning its critical gaze upon modernism, translation studies reflexively highlights some of its own most important intellectual roots and influences. Notably, for example, virtually all contemporary theorizing about translation, including the essays by DeMan and Derrida mentioned earlier, responds in one way or another to Walter Benjamin's evocative and deeply felt meditation, "Des Aufgabe des Ubersetzers" ("The Task of the Translator"), which first appeared as the introduction to his 1923 rendering into German of Baudelaire's *Tableaux parisiens*. Among his contemporaries, furthermore, Benjamin was not the first to consider that the scope of translation reaches far beyond just "the sterile equation of two dead languages" (73). A considerable array of modernist writers in Europe and the United States confronted the significance of translation as a literary mode, either as critics, as translators themselves, or, in certain rare circumstances like Benjamin's, as both critics and translators. Seven years earlier, in 1916, the poet, critic, and translator Ezra Pound was reflecting upon the role that the practice of translation plays in the development of a major literary culture; and in an essay titled "Elizabethan Classicists," he hypothesized that "A great age of literature is perhaps always a great age of translations; or follows it."[4] By 1929, any lingering doubts he might have harbored about the generative importance of the practice of translation in the rise of English literature had completely disappeared. Thus, in "How to Read," he summarily declared that, after the period of purely indigenous Anglo-Saxon works such as "The Seafarer" and *Beowulf*, "English literature lives on translation, it is fed by translation; every new exuberance, every new heave is stimulated by translation, every allegedly great age is an age of translations" (*LE*, 34–35).

Beginning at least as early as the summer of 1901, with Joyce's youthful renderings of two plays by Gerhart Hauptmann, *Before Sunrise* and *Michael Kramer*, and continuing all the way through to the publication in 1956 of Pound's deeply personal and idiosyncratic version of Sophocles' *Women of Trachis*, feats of translation not only accompanied and helped to give rise to, but sometimes even themselves constituted, some of the most significant modernist literary achievements. In addition to these examples at either end of the temporal bounds of the modernist period, several other major modernist writers engaged in translation, either as a sustained practice or at various, and sometimes crucial, points in their careers. Working on them between 1926 and 1927, at the very height of his powers as a poet, William Butler Yeats concluded his investigation into Greek tragedy as a model for the formation of a national, Irish dramatic culture by translating and producing on the stage both *King Oedipus* (1928) and *Oedipus at Colonus* (1934). Similarly, H. D. devoted considerable time and energy throughout her career to translating Greek poetry and drama, culminating in her 1938 translation of another classical Greek play, Euripides' *Ion*, and this lifelong practice profoundly affected her development as one of the most important women poets of her time. Another, Marianne Moore, published her translations of the moral fables of La Fontaine in 1954, and when asked if the act of translation had helped her as a writer, she replied, "Indeed, it did. It was the best help I've ever had."[5] H. D.'s husband, Richard Aldington, produced four volumes of poems by various Greek and Latin poets in *The Poets' Translation Series* published by the Egoist Press.[6] Extending to two sets of volumes with numbers in each by such other figures as H. D. herself, Edward Storer, F. S. Flint, and A. W. G. Randall, this series, as its very title suggests, bespeaks the fundamental interconnection between translation and other modes of literary production within the writing practices of the modernists. Comparably, William Carlos Williams translated poems by numerous French and Spanish writers, including Nicanor Parra, Silvina Ocampo, Pablo Neruda, Octavio Paz, Miguel Hernandez, Rafael Beltran Logroños, Mariano del Alcazar, Nicholas Calas, and even one poem, "The Cassia Tree," by the Chinese poet Li Bai.[7] And in addition to rendering numerous critical articles from French for publication in *The Criterion*, T. S. Eliot produced an English translation of St. John Perse's poem *Anabase*, which he considered "a piece of writing of the same importance as the later work of Mr. James Joyce, as valuable as *Anna Livia Plurabelle*."[8]

Nor was the practice of translation limited during this time to poets rendering poems or dramas, or focused primarily on the classics. Virginia Woolf produced versions of Dostoyevsky's *Stavrogin's Confession* and *The Plan of the Life of a Great Sinner* in 1922 in collaboration with S. S. Kosteliansky, as well as rendering under similar circumstances A. G. Goldenveizer's *Talks with Tolstoi* in 1923. And even though he took pains to hide the fact because he thought it wouldn't "do for [him] to appear to dabble in too many things,"[9] D. H. Lawrence also expended considerable effort as a translator. By himself he translated three novels by the Italian writer Giovanni Verga,[10] and in collaboration with Kosteliansky and Leonard Woolf, he also translated a work by the Russian writer I. A. Bunin, *The Gentleman from San Francisco and Other Stories*. Finally, Ford Madox Ford, who exerted a profound influence on the generation of modernists that followed him, rendered at least one novel from the French, Pierre Lotì's *L'Outrage des Barbares*, or *The Trail of the Barbarians*.

Ezra Pound, of course, exemplifies the modernist for whom translating constituted not just a sustained, but more important, a generative writing practice. By the time he declared the importance of translation to the evolution of English literature in "How to Read," he could have made a respectable case based virtually on his individual output alone By 1929, Pound had produced an extensive version of the poems of the fourteenth-century Italian poet Guido Cavalcanti in *Sonnets and Ballate of Guido Cavalcanti* (1912), an exquisitely rendered set of medieval Chinese lyrics based on the notes of Ernest Fenollosa in *Cathay* (1915), as well as a highly unconventional, and so critically reviled, treatment of the odes of the Latin poet Sextus Propertius in *Homage to Sextus Propertius* (1919). Over and above these major works of translation, he produced a version of the *Dialogues of Fontenelle* (1917), one of Rémy de Gourmont's *The Natural Philosophy of Love* (1922) and another of his *Dust for Sparrows* (1922), as well as one of *The Call of the Road* (1923) by the French writer Edouard Estaunié, and a rendering through an intermediary French source of the Confucian governmental classic, the *Ta Hio* (1928), or, as he later came to call it when he translated it again in 1945, *The Great Digest*.

In addition to these volumes specifically dedicated to his work as a translator, other significant translations Pound produced before 1929 include versions of some twenty poems by the Troubadour poet Arnaut Daniel published in *Umbra* (1920), and a rendering of the Anglo-Saxon poem "The Seafarer," first published in *Riposte* (1912). After 1929, the list becomes even more impressive in its diversity, both of languages and subjects. Such feats range from complete and fascinatingly incorrect versions of two more books in the Confucian canon of political and social thought, *The Unwobbling Pivot* (1947) and *The Analects* (1951), together with the *Shi Jing* (詩 經), to which he gave the rather verbose title, *The Classic Anthology Defined by Confucius* (1954), to a collection of *Love Poems of Ancient Egypt* (1962), as well as his rendering of the *Women of Trachis* mentioned earlier. From its very inception to even beyond what are normally considered its closing years, then, the age of modernism was, quite literally, an age of translations.

The sheer abundance of translations produced during the period gives concrete, textual expression to the interest on the part of modernist writers, most especially in Britain and the United States, in foreign cultures and languages as sources of both instruction and inspiration for renewing their own culture and expanding the possibilities of expression in English, an interest that also manifests in the explicitly multi-linguistic dimensions of so many major modernist texts. Pound titled poems in various languages, and in *Hugh Selwyn Mauberley* (1919) he rhymes words in French and Greek with ones in English. In *The Cantos*, he incorporates passages of Greek, Latin, Provençal, and Italian, as well as Chinese characters and Egyptian hieroglyphics as vital strands in the textual fabric of his "poem including history" (*LE*, 86). Similarly, Eliot employs passages from various foreign works in their original languages as epigraphs for many of his most important poems, and *The Waste Land* includes lines in German, French, Italian, Latin, and Hindi as crucial elements. Like Pound, Wallace Stevens titled many of his poems in French, and he once remarked, somewhat cryptically, that for him French and English were the same language. *Ulysses* contains numerous languages, which the characters in the novel vary in their ability to comprehend, and in *Finnegans Wake*, Joyce redefines the limits of English itself by investing it with the capacities of some sixty different languages, including such exotic specimens as Beche-la-Mar (a Melanesian pidgin), Samoan, Shelta, Gipsy, Norwegian, Kiswahili, and Bearlagair Na Saer. Even as avowedly American and nativist a poet as William Carlos Williams gave one of his volumes of poetry the Spanish title *Al Que Quiere!* (1917). In their efforts at cultural renewal, the modernists employed languages other than English with such frequency that Pound's famous injunction to "Make It New" seems in large measure to have meant "Make it Foreign."

The concern with and use of foreign cultures and languages bespeak a general modernist attitude to which Pound gave explicit articulation when he declared in "How to Read" that, "Different languages – I mean the actual vocabularies, the idioms – have worked out certain mechanisms of communication and registration. No one language is complete" (*LE*, 36). Twenty-six years later, with the publication of the "Rock-Drill" section of *The Cantos*, Pound reiterated this concern and made it a subject of his own *poetic* expression, declaring in Canto LXXXVI, "It can't be all in one language."[11] Indeed, much of the formal innovation in his poetry embodies an attempt to infuse English with the energies of other languages and their "mechanisms of communication and registration."[12] Thus, in "The Return," Pound not only announces the reappearance of Greek gods in the modern world, but he seeks to enact a recovery in English of the rhythmical possibilities embedded in the poetic meters of the Greek language itself. Comparably, in the second section of his own meditation on the poet's craft, "Little Gidding," Eliot invokes the "familiar compound ghost"[13] of two earlier masters, Swift and Yeats, in a section of fabricated English terza rima as a strategy for investing his own language with the possibilities and cultural authority of Dante's medieval Italian. And in this light, Marianne Moore's predilection for syllabic poetry can be seen as an attempt to shape English according to the rhythmic dimensions of French.

Collectively, modernist writers understood and employed translation as a kind of dynamic procedural lens through which they could view both the past as well as other cultures. Even more important, perhaps, translation also thereby served as a means to focus their images of these traditions in their own times and in ways that could serve their individual ideological and aesthetic purposes. As a mode of literary production, translation helped modernist writers to expand the range of cultural, linguistic, and generic fields in which they could actively participate; it helped them to determine and establish the defining boundaries of their own cultures; it provided a means by which to broaden their sources for material and inspiration, thereby enabling them to begin moving beyond the limits of a single-language literary practice and history to explore territories other than those already mapped by their literary antecedents as a way of expanding the very linguistic dimensions of individual national literatures. Through the practice of translation, modernist writers undertook to extend the limits of language itself, which in turn led them to discover new possibilities for their own expression.

For beyond simply producing a great many renderings of documents from various cultures and traditions, modernist writers also engaged in translation as a technique in the composition of their own "original" works. Fragments and even extended passages from a vast array of texts in a wide range of languages comprise constitutive elements in a number of modernist poems and novels, which themselves oftentimes take the process of translation as one of their subjects. Here again, Pound serves as the prime example. *The Cantos* opens with a translation of a Renaissance Latin version of the Nekuia episode in Homer's *Odyssey* and, in the inimitable words of Hugh Kenner,[14] Canto I "is not simply, as was Divus' Homer or Chapman's Homer or Pope's, a passing through the knot of a newer rope. It is *about* the fact that self-interfering patterns persist while new ways of shaping breath flow through them. It illustrates that fact, and its subject is in part that fact" (emphasis in the original). Indeed, translation figures so largely as both technique and subject in the remainder of Pound's poem, most notably in the "Malatesta" and "Chinese History" Cantos, that another critic has gone so far as to call *The Cantos* an "epic of translation."[15]

Similarly, Yeats blurred the distinction between original poetic composition and translation when he concluded both "A Man Young and Old" and "A Woman Young and Old," the two final sequences in arguably his two finest collections of verse, *The Tower* (1928) and *The Winding Stair and Other Poems* (1933), with poetic renderings of choral odes from *Oedipus at Colonus* and *Antigone* respectively. And in a lyric written in 1949, entitled, logically enough, "Translation," William Carlos Williams integrates the act of translation with his theory about writing as a form of sexuality, saying in the opening stanza of the poem,

> There is no distinction in the encounter, Sweet
> there is no grace of perfume
> to the rose but from us, which we give it
> by our loving performance.[16]

At a more conceptual level, many modernist texts encode translation into the very act of reading itself. The multi-linguistic fabric, allusiveness, and formal structure of such works as *The Cantos* and *The Waste Land* require readers to engage, often quite literally, in translation to derive any sort of meaning from the text. Analogously, readers of *Ulysses* must render the distinctive language of each chapter into a common idiom in order to reconstruct the narrative contained in what one critic has termed the "odyssey of style"[17] in the novel. In *Finnegans Wake*, this demand reaches down to the level of the most basic unit of the text, the level of the word. What Fritz Senn has said about Joyce's fiction could be applied with equal validity to a number of modernist texts: "Joyce's works consist of translation and glorify all cognate processes."[18] As both a compositional procedure and a conceptual structure, then, translation informs the entire range of modernist literary production, most especially poetry, but likewise some of the more extreme achievements in the novel.

Moreover, as the poem by Williams cited above suggests, translation constituted a subject of considerable critical reflection throughout the period. Modernist writers and translators repeatedly, if never systematically, theorized about both the larger cultural meaning and the proper methods of translation as a literary mode. They afforded it a place within the modernist critical framework equal in significance to that occupied by the more traditionally esteemed modes of poetry and prose fiction. As a result, they also assigned to translation a role of constitutive importance in the process of culture formation. This helps to explain the frequency with which the modernists both engaged in translation and employed it as at once a compositional and a conceptual strategy. Thus, when Pound declares in "How to Read" that "some of the best books in English are translations" (*LE*, 34), later specifying this assessment in the *ABC of Reading* by calling Arthur Golding's sixteenth-century version of Ovid's *Metamorphoses* "the most beautiful book in the language,"[19] he implicitly endorses the capacity of translation to function as an avenue of genuine aesthetic expression and as a source of enduring literary value.[20] Similarly, the lavish praise he offers to Lady Gregory's rendering of Irish folktales in *Cuchulain of Muirthemne* makes it clear that Yeats considered translation a means by which Ireland could establish its own particular identity amid the crowd of world contemporary, and even historical, cultures: "I think this book is the best book that has come out of Ireland in my time. Perhaps I should say that it is the best book that has ever come out of Ireland; for the stories it tells are a chief part of Ireland's gift to the imagination of the world – and it tells them perfectly for the first time."[21] And in laying out the plans for the stock company of the proposed Irish Literary Theatre in the *Samhain* of 1901, Yeats tacitly presents translation as a crucial instrument in the formation of a robust national cultural identity. By "making it a point of performing Spanish, and Scandinavian, and French, and perhaps Greek masterpieces rather more than Shakespeare," the Irish Literary Theatre, he proposes, "would do its best to give Ireland a hardy and shapely national character by opening its doors to the four winds of the world, instead of leaving the door that is towards the east wind open alone."[22] Operating from a different set of ambitions and concerns entirely, H. D. gives in her novel *Bid Me to Live (A Madrigal)* a fictionalized account of her own approach in translating Greek. With a series of metaphors that moves from a decidedly masculinist "attack on those Greek words" to a method of productive exchange in "bargaining with each word," and finally to an explicitly reproductive and feminine image as her thinly veiled fictional self-representation "brooded over each word, as if to hatch it," she adumbrates a theory in which translation serves as a method for critiquing and engendering alternatives to masculinist constructions of both knowledge and literary production. William Carlos Williams summarized this aspect of modernist thought on translation when he said in a letter to the French Surrealist poet and art critic, Nicholas Calas, a small number of whose poems he translated, "You know, all this fits well into my scheme. I don't care how I say what I must say. If I do original work all well and good. But if I can say it (the matter of form I mean) by translating the work of others that is also valuable. What difference does it make?"[23] No longer the bastard child in the family of literary genres, translation came over the course of the modernist period to function and be recognized as a distinctly vital and generative writing practice.

Together with legitimizing its cultural pedigree as a mode of writing, the modernists also reconfigured the parameters for the very practice of translation itself, cleanly decoupling its linguistic from its more expressly literary dimensions, and thereby making possible such subsequent achievements as the radical versions of the odes of Catullus by Louis and Celia Zukofsky, as well as the diverse efforts of contemporary poetic translators like Stephen Mitchell, W. S. Merwin, Kenneth Rexroth, Robert Hass, and others.[24] During the course of modernism, translation as a literary mode rose to a level within the generic hierarchy fundamentally different from that which it occupied during other periods of English literary history, and this difference manifests in both the scope and the methods of the modernists as they engaged in the practice of translation itself.

Before modernism, literary translation functioned primarily as a means for renewing and strategically deploying the authority of the classics, which explains why the most renowned translators in English of earlier eras – Golding and Chapman in the Elizabethan, Dryden and Pope in the Enlightenment, and Browning, Rossetti, and Swinburne in the Victorian – all derive their reputations specifically as translators from their renderings of various Latin and Greek writers and other figures explicitly connected with the classical tradition.[25] While the modernists certainly coveted the monumental authority of classical writers, especially Homer, they also explored alternative sources for such enabling models, employing translation as a strategy by which to underwrite their own cultural ambitions and advance their own aesthetic and ideological ends. In doing so, they expanded the geographical and temporal domain of literary translation to include works outside the Western tradition entirely, as well as more recent figures by no means assured of their place in the canon. Thus, long before he gave a conceptual rendering of Homer in *Ulysses*, Joyce sought to promote in Ireland his taste for nineteenth-century continental drama when he translated Gerhart Hauptmann, a relative contemporary, in his youthful version of *Vor Sonnenaufgang*. If Yeats and H. D. directed their efforts as translators exclusively to classical Greek drama and poetry, William Carlos Williams translated exactly contemporary poets writing in Spanish and French. Pound translated not only Sextus Propertius, but also Li Bai, and while *The Cantos* opens with a rendering of the Nekuia episode in *The Odyssey*, the poem also includes long passages culled from a Qing dynasty historical treatise. Indeed, some of Pound's most important translations include his deeply unorthodox, yet fascinating treatments of books from the Confucian tradition of political and social thought.

Without a doubt, however, the most dramatic indication of the change that took place during the modernist period in the dimensions of translation as a literary mode lies in the extent to which formal knowledge of the source language no longer constituted a requirement for its practice. Before the modernists, translators in English as well as other languages simply proceeded under the assumption that full comprehension of the source language represented a necessary condition for translation. Indeed, theorists of translation before the modernist period made such knowledge a formal requirement for the practice itself. Thus, in 1711, Dryden asserts that "The qualification of a translator worth reading must be mastery of the language he translates out of, and that he translates into," though he concedes that "if a deficience be to be allowed in either, it is in the original, since if he be but master enough of the tongue of his author as to be master of his sense, it is possible for him to express that sense with eloquence in his own, if he have a thorough command of that."[26] Exactly 150 years later, Matthew Arnold, the most influential theorist of translation during the Victorian period, took this requirement one step further, asserting that proper translation must include scholarship as a major component. In his famous essay "On Translating Homer,"[27] which began as a series of lectures at Oxford University in 1860, he argues:

> [The translator] is to try to satisfy *scholars*, because scholars alone have the means of really judging him. A scholar may be a pedant, it is true, and then his judgment will be worthless; but a scholar may also have poetical feeling, and then he can judge him truly; whereas all the poetical feeling in the world will not enable a man who is not a scholar to judge him truly. For the translator is to reproduce Homer, and the scholar alone has the means of knowing what Homer is to be reproduced. He knows him but imperfectly, for he is separated from him by time, race, and language; but he alone knows him at all. (emphasis in the original)

Ideally, for Arnold, translation unites the sensitivity and skills of a poet with the knowledge and learning of a literary scholar.

By contrast, modernist writers repeatedly engaged in translation, and sometimes achieved remarkable results, with partial, imprecise, faulty, and sometimes even no formal understanding of the languages in which the texts they translated were originally written. Moreover, as the case of Pound alone most clearly illustrates, modernist translators' knowledge of the source language had little to do either with their willingness to translate a given text or, indeed, the success of their translations. Joyce had at best a tenuous grasp of German when he undertook *Vor Sonnenaufgang*. After considering his translation of Hauptmann for performance at the Irish Literary Theatre and showing it to a friend versed in German, Yeats wrote to Joyce, chiding him lightly "that you are not a very good German scholar."[28] Yeats himself knew absolutely no Greek when he translated *Oedipus Rex* and *Oedipus at Colonus* in 1928, piecing together his versions from a number of preexisting renderings. H. D.'s knowledge of Greek remains a subject of considerable scholarly debate. And while Pound's formal training as a graduate student in comparative literature, as well as his individual gifts for languages, underlie his translations of Cavalcanti, Arnaut Daniel, and other Romance poets, by the time he began work on *Cathay* in 1914, he had absolutely no knowledge of Chinese. Indeed, as he continued over the course of his career to translate works from the Confucian tradition, he came to believe that his lack of knowledge, far from being a hindrance, actually represented a decided advantage in his attempt to reproduce even the mode of signification encoded within the very characters of the texts themselves. His adherence to the evocative, but vastly oversimplified theories of Ernest Fenollosa about the nature of the Chinese language merely allowed him to justify his own ignorance and, indeed, see it as a positive trait, one that made it possible for him to penetrate the layers of scholarship that had accumulated over time to arrive at a genuine, poetic understanding of Confucian political wisdom. Likewise, H. D. and Yeats explicitly rejected classical training as a barrier to authentic translation. And even though many of the translators themselves knew the languages from which they made their renderings, the editors of *The Poets' Translation Series* expressed the pervasive modernist distrust of scholarship when they described their intentions in the following terms:

> The object of the editors of this series is to present a number of translations of Greek and Latin poetry and prose, especially of those authors who are less frequently given in English.

> This literature has too long been the property of pedagogues, philologists, and professors. Its human qualities have been obscured by the wranglings of grammarians, who love it principally because to them it is so safe and so dead.... The translators will take no concern with glosses, notes, or any of the apparatus with which learning smothers beauty.... The first six pamphlets, when bound together, will form a small collection of unhackneyed poetry, too long buried under the dust of pedantic scholarship.[29]

Understandably, perhaps, such unorthodox beliefs and practices continue to raise objections, either as expressions of an imperialist arrogance or, at best, as convenient rationalizations that serve to mitigate personal failings. Nevertheless, this valorization of their own ignorance and the consequent willingness (and even insistence) to undertake renderings of texts for which they lacked command of the source language together fundamentally differentiate the modernist practice of translation from that of previous eras. Thus, during the modernist period, translation came into its own, serving as an expressly generative and literary mode of writing, rather than a principally linguistic operation limited in scope simply to reproducing the "meaning" of a foreign text. No longer governed by traditional conceptions of semantic fidelity and the constraints of linguistic knowledge, it functioned, and should be viewed, as a mode of literary production fundamentally comparable to and, indeed, deeply constitutive of the other major modernist forms of poetry and prose fiction.

From its earliest beginnings, modernism always sought to negotiate between a variety of conflicting impulses. Even as they sought to break away from the established modes and stances of their predecessors, modernist writers like Yeats, Pound, H. D., and Joyce turned to the ancient past for sources of inspiration and models of literary creativity. And even as they sought to bring literature to the forefront of culture, they produced texts expressing at best indifference, and sometimes outright hostility, to even the most attentive and devoted readers. And even as they sought to make English into a world language by producing works with expressly epic ambitions, they used a wide range of foreign languages and texts to extend the possibilities of both the literary forms they inherited and even the English language itself. As a strategy for negotiating these demands, translation became an immensely important literary practice, gaining over the course of modernism a significance in the realm of English literary culture that it had not possessed since the time of Dryden.

Throughout the modernist period, then, translation occupied a manifold conceptual space: it constituted an autonomous literary activity that inspired sustained and varied critical reflection; it functioned as a specific technique in the construction of texts in a variety of different modes, ranging from "original" works to so-called adaptations to "translations" proper, as that term has been traditionally understood, texts by which various writers both expanded the scope of modernism and explored issues of gender, politics, and language itself; and it embodied a comprehensive textual strategy for negotiating between the demands of transmission and transformation, between the authority of tradition and the demands of innovation, between the endowments of the past and the imperatives of the present. In their drive to develop and renew different formal and social possibilities, the modernists turned to translation and, in turn, reinvented it as a uniquely important mode of literary composition.

Notes

1   See Chamberlain (1992) and Johnson (1985).
2   Lefevere, 96–97.
3   Berman, 2.
4   Pound, *Literary Essays of Ezra Pound*, 232.
5   In an interview with Donald Hall, *Paris Review*, 1961. As cited in Moore, 263.
6   Such a series, published by the Egoist Press, also indicates the importance of little magazines like *The Egoist* in the development of modernism. For a thoroughly researched and historically nuanced account of this aspect of modernism, see Mark S. Morrison.
7   This is the same poet known through Pound's famous renderings as Li Po.
8   From the Preface to Eliot's translation, *Anabasis*, 10.
9   Letter from D. H. Lawrence to Kosteliansky, August 10, 1919.
10   These novels were *Mastro Don Gesualdo* in 1923, *Little Novels of Sicily* in 1925, and *Cavalleria Rusticana* in 1928.
11   This is, of course, one of Pound's several definitions of an epic, and one he repeatedly employed for *The Cantos*.
12   *The Cantos of Ezra Pound*, Canto LXXXVI, 563.

13   Eliot, l. 95.
14   Kenner, 149.
15   See Reid.
16   Williams, 198.
17   See Lawrence.
18   Senn, 38.
19   Pound, *The ABC of Reading*, 58.
20   Comparably, in the essay "Dateline" originally published in 1934, he bestows upon translation a critical function, placing it as the second of five categories of criticism, the remaining of which are criticism by discussion, criticism by exercise in the style of a given period, criticism via music, and, the most intense form among the group, criticism in new composition. See *LE*, 74–87.
21   Yeats, 3.
22   Yeats, 75–76.
23   WCW to Calas, December 4, 1940, Lilly Library, Indiana. As cited in Williams, 451–452.
24   A major exception to this general trend is Fitzgerald, whose version of the *Rubaiyat* exerted a profound influence over both his contemporaries and modernists such as Pound.
25   Even such unorthodox translators as Abraham Cowley (1618–1667) and Francis Newman (1805–1897), brother to the famous Cardinal, both knew well the Greek from which they made their renderings of Pindar and Homer respectively. For more on Newman and his debate with Arnold, see Venuti, 118–147.
26   From "The Life of Lucian," in Dryden.
27   Arnold 218.
28   Letter from Yeats to Joyce, 1904. As cited in Ellmann, 178.
29   Introductory Note to *The Poets' Translation Series* (London: The Egoist Press, 1915), 7–8.

References

Arnold, Matthew. (1961). "On Translating Homer." In *Poetry and Criticism of Matthew Arnold*, ed. A. Dwight Culler. Cambridge: The Riverside Press.

Berman, Antoine. (1984). *The Experience of the Foreign: Culture and Translation in Romantic Germany*, trans. S. Heyvaert. Albany: State University of New York Press.

Chamberlain, Lori. (1992). "Gender and the Metaphorics of Translation." In *Rethinking Translation: Discourse, Subjectivity, Ideology*, ed. Lawrence Venuti. New York: Routledge.

Dryden, John. (1962). *Of Dramatic Poesy and Other Critical Essays*, vol. 2, ed. George Watson. London: J. M. Dent and Sons.

Eliot, T. S. (1963). Four Quartets. "Little Gidding," l. 95. *Collected Poems: 1909–1962*. New York: Harcourt Brace and World.

Ellmann, Richard. (1959). *James Joyce*. New York: Oxford University Press, rev. edn 1983.

Johnson, Barbara. (1985). "Taking Fidelity Philosophically." In *Difference in Translation*, Joseph F. Graham. Ithaca, NY: Cornell University Press.

Kenner, Hugh. (1971). *The Pound Era*. Berkeley: University of California Press.

Lawrence, Karen. (1981). *The Odyssey of Style in Ulysses*. Princeton, NJ: Princeton University Press.

Lefevere, André. (1992). *Translation, Rewriting, and the Manipulation of Literary Fame*. New York: Routledge.

Moore, Marianne. (1961). *The Marianne Moore Reader*. New York: Viking.

Morrison, Mark S. (2001). *The Public Face of Modernism: Little Magazines, Audiences, and Reception, 1905–1920*. Madison: The University of Wisconsin Press.

Perse, St. John. (1938). *Anabasis*, trans. T. S. Eliot. New York: Harcourt, Brace and Company.

Pound, Ezra. (1960). *The ABC of Reading*. New York: New Directions.

Pound, Ezra. (1968). *Literary Essays of Ezra Pound*. New York: New Directions.

Pound, Ezra. (1986). *The Cantos of Ezra Pound*. New York: New Directions.

Reid, Richard. (1986). *Discontinuous Gods: Ezra Pound and the Epic of Translation*. PhD Dissertation, Princeton University.

Senn, Fritz. (1984). *Joyce's Dislocutions: Essays on Reading as Translation*, ed. John Paul Riquelme. Baltimore: The Johns Hopkins University Press.

Venuti, Lawrence, ed. (1992). *Rethinking Translation: Discourse, Subjectivity, Ideology*. New York: Routledge.

Williams, Williams Carlos. (1986). *The Collected Poetry of William Carlos Williams*, vol. 2, ed. Christopher MacGowan. New York: New Directions.

Yeats, W. B. (1962). *Explorations*. London: Macmillan.

13

Modernism, Mind, and Manuscripts

Dirk Van Hulle

Why have so many modernist writers kept their manuscripts? In her capacity as director of the manuscript department of the Bibliothèque Nationale de France, Florence Callu (1993) opened a chapter on twentieth-century manuscripts by noting that this is the beginning of a "golden age": "Commence alors l'âge d'or du manuscrit contemporain. Tout auteur – du plus modeste au plus grand – préserve la moindre note, le moindre 'tapuscrit', le moindre placard corrigé comme une relique" (65). Callu's use of the religious metaphor of relics is appropriate in this context if, as Peter Childs suggests, the "diagnosis of the individual" in literary modernism "came to substitute for religion" (60). If manuscripts are relics of the workings of the mind, it is understandable that many literary modernists preserved them, and this act of preservation can be linked to the content of their works. Manuscripts thus become part of a modernist project, described by Finn Fordham (2010) as "reformulating the self" or "the reconstruction of ideas of selfhood and identity," which is turned "Inside-Out" in his chapter on "Modernism and the Self": "Manuscripts – broadly understood – have been underestimated as a potential scene from which such reformulations can be both provoked and described" (35). The program of "reformulating the self" is presented as part of the so-called "shift from outside to inside" (Meisel 2006, 79) that is often associated with literary modernism.

Recent developments in post-cognitivist philosophy, however, question the inside/outside dichotomy with regard to descriptions of the mind. These developments are directly relevant to the study of modernism's preoccupation with the workings of the mind and representations of consciousness. In narrative theory, concepts from the cognitive sciences and from cognitive philosophy are usefully employed to develop a vocabulary for the analysis of stories, focusing mainly on the *reception* of literary texts. Genetic criticism has the expertise to investigate

A Handbook of Modernism Studies, First Edition. Edited by Jean-Michel Rabaté.
© 2013 John Wiley & Sons, Ltd. Published 2013 by John Wiley & Sons, Ltd.

the relevance of recent developments in cognitive philosophy for the *production* of literary texts. In "Re-Minding Modernism," David Herman (2011) suggests that modernist writers could be regarded as "*Umwelt* researchers in von Uexküll's sense – explorers of the lived, phenomenal worlds that emerge from, or are enacted through, the interplay between intelligent agents and their cultural as well as material circumstances" (266). The notion of "*Umwelt*" employed in this context is based on the Estonian biologist Jakob von Uexküll's coinage, applied to such organisms as the tick. An *Umwelt*, in this biological context, is the organism's model of the world. It consists of all the meaningful aspects of the world for any particular organism, for example, water, food, shelter, potential threats, or points of reference for navigation. Each organism has a unique history, so each organism also has a different *Umwelt*:

> Mit der Zahl der Leistungen eines Tieres wächst auch die Anzahl der Gegenstände, die seine Umwelt bevölkern. Sie erhöht sich im Lauf des individuellen Lebens eines jeden Tieres, das Erfahrungen zu sammeln vermag. Denn jede neue Erfahrung bedingt die Neueinstellung gegenüber neuen Eindrücken.

> [As the number of an animal's performances increases, so does the number of objects that populate its *Umwelt*. It increases in the course of the individual life of each animal that is capable of gathering experiences. For every new experience brings about the new attitude to new impressions.] (von Uexküll 1956, 69)

Especially the last sentence in this passage stresses the organism's constant interaction with its surroundings. An organism creates and reshapes its own *Umwelt* every time it interacts with the world. Because of this interaction, mind and world are inseparable. Instead of viewing the world as one entity that contained all living species, stemmatically relatable in a tree of life, von Uexküll came up with the suggestion of a variety of worlds-as-perceived. Von Uexküll's attempt to describe the tick's *Umwelt* is so defamiliarizing that Giorgio Agamben (2002) has called it a pinnacle of modern antihumanism, to be read next to *Ubu Roi* and *Monsieur Teste* (69).

In order to present a world as a world-as-perceived, writers need to be keen observers of the way intelligent agents experience the world. If modernist writers can be regarded as "*Umwelt* researchers," they necessarily start from their own *Umwelt* and their research in its turn becomes part of their *Umwelt*. While performing their research, they also construe their own *Umwelt*, typically by means of manuscripts, which can be regarded as part of what in cognitive philosophy is often referred to as the "extended mind" (Logan 2007; Menary 2010). The present essay investigates the role of manuscripts in these "construals."

The So-Called "Inward Turn"

One of the most conspicuous effects of modernist fiction is its attempt to find new ways of allowing readers to "enter" the minds of its characters. To a large extent, modernist writers themselves are responsible for creating this commonplace view of the mind as an interior space. Virginia Woolf's rhetoric in essays such as "Mrs. Brown and Mr. Bennett" or "Modern Fiction" not only aimed at creating a rift between her own generation and the previous one, but Woolf (1972) also insisted on the image of "entering" her characters' minds, under the famous motto: "Look within" (106). Although criticism has punctured this rhetoric, the image of "looking within" is persistent. For instance, in his introduction to James Joyce's book project *Stephen Hero*, Theodore Spencer describes Joyce's endeavor as an attempt "to place his centre of action as much as possible *inside* the consciousness of his hero" (Joyce 1969, 17; emphasis added). According to Woolf, "Mr. James Joyce" was the "most notable" exponent of the new generation of authors whose work distinguished itself from the previous generation's. To investigate how this effect of "entering" a mind is achieved, Joyce's writings may serve as a suitable case study.

With reference to criticism of Romanticism, Jerome McGann (1983) pointed out to what extent critics were influenced by the self-images of the Romantics and their writings were "dominated by a Romantic Ideology, by an uncritical absorption in Romanticism's self-representations" (1). To some extent a similar observation applies to twentieth-century criticism of modernism. The so-called "inward turn," which has become "something of a critical commonplace" (Herman 2011, 249), is based on a Cartesian model of the mind as an interior space. A good example of the critical response to that "inward turn" is the notion of "skullscape" that is frequently used in Beckett studies. For instance, Samuel Beckett's stage setting of *Fin de partie / Endgame* has been interpreted as the inside of a skull. The stage directions do start with a description of a *"Bare interior. Grey light. Left and right back, high up, two small windows, curtains drawn"* (Beckett 2009a, 5). From this "internalist" perspective, the play can be connected to Beckett's early novel *Murphy*, notably the famous chapter 6 about Murphy's mind. But Beckett's extreme examples of the "inward turn" entail a serious criticism of the Cartesian dualism between mind and body. Murphy aspires to pure Cartesianism: "For it was not until his body was appeased that he could come alive in his mind, as description in section six. And life in his mind gave him pleasure, such pleasure that pleasure was not the word" (Beckett 2009b, 4). Yet, after the realization that this extreme focus on the "inside" of the mind leads to solipsism, both the body and the mind of Murphy (in the form of his ashes) are eventually scattered among an "external" world that consists of such demented particulars as "the sand, the beer, the butts, the glass, the matches, the spits, the vomit" (171).

The Cartesian mind-body split in terms of an "inside" and an "outside" is not only mocked in *Murphy*, but also criticized by several cognitive philosophers. Daniel C. Dennett refers to Descartes' model as the "Cartesian theatre," suggesting the image of a small theater in the brain, where a tiny homunculus observes and interprets all the incoming sensory data (as if they were projected onto a screen) and where he makes decisions or sends out commands to the limbs – not unlike the way the "homunculus" Hamm commands Clov inside the bare interior of *Endgame*.

This homunculus would need a consciousness, which would in its turn necessitate another, even smaller homunculus inside that consciousness, etcetera, ad infinitum.

Instead of this scenario, Dennett suggests another metaphor, which he called the multiple-drafts model. In other words, the research object of genetic criticism serves as a model for the workings of the mind. In Dennett's multiple-drafts model, various sensory inputs from a certain event and various interpretations of these inputs happen at various times. The result is a succession of interpretations, which are comparable to multiple drafts of a narrative. Conscious experience thus appears as a process unfolding in time. The innovating aspect of this model is that it does not posit a clear boundary to separate a conscious experience from all other mental processing.

Another subdiscipline within cognitive sciences that criticizes a Cartesian model is "enactivism," which does not regard cognition as the representation of a pre-given world by a pre-given mind, but as the enactment of a world and a mind on the basis of performances. From this point of view, the modernists attempted, not to "look within," but to study the resulting *Umwelten*, focusing on what David Herman calls "the nexus between intelligent agents and the environments they seek to navigate" (2011, 264). Herman's analysis of the confession scene in *A Portrait of the Artist as a Young Man* is a convincing example of Joyce's complex representation of Stephen Dedalus's mental construals, marked by the interweaving of two systems of understanding:

> A soft whispering noise floated in vaporous cloudlets out of the [confession] box. It was the woman: soft whispering cloudlets, soft whispering vapor, whispering and vanishing. He beat his breast with his fist humbly, secretly under cover of the wooden armrest. He would be at one with others and with God. He would love his neighbor. (Joyce 2000, 154)

Thanks to Stephen's past interactions with similar environments (churches, chapels), he is familiar with the so-called "protocols" for inhabiting this ecosystem. But while he perceives this environment with his *religious* system of understanding (kneeling, waiting, preparing for confession), his *poetic* system of understanding interferes (the repetitious melopoeia of the "soft whispering" cloudlets and vapor) and the tension between these two systems "suggests the extent to which Stephen oscillates between them, switching back and forth between two ways of orienting himself within his environment via two competing sets of action possibilities" (2011, 259).

The vocabulary developed to describe the interaction between mind and environment in terms of "protocols" corresponds with Daniel Ferrer's important definition of modern manuscripts as "des protocoles pour la fabrication d'un texte": "C'est la diversité et la complexité des *instructions* composant ces protocoles qui font du brouillon un espace ouvert, échappant à l'implacable exigence de répétition à laquelle est soumis l'espace textuel" (Ferrer 2011, 182; emphasis added). The definition of modern manuscripts, not as texts but as protocols for making a text, regards them as "instructions," in function of an afterlife.

But these documents do not only function solely in view of an afterlife; they also have a life of their own, marked by a logic that functions along the lines of what cognitive philosophy calls *enaction*. Activity is central in the enactive approach to the so-called "extended mind," an approach that focuses on "how the manipulation of environmental vehicles constitutes cognitive processes" (Menary 2010, 21). This is relevant for the study of writing processes, for such an "environmental vehicle" can be a notebook or a draft – which opens perspectives for genetic criticism.

The Manuscript as "Environmental Vehicle"

In the enactivist paradigm of cognitive science, writing is "not a simple derivative transcription of spoken language" but "an integral part of cognitive operations that would be simply impossible on the sole basis of spoken language" (Stewart 2011, 23). While narratology makes these cognitive philosophical concepts operational for narrative analysis, genetic criticism can probe them to analyze the dynamics of the process of writing – which is always a process of *thinking and* writing. In "Writing as Thinking," Richard Menary (2007) employs his notion of "cognitive integration" to show that the creation and manipulation of "written vehicles" is part of our cognitive processing and to argue that "writing transforms our cognitive abilities" (621).

The eighteenth-century scientist and satirist Georg Christoph Lichtenberg already noted in his notebooks or "Sudelbücher": "jeder der je geschrieben hat, wird gefunden haben, dass schreiben immer etwas erweckt, was man vorher nicht deutlich erkannte, ob es gleich in uns lag" ["anyone who has ever written will have experienced that writing always awakens something that one had not previously recognized clearly, even though it was lying simply within us"] (Lichtenberg 1968, I.653, notebook J.19). The observation that the act of writing often facilitates the process of thinking is a well-known phenomenon in genetic criticism. In this process of "writing as thinking," the notion of *invention* plays a central role.

In *Logiques du brouillon: Modèles pour une critique génétique* (2011), Daniel Ferrer defines the discipline of genetic criticism as the science of written invention – "la science de l'invention écrite" (184). The etymology of "invention" (Lat. "in-venire") is to "come in." For Joyceans, this etymology is reminiscent of a famous anecdote about Samuel Beckett's contribution to the composition process of *Finnegans Wake* – which was at that point still called "Work in Progress." According to the biographer Richard Ellmann, Joyce was dictating to Beckett. When Joyce asked him to read what he had written, Beckett read it out loud and arrived at a passage that said: "come in." Joyce interrupted Beckett and asked him where this "come in" came from. " 'Yes, you said that,' said Beckett," according to the biographer. "Joyce thought for a moment, then said, 'Let it stand.' He was quite willing to accept coincidence as his collaborator" (Ellmann 1983, 649). Whether this anecdote is true or not, it keeps being recounted. While Joyce's biographer introduced it, Beckett's official biographer, James Knowlson, questioned it, arguing that "it has proved hard for scholars to find the unintended words in the finished text" (1996, 99). Of course, if we really wanted to verify this anecdote, it would not suffice to examine the finished text; we would need to check hundreds of manuscript pages. But that is not the point here. The point is the tenacity of the anecdote, possibly because it confirms a common view on Joycean "invention" as a form of "coming in."

This "coming in" presents us with a metaphor – or a "model" in the sense of the "modèles pour une critique génétique" in Daniel Ferrer's *Logiques du brouillon* – in which not so much the author is the in-ventor, but something else, coming in from somewhere else. If this "somewhere else" is to be conceived as an "outside," it is important that, whatever it is that "comes in," it enters the *manuscripts* rather than the mind of the author. If the "come in" model of "invention" suggests an out/in metaphor, it is the outside and inside of "exogenesis" and "endogenesis," not the in/out of the mind/body dualism à la Descartes.

Raymonde Debray Genette coined the terms exogenesis and endogenesis in her article "Génétique et poétique: le cas Flaubert" (1979). Whereas exogenesis relates to the gathering of external information and materials, endogenesis focuses on the actual writing of drafts, including the processing, assimilation, appropriation, or absorption of this external information in the author's own work. As Pierre-Marc de Biasi (1996) indicates, the border zone between these two domains is necessarily vague since "the exogenetic procedure contains within itself the principle of its own effacement by writing" (46).

In spite of the recent recognition within the cognitive sciences of the role of writing in cognitive processes, there is still some skepticism among theorists of genetic criticism, who feel it is necessary to distinguish their discipline from the cognitive sciences before trying to find a common ground, as explored in articles (Lumbroso 2005; Lebrave 2010), lectures (Bernini, Oxford, October 31, 2011) and genetic colloquia (Aachen 2010; Antwerp 2011, "Figures of Thought: Between Thinking and Writing"). The word "versus" in the title ("Kognitive Forschung versus *critique génétique*") of Louis Hay's contribution to the latter, for instance, indicates the apparent need for a clear delineation, before an interdisciplinary exchange of views can take place. The reticence is understandable if cognitive sciences are understood in the cognitivist sense of an internalist conception of mind. The task of the genetic critic, according to Louis Hay, is to act as a ferryman between the universe of the writer and that of the reader – "Il lui faut être le passeur entre l'univers des écrivains et celui des lecteur, faire que le livre, dans leur main, ne reste pas un objet, mais vive encore de toutes les vies qu'il a traversées" (Hay 2002, 30). The concrete, material objects (manuscripts) are the starting point of genetic criticism. "Face à des traces ostensibles (. . .) elle peut passer du régime de la spéculation à celui de l'observation et dire *comment les choses se sont faites*" (19).

On the other hand, Daniel Ferrer (2011) insists that the research object of genetic criticism is *not* material; what it studies is "l'objet immatériel qu'est le processus d'écriture" (185). Regarding this process of writing, Louis Hay and Almuth Grésillon have suggested a dichotomy between *écriture à programme* and *écriture à processus* (Grésillon 1994). The "intelligent agents" enacting these forms of *écriture* all belong to what the editorial theorist Siegfried Scheibe called "Papierarbeiter" or "paper workers," because only paper workers leave palpable traces (Van Hulle 2008, 47).

Scheibe's other category is called "Kopfarbeiter" or "mind workers" in the sense of writers who conceptualize their literary work in their "heads" before putting pen to paper – according to the traditional, cognitivist opinion that the head is where the mind resides. But if this traditional dichotomy does not hold, according to post-cognitivist theories, and the mind should be regarded as "extended," the so-called "paper workers" are actually the kind of authors whose manuscripts show the mind at work.

Evidently, genetic criticism is not the science that "enters the author's mind" and investigates what goes on "inside"; that is not its field of expertise. But if the mind is by definition "extended" and the manuscripts are considered as part of the writer's *Umwelt*, the workings of the writer's mind can be "triangulated" or "trilaterated." In this respect, modernist manuscripts could serve as a GPS of modernist studies, a useful tool for what Herman (2011) dubbed "Remapping Modernism / Modernist Remappings: New Geographies of Mind" (254) and the study of the way in which intelligent agents navigate their environments. Through the use of "reflectors" Henry James already tried to embed the characters' construals of events into the discourse of narration. If modernists can be said to have "sought to develop an even finer-grained representation of the form and flow of mental activities as they unfolded in time" (247), the techniques they devised are not limited to interior monologue and stream of consciousness, punctuated by "moments of being," "mémoires involontaires," or "epiphanies."

Non-Epiphanies

To some extent, Joyce already parodied his own method of the epiphany as soon as he had developed it. Gabriel Conroy's famous epiphany toward the end of "The Dead," marked by the two stylistic X figures of the double antimetabole "softly falling" / "falling softly" and "faintly falling" / "falling faintly," is parodied in the endings of the chapters of *A Portrait of the Artist as a Young Man*, most conspicuously at the end of chapter 4: "soft and slight / slight and soft" (Joyce 2000, 186). Joyce's gradual distancing from the notion of "epiphany" in the sense of a "sudden spiritual manifestation, whether in the vulgarity of speech or of gesture or in a memorable *phase of the mind* itself" – as Stephen defines it in *Stephen Hero* (Joyce 1969, 216; emphasis added) – does not necessarily mean that moments of crystallization or sudden comprehension cannot occur, but it suggests the realization that, if such privileged moments occur at all, they do so thanks to intense construal processes and they often have a supportive rather than a climactic function in these processes, as Scott Berkun (2010) has pointed out: "The myth of epiphany tempts us to believe that the magic moment is the grand catalyst; however, all evidence points to its more supportive role" (8). When Stephen speaks of a "memorable phase in the mind itself," the notion of a "phase" suggests a series of mental activities unfolding in time.

If one were to apply this epiphanoid paradigm to Joyce's own work, a most "memorable phase" would be his shift of focus from a preoccupation with epiphanies to a more empathetic form of "*Umwelt* research." This is a paradox because the shift was not a "sudden spiritual manifestation," but a gradual process. As the number of an animal's performances increases, according to von Uexküll, so does the number of objects that populate its *Umwelt* (69; cf. supra) and every new experience brings about a new attitude to new impressions. In the world of James Joyce, at least one new attitude is incarnated by Leopold Bloom. In the very first chapter in which he is introduced in *Ulysses*, he bends down to his cat and wonders what a cat's *Umwelt* looks like: "They call them stupid. They understand what we say better than we understand them. She understands all she wants to. Vindictive too. Cruel. Her nature. Curious mice never squeal. Seem to like it. Wonder what I look like to her. Height of a tower? No, she can jump me" (Joyce 1993, 45). Bloom effortlessly switches from the first "They" to the second "They," from an anthropocentric perspective ("They call them stupid") to a feline point of view ("They understand what we say...."). This is precisely the kind of mental experiment Jakob von Uexküll performs in order to "see the world through the eye of a fly," or, in more general terms, "eine Anschauung der Umwelt eines Tieres zu gewinnen" [to gain an impression of an animal's *Umwelt*] (39). The title of von Uexküll's work would, for that matter, make an excellent candidate in a Monty Pythonesque "Summarize *Ulysses* Contest": Streifzüge durch die Umwelten von Tieren und Menschen [A Stroll through the Worlds of Animals and Men].

From a genetic point of view it is interesting that this scene of Bloom and the cat on the opening page of chapter 4 of *Ulysses* was developed in several phases. Only at a late stage in the process of composition – in the bottom margin of the first page proofs – did Joyce add the crucial lines reflecting Bloom's mental research into the cat's *Umwelt*. And this addition in its turn consists of two writing phases, for within the autograph addition, Joyce added yet another perspective, the point of view of mice. "Vindictive too. Cruel. Her nature. Curious mice never squeal. Seem to like it. Wonder what I look like to her. Height of a tower? No, she can jump me" (*JJA* 22, 173). Bloom's empathetic ability to put himself in other positions is the accumulated result of multiple drafts or phases in Joyce's *Umwelt* research.

Joyce's development as an *Umwelt* researcher could be described in terms of a shift of emphasis from a narrow focus on "memorable phases" to the complex process of the numerous other phases that make up the mind. These phases are the equivalent of what Daniel Dennett described in terms of "multiple drafts." It is of course just a metaphor, but it is a metaphor not only *we* live by (as Lakoff and Johnson would put it), but especially a metaphor many literary modernists lived by, often only gradually realizing the many complex implications of this metaphor. If the use of "reflectors" was a way of embedding the characters' construals of events into the discourse of narration, Joyce's vaguening of the notion of character in *Finnegans Wake* can be interpreted as a method of embedding in the discourse of narration the *process* of "enaction" (rather than the *products* in the form of "construals"). "*Umwelt* researchers" such as James Joyce seem to have done important spadework for post-cognitivist researchers to be able to demythologize the myth of epiphany and understand the workings of the mind in a more enactive sense. Scott Berkun compares the notion of epiphany to working on a jigsaw puzzle. The last piece that is put into place is only significant because of all the others that have been put into place before; what matters, according to Berkun, is not so much "the magic moment" but "the work before and after" (8). Against this background, Joyce's procedure in his "Work in Progress" demythologizes the epiphany, and to a large extent his manuscripts enable us to reconstruct some of that work.

Case study

A suitable case to examine the topical issue regarding the interplay of modernism, mind, and manuscripts is a note that eventually turned out to be important in the development of *Finnegans Wake*. When James Joyce took notes from a newspaper in a notebook shortly after finishing *Ulysses*, he did not yet have a clear idea of what his next work was going to be. To a journalist he claimed that he was going to write a "history of the world," but if and how this was going to take shape was far from established. When he read the *Daily Sketch* of December 14, 1922, he came across a petition regarding a murder trial (a source text discovered by Vincent Deane). A man called Frederick Bywaters had murdered the husband of his beloved Edith Thompson. In spite of an appeal and petitions for reprieve, the murderer was eventually hanged on January 9, 1923, and so was Edith Thompson, as she was considered an accessory to the murder. From the petition for reprieve that appeared in the *Daily Sketch*, Joyce excerpted several opinions, notably the following one:

> Three soldiers were walking together in Fleetstreet: one gave an opinion in which all concurred. It was the woman who was to blame. Bywaters played a bad part in the crime, but he was coerced. He proved himself a man afterwards. (*Daily Sketch*, 14 December 1922; qtd. in Deane, Ferrer, and Lernout 2001, 10)

When Joyce excerpted this passage (almost literally) in his notebook (VI.B.10, p. 71), it was simply a note among numerous others. Not until October 1923, almost one year later, did Joyce realize that it might be interesting for his new work. He started writing sections of this "Work in Progress" in a copybook that opens with the word "Guiltless" (preserved in the British Library, BL MS 27271b). This first word already indicates how Joyce was conceptualizing his new work at that moment: if his next book was going to be a history of the world it would be a history as perceived and construed by people. The protagonist of his "Work in Progress" might or might not have been involved in some vague crime, but it was crucial that the text would never plainly state the truth about what actually happened. The whole book can be regarded as a tangle of interrelated construals. Once a character claims that the protagonist is "Guiltless," that very construal can be interpreted as a sign that at least something fishy must be going on. From the lack of sufficient information each character construes his or her own narrative. And these construals are constantly readjusted as soon as new elements in the character's surroundings are picked up or overheard.

As soon as Joyce saw the potential of the note on the three soldiers and assimilated it in his text, it became an intertextual note. The first-draft version reads:

Three soldiers of the Coldstream Guards were walking in Montgomery street. One gave an opinion in which all concurred. It was the women, they said; he showed himself a man afterwards. (BL MS 47471b, page 3recto)

As the work "progressed" and the plot thickened, so did the phrasing of the passage:

Three tommix, soldiers, free, cockaleak and cappapee, of the Coldstream. Guards were walking, in (*pardonnez-leur, je vous en prie, eh?*) Montgomery Street. One voiced an opinion in which on either wide (*pardonnez!*), nodding, all the Finner Camps concurred (*je vous en prie, eh?*). It was the first woman, they said, souped him, that fatal wellesday, Lili Coninghams, by suggesting him they go in a field. Wroth mod eldfar, ruth redd stilstand, wrath wrackt wroth, confessed private Pat Marchison *retro*. (Terse!) (Joyce 1939, 58)

The intertext is still recognizable, but no matter how important the source text once was, the "thickening" elements are just as important, since they indicate the degree of interaction between exogenesis and endogenesis. The note plays an important role as a point of interplay between the two domains.

Among Joyce's notes, and among notes by other modernists as well, there are at least two different kinds of jottings: intertextual notes and conceptual notes. Conceptual notes are intuitively considered more important in literary studies than intertextual ones. In 1995, David Hayman denoted "source hunting" as "philological spadework," making a clear distinction between those "who limit themselves to the philological tasks" and "we others" (8). Hayman may have been right in urging "source hunters" to use "the implications of such findings (. . .) to disclose something about the text and its procedures," but at the same time an emphasis on the critical interpretation of notes should not lead to a neglect of the philological spadework (8). Confronted with handwritten notes, it is tempting to regard them as conceptual notes rather than "merely" intertextual ones. First of all, philological "spadework" or "source hunting" requires diligent research that can be extremely time-consuming; moreover, intertextual notes may turn out to be simply excerpts from an uninteresting newspaper article that eventually did not make it into the published text. If, on the other hand, one prefers to treat them as conceptual notes, one regards them as potentially important steps in the conception of the literary work. In 1999, David Hayman suggested the term "epiphanoiding" for a particular, Joycean form of conceptualizing his work. As an example, he quoted a series of notes from the same notebook VI.B.10 (pp. 77 and 78):

It's [a] comedy or smthg. Lord, I'm tired yawning (. . .)
child to father – Aren't we a pair of young rascals
Joycey (DB) / tugs at heartstrings
~~Jackie Coogan believes in caveman attitude to W~~ (qtd. in Hayman 1999, 37)

Hayman regarded this as an "epiphanoid" and interpreted it as follows: "The first item probably records [Joyce's wife] Nora's reaction to a book, but its glory derives from its wit and from the absurdity of her colloquial phrasing, her being 'tired yawning'" (37). In the transcription by the editors of the *Finnegans Wake Notebooks at Buffalo*, however, the first line does not read "It's [a] comedy or smthg" but "It's windy or smthg" (Deane et al. 2001, 94), which makes Hayman's interpretation less plausible. Regarding the other entries quoted above, Hayman admitted that they may have been taken from "a newspaper" (as Vincent Deane suggested to him), but nonetheless he proposed that "Joyce is treating it as a personal epiphanoid"; even with regard to the last item relating to Jackie Coogan, the child star from the silent movie *The Kid*, Hayman wrote that he was "tempted" to treat it as an epiphanoid "because its implications are personal and wry in a way characteristic of Joyce's wit" (38–39).

As Vincent Deane has shown, these items do not just derive from "a newspaper" but from the same newspaper as the Bywaters notes, the *Daily Sketch* of December 21, 1922, the day that was set for the (unsuccessful) appeal in the Bywaters case. "Joycey" for instance is based on the *faits divers* page, mentioning that "Many of my friends are going to the Côte d'Azur by sea [. . .] Vi Lorraine (Mrs Edward Joicey) is making this journey next week" (qtd. in Deane et al. 2001, 95). The note was taken from a section in the newspaper called "Echoes of the Town and Round About." It is telling that these trivialities are presented as "Echoes" – not the direct sound, but an indirect, roundabout reverberation. From the same page Joyce took the note about Coogan's belief in "the cave-man attitude to women" (qtd. in Deane et al. 2001, 95). In the endogenetic writing process (more specifically in his first draft), Joyce used this line in the same paragraph as the three soldiers. And he opened the previous paragraph with a line based on yet another note from VI.B.10 (p. 39): "these data, did we possess them, are too complex." In the first draft, this became: "The data, did we possess them, are too few to warrant certitude" and in the first typescript Joyce crossed out the word "data," replacing it by "unfacts" (British Library MS 47472–150; *JJA* 45, 189).

The data James Joyce himself worked with were sentences he snatched from his surroundings, such as one of the three soldiers' opinion in which all concurred: "It was the woman. He proved himself a man afterwards" (qtd. in Deane et al. 2001, 86) In the first draft, Joyce subtly changed the "woman" into plural "women" and "proved" into "showed": "he showed himself a man afterwards." One of the vague accusations made against the protagonist of *Finnegans Wake* is his so-called crime in Phoenix Park, Dublin. Judging from hearsay, this may have consisted in exposing himself to two girls or women. Taken out of its original context and placed in the new context of gossip and scandalmongering, the line with the changed verb ("he showed himself a man afterwards") suddenly became very ambiguous. But if exposing himself was the actual crime, the information was too explicit to run the gossip factory and in the typescript Joyce turned the "data" into an "unfact" by crossing out the line "He showed himself a man afterwards." (BL MS 47472–150;

JJA 45, 189). The whole book, Joyce's "history of the world," thus turns around a void – "In the buginning is the woid" (Joyce 1939, 378.29).

(De)composition, Bricolage, and Worldmaking

To the extent that *Finnegans Wake* can be read as a huge speculation about the protagonist's crime in the park, the idea of taking away the piece of the puzzle that allows one to suddenly see the whole picture ("he showed himself a man") is an excellent way of drawing attention to what Berkun called "the work before and after." This cancellation is an interesting example of the role of decomposition in the composition process. In *Logiques du brouillon*, Daniel Ferrer describes the subject of genetic criticism as a "dialectique de l'invention écrite" (185), that is, invention consists of a dialectics between composition and decomposition. Ferrer suggests that this notion of invention opens up the possibility of a larger relevance of genetic studies as genetic criticism could make an important contribution to the study of invention in our everyday lives, and even of the invention *of* our everyday lives (181). Especially Ferrer's exploration of possible worlds toward the end of his book is an important step in that direction. Notably the notion of bricolage could serve as a catalyst in order to find possible points of common interest between post-cognitivist philosophy and genetic criticism, especially against the background of modernism's preoccupation with consciousness. Modern manuscripts could be regarded as part of an *Umwelt* and reflect various "Ways of Worldmaking." And as Nelson Goodman already noted in 1978, "worldmaking (. . .) always starts from worlds already on hand; the making is a remaking": "The many stuffs (. . .) that worlds are made of are made along with worlds" (6).

A *Portrait of the Artist as a Young Man* is thus a remaking of *Stephen Hero*, and *Finnegans Wake* is made of such "stuff" as *faits divers* from newspapers like the *Daily Sketch*. The source may be trivial, but precisely the triviality seems important: Joyce's notes from the *Daily Sketch* illustrate his research into the "nexus between intelligent agents and the environments they seek to navigate" (Herman 2011, 264). The cluster of notes is neither an "epiphanoid" nor a "conceptual note," and yet it is important because it is an excellent illustration of the workings of the extended mind. If modernists can be regarded as "*Umwelt* researchers" (266), and if genetic criticism has the potential to make a contribution to the study of invention in our everyday lives, and even of the invention *of* our everyday lives (Ferrer 2011, 181; cf. supra), it might be possible to find common points of interest between the narratologist's and the genetic critic's views precisely in the area of post-cognitivist research: the extended mind as it functions, both in (i) the researcher's *Umwelt* (the writing as process) and in (ii) the *Umwelt* research (the writing as product).

(i) The researcher's *Umwelt*: although it is impossible to "enter" the mind of James Joyce in the cognitivist sense, it is possible to make a triangulation between the newspaper article, the note, and the first "construal" (the first-draft version). More notebook research on the period between December 14, 1922 and October

1923 might result in a more precise account of the way the first draft was construed. This triangulation could lead to a more precise mapping of what in a German-speaking context is more readily referred to as "conceptualization" than in a Francophone context or in an Anglophone context, which may prefer the notion of "crystallization." The more important question for modernism studies, however, is what this yields for modernist writings as "*Umwelt* research."

(ii) The *Umwelt* research: if the modernists' aim was not so much to "look within" – as Woolf formulated it – but to explore and map *Umwelten*, the anti-Cartesian multiple-drafts model suggested by Dennett may be an interesting model to find correspondences between the researcher's *Umwelt* (the process of "writing as thinking") and the *Umwelt* research (in the published text or the writing as product). The post-Cartesian, enactivist framework sheds new light on modernist narratives and the way they create the effect of a fictional world as it is perceived and experienced. Even though Virginia Woolf presented the endeavor to represent consciousness in terms of an inward/outward opposition, many modernists were remarkably sensitive to the process-like nature of the mind and its inseparability from its surroundings. The nexus between the mind and its environment is a constant process of interaction that helps constitute the mind in the first place. This process is sometimes more evident in modernists' manuscripts than in their published texts, and given the literary modernist preoccupation with the mind, it is therefore no wonder that so many of them did preserve their manuscripts.

References

Agamben, Giorgio. (2002). *L'Ouvert: De l'homme et de l'animal*. Paris: Éditions Payot & Rivages.

Beckett, Samuel. (2009a.) *Endgame*. London: Faber and Faber.

Beckett, Samuel. (2009b.) *Murphy*. London: Faber and Faber.

Berkun, Scott. (2010). *The Myths of Innovation*. Sebastopol: O'Reilly Media.

Bernini, Marco. (2011). "Supersizing Narrative Theory: Towards a Cognitive Approach to Form, Content, Intention and Interpretation." Paper delivered at Oxford University, October 31.

Callu, Françoise. (1993)."La Transmission des manuscrits." In *Les Manuscrits des écrivains*, ed. Anne Cadiot and Christel Haffner (pp. 54–67). Paris: CNRS editions/Hachette.

Childs, Peter. (2008). *Modernism*, 2nd edn. New York: Routledge.

Deane, Vincent, Daniel Ferrer, and Geert Lernout, eds. (2001). *The Finnegans Wake Notebooks at Buffalo: VI.B.10*. Turnhout: Brepols.

de Biasi, Pierre-Marc. (1996). "What Is a Literary Draft? Towards a Functional Typology of Genetic Documentation." *Yale French Studies* 89: 26–58.

Debray Genette, Raymonde. (1979). "Génétique et poétique: le cas Flaubert." In *Essais de critique génétique* (pp. 21–67). Paris: Flammarion.

Ellmann, Richard. (1983). *James Joyce*, rev. edn. Oxford: Oxford University Press.

Ferrer, Daniel. (2011). *Logiques du brouillon: Modèles pour un critique génétique*. Paris: Seuil.

Fordham, Finn. (2010). *I Do, I Undo, I Redo: The Textual Genesis of Modernist Selves*. Oxford: Oxford University Press.

Goodman, Nelson. (1978). *Ways of World-making*. Hassocks, UK: The Harvester Press.

Grésillon, Almuth. (1994). *Éléments de critique génétique: lire les manuscrits modernes*. Paris: Presses universitaires de France PUF.

Hay, Louis. (2002). *La Littérature des écrivains*. Paris: Corti.

Hayman, David. (1995). "Genetic Criticism and Joyce: An Introduction." In *Probes: Genetic Studies in Joyce*, ed. David Hayman and Sam Slote (pp. 3–18). Atlanta, GA: Rodopi.

Hayman, David. (1999). "Epiphanoiding." In *Genitricksling Joyce* (*European Joyce Studies* 9), ed. Sam Slote and Wim Van Mierlo (pp. 27–41). Atlanta, GA: Rodopi.

Herman, David. (2011). "Re-Minding Modernism." In *The Emergence of Mind: Representations of Consciousness in Narrative Discourse in English*, ed. David Herman (pp. 243–271). Lincoln: University of Nebraska Press.

Joyce, James. (1939). *Finnegans Wake*. London: Faber and Faber.

Joyce, James. (1969). *Stephen Hero*. London: Jonathan Cape.

Joyce, James. (1978–1979). *The James Joyce Archive*, ed. Michael Groden et al. New York: Garland [abbreviated as *JJA*].

Joyce, James. (1993). *Ulysses*, ed. Hans Walter Gabler with Wolfhard Steppe and Claus Melchior. Afterword by Michael Groden. London: The Bodley Head.

Joyce, James. (2000). *A Portrait of the Artist as a Young Man*. London: Penguin Classics.

Knowlson, James. (1996). *Damned to Fame: The Life of Samuel Beckett*. London: Bloomsbury.

Lebrave, Jean-Louis. (2010). "La critique génétique et les sciences cognitives." *Genesis: manuscrits, recherche, invention* 30: 131–150.

Lichtenberg, Georg Christoph. (1968). *Schriften und Briefe, Volume I: Sudelbücher I*. München: Carl Hanser Verlag.

Logan, Robert K. (2007). *The Extended Mind: The Emergence of Language, the Human Mind, and Culture*. Toronto: University of Toronto Press.

Lumbroso, Olivier. (2005). "Éléments pour une critique génétique cognitiviste: L'imagerie mentale chez Zola." *Poétique* 141: 320.

McGann, Jerome. (1983). *The Romantic Ideology*. Chicago: The University of Chicago Press,

Meisel, Perry. (2006) . "Psychology." In *A Companion to Modernist Literature and Culture*, ed. David Bradshaw and Kevin Dettmar (pp. 79–91). Oxford: Blackwell.

Menary, Richard. (2007). "Writing as Thinking." *Language Sciences* 5: 621–632.

Menary, Richard, ed. (2010). *The Extended Mind*. Cambridge, MA: MIT Press.

Stewart, John. (2011). "Foundational Issues in Enaction as a Paradigm for Cognitive Science." In *Enaction: Toward a New Paradigm for Cognitive Science*, ed. John Stewart, Olivier Gapenne, and Ezequiel A. Di Paolo (pp. 1–32). Cambridge, MA: MIT Press.

Van Hulle, Dirk. (2008). *Manuscript Genetics: Joyce's Know-How, Beckett's Nohow*. Gainesville: Florida University Press.

von Uexküll, Jakob. (1956). *Streifzüge durch die Umwelten von Tieren und Menschen: Ein Bilderbuch unsichtbarer Welten*. Hamburg: Rowohlt.

Woolf, Virginia. (1972). *Collected Essays*, vol. 2 (pp. 103–110). London: Hogarth Press.

14

Modernism and Visual Culture

Laura Marcus

"The frenzy of the visible" (Jean-Louis Comolli); "the society of the spectacle" (Guy Debord); "the tyranny of the eye" (Roland Barthes): these are just a few of the terms and phrases coined or deployed by theorists in recent decades to define modernity in relation to visibility, visuality, and perception. One of the most striking aspects of many theorizations of visuality and visual culture is, as these terms indicate, the ambivalence toward the primacy, or hegemony, of the visual. This negative critique is often identified with the theoretical perspectives of the second half of the twentieth century, influenced substantially by the work of Michel Foucault, whose writings on surveillance and the "panoptical" regime of the nineteenth century identified acts of looking with the exertions of power. Critiques of "ocularcentrism" (or the domination by vision) are the central topics of Martin Jay's compendious study *Downcast Eyes: The Denigration of Vision in Twentieth-Century French Thought* (1993), which begins with a discussion of "the ubiquity of visual metaphors," showing "how ineluctable the modality of the visual actually is, at least in our linguistic practice" (1). The question of vision goes far beyond literal acts of perception, of seeing and being seen, reaching into our inherited models of knowledge, thought, and ideation. The trajectory of Jay's study, however, is the tracing through of the "antiocularcentrism" that marks so much modern philosophy, aesthetic theory, and artistic practice.

As Jay's nod to James Joyce's "the ineluctable modality of the visible" suggests, modernist cultural practice plays a particularly important role in the exploration of visuality and culture, bringing together explicit, and at times violent, optical imagery with the indirections of mediated or internalized concepts of "an inner eye" or "mind's eye." At the same time, it should be noted that many modernist writers turned with exceptional frequency and fullness to the visual arts, in their endeavors

A Handbook of Modernism Studies, First Edition. Edited by Jean-Michel Rabaté.
© 2013 John Wiley & Sons, Ltd. Published 2013 by John Wiley & Sons, Ltd.

to define and work through questions of aesthetics and ideology, including issues concerning representation and mimesis, the nature of "the image," realism and anti-realism, temporality and consciousness, organic form, and artistic and cultural evolution. To this extent, literary modernism *is* a visual culture (Beasley 2007, 4).

W. J. T. Mitchell (1995), whose work has focused on iconography and sign systems within culture, as well as on the relationships between visual and verbal representations, has defined "visual culture" as "a new social/political/communicational order that employs mass spectacle and technologies of visual and auditory stimulation in radically new ways" (207). This broadens out the term from its more narrowly academic use as an extension of the territory of the fine arts (to take in architecture and design as well as painting and sculpture) and foregrounds its technological aspects. Implicit in Mitchell's definition is the argument put forward in one of its most influential forms by Walter Benjamin who, writing in the 1930s, made the argument that modern life was now thoroughly saturated, and "reality" fully mediated, by technological forms. The technology to which Benjamin pointed most emphatically, in his "The Work of Art in the Age of its Mechanical Reproducibility," was film, a focus which this chapter will share. It will also touch on developments in painting, in its discussion of relationships between the visual arts (to include painting, photography, and film) and modernist literature. Photography and film, which, respectively, came into being in the mid-nineteenth century and at that century's close, had a profound impact on the visual arts, displacing, for example, the value of artistic realism. They also served to make newly vulnerable the human organ of sight. In their power to extend human vision (in what Sigmund Freud understood to be a form of prosthesis) or to penetrate more deeply into reality than could the human eye (as Walter Benjamin has it), the technologies of the visual also exposed the human eye's frailties, partialities, and limitations.

In his introduction to his collection of essays *Signatures of the Visible*, Fredric Jameson wrote that the experiences of cinema and cinema-going might underlie the thought and writing of the twentieth century in ways we have not yet understood. Jameson (1990) instanced Jean-Paul Sartre's claim for his own theory of "contingency," "derived from the experience of film, and in particular from the mystery of the difference between the image and the world outside," and asks whether this might not be true even for artists and writers who have less obvious connections to film and to movie-going. "Did human nature," Jameson asks, "change on or about December 28, 1895?" (the date of the first screening of films by the Lumière brothers) (5). "Or was some cinematographic dimension of human reality always there somewhere in prehistoric life, waiting to find its actualization in a certain high-technical civilization? (and thereby now allowing us to reread and rewrite the past now filmically and as the philosophy of the visual)?" (5). Jameson poses these questions rhetorically. The awareness that it would be impossible to give answers to them that would carry any conceptual or historical weight does not diminish the desire to understand the impact and import of the coming of film – on literature, philosophy, human perception, the history of dreaming. It is a desire that is not, as Jameson seems to suggest, particular to the late twentieth century (at the close of "the century of cinema" and thus at the point where film might find "its philosophy as well as its history posthumously"), but one that emerges alongside the new medium. This is in part because film seemed, to its first viewers, to be a reproduction or doubling of the world itself – "a recreation of the world in its own image," in André Bazin's words – and thus engendered models or "film fables" (to borrow the title of Jacques Rancière's 2001 book) of origin and evolution that were both fantastical or utopian and historical through and through (Bazin 1967, 21).

"The film arrived," Robert Richardson (1969) wrote in his study *Literature and Film*, "as a new answer to certain literary searches, such as Hardy's for a mobile point of view, or the Imagists' concern with vividness and picturization" (1969, 34). There are a number of problems with the teleological nature of this argument, as well as with its overly literal understanding of "the visible." As Rancière (2007) suggests in *The Future of the Image*, "words make seen what does not pertain to the visible" (12). The focus on "vision," nonetheless, and the ways in which it is "framed" through the sectional or mobile gaze of narrator or character, in both film and literary texts, make their own contribution to that writing of the history of "the image" in culture for which Rancière and others have been calling.

* * * *

In his preface to *The Nigger of the "Narcissus"* (1897), Joseph Conrad wrote that, as artist, he aspired "by the power of the written word to make you hear, to make you feel . . . before all, to make you *see*. That – and no more, and it is everything. If I succeed, you shall find there according to your deserts: encouragement, consolation, fear, charm – all you demand – and, perhaps, also that glimpse of truth for which you have forgotten to ask" (1925, x). "Before all, to make you *see*" seems to indicate both a hierarchy, in which vision becomes the most important of the senses, and a temporal model, in which vision has primacy. Yet "to make you *see*" comes at the end of the sentence, after the invocation of hearing and feeling. We might pause on the italicization of the "*see*" in the Conrad quotation – "to make you *see*." Writers and critics frequently place in italics words connected to sight and seeing, as if they were reaching toward the representation of visuality by means of typography – you "*see*" the emphasis, and the word comes closer to being an image. Visuality, we might say, becomes visible, as it does in Conrad's letter to William Blackwood, when he was in the early stages of writing *The Rescue*: "I aim at stimulating vision in my reader. If after reading *Part 1st* you don't *see* my man (Tom Lingard) then I've absolutely failed" (September 6, 1897) (Conrad 1983, 381). T. S. Eliot (1936), in footnote 218 of his Notes to *The Waste Land*, wrote: "What Tiresias *sees*, in fact, is the substance of the poem" (80). This is also an attempt to get beyond "mere" sight into a model of inner vision, in the face of Tiresias's blindness and his role as "seer." So *sees* in Eliot should perhaps be "sees," leading us to the question of blindness and insight, and to the figurative dimensions of sight and vision. The question then arises: to what extent could it be legitimate to interpret Conrad's emphases in relation to the eye, rather than the mind's eye, and to make vision the first sense (a "before all") rather than to understand it as transcendence (an "above all")? This corresponds to the critical move made by modernism's "visual turn" and to the correlation between modernist literature's models of "presented vision" and the visual and optical technologies of the same period, in particular the new medium of film.

In contrast to the critics for whom vision has a more metaphorical sense, Fredric Jameson offers an account of Conrad that emphasizes "vision" as literal perception, isolated from the other senses. Jameson (1981) analyses Conrad's "aestheticizing strategy" as the "designation of a strategy which for whatever reason seeks to recode or rewrite the world and its own data in terms of perception as a semi-autonomous activity" (230). Conrad's construction of point of view would seem to share with Henry James and other nineteenth-century novelists a "theater-goer's position with respect to the content of the narrative," in its deployment of terms such as "scene," tableau, spectacle. Yet, Jameson argues, "Conrad displaces the theatrical metaphor by transforming it into a matter of sense perception, into a virtually filmic experience" (232).

Film has entered the discussion of Conrad's fiction in a further route, by means of the familiar phrase, "to make you *see*." In 1913, the American pioneer film-director D. W. Griffith is reported by an interviewer to have stated: "The task I'm trying to achieve is above all to make you see." Griffith's echo of Conrad's phrase has been deployed to secure a relationship between film and literature. Mid-twentieth-century critics exploring the film–literature relationship have divided between those who see compatibility, hostility, or interchangeability between "the percept of the visual image and the concept of the mental image" (Bluestone 1968, 2). Most recently, David Trotter's *Cinema and Modernism* quotes the Conrad–Griffith association around "to make you see" to reinforce his argument that Griffith went to literature not just for narrative structuring devices but for "its understanding of the 'systems of time and space' which constitute the lived world"(Trotter 2007, 51). Trotter's study takes its stand against critical assumptions that the relationship between literature and film can be defined through a set of exchangeable techniques. Film, he argues, comes into being as a recording medium: literature is a representational medium, even if it is one which, with the advent of modernism, constructs as its axiom "literature as (recording) medium *before* literature as (representational) art": "an axiom or medium sprung, at that particular moment in history, by the sudden preeminence of a medium which was from the outset, and remained at least for the ten years or so after its invention in 1895, a medium rather than an art" (5).

We are, in fact, talking, he suggests, about parallel developments, whose shared term is (in a revision of Foucault's "will to power" and Jameson's "will to style") a "will to automatism," the "automatism of the camera-eye's view," "the instrumentality of a non-living agent": "My hypothesis," Trotter writes, "is that some modernist writers found in film's neutrality as a medium a stimulus to the reintroduction or re-enactment of the neutrality of literature, or in some cases of writing itself, as a medium. It was not cinema which made literary modernism, but cinema's example" (9). The will to automatism was, Trotter argues, "the instrument by which writers and film-makers explored the double desire at once for presence to the world and for absence from it" (11). The argument extends the film theorist Christian Metz's definition of cinema as "the presence of an absence," an understanding that has shaped film aesthetics from cinema's earliest years, as in Georg Lukács' account, in 1913, of a defining lack of "presence" in film, through to the influential film-philosophy of Stanley Cavell. As Cavell (1979) has written: "I was led to consider that what makes the physical medium of film unlike anything else on earth lies in the absence of what it causes to appear to us; this is to say, in the nature of our absence from it; in its fate to reveal reality and fantasy (not by reality as such, but) by projections of reality, projections in which reality is freed to exhibit itself" (166).

* * * *

An issue of significant interest in the history of conceptions of film–literature relationships is their fluctuating appearances throughout the past hundred or so years. To summarize, we have explorations of the relationship in the 1920s and 30s, often written by scenario-writers and others involved in literary adaptation as well as by theorists and practitioners of documentary exploring the relative merits of film and literature in representing reality. There were also experiments, in the work of a number of 1920s and 1930s writers, in producing formal equivalences to the camera-eye and cinematic movement in their fiction: this was explored in a number of significant essays of the period. Sergei Eisenstein's essay "Dickens, Griffith and the Film To-Day," first published in Russian in 1944, remains one of the key contributions to the field, and was highly influential on the criticism to come; in particular, in its focus on "montage" as a way of linking the novel and film, as well as its argument that filmic methods, and a filmic way of perceiving the world, preceded the invention of cinema as technology.

A much more obscure essay, now long-forgotten but cited by a number of commentators in its time, was the British critic G. W. Stonier's "The Movie," published in his 1933 collection *Gog Magog*. This perceptive essay noted aspects of the cinema that have become central to more recent film aesthetics. These include the importance of contingency and of the accidental or, in Stonier's term, the *"irrelevant"* detail; the particular or peculiar combination in cinema of documentary realism and aesthetic abstraction, to create "a new version of visible fact" (Stonier 1933, 180); film's "momentaneity" (186) and its "elasticity of size and distance" (187). This last attribute, Stonier argued, was to be found in the work of modernist writers including Joyce, Wyndham Lewis, Dos Passos, and Céline in which "the distance between the writer and the reader is liable to shift; the puppets do not move in uniform scale." Stonier noted the importance of the close-up (which for early theorists of film was the technique by which cinema came into its own as an art, liberating itself from theatrical representation) and "the substitution of a part of an image for the whole of it" ("the picture of feet crossing on a pavement: a seagull and a masthead; a hat floating among drift-weed; cigarette-smoke spiralling

up a window"). Such devices in films "has brought home their value afresh to
the writer: he sees now their particular *visual* property" (188). Stonier closes his
discussion with intimations that "the *silence* of the movie has affected the *silence* of
literature . . . This important quality in modern writing, produced by the absence
of the voice in what is written, has been altered, deflected ever so slightly, by the
far-reaching use of silence in films" (188). Finally, there is "the influence merely
of the analogy between the brain's flicker and a film. Bergson has described the
stream of consciousness as an interior cinema. With or without knowing it, many
writers have seen this comparison, and it has influenced their work" (188–189). His
observations are at once acute and tentative and speculative, pointing to a difficulty
in pinning down the nature of the influence and impact of cinema on literature
which inheres in discussions today.

Detailed discussions of film and literature do not appear again in any very
substantial way until a cluster of texts was published in the 1960s and 70s. These
years also saw the publication of some of the most influential texts of film aesthetics
and ontology, notably Stanley Cavell's *The World Viewed* (1971/1979). A little earlier,
Siegfried Kracauer's *Theory of Film: The Redemption of Physical Reality* had appeared
(published in 1960), following on from the Hungarian writer and film theorist Béla
Balázs' *Theory of the Film* (1952), both texts which gathered up and translated earlier
materials (from the 1920s and 30s). For Kracauer, it was the penetration and the
disclosure of physical reality, as a form of seeing again or seeing anew, which was
made central to the medium: Balázs (1952) also explored this dimension of film,
along with its power to show us not only the "face of objects," the "physiognomy
of things," in "a mighty visual anthropomorphism," but the human face, which, in
the final years of the silent film, "had grown more and more visible" (73). Cavell's
film-philosophy, as articulated in *The World Viewed*, took up Kracauer's model
of film reality (which for Cavell meant the unfolding of the world's reality in its
own image rather than our own) and Balázs' concept that film returns to us "the
inner and fixed lives" (in Cavell's phrase) of objects (Cavell 1979, 43). We find an
extension of this work not only in David Trotter's exploration of the "automatism"
of modernist film and literature, but also in the current critical focus on the "object
matter" of literary texts (Bill Brown) or "the ideas in things" (Elaine Freedgood), in
which the focus on commodity culture comes together with more physiognomical
(in Balázs' terms) approaches to the lives of objects.

Arnold Hauser's influential account of "The Film Age," published in 1958 as the
closing section of his *Social History of Art*, gave a further impetus to the film-literature
writings of the mid-twentieth century. In the 1950s, when Hauser was writing, and
in the spate of texts on the film–literature relationship that appeared in the 1960s
and 1970s, modernist writers became central figures for the exploration of past and
potential relationships between the novel and the cinema. As Hauser's argument
suggests, it was as if modernist fictional experiments with the representation of
time and space could serve as models for a cinema that had, it was suggested, lost
sight of its own radical and experimental possibilities, embedded and embodied in
its very medium, and was seeking out forms of representation and narration that

might be characterized as "realist." Modernist literature, it was suggested, thus had the potential to re-animate the film medium, and to bring it back to an awareness of its extraordinary capacities, arising out of its machinic nature, "to describe," in Hauser's words, "movement, speed and pace" (Hauser 1962, 243).

Writers including Woolf, Joyce, Proust, and Stein thus had a crucial role to play in the conceptualization of film–literature relationships at this juncture in literary and cultural history. In the middle and later decades of the twentieth century, narrative theory was preoccupied with the representation of time and space; visual–verbal relationships became central to structuralist approaches to narrative; and the anti-metaphysical tenets underlying the *nouveau roman* were concentrated in a fascination with the world of objects and material presences, with movement and gesture, and with the realization of a new clarity in vision and perception, untrammeled by anthropomorphism, sentiment, and habit. The analysis of film seemed to offer, to the literary critic above all, new ways of thinking through the terms of humanism and antihumanism, subjectivity and objectivity.

The fascination with subject–object, word–image, literature–film relationships in the 1960s and 70s then appeared to cede to, or become submerged beneath, the focus on textuality, and literary-theoretical interest in film, where it did emerge, tended to be concerned specifically with its graphic or hieroglyphic dimensions. It is the most recent decades that have seen a surge of interest not only in film–literature relationships, but more generally in the visual cultures of the modern period – including optics, photography, cinema – and their impact on literature. This is part, at least, of "modernism's visual turn." In the field of cinema and literature specifically, there have been a number of important recent books, most of them focused on modernist literature and avant-garde cinema and to a significant extent concerned with the "machinic modernism" which Hauser identified. Few of these studies express much interest in the work in the field produced in the middle decades of the twentieth century. It would seem, then, that the very visibility of cinema, as a structuring element in the creation and construction of literary texts, has itself been a flickering one, disappearing and reappearing in the cultural and conceptual field. Moreover, readers, it is implied, have to learn anew how to recognize the cinematic dimensions of the literary work.

Recent work in the field of film and literature has come together with the greatly increased interest in film studies with early cinema and the early history of the medium. To a large extent I share David Trotter's view that a term such as "cinematographic," when applied to literary texts, is insufficiently precise unless referred back to film's particular stages of development and writers' awareness of these. Yet there is also scope for a level of abstraction where the concept of the cinematic or "cinematicity" is concerned. We have writers' own generalized concepts of "the cinema mind," suggested by Conrad's argument, in a lecture he gave on "Author and Cinematograph" in 1923, that "the creator in letters aims at a moving picture – moving to the eye, to the mind, and to our complex emotions" (Schwab 1965, 344).

One dimension of modernism's "visual turn," as I have suggested, has been the mapping of questions of modernist visuality onto optical technologies – in particular, photography and early film. Following Conrad's hints, however, we might pause to reconsider the question of the novel as a "moving picture." Conrad's "Notes" for his "Author and Cinematograph" lecture seem less concerned with the relationship between literature and film as a question of "adaptation" than with the novel as (always having been) a form of cinema, whose motion and emotion are actualized by the reading process. The idea of continuous motion was clearly crucial to Conrad's conceptions of his novelistic practice, and colored many of his comments on visual media: "When writing I visualize the successive scenes as always in motion – a flow of closely linked effects, so that when I attempt to arrest them in my mind at any given moment the first thought is always: that's no good" (August 16, 1917) (Conrad 2002, 117). Similarly, his recorded comments on film nearly always return to the issue of motion. At least some of Conrad's expressed reservations toward the cinema (which have affinities with Henri Bergson's account of the limitations of the "cinematographical" mechanism of our ordinary knowledge, the cinematograph being composed of separate and unconnected instants and thus producing only the illusion of movement) seemed to concern its alleged failure to represent a smooth flow of actuality in motion: hence his recorded antipathy toward both slow-motion and the speeding up of action through cutting. This antipathy was at one with Conrad's idealizations of the literary "moving picture" and his models of visualization and actualization. Similar representations can be found in the work of D. H. Lawrence who, in his *Etruscan Places* (1932), wrote: "a man who sees, sees not as a camera does when it takes a snapshot, not even as a cinema-camera, taking its succession of instantaneous snaps; but in a curious rolling flood of vision, in which the image itself seethes and rolls; and only the mind *picks out* certain factors which *shall* represent the image seen" (1960, 171).

A different version of "the cinema mind" is at play in Virginia Woolf's reference to ideas and images moving across "the screen of my brain" or James Joyce's (in a letter to Harriet Weaver) to his "prolonged cinematographic nights" after his eye operations: "Whenever I am obliged to lie with my eyes closed I see a cinematograph going on and on and it brings back to my memory things I had almost forgotten" (Joyce 1966, 216). A strong association was drawn between cinema and mental life in the work of early film theorists, and in particular those informed by the psychology and philosophy of the period, so that from cinema's early years onward a connection was made between literature, film, and the mental apparatus, and (analogous to the concerns of Impressionist aesthetics) with the relationship between eye and mind or brain in the film's reception. Writers (as well as film theorists and indeed filmmakers) entertained their own visions of what cinema might or might not be, might or might not become. From the point of cinema's origins (with Edison, Méliès, and the Lumières) onward, there is a strongly utopian dimension to conceptions of film; conceived or fantasized, indeed, during cinema's most dim and flickering stages, as having not only the power to reproduce the world but to extend human life itself.

The "new modernist studies" has driven extensive work on the impact of the coming of film on a range of writers, including Gertrude Stein, Dorothy Richardson, James Joyce, Virginia Woolf, Wyndham Lewis, H. G. Wells. There has also been growing interest in those mid-century British writers – among them Graham Greene, Patrick Hamilton, Jean Rhys, Aldous Huxley, Henry Green, Elizabeth Bowen – whose fiction represents the experience of cinema-going as a form of modern pleasure or distraction continuous with everyday life. In this blurring of the distinction between what is on the screen and what is projected by consciousness – "my film-mind," as Rhys's heroine Sasha terms it in the novel *Good Morning, Midnight* (1939) – lie the seeds of the understanding (which it is perhaps inevitable that we can only glimpse rather than capture) that, for the moderns, experience and representation are mediated through and through by the technologies of the times.

*   *   *   *

Recent years have also seen the development of what we might call a Romanticist film theory, or way of writing about film; an absorption in and by fragments and ruins, and a preoccupation with the relationship between film (or photographic) and memory images. Recent works of film theory such as Victor Burgin's *The Remembered Film* (2004) and Laura Mulvey's *Death 24x a Second: Stillness and the Moving Image* (2006) point both to our nostalgic relationship to film fragments and to the ways in which new technologies are remaking our relationship to film images and sequences. Like Burgin, Mulvey makes the argument that "video and digital media have opened up new ways of seeing old movies," creating "the possibility of returning to and repeating a specific film fragment. Return and repetition necessarily involve interrupting the flow of film, delaying its progress, and, in the process, discovering the cinema's complex relationship to time" (Mulvey 2006, 8). Mulvey's interest in "stillness" in the cinema leads her to the cinema of the past as well as to "new mechanisms of delay." Dziga-Vertov's *Man with a Movie Camera* (1928) forms a central paradigm for her discussion, and in particular the sequence in which the frenzied movement of the film halts to show its editor, Elizaveta Svilova, in the editing suite, cutting the still frames which we have seen, or will see, in their animated form. Death emerges for Mulvey out of the presence of preserved time; in the porous boundaries between life and death and in cinema's mechanical animation of the inanimate.

The interruption or remaking of the flow of images and of sequences has in fact been present from the very early days of film and writing about film, as in the Surrealists' aleatory acts of cinema-spectatorship (the day spent entering one cinema after another, in the days of continuous performance, to watch just a part of whatever was being screened and thus composing or compiling a new film-in-the-head from the different film narratives they had seen). Much film writing of the 1910s and 20s committed to "film as an art" shared with Surrealism this desire to "liberate" images or sequences from, in Paul Hammond's words, "the narrative that held them prisoner" (Hammond, 2000, 8). For Jacques Rancière this "work of de-figuration," which entails extracting one film fable from the body of another, "making a film on the body of another," is as strongly present in the film writings of Gilles Deleuze (where it functions as an "ontological restitution") or of Jean-Luc Godard (in his *Histoire(s) du cinema*) as it is in the work of the early film theorist Jean Epstein (Rancière 2006, 7).

In a retrospective account of cinema-spectatorship in the first decades of the twentieth century, "As in a Wood," the Surrealist writer and artist André Breton wrote:

> We saw in the cinema then, such as it was, a lyrical substance simply begging to be hauled in en masse, with the aid of chance. I think that what we valued in it most, to the point of taking no interest in anything else, was its power to disorient.... The marvel, besides which the merits of a given film count for little, resides in the devolved faculty of the first-comer [the first person to come along, anyone] to abstract himself from his own life when he feels like it, at least in the cities, as soon as he passes through one of the muffled doors that give on to the blackness. From the instant he takes his seat to the moment he slips into the fiction evolving before his eyes, he passes through a critical point as captivating and imperceptible as that uniting waking and sleeping.... How come that the solitary spectator I have in mind, lost in the middle of these faceless strangers, at once takes up with them that adventure which is not his and is not theirs? (Hammond 2000, 373–340).

The passage contains much that defined Surrealist film-going: the celebration of the chance or "aleatory," which in turn, Breton suggests, precludes that "judgement" associated with a Kantian aesthetic: the cinema spectator's entry into a liminal or threshold space between sleeping and waking which recalls a Benjaminian fascination with states of "reduced attentiveness"; a "disorientation," "abstraction," and dispersal of subjectivity which would, though in rather different terms, be taken up by Benjamin and Kracauer in their accounts of the "cult of distraction" produced by the cinema and identified, as they would identify it, as an essentially urban phenomenon. The cinema trains the spectator, Benjamin suggested, in the transformed mode of perception demanded by modern life. For Siegfried Kracauer, "distraction" – originally a negative attribute, opposed to contemplative concentration – took on a positive aspect as it became anchored in a non-bourgeois mode of visual and sensorial experience, a form of attention or inattention appropriate to the fragmentary, discontinuous nature of the modern visual media.

The film spectator, in the contexts Breton described, was as "anonymous," as "untitled," as the film, or the part of the film, that he or she saw. Entering a film, and leaving it, in a temporality and logic determined only by the spectator's desire for the spectacle and the exhaustion of that desire, was the Surrealists' way of disrupting linear narratives and of producing their own form of "film," composed not only of an aggregate of the films seen on the occasions of their wandering, but of the interface between the city and the cinema, so that film-spectatorship itself becomes a form of *flânerie*. While Surrealist film-spectatorship was at one level a counter-cinema, or the construction of an alternative cinema in its modes of fragmented and "chance" viewing, it was also a way of mirroring the properties of the new medium, with its radically new relations of time and space.

Cinema's "drive to narrative" (as Stephen Heath and others have defined it), exemplified in the development from the first *actualité* films to the narrative cinema which would come into being a decade or so later, developed alongside film theory's drive against it. Film viewing was frequently represented as a form of spectatorship working against the grain of the narrative film, either to extract "essence" or "beauty" from the narrative flow or to construct in imagination an entirely different film. *Photogénie* (perhaps the most significant concept in French avant-garde criticism of the first decades) escapes definition, the filmmaker and theorist Jean Epstein wrote, though other theorists variously defined it as a form of defamiliarization, as a seeing of ordinary things as if for the first time, and as the power of the camera to transform image-objects. For Epstein it was a temporal category, defined as "a value on the order of the second," as a sublime instant, though what it flashes up also exists in an impossible or illusory time, that of the present (Abel 1988, 236). In a very wide range of critical contexts, we find similar emphases on the film "fragment," on the essentially metonymic nature of film, and on the "glimpse" of beauty.

Decades later the film theorist Paul Willeman (1994) would echo this preoccupation:

> For the cinephile, there is a moment in a film (and it happens more often in certain kinds of films) when cinema, in showing you one thing, allows you to glimpse something else that you are not meant to see: the film allows you to think or to fantasise a "beyond" of cinema, a world beyond representation which only shimmers through in certain moments of the film. Where you see it shimmering is largely, but not exclusively up to you. The cinephiliac claim is that cinema can do this. (241)

Willeman's assertion, and the "cinephiliac claim" more generally, echoes the writings of Sergei Eisenstein, among others, on the "fourth dimension" of the cinema, in a model of aesthetic transcendence also to be found in the work of modernist artists such as Wassily Kandinksy and Kazimir Malevitch. Here we encounter a valuation of "intuition" whose modernist roots lie, in part, in the philosophies of William James and Henri Bergson. The work of these thinkers had a significant impact on the work of early twentieth-century artists and writers, including Gertrude Stein and her circle in Paris. Bergson's thought was also foundational for the Vorticism of the 1910s in Britain, where it was taken up strongly by T. E. Hulme and, in more ambivalent and contestatory ways, by Wyndham Lewis and Ezra Pound, whose engagements with the visual arts and with the nature of the image (as practitioner-theorist and poet-theorist respectively) were among the most profound of their modernist contemporaries.

The avant-gardism of cinematic spectatorship, exemplified in Surrealist practices, cut across the divisions, which would later become so impermeable, between art/experimental and popular/mainstream cinema. Surrealist writers and artists, including Philippe Soupault and Louis Aragon, celebrated US film; above all the films of Chaplin (or Charlot), who became identified with the cinema itself, at one with its workings. As Aragon wrote in 1918:

> [Chaplin] alone has sought the intimate sense of cinema and, endlessly persevering in his endeavours, he has drawn comedy towards the absurd and the tragic with equal inspiration. The elements of the décor which surround Charlie's persona participate intimately in the action: nothing is useless there and nothing indispensable. The décor is Charlie's very vision of the world which together with the discovery of the mechanical and its laws, haunts the hero to such an extent that by an inversion of values each inanimate object becomes a living thing for him, each human person a dummy whose starting-handle must be found. (Hammond 2000, 52–53)

Such reversals of human and machinic attributes, of the worlds of subject and object, lay at the heart of much of the avant-garde filmmaking of the first decades of the century, in the work of Surrealists, Dadaists, Futurists, and Constructivists. Their films frequently returned to the devices of the cinema in its very first years, celebrating speed and motion, often through extended, and frequently absurdist, chase-sequences. The Surrealists' rediscovery of the work of Méliès returned film to an originary magic and to acts of metamorphosis, of objects and persons. Fernand Léger's "Dadaist" film *Ballet Mécanique* (1924) is composed of machine imagery, the movements of everyday objects, and the repetitive movements of human figures, opening and closing with a fractured and recomposed representation of the figure of Chaplin. The reflexivity of such projections of film motion is matched by the focus on acts of vision, and a punitive stance toward the voyeurism enabled by optical technologies (from telescopes and binoculars through to the film camera itself) which was present in the very earliest narrative films. Attacks on the eye in experimental film are at their most extreme in Luis Bunuel's *Un Chien Andalou* (1929), in which the slitting of an eyeball presents, in shocking ways, the ambivalence toward vision, the "antiocularcentrism," of modern cultural thought.

The critique of "retinalism" runs from the nineteenth century, where it is identified with photography as well as with the art of the Impressionists (defined in terms of a purely visual receptivity making its appeal, through the wash of color, to the viewer's eye, in isolation from other sensory or conceptual arena) through to modernism. The art works, or installations, of Marcel Duchamp have been identified as the most radical inheritor of this anti-retinal anti-aesthetic. "Doubts about vision," the art historian T. J. Clark (1984) has written, "became doubts about almost everything involved in the act of painting: and in time the uncertainty became a value in its own right: we could say it became an aesthetic" (2). Clark's recent work on modernist painting offers new, and often unexpected, terms for its experiments. The "language" of Cubism, in which Clark finds "a quality of insistence and repetitiveness . . . that sets it apart from all other modernisms," "effects a point-by-point reframing and rearticulation of painting's pursuit of likeness, which reveals this pursuit and its procedures as the unlikely things they always were" (Clark 1999, 191; 221).

As with the question of film and literature, one should not be too ready to collapse the terms of painting and writing into each other, but it is undoubtedly the case that modernist writers (including and especially Wyndham Lewis, Ezra Pound, D. H. Lawrence, Samuel Beckett, Virginia Woolf, and Gertrude Stein) used the visual arts as a way of defining their own aesthetic practices, of working through questions of aesthetics more generally, and of constructing models of culture, history, and subjectivity. The staging of a radical transition in representational modes, from Impressionism to what would be termed Post-Impressionism in the early 1910s, with artists including Cézanne, Matisse, Picasso, Van Gogh, and Gauguin central to it, was of profound importance for a number of modernist writers. D. H. Lawrence wrote extensively on Cézanne, debating with the Bloomsbury art theorists Roger Fry and Clive Bell over their "formalist" views of the artist's work. Lawrence insisted on the bodily, material aspect to Cézanne's still lives, in particular, which he pitted against the "modern" media of photography and film. Turning the arguments of Cézanne's detractors on their heads, Lawrence (1936) represented Cézanne's spatial "distortions" and multiperspectivalism as crucial counters to the bloodless "camera-eye" vision of modernity and (in an echo of Bergson) to "a kaleidoscope of inert images, mechanically shaken," whose cinematographic basis he saw as characteristic of an overly visual modern "consciousness," "made up, really, of inert visual images and little else" (526). For Lawrence, the greatest art was, paradoxically, resistant to pure visuality, and he turned (as did so many of his contemporaries) to the art of the "primitives" for a number of his examples. He implicitly evoked a model of "haptics" ("touching with the eye") in aesthetic response: a concept explored in the work of late nineteenth- and early twentieth-century art theorists but given, by the philosopher Maurice Merleau-Ponty in particular, a phenomenological twist which has become highly influential on art and film theories today.

Virginia Woolf at times represented the visual arts, and the visual image, as infinitely less complex and multi-sensorial than writing, the word, and the verbal "image," but she nonetheless turned to painting, and subsequently to film, as ways of working through her own literary innovations and strategies. Her early short stories (including "The Mark on the Wall," "Kew Gardens," and "An Unwritten Novel") were experiments in breaking with traditional literary forms which engaged strongly with painting and theories of the visual arts, in particular those of Bell and Fry. Her short fiction also opens up questions of thought, mediation, relations between self and other, empathy, sensation, emotion, affect, and becoming. Explorations of vision and visuality in the short stories are frequently intertwined with questions of the nature of consciousness and, more particularly, with the concept of "reflection," which conjoins the definitions of the word as both meditation and mirroring. The short stories (such as "Green and Blue" or "Solid Objects") took on some of the qualities of the "object" for the artist, functioning as the arena in which Woolf tested out the visuality of writing, and the connections between word and (mental) image.

The visuality of Woolf's prose was identified by a number of early critics and commentators not only as painterly (as Rebecca West observed in a 1922 review of *Jacob's Room*, which she described "not as a novel but as a portfolio") but also as cinematographic (Majumdar and McLaurin 1975, 101). Winifred Holtby (1978), in one of the first studies of Woolf's work, identified "expansion and contraction," as well as "the changing positions and gestures of the characters," as film-influenced prose (117–118). *Jacob's Room*'s experiment, its breaking with traditional narration and its fragmentary mode of characterization, would indeed seem to be effected through a self-conscious play with film form (in its perceived limitations as well as its potentialities), which takes in both a Bergsonion critique of cinema as seriality and succession rather than duration and flow and the concept of the film-world as a doubled reality, created by the play of light and shadow. The imbrications of the painterly and the cinematographic are heightened in Woolf's 1927 novel *To the Lighthouse*, where they are also brought together with an understanding of a photographic aesthetic, including the pictorialism of the Victorian photograph. The structure of the novel, which begins and ends with the artist Lily Briscoe's attempts to paint her "vision" of the mother of the house, Mrs Ramsay, both in her life and after her death, takes the form of a triptych. In the first part of the novel, "The Window," characters are shown in the act of looking and of being looked at. In the central section, "Time Passes," the house, empty after Mrs Ramsay's death, is represented in the absence of a seeing human eye: "Now, day after day, light turned, like a flower reflected in water, its clear image on the wall opposite" (Woolf 1992, 141). The final part of the novel, "The Lighthouse," alternates between the view from the shore and the view back to the shore from the sea. This form of movement had become the keynote of D. W. Griffith's narrative cinema, in its use of parallel editing to represent both simultaneity and human loss and longing.

Following through the theme of literature and painting, there are without doubt connections between the art of Cézanne, Picasso, and Braque in the 1910s and the prose of one of the most radical and uncompromising of modernists, Gertrude Stein, in whose work, as Mark Antliff and Patricia Leighten (2001) argue, "the rhythmic play of repetition and difference acts to undercut the separation of one thought from another" (108). Stein's prose portrait of Picasso, written in 1909 and functioning as a response to Picasso's visual portrait of Stein (1905–06), works to "unfold her assessment of [him] – and to view his art – as a series of unending permutations" (106). It should, moreover, be noted that words and images are fundamentally imbricated and intertwined in both experimental film and painting (playing on the subtitles, intertitles, and inserted "leaders," in the form of newspaper clippings, advertising slogans, and the hieroglyphs of urban signs, which punctuate film in its silent era and beyond).

Stein's relationship to painting – she and brother Leo were amongst the significant collectors of modernist art in the early twentieth century – is well documented. There has also been some exploration of the significance for her writing of film, the *modus operandi* of which is not only juxtaposition by means of cutting and "montage," but the putting into motion, at the level of projection, of a series of still frames whose differentiations mark the flow of time in fractions of a second. This mode of repetition with difference is at one with Stein's ways of proceeding, while the tense of cinema, like that of her prose, could be parsed as "a continuous present." As Stein (1967) wrote in "Portraits and Repetition":

> I was doing what the cinema was doing, I was making a continuous statement of what that person was until I had not many things but one thing . . . I, of course did not think of it in terms of the cinema, in fact I doubt whether at that time I had ever seen a cinema but, and I cannot repeat this too often, any one is of one's period and this our period was undoubtedly the period of the cinema . . . And each of us in our own way are bound to express what the world in which we are living is doing. (106)

References

Abel, Richard. (1988). *French Film Theory and Criticism: 1907–1939, Volume 1: 1907–1929*. Princeton, NJ: Princeton University Press.

Antliff, Mark and Patricia Leighten, eds. (2001). *Cubism and Culture*. London: Thames and Hudson.

Balázs, Béla. (1952). *Theory of the Film: Character and Growth of a New Art*, trans. Edith Bone. London: Dennis Dobson.

Bazin, André. (1967). *What is Cinema?* Vol. 1, trans. Hugh Gray. Berkeley: University of California Press.

Beasley, Rebecca. (2007). *Ezra Pound and the Visual Culture of Modernism*. Cambridge: Cambridge University Press.

Benjamin, Walter. (2002). "The Work of Art in the Age of its Mechanical Reproducibility." In *Walter Benjamin: Selected Writings Volume 3: 1935–1938* (pp. 101–133). Cambridge, MA: Harvard University Press.

Bluestone, George. (1968). *Novel into Film: the Metamorphosis of Fiction into Cinema*. Berkeley: University of California Press.

Burgin, Victor. (2004). *The Remembered Film*. London: Reaktion Books.

Cavell, Stanley. (1979). *The World Viewed: Reflections on the Ontology of Film*, enlarged edn. Cambridge, MA: Harvard University Press.

Clark, Timothy J. (1984). *The Painting of Modern Life: Paris in the Art of Manet and his Followers*. Princeton, NJ: Princeton University Press.

Clark, Timothy J. (1999). *Farewell to an Idea: Episodes from a History of Modernism*. New Haven, CT: Yale University Press.

Conrad, Joseph. (1925). *The Nigger of the "Narcissus."* Edinburgh: John Grant.

Conrad, Joseph. (1983). *The Collected Letters of Joseph Conrad*, Vol. 1, ed. Frederick Karl and Laurence Davies. Cambridge: Cambridge University Press.

Conrad, Joseph. (2002). *The Collected Letters of Joseph Conrad*, Vol. 6, ed. Laurence Davies, Frederick R. Karl, and Owen Knowles. Cambridge: Cambridge University Press.

Eliot, T. S. (1936). *Collected Poems 1909–1935*. London: Faber and Faber.

Hammond, Paul. (2000). *The Shadow and its Shadow: Surrealist Writings on the Cinema*. San Francisco: City Lights Books.

Hauser, Arnold. (1962). *The Social History of Art, Volume 1V; Naturalism, Impressionism, The Film Age*. London: Routledge.

Holtby, Winfred. (1978). *Virginia Woolf: A Critical Memoir*. Chicago: Academy Press.

Jameson, Fredric. (1981). *The Political Unconscious: Narrative as a Socially Symbolic Art*. Ithaca, NY: Cornell University Press.

Jameson, Fredric. (1990). *Signatures of the Visible*. New York: Routledge.

254 Laura Marcus

Jay, Martin. (1993). *Downcast Eyes: The Denigration of Vision in Twentieth-Century French Thought*. Berkeley: University of California Press.

Joyce, James. (1966). *Letters of James Joyce, Volume* 1, ed. Stuart Gilbert. New York: Viking.

Kracauer, Siegfried. (1960). *Theory of Film: The Redemption of Physical Reality*. Oxford: Oxford University Press.

Lawrence, D. H. (1936). *Phoenix: The Posthumous Papers 1936*. London: William Heinemann.

Lawrence, D. H. (1960). *Mornings in Mexico and Etruscan Places*. Harmondsworth: Penguin.

Majumdar, Robin and Allen McLaurin, eds. (1975). *Virginia Woolf: The Critical Heritage*. London: Routledge and Kegan Paul.

Mitchell, W. J. T. (1995). "What is Visual Culture?" In *Meaning in the Visual Arts: Views from the Outside*, ed. Irving Lavin (pp. 207–217). Princeton, NJ: Institute for Advanced Study.

Mulvey, Laura. (2006). *Death 24x a Second: Stillness and the Moving Image*. London: Reaktion Books.

Rancière, Jacques. (2006). *Film Fables*, trans. Emiliano Battista. London: Berg. (Original work published 2001: *La Fable cinématographique*, Editions Seuil).

Rancière, Jacques. (2007). *The Future of the Image*, trans. Gregory Elliott. London: Verso.

Rhys, Jean. (1969 [1939]). *Good, Morning Midnight*. Harmondsworth: Penguin.

Richardson, Robert. (1969). *Literature and Film*. Bloomington: University of Indiana Press.

Schwab, Arnold T. (1965). "Conrad's American Speeches and His Reading from *Victory*." *Modern Philology* 62 (May): 342–370.

Stein, Gertrude. (1967). *Look at Me Now and Here I Am: Writings and Lectures 1911–45*, ed. Patricia Meyerowitz. Harmondsworth: Penguin.

Stonier, G. W. (1933). *Gog Magog*. London: J. M. Dent.

Trotter, David. (2007). *Cinema and Modernism*. Oxford: Wiley-Blackwell.

Willeman, Paul. (1994). *Looks and Frictions: Essays in Cultural Studies and Film Theory*. London: British Film Institute.

Woolf, Virginia. (1992). *To the Lighthouse*. Harmondsworth: Penguin.

15

More Kicks than Pricks
Modernist Body-Parts

Maud Ellmann

"Scraps, orts, and fragments." This Shakespearean phrase reverberates throughout Virginia Woolf's posthumous novel *Between the Acts* (1941), set during the build-up to World War II.[1] In this work, Miss La Trobe's twee village pageant climaxes in a modernist experiment called "Ourselves," in which juvenile performers flash reflective objects at the audience, breaking its collective body into pieces: "Here a nose... There a skirt... Then trousers only... Now perhaps a face... Ourselves? But that's cruel. To snap us as we are, before we've had time to assume... And only, too, in parts... That's what's so distorting and upsetting and utterly unfair."[2] This slapstick scene recalls Hamlet's advice to the players to hold the mirror up to nature (*Hamlet* III ii). What is ominous, however, is that the children's makeshift mirrors dismember the bodies they reflect, producing the hallucination of carnage.

In this way the scene suggests a sinister complicity between the fracturing effects of modernism and those of aerial bombardment. Both "snap us as we are"; the word "snap," in this context, could mean to break apart as well as to capture, thus evoking the term "snapshot," which was used of guns before it was extended to cameras. In the pageant, the children's reflective shards catch momentary snapshots of the audience, shots that snap these viewers into smithereens. Lest the audience should miss the analogy between violence and representation, Miss La Trobe's megaphone booms: "Consider the gun-slayers, bomb droppers here or there. They do openly what we do slyly." The sly insinuation is that art and bombing are in league: both "shiver into splinters the old vision, smash to atoms what was whole."[3] A continuation of war by other means, art explodes the illusion of bodily integrity, reducing it to splintered body-parts.

A body-part normally implies a whole; it is part *of* the potential unity we call "the" body. The definite article is misleading, however, since it presupposes an integrity

A Handbook of Modernism Studies, First Edition. Edited by Jean-Michel Rabaté.
© 2013 John Wiley & Sons, Ltd. Published 2013 by John Wiley & Sons, Ltd.

that never exists. Jean-Luc Nancy has argued that "there is no whole, no totality of the body":

> Stains, nails, veins, hairs, spurts, cheeks, sides, bones, wrinkles, creases, hips, throats. The parts of the corpus do not combine into a whole, are not means to it or ends of it. Each part can suddenly take over the whole, can spread out over it, can become it, a whole – that never takes place.

"There is no body," Nancy reiterates, only shifting constellations of body-parts.[4] Far from unified or self-contained, the body is constantly leaking, bleeding, bruising, swelling, flaking, breaking, rotting, its boundaries assaulted from without and from within. The skin, rather than a smooth, unbroken surface, impervious to the turmoil of the entrails, actually consists of thousands of tiny orifices, sucking, gasping, belching, oozing, farting, stinking – as Gulliver discovers to his horror in Brobdingnag where the giantesses' breasts are monstrously enlarged.

These giantesses hark back to the medieval grotesque body, defined by Bakhtin as an unfinished and open body without clearly delimited boundaries.[5] It has been argued, notably by Norbert Elias, that the open body of the Middle Ages was superseded by the closed body of the Renaissance – *homo clausus* – fortressed by muscles and encased in skin.[6] According to this argument, the medieval imagination was obsessed with the body's holes and orifices, along with its bumps and sores, whereas the Renaissance shifted attention to the skin and musculature.

There has been much dispute about the historical boundaries assigned to these bodily alternatives; it is likely, for instance, that the closed body pre-dates the Renaissance, and that the open body has never been superseded. From a psycho-analytic perspective, the repression of the open body by the closed recurs in every childhood. Lacan's theory of the mirror stage implies that every infant begins as a medievalist and ends up trapped in a Renaissance body. Prior to the mirror stage, the infant's body is experienced as a *corps morcelé* – "a heterogeneous mannequin, a baroque doll, a trophy of limbs" – an image reminiscent of Surrealist assemblages of body-parts, or the scattered limbs, skirts, and noses reflected in the broken mirrors of *Between the Acts*.[7] Unlike these fragmented reflections, the Lacanian mirror confers a deceptive wholeness on the body-in-pieces. The infant, by identifying with this mirror-image, undergoes a fundamental alienation from the body, whose chaotic incoherence is repressed. This misrecognition results in "the assumption of the armor of an alienating identity, which will mark with its rigid structure the subject's entire mental development."[8]

This contrast between fragmentation on the one hand, and paranoid rigidity on the other, invites comparison to two conflicting tendencies in modern art. In the aftermath of World War I, Surrealism specialized in macabre bouquets of body-parts, such as Hans Bellmer's mangled dolls.[9] Yet in the same period, as Ana Carden-Coyne has shown, a classical revival in the arts emphasized the body's defensive musculature.[10] Both these developments in the visual arts could be understood as contradictory reactions to the mud and mutilation associated with the battlefields of World War I. For reasons of space, the present chapter focuses on modernist images of dismemberment, rather than the struggle for reintegration expressed in the classical ideal, but each of these tendencies exacerbated the excesses of the other.

Generally speaking, the fragmented bodies of modernism reflect the break-up of traditional aesthetic forms. In *The Waste Land*, for example, the *disjecta membra* scattered through the text – teeth, bones, knees, hands, fingernails – provide a corporeal analogy for Eliot's techniques of parataxis, bricolage, and metrical disruption. Although characteristic of modernism, this self-reflexive use of body-parts is only one way that these bits and pieces are represented in the artworks of this period. To investigate some of these representations, I begin with the opening of Proust's *A la recherche du temps perdu*, which shows how body-parts can "suddenly take over the whole," in Nancy's words. I then turn to Anglophone modernism, specifically to Joyce, Conrad, and Woolf, to examine how their images of dismemberment correspond to the *corps morcelés* of Surrealism, as well as to the broken bodies of the battlefields of World War I. In the iconography of the Great War, as Trudi Tate has pointed out, the body-part most frequently represented is the foot, which often features as the only vestige of exploded bodies.[11] Why the foot, as opposed to other severed remnants?

The second half of this chapter tackles this question by tracing the modernist obsession with the foot from the iconography of World War I to the pedestrian epics *Ulysses* and *Molloy*. The fact that both these epics belong to the canon of Irish modernism suggests that there is something peculiarly Irish, as well as modernist, about the plodding insistence of the foot. As we shall see, there are more kicks than pricks in Irish modernism, more "feet in marmalade" than rising phalluses: "I trundle along rapidly now on my ruined feet / Flush with the livid canal," Beckett writes in his walking poem "Enueg II" (1935).[12] Beckett's works abound with "ruined feet," inventoried in *First Love* as "the corn, the cramp, the kibe, the bunion, the hammer toe, the nail ingrown, the fallen arch, the common blain, the club foot, duck foot, goose foot, pigeon foot, flat foot, trench foot and other curiosities."[13] The conclusion of this chapter therefore considers why the foot – especially the abject, ailing, damaged foot – obtrudes so insistently in Irish modernism. As we shall see, the Irish foot is more than just a footnote to modernism; it is pedimental to the movement as a whole.

* * * *

The famous opening paragraphs of *Swann's Way* (1913) describe how the narrator's sense of self dissolves in sleep, having lost its bearings in the body and the bed. In order to remember who he is, the narrator has to re-collect himself – both physically and psychically – by ascertaining the position of his body-parts. "Not knowing where I was," Proust writes, "I could not be sure at first who I was."

> My body, still too heavy with sleep to move, would make an effort to construe the form which its tiredness took as an orientation of its various members, so as to induce from that where the wall lay and the furniture stood . . . . Its memory, the composite memory of its ribs, knees, and shoulder-blades offered it a whole series of rooms in which it had at one time or another slept . . . . [14]

This "composite memory" resembles Paul Schilder's concept of the body-image, which develops through "contact with the outside world" and incorporates the body's experience of its environment, such as walls, furniture, and bedlinen.[15] For Proust's somnolent narrator, however, these familiar landmarks disappear, causing the disintegration of his bodily gestalt. Waking in the dark, the narrator has to pull himself together by reassembling his scattered body-parts, like Isis gathering the limbs of the dismembered god Osiris.

Note that it is not the mind but the body-parts themselves that bring about this resurrection, by means of the haptic memory accumulated in the ribs, knees, and shoulder-blades. These bones and joints remember how they have disposed themselves in other beds, and how those beds have disposed themselves in other rooms:

> Even before my brain . . . had collected sufficient impressions to enable it to identify the room . . . it, my body, would recall from each room in succession what the bed was like, where the doors were, how the daylight came in at the windows, whether there was a passage outside . . . (Proust, 5)

The product of its mise-en-scène – part flesh, part furniture – the body has to be reconstituted by reference to the objects which have left their traces on the senses. When these props disappear into the darkness, the body falls apart, its parts assuming an uncanny independence of the whole. Liberated from the body as a unified gestalt, the limbs dream up alternative scenarios.

> Sometimes, too, just as Eve was created from a rib of Adam, so a woman would come into existence while I was sleeping, conceived from some strain in the position of my limbs. (Proust, 4)

Such dreams, Proust implies, are engendered by the joints and muscles, bypassing both the mind and the body-as-a-whole. Whereas Freud attributes dreams to the return of the repressed, Proust attributes them to irritation in the body-parts. These parts, dismembered by the state of sleep – as Adam's rib was extricated from his sleeping body – acquire an autonomous life, producing Eves out of contortions of the limbs.

In this context, it is worth noting that the English language grants little agency to body-parts; we say "my arm," "his leg," as if these limbs were enslaved to their respective owners. The French, by contrast, say "le bras," "le jambe," and the definite article seems to confer a modicum of independence on the limb.[16] Perhaps encouraged by the grammar of his language, Proust endows body-parts with the capacity to act, remember, dream, or even conjure up an Eve without deferring to the conscious mind. Joyce strives for a similar effect in describing Bloom's sad steps in the "Lestrygonians" episode of *Ulysses*: "His slow feet walked him riverward . . . ."[17] Here it is the feet that do the walking, retracing their familiar route without the guidance of Bloom's distracted consciousness.

I shall return to feet, but first it is important to investigate the general phenomenon of broken bodies in the artworks of this period. As we have seen, Eliot's wasteland is cluttered with body-parts, including bones, carious teeth, the broken fingernails of dirty hands, and "other withered stumps of time." These withered stumps could refer to either the fractured quotations scattered through the text or the unburied body-parts scattered through the "Unreal City." Littered with dead men's words, as well as dead men's bones, *The Waste Land* could be seen as the fallout from a blast that exploded both the graveyard and the library.[18] A comparable explosion takes place in Conrad's novel *The Secret Agent* (1907), when the innocent dupe Stevie is "blown to small bits: limbs, gravel, clothing, bones, splinters – all mixed up together," as Inspector Heat reports. "I tell you they had to fetch a shovel to gather him up with." To the Inspector it seems "impossible to believe that a human body could have reached that state of disintegration without passing through the pangs of inconceivable agony."[19] While Conrad's Stevie is blown to pieces, Beckett's narrator in *The Unnamable* seems resigned to a continuous dismemberment, a kind of explosion in slow-motion. "Why should I have a sex, who have no longer a nose? All those things have fallen, all the things that stick out, with my eyes my hair, without leaving a trace . . . ."[20] Similarly Woolf's anti-war treatise *Three Guineas* (1938), as Marina Mackay has pointed out, is punctuated by the "stunned reiteration . . . of blown-to-bits houses and bodies," anticipating the dismemberment inflicted by the mirrors in *Between the Acts*.[21]

In contrast to Woolf's scraps, orts, and fragments, Joyce's description of *Ulysses* as the "epic of the human body" implies an aspiration to corporeal completeness.[22] His schemata for *Ulysses* assign a different body-part to each of the novel's episodes, presumably for the purpose of anatomical exhaustiveness. On careful inspection, however, this body "doesn't quite add up" – as Paul Muldoon describes the mutilated remnants of the victim of a bomb-blast.[23] Several vital organs are omitted, including such essentials as the liver, the intestines, and the pancreas. If the body-parts allotted to the episodes were patched together, the mishmash would resemble Lacan's "heterogeneous mannequin": a jumble of kidneys, genitals, heart, lungs, esophagus, brain, blood, ear, muscles, bones, eye, nose, womb, nerves, skin, skeleton, unspecified "juices," flesh, and fat. Thus Joyce's schemata tease his readers with the prospect of a unified body – and a unified epic – while gleefully dismembering both the fleshly and the literary corpus.

In the "Hades" episode of Ulysses, Bloom imagines the cemetery as a landfill of discarded body-parts: "Lots of them lying around here: lungs, hearts, livers. Old rusty pumps." The skeptical hero scoffs at "that last day idea," when all these organs will be spewed out of their graves: "Get up! Last day! Then every fellow mousing around for his liver and his lights and the rest of his traps. Find damn all of himself that morning" (*U* 6: 678–681). Since several of those "traps," including the liver, are excluded from the schemata of *Ulysses*, Bloom's vision of the risen corpse, mousing around for his lost organs, could be seen as a parody of readers who attempt to reconstruct the corpus of this epic from its disconnected body-parts. Moreover, Bloom describes body-parts as "rusty pumps," as if they were mechanical prostheses, constructed out of iron as opposed to flesh and blood. In a much-cited passage from *Civilization and Its Discontents* (1929), Freud argues that man has "become a kind of prosthetic God. When he puts on all his auxiliary organs he is truly magnificent; but those organs have not grown on to him and they still give him much trouble at times."[24] Joyce's "Hades" could be seen as the junkyard of this prosthetic God, deserted by his biological as well as his auxiliary organs – those rusty pumps that challenge the distinction between organic and mechanical.

While prosthetic organs play a conspicuous role in modernism, as Tim Armstrong has shown,[25] the obsession with "piecing out the body" goes back at least as far as the sixteenth century. David Hillman and Carla Mazzio find evidence of this obsession in a range of early modern social and symbolic practices, including "punitive dismemberment, pictorial isolation, poetic emblazoning, mythic *sparagmos*, satirical biting, scientific categorizing, or medical anatomizing."[26] Some of these practices persist in modernism, including the technique of pictorial isolation, which has been enhanced by innovations such as cinematic close-up and photographic cropping. The poetic blazon, which dismembers the beloved to extol her body-parts, also reappears in modernism, usually in the satiric mode of Shakespeare's sonnet "My mistress's eyes are nothing like the sun." In William Carlos Williams's anti-blazon "Portrait of a Lady" (1920/1934), for instance, the poet's extravagant comparisons peter out before they reach above the lady's thighs; in Beckett's *Murphy* (1938), the leading lady Celia is introduced with a maniacal catalogue of body-parts that includes the vital statistics of her forearm – 9 1/2 inches.[27]

Although punitive dismemberment has receded from the modern arsenal of discipline, it has been superseded by the grisly spectacles of modern warfare, where bodies are "blown into fuckin' bits," to quote a soldier in Frederic Manning's World War I novel *The Middle Parts of Fortune* (1916). This body-in-bits differs from the traditional image of the body-in-parts, since a body-part is a functional component of the body, which retains its integrity even if it is amputated from the whole. A body-bit, by contrast, implies the destruction not just of the whole but of the part. This is the kind of disintegration that we find in Conrad's *The Secret Agent*, or in Edmund Blunden's *Undertones of War*, where a "young and cheerful lance corporal" is suddenly transformed by a grenade into "gobbets of blackening flesh" sprayed over the earthwalls of his firebay. His eyeball, flung under a duckboard, is the only body-part distinguishable from the gore. As Manning's soldier puts it: "'e were just blown to buggery . . . .'e were a chum o' mine, sir, an' I seen 'im blown into fuckin' bits."[28]

Technological innovations in weaponry in World War I meant that bodies could be blown to buggery more thoroughly than ever before.[29] For this reason many casualties could not be identified for burial, their bodies too scrambled to be reassembled for the grave. Some combatants' bodies completely disappeared; some splattered across the trenches, showering blood and guts on their comrades-in-arms. Others deposited grotesque remains, such as the eyeball in the scene quoted above; more frequently, a dismembered foot is the body-part that marks the absence of a decimated combatant.

In Britain alone, over 240,000 men returned from World War I with total or partial limb amputations; 60,500 were wounded in the head or eyes, while another 89,000 sustained serious damage to other parts of their bodies. Carden-Coyne has pointed out that the "numbers of men living with disfigurement, chronic ailments, and disability highlighted the paradox of modern technology with its capacity to inflict horrific injuries while enabling medics to keep the wounded alive." After the war, images of mutilated bodies pervaded visual and literary culture, as well as medical texts and humanitarian publicity, provoking horror and fascination in equal measure. The wounded body and the military hospital became "theatrical sites," while "a growing entertainment industry . . . placed war's shocking culture as the central attraction."[30]

These spectacles of amputation and disfigurement, as I suggested earlier, provoked two contradictory reactions in the visual arts, producing the dismembered bodies of Surrealism on the one hand, and the fortressed bodies of the classical revival on the other.[31] These tendencies in turn reflected wider cultural reactions to the war, where lascivious interest in mutilation was counterbalanced by fantasies of miraculous repair. In medicine, such fantasies boosted the development of plastic surgery; in the arts, a revival of the classical ideal of human beauty; in popular culture, a craze for body-building.[32] Through the cultivation of musculature, body-building strove to transform the male body into a bullet, as firm, metallic, and hygienic as the new machineries of war, that "storm of steel" which had exposed the frailty of flesh as never before.[33]

Meanwhile Surrealism mocked these fantasies of wholeness by promoting an aesthetics of dismemberment. Hal Foster, in *Prosthetic Gods*, has suggested that the cut-up female bodies of Surrealism, such as Brassaï's photographs or Bellmer's dolls, served as a displacement of the all-too-visible reality of male dismemberment. Foster poses the question: "Are these surrealist transgressions of the body related to actual transgression of the body during the period . . . ?"[34] The likely answer is yes, since these Surrealist images displace onto the female body the mutilation inflicted on the male, possibly to punish women for their supposed exemption from the horrors of the battlefield. During and after the Great War, women, as well as male non-combatants, were often scapegoated for the carnage; as Amy Lyford has shown, the heroic masculine sacrifices of the men at the front were frequently contrasted with the decadent ingratitude of the women – and unfit men – who remained at home.[35] In this context the dismemberment of female bodies in Surrealism could be seen as retaliation for the gruesome injuries endured by men.

To take an example, Brassaï's famous photograph "Nude 115" (1936) crops off the woman's head, arms, and legs, so that only her trunk and buttocks remain visible, forming a white stain in the surrounding darkness. In a technique that became a Surrealist trademark, the limbless upright body is rotated horizontally so that the woman's form assumes the appearance of a phallus.[36] A similar visual pun emerges in Brâncuşi's *Princess X* (1915–16), a sculpture removed from the Salon des Indépendants in 1920 on the grounds of "phallic obscenity" – although Brâncuşi insisted that the object was a female bust, which had been mistaken for male genitalia.[37] Such images partake of the ambivalence of the Freudian fetish: on the one hand, the fear of castration is displaced onto the dismembered female body, but this body is simultaneously transformed into a phallus, a "monstrous enlargement" of the imperiled organ.[38]

Viewers today have grown accustomed to techniques of photographic cropping and cinematic close-up, so that the part is readily accepted as an index of the whole. But Surrealist images of body-parts resist this synecdochic inference. Instead of synecdoche, Brassaï's photographs elicit the kind of metaphoric substitution that Freud associates with anal eroticism, in which body-parts are treated as symbolic equivalents.[39] In "Nude 115," buttocks become testicles, just as Freud argues that the penis can morph into a baby or a turd. Whether Freud has a Surrealist imagination, or Brassaï a Freudian unconscious, it is clear that these contemporaries are working along parallel lines.

Like Brassaï's photographs, Bellmer's *poupées* could be understood as an attack against the female body in revenge for the emasculation of the male. These dolls, as Lyford has pointed out, "look as if they could be Surrealist mannequins made by the prosthetic industry; their deformed yet interlocking parts reflect a chilling combination of mass-market eroticism and wartime bodily trauma."[40] In one of Bellmer's photographs (*Self-Portrait with the Doll*, 1934), the spectral figure of the artist bends down towards a *poupée*, whose ravaged form anticipates Deleuze's notion of the body-without-organs.[41] Teetering on prosthetic legs, her torso is hollow and eviscerated, its inner organs replaced by rods and screws, reminiscent of the machine-woman of Villiers's science fiction novel *L'Eve future* (1886). Other *poupées* show the female body reduced to an abject heap of breasts, buttocks, hair, and genitals; one *poupée* has numerous breasts, bubbling up like boils over her fragmented body (*La Poupée*, 1935). From a Freudian perspective, these breasts could be interpreted as multiplied phallic symbols that serve as a defense against castration; from a Kleinian perspective, they evince both destructive and reparative impulses, their plurality implying over-compensation for infantile attacks against the breast. In either case, these dolls reveal conflictual reactions to femininity: on the one hand a punitive attack against the female body, but on the other an attempt at restitution, in which the mutilated body-parts are patched together with the anatomical naïvety of a penitent child.

Schilder's theory of the body-image suggests that these fantasies of corporeal disintegration may serve a therapeutic purpose. "There is a tendency towards the dissolution of the body-image," Schilder argues, because this image is "the result of an effort and cannot be completely maintained when the effort ceases." While the body-image aspires to a certain equilibrium, it never achieves this stability once and for all; on the contrary, "whenever a gestalt is created the gestalt tends immediately to change and to destruction." Nonetheless Schilder insists that "we destroy in order to create anew." The body-image has to be constantly demolished in order to adapt to changing stimuli; otherwise there is a risk of being "bound and tied down" by this bodily gestalt, as by a straitjacket. For this reason we resist this rigidity by "playing" with the body image, altering it with clothes, decoration, jewelry, or more invasive fashions such as piercing and tattoos.[42] Schilder's theory would imply that the widespread obsession with dismemberment after World War I expresses a need to smash the body-image in order to restore its vital pliability. What seems like a perverse fascination with mutilated body-parts may also represent an effort to escape the risk of petrifaction of the body-image.

Of all the broken body-parts of World War I, it is the feet that come to signify the horrors of trench warfare. These gory remnants arouse a range of ambivalent responses in the art and literature of the Great War, in which pity and terror converge with schadenfreude, voyeurism, sadomasochistic titillation, and sardonic humor. From a Schilderian perspective, these guilty pleasures may derive from shattering the armor of the body-image, albeit at a safe remove. Furthermore, Emerson argues that disconnected objects are intrinsically funny: "Separate any object . . . from the connection of things, and contemplate it alone, standing there as absolute nature, it becomes at once comic; no useful, no respectable qualities can rescue it from the ludicrous."[43] The next section of this chapter shows how the separated foot elicits both hilarity and horror.

Podiatric Modernism

"A generation that had gone to school in horse-drawn streetcars now stood in the open air, amid a landscape in which nothing was the same except the clouds and, at its center, in a forcefield of destructive torrents and explosions, the tiny, fragile human body."[44] So Walter Benjamin describes the wasteland of World War I. In many representations of this wasteland, all that remains of the tiny frail human body are the feet, or more specifically the boots, choked with remnants of dismembered flesh. Percy Smith's chilling etching "Death Awed" portrays the figure of Death brought to a halt by a pair of boots with splinters of bone protruding from the shafts, the rest of the body having disappeared into the desolate landscape.[45] It is striking that Smith depicts two boots rather than one – probably because a pair evokes the absent human form more palpably. The boots' position, one standing, one fallen, reflects the position of Death's bony feet, one standing higher than the other in the composition. Although bootless and fleshless, Death's feet are still attached to a vertical, coherent biped, whose draped skeleton provides a mirror-image for the body missing from the gory boots.

Dismembered boots also crop up in Barbusse's World War I novel *Under Fire* (1916), but in this novel the effect is more grotesque than pathetic. A French soldier recounts his attempt to wrench the boots off a German corpse:

Old man, he was there, his arse in a hole, doubled up, gaping at the sky with his legs in the air, and his pumps offered themselves to me with an air that meant they were worth my while. 'A tight fit,' says I. But you talk about a job to bring those beetle-crushers of his away! I worked on top of him, tugging, twisting and shaking, for half an hour and no lie about it. With his feet gone quite stiff, the patient didn't help me a bit. Then at last the legs of it – they'd been pulled about so – came unstuck at the knees, and his breeks tore away, and all the lot came, flop! There was me, all of a sudden, with a full boot in each fist. The legs and feet had to be emptied out . . . . we shoved our arms inside the boots and pulled out of 'em some bones and bits of sock and bits of feet.[46]

The horror of this scene is offset by its charnel humor. The corpse's absurd position, with its arse in a hole and its legs in the air, anticipates some of the postural contortions of Beckett's *Trilogy*, while the tussle with the boots looks forward to *Waiting for Godot*, where Estragon spends much of the play struggling to remove his boots.[47] When he finally succeeds in pulling off one boot, he is surprised to find it empty, whereas Barbusse's soldier is surprised to find it full. "Nothing," Estragon laments, "There's nothing to show." Vladimir retorts, "That's man all over for you, blaming on his boots the faults of his feet."[48]

In each of these cases, the distinction between foot and boot is strangely blurred: the effect could be compared to Magritte's Surrealist painting "The Red Model" (1934), which depicts two boots metamorphosing into feet, their leather shafts descending into fleshly toes. In Beckett's and Barbusse's works, the muscular difficulty of removing boots evokes the cognitive difficulty of detaching the idea of feet from their prosthetic coverings. Heidegger's inspired misprision of Van Gogh's painting "The Old Shoes," in which the philosopher invents a peasant-woman to fit into these empty shoes, interpreting the footgear as a metonymy for peasant life, also testifies to the difficulty of imagining a shoe without a foot.[49] Likewise Beckett's Estragon seems to lose his foot by pulling off his boot – "there's nothing to show" – thus suggesting that the boot confers existence on the foot.

In the scenes from World War I discussed above, all that remains of the "foot soldier" is the footed boot – as opposed to the booted foot. Boots make the soldier, these images imply; if "society is founded upon cloth," in Carlyle's words, battlefields are founded upon shoe-leather and shoe-rubber.[50] Yet boots often fail in modern warfare: one of the greatest miseries of World War I was trench foot, brought on by inadequate supplies of socks and boots. Bearing in mind the horrors of trench foot, it is no wonder that Barbusse's soldier, apparently immunized to nausea, goes to such disgusting lengths to yank the "beetle-crushers" off the putrefying corpse. If boots make trench warfare possible, they nevertheless offer meager protection to the "tiny frail human body" caught up in the storm of steel.

In Smith's etching, the fallen boot metonymically evokes the fallen soldier, and metaphorically the fall of man. Similarly Georges Bataille argues that the foot is "psychologically analogous to the brutal fall of man," because this organ grounds the body in the earth, mocking the head's aspirations to the sky.[51] In his famous essay "The Big Toe" (1903), Bataille points out that our faces rise up into the light, whereas our feet sink back into the mud; hence we speak of having "feet of clay." The "indelible" division of the universe into a subterranean hell and a celestial heaven implies that feet are closer to the devil, whose cloven feet attest to his kinship to the earth as well as to the animal.[52] Yet Bataille also stresses that the big toe is "the most *human* organ of the body" because of its striking difference from the ape's equivalent digit, which bears a closer resemblance to the human thumb. Prehensile and opposable, the ape's big toe, with its capacity to grip, enables the animal to live in trees. By contrast, the human animal turns *himself* into a tree, the big toe providing the foundation for the full-body erection "of which man is so proud." The lowly big toe, doomed in its "imbecilic way . . . to corns, calluses, and bunions," nonetheless supports the priapic splendor of the upright human form.[53]

It is humbling to think that human verticality depends on this squat, debased, diminutive appendage; the big toe is a clumsy parody of the dexterous thumb. Indeed Bataille marvels at the laughter "commonly produced by simply imagining the *toes*." While "the fingers have come to signify useful action and firm character," the toes connote "stupor and base idiocy."[54] The big toe stands *for* what it stands *in* – dirt, excrement, decay, mortality. Yet its amputation is drastically disabling; hence the big toe is the body-part most frequently sacrificed to evade military service. In Evelyn Waugh's *Brideshead Revisited* (1945), Sebastian's German lover Kurt has shot off his big toe to get out of the army, but the unhealed wound weeps continuously, as if all the grief of his calamitous century had taken refuge in this gory stump.

Bataille's 1903 essay was republished in the Surrealist journal *Documents* in 1929, where it was illustrated by Jacques-André Boiffard's close-up photographs of big toes. These photographs magnify the big toe to grotesque proportions, exaggerating all its wrinkly, knobbly, hang-nailed blemishes. They also phallicize the toe, like Brassaï's images of female body-parts, an effect achieved by close-up and cropping. Suspended in mid-air and glowing in the dark, these airborne big toes unflatten and unground the foot, endowing it with a priapic autonomy and assertiveness. They also remind us that the big toe is often sexualized, both in practice and in representation. When the British Minister of Culture David Mellors was fired for his adulterous shenanigans in 1992, *The Sun* sported the immortal headline "TOE JOB TO NO JOB." Perhaps the sexiest big toe in modernism appears in Buñuel's Surrealist masterpiece *L'Age d'or* (1930), in which the leading lady performs a salacious toe-job on a garden statue.

Despite its sex appeal, the big toe has received little attention from psychoanalysis, in which foot-fetishism is generally understood as a displacement of castration phobia. This neglect of the foot is all the more surprising since Freud's most famous theory, the Oedipus complex, is based on a hero whose name means "swell-foot." An exception to this neglect is Wilhelm Stekel, a follower of Freud's who strayed from psychoanalytic orthodoxy by insisting that the widespread prevalence of foot-fetishism justified the promotion of the foot to the status of a secondary sex organ.[55] Freud, by contrast, concedes no erotic power to the foot per se. Indifferent to the use-value of the foot, Freud considers only its exchange-value, its function as a stand-in for the mother's missing penis.[56] In this respect Freud differs sharply from Bataille, who insists on the ignominious, asexual materiality of feet, especially the lumpish big toe. Sometimes a big toe is just a big toe, Bataille implies. "Always more or less damaged and humiliating," the big toe signifies the brute solidity of matter, like the stone that Samuel Johnson kicked to disprove the idealist philosophy of Bishop Berkeley, no doubt stubbing his big toe in the demonstration.[57]

In my view, it is Bataille's literalism, as opposed to Freud's symbolic displacements, which predominates in modernist representations of the foot. To risk a sweeping generalization, the modernist foot testifies to the disenchantment of the world, the subordination of spirit to matter, grace to gravity.[58] Thus Beckett's Molloy speaks of "my feet obscenely resting on the earth" – obscene because the earth consists of "flesh, fur, and faeces."[59] "Man's secret horror of his foot," Bataille contends, derives from this obscene proximity to earth and death, to the dust to which our dust eventually returns. For this reason feet often serve as a metonymy for death, as in Wallace Stevens' elegy for his mother, "The Emperor of Ice Cream": "If her horny feet protrude, they come / To show how cold she is, and numb."[60] Although the terms "horny" and "protrude" carry sexual and even demonic innuendos, these are overpowered by the terse monosyllables "cold" and "numb," which identify the feet with the chill rigidity of lifeless matter.

According to Bataille, it is our secret horror of the foot that produces the desire to conceal its shape and length, often at the cost of podiatric torture. Although Bataille ignores the question of gender, it is usually women's feet which are condemned to represent transcendence of the earth, with all the agony entailed. The Chinese practice of footbinding, for example, drastically reduced the female foot's protension, whereas Western stilettos stretch its height and curve, disguising the foot's ignoble lowness and flatness. In the art of ballet, as Peter Stallybrass has pointed out, the foot virtually disappears, due to the refinement of the toe-shoe in the later nineteenth century. Twirling *en pointe*, the ballerina barely seems to touch the earth; her body is lifted effortlessly off the floor, creating the illusion of weightlessness. Virtually footless and impervious to gravity, the ballerina embodies the fantasy of an ungrounded subject, transcending material contingencies. In the circus, it is aerial acrobats who enact this fantasy, flying free of the feet that bind them to the earth; clowns, by contrast, constantly fall down, often tripped up by their own enormous shoes, in a comic exaggeration of footedness and groundedness. This falling literally lands them in the shit; the original purpose of clowns was to shovel up the dung of the animal performers in the circus.[61]

Stallybrass's discussion of the role of feet in circus-culture casts a revealing light on "Circe," the circus episode of Joyce's *Ulysses*, where feet and shoes also play a pivotal role. In this episode Bloom metamorphoses into both a clown and an animal performer, as well as a shoe-fetishist and a dung-devourer. All these shape-changes entail falling and debasement, both literally and figuratively, thus aligning Bloom with the earthbound, tumbling circus clown. The "Circe" episode comes to a climax when Bella Cohen, masculinized as Bello, forces Bloom to cower under her hoof. "You will fall," Bello taunts. "You are falling. On the hands down!" Bloom obediently "*sinks on all fours, grunting, snuffling, rooting*" at the tyrant's feet (*U* 15: 2848–2853). Confirming Bataille's view that the foot is "psychologically analogous to the fall of man," Bella's foot brings about Bloom's fall, transforming the upright biped into a prone four-footed swine.

This sadomasochistic ritual exploits a familiar association of feet with power; one well-known instance is Psalm 110, where the Lord promises to "make thine enemies thy footstool."[62] To kiss someone's foot is to abase oneself, to cringe and curry favor; to put one's foot down is to quash dissent; to conquer a country is to crush it underfoot. In these figures of speech, the lowest part of the anatomy is used to lower others, to reduce them to the dirt we trample on. Christ overturns this hierarchy, however, by washing his disciples' feet, thus adopting the position of the powerless. Bloom, who is often aligned with Christ, mocks this gesture of humility by groveling at Bella's feet, for Bloom, unlike the savior, gets a perverse kick out of this self-abasement: "Enormously I desiderate your domination." His kinky pleasure in humiliation, compounded with his delectation of the well-shod foot – "To be a shoefitter in Mansfield's was my love's young dream, the darling joys of sweet buttonhooking" – suggests a parody of the Christ story, in which the foot-washer is outed as foot-fetishist, the martyr as masochist (*U* 15: 2813–2814).

It is intriguing that D. H. Lawrence, deploring what he sees as the moribund excesses of the modernist novel, singles out the foot – or more specifically the toe – as the focus of his censure. "'Did I feel a twinge in my little toe, or didn't I?' asks every character in Mr Joyce or Miss Richardson or Monsieur Proust."[63] There is some justice in this taunt, particularly with regard to *Ulysses*, where Bloom's pedestrian odyssey actually produces such a twinge, though in his big toe rather than his little one. While Lawrence's attention to the body is restricted to the melodrama of the loins, Joyce exploits the comedy of the extremities, including the ridiculous big toe. In the manically loquacious "Ithaca" chapter of *Ulysses*, no fewer than one hundred and forty-seven words are devoted to Bloom's great toenail:

> Sensible of a benignant persistent ache in his footsoles he extended his foot to one side and observed the creases, protuberances and salient points caused by foot pressure in the course of walking repeatedly in several different directions, then, inclined, he disnoded the laceknots, unhooked and loosened the laces, took off each of his two boots for the second time, detached the partially moistened right sock through the fore part of which the nail of his great toe had again effracted, raised his right foot and, having unhooked a purple elastic sock suspender, took off his right sock, placed his unclothed right foot on the margin of the seat of his chair, picked at and gently lacerated the protruding part of the great toenail, raised the part lacerated to his nostrils and inhaled the odour of the quick, then with satisfaction threw away the lacerated ungual fragment. (*U* 17: 1480–1491).

This is a comedy of scale, whose effect relies on disproportion: the style is Brobdingnagian, the action Lilliputian. As Lukàcs protests in *The Meaning of Contemporary Realism*, Joyce overturns the "hierarchy of significance" established in the nineteenth-century novel, where nobody peels off their toenails.[64] If such a trifle as a "lacerated ungual fragment" were to obtrude into a classic realist narrative, this nail-paring would have to serve an ulterior purpose, either as a clue to an unfolding mystery or as a Barthesian "reality effect." In "Ithaca," however, any such reality effect is undercut by the logorrhea of the narrator; instead the words stick out, like Bloom's protruding toenail, "effracting" their referential function. Furthermore, Bloom's pedicure parodies Stephen Dedalus's grandiose vision of the artist's manicure: "the artist, like the God of creation, remains within or behind or beyond or above his handiwork, invisible, refined out of existence, indifferent, paring his fingernails."[65] Although "there's a touch of the artist about old Bloom," there's nothing godlike in the way he picks his toenails (*U* 10: 582–583). On the contrary, this gesture demythologizes Bloom, bringing the would-be Homeric hero rudely down to earth – the debased domain of the big toe.

Most of the feet discussed in this chapter belong to male rather than female characters, and derive from the male authors of high modernism. Yet it would be mistaken to assume that female writers were indifferent to feet, or that the female foot had been excluded from the modernist canon. However, women's feet assert themselves in very different ways from those of men. John Berger's famous study of the iconography of gender, *Ways of Seeing*, argues that "men act and women appear."[66] The same formula, I would argue, applies to their respective feet. In *Ulysses*, male feet "act" in the form of flânerie, albeit of a down-at-heels variety, whereas female feet "appear" as fetishes – in the shoe-fitting fantasy of "Circe" – or as counter-fetishes, in the case of Gerty McDowell's anaphrodisiac limp. In "Penelope," we learn that Blazes Boylan flirted with Molly by complimenting the shape of her feet; Bloom, on the other hand, is excited by her muddy boots: "hed like me to walk in all the horses dung I could find but of course hes not natural like the rest of the world . . ." (*U* 18: 267–268). In poignant contrast to Molly's titillating feet, Gerty's limp demolishes Bloom's voyeuristic fantasy: "a defect is ten times worse in a woman," he reflects (*U* 13: 774–775). Perhaps a defective foot is ten times worse for Bloom than other flaws, and a low part ten times lower on his scale of values.

For the most part, women's feet in *Ulysses* are portrayed as objects of desire rather than vehicles of mobility; indeed Gerty's foot fails her when she tries to walk, despite the allure of her "wellturned ankle" and "higharched instep" (*U* 286: 98; 287:168). In Joyce's Dublin, as in Baudelaire's Paris, flânerie is a privilege largely reserved for men; women either loll in bed (Molly), or dally at the beach (Gerty), which is geographically marginalized from the streets. Meanwhile Bloom's perambulations confirm Raymond Williams's contention that the dominant literary perspective on the modern city is that "a man walking, as if alone, through its streets."[67]

A rare exception to the male flâneur may be found in Virginia Woolf's essay "Street Haunting," where the narrator assumes the role of flâneuse in order to enjoy "the greatest pleasure of town life in winter: rambling the streets of London."[68]

Yet even Woolf depicts women's feet as agents of transfiguration, rather than transportation; their use-value is subsumed into commodity-fetishism. A phantasmagoric scene in "Street Haunting" begins in a shoe-shop, in which a dwarf exhibits her incongruously well-formed foot. "Look at that! Look at that! she seemed to demand of us all, as she thrust her foot out, for behold it was the shapely, perfectly proportioned foot of a well-grown woman. It was arched; it was aristocratic." A modern-day Cinderella, this dwarf pirouettes in front of "a glass which reflected the foot only," trying on shoe after elegant shoe. When she leaves the orbit of the mirror, however, this flattering illusion crumbles: "by the time she had reached the street again she had become a dwarf." At this point her deformity seems to spread contagiously across the urban crowd, making every passer-by look maimed, humped, stunted, twisted: "all joined in the hobble and tap of the dwarf's dance."[69] Well-heeled shoppers are magically transformed into derelicts and beggars, lurching in a spastic carnival; it is as if Mrs Dalloway's Bond Street had suddenly turned into Joyce's Nighttown, with its stunted crones and gobbling idiots.

Woolf's "company of the maimed and the blind" could also be compared to Beckett's netherworld of tramps and *mutilés de guerre*. The difference lies in the solitude of Beckett's pedestrians, as opposed to the jostling throngs of "Street Haunting" or "Circe." Another difference is that Joyce and Woolf pay little attention to the podiatric risks of flânerie, which dog the footsteps of Beckett's wanderers. Bloom concludes his peripatetic day unscathed apart from "a benignant persistent ache in his footsoles" (*U* 17: 1480). Woolf's street haunter never even mentions her own feet; only the dwarf's unlikely foot attracts her interest. Apparently Woolf's concern for women's oppression stops short of their footwear; although deploring the material constraints on women's writing, she ignores the high-heeled impediments to women's walking.

In Beckett, by contrast, it is feet themselves that thwart the act of walking. To vary one of his most quoted statements, Beckett's works imply that there is nothing with which to walk, nothing from which to walk, no power to walk, no desire to walk, together with the obligation to walk.[70] Feet necessitate walking but also render it impossible.

The next part of this chapter turns to Beckett's feet – both his own and those of his limping protagonists – in order to explore the implications of feet and walking in Irish modernism.

Walking Wild

To kick in with a biographical anecdote, Deirdre Bair reports that Beckett, as a young Irish émigré in Paris, tried to follow in Joyce's footsteps by literally standing in his shoes. Such was his admiration for the older writer that Beckett imitated Joyce's dandyish footwear, wearing shoes too narrow for his feet, at the cost of considerable discomfort – no doubt blaming on his feet the defects of his shoes.[71] Ezra Pound, by contrast, made the crass mistake of overlooking Joyce's expensive taste in footwear. In 1920 T. S. Eliot, accompanied by Wyndham Lewis, presented Joyce with a mysterious package from Ezra Pound, which turned out to contain a pair of old shoes, probably resembling the wrinkly brogues of Van Gogh's shoe paintings. Affronted by this charitable offering, Joyce retaliated by wining and dining the emissaries with princely extravagance, footing the bill in retribution for the mortifying footwear. As Lewis recalls, "We had to pay his 'Irish pride' for the affair of the old shoes. That was it! He would not let us off. He was entirely unrelenting and we found it impossible to outmaneuver him." The fact that the term "brogue" refers both to a stout shoe and to an accent from the Celtic fringe may have aggravated the offense to Joyce's pride.[72]

Commenting on this famous anecdote, Steven Connor argues that "Joyce defines his own deracinated, cosmopolitan avant-gardism against the counter-image of the Irish boot. More than any other item of footwear, the boot testifies to the slovenly indistinction of the subject and the subjacent ground it occupies."[73] It is to avoid this indistinction that Joyce's Gabriel Conroy rejects boots for galoshes in "The Dead." Having spurned the Irish nationalism associated with the West, Gabriel sports continental galoshes imported from the East, as if to immunize his feet against the Irish sod.

In *Ulysses*, the impecunious Stephen has been forced to borrow Buck Mulligan's boots, along with his trousers. This secondhand footwear chafes against Stephen's pride more than his shins – much as Pound's tactless present irritated Joyce. "My two feet in his boots are at the end of his legs," Stephen broods in "Proteus," as he listens to these boots beating a tattoo into the seawrack. It is with such footsteps that "rhythm begins," generating the so-called "feet" of poetic meter. Stephen proceeds to scan his footsteps: "Acatalectic tetrameter of iambs marching" (*U* 3: 16–24). This passage implies that poetry, despite its spiritual flights, has feet of clay, its music originating in the thud of footfalls. To make matters worse, Stephen's feet – both metrical and corporeal – are shod in someone else's boots, trapped in secondhand "brogues." Since Stephen regards the English language as a borrowed tongue, it is worth noting that the word "tongue," like the word "brogue," pertains to shoes as well as speech, thus implicating footwear in Stephen's struggle with the language of imperialism.

Other common expressions link podiatric to linguistic difficulties: to put your foot in it is to say the wrong thing, committing a *faux pas*, a false step. This expression conflates walking with talking, or specifically mis-stepping with misspeaking. Such double meanings often recur in Beckett's work, where walking and talking are both presented as perilous enterprises, subject to multiple impediments of speech and gait; the word "impediment," incidentally, derives from the Latin *impedere*, which means to shackle the feet. Molloy, having lost his bicycle and suffering from premature rigor mortis in his legs, resorts to rolling in the muck, like the nameless creatures crawling in primeval slime in *How It Is* (1961/1964). What goes for walking also goes for talking; Beckett's talkers stop and start, "stumbling and mumbling, tumbling and bumbling," the rhythm of their speech as epileptic as their gait.[74] In *Not I* (1972), Mouth's jerky utterances echo the spurts of ambulation they describe: "a few steps then stop . . . stare into space . . . then on . . . a few more . . . stop and stare again . . . so on . . . drifting around . . ."[75] These halting steps evoke the French title of *Footfalls*, *Pas*, which means "not" as well as "footstep" or "footprint" (an ambiguity also exploited by Blanchot and Derrida).[76] This pun implies that the "pas" or pace is negated in its own performance. Just as I am "not I" (the French title is *Pas Moi*), so stepping is a form of stopping. Beckett's walkers are compelled to "go on," to keep their feet and narratives in motion, even though these journeys are impossible: "I can't go on, I'll go on."[77]

This principle of "pas" or "not-step" also applies to writing, which advances only to retreat, backtracking with every forward motion. Since walking is a way of making tracks, inscribing footprints, it constitutes a form of writing – a form that human beings share with animals, as Derrida has pointed out.[78] Beckett's tramps and indigents, hobbling on sticks and crutches, shadow forth the writer stumbling with his pen. "I shall not say this again, when not mentioned my stick is in my hand, as I go along," says the writer in *From an Abandoned Work*.[79] This "going along" corresponds to other allegories of writing in Beckett's work, as Phil Baker has observed, "such as the conflation of Malone's pencil and Lemuel's axe at the end of *Malone Dies* or the crawling slog across the lines of an exercise book which is, at one level, *How It Is*."[80] In each of these cases, going on – whether in the form of walking, talking, or writing – is constantly arrested, diverted, retracted, or reversed, leaving only "pas" or vanishing traces.

Joyce's works also implicate walking in writing. "Scribbledyhobble," the title of Joyce's notebook for *Finnegans Wake*, combines hobbling with scribbling, implying that both are forms of staggering along, whether with a cane or with a pen. In *Ulysses*, likewise, walking-sticks double for pens: Stephen the aspiring writer carries an ashplant cane, while Bloom uses a stick to scrawl an unfinished sentence in the sand, thus transforming this potential walking-aid into a writing tool. This unfinished sentence – "I AM A" – could be completed with several predicates, most obviously "cuckold," as suggested by the cuckoos whose eponymous refrain concludes the "Nausicaa" episode: "*Cuckoo Cuckoo Cuckoo*" (*U* 13: 1258–1306). "Jew" is another possible predicate, given that Bloom lays claim to Jewishness as well as Irishness in his confrontation with the Citizen in "Cyclops."

Sander Gilman, in *The Jew's Body*, argues that the Jewish foot has provided a target for anti-Semitic prejudice since the nineteenth century, when Jews came to be suspected of flat-footedness, a symptom associated with their sinister work as urban merchants. As "the city-dweller par excellence," the Jew plods the pavement, rather than the countryside, and his flat foot therefore marks his estrangement from the organic community. At the same time, flat-footedness reveals the lowness of his moral character, aligning the Jew with the devil, who is also associated with a malformed foot and relegated to the lowest regions of the earth. Paradoxically the Jew's flat foot is too grounded – since it lacks an arch to lift it off the dirt – but also too ungrounded, since it is deracinated from the native soil and trudges on the city's artificial surfaces. For this reason, as Steven Connor has argued, the Jew's foot encapsulates the geopolitical contradictions of modernity, which is associated on the one hand with the establishment of nations, and on the other with the mass displacement of populations. In this context, the Jew comes to be imagined "as the creature and embodiment of modernity because of a lack of grounding, condemned to wander over the surface of the earth without ever being able to establish a relation to any one portion of it."[81] Flattened by excessive wandering, the Jew's foot cannot find a toehold in a nation.

"Flatfoot" is one of many insults hurled at Bloom by Bello in the "Circe" episode: "How many women had you, eh, following them up dark streets, flatfoot, exciting them by your smothered grunts, what, you male prostitute?" (*U* 15: 3155–3157, [13: 1259]). The *Oxford English Dictionary* defines "flatfoot" as "a person with flat feet," citing this passage from "Circe" as confirmation; other definitions include foot soldier, sailor, or policeman, which are all vocations that depend on footwork. In Bloom's case, the term also evokes the flat-footedness attributed to Jews. Bloom is both the wandering Jew and the wandering Odysseus, who is searching for a promised homeland, although he is diverted – like his mythic antecedents – by distractions along the way. His feet eventually walk him back to 7 Eccles Street, just as they walked him riverwards in "Lestrygonians," but the home that he reclaims is not the same home that he left in "Lotus-Eaters." In the meantime Molly has rearranged the furniture, and Blazes Boylan has left his imprint on the bed, along with telltale flakes of Plumtree's potted meat. The weakness of Bloom's foothold in the home is underscored by the soreness of his wandering feet, the "benignant persistent ache in his footsoles" which also evokes the fallen arches of the flat-footed Jew.

In the "Nestor" episode, the anti-Semitic Mr Deasy decries the Jews as "wanderers on the earth." Yet the same is true of the Irish, driven into diaspora by famine and oppression. Hence Beckett's wanderers sport the most typical of Irish surnames, Murphy and Molloy; their feet, meanwhile, suffer from much worse deformities than those of the supposedly flat-footed Jew. In the course of his circular, inconsequential journey, Molloy loses half his toes, along with his crutches and his bicycle. "I fix at this period the dastardly desertion of my toes," he remembers – a bewildering betrayal since "I thought they were in excellent fettle, apart from a few corns, bunions, ingrowing nails, and a tendency to cramp."[82] Before their defection, these toes enjoy a pedicure of sorts from the woman Molloy calls Lousse or Edith: "Our commerce was not without tenderness, with trembling hands she cut my toe-nails and I rubbed her rump with winter cream." But "this idyll was of short duration," Molloy recalls, for it was followed by "the sudden loss of half my toes," possibly purloined by Lousse herself. But Molloy cannot remember when this catastrophe occurred, or which foot was affected, left or right (*M* 51–52). Lying in bed, in a passage reminiscent of the awakening narrator in Proust's *Recherche*, Molloy disintegrates into his body-parts:

> And when I see my hands, on the sheet, which they love to floccillate already, they are not mine, less than mine, I have no arms, they are a couple, they play with the sheet, love-play perhaps.... And with my feet it's the same, sometimes, when I see them at the foot of the bed, one with toes, the other without.... But my feet are not like my hands, I do not bring them back to me, when they become my feet again, for I cannot, but they stay there, far from me, but not so far as before. End of the recall. (*M* 61)

The *Oxford English Dictionary* defines floccillation as carphology, that is, "the movements of delirious patients, as if searching for or grasping at imaginary objects, or picking the bed-clothes." In Proust, as we have seen, the narrator's body-parts patch themselves together through their tactile memories of beds and rooms. But Molloy's feet and hands lack these somatic landmarks, having been deprived of any recognizable environment. His hands floccillate, his arms make love to one another, his feet recede into the distance, ignoring his attempts to call them back.

He contemplates his body as an alien collection of appendages, each twitching in its own delirium. His feet, in particular, are far too distant to obey his mind.

Is there something distinctively Irish, as well as modernist, about this obsessive concern with feet? To borrow Bloom's equivocating answer: "Nes. Yo" (*U* 15: 2766). Although feet are associated with the Irish sod, they also serve as agents of de-nationalization. Indeed the restless feet of Joyce's and Beckett's wanderers seem to kick against the current critical compulsion to repatriate these authors in their homeland. What does it mean to be an "Irish writer," especially during the early decades of the twentieth century when most of the literary talent fled the island? Is proof of residence required? To exclude all those who lived abroad would reduce the major Irish writers of this era to a party in a phone booth – though it would be a good party. On the other hand, there is nothing more typical of Irishness than exile and hybridity: to be Irish is to be not Irish, just as to be I is to be not I. Beckett's backtracking travelers intimate that going is not going, that exile is a way of turning back. Similarly Joyce hot-footed it from Ireland only to scribbledyhobble his way home, returning with his pen to the country he abandoned with his feet.

In geographical reality, it is impossible to walk away from Ireland: hence Stephen Dedalus dreams of flying, not of walking. Given that the island cannot be escaped on foot, and that modernism owes so much to technological innovations in transportation, there is something counterintuitive about the prominence of feet in Irish modernism. In 1904 Ireland's public transportation system was surprisingly advanced, in contrast to the living conditions of the populace, but Joyce's heroes never board the trams that screech through Dublin. Throughout *Ulysses*, trams and trains assert themselves as urban music rather than as vehicles of transportation: "frseeeeeeeeeeeeeeeeeeeefrong that train again . . ." (*U* 18: 874, [18: 596]).

Beckett's deserted landscape, on the other hand, is virtually bereft of transportation; the only vehicle available to Molloy, apart from his ruined feet, is a dilapidated bicycle. This lonely, unidentifiable terrain, deprived of the gleaming structures of modernity, suggests the aftermath of a nuclear holocaust. At once premodern and post-apocalyptic, this is a world in which technology has been annihilated by technology, leaving only cripples to hobble among the ruins. If cars and airplanes are characteristic of modernity, so are refugees and urban derelicts, and it is the plight of these unwilling pedestrians – the migrant casualties of capitalism – which is evoked by Beckett's tramps.

Although Irish modernism tends to be identified with émigrés like Beckett and Joyce, exile also takes place at home, as the lonely wanderers of Jack B. Yeats's paintings intimate. Similarly Synge's *Playboy of the Western World* (1907) opens with Christy Mahon rubbing his blistered feet after "walking wild eleven days."[83] Walking wild occurs in the city as well as in the countryside; in James Stephens's novel *The Charwoman's Daughter* (1912), Mary Makebelieve flees the slums by stravaging around the streets of Dublin, thus anticipating Bloom's urban odyssey. Later Beckett's Molloy goes walking wild through a wilderness both Irish and un-Irish, both *heimlich* and *unheimlich*, dotted with familiar place-names that dissolve as soon as they are posited; in Gertrude Stein's much-quoted phrase, "there is no there there."[84] This de-nationalized terrain offers little solid ground for the mismatched feet that stagger on it, feet that are always out of step with their own counterparts. Like Lévi-Strauss's autochthonous warriors, Beckett's bipeds are fatally dissymmetrical:

> For when the two legs shorten at the same time, and at the same speed, then all is not lost, no. But when one shortens, and the other not, then you begin to be worried. Oh not that I was exactly worried, but it was a nuisance, yes, a nuisance. For I didn't know which foot to land on, when I came down. (*M* 71)

Lacking a foot to land on, and a leg to stand on, Molloy's plight could be compared to that of the flat-footed Jew, uprooted from the native soil yet also mired in urban filth. In Beckett, the impossible activity of walking, in which one foot teeters on the quaking sod while the other is suspended in mid-air, corresponds to the conflict embodied in the Jewish foot – both groundless and grounded to excess – a conflict endemic to the exilic condition. For Beckett's characters, two feet never make a pair; instead they remain odd, unbalanced, misaligned, like the single rusty boot washed up by the sea in Joyce's "Proteus."[85] It is tempting to link Beckett's lopsided cripples to the partitioned state of Ireland, which also has a foot in two camps, the crumbling empire and the struggling republic – but this is to attribute too much thereness to Beckett's indeterminate geography. More cautiously, I would suggest that the oddness of feet – both earthbound and airborne, both chthonic and deterritorial – evokes the paradoxical condition of Irish exile, whether foreign or indigenous. Like Molloy, the exile doesn't know which foot to land on, or which land to set foot on, since going is a means of coming back.

> For what is the shadow of the going in which we come, this shadow of the coming in which we go .... I now go with my purpose as with it then I came, the only difference being this, that then it was living and now it is dead, which is what you might call the English call six of one and half a dozen of the other, do they not, or might you not? Or do I confuse them with the Irish?[86]

Notes

1 Virginia Woolf, *Between the Acts*, 127, 128, 131, 146. The phrase is adapted from Shakespeare's *Troilus and Cressida* V ii 161–163; see Julia Briggs, *Reading Virginia Woolf* (Edinburgh: Edinburgh University Press, 2006), 23 n.12. I would like to thank David Hillman and Judith Farquhar for their careful reading and insightful comments on this chapter.
2 Woolf, *Between the Acts*, 125.
3 Woolf, *Between the Acts*, 127.
4 Jean-Luc Nancy, "Corpus," 31.
5 Mikhail Bakhtin, *Rabelais and His World*, 26, 317–318, 339.
6 Norbert Elias, *The Civilizing Process: Sociogenetic and Psychogenetic Investigations*, 472; see also David Hillman, *Shakespeare's Entrails*, 7.
7 Quoted in Malcolm Bowie, 27. According to Lacan, the fantasized *corps morcelé* includes "images of castration, mutilation, dismemberment, dislocation, evisceration, devouring, bursting open of the body." In dreams, this "fragmented body ... appears in the form of

disjointed limbs, or of those limbs represented in exoscopy, growing wings and taking up arms for intestinal persecutions – the very same that the visionary Hieronymus Bosch has fixed, for all time, in painting." See Lacan, *Ecrits: A Selection*, 11, 4.

8   Jacques Lacan, *Ecrits*, 4. See also Gail Weiss, *Body Images: Embodiment as Intercorporeality*, 12.

9   It is worth noting that Lacan himself was closely associated with the Surrealist movement, which inspired his concept of the *corps morcelé*.

10 Ana Carden-Coyne, *Reconstructing the Body: Classicism, Modernism, and the First World War*, 38–39.

11 Trudi Tate, *Modernism, History and the First World War*, 78.

12 Samuel Beckett, *Collected Poems in English and French*, 13. See also Marjorie Perloff, "Beckett the Poet," in *A Companion to Samuel Beckett*, ed. S. E. Gontarski (Oxford: Blackwell, 2010), 212–215, where Perloff places "Enueg" in the tradition of the "walking poem."

13 Samuel Beckett, "Enueg I," in *Collected Poems*, 10; Beckett, *First Love*, 33; see also Ulrika Maude, *Beckett, Technology and the Body*, 92.

14 Marcel Proust, *Swann's Way*, 5.

15 See Paul Schilder, *The Image and Appearance of the Human Body: Studies in the Constructive Energies of the Psyche*, 11, 64.

16 See Derek Attridge, *Peculiar Language: Literature as Difference from the Renaissance to James Joyce* (London: Routledge, 2004), 160; see also Ulrika Maude, " 'A Stirring Beyond Coming and Going': Beckett and Tourette's," 157.

17 James Joyce, *Ulysses*, ch. 8, line 10. Henceforth cited as *U*, followed by chapter and line numbers. Freud notes the uncanny power of "dismembered limbs, a severed head, a hand cut off at the wrist . . . feet which dance by themselves," especially when these body-parts "prove capable of independent activity." Predictably (though not implausibly), he argues that "this kind of uncanniness springs from its proximity to the castration complex." See "The 'Uncanny,' " (1919) in *The Complete Psychological Works of Sigmund Freud*, Standard Edition, 244. Henceforth cited as *SE*.

18 T. S. Eliot, *The Waste Land* (1922), III.207; II.116; V.339; III.303; II.104, I.71–75.

19 Joseph Conrad, *The Secret Agent*, 83, 202.

20 Samuel Beckett, *The Unnamable* (1953/1958), in *Three Novels*, 299.

21 Marina Mackay, *Modernism and World War II*, 29.

22 Frank Budgen, *James Joyce and the Making of "Ulysses," and Other Writings* (Oxford: Oxford University Press, 1972), 21.

23 Paul Muldoon, "The More a Man Has the More a Man Wants," in *Quoof*, 53.

24 Sigmund Freud, *Civilization and Its Discontents*, SE Vol. 21, 91.

25 See Tim Armstrong, *Modernism, Technology, and the Body: A Cultural Study*, ch. 3: "Prosthetic Modernism," 77–105; see also Yoshiki Tajiri, *Samuel Beckett and the Prosthetic Body: The Organs and Senses in Modernism*.

26 David Hillman and Carla Mazzio, *The Body in Parts: Fantasies of Corporeality in Early Modern Europe*, xi.

27 Williams, "Portrait of a Lady," in *Collected Poems of William Carlos Williams*, Vol. 1, 129; Samuel Beckett, *Murphy*, 10.

28 Edmund Blunden, *Undertones of War*, 46; Frederic Manning, *The Middle Parts of Fortune*, 21; see Tate, *Modernism, History and the First World War*, 78.

29 Joanna Bourke, *Dismembering the Male: Men's Bodies, Britain and the Great War*, 31–35.

30 Carden-Coyne, 73, 83, 87.

31 Hal Foster, *Prosthetic Gods*, 131.

32   See Carden-Coyne, 178, on the development of plastic surgery during the post-war period, and 38–39 and 163–164 for the revival of classical aesthetics. For discussions of body-building during this time, see Bourke, 138–140 and Carden-Coyne, 166–170 and 179–183.

33   See Ernst Jünger's World War I memoir *Storm of Steel*, first published as *In Stahlgewittern* (1920), trans. Michael Hoffman (London: Penguin, 2007).

34   Hal Foster, "Armor Fou," 65.

35   Amy Lyford, *Surrealist Masculinities: Gender Anxiety and the Aesthetics of Post-World War I Reconstruction in France*, 11.

36   For "Nue 115," see the website for the Metropolitan Museum of Art http://www.metmuseum.org/collections/search-the-collections?ft=brassai&rpp=60&pg=1 (accessed December 1, 2012).

37   For "Princess X," see the website for the Philadelphia Museum of Art http://www.philamuseum.org/collections/permanent/51035.html (accessed December 1, 2012).

38   Foster, *Prosthetic Gods*, 249, 226–227.

39   Sigmund Freud, *On Transformations of Instinct as Exemplified in Anal Erotism*, SE Vol. 27, 126–127.

40   Lyford, *Surrealist Masculinities*, 15.

41   The Body without Organs is a term that Deleuze and Guattari borrow from Antonin Artaud to describe an assemblage or body with no underlying organizational principles, and hence no organs, which is continually constructed and deconstructed. Another source is Daniel Paul Schreber (*Memoirs of my Nervous Illness*, 334), who claims to have "lived for a long time without stomach, without intestines, bladder, almost without lungs...." See Gilles Deleuze and Félix Guattari, *A Thousand Plateaus: Capitalism and Schizophrenia*, ch. 6 and *passim*. For Bellmer's *Self-Portrait with the Doll*, see the website for the Los Angeles County Museum of Art http://collectionsonline.lacma.org/mwebcgi/mweb.exe?request=record;id=109721;type=101 (accessed December 1, 2012).

42   Schilder, 287, 191, 206.

43   Ralph Waldo Emerson, "The Comic," 83–84.

44   Walter Benjamin, "Experience and Poverty," 732.

45   *Death Awed* is one of a series of etchings by Percy Smith entitled *Dance of Death* and completed from 1914 to 1918. For a reproduction, see http://cas.awm.gov.au/item/ART50278 (accessed December 1, 2012).

46   Henri Barbusse, *Under Fire*, 13.

47   Beckett, *Waiting for Godot*, Acts I and II, 7–8, 34, 58.

48   Beckett, *Waiting for Godot*, Act I, 8.

49   See Martin Heidegger, "The Origin of the Work of Art," in *Basic Writings*, 162–164. For the debate inspired by Heidegger's analysis, see Meyer Schapiro, "The Still Life as a Personal Object – A Note on Heidegger and Van Gogh" and "Further Notes on Heidegger and Van Gogh," in *Theory and Philosophy of Art: Style, Artist, and Society, Selected Papers Vol. IV*, 135–142; 143–151; Jacques Derrida, "Restitutions of the Truth in Pointing [*pointure*]," in *The Truth in Painting*, 255–382. Fredric Jameson cites this discussion in distinguishing Van Gogh's modernist footwear from Andy Warhol's *Diamond Dust Shoes* in *Postmodernism*, 6–10.

50   Thomas Carlyle, *Sartor Resartus*, 41.

51   Georges Bataille, "The Big Toe," in *Visions of Excess: Selected Writings, 1927–1939*, 22. Originally published in *L'Anthropologie* 1903, 733–736.

52 In his famous interpretation of the Oedipus myth, Claude Lévi-Strauss points out that the patronymics in Oedipus's lineage have to do with "*difficulties in walking straight and standing upright*," which the anthropologist attributes to the persistence of the belief in the autochthonous origins of man. "It is a universal characteristic of men born from the earth that the moment they emerge from the depth they either cannot walk or they walk clumsily." See Claude Lévi-Strauss, *Structural Anthropology*, 213–215.

53 Bataille, *Visions of Excess*, 21–22.

54 Bataille, *Visions of Excess*, 22.

55 See William Rossi, *The Sex Life of the Foot and Shoe*, 14–15.

56 Freud, "Fetishism" (1927), Standard Edition, Vol. 21, 147–158.

57 Bataille, 22.

58 The association of feet with desacralization goes back at least as far as Caravaggio, who was notorious for painting profane feet in sacred scenes: examples include *Death of the Virgin* (1606), which scandalized the Carmellites with its undignified exposure of the Virgin's bare and swollen feet, and the *Madonna of Loreto* (1604), where the soles of the pilgrims' bare, dirty feet stick out towards the viewer.

59 T. S. Eliot, *East Coker*, Pt. I, line 7, in *Four Quartets, Complete Poems and Plays*, 123.

60 Bataille, 21; Wallace Stevens, "The Emperor of Ice Cream," in *The Collected Poems of Wallace Stevens*, 64.

61 Peter Stallybrass, "Footnotes," in *The Body in Pieces*, ed. Hillman and Mazzio, 313–314.

62 Peter Stallybrass, "Footnotes," 314.

63 D. H. Lawrence, "The Future of the Novel [Surgery for a Novel – Or a Bomb]," in *Study of Thomas Hardy and Other Essays*, 151. My thanks to David Trotter for alerting me to this reference.

64 Georg Lukács, *The Meaning of Contemporary Realism*, 34.

65 Joyce, *A Portrait of the Artist as a Young Man*, 217.

66 John Berger, *Ways of Seeing* (London: Penguin, 1990), 47.

67 Raymond Williams, *The Country and the City* (Oxford: Oxford University Press, 1975), 233.

68 Virginia Woolf, "Street Haunting" (1927), in *Selected Essays*, ed. David Bradshaw (Oxford: Oxford University Press, 2008), 177.

69 Virginia Woolf, "Street Haunting," 179–180.

70 See Beckett, *Proust and Three Dialogues with Georges Duthuit* (London: John Calder, 1965), 103.

71 Deirdre Bair, *Samuel Beckett: A Biography* (New York: Simon & Schuster, 1990), 71.

72 Wyndham Lewis, *Blasting and Bombardiering* (Berkeley: University of California Press, 1967), 29.

73 Steven Connor, *Scribbledehobbles: Writing Jewish-Irish Feet.*

74 Mary Bryden, *Gilles Deleuze: Travels in Literature*, 136.

75 Samuel Beckett, *Not I* (1972), in *Collected Shorter Plays* (London: Faber, 1984), 216. The title of the French edition (*Pas Moi*, 1975) also puns on "pas."

76 Blanchot puns on "pas" in his titles *Faux pas* (1943) and *Le pas au-delà* (1973); see also Jacques Derrida, "Pas," in *Parages*, 9–116; English version *Pace Not(s)*, trans. John P. Leavey, in Derrida, *Parages*, ed. John P. Leavey (Stanford: Stanford University Press, 2011), 11–102. See also Marinetti's short play "Feet" or "The Bases" ("Le Basi," 1915), which is a probable source for Beckett's *Footfalls*, in *Futurism: An Anthology*, 494.

77 Samuel Beckett, *The Unnamable*, 407.

78   Jacques Derrida, *The Animal That Therefore I Am*, 33.

79   Samuel Beckett, *From an Abandoned Work*, in *Samuel Beckett: The Complete Short Prose, 1929–1989*, 161.

80   Phil Baker, *Beckett and the Mythology of Psychoanalysis*, 166.

81   Connor, "Scribbledyhobbles."

82   Samuel Beckett, *Molloy* (1951/1955), in *Three Novels*, 75. Henceforth cited as *M*.

83   J. M. Synge, *Playboy of the Western World*, Act 1, 86.

84   Gertrude Stein, *Everybody's Autobiography*, 298.

85   This single boot is reminiscent of the single footprint that Robinson Crusoe discovers in the sand; see Daniel Defoe, *The Life and Adventures of Robinson Crusoe*, ed. Doreen Roberts (1719; Hertfordshire: Wordsworth Editions Ltd., 1995), ch. 18, 117–118.

86   Beckett, *Watt* (1953; London: Picador, 1988), 64.

References

Armstrong, Tim. (2004). *Modernism, Technology, and the Body: A Cultural Study*. Cambridge: Cambridge University Press.

Attridge, Derek. (2004). *Peculiar Language: Language as Difference from the Renaissance to James Joyce*. London: Routledge.

Bair, Deirdre. (1990). *Samuel Beckett: A Biography*. New York: Simon & Schuster.

Baker, Phil. (1997). *Beckett and the Mythology of Psychoanalysis*. New York: St. Martin's Press.

Bakhtin, Mikhail. (1984). *Rabelais and His World*. Bloomington: Indiana University Press.

Barbusse, Henri. (1960 [1916]). *Under Fire*, trans. W. Fitzwater Wray. London: J. M. Dent.

Bataille, Georges. (1985). *Visions of Excess: Selected Writings, 1927–1939*, ed. Allan Stoekl, trans. Allan Stoekl, Carl R. Lovitt, and Donald M. Leslie. Minneapolis: University of Minnesota Press.

Beckett, Samuel. (1954 [1952]). *Waiting for Godot*. New York: Grove Press.

Beckett, Samuel. (1957 [1938]). *Murphy*. New York: Grove Press.

Beckett, Samuel. (1974). *First Love and Other Shorts*. New York: Grove Press.

Beckett, Samuel. (1977). *Collected Poems in English and French*. New York: Grove Press.

Beckett, Samuel. (1988 [1953]). *Watt*. London: Picador.

Beckett, Samuel. (1995). *Samuel Beckett: The Complete Short Prose, 1929–1989*, ed. S. E. Gontarski. New York: Grove Press.

Beckett, Samuel. (2009). *Three Novels: Molloy, Malone Dies, The Unnamable*. New York: Grove Press.

Bellmer, Hans. (1934). *Self-Portrait with Doll*. Los Angeles County Museum of Art. At http://collectionsonline.lacma.org/mwebcgi/mweb.exe?request=record;id=109721;type=101 (accessed December 1, 2012).

Benjamin, Walter. (2005). "Experience and Poverty." In *Selected Writings*, vol. 2, ed. Michael W. Jennings et al. (pp. 731–736). Cambridge, MA: Harvard University Press.

Blanchot, Maurice. (1973). *Le pas au-delà*. Paris: Gallimard.

Blanchot, Maurice. (2002 [1943]). *Faux Pas*, trans. Charlotte Mandell. Stanford: Stanford University Press.

Blunden, Edmund. (2000 [1928]). *Undertones of War*. London: Penguin.

Bourke, Joanna. (1999). *Dismembering the Male: Men's Bodies, Britain, and the Great War*. London: Reaktion Books.

Bowie, Malcolm. (1993). *Lacan*. Cambridge, MA: Harvard University Press.

Bryden, Mary. (2007). *Gilles Deleuze: Travels in Literature*. Basingstoke: Palgrave Macmillan.

Carden-Coyne, Ana. (2009). *Reconstructing the Body: Classicism, Modernism, and the First World War*. Oxford: Oxford University Press.

Carlyle, Thomas. (1987 [1833–34]). *Sartor Resartus*. Oxford: Oxford University Press.

Connor, Steven. *Scribbledehobbles: Writing Jewish-Irish Feet*. At http://www.stevenconnor.com/scribble/ (accessed December 1, 2012).

Conrad, Joseph. (1948 [1907]). *The Secret Agent*. London: Methuen & Co. Ltd.

Deleuze, Gilles and Felix Guattari. (1987 [1980]). *A Thousand Plateaus: Capitalism and Schizophrenia*, trans. Brian Massumi. Minneapolis: University of Minnesota Press.

Derrida, Jacques. (1986). *Parages*. Paris: Éditions Galilée.

Derrida, Jacques. (1987). *The Truth in Painting*, trans. Geoff Bennington and Ian McLeod. Chicago: University of Chicago Press.

Derrida, Jacques. (2008). *The Animal That Therefore I Am*, ed. Marie-Louis Mallet, trans. David Wills. New York: Fordham University Press.

Elias, Norbert. (2000 [1939]). *The Civilizing Process: Sociogenetic and Psychogenetic Investigations*. Oxford: Blackwell.

Eliot, T. S. (1971). *The Complete Poems and Plays, 1909–1950*. New York: Harcourt, Brace & World.

Emerson, Ralph Waldo. (2010 [1875]). "The Comic." In *The Collected Work of Ralph Waldo Emerson*, Vol. 8: *Letters and Social Aims*, ed. Glen M. Johnson et al. (pp. 82–92). Cambridge, MA: Harvard University Press.

Fischer, Gerhard, ed. (1996). *'With the Sharpened Axe of Reason': Approaches to Walter Benjamin*. Oxford: Berg.

Foster, Hal. (1991). "Armor Fou." *October* 56: 64–97.

Foster, Hal. (2004). *Prosthetic Gods*. Cambridge, MA: MIT Press.

Freud, Sigmund. (1917). *On Transformations of Instinct as Exemplified in Anal Erotism*, in *The Complete Psychological Works of Sigmund Freud*, Standard Edition, 24 vols, trans. James Strachey. London: Hogarth, 1953–1974. Vol. 27, 125–134.

Freud, Sigmund. (1919). "The 'Uncanny'." SE Vol. 17, 217–256.

Freud, Sigmund. (1927). "Fetishism." SE Vol. 21, 147–158.

Freud, Sigmund. (1930). *Civilization and Its Discontents*, in Standard Edition, Vol. 21, 57–146.

Heidegger, Martin. (1977). *Basic Writings*, ed. David Farrell Krell. New York: Harper & Row.

Hillman, David. (2007). *Shakespeare's Entrails: Belief, Scepticism, and the Interior of the Body*. Basingstoke: Palgrave Macmillan.

Hillman, David and Carla Mazzio. (1997). *The Body in Pieces: Fantasies of Corporeality in Early Modern Europe*. New York: Routledge.

Jameson, Fredric. (1991). *Postmodernism*. Durham, NC: Duke University Press.

Joyce, James. (1961 [1922]). *Ulysses*. New York: Random House.

Joyce, James. (2003 [1916]). *A Portrait of the Artist as a Young Man*, ed. Seamus Deane. New York: Penguin Classics.

Jünger, Ernest. (2007 [1920]). *Storm of Steel*, trans. Michael Hoffman. London: Penguin.

Lacan, Jacques. (1977). *Écrits: A Selection*, trans. Alan Sheridan. New York: Norton.

Lawrence, D. H. (1962). *The Complete Letters of D.H. Lawrence, Vol. 2*, ed. Harry T. Moore. New York: Viking Press.

Lawrence, D. H. (1985). *Study of Thomas Hardy and Other Essays*, ed. Bruce Steele. Cambridge: Cambridge University Press.

Lévi-Strauss, Claude. (1983). *Structural Anthropology*, vol. 2, trans. Monique Layton. Chicago: University of Chicago Press.

Lewis, Wyndham. (1967). *Blasting and Bombardiering*. Berkeley: University of California Press.

Lukács, George. (1963). *The Meaning of Contemporary Realism*, trans. John and Necke Mander. London: Merlin Press.

Lyford, Amy. (2007). *Surrealist Masculinities: Gender Anxiety and the Aesthetics of Post-World War I Reconstruction in France*. Berkeley: University of California Press.

Mackay, Marina. (2007). *Modernism and World War II*. Cambridge: Cambridge University Press.

Manning, Frederic. (1979 [1929]). *The Middle Parts of Fortune*. New York: New American Library.

Marinetti, Filippo Tommaso. (2009 [1915]). "Feet" ("Le Basi"). In *Futurism: An Anthology*, ed. Lawrence Rainey et al. (p. 494). New Haven, CT: Yale University Press.

Maude, Ulrika. (2008). "'A Stirring Beyond Coming and Going': Beckett and Tourette's." *Journal of Beckett Studies* 17: 153–168.

Maude, Ulrika. (2009). *Beckett, Technology, and the Body*. Cambridge: Cambridge University Press.

Muldoon, Paul. (1983). *Quoof*. London: Faber and Faber.

Nancy, Jean-Luc. (1994). "Corpus," trans. Claudette Sartiliot. In *Thinking Bodies*, ed. Juliet Flower McCannell and Laura Zakarin (pp. 17–31). Stanford: Stanford University Press.

Proust, Marcel. (1934). *Remembrance of Things Past*, trans. C. K. Scott Moncrieff. Vol. 1: *Swann's Way*. New York: Random House.

Rossi, William. (1977). *The Sex Life of the Foot and Shoe*. London: Routledge.

Schapiro, Meyer. (1994). *Theory and Philosophy of Art: Style, Artist, and Society, Selected Papers*, vol. IV. New York: George Braziller.

Schilder, Paul. (1935). *The Image and Appearance of the Human Body: Studies in the Constructive Energies of the Psyche*. London: Kegan Paul.

Schreber, Daniel Paul. (2000). *Memoirs of my Nervous Illness*, trans. Ida Macalpine and Richard A. Hunter. New York: New York Review of Books.

Shakespeare, William. (2006). *Hamlet*. London: Arden.

Stein, Gertrude. (1993 [1934]). *Everybody's Autobiography*. Cambridge, MA: Exact Change.

Stevens, Wallace. (1990). *The Collected Poems of Wallace Stevens*. New York: Vintage Books.

Synge, John Millington. (1994 [1907]). *The Playboy of the Western World*, ed. Malcolm Kelsall. London: A & C Black.

Tajiri, Yoshiki. (2007). *Samuel Beckett and the Prosthetic Body: The Organs and Senses in Modernism*. London: Palgrave Macmillan.

Tate, Trudi. (1998). *Modernism, History, and the First World War*. Manchester: Manchester University Press.

Weiss, Gail. (1999). *Body Images: Embodiment as Intercorporeality*. New York: Routledge.

Williams, William Carlos. (1991). *Collected Poems of William Carlos Williams, Vol. 1: 1909–1939*, ed. Litz, A. Walton and Christopher MacGowan. New York: New Directions.

Woolf, Virginia. (2008). *Between the Acts*, ed. Melba Cuddy-Keane. Orlando, FL: Houghton Mifflin Harcourt.

16

Materialities of Modernism
Objects, Matter, Things

Bill Brown

The task of art, Emmanuel Levinas argued, is a matter of "extracting the thing from the perspective of the world": presenting things in their "real nakedness," uncovering "things in themselves" (2001, 46). He thus assigns to art the role of overcoming the epistemological limits established by Kant (that is, the role of evading the spatiotemporal grid and causal logic that determine human perception), but not, it may seem, without specifying art's function in the context of a degraded twentieth century. A Lithuanian Jew who had been naturalized as a French citizen and had fought against Germany in World War II, Levinas began to draft *Existence and Existents* (1947) during his years of internment in Hanover; from there he imagined that the "common intention" of "modern painting and poetry" is "to present reality as it is in itself, after the world has come to an end" (50). But "the end of the world" did not mean for him the destruction perpetrated by two wars; it meant, rather, the "destruction of representation," of "realism," and of the "continuity of the universe" (50). Indeed, even if Levinas could glimpse such an end (and thus the emergence of being), it was, rather, the world's persistence (exacerbated by two wars) that proved to be an intractable problem: that's why the thing must be *extracted* from the world. And that's why so much of modernism (visual, plastic, and literary) can be understood to name the provocation of aesthetic events meant to release things – or thingness – from the fetters of modernity.

Although modernity entails industrialization and urbanization, bureaucratization and massification (the emergence of mass culture), the grand sociological accounts of modernity – by Émile Durkheim, Max Weber, and Georg Simmel – concur in considering the increase in abstraction to be an overarching characteristic of the modernizing world. Simmel took the medium of money to be the master trope for, and the dominant force of, the increasing abstraction and rationalization of

A Handbook of Modernism Studies, First Edition. Edited by Jean-Michel Rabaté.
© 2013 John Wiley & Sons, Ltd. Published 2013 by John Wiley & Sons, Ltd.

the social and psychological realms, not just because (as Marx would have it) the particularities of any object or action disappear within the regime of value (all qualities being translated into quantities), but also because it facilitates the preponderance of calculation (Simmel 1990, esp. ch. 6). Among those who heard Simmel lecture (such as Ernst Cassirer, Walter Benjamin, Ernst Bloch, and Siegfried Kracauer), Georg Lukács both absorbed the claim and embedded it within the Marxist paradigm that Simmel himself eschewed. Describing the effects of the commodity form once it saturates society, he concludes (in 1923) that "reification" (*Versachlichung*: objectification or thingafication) is "the necessary, immediate reality" of anyone inhabiting capitalist society; indeed, "the structure of reification progressively sinks more deeply, more fatefully and more definitively into the consciousness of man" (197, 93). As one recent commentator puts it: persons, feelings, talents, ideas – "these get experienced as thing-like objects as soon as they come to be viewed according to their potential usefulness in economic transactions" (Honneth 23, and see Bewes). But for Lukács, the ramifications of reification extend to the object world, destroying its "original and authentic substantiality": "rational objectification," he writes, "conceals above all the immediate – qualitative and material – character of things as things" (92).

But what precisely is this qualitative and material character of things? By what means – within the modern world – could one gain access to this concealed character? Martin Heidegger (who had a considerable impact on Levinas) spent a good portion of his philosophical career in pursuit of that question – *The Question of the Thing* – as he named it in 1936. He had wondered, in 1927, about "grasping" a specifically "thingly character" (*Being in Time*, 98). This became an inquiry after "the thing-being of the thing," as he put it in his 1935 lecture on "The Origin of the Work of Art" (29–30), which necessitates "thinking of the thing as thing," focusing on the "thingness of the thing" as he insists in his 1950 lecture on "The Thing," differentiating it from the *object* of human perception, let alone scientific attention (29–30). Obsessive as Heidegger may thus seem, modernism was no less obsessed. And however successfully modernism has been understood as an engagement with the subject (consciousness and the unconscious) or as an investigation of the formal and material properties of specific media, it has increasingly been recognized as an inquiry into the fate of the object world, an account of how objects produce subjects, and an effort to encounter or effect a kind of thingness (Asendorf, Larrissy, Mao, Brown 2003). Indeed, at the outset her book on the *Machine Art* exhibition at MOMA (1934), Jennifer Marshall, imagining the syllabus for a course on "Ordinary Objects in Interwar Modernism," concludes with the quip that "the role of things in American modernism was significant enough to have accounted for most of it" (xv).

That role extends beyond the historical frame of the wars, and beyond the geographical scope of the United States. For in the "thing-poems" (Dinggedichte) that he published in *New Poems* (1908), Rainer Maria Rilke began to express what he reports elsewhere as his lifelong devotion to objects. Rodin and Cézanne had offered him an education, he said repeatedly, in *things*; in 1903, the year after his first meeting with Rodin, he writes of his sense of being forsaken as a child, "but then," he adds, "when people remained alien to me, I was drawn to things, and from them a joy breathed upon me" (*Letters*, 102). In his lecture on the sculptor in 1907 he begins by insisting that "it is not people about whom I have to speak, but things" *(Prose, 131)*. "You still need things," he tells his audience, "things" await "your confidence, your love, your dedication" (132). The second of his *Duino Elegies* (1922) makes it clear how fleeting and insubstantial a human being is in contrast to the being-of-things – at once stable and agential:

> Look: the trees exist; the houses
> That we live in still stand. We alone
> Fly past all things, as fugitive as the wind.
> And all things conspire to keep silent about us, half
> Out of shame, perhaps, half as unutterable hope.   (13)

To defend his "pathological fixation" on things he claimed that they are the "little batteries of life" – the phrase Christoph Asendorf borrowed for *Batteries of Life: On the History of Things and Their Perception in Modernity* (1984), an account that stretches from Descartes to the first two decades of the twentieth century (192). But, as in Marshall's history, the 1920s proves to be the decade of the most widespread fixation. In *One-Way Street* (1928), Walter Benjamin can begin to sound like Rilke – "warmth is ebbing from things," he writes – but he presents an antagonism between the human and the object worlds that proves more difficult to overcome: "Objects of daily use gently but insistently repel us. Day by day, in overcoming the sum of resistances – not only the overt ones – that they put in our way, we have an immense labor to perform. We must compensate for their coldness with our warmth if they are not to freeze us to death" (453–454). In 1942 Francis Ponge published a collection of prose poems, *Le parti pris de choses*, on behalf of "taking the side of things"; in 1956, Alain Robbe-Grillet declared that "*Les choses sont là*," when he described the *nouveau roman* in 1956, insisting that photographic and filmic media had taught the novel about the sheer presence of things, which would now "renounce their pseudo-mystery" (19, 21, 22). While Heidegger is concerned with an ontological amplitude (Being) that is irreducible to the ontic (mere beings), and while Levinas is particularly fixated on a "paroxysm of materiality" that exceeds any recognizable object form (51), for literature the object form of things, and the human relation to them, remains the more explicit topic of both thematic and formal attention. This is because, as one of Virginia Woolf's characters puts it, in *Between the Acts* (1941), "We live in things" (70).

In the 1920s things also appear as an object of explicitly political attention. One of the great theorists of Soviet Constructivism, Boris Arvatov, believed that the "peculiar ideologism" of Marxist thought had sacrificed materialism, which should centralize material culture, the "production and consumption of material values" (119–120, and see Kiaer). In "Everyday Life and the Culture of the Thing," he argues that "the most defining of the social relations" is "the relation of the individual and the collective to the Thing" (121). Though the Soviet revolution had not yet enabled society to "eliminate[. . .] the rupture between Things and people that characterized bourgeois society," success lay in imbuing the "proletariat" with the "deepest sense of Things" (121). While Lukács himself had argued that "the transformation of things into a process" can provide "a *concrete* solution to all the *concrete* problems created by the paradoxes of existent objects" (203), he anticipates nothing like Arvatov's concentration on material culture or his faith in modern technology and the "positive side" of "the concept of 'Americanism' ": " 'Thing-ness" (127).

Even such an abbreviated array of concerns about things and the human relation to them can provide a different perspective on the most familiar modernist texts. The absurdly meticulous inventory in the Ithaca episode of *Ulysses* (1922), prompted by a catechistic interrogation, can be understood as a response to what Raymond Williams called the "magic system" of advertising, a system registered by the "final" of Bloom's nocturnal "meditations": "Of some sole unique advertisement to cause passers to stop in wonder, a poster novelty with all extraneous accretions excluded, reduced to its simplest and most efficient terms not exceeding the span of casual vision and congruous with the velocity of modern life" (592). The poster novelty squares with the modern shift in advertising when information about a product (about its constituent parts, about its function, about its reliability) gives way to mere allure and efficiently coded associations with a lifestyle – a shift that prompted Williams to conclude that the problem is not that "our society is too materialist"; rather, "quite evident[ly] . . . our society is not materialist enough" (185, see also Wicke). The episode's relentless accumulation of details might then be understood as a mode of being "materialist enough": "What did the first drawer unlocked contain? A Vere Foster's handwriting copybook, property of Milly (Millicent) Bloom, certain pages of which bore diagram drawings, marked *Papli*, which showed a large globular head with 5 hairs erect, 2 eyes in profile, the trunk full front with 3 large buttons, 1 triangular foot . . . " (592). And yet so much of the catalogue is hyperbolically and comically hyperrationalist – "A contract with an inconsiderate contractee for the delivery of 32 consignments of some given commodity in consideration of cash payment on delivery per delivery at the initial rate of 1/4d to be increased constantly" – that whatever thingness things may possess gets obscured – in this case, by the abstracting discourse of calculation (590). This is a far cry from Joyce's effort to convey the sensuous encounter with the object world: "Most of all he liked grilled mutton kidneys which gave to his palate a fine tang of faintly scented urine" (45).

While the Ithaca episode may thus be read as an experiment in how linguistic and numerical representation can seem to materialize or dematerialize the object world, the Circe episode provides a hallucinatory drama where the inanimate object world comes to life and assumes a voice of its own. At one point, "*A cake of new clean lemon soap arises, diffusing light and perfume.*" The soap goes on to declare, "We're a capital couple are Bloom and I. / He brightens the earth. I polish the sky" (360). Jacques Rancière may be right to say that, in the pages of Flaubert and Balzac, "mute things speak better than any orator," but in Ulysses they are more simply unmuted (18). Given the chapter's reference to the economic system – when Bloom appears as chief magistrate he denounces those "laboursaving apparatuses, supplanters, bug bears...produced by a horde of capitalistic lusts upon our prostituted labour" (391) – it is possible to attribute the various metamorphoses within the chapter to the fetish character of the commodity as Marx explains it ("contain[ing] within itself," according to Lukács, "the whole of historical materialism" [170]). Indeed, the overarching metamorphosis that Marx repeatedly points out – "the personification of things and the reification of persons" (*Personifizierung der Sachen und Versachlichung der Personen*) – seems particularly appropriate to this brothel scene within Nighttown (Marx, 209). But the untoward animation of things can also be read as a kind of surrealist flamboyance (Joyce wrote the episode while living in Paris in 1920) that discloses a life of things beyond our quotidian encounter with them – a life that does not depend on the commodity form.

More simply, as the narrating Marcel puts it within the Overture to Proust's *Swann's Way* (1913), "Perhaps the immobility of the things that surround us is forced upon them...by the immobility of our conception of them" (6). When Rilke writes of a statue that "there's no place" within its "surfaces...that does not see you," he transforms the object into a new kind of subject (*New Poems*, 143). Indeed, the animism that E. B. Tylor had described at such length in the second volume of *Primitive Culture* (1871) survives modernity's disenchantment of the world, at least in the pages of Rilke and Proust and Joyce. Which is to say nothing of Surrealist fiction and film. Bruno Latour, the anthropologist who has recently prodded the social sciences to refocus their attention on the object world, has defined modernity itself as the project that established different "ontological zones," radically distinguishing – despite their *de facto* imbrication – the human from the nonhuman (11). This is why it has been possible for humanists to say that modernism, insofar as it animates the inanimate and gives voice to things, always knew that modernity was a kind of ruse (Brown 2004, 12). When, in *The Gift* (1925), the anthropologist Marcel Mauss surveys systems of exchange wherein objects have spirit, voice, and agency, he contends that "it is our western societies who have recently made man an 'economic animal,'" for which the object world has been disenchanted into alienable property; he goes on to insist that "we are not yet all creatures of this genus" (76).

In the absence of such animation, it is nonetheless the premodern or nonmodern object – the unreified object – that becomes a focus (if not a fulcrum) within narrative prose fiction, just as "primitive" objects came to rejuvenate the visual and plastic arts of the West. As Picasso himself came to tell the story, he "knew [he] had found [his] way" in 1907 by realizing, from the "masks and other objects" at the Trocadéro, that art is "a kind of magic," a "way of seizing power" (Flam, 425). In his preface to the Omega workshops catalogue of 1914, Roger Fry, riding the wave of interest in African artifacts, insisted that, with sufficient "contemplation," you can see how "a pot or a woven cloth made by a negro savage of the Congo" has "greater value and significance" than "a piece of modern Sevres china or a velvet brocade from a Lyons factory." Such value derives not simply from the form of the object but also from the (supposed) joy in its creation, which the artists of the collective (manufacturing textiles, furniture, and ceramics) mean to retrieve, "by allowing free play to the delight in creation in the making of objects of common life." In opposition to the "wonder of modern civilization" and the "pretentious elegance of the machine-made," they "try to keep the spontaneous freshness of primitive or peasant work" (201). As D. H. Lawrence makes clear in the most notoriously primitivist English novel, *The Plumed Serpent* (1926), the rejuvenation of human body and spirit (along with the reincarnation of the old gods) necessitates a rejuvenated object culture. During her trip to Mexico, Kate Leslie dismisses the "banalities" of Mexican furnishing (108), but she is no less oppressed by a collection of "Aztec things, obsidian knives, grimacing squatting idols" (35); at a market where the native people (from Ixlahuacan and Jaramay and Las Zemas) exhibit their "big red pots, bulging red ollas for water-jars, earthenware casseroles and earthenware jugs," she feels only the "strange, black resentment" of those who have succumbed to the modern traffic in goods, part and parcel of the "world gone ghastly" (229–230). She escapes from that world only by accompanying Don Ramón to his cult of Quetzalcoatl. He himself denounces the prospect of "every peon in Mexico wear[ing] an American suit of clothes and shiny black shoes" (359). At the workshops in his community, though, smiths and weavers delight in fabricating the material culture that is meant to accompany his spiritual and corporeal revolution: "In the shadow of the mud shed, the pure colours of the lustrous wool looked mystical, the cardinal scarlet, the pure, silky white, the lovely blue, and the black, gleaming in the shadow of the blackish walls" (321). However infamously volkish the politics of Lawrence's novel may be, they should not obscure what the novelist shares with the Constructivists, with the Bauhaus, with Le Corbusier: the conviction that social change must be accompanied by (if indeed it is not precipitated by) new object relations. It is the conviction that underlies Le Corbusier's overarching question: "Well might we write: Architecture or Revolution" (299).

While *The Plumed Serpent* can thus be cast at the periphery of a modernist effort (indebted to Ruskin as to William Morris) to rethink production (Mao), it is the phenomenological encounter with the premodern object itself that catalyzes the transformation of the individual in Willa Cather's *The Song of the Lark* (1915). The artistic scene of Chicago has left Thea Kronborg uninspired, but the cliff dwellings of Arizona, from which she has taken respite from the city, provide the environment – with "fragments of pottery everywhere" – for the epiphany that convinces her of her artistic mission as a singer (254). With "her power to think converted into a power of sustained sensation," she bathes within the "ritualistic" atmosphere provided by a canyon pool; from there, she discovers a new way of imagining art: "The stream and the broken pottery: what was any art but an effort to make a sheath, a mold in which to imprison for a moment the shining, elusive element which is life itself" (251, 254). Pottery surfaces as the metonymic master trope for the capacity to give vitality form. When Cather effectively rewrites the discovery of the Southwestern mesas in *The Professor's House* (1925), the pots found by Tom Outland in the "Cliff City" of "some extinct civilization, hidden away for centuries" – artifacts that he considers to be the inalienable property of the nation – appear in absolute contrast to the objects acquired in an irrepressible shopping spree (in Chicago and Paris) during which a young couple flamboyantly work to furnish their new country home (202). While the Professor's most familiar objects – the "old walnut table" and the "cane-backed office chair" – provide artifactual relief from the hubbub of the modern world (16), for the orphaned Outland the unreified objects he finds within the "little cliff-hung villages" provide metonymic access to ancient ancestors and to a spiritualized American identity (16, 202; see Brown 2003, 127–132).

In her program essay on modern fiction, "The Novel Démeublé" (1913), Cather zeroes in on a different question of the thing: on the fact that the nineteenth-century novelist (most notably Balzac) had come to resemble an "interior decorator" who stresses "the importance of material objects and their vivid presentation" to the point of rendering the novel "overfurnished" (47, 43). "How wonderful," she writes, "if we could throw all the furniture out of the window" (51). But modernists were more inclined to pursue the same path as Cather did, not dispensing with things so much as dramatizing how oppressive the object world could be. In *The Last September* (1929), Elizabeth Bowen uses built space to convey the weight of the past: "The pale room rose to a height only empty mirrors followed above the level of occupation; this disproportionate zone of emptiness dwarfed at all times figures and furniture. The distant ceiling imposed on consciousness its blank white oblong, and a pellucid silence, distilled from a hundred and fifty years of society, waited under the ceiling" (22–23). As a boy, the protagonist of Thomas Mann's *Magic Mountain* (1924), Hans Castorp, is fascinated by the objects that his grandfather shows him in the "rococo china cabinet made of rosewood, with yellow silk curtains pulled across the inside of its windowpanes," but the objects there are lifeless: "Inside were all manner of disused and fascinating objects: a pair of silver-branched candlesticks, a broken barometer in a wooden case with allegorical carving, an album of daguerreotypes, a cedar-wood case for liqueurs, a funny little Turk in flowing silk robes, under which was a hard body with a mechanism inside. Once, when you wound him up, he had been able to leap about all over the table, but he was long since out of repair" (20). Life has gone out of this object world. Even the family baptismal bowl and plate, while providing the boy with the sense of generational continuity, give him the feeling of "dizzying, everlasting sameness" (22).

Just as pottery could provide relief from such sameness for Cather (and just as it served as an iconic component of the modernist attraction to the American Southwest), so too it served as a rejuvenating object of aesthetic attention for Herbert Read, the poet and literary critic who, following his military service in the war and subsequent service at the Treasury, was transferred (in 1922) to the post of Assistant Keeper of Ceramics at the Victoria and Albert Museum. The book he co-authored with Bernard Rackham on *English Pottery* (1924) interrupted the many histories that had narrated a steady progress in ceramic art from the coarse to the elegant, from "mere peasant work" to the work of Wedgwood, with no "account of the nature of pottery" – which, in Read's understanding, had been steadily compromised since the eighteenth century. Drawing attention to very early work, and objecting to much of the subsequent painted decoration, the authors pronounce that "pottery is, at its best, an abstract art," which should be recognized as "plastic art in its most abstract form" (1–7). And for Read, on his way to becoming the century's first great expositor of modern sculpture, pottery catalyzed (or, say, materialized) a new conceptualization of art. "Pottery is pure art," he goes on to write, in *The Meaning of Art* (1931); "it is freed from any imitative function" (41–42). In this historical survey, committed to understanding "all art" as "the development of formal relations" and to understanding "aesthetic sensibility" as that which "corresponds to the element of form in art," modernist abstract art enjoys special attention; pottery appears as "the simplest and the most difficult of all arts. It is the simplest because it is the most elemental; it is the most difficult because it is the most abstract" (40–41).

Within the book, Read also refuses to distinguish between the artist and the artisan – "The distinction between the 'fine' and 'applied' arts is a pernicious one" (49) – and that refusal becomes the argumentative force of *Art and Industry* (1934), his manifesto on behalf of industrial design. In an argument that resonates more with Walter Gropius than with William Morris, he argues that once we "recognize the abstract nature of the essential element in art" (41) we can appreciate how industrially produced useful objects can "appeal to the aesthetic sensibility as *abstract art*," with an "appeal" that is "rational and irrational," which is to say "appreciated by intuitional modes of apprehension" (36). For Read, then, pottery exemplifies the resolution not only of artist and artisan, but also of art and industry, all the while epitomizing "pure art" not on the grounds of some autonomy from the regimes of use and exchange but on the grounds of its autonomy from mimetic representation. Within a kind of homeopathic logic, concrete abstraction appears as a source for rehabilitating the modern world.

Writing of "intuitional modes of apprehension," Read signals his debt to Henri Bergson, whose work he encountered before the war through his association with T. E. Hulme, who translated *An Introduction to Metaphysics* (1903) in 1913; there, Bergson posits that thinking about objects can be displaced by "adopting the very movement of the life of things" (40). This *Introduction* paves the way for *Creative Evolution* (1907), where he goes on to argue that *concepts* prevent philosophers from engaging with *objects* – from recognizing the mind's capacity "to think matter." The "intellect feels at home among inanimate objects," he writes, and "more especially among solids, where our action finds its fulcrum and our industry its tools" (ix). This is the book that became a kind of bible for the later generation of sculptors who sought to liberate the latent vitality of their material. A vitalist sculptor like Henri Moore, Read went on to write, "believes that behind the appearance of things there is some kind of spiritual essence, a force of immanent being which is only partially revealed in actual living forms" (*Moore* 73). But in the (overlooked) book on English pottery, he had already argued that "a good vessel possesses *vitality*": "The eye registers and the mind experiences in the contemplation of energetic lines and masses a sense of movement, rhythm, or harmony which may indeed be the prime cause of all aesthetic pleasure" (7). The life of things could be registered not by their animation but by their inherent vivacity.

Although Read had an anarchist antipathy to modern society and culture, he differentiates his basic argument from Morris's vilification of machinery, and he shares none of Heidegger's technophobia. Still, he had no patience for the technophilia that attracted a different branch of modernism, manifest in the inspiration that engineering provided for Hart Crane's epic poem, *The Bridge* (1930), in the machine aesthetics of Vorticism (which helped to ground Wyndham Lewis's antihumanism), and in the widespread fascination with the airplane, from Kafka's "The Aeroplanes at Brescia" (1909) to Marinetti's "Manifesto of Aeropoetry" (1931), and other Italian Futurist manifestos (on behalf of Aeropainting, Aeromusic, Aeroplastic, Aeroceramics, and Aeroxlography). (On technology and the machine aesthetic, see Burstein, Foster, and Danius.) As Wanda Corn has said of the visual arts, there are two strains of modernist engagement with object culture: an art that means to "save the world from the enslavement to things," and an art that imagines a "harmonious alignment with the new world of glass, steel, and geometry" (17–18; see also Orvell). In Proust's case, that alignment takes the form of casting the new invention within a mythological mold: his eyes "tear-filled," "as deeply moved as an ancient Greek on seeing for the first time a demi-god," Marcel encounters "not two hundred feet above [his] head, against the sun,... two great wings of flashing metal." His first sight of an airplane makes him feel that he has access to "all the routes in space, in life" (*Cities of the Plain* 1062). In Benjamin's case, the alignment takes the form of imagining a collective innervation of the filmic apparatus that would provide new access to the structures of the material world ("Work of Art").

Most paradigmatically, though, the modernist poet, whether addressing natural or technological objects, feels the need to rescue them – to extract them in their real nakedness, as Levinas would have it – not from consumer culture so much as from rationalism, symbolism, and language itself. Hannah Arendt was right to say that "for Rilke, things have a higher rank in existence than do human beings" (7), but Rilke retained faith in the capacity of language to intensify the object world: in the ninth of the *Duino Elegies*, he asks a rhetorical question: "What if we're only *here* to say *house*, / bridge, fountain, gate, jug, fruit, tree, window"? Nonetheless, such a role confers on things a new ontological amplitude: "but for *saying*, understand, / oh for such saying as the things themselves / never dreamt so intensely to be" (57). Fernando Pessoa provides an ascetic alternative. In 1914 he invented a poet (one of what he called his "heteronyms"), Alberto Caeiro da Silva, who is said to have recorded *The Keeper of Flocks* between 1910 and 1912. Stridently anti-metaphysical, anti-rational, and anti-religious, the lyrics comprise a meditative argument against the significance of things.

> Because the only hidden meaning of things
> Is that they have no meaning at all.
> This is stranger than all the strangenesses,
> And the dreams of all the poets,
> And the thoughts of all the philosophers –
> That things really are what they appear to be
> And that there is nothing to understand.   (97)

The recognition of things depends on our capacity to "unlearn" – on "Knowing how to see without thinking" (65). A chief impediment to that recognition is language itself – "the language of men / Which gives personality to things, / And imposes a name on things" (71). Whereas, for Rilke, the act of naming confers greater being, for Pessoa that act prevents things from being what they are, for "things have neither name nor personality" (71).

And yet, for all Caeiro's repudiation of language and the "dreams of poets," his objects of fascination – sky, trees, grass, wind, rivers – seem paradigmatically "poetic," as does his self-appellation as a shepherd, "a keeper of sheep," despite the fact that he does not keep sheep: "I never kept sheep / But it's as if I'd done so" (32, 3). However resistant to analogy or metaphor, Caeiro frames his endeavor metaphorically. Sharing many of Pessoa's concerns, William Carlos Williams nonetheless produced very different lyric results. He recognized the need to "escape from crude symbolism, the annihilation of strained associations" (*Spring and All*, 102). And he was appalled by the way that "categories" trap things within "corners of understanding" – by the fact that, "reinforced by tradition, every common thing has been nailed down" (*A Novelette* 295). But his eye was drawn not just to such pastoral objects as the famous "red wheelbarrow"; it was drawn as well by the quotidian artifacts of domestic life.

> The red paper box
> hinged with cloth
> is lined
> inside and out
> with imitation leather (*Poems*, 260)

It is the *imitation leather* that affirms the status of this object beyond realm of the "poetic," just as it affirms the prospect that any object might be redeemed by the right kind of attention.

His playful allusion to Rodin in the title of "The Thinker" similarly deflates the grandiosity of art while the poem expands its purview:

> My wife's new pink slippers
> have gay pompons.
> There is not a spot or a stain
> on their satin toes or their sides.
> All night they lie together
> under her bed's edge. (Poems, 220)

In such poems, Williams enacts a kind of redemptive reification, resignifying the mundane (indeed, the silly) not through rhetorical inflation but through an untoward engagement: "I talk to them / in my secret mind / out of pure happiness" (220). Such engagement compensates for the object world's coldness with human warmth.

For the Benjamin of *One-Way Street*, it is children who, by producing "their own small world of things," exempt themselves from modernity's pathological subject–object relations: they are "irresistibly drawn by the detritus generated by building, gardening, housework, tailoring, or carpentry. In waste products they recognize the face that the world of things turns directly and solely to them"; they bring together, "in the artifact produced in play, materials of widely differing kinds in a new, intuitive relationship" (449–450). When Virginia Woolf narrates the story of a man who re-centers his life around a piece of beach glass, she describes a small world of things in the context of the material scarcity provoked by World War I (Brown 1999). And it didn't take Benjamin long to see how artists too could develop a childlike intuition: how the "materialist, anthropological inspiration" of the Surrealists allowed them to see "the revolutionary energies that appear in the 'outmoded,'" and to figure out the "trick by which the world of things is mastered," which "consists in the substitution of a political for a historical view of the past" ("Surrealism," 209–210).

But mastering things can take the form of submitting to them, subjecting oneself to the point where subject and object, human and nonhuman, seem to converge. This is the form that mastery takes when, with a kind of enchanting austerity, Ernst Bloch stages his meditation on the pitcher (*Krug*) at the outset of *The Spirit of Utopia* (1921), which he had drafted during the war (1915–16). His materialist phenomenology releases the subject from the subject/object mise-en-scène by realizing an exchange of bodies with the object at hand. But this becoming-the-pitcher begins with a mere being-by it: "I am by the pitcher. Thus it leads inside, stands before the wall in the room. The wall is green, the mirror is golden, the window is black, the lamp burns brightly. But the pitcher is not simply warm, let alone so indisputably beautiful as other fine old artifacts" (7).

Preferring "the clumsy, brown implement" with "almost no neck, a wild man's bearded face" to any of the "expensive pitchers" (8), Bloch begins by granting the object its physical character. He means to interrupt that reified world and to grant the pitcher its immediate character as a thing. But even as the object seems to summon up its rustic origins – "the bearded aspect of the forest spirit still peers out at us" (8), it also summons the attentive subject at hand: "whoever looks long enough at the pitcher soon begins to carry its color and form with him" (9).

> I could probably be formed like the pitcher, see myself as something brown, something peculiarly organic, some Nordic amphora, and not just mimetically or simply empathetically, but so that I thus become for my part richer, more present, cultivated further toward myself by this artifact that participates in me. (9)

This participation of the object in the subject signals something other than a phenomenology of perception, and something other than the metaphysical thingness of things that Heidegger would come to imagine, in "The Thing," at the close of his meditation on the jug (*Krug*). The participation of the thing in the body, which is the body's participation in the thing, confers above all a greater presence, which is self presence.

Theodor Adorno, skeptical of the "cult of things" that he associated above all with Rilke, nonetheless found Bloch's meditation mesmerizing. He considered Rilke's effort "to bring the alien objects into subjectively pure expression" to be a thoroughly unconvincing compensation. The "aesthetic weakness" of the poet's mixture of "religion and decorative handicraft" lies in the fact that "the genuine power of reification" cannot be "painted over with a lyric aura" (Adorno 1989, 158). But writing in 1965, Adorno recalls having read *The Spirit of Utopia* in 1921, at the age of seventeen, and cherishing Bloch's mode of engagement with the inanimate object world (especially in contrast to Georg Simmel's, whom he nonetheless credits with returning "philosophy to concrete subjects," and away from epistemology) (Adorno 1992, 213). With his thought "losing itself unreservedly in the material itself," Bloch accomplishes what Simmel could not: "the need to disappear into the object" (Adorno 1992, 213, 215). "What Bloch is after is this," Adorno writes: "if one only really knew what the pot in its thing-language is saying and concealing at the same time, then one would know what ought to be known and what the discipline of civilizing thought, climaxing in the authority of Immanuel Kant, has forbidden consciousness to ask" (219). In this more unpredictable encounter with things, the pay-off amounts to novelty itself: "This secret would be the opposite of something that has always been and will always be, the opposite of invariance: something that would finally be different" (219).

Adorno does not explicitly differentiate Bloch's encounter from Heidegger's famous lecture on the jug (*Krug*) – more specifically the void around which the jug is thrown, which comes to gather and stay the fourfold. That difference lies most obviously in Bloch's narrated patience to stare "long enough" at an object described in detail, in contrast to Heidegger's etymologically derived assertion that the thing gathers earth and sky, deities and mortals. Indeed, Adorno relishes his memory of *The Spirit of Utopia* as a physical object – a "dark brown volume of over 400 pages, printed on thick paper" (213), and such pleasure in the sensuous qualities of print points to an altogether different strategy whereby literary modernism worked to dramatize the thingness of things – to dramatize its own thingness: the design of books and journals as objects (the two issues of the Vorticist *Blast* [1914–15], for instance), or the effort to insist on the material presence of language itself, from Pound's use of the Chinese ideogram to the typographical experiments of the Futurists, Dadaists, and Surrealists (Drucker, Davidson).

The artist, as Williams declared, is "AT WORK MAKING OBJECTS" (*Spring and All*, 112). Though his declaration concerned a visual artist (Juan Gris), Williams also recognized how literary artists such as Gertrude Stein interrupted the transparency of language to confer on words and sentences their own status as objects. Her "words, in writing, . . . transcend everything"; as anticipated by Lawrence Sterne, "the feeling is of words themselves, a curious immediate quality quite apart from their meaning" ("Stein," 350, 347). Unwilling as Stein was to eradicate sense altogether (as did her Formalist contemporary Victor Khlebnikov), in the "Objects" section of *Tender*

Buttons (1914) her compositions enigmatically play with referentiality, evading sense while promoting sound to the point of turning the pieces into aural objects. Thus, in "Dirt and Not Copper":

> Dirt and not copper makes a color darker. It makes the shape so heavy and makes no melody harder.

> It makes mercy and relaxation and even a strength to spread a table fuller. There are more places not empty. They see cover. (464)

It is the opacity of the prose that enables the composition to emerge as a thing among things.

While various transformations of the modernist attention to objects proliferate after World War II in Pop, Minimalism, Earth Art, and what Donald Judd called "specific objects" (inhabiting neither the form of painting nor that of sculpture), Stein's impact persists in the language art of the 1960s. She is invoked by Carl Andre, who eliminates narrative and grammar on behalf of dramatizing the materiality of the sign. And she is invoked by Vito Acconci, for whom the "page has to be narrowed in on, treated as a chamber space separated from its surroundings," which means using "language to cover a space rather than [to] uncover meaning" (quoted in Kotz, 164, 167). Whatever thingness might be conveyed or summoned up by words, this gives way to the thingness of them.

References

Adorno, Theodor. (1989). "Lyric Poetry and Society," trans. Bruce Mayo. In *Critical Theory and Society* (pp. 155–171), ed. Stephen Bronner and Douglas Kellner. London: Routledge.

Adorno, Theodor. (1992). "The Handle, the Pot, and Early Experience." In *Notes to Literature*, Vol. 2, trans. Shierry Weber Nicholson. New York: Columbia University Press.

Arendt, Hannah and Gunther Stern. (2007). "Rilke's *Duino Elegies*." In *Reflections on Literature and Culture*, ed. Susannah Gottlieb (pp. 1–23). Stanford: Stanford University Press.

Arvatov, Boris. (1996). "Everyday Life and the Culture of the Thing (Toward the Formulation of the Question)," trans. Christina Kiaer. October 75 (Winter): 119–128.

Asendorf, Christoph. (1993). *Batteries of Life: On the History of Things and Their Perception in Modernity*, trans. Don Renau. Berkeley: University of California Press.

Benjamin, Walter. (1996). *One-Way Street*, trans. Edmund Jephcott. *Selected Writings Volume 1: 1913–1926*, ed. Marcus Bullock and Michael W. Jennings. Cambridge, MA: Harvard University Press.

Benjamin, Walter. (1999). "Surrealism: The Last Snapshot of the European Intelligentsia," trans. Edmond Jephcott. In *Selected Writings: Volume 2: 1927–1934*, ed. Michael Jennings, Howard Eiland, and Gary Smith (pp. 207–221). Cambridge, MA: Harvard University Press.

Bergson, Henri. (2007). *An Introduction to Metaphysics*, trans. T. E. Hulme. London: Palgrave.

Bergson, Henri. (1998). *Creative Evolution*, trans. Arthur Mitchell. Mineola, NY: Dover.

Bewes, Timothy. (2002). *Reification, or the Anxiety of Late Capitalism*. London: Verso.

Bloch, Ernst. (2000). *The Spirit of Utopia*, trans. Anthony A. Nassar. Stanford: Stanford University Press.

Bowen, Elizabeth. (2000). *The Last September*. New York: Random House.

Brown, Bill. (1999). "The Secret Life of Things (Virginia Woolf and the Matter of Modernism)." *Modernism/ Modernity* 6.2 (April): 1–28.

Brown, Bill. (2003). *A Sense of Things: The Object Matter of American Literature*. Chicago: University of Chicago Press.

Brown, Bill, ed. (2004). *Things*. Chicago: University of Chicago Press.

Burstein, Jessica. (2012). *Cold Modernism: Literature, Fashion, Art*. University Park: Penn State University Press.

Cather, Willa. (1925). *The Professor's House*. New York: Knopf.

Cather, Willa. (1936). "The Novel Démeublé." In *Not Under Forty* (pp. 43–51). New York: Knopf.

Cather, Willa. (1999). *The Song of the Lark*. New York: Penguin.

Corn, Wanda. (1999). *The Great American Thing: Modern Art and National Identity, 1915–1935*. Berkeley: University of California Press.

Crane, Hart. (1992). *The Bridge*. New York: Liveright.

Danius, Sara. (2002). *The Senses of Modernism: Technology, Perception, Aesthetics*. Ithaca, NY: Cornell University Press.

Davidson, Michael. (1997). *Ghostlier Demarcations: Modern Poetry and the Material Word*. Berkeley: University of California Press.

Drucker, Johanna. (1997). *The Visible Word: Experimental Typography and Modern Art, 1909–1923*. Chicago: University of Chicago Press.

Flam, Jack and Miriam Deutch, eds. (2003). *Primitivism and Twentieth-Century Art: A Documentary History*. Berkeley: University of California Press.

Foster, Hal. (2004). *Prosthetic Gods*. Cambridge, MA: MIT Press.

Fry, Roger. (1996). "Preface to the Omega Workshops Catalog." In *A Roger Fry Reader*, ed. Christopher Reed (p. 201). Chicago: University of Chicago Press.

Heidegger, Martin. (1962). *Being and Time*, trans. John Macquarrie and Edward Robinson. New York: Harper & Row.

Heidegger, Martin. (2001). "The Origin of the Work of Art." In *Poetry, Language, Thought*, trans. Albert Hofstadter (pp. 15–86). New York: Harper & Row.

Heidegger, Martin. (2001). "The Thing." In *Poetry, Language, Thought*, trans. Albert Hofstadter (pp. 161–184). New York: Harper & Row.

Honneth, Axel. (2008). *Reification: A New Look at an Old Idea*. New York: Oxford University Press.

Joyce, James. (1986). Ulysses, *ed.* Hans Walter Gabler. New York: Random House.

Judd, Donald. (1975). "Specific Objects." *Donald Judd: Complete Writings 1959–1975* (pp. 181–89). Halifax: The Press of the Nova Scotia College of Art and Design.

Kafka, Franz. (1992). "The Aeroplanes at Bresica." *The Transformation ('Metamorphosis') and Other Stories*. Trans. Malcolm Pasley (pp. 1–10). London: Penguin.

Kiaer, Christina. (2005). *Imagine No Possessions: The Socialist Objects of Russian Constructivism*. Cambridge, MA: MIT Press.

Kotz, Liz. (2007). *Words to Be Looked At: Language in 1960s Art*. Cambridge, MA: MIT Press.

Larrissy, Edward. (1990). *Reading Twentieth-Century Poetry: The Language of Gender and Objects*. Oxford: Blackwell.

Latour, Bruno. (1993). *We Have Never Been Modern*, trans. Catherine Porter. Cambridge, MA: Harvard University Press.

Lawrence, D. H. (1992). *The Plumed Serpent*. New York: Vintage.

Le Corbusier. (2007). *Toward an Architecture*, trans. John Goodman. Los Angeles: Getty Publications.

Levinas, Emmanuel. (2003). *Existence and Existents*, trans. Alphonso Lingis. Pittsburgh: Duquesne University Press.

Lukács, Georg. (1971). *History and Class Consciousness: Studies in Marxist Dialectics*, trans. Rodney Livingstone. Cambridge, MA: MIT Press.

Mann, Thomas. (1996). *The Magic Mountain*, trans. John E. Woods. New York: Vintage.

Marinetti, F. T. (1931). "Manifesto dell'aeropoesia." *La Gazzetta del Popolo*, Oct. 22.

Marx, Karl. (1990). *Capital*, vol. 1, trans. Ben Fowkes. London: Penguin.

Mauss, Marcel. (1990). *The Gift*, trans. W. D. Halls. New York: W. W. Norton.

Orvell, Miles. (1989). *The Real Thing: Imitation and Authenticity in American Culture, 1880–1940*. Chapel Hill: University of North Carolina Press.

Pessoa, Fernando. (1997). *The Keeper of Sheep*, trans. Edwin Honig and Susan M. Brown. Riverdale- on-Hudson, NY: Sheep Meadow Press.

Proust, Marcel. (1981). *Swann's Way*, trans. C. K. Scott Moncrieff and Terrence Kilmartin. New York: Random House.

Proust, Marcel. (1981). *Cities of the Plain*, trans. C. K. Moncrieff and Terrence Kilmartin. New York: Random House.

Rancière, Jacques. (2004) "The Politics of Literature." *SubStance*, 33.1: 10–24.

Read, Herbert. (1934). *Henry Moore, Sculptor*. London: A. Zwemmer.

Read, Herbert. (1961). *Art and Industry*. Bloomington: Indiana University Press.

Read, Herbert and Bernard Rackham. (1972). *English Pottery*. Wakefield, UK: EP Publishing.

Read, Herbert. (1972). *The Meaning of Art*. London: Faber and Faber.

Rilke, Rainer Maria. (1969). *The Letters of Rainer Maria Rilke 1892–1910*, trans. Jane Bannard Greene and M. D. Herter Norton. New York: W. W. Norton.

Rilke, Rainer Maria. (1978). *Where Silence Reignsn Selected Prose*, trans. G. Craig Houston. New York: New Directions.

Rilke, Rainer Maria. (1998). *New Poems*, trans. Stephen Cohn. Evanston, IL: Northwestern University Press.

Rilke, Rainer Maria. (2009). *Duino Elegies and the Sonnets to Orpheus*, trans. Stephen Mitchell. New York: Vintage.

Robbe-Grillet, Alain. (1965). "A Future for the Novel." In *For a New Novel*, trans. Richard Howard. New York: Grove Press.

Simmel, Georg. (1990). *The Philosophy of Money*, trans. Tom Bottomore and David Frisby. London: Routledge.

Stein, Gertrude. (1962). *Tender Buttons. Selected Writings of Gertrude Stein*, ed. Carl Van Vechten (pp. 459–510). New York: Vintage Books.

Tylor, E. B. (1871). *Primitive Culture: Researches into the Development of Mythology, Philosophy, Religion, Art, and Custom*, 2 vols. London: John Murray.

Wicke, Jennifer. (1988). *Advertising Fictions: Literature, Advertisement, & Social Reading*. New York: Columbia University Press.

Williams, Raymond. (1980). *Problems in Materialism and Culture*. London: NLB.

Williams, William Carlos. (1966). *The Collected Earlier Poems*. New York: New Directions.

Williams, William Carlos. (1970 [1926]). *Spring and All*. In *Imaginations*, ed. Webster Schott (pp. 85–154). New York: New Directions.

Williams, William Carlos. (1970 [1932]). *A Novelette*. In *Imaginations*, ed. Webster Schott (pp. 272–206). New York: New Directions.

Williams, William Carlos. (1970). "The Work of Gertrude Stein." In *Imaginations*, ed. Webster Schott (pp. 346–352). New York: New Directions.

Woolf, Virginia. *Between the Acts*. (1969). New York: Harcourt Brace.

17

Glamour's Silhouette
Fashion, Fashun, and Modernism

Judith Brown

> *For fashion was never anything other than the parody of the motley cadaver,*
> *provocation of death through the woman and bitter colloquy with decay whispered*
> *between shrill bursts of mechanical laughter. That is fashion. And that is why*
> *she changes so quickly; she titillates death and is already something different,*
> *something new, as he casts about to crush her.*
>
> (Walter Benjamin, *The Arcades Project*, 63)

Browsing once at Paul Smith's – the upscale men's fashion boutique – I held up two ties and asked the clerk for an opinion. The "fashion forward," he helpfully suggested, might choose the skinny tie, thus pointing me away from the wider one considered classic in the slender memory of the fashion industry. *Fashion forward*: in this winning, even modish phrase, is inscribed both a paradox (the forward must go backward to an earlier tie-time) and an inaccuracy. For fashion has no forward, but only a present, a present that asserts itself with what Roland Barthes (1983) calls the "absolute, dogmatic, [and] vengeful present tense in which Fashion speaks" (273). Fashion, of course, casts its gaze backward, but only with a glance that is murderous in intent and whose inclination is "the same as that of vendettas": "Fashion's *today* is pure, it destroys everything around it, disavows the past with violence, [and] censures the future" (273, 289).

Why, one might wonder, does fashion speak in this language of pure aggression? After all, fashion with its bodices and hemlines, its lapels and cuffs, delivers us into a realm of pleasure and decadent excess, where surface is layered upon surface, and limp material is transformed into the striking forms of *haute couture*. Memory itself, it would seem, threatens the fullness of this realm which must, at all costs, defend itself from the competing forces of other times and other tenses. Barthes isn't the only theorist who has noted fashion's mean spirit: many others, including Georg

A Handbook of Modernism Studies, First Edition. Edited by Jean-Michel Rabaté.
© 2013 John Wiley & Sons, Ltd. Published 2013 by John Wiley & Sons, Ltd.

Simmel and Walter Benjamin, have observed that it is bound up with negation, destruction, and even death. Benjamin's "bitter colloquy" tells us that there is a struggle at the heart of fashion, a terrible dialectic, in which death will whisper its dark message via the mechanized bodies of modernity itself. The surprising insight that quickens the journey from cat-walk to coffin has to do with modern temporality, fashion's beginnings and endings, cycling constantly and efficiently from season to season, always maintaining a hold on the contemporary. In Simmel's work, fashion revolves around the antagonistic forces of creation and destruction that silently structure the sartorial world: "As fashion spreads," he writes, "it gradually goes to its doom. The distinctiveness which in the early stages of a set fashion assures for it a certain distribution is destroyed as the fashion spreads, and as this element wanes, the fashion also is bound to die" (1971, 302). The battleground is time itself, a no man's land of sorts, where the borders of past and future are contested: "Fashion always occupies the dividing-line between the past and the future, and consequently conveys a stronger feeling of the present . . . What we call the present is usually nothing more than a combination of a fragment of the past with a fragment of the future" (303). Situated where past meets future on the slimmest of frontlines, fashion figures the tumultuous and evanescent present itself.

There's a trace of modernism in both the invocation of doom and the sense that the clutching hand of the past threatens the vitality of the present. The modernist quest for the new demanded, too, a release from the chokehold of tradition and the conventionality that both pampered and stupefied. Modernists insisted that the past be rejected in favor of an expression, even if "spasmodic," more relevant to the present moment (and, while Virginia Woolf asks for our forbearance as readers – "tolerate the spasmodic," she pleads in "Modern Fiction" – the fashion industry might make even greater demands on our tolerance of the awkward). Modernism, too, embraced the ephemeral, the transitory, and the inevitability of loss, building an aesthetics on the fragility of experience itself, the aching recognition that time passes. Fortunately, consolations could be gleaned from the wreck of modern life and, for the modernists, the consolation was artistic expression, the often beautiful, lyric, and wrenching acknowledgment that every moment is already a lost moment (what Heidegger calls a "falling into lostness"[1]). Modern writing might, at the very least, maximize the sensuality of the fleeting present, slow down the stream of time, and submerge its reader in a fully realized, even enchanted, moment.

It is at this nexus of fleeting pleasure and the knowledge of pain, of impossible beauty and the enchantment of surfaces that we might locate glamour. Indeed, fashion has always walked hand in hand with glamour: fashion names the material form, and glamour its aesthetic effect, each captured in a fragment of time. We might situate modern temporality here in the conflicted recognition of the layers of time and the fierce desire for only the now, the new, the novel. "Fashion is the supreme expression of that contemporary spirit," writes Ulrich Lehmann (2000), "It changes constantly and remains necessarily incomplete; it is transitory, mobile, and fragmentary. This quality ties it in with the pace and rhythm of modern life" (xi).

Modernist writers have long been associated with harnessing this rhythm, creating a new language in tune with modern experience, and in so doing making a decisive break from the past. Yet while modernism might mark the rejection of diachronic models of time in favor of the synchronic, the immediate, and the experiential quality of lived time, it also marks the inescapability of the old model, hurrying us toward an unspoken fate (HURRY UP PLEASE IT'S TIME). The clock towers chime through Clarissa Dalloway's preparations, through Quentin Compson's last moments of life, and through Leopold Bloom's peripatetic day.[2] These demanding hours, however, provide the context for the suspended moment pulled out of the rush and not burdened by its responsibility. Glamour emerges in that stilled moment plucked from the stream, where the material world might recede, if only for an instant.

Glamour, I want to argue here, emerges from the combination of attributes that make up modern fashion, from its beauty to its evanescence to its suggestion of a life lived without the tedium of the mundane, or the necessity of work ("Our dress," Thorstein Veblen writes, should "make plain to all observers that the wearer is not engaged in any kind of productive labour" 4). It is glamour that delivers us into a glistening, ethereal, and even magical world, far above the demands of everyday lives; and it is glamour that frames our desire for something better, more luminous and exquisite, resting always just out of reach, in sight but unattainable. Glamour, whether invoked by the cat-walk, the glossy pages of a fashion magazine, or the formal capacities of art, maintains a promise that, although perpetually disappointed, sustains an illusion. Glamour and fashion thus speak the same language, or at least share a vocabulary, although glamour pulls away from materiality itself, and the constraints of the body (one of fashion's necessary limitations). The temporality of fashion demands the now, the immediate, the present at the expense of the past and future (even if this temporality is fictive). Glamour drifts away from grammatical tense altogether, inhabiting and expanding the present moment, yes, but also relying on the conditional tenses of past and future, the what if, the what could have been and the what might be.

Glamour, like fashion, has a history that long pre-dates the modern era. Yet, unlike fashion, glamour doesn't have a documented archive, or a clearly demarcated history across periods, social groups, or genre (daywear, eveningwear, etc.). While we might locate the effects of glamour across a broad sweep of history (as critics such as Gundle and Dyhouse have done), it finds, arguably, its most idealized form in the early twentieth century, emerging in the convergence of high and low cultures, in the ubiquity of mass-produced images or industrial design, and in the fascination with celebrity culture. Glamour, as I have argued at greater length in *Glamour in Six Dimensions: Modernism and the Radiance of Form*, feeds on a desire that is modern in its lineaments: it has its own recognizable aesthetic that finds its ideal conditions in the clean (synthetic, cold, abstract) lines of high modernism and provides a way of reading the modern cultural landscape, enriching and enchanting the products of mass culture.

Fashion, glamour, and modernism: the three terms thus sit companionably together, speaking a shared vocabulary, shining a dark light on the elite and popular culture of the early twentieth century. Fashion, one might say, establishes a material form, a kind of sartorial silhouette for the less tangible and more resonant effects of glamour. Silhouettes are, after all, simplified outlines with dark interiors (or, you could say, they are all surface without interiors at all), streamlined versions of something else: the silhouette is a blank form, even if seductively shaped. The silhouette, especially in the world of fashion, stands for the copy, as well as the possibility of form delivered in the contrasting values of light and dark. The silhouette heightens the element of form itself – Henri Focillon (1992) writes that "what fashion calls line or style is perhaps but a subtle compromise between a certain physiological canon... and a pure fantasy of shapes"; it is the inventor of "an artificial humanity" (86, 85).

One need think only of the new lines of women's fashion of the 1920s – what Clive Bell (1949) called tubular ("The feminine dress of about the year 1928 was a sack-like envelope which left arms and neck free, terminated in a kilt, and reduced the feminine silhouette to a flat tube," he writes in *On Human Finery*), for example, that articulated a radical expansion of possibility in its movement toward reduction and artifice (102). Women's roles were changing, industry was finding its way into domestic spaces through the new language of industrial design, and the simplified lines of a streamlined and modernizing generation were altering the contours of daily life. "Between 1900 and 1912," Anne Hollander (1994) writes, "women's clothes... were gradually reduced in scale so that the dressed bodies of men and women appeared equal in physical scope. Women's clothes also began to aim at creating a visual unity of bodily form" (127). Rather than breaking the female figure into voluminous tops and bottoms, joined at the narrow point of a cinched waist, the new fashion unified the body, creating a harmonious line moving from head to toe: "A woman could seem like a sleek new streamlined machine, that universal object of longing" (144).

This new silhouette Hollander describes as "reduced, abstract, and similar"; her terms evoke an aesthetics that we associate with modernism more generally: the simplified or reduced line (think Imagism or the slim modernist novel), the fascination with abstraction (the provenance of modernist poetry, as well as Gertrude Stein), and the recognition that the modern era was an era without originality (one of Eliot's great themes) (145). In the terms she chooses, Hollander brings together the two principles of fashion: its status as an art-form (its transformative power through a reduced and abstract aesthetics) and its status as a commodity (the similarity or reproducibility of the copy). The manufacture of copies in the new ready-to-wear garment industry positioned the articles of fashion as commodities, conveniently available without the necessity of expensive dressmakers and tailors. Mass production enabled mass consumption, facilitating the sweeping trends of the fashion world and their necessary obsolescence in order to maintain the pace of the industry. Fashion may have been aligned with the artistic production of the modernists and their complex relationship to time past and time present, but it was also governed by the guiding principle of capitalism: profit. Profit and aesthetics combine in a way that speaks to the fantasy lives of the consumer, as Elizabeth Wilson

(2009) suggests in her essay, "Magic Fashion": besides thinking about clothing as sexual fetish, she writes, "the fetish, including fetish garments, may also stand in for other, more nebulous desires: for power, for social affirmation, for spiritual certainty, as well as, of course, as Marx brilliantly demonstrated, representing the machinery of capitalism" (288). In this way, subjects and objects merge as women take on the shape of machines, and machines become the object of desire. "In the process of displacing nature's transiency onto commodities," writes Susan Buck-Morss (1991) in her analysis of Benjamin, "the life force of sexuality is displaced there as well. For what is it that is desired? No longer the human being: Sex appeal emanates from the clothes that one wears. Humanity is what you hang your hat on" (100). In fashion, as she famously paraphrases Benjamin, "the phantasmagoria of commodities presses closest to the skin" (97).

There is no escape from the machinery of capitalist production, as twentieth-century history demonstrates, but we might find ways to read its effects that evade the over-determination of that narrative, and our position as helpless consumers of its totalizing effects. Glamour offers us one such alternative narrative. Certainly, glamour is bound up in the structures of capital, as Stephen Gundle (2009) notes: "If properly employed, this undertheorized term can account for the particular seductive appeal that capitalism was able to take on in the early stages of mass consumption, helping it to bypass arguments about exploitation, imperialism, inequality, and alienation" (261). Glamour can mystify, providing a streamlined vehicle for nefarious ideologies and totalitarian systems (one need only think of Conrad's Kurtz, or Leni Riefenstahl's fascist aesthetics, to see glamour in its worst guise). Yet, when read solely through its service to capitalism and its system of commodity production or its affinities with the rise of fascism, we lose glamour's aesthetic power, as well as its range of pleasures from the disruptive, to the unproductive, to the immoral or revolutionary, none of which will be neutralized in the face of politics or profit-driven industry. We give up something vital when we castigate glamour and the illusions to which we happily fall prey. "Any attempt to explore the magical properties of dress," writes Wilson, "may seem a puny and even trivial commentary on the unnerving world of consumption with its illusory and disorienting powers of enchantment" (2009, 290). Yet that disquieting world might also offer relief, a turn to other pleasures that allow us to re-create ourselves, to imagine other desires unconstrained by historical circumstance, both in and out of time. To venture into the aesthetic realm is to cut ourselves free, at least momentarily, from real conditions, making space for new kinds of subjectivity, new languages that might lead to new modes of being.

Modernist writers might be situated here, in the recognition of those narratives that control modern subjects, and in the possibility of remaking them on the page, of reimagining human possibility itself through aesthetics. Modern writers, I argue, were thinking through the delicate weave of glamour and modernism, or the intricacies of modern aesthetics and the seductions and coercions of capitalism, meditating on the complex desires arising from their combination. Conrad, Woolf, and Lawrence, for example, overtly placed Western systems of thought (governing empire, gender, and industry respectively) in direct competition with modern modes of writing, and this might be said to characterize a whole generation of modernist writers.

Where does fashion fit in? Plenty of fashionable characters parade through modern novels: the list might include Brett Ashley (in her yacht-like lines), Jay Gatsby (in his gorgeous shirts), Jake Brown (in his English suit), Gudrun Brangwen (in her look-at-me outfits), and Robin Vote (in her dashing trousers). Nella Larsen seemed particularly attuned to the woman of fashion, both in the character of Helga Crane, who impulsively spends the last of her savings on a beautiful purse, and in Irene Redfield's careful self-fashioning as an upstanding citizen and woman of good taste.[3] All of these emphatically modern characters are clothed with care by their writers, but to what end? The easiest and most plausible explanation is one to do with the contemporary moment: characters clothed in the latest fashion represent the height of modernity, and allow the novel to speak in a vernacular as immediate as the modern moment. Fashion provides important information including a character's cultural location, self-presentation, and desires.

Modern novels also stage the ways that fashion gives rise to glamour. The details of a character's dress can open up to larger formal and thematic questions that motivate a text from modern surfaces to the role of self-fashioning, to the necessary and pleasurable risks that attend any step away from conventional categories. In what follows, I consider two literary examples to reflect on how fashion is used in narrative to express the impulse to creation and destruction, the dynamics of individual and group identity, and the high stakes of visibility. Finally, I want to think through the idea of touch and clothing: Hollander (1994) argues that modern dress accentuates a quality of touchability as opposed to the armor presented by earlier dress forms (one need only summon a vision of the Victorian silhouette to appreciate the degree to which Victorian costume made the body impregnable): "By 1920," Hollander claims, "women's clothes not only showed women's structure, they also began to suggest how the female body actually felt to its owner and how it might feel to the touch of others" (134). Touch, at least in this formulation, enters the realm of fashion through fantasy, through an act of imagination. Barthes (1983) pushes this idea further, making explicit the link to language: "We can expect clothing to constitute an excellent poetic object," he writes:

> first, because it mobilizes with great variety all the qualities of matter: substance, form, color, tactility, movement, rigidity, luminosity; next, because touching the body and functioning simultaneously as its substitute and its mask, it is certainly the object of a very important investment; this "poetic" disposition is attested to by the frequency and the quality of vestimentary descriptions in literature. (236)

While Barthes aims his analysis at the descriptive copy of fashion magazines, not finding adequate material in fictional prose, I turn my attention to two instances of fashion as represented in modern novels. Each imagines its way around the poetic possibilities of fashion and contributes to our understanding of modern surfaces, human individuality, and the glamorous fantasies to which these give rise.

Nella Larsen's novel *Passing* (1929) places us squarely within the world of the fashionable black middle class: Irene Redfield, the novel's protagonist – stolidly conventional, community minded, and socially engaged – values appearances and material signs of success above all else; she is a model of repression, resolutely averting her gaze from anything that might disturb her highly valued sense of equanimity. She's married well (to a handsome doctor), has two children, and works energetically to maintain her sense of middle-class safety. Safety, the reader will discover, becomes the tipping point for Irene, a frantic obsession in her otherwise carefully ordered world. Disturbance will come in the figure of her childhood friend, Clare Kendry, who appears as both women are passing at a tony all-white café. The encounter is riven with ambivalence for Irene who is overtly censorious about the act of passing (although here ceding to its convenience), while Clare shares no such compunction: the morality that confines Irene has no hold on Clare who has stepped clear of her past and unapologetically lives her life as a white woman.

Clare is striking for a number of reasons in this introduction, not least of which is her seeming capacity to transcend her immediate environment. While Irene perspires, feeling "damp and sticky and soiled from contact with so many sweating bodies" (1997, 12), Clare seems to float untouched by the oppressive heat: "A waiter passed her, followed by a sweetly scented woman in a fluttering dress of green chiffon whose mingled pattern of narcissuses, jonquils, and hyacinths was a reminder of pleasantly chill spring days" (14). Irene sizes up the woman who fragrantly embodies the dress she wears, "just right for the weather, thin and cool without being mussy"; the very "rightness" of her clothing will become a mark of suspicion in the narrative, a sign of her adaptive nature, her questionable ability to fit seamlessly into any environment, to become the clothes she wears (14). Everything about Clare points "in the same glamorous direction" and a whiff of scandal always accompanies her name (19).

As Irene scans her memory, delivering up fragments – a young Clare piecing together a red dress (having stolen the money to buy it); Clare weeping theatrically; Clare cat-like and selfish – she assembles her case against the beautiful woman, a judgment to which she'll cling, albeit ambivalently. For Clare is all charm, as "fair and golden" as a "sunlit day" (72), gravity-defying and irresistible: she has an "intangible quality, too vague to define, too remote to seize" (17). We learn that Clare has transcended the material grind and racial designation of her early life when she marries the wealthy, white John Bellew, who knows nothing of her racial background. Clare's marriage offers access to a world of privilege that she breezily accepts and wears as easily as her furs, her priceless velvet, or her Parisian fashions. In fact, she wears her privilege gorgeously and makes Irene feel, by contrast, her frumpy inadequacy: "Clare, exquisite, golden, fragrant, flaunting, in a stately gown of shining black taffeta, whose long, full skirt lay in graceful folds about her slim golden feet; her glistening hair drawn smoothly back into a small twist at the nape of her neck; her eyes sparkling like dark jewels. Irene, with her new rose-coloured chiffon frock ending at the knees, and her cropped curls, felt dowdy and commonplace" (74).

Clare's most significant fashion accessory is, of course, her "ivory mask": her face itself in its golden pallor withholds information – whether racial or emotional – while it presents the stylized exoticism so much in vogue in the period. She is, in ways, a picture of Africa inverted as she draws upon its distant allure, its connotations of sexuality and danger, while free-floating from place and material form itself. She suggests darkness through her luminous face, drawing admirers with mesmeric power and what Anne Cheng (2011) calls "the dream of a second skin – of remaking one's self in the skin of the other – . . . a mutual fantasy, one shared by both Modernists seeking to be outside of their own skins and by racialized subjects looking to escape the burdens of epidermal inscription" (13). We might wonder where to place Clare on this spectrum of racial possibility: she travels its length, unbothered by its gradations, not so much taking what she wants (the "having way" condemned by Irene) so much as absenting herself from want, re-creating herself in the shape of other's desire. She is, after all, a disappearing figure, a negative space, a blank promise: "Beyond the aesthetic pleasure one got from watching her, she contributed little, sitting for the most part silent, an odd dreaming look in her hypnotic eyes. . . . And, no matter how often she came among them, she still remained someone apart, a little mysterious and strange" (1997, 80).

Why is her shimmering blankness the very source of her danger, one might wonder? Irene tries to pin all kinds of moral lapses on her, but at the center is not fear of loss, or anxiety about her own desire, but Clare's capacity to engulf Irene in a world of endless, seamless surface. She is a moving silhouette, allowing her admirers to fill in the details, shaping herself to the desires of all who gaze upon her. For Irene, her Negro eyes are the only hope for safety, situating Clare in a known past, finding in her a still point of identification. For Irene, the past is a place of comfort where her family coheres, where she controls the narrative and where change no longer threatens. But Clare brings with her all the evanescence, the terrifying instability of the present. "Really, 'Rene, I'm not safe," she declares, as if she is the "provocation of death" that Benjamin aligns with fashion (81). Clare is, we understand, a deathly presence throughout – she is cold, hard, indifferent, and transcendent in her ivory death mask – yet she is realized so perfectly in silks and chiffons, in velvets and pearls: what better "parody of the motley cadaver" – Benjamin's lively phrase with which I began this essay – than this?

The act of passing itself, in its relationship to the immediate present and its startling risk, represents for Irene the turning away from the past, the cutting oneself free, and an opening up to the shifting unknown. Passing, of course, is also a euphemism for dying. To pass is to die, to pass over some threshold into a new formation, to transform, or change from one state to another. Passing, you might say, suggests movement into a weightless condition, a defiant coolness in the heavy heat of summer, a merging with the object world. This is a novel about racial passing, but it is as much a novel about dying, or at least the condition of deathliness. The fashions that have allowed Clare to fit perfectly ("And Clare was wearing a thin floating dress of the same shade of blue, which suited her and the rather difficult room to perfection") have been in the service of passing, of transforming, of embracing one's objecthood and thus embracing one's death (33).

Like Pearl Fulton, Katherine Mansfield's luminously named and dangerously seductive character in "Bliss," Clare gleams in name and presence with cold light. This is a kind of attenuated whiteness that stretches thin, covering all aspects of privilege: one might think of this whiteness as a brilliant and expensive covering or surface that refracts light and drifts free from the material body itself. Clare in her whiteness is paired with cold foggy mornings and with precious metals (her laughter tinkles or rings like bells). The whiteness that clings to her is not sentient; it doesn't bestow life, but death in the form of impossible illusion. It might partake of the power and privilege that racist culture arbitrarily grants, but it enshrouds her in its chilling transcendence, a glamorized whiteness that cannot sustain life. Although Clare's desire to stand alone, to step free from limitation, is fully human, the form it takes in Larsen's novel can only rob her of life. Death follows Clare; she wears it, although even her death will be a hazy affair, rendered in Irene's ambiguous prose. We know that she had "arrived, radiant in a shining red gown" to a party in Harlem and was discovered there by her husband who had begun to suspect her claim to whiteness (105). In a flash of an eye, he rushes at her: "Clare stood at the window, as composed as if everyone were not staring at her in curiosity and wonder, as if the whole structure of her life were not lying in fragments before her. She seemed unaware of any danger or uncaring. There was even a faint smile on her full, red lips, and in her shining eyes" (110). Hardly sentient, Clare stands apart, even as she is the object of fascinated and enraged attention. Then: "One moment Clare had been there, a vital glowing thing, like a flame of red and gold. The next she was gone" (111). Clare defies limitation and passes, as if by magic, through the open window, exceeding its frame at last, surpassing its material limit. For Irene, whose desire for Clare's expulsion has been plain, the present itself has been expelled in all its transient possibility: the death of the present in the form of Clare will allow Irene to cling persistently to the safety of the past, a conservative will to morality that defies its own desire.

Clare's fashion, her act of passing, her evanescence and indifference combine to create the effect of glamour ("all pointing in the same glamorous direction," recall). Glamour is both an elusive and a generative form with the magical ability to shape and reshape the objects before us, making them more tantalizing by pressing them into an inhuman dimension. Glamour draws from a crossing of attributes, an impossible longing in the form of a fantasy, or one's ability to transcend historical and cultural time. There is risk here, the risk of falling, of loss, and even death, but there is pleasure in the promise of losing the self, and this is a pleasure that Irene can only ambivalently experience through Clare who is now the haunting word, the absent object, the blank surface whose instability unplots Irene's carefully plotted world.

Clare, despite her wardrobe and the material fantasies she generates, has been, from the opening lines of the novel, figured as an abstract threat:

After her other ordinary and clearly directed letters the long envelope of thin Italian paper with its almost illegible scrawl seemed out of place and alien. And there was, too, something mysterious and slightly furtive about it. A thin sly thing which bore no return address to betray the sender . . . Furtive, but yet in some peculiar, determined way a little flaunting. Purple ink. Foreign paper of extraordinary size. (9)

The letter – too slim, its color too bold, its adornment too obscure and alien – speaks in a foreign and threatening tongue that will, eventually, cause Irene's breakdown, a breakdown in reason that is already prefigured in the sentence fragments that end the letter's description. Perhaps it's most fitting that Clare is introduced in the form of an object bearing a beautiful if difficult inscription. Clare, even in her mystified death, is best expressed through metaphor: she is spark and dying ember, a cameo (in all of its senses: a beautiful ornament; a figure positioned against a background of a different color; a celebrity figure making an unexpected and thrilling appearance), a silhouette, a foreign letter in extravagant script. She is antithesis and hyperbole, or the mobility of language itself. Clare's mobility, her capacity to seduce, to engender fascination, to elude one's grasp, is her most unsettling quality. She frustrates desire even as she creates and prolongs it. Like metaphor, she is a vehicle with shifting signification, who destabilizes any environment she enters and produces a sort of vertigo that will be realized in her finale, the fall from a fourth-floor window.

What Irene finally must repress is the memory of touch, the "vision of her hand on Clare's arm"; touch itself is a necessary repression not only because of potential incrimination – did she push Clare to her death? – but because Clare, in Irene's glamorizing fantasy, must remain untouchable (112). Touch is therefore transmuted to vision, and here a vision in which Irene might find some distancing comfort. From humanizing touch to the more distant visual image: this last encounter with Clare is a necessary fabulation, an expression of the nulling effects of modernity through the cold, the indifferent, the abstract, and the deathly. Clare, in Irene's fantasy, lives outside the limits of her body, and thus cannot be touched: the image Irene summons and represses covers a deeper repression, then, that of tactility itself. Touch, the skin to skin encounter, must be undone so that the body might be lifted from hard reality and transmuted into something more luminous.

It is on this question of touch that I want to turn to a starkly different landscape than middle-class Harlem, or the dizzying heights of privilege enjoyed by Clare. If touch defines the limits of the body, and Clare is rendered untouchable by the glamorizing gaze of Irene, how might we read an Untouchable boy's fascination with fashion? Mulk Raj Anand's novel *Untouchable* (1935), set in an "outcastes' colony" of India, imagines the condition of sentience itself in the figure of Bakha, the street-sweeper whose body is abstractly understood as belonging to the race of Untouchables. Sentience, to the Untouchable, is a secret condition, a dirty reality that must be suppressed under the threat of violence. Bakha exists in an economy of absolute denial: he must remain vigilantly self-conscious, so that others may not become conscious of his presence. Like Clare, Bakha courts danger through visibility and the invisible threat of pollution (a fear of racial contagion that also defines the world of *Passing*). This, we learn, is a delicate negotiation as he balances the need for visibility (so that no one will touch him) with invisibility (so that no one will be reminded of him): he is a potentially catastrophic figure for those he might pollute. Unlike Clare, however, Bakha lives in desperate poverty, abused by both family and the community to which he belongs. Humiliation lurks around every corner, but none so terrible as when he forgets himself and his status for a moment, and is beaten as a consequence. Untouchability rests precariously on a structural paradox in this novel: the body deemed untouchable is that body that comes closest to the intimate muck of human life, the body most in touch with what it means to be human. Bakha is both an abstract principle and a fully sentient being (indeed, it is the description of the latter that forms the radical politics of Anand's novel). Touch will remain a prohibited category for the boy who is granted no appetite, no desire, and no contact with the class for whom he is indispensable; yet the novel will devote a great deal of descriptive energy to Bakha's inarticulate desires. Its single-day episodic structure takes us through the events of his day and delivers us again and again to scenes of prohibited pleasure, from the syrupy sweetness of jalebis on his tongue, to the hot sun on his upturned face in a moment of rest, to the joy of playing hockey, or the comfort of hot chai; even the satiation of hunger is a luxury to which Bakha is unaccustomed. These scenes of sensual pleasure are inevitably concluded by the cries of "polluted, polluted!" as he is forced to leave reverie and reenter the reality of untouchability. Anand offers a radically intimate view of Bakha's physical pleasure, making visible that which his social world has condemned to inhumanity.

Bakha's greatest pleasure, we learn, is the "regulation overcoat, breeches, puttees and ammunition boots of the military uniform that clothed him" (1940, 10). Bakha too wants to be lifted away from his lived reality and is under the spell of the uniform of the sahibs: Bakha "had been caught by the glamour of the 'white man's' life" and "could sacrifice a good many comforts for the sake of what he called 'fashun,' by which he understood the art of wearing trousers, breeches, coat, puttees, boots, etc., as worn by the British and Indian soldiers in India" (9, 10). Whiteness and its imitation open a realm of possibility to Bakha, since – and Anand is aware of the irony here – the fantasy of imperial fashion offers him the possibility of touch ("He had hungered for the touch of them"), of performing a singular human identity forbidden him in the outcaste colony (11). Glamour, in the guise of whiteness, once again offers its enchantments even if, as we've seen before, it is an enchantment that cannot sustain life. One might offer a reading of Bakha's misguided fascination, his ideological abduction by imperial discourses and the necessary dehumanization on which empire is predicated. Yet Bakha's longing for human recognition through sartorial forms is not dismissed or condemned by Anand who foregrounds instead the artifice of British dress and the artifice of the humanity it constructs: "Bakha was a child of modern India. The clear-cut styles of European dress had impressed his native mind. This stark simplicity had furrowed his old Indian consciousness and cut deep new lines where all the considerations which made India evolve a skirty costume as best fitted for the human body, lay dormant" (10). Bakha's sartorial desires – if only in fantasy – remove him from the violence of tradition and place him in proximity to the new (a relative term in relation to the dhoti worn by his fellow outcastes), although at the expense of practicality. Through the "clear-cut" lines of the uniform, he might reject tradition and write himself into the modernizing world. He hardly knows this: Anand carefully shapes Bakha's dim and slowly awakening consciousness, presenting him as a subject in transition who might, one day, disturb the accepted order of things.

Bakha's interiority, above all, stages the antagonism between individual and group identity (which Simmel claims is the basis of fashion (2009, 14–15)). The boy's fascination with fashion is the dream of individual identity for a person to whom it is forbidden: fashion brings with it the fantasy of touch, of singular human experience within the wider circles of social inscription that would annul its expression. Imitation is the necessary ground of individuation as Bakha negotiates the poles of the individual who wants to impress upon others his difference, and his impulse to belong to a group. He'll attempt to find group identity, however, in the sahibs he imitates (the "boys of the outcaste colony called him Pilpali sahib (imitation sahib)") and he'll base this imitation on the formal lines of dress: "But he kept up his new form, rigidly adhering to his clothes day and night and guarding them from all base taint of Indianness, not even risking the formlessness of an Indian quilt, though he shivered with the cold at night" (12).

The unattainable object of Bakha's fantasy is a solar topee; the English hat becomes an illuminated object of wonder: "A hat with its curious distinction of shape and form, with the peculiar quality of honour that it presents to the Indian eye because it adorns the noblest part of the body, had a fascination such as no other item of European dress possessed" (101). Again, form offers Bakha a way out of his grinding daily activity. The hat suggests protection from the harshness of environment and also the site of reason that enlivens his imagination. "Ever since he was a little child he had contemplated it with the wonder-struck gaze of the lover and devotee" (102). Fashion here is both spiritual and carnal and has the capacity to bestow on its wearer the recognition and worth of a lover; it lifts one out of the muck, and allows one spiritual transcendence. Bakha's commitment to British dress suggests, after all, a commitment to his own autonomy and a demand for its recognition. Bakha's desire, in Simmel's terms, demonstrates "the tendency towards social equalization with the desire for individual differentiation and change" (1971, 296). The emblem of the solar topee marks Bakha's growing awareness of injustice and a recognition that fashion itself plays a role in larger questions of selfhood and equality:

> He didn't like his home, his street, his town, because he had been to work at the Tommies' barracks, and obtained glimpses of another world, strange and beautiful; he had grown out of his native shoes into the ammunition boots that he had secured as a gift. And with this and other strange and exotic items of dress he had built up a new world, which was commendable, if for nothing else, because it represented a change from the old ossified order and the stagnating conventions of the life to which he was born. (1940, 78)

"Fashion is one of the faces of modern artifice," writes Gilles Lipovetsky (1994), "of the effort of human beings to make themselves masters of the conditions of their own existence" (24). A new form of individuality is emerging, enabled by the dream of the solar topee and by the pleasure of clothing: surprisingly this human autonomy is not only expressed by, but also created in the sartorial surface. The national autonomy that is the dream of this novel is founded on the dream of individual autonomy, founded on the surface, and here on the "groundless surface" that is fashion (Svendsen, 16), or as Bakha would have it, "fashun."

Anand asks us to consider the material condition of fashion through its very inscription on the page as what Bakha "called 'fashun,' by which he understood the art of wearing trousers," etc. (1940, 10). Fashion as fashun: why does Anand rewrite the writing of fashion itself? Fashun: his imitation of the word "fashion" itself embeds negativity, altering the structure of the word itself. The "un" marks dissolution and signals opposition, contrariness, negation, privation, and absence. Fashion is undone in Bakha's formulation: perhaps he cannot invoke fashion without changing it, inverting it, undoing its assumptions. This suggests something like colonial mimicry, certainly, but also something more. Can we take fashion and make it fit into a different social structure? Only with the addition of "un," Anand suggests, as he places structural instability in the word, and thus in language. We might here be reminded of Clare, a ghostly presence now, making or unmaking the comfort of what we think we know. Perhaps then fashun speaks most vividly of modernism and its dream of demolishing past edifices, from the grounds of empiricism, to empire, to the novel form that the modernists worked so strenuously to unmake.

The narrative of *Untouchable* is placed explicitly in the larger context of the modernizing world as it reaches its conclusion. Bakha has stumbled upon a large gathering of people, assembled to hear the words of Gandhi himself. He hears, from some of those gathered, of possibilities that were until that moment unimaginable. For Bakha hears of the dream of modern plumbing, the wonders of the toilet that offer to the Untouchable the dream of a reinvented life: "When the sweepers change their profession," argues a bystander, "they will no longer remain Untouchables. And they can do that soon, for the first thing we will do when we accept the machine, will be to introduce the machine which clears dung without anyone having to handle it – the flush system" (155). It is an unexpected turn as now glamour circulates around the clean, cold lines of modern plumbing. We understand by the end of the novel that his glamorizing fantasy will be placed elsewhere, onto the machine and the dream of modernity that might grant a distancing of the human body. Any object can hold promise, no matter how unexpected; the deadly whiteness of the sahib will be transmuted to the whiteness of the porcelain surface. Fashion, glamour, and modernism: once again the terms bind together if only for a fleeting instant. Fashions change, go to their doom, the uniform will not endure. Bakha will witness the burning of foreign clothes; "The prospect of never being able to wear the clothes that the sahibs wore . . . was horrible" (150, 157). Yet a new horizon of possibility emerges as a faint glimmer in Bakha's dim consciousness:

> The sun descended. The pale, the purple, the mauve of the horizon blended into darkest blue. A handful of starts throbbed in the heart of the sky.

> He emerged from the green of the garden into the slight haze of dust that rose from the roads and the paths.

> As the brief Indian twilight came and went, a sudden impulse shot through the transformations of space and time, and gathered all the elements that were dispersed in the stream of his soul into a tentative decision. (157)

Space and time here shift and transform as the gorgeous display of the natural world meets the transformative possibilities of the modern. Bakha – the site of change itself – moves dimly away from the glamorizing whiteness offered up to him in the sign of the British costume that had clothed his body, allowing him an experience of the humanizing possibility of dress, of the meaning it bestowed upon him through its touch. We imagine that this fantasy will be displaced by another, the promise of modernity, the machine, and the earthly toil these might mitigate. Glamour will be a necessary category for survival, even if it offers only a diffuse promise, a distant hope for change in the clean, cold lines of modern form.

Our glamorizing capacity is vast as it draws on our particular cultural longings (for beauty and wealth perhaps, as well as human recognition), and on our distinctively individual landscapes. We might not always be able to predict what objects will gather glamour about them – this is its power to alight on a surface and to lift it from the everyday, to enchant a moment, an image, or a mere object. Glamour perhaps explains the appeal of a foggy day, a curtain of smoke, the gelatin-smear of a camera lens, layers of voile, or even a modern toilet; it delivers the world in soft focus and without blemish, and conceived without the harshness of time traveling on a linear path. If it depends on murder, on the necessary repression of past and future, it's the price we're willing to pay, at least in our fantasies. Fashun thus emerges as the perfect marriage of fashion and glamour: it both carries with it a negative aesthetic, a capacity for self-cancelling, and the undoing of one moment into the next, and carries within it the power of desire, of the sentient body imagining another and more exquisite state, freed from the filth of embodied experience. Social change, improbably spoken by the fabrics we wear next to our skin, is achieved – at least in the discourse of fashion – by holding resolutely to desire, by living in the present, even as that present tears us away from the past and refuses us a future. Fashion, as Benjamin intimates, tells us something about the deadly forces that shape us as we browse at Paul Smith's, at a Paris boutique, or in the village bazaar. Our glamorizing fantasy may make us believe, if only for a moment, that we've defeated death, even as we wear it, swathed in the fabrics of our dreams.

Notes

1   See David Couzens Hoy, *The Time of Our Lives: A Critical History of Temporality* (Cambridge: MIT Press, 2009), 58 and Leo Charney, "In a Moment: Film and the Philosophy of Modernity" in *Cinema and the Invention of Modern Life*, Leo Charney and Vanessa Schwartz, eds. (Berkeley: University of California Press, 1995), 281.

2   These examples are drawn from T. S. Eliot's *The Waste Land* (1922), Virginia Woolf's *Mrs. Dalloway* (1925), William Faulkner's *The Sound and the Fury* (1929), and James Joyce's *Ulysses* (1922).

3   These characters appear in the following novels: Ernest Hemingway's *The Sun Also Rises* (1925), F. Scott Fitzgerald's *The Great Gatsby* (1925), Claude McKay's *Home to Harlem* (1925), D. H. Lawrence's *Women in Love* (1920), Djuna Barnes' *Nightwood* (1938), and Nella Larsen's *Quicksand* (1928) and *Passing* (1929).

References

Anand, Mulk Raj. (1940). *Untouchable.* London: Penguin.

Barthes, Roland. (1983). *The Fashion System*, trans. Matthew Ward and Richard Howard. Berkeley: University of California Press.

Bell, Clive. (1949). *On Human Finery.* New York: A. A. Wyn.

Benjamin, Walter. (1990). *The Arcades Project*, trans. Howard Eiland and Kevin McLaughlin. Cambridge, MA: The Belknap Press of Harvard University Press.

Brown, Judith. (2009). *Glamour in Six Dimensions: Modernism and the Radiance of Form.* Ithaca, NY: Cornell University Press.

Buck-Morss, Susan. (1991). *The Dialectics of Seeing: Walter Benjamin and The Arcades Project.* Cambridge, MA: MIT Press.

Cheng, Anne Anlin. (2011). *Second Skin: Josephine Baker and the Modern Surface.* New York: Oxford University Press.

Dyhouse, Carol. (2010). *Glamour: Women, History, Feminism.* London: Zed Books.

Focillon, Henri. (1992 [1934]). *The Life of Forms in Art.* New York: Zone Books.

Hollander, Anne. (1994). *Sex and Suits: The Evolution of Modern Dress.* New York: Kodansha International.

Gundle, Stephen. (2008). *Glamour: A History.* New York: Oxford University Press.

Gundle, Stephen. (2009). "Hollywood Glamour and Mass Consumption in Postwar Italy." In *Fashion: Critical and Primary Sources. Volume 4: The Twentieth Century to Today*, ed. Peter McNeil (pp. 261–282). New York: Berg.

Larsen, Nella. (1997 [1929]). *Passing.* New York: Penguin.

Lehmann, Ulrich. (2000). *Tigersprung: Fashion in Modernity.* Cambridge, MA: MIT Press.

Lipovetsky, Gilles. (1994). *The Empire of Fashion: Dressing Modern Democracy*, trans. Catherine Porter. Princeton, NJ: Princeton University Press.

Mansfield, Katherine. (1920). *Bliss, and Other Stories.* New York: Knopf.

Simmel, Georg. (1971). "Fashion." In *Georg Simmel: On Individuality and Social Forms*, ed. Donald N. Levine (pp. 294–323). Chicago: University of Chicago Press.

Simmel, Georg. (2009). "The Philosophy of Fashion." In *Fashion: Critical and Primary Sources. Volume 4: The Twentieth Century to Today*, ed. Peter McNeil (pp. 14–37). New York: Berg.

Svendsen, Lars. (2006). *Fashion: A Philosophy*, trans. John Irons. London: Reaktion Books.

Veblen, Thorstein. (2009). "Dress as an Expression of the Pecuniary Culture." In *Fashion: Critical and Primary Sources. Volume 4: The Twentieth Century to Today*, ed. Peter McNeil (pp. 3–13). New York: Berg.

Wilson, Elizabeth. (2009). "Magic Fashion." In *Fashion: Critical and Primary Sources. Volume 4: The Twentieth Century to Today*, ed. Peter McNeil (pp. 283–292). New York: Berg.

Woolf, Virginia. (1986). "Modern Fiction." In *Essays of Virginia Woolf*, vol. 4, 1925–1928, ed. Andrew McNeillie (p. 160). London: Hogarth Press.

Further Reading

Barthes, Roland. (1983). *The Fashion System*, trans. Matthew Ward and Richard Howard. Berkeley: University of California Press.

Benjamin, Walter. (1990). *The Arcades Project*, trans. Howard Eiland and Kevin McLaughlin. Cambridge, MA: The Belknap Press of Harvard University Press.

Blau, Herbert. (1999). *Nothing in Itself: Complexions of Fashion*. Bloomington: Indiana University Press.

Brown, Judith. (2009). *Glamour in Six Dimensions: Modernism and the Radiance of Form*. Ithaca, NY: Cornell University Press.

Cheng, Anne Anlin. (2011). *Second Skin: Josephine Baker and the Modern Surface*. New York: Oxford University Press.

Lehmann, Ulrich. (2000). *Tigersprung: Fashion in Modernity*. Cambridge, MA: MIT Press.

Lipovetsky, Gilles. (1994). *The Empire of Fashion: Dressing Modern Democracy*, trans. Catherine Porter. Princeton: Princeton University Press.

Miller, Monica. (2009). *Slaves to Fashion: Black Dandyism and the Styling of Black Diasporic Identity*. Durham, NC: Duke University Press.

Simmel, Georg. (1971). "Fashion." In *Georg Simmel: On Individuality and Social Forms*, ed. Donald N. Levine (pp. 294–323). Chicago: University of Chicago Press.

Svendsen, Lars. (2006). *Fashion: A Philosophy*, trans. John Irons. London: Reaktion Books.

Wilson, Elizabeth. (2003). *Adorned in Dreams: Fashion and Modernity*. Newark, NJ: Rutgers University Press.

18

Otherness and Singularity
Ethical Modernism

Marian Eide

In 1999 Lawrence Buell introduced an excellent collection of essays for *PMLA* with this claim: "Ethics has gained new resonance in literary studies during the past dozen years" (7). In modernist studies, however, the turn to ethics over the next dozen years was slow if not imperceptible.[1] My argument in this essay, however, is that modernist literary experimentation, with its emphasis on revolution, cleared the way for a critical burgeoning of ethical theory in the mid- to late twentieth century. Modernists made readers aware of the inequities created by conformity to prevailing moral norms, and their ambitious social and political experiments opened the way for a reconsideration of classic ethics. My claim is not that modernist literature directly influenced ethical theory; rather I am noting that issues addressed during the modernist period cleared paths for innovations in ethics. Late-century ethical theory presents literary critics with an opportunity to register the latent ethical systems our scholarly attention can bring into presence in modernist texts. I am not suggesting that we treat literature as a site for applied ethics; rather I am arguing that literature gives us an opportunity to texture the challenges we pose to ethical theory. To read literature as an opportunity to *apply* ethical theory runs the risk of simplifying both the philosophical and literary interventions in order to facilitate the fit between the two. However, placing these genres in conversation poses new challenges and opens potentials in each.

In the twentieth century, four major ethical models emerged from the classical modes of moral philosophy. Vital debate in the field of ethics from the mid-twentieth century was fueled in large part by the innovative and influential writings of Emmanuel Levinas and invigorated by the writings of Jacques Lacan, Michel Foucault, and Alain Badiou. Of these, Levinas's work has had the most marked impact on literary studies. After surveying his thought and its potential for understanding

A Handbook of Modernism Studies, First Edition. Edited by Jean-Michel Rabaté.
© 2013 John Wiley & Sons, Ltd. Published 2013 by John Wiley & Sons, Ltd.

modernism, I will make a case for considering the other three ethical systems in the context of modernist studies. I will then identify some of the ways in which modernist literary scholars might engage with ethical theories of the late twentieth century.

The Other

Emmanuel Levinas's radical claims in his 1961 essay "Ethics As First Philosophy" made ethics the ground on which all other philosophical constructs were to be built. Levinas argued that ethics is not bound by principles of moral good or codes of conduct; rather we exist in the ethical challenge. For Levinas responsibility is the foundational human condition; responsibility carries within it the necessity of being responsive or responding to the call or claims of an other. Living in the face of God as Other (for Levinas was also or even primarily a philosopher of Judaism), one also registers the face of the human stranger as the other to whom one is called to respond. The other is a stranger in the sense that, while she or he could be my wife or my brother, this other's difference from me demands recognition; I must meet the other in his or her habitat, in the rich context in which the other's human singularity is visible. Levinas's ethical demand of responsibility is both utopian and limitless: I am always responsible, I am more responsible than any other, and in fact, I am responsible for the other's responsibility.

In the context of these claims, as Judith Butler (2004) notes, readers have worried: "It is possible, even easy to read Levinas as an elevated masochist" (140). Does the ethical subject make himself or herself a victim to the whims and demands of the other, even to an enemy? Do ethics require responsibility toward the most egregious of acts from the other? In making myself responsible to the other, do I have to abase myself to my utopian goal to the extent that I would allow the other to harm and even to destroy me? How, for example, are we to respond to the political leader responsible for untold suffering (and each of us can provide an embarrassingly rich catalogue of such figures from the modernist period alone)? Is the human monster also my other? Levinas's system is categorical: yes, we are responsible even to the tyrant. Responsibility is not a decision one makes, nor is it a contract into which one enters; rather it is our condition of being: I am and therefore I am responsible. However, Levinas (1998) wishes to emphasize that responsibility is not necessarily enslaving:

> In the light of a face we have sought to bring out the relationship that is nontyrannical, and yet transitive. We have sought to set forth exteriority, the other, as that which is nowise tyrannical and makes freedom possible, opposes us because it turns itself toward us. This exteriority is beyond the violence of brutality, but also that of incantation, ecstasy and love. (23)

Even in the transitive, in the place of dependence between subject and object, Levinas locates the possibilities of freedom, ecstasy, and love.

How are we to understand this tension between the possibility of ethics as elevated masochism and the other as the condition of freedom? I would like to argue that the sadomasochistic sexual game – as it was narrated in modernist fictions – clarifies the ethical exchange of responsibility. Reading James Joyce's *Ulysses* (1922, 1986), for example, one finds that masochism on a psychological or social level is a game that runs parallel to sexual games in which the masochist is understood to hold the power over the pacing and potency of the exchange. From the beginning of his day when he serves his wife breakfast in bed and enjoys her gently barbed conversation ("O rocks tell us in plain words"), through his day-long pained avoidance of her lover and recurring, painful thoughts of her adultery, into his late-night encounters with sex workers in Nighttown who scourge him and place him on trial, to his late-night hosting of Stephen Dedalus, who insults him with anti-Semitic song, Leopold Bloom enters into a series of masochist games consciously, willingly, and often with pleasure (1986, 50). While readers may wonder (to quote his correspondent, Martha), "Are you not happy in your home you poor naughty boy," Bloom remembers his correspondent's epistolary threat ("Remember if you do not I will punish you.") with pleasure enhanced by his consciousness of the mundanity of their shared sentimental game (1986, 61, 62). Because it reverses the conventional domestic gender divisions in which women are asked to be masochists to men's sadism, Bloom's masochistic bargain with his wife and his community is seen in high relief and raises potent ethical questions about responsibility and the necessity of care.[2]

Joyce's fiction frames Levinas's ethics as a system of compassion and generosity, and also of a goodness that displaces the self, that decenters the primacy of self as transitive in a way that, while it is morally good, is also deeply pleasurable. Focusing on Bloom's masochism, I do not wish to diminish the hazards of his place in the ethical conundrum. For, throughout Bloom's day, he is repeatedly called upon by the face of the Other, and by myriad others; he is consistently responsive and responsible, evacuating his place in the sun in a utopian acknowledgement of the primacy of the other even when that other (like the Citizen) threatens, cajoles, hates, or assaults him. Trying to do a good turn for the grieving Dignam family left destitute by their patriarch's sudden death, he is treated to his community's bigoted suspicions even as he calls upon his fellows to take up responsibility for the others among them, for the Dignam family. The Citizen, an exaggerated allegorical substitute for the Irish nationalist, is particularly violent and hostile in the face of Bloom's charitable efforts. However, while Bloom is responsive to the Citizen, he does not merely make himself a hostage of the Citizen's aggression. Masochist, he may be, but he is also ethical in the Levinasian sense: he sees himself as responsible for the Citizen's responsibility. While he must participate when the Citizen calls on him, he cannot merely abase himself; he must also guide the Citizen to himself becoming responsible in the face of Bloom's otherness. Joyce's playful connections between the social and the sexual make evident the ecstatic (decentered) possibilities for a self made hostage to demands from the other. His version of responsibility challenges Levinas's ethics on the ground of reciprocity. Bloom's masochistic pleasure does not reduce his altruism to mere self-interest but opens the possibility for an asymmetrical ethical reciprocity.

Care of the Self

While for Levinas, ethics is the condition of being, for other writers in the twentieth century the ethical is a product of an invented or created self. Oscar Wilde posed this possibility in his revision of the *Bildungsroman*, which he wrote as a novel of self-production. At the turn into the twentieth century, he returned to models from antiquity to describe the love between men that "dare not speak its name" as Socratic love. In narrative argument, he suggested that life practices form, rather than merely reflect, individual morality and, further, that beauty signals the moral good. *The Picture of Dorian Gray* (1891) demonstrates this principle: as Dorian's unnamed sensual experiments horrify his community, those practices are written on his surrogate body (his portrait) while his own body benefits from a wish to change places with this picture and remain eternally beautiful and young. Dorian's portrait makes visible the hideous moral interior produced by degraded social and personal practices.

Responding to Wilde in *The Portrait of an Artist as A Young Man* (1916), Joyce also located the production of an ethical self in life practices. Stephen Dedalus attempts to reform the sexual experiments of his precocious sixteenth year by repeated confessions and self-prescribed practices of renunciation. Through Stephen's experience, Joyce explored the discipline exerted by institutions (most explicitly the church and the school) on their subjects. He also investigated the process through which subjects can enact rebellion, can resist (to use Buell's phrase) "institutional constraints on selfhood." Mortifying his body through an assault on the senses, Stephen both magnifies Roman Catholic penance and, on a literary level, performs a satiric inversion of Dorian's sexual experiments alongside a Christian disciplinary *reductio ad absurdum*. "Each of his senses was brought under a rigorous discipline," the narrator observes (1916, 150). Stephen mortifies his sight by walking with downcast eyes, avoiding the pleasure of looking at women, and averting his gaze abruptly while reading. His hearing is punished by the sound of his own changing voice, and by intentional exposure to obnoxious sounds like sharpening knives. He denies himself the pleasure of music, neither singing nor whistling. Finding that he likes the odors most people avoid, Stephen makes "many curious comparisons and experiments" before finding that he is "revolted" by "a certain stale fishy stink like that of longstanding urine," which he then seeks out to assault his sense of smell (151). His tastes are thwarted by fasting as well as a conscious mental diversion from the enjoyment of food. He mortifies his touch with exposure to cold, itching, and pain. He denies his body comfort in long periods of kneeling and rigidly maintained postures.[3]

Stephen's penitence exaggerates church rituals to the point of absurdity; Joyce presents these renunciatory experiments in a decadent literary mode indicating the extent to which Stephen's project is aesthetic rather than pious.[4] Focusing so completely on the mortification of his senses and the discomfort of his body, he is diverted from the devotion of the soul. In *Ulysses*, Buck Mulligan registers his roommate's ethical rebellion when he notes that Stephen has "the cursed Jesuit strain . . . only it's injected the wrong way".[5] Mulligan suggests that Stephen disrupts church doctrine by diverting its moral demands in sensual experiments.

Michel Foucault followed the path worn by Joyce's interests in institutional disciplines and rebellious life practices. In projects from *Discipline and Punish* to *Madness & Civilization*, his historical and sociological studies demonstrated the extent to which each person is subject to institutional discourses. He argued, for example, that in the nineteenth century, building on models provided by Jeremy Bentham, European countries shifted in their punishment methods; criminals who had been subject to physical retribution were instead housed in prisons where they lived under constant, unseen observation. As a result, prisoners began to interiorize the disciplinary consciences established by the state; as such, punishment shifted from temporary physical pain into permanent discursive discipline experienced as surveillance.

At the end of his career Foucault embarked on a major project tracing sexuality's genealogy. In the third volume of this *History of Sexuality* (1986) he referred, like Wilde, to the classical period in Ancient Greece. He noted the attention Greek thinkers paid to the mode or manner of life, to its rituals and practices. Ultimately, he argued that these practices were the disciplines through which individuals produced a self that could speak the truth, a concept referred to in Greek as "*parrhesia*" (62–63).[6] *Parrhesia* was invoked in the Socratic dialogues to describe individuals who confronted people in power with difficult truths. Socrates himself focused the concept on conversations between individuals in which the truth-teller has less power or is of lower rank.

In a series of seminars at Berkeley late in his career, Foucault developed a theory of self-care as the foundation for ethics as *parrhesia*. "How does a *Parrhesiastes* take care of herself?" he asks. "To take care of herself, she must change her practices of life so as to know herself" (Foucault 2001, 106–107). Lest readers assume these practices involve conventional procedures of good living, Foucault provided the example of Diogenes who spoke truth to Alexander the Great's power, but whose life practices followed no recognized etiquette. "Cynic *Parrhesia*," he notes, "in its scandalous aspects also utilized the practice of bringing together two rules of behavior which seem contradictory and remote from one another. For example, regarding the problem of bodily needs . . . . Since Diogenes ate in the agora, he thought that there was no reason why he should not also masturbate in the agora; for in both cases he was satisfying a bodily need" (2001, 122). Depending not on the production of general principles but on a recognition of disciplinary practices that form particular lives, Foucault argued that in the Greek classical age, "their theme was to constitute a kind of ethics which was an aesthetics of existence" (Foucault 1997, 255). That aesthetic was to recur in the modernist period in the decadent's aesthetic life experiments.[7]

Through practices of *parrhessia*, uncomfortable insights are broached. When the *Parrhesiastes* presents those in power with difficult truths, her own moral practices are open to scrutiny. In order to deliver *parrhesia*, the speaker has to say what she knows to be true and the only way to know this truth is through "the possession of certain *moral* qualities" (Foucault 2001, 15). As a result the truth-teller must maintain a discipline of self-care that is also good living, but must do so in ways that are original, that pursue ethical practice as both conscious and consistent. While one who speaks truth to power will "risk death to tell the truth instead of reposing in the security of a life where the truth goes unspoken," he will also choose a specific relation with the self, a specific interior life in which "he prefers himself as truth-teller rather than as a living being who is false to himself" (106–107). Life practices that loosened conventional constraints, Foucault argued, made possible an ethical relation to power.

In *Portrait*, Joyce presents a slightly different possibility: that the disciplines demanded by institutions might themselves produce rebellious subjects. Stephen's piety piques the interest of his school director, who invites him to pursue a vocation in the clergy, a vocation Stephen refuses. While he does not *speak* truth to power in this meeting, he nonetheless finds himself capable of withstanding the appeal of the ministry, which in the novel appears primarily as an appeal to the power of the priesthood: "the power of the keys, the power to bind and to loose from sin, the power of exorcism, the power to cast out from the creatures of God the evil spirits that have power over them, the power, the authority, to make the great God of Heaven come down upon the altar and take the form of bread and wine" (1916, 158). Refusing this "awful power" – that in the priest's imagination rivals that of the archangels, of the Blessed Virgin, and (at least in the moment of transubstantiation) of God Himself – Stephen positions himself, in conjunction with his rigorous bodily "comparisons and experiments," to take care of himself such that he can follow the path of the *parrhesiast*. In *Ulysses*, he resists the British imperialist assumptions of his new roommate, Haines, and refutes his supervisor's anti-Semitism. Stephen's care of the self is less ascetic in the pages of *Ulysses* than in the earlier text in which he made it his mission to "forge in the smithy of my soul the uncreated conscience of my race" (255). In *Ulysses* he is seen drinking, consorting with prostitutes, spending his salary in the pursuit of immediate pleasures, in essence masturbating in the agora. While he has few opportunities to speak to people in actual power, he takes multiple opportunities to speak against injustice.

But while he challenges power, he may not be equally able to challenge himself. One conspicuous moment of moral crisis in *Ulysses* occurs when Stephen meets his younger sister among the used book stalls on Bachelor's Row. Readers glimpse his interior monologue and know that he sees the desperate straits in which she lives:

> she crouched feeding the fire with broken boots.... She is drowning. Agenbite. Save her. Agenbit. All against us. She will drown me with her, eyes and hair. Lank coils of seaweed hair around me, my heart, my soul. Salt green death. (1986, 200)

Imagining his sister both as an Ophelia and as a siren with the power to drown him in the seas of her miserable poverty is not one of Stephen's most admirable fantasies. Nor does spending salary money on bacchanalian adventures in the face of his siblings' material suffering light him in conventionally moral hues.

While Joyce could be suggesting that the moral drive produced by the ascetic project in *Portrait* is betrayed by the lack of discipline in *Ulysses*, Foucault's example provides an alternate reading. In his continued experiments on his body, Stephen produces a self that will not make the gesture of immediately assuaging moral conscience ("agenbite of inwit") if it will prevent him from pursuing the larger project of moral reform on a national level. His salary would do little to change the conditions in his father's impoverished home. On a wider scale, he also cannot change his country, as he observes, so he makes it his mission to change the subject: " – We can't change the country. Let us change the subject." (1986, 527). Avoiding a conversational dead end, Stephen also puns on the project of changing subjectivity; the only way to influence national or familial conditions would be this radical or root transformation. His care of the self, his experiments on the body, are performed in the service of such transformation in the production of *parrhessia* or an ethical subject.

If Stephen speaks the truth in the confines of the cabman's shelter in the company of drivers and sex workers or in the newsroom and pub among journalists, he does not deliver truths to the sovereign. The circulation of the Vice Regal cavalcade through the city of Dublin during the "Wandering Rocks" episode is a reminder of the presence of a power to whom Stephen does not address his insights. However, with this gesture, Joyce indicates the extent of the tyranny suffusing Dublin in which subjects are not precisely citizens, in which the individual has no voice in the polity. Foucault makes this diagnosis explicitly when he remarks that while *parrhessia* is a duty for those who practice the care of the self such that ethical truths are known, those truths can only be registered in a well-run polity where *parrhessia* is both a duty and a kind of game played between sovereign and citizen in which it is understood that there will be no punishment for telling the truth. If such a contract between unequal partners is impossible, then the sovereign is a tyrant and the citizen a slave. But for the Greeks, the impossibility of *parrhesia* turns a citizen into a slave." Joyce's subjects are not the slaves of tyrants, but their truths are experienced and expressed at such a remove from the centers of imperial power as to be more symbolic than actual.

Moral Goods

The material concerns that form Stephen's ethical practice occupy Virginia Woolf as well. Throughout her writings she makes the case that the moral good, as it has been normatively defined, works in the service of the powerful to maintain the status quo and to justify marginalization by limiting access to both the public good and material goods. Moral capacities that serve normative arrangements earn individuals both social and monetary capital; however, rejecting one part of this equation entails losses in the other. *Mrs. Dalloway* (1925) meditates on this power imbalance through the doctrine of proportion that is inflicted like a punitive medicine on the eponymous character and her doppelganger, the shell-shocked veteran, Septimus Smith. Both figures threaten the status quo with their neurotic wounds, disabilities received in the service of the powerful. They are counseled to adhere to a sense of proportion that would excise their puny protests. The very mise-en-scène of the novel protests this service to the goods in the name of being good: "Shredding and slicing, dividing and subdividing, the clocks of Harley Street nibbled at the June day, counselled submission, upheld authority, and pointed out in chorus the supreme advantages of a sense of proportion . . ." (1925, 155). By contrast, in *To the Lighthouse*, Mrs. Ramsay, by setting an example of the moral good, earns immense social capital both in her large family and in the larger community. Those around her who refuse the prevailing moral system are impoverished by their protests.

Woolf (1921) pursues this problematic with increasing specificity and complexity in "Solid Objects," which opens on a young man, John, with bright political career prospects walking with a colleague and friend along the shore where he unearths and is captivated by a piece of beach glass. His delight in this object subsequently derails his more practical goals into an obsession with assembling discarded objects into a collection of found art. As his collection of found objects grows, John's distinctions, his aesthetic parameters, become increasingly exacting. His concern with accidental art guides him away from the more material concerns his friend pursues, while contributing to a frenzied system in which pursuit of the aesthetic good becomes more and more demanding.

Woolf observes in this connoisseur of the rejected that the obsessive pursuit of achievement and advancement trained into British men of the elite classes cannot be entirely relinquished but only redirected. In his collecting practices John does not abandon but channels the demands of his class into the increasingly discerning demands of the connoisseur as "his standards became higher and his taste more severe" (1921, 85). However, transferring these demands onto the eccentric and away from the normative earns John the pity of his peers, and his constituents frown on his found art collection and read its display as a sign of deteriorated political capacities as if his unusual assessment of material goods were an impediment to the moral or public good.

While modernist narratives like Woolf's have provided an extraordinarily rich home for the study of Jacques Lacan's writings, modernist scholarship is primarily devoted to his work on gender and sexuality and his theories of language and consciousness. His powerful critique of moral philosophy, beginning with the seminar on ethics during the 1959–1960 academic year, has received less attention. However, two particular claims echo Woolf's concerns: that our devotion to being good primarily serves the accumulations of material goods and that the more we feed the superego with moral propriety, the more it demands and the finer are the distinctions it makes in pursuit of absolute moral goodness or purity. More explicitly, Lacan (1986) argued that Aristotle's influential work presents "the morality of the master, created for the virtues of the master and linked to the order of powers" (315). Further, this version of morality – "since Plato, certainly since Aristotle, and down through the stoics, the Epicureans, and even through Christian thought itself in Saint Thomas Aquinas" (221) – primarily serves power; its vision of the service of the Good disguises its actual demand that each of us serve "the goods," while asking our desires to "come back later" (315). Interpreting Freud's modernist-era *Civilization and Its Discontents*, Lacan concluded "everything that is transferred from *jouissance* to prohibition gives rise to the increasing strengthening of prohibition. Whoever attempts to submit to the moral law sees the demands of his superego grow increasingly meticulous and increasingly cruel" (176). The converse, however, is not allowed: "Whoever enters the path of uninhibited *jouissance*, in the name of the rejection of the moral law in some form or other, encounters obstacles whose power is revealed to us every day..." (177). It is the analyst's ethical responsibility to witness honestly to this *jouissance*.

"Solid Objects" poses a challenge to Lacan's ethical theory on the question of pleasure. John's collection to which he devotes his "increasingly meticulous attention" has the obscene appearance of *jouissance* for those around him who participate in the construction of obstacles to its social spread. In this meticulous attention John also falls victim to what Douglas Mao (1998) describes as a "profound possession *by* things" (27). While John seems to choose pleasure in beauty over obligation to the political, it is difficult to tell whether he is relinquishing the dynamics of the goods or the Good. When John first appreciates his beach glass, the narrator describes the look of childlike pleasure on his face as "delight" in the power he has to offer this object, as if it were animate, "a life of warmth and security," in which it may "leap with joy when it sees itself chosen from a million like it, to enjoy this bliss instead of a life of cold and wet...." (Woolf 1921, 82). The narrator does not claim to actually *know* the content of John's thoughts, but she equates his delight in acquiring a material object, however non-commercial, with an ability to do good, to house the homeless, to give the forgotten the joy of being chosen. In trading between the ornamental and the instrumental, Woolf at the same time conflates and distinguishes the two. Can we know when our pleasure at doing good is only an instrument of power's investments in the goods? Are our desires authentic or are they intercepted by power in its guise as the moral good? While his collection first distracts and then disqualifies John from the political life with all its attendant service to the goods in the name of the Good, Woolf suggests that these discarded goods appeal to John's judgment through the potential of a childlike moral rectitude. Lacan's appealing ethical dictum that one act always "in conformity with the desire that is in you" and that " 'giving ground relative to one's desire' is always accompanied in the destiny of the subject by some betrayal," is crossed through in Woolf's account with the elusive obedience of desire itself (1986, 314, 321).

The Event

At the close of the century, Alain Badiou pondered Levinas's system as an ethics that had failed to bring about a public good. In his book *Ethics: An Essay on the Understanding of Evil* (2002), he outlines his concerns about the *application* of Levinasian ethics in contemporary social and political discourses. He posits that the ethical subject needs a truth to live by. In formulating this truth, Badiou adapts the concept of singularity within Levinas's system, recognizing its potential to produce the kinds of eternal truths that would make possible a public ethics. Modernism's ugly underbelly prepared the way for Badiou to see that mistaking a singularity for a part of a pattern, or to use Badiou's vocabulary addressing an *event* as part of a historical sequence, or folding *truth*, which is revolutionary and singular, into a repetition of pattern, produces evil. Modernism's simultaneous commitments to classical revival and formal innovation made the sustained recognition of singularity (or Badiou's fidelity to the event) difficult.

For Badiou, ethics should be understood as singular. To explain singularity, Badiou imagines a physician on a panel determining governmental health care policy. That physician when imagining the treatment of cancers in the aggregate may make certain policy decisions: perhaps that government only fund care for treatable cancers in order to make the best use of bursary, or that only taxpayers are eligible for services. But if that doctor is in the presence of a particular person with a vexing cancer, she has no need for an ethical code; she just needs to see the situation clearly and in its particularity as a singular event. She will then care for this person to the limit of her ability and her means (or to use Badiou's phrase, "to the rule of maximum possibility"). For Badiou, there is no ethics in general. There is only the singularity of the situation and our commitment to it.

The event is an exception to the sequence of everyday life. It does not evolve from the current situation, but interrupts it in a way that shows the void at the center of experience as it is. Badiou provides one example of the event that is particularly apropos for literary readers: when one day a denizen of Socrates's mythical cave emerges into the light, he struggles as his eyes adjust to the sunlight, but finally realizes that the things he has been seeing all his life were merely shadows projected on a wall. For this man, fidelity to the event requires his willingness to return to the cave and tell others about the world of light even if they mock him or try to kill him for attempting to set them free. For Socrates, the sun metaphorizes the good, and a person who is able to see the good is compelled to testify to it in all circumstances no matter the costs, for "the thing seen last, and seen with great difficulty, is the form or character of the good. But when it is seen, the conclusion must be that it turns out to be the cause of all that is right and good for everything" (2002, 59).[8] Similarly, for Badiou, one cannot return to ordinary practices after experiencing an event. To be ethical one has to act with fidelity to that event as the essential truth of one's existence, for an event constitutes a moment in which everything changes.

Additionally, Badiou argues that subsuming an event into the sequence of the ordinary is evil: "to believe that an event convokes not the void of the earlier situation, but its plenitude, is Evil in the sense of simulacrum, or terror" (71). His ethic demands that the radical break be acknowledged, not understood as the final item in a set (to adopt his mathematical metaphor) that completes this set, but the item that undoes the logic of the set itself, for to subsume the item into the set is to produce a *"simulacrum of truth"* comparable to the shadows on the wall of Plato's cave; it has all the formal traits of truth without truth's actual substance (73). To draw on a recent example: to pretend that the violent events that took place on September 11, 2001 were not singular – or, worse, to describe those attacks as singular while treating them as the latest of a series of occurrences in which the collapse of the World Trade Center towers is an invasion comparable to Pearl Harbor – is unethical, creates a mere simulacrum of truth, and results in evil. In fact, "fidelity to the simulacrum . . . has as its content war and massacre" (74) and to act on the event as the latest in a set of historical incidents that demand similar national responses is to exercise "fidelity to the simulacrum," an act that is "necessarily the exercise of terror" (77).

Modernism, with its contradictory emphases on revolution and innovation, on the one hand, and on allusion, renaissance, pattern, and recurrence, on the other, may have prepared its readers poorly for the singularity of what Badiou designates as the event. Joyce's *Finnegans Wake*, for example, is written as a cycle in which the ending folds back into the beginning like a serpent biting its tail; it is the most structurally explicit of the modernists' claims for recurrence. The deeply allusive poetry of high modernists like Ezra Pound and T. S. Eliot suggests that the past is always relevant as a spiraling recurrence with slight changes or shifts in the present that "make it new." Even Woolf's emphasis on the ordinary and routine suggests the inevitability of repetition within oppressive structures that demand their own constant reflection. W. B. Yeats's poetic vision, however, may provide the most striking example of modernism's failure to recognize the event. Several months after men and women of his acquaintance took up arms against the seemingly invincible British Empire in an insurgent bid for Irish independence, Yeats wrote one of his most riveting lyrics. The poem was inspired by this singular revolutionary action, which entered the historical record under the name of his powerful verse.[9] "Easter 1916" recognized the singularity of this event even within a ballad structure with a repeated refrain: "All changed, changed utterly: / A terrible beauty is born." Yeats's metaphor of birth insists on the uniqueness brought forward in the previously line by the equally insistent modification on change as *utter* change. The oxymoronic tension in "terrible beauty" indicates the straining in language as it signifies newness beyond representational capacity but within codes that more easily signal the familiar. The poem registers the transformative significance of the Easter Rising through a parallel transformation in formal, literary terms in which these soldiers' actions shift the genre from comedy to tragedy. If "all the world's a stage, / And all the men and women merely players," as Shakespeare suggested, then players on this stage have changed the genre mid-scene. Each "has resigned his part / In the casual comedy," and the shift in genre has changed the actors themselves in turn. Yeats ends his lyric with the necessity of communal fidelity to the truth of the militants' sacrifice by declaiming the names of the leaders who: "Now and in time to be, / Wherever green is worn, / Are changed, changed utterly: / A terrible beauty is born."

Yet Yeats's own fidelity to the truth of the revolution was shortly compromised: the singularity of 1916's effort was folded into the theory of historical repetition metaphorized in the perning gyres of "A Vision" on which he was at work in 1919. The ambivalence about the militant leaders that empowered his 1916 verse had hardened into critique within a model of historical repetition. Their sacrifice was no longer a singular event to be remembered wherever green was worn; rather the certainty with which they gave their lives to a cause was a signal indication of their moral failure and, further, a general descent into anarchy, an imbalance in forces that would lead through revolution to a returning stabilization exemplified in "The Second Coming" (1919) by the predictable biblical moment of revelation, when

> Turning and turning in the widening gyre
> The falcon cannot hear the falconer;
> Things fall apart; the centre cannot hold;
> Mere anarchy is loosed upon the world,
> The blood-dimmed tide is loosed, and everywhere
> The ceremony of innocence is drowned;
> The best lack all conviction, while the worst
> Are full of passionate intensity.

The poem situates political revolution in the context of mythic revolution and upheaval from the Homeric to the biblical to indicate that nothing changes utterly, but that change is merely a part of sequence in which even the second coming of the savior is neither an event nor an end, but a mere shift in the gyrating course of cyclical history.

By 1928 the joined forces of this Irish revolution had succumbed to internal fissions and took opposing sides in civil war; Yeats's *The Tower* presents 1916 not as an event but as a mere novelty adapted within the historical cycle of violent recurrence. The Easter Rising is subsumed into recurrent comedy when even in the midst of this war's tragedies, it is Falstaff who takes center stage in "The Road at My Door": "An affable Irregular, / a heavily-built Falstaffian man, / Comes cracking jokes of civil war / As though to die by gunshot were / The finest play under the sun." Describing his contemporary Falstaff whose very life is hostage to a Republican ideal, Yeats poses a challenge to moral certainty that Levinas (2010) echoed at the end of his life: "one has to think sometimes of all the harm that the truth can bring about" (17).

Conclusion

In the twentieth century four major new models for ethics emerged that were departures from classical modes of ethical engagement. The modernist period presaged and contributed to the ground that made these innovations possible by creating shifts in public or collective thought on morality. Reading modernist literature beside ethical theory enriches our understanding of each and presents possibilities for new avenues of exploration.

Notes

1 While a series of recent dissertations in this field and a double session on "Modernism and Ethics" at the 2011 Modernist Studies Association Meeting indicate that the turn to ethics is gaining momentum, books and journal articles explicitly devoted to the topic are scarce. A conspicuous exception to this generalization is Lee Oser's *The Ethics of Modernism: Moral Ideas in Yeats, Eliot, Joyce, Woolf, and Beckett*. As Oser takes no explicit recourse to twentieth-century ethical theory, his book has not opened this particular methodological path. More recently Jessica Berman's *Modernist Commitments: Ethics, Politics, and Transnational Modernism* makes the case for an ethical ground in modernist literary politics.

2 Bloom's game also reminds readers of the masochist's moral mantra that it is better to give than to receive, a truism that was brought home to me recently by students in a first-year seminar on the concept of "the Good." When asked to write about the idea of feeling good, almost to a person they described feeling good as a result of doing someone else good; not one person described feeling good because someone else had done her good or given him something good. I realized that in the ethical game of sadomasochistic exchange, it is once again the masochists who are having all of the fun; doing good feels good while receiving the good may make the recipient feel powerless, indebted, and even sadistic.

3 James Joyce, *Portrait of the Artist as a Young Man*, 150–151.

4 His abstentions emerge as a masochistic version of Jean Des Esseintes's sensual experiments in Joris-Karl Huysmans's *À rebours* rather than in the Roman Catholic tradition of spiritual discipline.

5 James Joyce, *Ulysses*. I prefer using Hans Walter Gabler's 1986 edition, here p. 7.

6 Meaning "literally saying everything." *Parrhesia* could be used pejoratively to describe people who cannot be discrete and whose words can be dangerous for the community. But *parrhesia* is usually distinguished from *authuroglossos*, or a tongue with no door. Foucault uses the term to indicate speech of consequence.

7 Many readers categorized these arguments as a radical shift in Foucault's concept of discipline, from a model of the subject produced by discursive impositions to a set of practices that produce interiority as ethical existence. However, Lawrence Buell elegantly observes that Foucault's late work was actually a "redirection of emphasis," noting that "the spirit of Foucault's work was always one of irony and at times Nietzschean outrage against institutional constraints on selfhood" (Buell 1999, 9–10), "his longstanding concentration on the power-knowledge problematic and on the construction of social selves by discursive macroinstitutions to the care of the self conceived as an ethical project, a movement quickened by the perception that for privileged men of Greek and Roman antiquity 'reflection on sexual behavior as a moral domain was not a means of internalizing, justifying, or formalizing general interdictions imposed on everyone' but 'an aesthetics of existence' (*Uses of Pleasure* 252–253), indeed an 'ethics of pleasure' (*Care* 239)" (Buell 1999, 9–10).

8 Plato, *The Republic*, 223. Badiou writes: "This is what Plato had already anticipated, when he indicated that the duty of those who escape from his famous cave, dazzled by the sun of the Idea, was to return to the shadows and to help their companions in servitude to profit from that by which, on the threshold of this dark world, they had been seized." Alain Badiou, *Ethics: An Essay on the Understanding of Evil*, 59.

9 The poem was completed, according to Richard J. Finneran's edition, on September 25, 1916.

References

Badiou, Alain. (2002). *Ethics: An Essay on the Understanding of Evil*, trans. Peter Hallward. London: Verso.

Berman, Jessica. (2011). *Modernist Commitments: Ethics, Politics, and Transnational Modernism*. New York: Columbia University Press.

Buell, Lawrence. (1999). "Introduction: In Pursuit of Ethics." *PMLA* 114.1 (January): 7–19.

Butler, Judith. (2004). *Precarious Lives: The Powers of Mourning and Violence*. New York: Verso.

Foucault, Michel. (1997). *Ethics: Subjectivity, and Truth*, ed. Paul Rabinow, trans. Robert Hurley and others. New York: The New Press.

Foucault, Michel. (2001). *Fearless Speech*, ed. and trans. Joseph Pearson. Los Angeles: Semiotext(e).

Joyce, James. (1916). *A Portrait of the Artist as a Young Man*. New York: Penguin.

Joyce, James. (1922, 1986). *Ulysses*, ed. Hans Walter Gabler. New York: Random House.

Lacan, Jacques. (1986). *The Ethics of Psychoanalysis* 1959–1960, ed. Jacques-Alain Miller, trans. Dennis Porter. New York: Norton.

Levinas, Emmanuel. (1998). *Collected Philosophical Papers*, trans. Alphonso Lingis. Pittsburgh: Duquesne University Press.

Levinas, Emmanuel. (2001). *The Emmanuel Levinas Reader*, ed. Seán Hand. Oxford: Blackwell.

Mao, Douglas. (1998). *Solid Objects: Modernism and the Test of Production*. Princeton, NJ: Princeton University Press.

Oser, Lee. (2007). *The Ethics of Modernism: Moral Ideas in Yeats, Eliot, Joyce, Woolf, and Beckett*. Oxford: Oxford University Press.

Plato. (2000). *The Republic*, ed. G. R. F. Ferrari, trans. Tom Griffith. Cambridge: Cambridge University Press.

De Saint Cheron, Michaël, ed. (2010). *Conversations with Emmanuel Levinas*, trans. Gary D. Mole. Pittsburgh: Duquesne University Press.

Woolf, Virginia. (1921). *A Haunted House and Other Stories*. London: Harcourt.

Woolf, Virginia. (1925). *Mrs. Dalloway*. London: Hogarth Press.

Yeats, W. B. (1996). *The Collected Poems of W.B. Yeats*, ed. Richard Finneran. London: Scribner.

Further Reading

Attridge, Derek. (2004). *The Singularity of Literature*. New York: Routledge.

Claire Katz. (2003). *Levinas, Judaism, and the Feminine: The Silent Footsteps of Rebecca*. Bloomington: Indiana University Press.

Levinas, Emmanuel. (1969). *Totality and Infinity: An Essay on Exteriority*, trans. Alphonso Lingis. Pittsburgh: Duquesne University Press.

Levinas, Emmanuel. (1998). *Otherwise Than Being: Or Beyond Essence*, trans. Alphonso Lingis. Pittsburgh: Duquesne University Press.

Rabaté, Jean-Michel. (2001). *Jacques Lacan: Psychoanalysis and the Subject of Literature*. New York: Palgrave.

Rancière, Jacques. (2009). *Aesthetics and Its Discontents*. London: Polity.

19

Phenomenology and Affect
Modernist Sulking

Sara Crangle

In *The Expression of the Emotions in Man and Animals* (1872), Charles Darwin locates the origins of human sulking in our primate ancestors. In experiments, Darwin encouraged sulking in chimpanzees by offering them something appealing, like an orange, and then taking it away. Darwin (2009) describes the expression that followed: "A firmly closed mouth, in addition to a lowered and frowning brow, gives determination to the expression, and may make it obstinate and sullen" (209). We frown from the first few days of life, Darwin points out, and never learn to control this expression as we do weeping, for instance. Frowning Darwin considers a product of our evolutionary need to look into the distance, scanning the horizon for danger; we also frown when contemplating a difficult or obscure line of thought. A mouth resolutely shut indicates attentiveness, decisiveness, and may precede physical exertion, but pouting, or what Darwin delightfully calls "making a snout," is a behavior he restricts to European children and adults of all other races (212–213). Frowning falls within Darwin's survivalist remit; sulking proper he demarcates as childish and "primitive." While Darwin's suggestion that non-European adults sulk was popular in the nineteenth century – witness "[t]he silent sullen peoples" of Kipling's "The White Man's Burden" (1897–1899) – the conviction remains that sulking is an emotional state most prevalent in childhood.

Modernist literature paints a different picture of sulking: for modernist writers, sulking is a predominantly adult behavior. As early as *Middlemarch* (1872), grown men sulk when they don't get their own way; George Eliot's Will Ladislaw "w[ears] rather a pouting air of discontent" on meeting the recently betrothed Dorothea Brooke, with whom he is instantly besotted (1994, 79). In 1914, Mina Loy (2011) embarks upon a dramatic satire of Futurism in which the male protagonist woos his lover by alternately withholding himself and using petulant phrases such as "you

A Handbook of Modernism Studies, First Edition. Edited by Jean-Michel Rabaté.
© 2013 John Wiley & Sons, Ltd. Published 2013 by John Wiley & Sons, Ltd.

don't love me because I am not handsome" (210). A bout of sulking marks the outset of Joyce's *Ulysses* (1922) where Stephen Dedalus distances himself from Buck Mulligan's early morning jollity. After repeatedly asking Stephen what is wrong, Buck is told that he has been too glib, in the past, about Stephen's mother's death. Buck rejoins, incredulous, "You crossed her last wish in death yet you sulk with me . . . . Absurd!" (Joyce 1993, 7–8). But Stephen, being Stephen, remains affronted. The adult sulker persists in narrative time and across the period: Woolf's final novel, *Between the Acts* (1941), features ribald Mrs. Manresa, who flirts with another woman's husband, namely Giles Oliver, he who jerks chairs and rages inwardly about the passive social and political responses to the imminent threat of World War II. Manresa watches his moody antics throughout the day, and tells herself, "I am the Queen, he my hero, my sulky hero"; in turn, the narrator tells us, her "surly knight remained in attendance" (1972, 78–79).

As in life, fictional sulking involves resentment, distancing, nonverbal communication, and obstinacy; a perceived power imbalance is usually at stake. Once underway, sulking is most quickly resolved by the receipt of another's empathy, which levels the playing field in that it involves treating the sulker as an equal. But modernist narrators do not tend to sympathize with their sullen characters. Instead, sulking is used to parody those who falsely believe themselves personally aggrieved, and in this period, that self-absorbed self tends to be not only adult, but white and male. The rare women who sulk usually possess distinctly masculine traits: witness Bertha Lunken of Wyndham Lewis's *Tarr* (1918–1928), who is a frequent sulker, and is described as heroic and handsome, with a body like "a self-indulgent athlete's" (43). A persistently male self-indulgence is at the heart of this modernist affective critique, one that is arguably feminist in that it extends to paternalistic structures like the family, the gentry, and the military. This critique can be extended to modernist aesthetics. In order to succeed, the sulker needs the very society he or she rejects; if no one notices, a sulk is just a bad mood. As a consequence, sulking involves risk, in that the targeted audience may or may not choose to appease the sulker. In turn, risk and dichotomy mark the literature in which sulking arises: writers who portray sulking often wrestle with a rejection of nineteenth-century literary sentimentality via confrontational or hard-to-read bids to promote modernist impersonality; an empathetic audience is far from certain. And, because it so insistently embodies feeling and T. S. Eliot's much-touted "escape from emotion," sulking encapsulates, to some degree, the modernist inability to wholly shuck the past (961).

Again and again, modernists show us how sulking replicates itself in successive generations, however rebellious, however self-aware. Sulking is passed on, and we know this from Woolf's *To the Lighthouse* (1927), which opens upon the youngest Ramsay child, who is nicknamed "James the Sullen."[1] James we find in a quiet, protracted battle with his Victorian father, himself an incessant sulker. Mr. Ramsay displays a propensity for confronting people with quivering, anguished silences, which are described as unsettling, insistent demands for sympathy. James loathes but mimics his father: when a boy, he petulantly turns away as his father tries to tickle him; come adolescence, James and his sister vow to resist their father's tyranny by proffering sullen cold shoulders as they journey, against their will, to the lighthouse (1992, 44). As James effectively steers their little boat, his father compliments him, and Woolf's narrator observes:

> There he sat with his hand on the tiller sitting bolt upright, looking rather sulky and frowning slightly. He was so pleased that he was not going to let anyone take away a grain of his pleasure. His father had praised him. They must think that he was perfectly indifferent. (278)

James feels pleasure; he has been affirmed by the tyrant he aims to reject, and proves as susceptible as that tyrant to empathy. But James insists on appearing capable of performing the rejection, of breaking away from his forebear, and therefore aims to be indifferent, aloof. In this instance lies the impossible sentiment and impersonality that wracks a modernist heir to Victorian tradition; what results is sulkiness, an emotion as tenacious and conflicted as its legacy.

In order to best represent the dichotomous modes of sulking, what follows will draw on the modernist literatures of Radclyffe Hall and Richard Aldington. Although discernibly modernist in content, Hall's novels are melodramatic and realist by turns, thereby bearing a close resemblance to a Victorian literary lineage. By contrast, Aldington is aligned with a distant, "characteristically modernist irony" reductively if usefully considered a product of the World War I; Aldington is also associated with figures like Pound and Eliot, who are, as per Maud Ellmann's well-known work, the major proponents of a poetics of impersonality (Gilbert 1983, 426). Although radically different in style and intent, the figure of the adult sulker informs Hall's and Aldington's narratives to similar effect; both use sulking to excoriate the masculine ego, and as a form of feminist protest, claims perhaps more surprising in Aldington's case.[2] These disparate writers address a binary-laden emotional state, one reliant on a self and a significant other, distance and proximity, feeling and aloofness. Maurice Merleau-Ponty's phenomenology will act as a synthesizing agent in this discussion of polarities both literary and emotional; as he writes, "the chief gain from phenomenology is to have united extreme subjectivism and extreme objectivism in its notion of the world" (2002, xxii).

The prominence of the adult sulker in modernist literature may be tied to a widespread recovery of childhood experience across the period. In *Strange Dislocations: Childhood and the Idea of Human Interiority, 1780–1930*, Carolyn Steedman (1998) argues on behalf of a cultural shift that occurs in the long nineteenth century, whereby the child comes to represent the inner being of the adult, "so that the child-figure becomes a central vehicle for expressing ideas about the self and its history" (5). The belief that the child shapes the adult is of course aided and abetted by the psychoanalytic recovery of youthful experience, a discourse Steedman describes as helpfully cohering Victorian views on childhood throughout the first two decades of the twentieth century (1998, 4). Alongside the burgeoning field of psychoanalysis existed a growing conviction that the child's point of view could offer an abundant source of novelty, and novelty is of course a renowned modernist aesthetic and intellectual priority.[3] Childhood, "making it new," and a working with and away from established discourses like philosophy and psychoanalysis are concerns that direct the thinking of Merleau-Ponty, a French phenomenologist who spent part of his career as a lecturer in child psychology and education at the Sorbonne (1949–1952). In his foundational work, *Phenomenology of Perception* (1945), and throughout his oeuvre, Merleau-Ponty maintains the view that modernist art and literature, particularly in their most difficult and avant-garde guises, run parallel to phenomenology in enabling "us to rediscover the world in which we live, yet which we are always prone to forget"; Merleau-Ponty describes this rediscovery as a generation of "'wonder'" (2004, 39; 2002, xv).[4] If high modernist literature wrestles with the conventions of realist narrative and omniscient narration, phenomenology is a method that counters what Merleau-Ponty calls the "God-like survey" of traditional philosophy, and regards the world of appearances from an intuitive standpoint, one that holds judgment and absolutism at bay while privileging the never-ending processes of perception, attentiveness, and an often literary description (1964b, 9). Merleau-Ponty's main contribution to phenomenological thinking is to remind us that we inhabit a body that shapes and informs all of our interpretations; we are not just subjects, we are "incarnate subject[s]" (2002, 215). In order to freshly comprehend the body as central to our grasp of the world, Merleau-Ponty returns, recurrently, to the experiences and feelings of childhood. For Merleau-Ponty, the child's perspective undermines a too-easy confidence in adult intellectual superiority and coherence. In a radio lecture published in 1948, he conveys the fundamental relationship between his phenomenology and the child:

> the way we relate to the things of this world is no longer as a pure intellect trying to master an object or space that stands before it. Rather, this relationship is an ambiguous one, between things who are both embodied and an enigmatic world of which we catch a glimpse (indeed which we haunt incessantly) but only ever from points of view that hide as much as they reveal, a world in which every object displays the human face it acquires in a human gaze.

> Yet we are not alone in this transfigured world. In fact, this world is not just open to other human beings but also to animals, children, primitive peoples and madmen who dwell in it after their own fashion; they too coexist in this world. Today we shall see that the rediscovery of the world of perception allows us to find greater meaning and interest in these extreme or aberrant forms of life and consciousness. So much so that the whole spectacle that is world and human life itself takes on a new meaning as a result. (2004, 70)

The child and the "primitive" exhibit "extreme or aberrant forms of life and consciousness"; if it sounds as if Merleau-Ponty has been reading Darwin, that's because he has: in *Phenomenology of Perception* he directly cites Darwin's chimpanzees' "knitting of the brows" as an early survivalist behavior that human beings transform into figurative, which is to say communicative, significance, a process he considers "neither more nor less miraculous than the emergence of love from desire, or that of gesture from the unco-ordinated movements of infancy" (2002, 225). Merleau-Ponty interrogates how the body senses, and then communicates its thoughts *and* its feelings; like his predecessor, Heidegger, he wants to reconstitute affectivity "as a distinct form of consciousness" (2002, 179).[5] With this aim in view, love, desire, anger, and shame are emotive states that arise in his work; sulking also emerges as a singular focal point.

In his essay "The Child's Relations with Others" (1964a [1960]), Merleau-Ponty identifies sulking as a fundamental aspect of human development. His central assertion is that affectivity grounds our understanding of others. Via the much-discussed Lacanian mirror stage, Merleau-Ponty argues that our comprehension of our own reflection is not rooted in logic. We retain, in looking at ourselves, a sense of our image as a doubled being, and this irrational belief extends into adulthood, where we avoid standing on the image of a face if it has fallen to the floor because we invest that image with human properties. This aversion reveals that our intellect does not control our grasp of reflection; instead, the perception is driven by feeling for others, and the very longevity of this emotion tells us that, "Childhood is never radically liquidated" (138). Feelings of reciprocity are learned from seeing ourselves as others see us, and this reciprocity grounds our intelligence; the relationship is not causal, but it is pivotal. Because our affective relationships remain fundamental, Merleau-Ponty dedicates much of his essay to describing how we learn to communicate. Separation is the catalyst for communication, which is perhaps why the first form of affective communication he discusses is negative and conflict-laden. Merleau-Ponty describes how an older child will parade a toy before a younger child, generating sensations of exclusion. What ensues is a power game in which the despot (Merleau-Ponty's name for the child with toy) engages in deliberate cruelty, a process only possible because this child is aware of what privation feels like; a slight sympathy is inevitably involved. In the meantime, the child without experiences disorientation and "de-centering"; this child wants to be the other, or to have what the other owns. Jealousy creates "a total affective situation" in which the longing child is overcome by "the complementary life . . . without yet knowing how to isolate or affirm his [or her] own" (144). What results is what Merleau-Ponty calls "the system 'me-and-other' " – a blurring of identity so complete that he likens it to a unity (146, 153). As the ego develops, the child is less likely to confuse the boundaries between self and other so completely. When this maturation occurs, all-encompassing infantile jealousy turns into a more self-aware sulking; sulking Merleau-Ponty defines as "the attitude of the child who renounces what it wanted to be and who consequently accepts the anguish of a repressed action" (143).

In emphasizing renunciation and acceptance, Merleau-Ponty likens the sulker to a martyr. The comparison makes sense: while the most admirable martyrs are those who suffer for a cause or a belief, in contemporary usage, the term also refers to an individual who is demonstrative about their suffering in the hopes of gleaning nothing more than a bit of sympathy. Audience is implied in the etymology of the word; in the Greek and Latin from which it emerges, "martyr" means "witness."

The comparison is echoed in literature: there is no shortage of sulkers-cum-martyrs in Radclyffe Hall's narratives. Her 1926 bestseller, *Adam's Breed*, features Gian-Luca, a boy raised in London by a stern, unaffectionate grandmother who blames her grandson for the loss of her daughter, who died in childbirth. His grandmother abandons her faith, and teaches her grandson that he must aim to be completely self-sufficient. Gian-Luca's story is one of increasingly holding himself apart from society; he lives a life without much in the way of sympathy or acceptance, and yields constantly to sulking. As an adolescent he finds himself infatuated with his employer's wife, and in her presence, he clumsily oscillates between over-eager lasciviousness and "sound[ing] sulky and gruff when he wished to be polite" (1985, 133). When World War I is declared, he sullenly announces that he, the child of an Italian immigrant, does not want to fight for either Italy or England because in his own view, he has no country (203). When Gian-Luca marries, his devoted wife can never dote on him enough. She is more mother than lover to her husband; Gian-Luca sulks, for instance, when she is not home when he returns from work, and in response, she "reassure[s] him as though [he] were a child" (187). As Gian-Luca withdraws still further from society – refusing to socialize, eat, and eventually work – his wife finds herself chastised by their associates: husbands, she is told, should never be allowed to sulk (253). Gian-Luca's distance from the world around him is fully effected by the novel's end, where he abandons his life in London and retreats to the New Forest. Here he becomes a Christ figure: he befriends humble creatures (beggars, gypsies, and animals), gives away his belongings, goes barefoot, fasts for weeks on end, has a vision of God, and dies. In case the reader misses this staggering array of biblical references, we're told that in death, the outcast Gian-Luca "returned to his country after thirty-four years of exile" (378). After the death that marks his new relationship with God, he is laid in a stable, like Christ at birth. In the New Testament, Christ's martyring completes his narrative: he is brutally sacrificed to further a religion that emphasizes humility and the renunciation of material and bodily desires. But Gian-Luca's martyring signals a distinctly twentieth-century need that exceeds dominant, progressive narratives of financial well-being or secular, rational independence; Gian-Luca longs for the emotional sustenance that is sympathy, be it human or spiritual. Deprived of compassion as a child, no subsequent sympathy but God's can touch Gian-Luca; his sulk is lifelong, and his acceptance of his anguish comes too late for a body so deliberately starved of the nourishment it craves.

   Gian-Luca is quite exceptional in being a sulking martyr who is male and venerated: in Hall's and Aldington's work, women are the most prevalent sulking martyrs, and their fate is not nearly as triumphant. Hall's most famous novel, *The Well of Loneliness* (1928), focuses on Stephen Gordon, a girl whose parents wanted a boy. Stephen becomes an *über*-tomboy as a child and what the narrator calls a "sexual invert" as an adult. This most stereotypically masculine of females sulks as a child when forced to visit her objectionable neighbors, the Antrims, against her will.

She envies their boy his privileges and despises their very feminine girl-child; both children are despots who tease her relentlessly because she evades straightforward gender categories. On the way to their house, Stephen journeys in obstinate silence. But then, Stephen turns her "sulky eyes" upon the beautiful Wye Valley, and "the joy of that seeing" absolves "her apprehension and sense of injustice." It is not just her local landscape that Stephen loves, but the fact that she associates it with her father, who is the most sympathetic figure in her life. "Stephen's eyes turned again; she could not stay sulky, for these were the woods where she drove with her father" (46). Here, sulky Stephen seeks sympathy, and finding it, sulks no more. While Stephen receives some of the sympathy that evades Gian-Luca, this childish sulking portends another adult martyrdom: Stephen's father dies young, leaving her with a mother who refuses to associate with her daughter after realizing that Stephen is sexually attracted to other women. When Stephen finds love at long last, she discovers that she cannot bear subjecting her partner to their social status as outcasts, and so stages a betrayal that drives her lover into the arms of a man. Stephen thus undertakes an emotional and spiritual suicide in the interests of "saving" another, but sacrifices her own happiness to uphold the status quo of heteronormativity, meaning that her martyrdom is both a critique of early twentieth-century sexual restrictions and a resounding defeat. There is no paternalistic homecoming for Stephen as there is for Gian-Luca. Instead, the last pages of the novel show her alone, begging for the acknowledgment of a god who does not reply; she is left without the sympathy of fathers celestial or terrestrial.

In Hall's *The Unlit Lamp* (1924), Joan Osborne suffers a similar fate. Joan is a "masculine" figure in being intellectual and careerist; as an adolescent, she longs to go to Cambridge and study to become a doctor. She is also in love with a woman: her former tutor Elizabeth. When Elizabeth is courted by a local man, Joan finds herself in an uneasy and unwinnable competition for Elizabeth's attention. This competition culminates in a literal race to the finish: one blustery day, suitor Lawrence insists on accompanying Elizabeth and Joan on their customary walk, and Elizabeth's hat blows off.

> [A]fter it went Joan, with Lawrence at her heels. She could hear him pattering persistently behind her. For some reason the sound of his awkward running infuriated her; his steps were short for a man's, as though he were wearing tight boots. She felt suddenly that she must reach the hat first or die; must be the one to restore it to its owner. She strained her lanky legs to their limit; her skirts flew, her breath came fast, she was flushed with temper and endeavour.... Several people stood still to laugh....

But just as Joan reaches the hat, she trips and falls flat, giving Lawrence his needed advantage.

> 'I've won!' laughed Lawrence provokingly. 'You're not hurt, are you?'
> She was, having slightly twisted her ankle, but she lied sulkily.
> 'No, of course not.' (223)

Joan is *almost*, but not quite, masculine enough to trounce Lawrence, who is effeminized by his tight, hobbling boots and undersized stride. As a result of her boyishly competitive behavior, culminating in a self injured physically and emotionally, Joan is forced to limp away home, leaving Lawrence to propose to Elizabeth, who accepts him, sealing the end of the intimacy Joan and Elizabeth have shared for years. Joan's sulk admits defeat on the widest possible scale; she is a female sulker who does not get what she wants, and like Stephen Gordon, is sacrificed to the expectations of an unsympathetic paternalistic culture.

This self-same culture blocks Joan's progress at every turn. The central question of the book is posed by the narrator at one juncture: "Why can there never be any real happiness for Joan Ogden, never any real fulfilment, never any joy that was quite without blemish?" (256). In essence, Joan is less sulker than martyr to a family of sulkers, her demanding sister Milly included; when both girls reach maturity and it becomes apparent that their father, a retired colonel, has squandered their inheritance, Milly is told that she cannot go to London to study music. But Milly sulks and their parents reverse their decision, even as Joan feels compelled to stay home (136).[6] Joan's less traditional goals prove irrecoverable: she cannot become a doctor because her parents have neither the will nor the money to support her. After her father's death, Joan spends the next twenty years taking care of her mother, a domineering hypochondriac. Joan promises herself that she will break free of familial obligation over and over, but repeatedly fails, even as she becomes increasingly aware that the era of the New Woman, with its promises of liberation and independence, has entirely passed her by. When her mother dies, Joan is alone, impoverished, and unskilled, and takes up a post as nurse for her orphaned cousin, Rupert Routledge, who lives with a staff of caretakers in the suburbs of a south-eastern English village. The novel concludes as Joan meets Rupert for the first time in his nursery; he is looking for his favorite doll, which Joan locates. His housekeeper Mrs. Keith prompts him to thank Joan, but he resists:

> [Rupert] looked sulky. 'I shan't thank her; she hid my dolly. I know she did!'
> 'Oh, you must thank her, Master Rupert. It was her who *found* your dolly for you. Come now, be good!'
> But the patient stamped his foot. 'Take her away!' he ordered peremptorily. (318)

Joan's martyring to an incompetent and petulant family takes on a sublime grotesquery in this final scene: for, although Rupert Routledge lives and behaves like a boy, he is in fact sixty-five years old. Dropped on his head as a baby, Rupert never matured past the age of six; he will forever remain a sulky man-child afraid to sleep alone, and who, left unsupervised, eats to the point of making himself sick. Having had Rupert's incessant daily needs explained to her in minute detail, Joan responds cheerfully, telling Mrs. Keith, "Oh, I shall soon get into it all, I expect. I'm used to invalids, you see." These chilling words of acceptance are the last lines of the book.

Joan's response to sulking is truly, in Merleau-Ponty's terms, "the attitude of [one] who renounces what it wanted to be and who consequently accepts the anguish of a repressed action."

Hall's portrayal of ambitious women who are martyred to the sulking of others carries over into Aldington's novel *Women Must Work* (1934b): here, protagonist Etta Morison wants nothing more than to get away from her small town and to get a job, but, as for Joan Osborne, paternal values impede her every step toward independence. The pressures at stake for Etta are detailed via the insular microcosm of her family's rituals early on in the book:

> Tom Morison made a great point of Sunday afternoon tea. At all times he liked to drink quantities of strong Indian tea with plenty of milk and sugar – Sergeant Major's tea, in fact. And at the proper season he derived additional satisfaction from seeing his muffins toasted at the drawing-room fire on a twisted brass toasting fork purchased at the Oriental Bazaar. This task, originally performed by Mrs. Morison, had now been allotted to Etta. There was no practical reason why the muffins should not have been toasted in the kitchen, but Mr. Morison's insistence on the muffin rite and his delight therein may probably be traced to an unconscious symbolical exercise of power – he was asserting the patriarch's rite to the services of all the females of his community. At the same time he tasted the only other discoverable reward of the modern family man, which is to contemplate the domestic prison he has given his life and his freedom to create, and to believe hopefully that he and his dependents are housed, clothed, fed, and generally provided for a little better and more tastefully than his neighbours. (20–21)

The satirical plays here are multiple: the English Empire is a source of security and comfort and the women of the home are in their subservient place, even as the reader knows we're on the verge of World War I, and that daughter Etta is on the cusp of rebelling. At first, Etta's rebellion is minor and sullen; on this particular afternoon, Etta is deeply engaged in a book, and begs off her serving duties. Her position is literally and symbolically aloof: invited to toast the muffins, she "sat down in a small chair as far from the fire as was possible without entirely deserting the family circle" (22). Proximity and distance define this moment of sulky rebellion, which her parents label a mark of her belief in her own superiority and a consequence of being "spoiled." Their goads have their effect: Etta defends herself by stating that she wishes she were not provided for, as she would like to work as hard as her father and provide for herself. The conversation escalates as her parents express alarm at her desires for education and work, and the possibility that she might be a suffragette. Etta is told to play them a tune on the piano, and, though weeping, obliges. Our narrator tells us:

> Etta's parents hadn't seen her tears at the piano, she took good care of that. Suppose they had seen, they would have thought them tears of petulant resentment and self-pity. And they would have wounded her still more deeply by patronising compassion, a blundering sympathy. (32)

"Patronising compassion" and "blundering sympathy" are the best responses a female sulker can expect; each of these oxymoronic affective states undoes its own good intentions. In fact, Etta is not sulking at the piano, but is reproaching herself for announcing her long-cherished desires in the wake of upsetting her father, a man too comfortably confident that he is better off than his neighbors to see that his kingdom is less fortress than prison.

Self-reproach in the wake of paternalistic betrayal becomes a constant motif in *Women Must Work*, where Etta encounters a stream of sulky patriarchs and finds herself martyred to each in turn. Tenaciously, she gets herself to London and secures a secretarial job where she makes scarcely a living wage. Frustrated but determined, she approaches her employer, Mr. Drayton, and asks for clear terms and conditions by which she might increase her salary. When she meets his demands, no raise is forthcoming, and she confronts him again. He complains "sulkily" that the decision lies in the hands of his immediate superior, and that he can do nothing about it; his claim is a lie, and Etta tells him so (1934b, 106). The situation goes unresolved, and then resolves itself all too horrifically: Drayton asks Etta out for dinner, and, in the midst of proclaiming himself a sentimentalist who was "pretty far gone on her" proposes that she become his kept woman (121). An accomplished paternalistic sulker, Drayton is confident that his call to contractually agreed "sentiment" will appeal to Etta, and tells her so (122). When Etta tries to leave the restaurant, he forces himself into her cab and tries to rape her. Etta's response is self-disgust at having so egregiously misread his intentions throughout her employment. Later, saved from Drayton's clutches by a promoter of women's rights who hires her as an assistant, Etta falls in love with her employer's nephew, Ralph Lawson. Fearful of losing her job should she go out with Ralph, Etta suggests that they resist their feelings; when Ralph responds "sulkily," she calls him childish for not understanding the rare privileges of her current post (180). Ralph's self-centered sulking foreshadows the demise of their love: they are secretly engaged as Ralph heads off to war, but when he returns on leave, it is to find Etta distressed because her brother has been wounded on the front. Frantic with desire, Ralph cannot understand her reticence to go to bed with him in the wake of this news; they part in the midst of a furious row that keeps them forever separated. Instead, Etta seeks solace in Francis Leigh, an older, married man who is a writer of experimental verse, an interest Etta does not understand, but justifies via "the theory that men are big children – they must have their playthings. And Francis's playthings showed his fine sensitive nature" (270). Francis proves more calculating than Drayton: when wooing a woman, he is aware that "a certain amount of sentiment was needed, [but] he didn't believe in pitching the note too high" (261). Etta succumbs to his contrived charms and decides to have a baby by him, but her announcement of her pregnancy is unwelcome: Francis is shocked by Etta's plan to raise a baby in the countryside, calling it " 'a sentimental schoolgirl's dream' " and offering her money for an abortion (280). When Etta refuses, Francis goes into another room, and "sit[s] sulkily in one of the armchairs" (282). This sulking announces the end of their relationship; Francis will have nothing more to do with her, and Etta in turn spends the rest of her adult life working her way up the ladder of an advertising firm, and raising her daughter Anne alone from a distant, work-harried vantage, without a shred of "sentimentalism" (320–321). Etta succeeds professionally, but becomes a woman defined by the worst attributes of paternalism: she is power hungry, rich, and unfeeling. Unfeeling, that is, until the very end of the book, where, surveying the enormous new home she has just purchased, Etta breaks down in hysterics. She thus brings to fruition her father's self-satisfied reflection, at the conclusion of the introductory family row about her ambitions, that "there are times when all women are hysterical" – hence their concerns need not be taken seriously (35). Over the course of her life, Etta does her utmost to acknowledge and eventually adopt masculine authority, but her full-scale rejection of empathy ultimately decimates her. *Women Must Work* is Aldington's scathing indictment of the limitations of paternalism and liberal feminism alike: powerful, autonomous men make demands on Etta's sentiment and sulk like children in need of sympathy; realizing early on that these tactics will not work for her, Etta drives herself so hard that she eventually yields to a pent-up and unmistakably "feminine" hysteria.[7]

Like Hall's Joan Osborne, Aldington's Etta Morison is a woman who has a brief and unsuccessful foray into sulking in her youth, and who then becomes the victim of others' sulking, rather than the active agent in the sulking relationship. And the word "relationship" is crucial: while the sulker can be akin to a solitary martyr, in general, Merleau-Ponty's argument that sulking is a renunciation and an acceptance of repressed activity accurately describes the initial stage of sulking, but neglects to elucidate the subsequent and requisite response of the other. This response is definitive: sulking is an affective state wholly reliant upon immediate interaction or attentiveness; the sulker requires a witness. In this regard, sulking is quite unusual: if we think of emotions such as shame, anger, or happiness, the other does not necessarily need to be present in order to enable or define the terms of these emotions. One can be angry without the source of anger nearby, but a while a solitary sulker might be seen as unhappy, dissatisfied, perhaps melancholic – s/he is not really sulking. But while Merleau-Ponty's definition of sulking is limited to the viewpoint of the individual, his discussion of sulking is built upon the subject's interaction with the other, which is, in turn, central to his oeuvre. For Merleau-Ponty, human beings exist as a "network of relationships" in which our associations with others are particularly difficult to define (2002, xxiii). As he writes, we cannot and "do not live [live the lives of others]; they are definitively absent.... But that distance becomes a strange proximity as soon as one comes back home to the perceptible world" (1964b, 15). The strangeness of this proximity is ineradicable, but the distance it implies is collapsed in part by consciousness and perception: "As soon as glances meet, we are no longer wholly two, and it is hard to remain alone" (1964b, 231). In short, in his description of self and other, Merleau-Ponty continually reconstitutes the very terms of alienating division and sympathetic cohesiveness necessary to the sulking relation: "Perhaps it is distance which constitutes the reality another person has for us.... But that distance would also rehabilitate us if we could only see ourselves from there" (1964b, 27). Sulking begins with an aggrieved self but demands recognition and interpretation; the sulker wants the witness to take up and empathize with his or her position.

While acknowledging that in understanding others, we are inevitably limited to the perspectives supplied by our own bodies, Merleau-Ponty is nevertheless fascinated by the process of interpreting human behavior, given that "there is not a human word, not a gesture, even one which is the outcome of habit or absent-mindedness, which has not some meaning" (2002, xx). He extends this interpretive delight to emotion, and argues that it begins at an early age:

> I never become aware of my own existence until I have already made contact with others; my reflection always brings me back to myself, yet for all that it owes much to my contacts with other people. An infant of a few months is already very good at differentiating between goodwill, anger and fear on the face of another person, at a stage when he could not have learned the physical signs of these emotions by examining his own body. This is because the body of the other and its various movements appear to the infant to have been invested from the outset with an emotional significance. (2002, 86)[8]

Merleau-Ponty believes that our perceptual solipsism is as inevitable as the social realm; in his opinion, in all of our thinking, feeling, and being, "I assume the existence of a community . . . and I address myself to it." It is impossible to exist without this outwardly directed address, because:

> The refusal to communicate . . . is still a form of communication. Multifarious freedom, my thinking nature, the inalienable ground, existence without qualification, which in me and in others mark the bounds of sympathy, do call a halt to communication, but do not abolish it. (2002, 420)

The refusal to communicate calls attention to the boundaries of the self and other and the sympathies each possess: in so doing, that very refusal becomes a form of communication. Refusal surfaces in the sulker's communicative aloofness, and can also form the non-response of the witness to a sulker. Joan's and Etta's tentative bouts of petulance, for instance, end with an all-too-clear demarcation of the limited sympathies of their immediate others, while the sulking men with whom they come into contact – infantile old man Rupert, lecherous Mr. Drayton, the romantics Ralph and Francis – either find the boundaries of sympathy more flexible, or force them to the breaking point. But the interpretive and responsive challenge posed by male sulking is not always so violently engendered, nor so destructively borne out.

Aldington's *Death of a Hero* (1929) portrays sulking as violent and farcical, but also, importantly, as a refusal to communicate that is both protest and creative process. Our hero is George Winterbourne, a child of the British upper middle classes, whose Victorian father is "an inadequate sentimentalist" who was consistently "selfishly unselfish (*i.e.* always patting himself on the back for 'renouncing' something he was afraid to do or take)" (2). Given his father's love of sentiment and affirming self-renunciation, it is perhaps no surprise that son George, like his fictional peer James Ramsay, is an inveterate sulker. At times, George's sulking is absurd: when he returns home from the front, he goes out for dinner with his wife, his soon-to-be-mistress Fanny, and their Cambridge scholar friend, and finds himself irked by their references to contemporary intellectual figures that George, culturally ostracized by serving overseas, does not recognize. After a solid attempt at intellectual banter of his own, George finds himself rebuffed, and decides to sit silently aloof at the table. Only Fanny notices his petulance:

> Now Fanny was quite a subtil little beast of the field, and saw that George was a bit sulky, and guessed why. Vapourish airs were indifferent to her . . . . There was a sort of physical indifference in Fanny which at first sight looked like mere hardness, and wasn't . . . . So Fanny began to talk to George quite naturally and gaily. He was suspicious, and gave her three verbal bangs in quick succession. She took them with unflinching good-humour, and went on talking and trying to find out what he was interested in. George pretty soon melted to her gaiety – or perhaps it was the gem-like eyes. (143)

Fanny is the ideal female respondent to a male sulker: receptive, willing to accept rebuff, as tenacious as the man himself, and entirely empathetic. She is indifferent on the surface only, and recognizes George's harshness as a similar posturing: beneath it, she sees that he is actively seeking her sentiment. So ideal a witness is Fanny to sulking that even Aldington's narrator seems smitten: the overwrought "perhaps it was the gem-like eyes" is an unusual stylistic foray in *Death of a Hero*, which reserves sincerity and admiration for few topics amidst its otherwise scabrous satire. As per Merleau-Ponty, the language of sulking here is readable if unspoken; each party interprets the other's complex emotive cues while carrying on an innocuous public conversation. This scene plays out stereotypes of modernist sulking: the male, briefly knocked off the course of his assumed superiority, behaves childishly, thus receiving quasi-maternal sympathy from a nearby woman.

Less stereotypical is George's encounter with avant-garde artist Frank Upjohn. Upjohn wants George, then dabbling as a journalist, to write about the Suprematist Movement of which he is a disciple. But George is baffled by the two examples of the movement given him to view: "One was a beautiful scarlet whorl on a background of the purest flake white. The other at first sight appeared to be a brood of bulbous yellow chickens . . . but on closer inspection the chickens turned out to be conventionalised phalluses" (85). Impatient with George's feeble attempts at interpretation, Upjohn throws himself on his sofa in a huff, eating candied apricots in a silence reinforced by his gestured dismissal of George's attempts to speak. In a manner that rather perfectly embodies the attraction and repulsion such sulks must maintain – in which regard, the affective state to which sulking is most readily aligned may well be disgust – the pout comes to an end when "Mr Upjohn, after coughing once or twice, swung himself from his couch with incredible swiftness, hawked vigorously, flung open a window with unnecessary violence and spat voluminously into the street" (86).[9] Upjohn expels abject object and mood simultaneously; turning back from the window, he enthusiastically invites George out to a party. George follows him there, "half amused by [the] childish swagger and self-conscious bounce" Upjohn affects along the way (87). Surveying the prewar bohemian party, the narrator tells us that Upjohn's earlier petulant silence will prove prophetic; from among this alternative society will emerge "one of the brightest of the post-war reputations . . . created by a young man who had the self-restraint to sit through forty-five literary parties without saying a word" – his peers, we are assured, will consider him brilliant (92). While rejecting this group as self-indulgent, George nevertheless engages in the petulant behavior it admires; he separates himself from everyone while feeling "hate-obstinate" (94). All of this sulking parodies the avant-garde: Upjohn wants to be the forerunner of an obscure movement and to have a wide audience sympathetic to his difficult art; when unappreciated, he pouts. As with Francis Leigh of *Women Must Work*, Aldington's portrayal of experimental artists given to sulking is a quiet dismissal of a modernist aesthetics based on a renunciation of subjective emotion.[10] His satire extends to the uncomprehending or ostracized audience, who, like George, may feel that the exclusive knowingness of a particular experimental set presents a power imbalance worthy of a petulant response.[11]

For Aldington, artistry lies in a willingness to question tradition *and* embrace emotion, and in this regard, sulky George Winterbourne proves emblematic. As a boy, George's parents and boarding school instructors long for him to become "manly." But George is disgusted by hunting and Officers' Training Corps; instead, he reads Keats and Shakespeare avidly, falls in love with Primitivism and the Pre-Raphaelites, and determines to teach himself how to paint. Commanded to take part in O.T.C., he skulks off to a geography class, and a prefect comes to retrieve him to the gymnasium, along the way berating George for not doing as he was told. But

> George made no answer. He just went hard and obstinate, hate-obstinate, inside. He was so clumsy and so bored – in spite of infinite manly bullyings – that the O.T.C. was very glad indeed to send him back to Geography class after a few drills. He just went hate-obstinate, and obeyed with sullen, hate-obstinate docility. He didn't disobey, but he didn't really obey, not with anything inside him. He was just passive, and they could do nothing with him. (58)

Fueled by sulking, George passively protests; when confronted by his superiors, he maintains this guise while "silently reciting to himself the Ode to a Nightingale, as a kind of inner Declaration of Independence" (59). In the process, he gains a reputation "in the School for sullen and obstinate behaviour" and is beaten and forced to pray for forgiveness and manliness by his "bullying, urbane Head" – as these rituals make no change in George's behavior, he finds himself increasingly left to his own devices (59–60). George stays his course: there is no one at his school in whom he can confide, so petulant George locates sympathy in books and art, reading "most of the poets from Chaucer onwards" (60). And as the narrator tells us, his motivation is as political as it is aesthetic, as successful as it is tenacious:

> George, though he didn't realise it then, wasn't going to be a bit of any damned Empire's backbone, still less a part of its kicked backside. He didn't mind going to hell, and disgracing himself and his parents and his House and The School, if only he could go to hell in his own way. That's what they couldn't stand – the obstinate, passive refusal to accept their prejudices, to conform to their minor-gentry, kicked-backside-of-the-Empire code. They worried him, they bullied him, they frightened him . . . but they didn't get him. (61)

Via sulking, George breaks free of paternalistic standards in a manner that Etta Morison can only dream of. He also refutes a "manly" engagement in textbook intellection and a coarse approach to intimacy: while his friends engage in what the narrator generalizes as "Smut" George is inflamed by poetry; his teachers dismiss him as "dull-minded as well as obstinate and unmanly" – he is feminized by his docile, passive protest, by his bid to create his own aesthetics that includes tradition, avant-gardism, and by his ready embrace of sentiment (60). The leap from childish sulker to feminine lover of sentiment is not hard to comprehend: as Jerome McGann points out, any display of sentimentality is associated with women, idiots, and children, or "creatures who 'think' through their feelings" (13). George is, in short, the ideal sulker: one who can tenaciously manage any number of disparate affective states, desires, and aesthetic and political aims, whilst remaining estranged from, but determinedly proximate to, the world around him.

Like Hall's Gian-Luca, George Winterbourne ultimately dies in a manner that suggests suicide, but where *Adam's Breed* is ultimately a conventional, if oddly melodramatic, account of a sulky boy seeking parental love and religious fulfillment, Aldington's *Death of a Hero* only occasionally forays into a veneration of traditional paternalistic norms. Aldington's descriptions of men on the front are not shy of nostalgically honoring the masculine heroism of war, but the novel nevertheless centers on a protagonist whose behavior is not one-sidedly heroic, but synthesizes foolishness and reason, skepticism and sentiment, emotional distance and unabashed longing. George is conscious of the power of his sullen obstinacy and the requisite passivity it involves. He pursues what Merleau-Ponty defines as an adult form of sympathy, which is one that, unlike childish sympathy, does not blend self and other in a total affective situation, but instead, maintains "the differences between myself and the other," even as it brings together traits typically divided along masculine and feminine lines ("Child's" 120). If sulking involves risk, George has undertaken some methodical calculations: courtesy of an adolescence spent sulking, "they didn't get him." But generally speaking, sulkers do not want to remain aloof for years on end; most sulkers trust or hope that someone nearby will soothe their perceived wound. This very risk means that the innumerable petulant patriarchs of modernist literature are often unwittingly laughable figures. But while we might laugh at these figures, we can perhaps extend the terms of George's passive protest to their behavior, and interpret it as a refreshingly public display of susceptibility. For grown men, sulking is a chance to shuck one's guise of impenetrability, to allow one's self to be visibly weak. Their sulks – like the tentative petulance of Hall's Stephen Gordon and Joan Osborne, and Aldington's Etta Morison – are forays into an inversion of outdated gender roles, a response to power imbalances that have unduly affected men and women alike. By extension, in portraying absurdly childish avant-garde artists who sulk when misunderstood, Aldington uncovers the emotional vulnerability at the very sensitive heart of so-called modernist avant-garde "impersonality" with its demand for newness and aggressive rejection of what came before. According to Marjorie Perloff, the modernist confrontation with the past was prematurely cut off by global catastrophes – World War I, the Great Depression, World War II. Indeed, Perloff describes modernism as an "embryonic phase" which we are still struggling to understand (3). Writing in 1960, Merleau-Ponty foresees Perloff's assessment of the enormity and destructiveness of the changes that have taken place in the wake of World War II; in a discussion about engaging in phenomenology amidst the ruins of conventional beliefs in democracy, humanism, and heroism, Merleau-Ponty states: "In the din of demolitions, many sullen passions, many hypocrisies or follies, and many false dilemmas also disappear" (1964b, 23). While Merleau-Ponty considers this abandonment of tradition a sign of hope, his own work demonstrates how a return to those self-same "sullen passions" of old is arguably in order. For if modernists remain renowned for distancing techniques such as oblique, complex narration, and the effacement of sentiment, then the numerous "childish" sulkers of modernist literature may well remind us of the very aesthetic and theoretical infancy of which they are a part, and perhaps, expose the emotional vulnerability so scarcely repressed by modernist iconoclasm.

Notes

1   Lily Briscoe and Mr. Bankes share a private joke of calling each Ramsay child after the kings and queens of England; while Bankes gives James the nickname "James the Ruthless," for Lily, James is "(certainly the Sullen)" (32; 201).

2   Sandra M. Gilbert holds up Aldington's most famous text, *Death of a Hero*, as an example of a widespread backlash against women's independence following World War I, which was rooted in the fear that the war was "a festival of female misrule" in men's absence (437). According to Gilbert, "Aldington is explicit about what he sees as the grotesque sexual permission the war has given . . . women" (438). I feel Gilbert's analysis is too narrow: Aldington reveals a considered awareness of and sensitivity toward the constraints of femininity and masculinity in this text and elsewhere, as this chapter will discuss.

3   In "The Painter of Modern Life" (1863), Baudelaire proclaims that genius is childhood recovered at will, because: "The child sees everything in a state of newness; he is always drunk" (8).

4 An example of this association arises in a lecture entitled "Exploring the World of Perception: Space" where Merleau-Ponty writes:

> It has often been said that modern artists and thinkers are difficult. Picasso is harder to understand, indeed to love, than Poussin or Chardin; the same is said of Giradoux or Malraux, as opposed to Marivaux or Stendhal.... If modern thought is difficult and runs counter to common sense, this is because it is concerned with truth; experience no longer allows it to settle for the clear and straightforward notions which common sense cherishes because they bring peace of mind. (*World of Perception* 49)

5 Heidegger's phenomenological approach is predicated upon a return to the overlooked concept of "Being" as distinct from human beings; "Being" he labels Dasein, a term referring to existence as an entity unto itself. This distinction Heidegger labels "the ontological difference"; his key work, *Being and Time*, is dedicated to an articulation or uncovering of Dasein. For Heidegger, one of the fundamental qualities of Dasein is attunement, or mood. Moods, Heidegger writes, make us aware of Dasein; a bad mood, for instance, can make us feel existence as a burden. Although noting that moods have been a subject of philosophical inquiry since antiquity, Heidegger believes that that inquiry has scarcely improved upon the work of Aristotle. "On the contrary," he writes, "the affects and feelings fall thematically under the psychic phenomena, functioning as a third class of these" (*Being and Time* 131). For Heidegger, phenomenology should be credited with creating a freer view of affectivity.

6 Milly's success wrought by petulance does not last long: she dies of consumption before completing her studies. That said, in Joan's recollection in later years, Milly continues to be defined by her propensity to sulk; she had, Joan thinks, "golden hair that was inclined to curl naturally, rather a sulky mouth at times, and a short straight nose" (280).

7 While Etta's concerns are treated seriously by Aldington's narrator, other female sulkers in his texts do not receive sympathy. The opening sentence of *The Colonel's Daughter* (1931) reads: "Georgina Smithers, daughter and only surviving child of Lt.-Col. Frederic Smithers and Alvina his wife, was in a pet" (3). Part of a deteriorating gentry with neither the money nor the motivation to secure Georgina a good future, petulant Georgina's initial strop is based on having to run yet another errand for her mother. Georgina is bored and boring; she is also mannish in feature and bullish behavior. In Aldington's *All Men are Enemies* (1934a), Antony Clarendon is in an unhappy marriage with a woman who frequently uses sulky behavior in a bid to control him; as he does not love or empathize with her, she is unsuccessful. That said, Tony admires her indifference and self-control; again, she is a sulking woman with masculine traits (173).

8 The following is an example of how Merleau-Ponty argues on behalf of an emotive understanding of others reliant upon the self: "I perceive the grief or the anger of the other in his conduct, in his face or hands, without recourse to any 'inner' experience of suffering or anger, and because grief and anger are variations of belonging to the world, and equally applicable to the other's conduct, visible in his phenomenal body, as in my own conduct as it is presented to me" (*Signs* 415).

9 In *Ugly Feelings*, Sian Ngai argues that disgust keeps the boundary between subject and object wholly alive, unlike most other forms of negative affect. By contrast, in *The Cultural Politics of Emotion*, Sara Ahmed suggests that disgust blurs the boundaries between subject and object; for Ahmed, disgust is something repulsive that fills up or

overtakes the disgusted self, who then struggles to eject or reject the disgusting. These contrary views – disgust divides, disgust conflates – are in fact central to the way disgust works, which is to say that disgust relies on a simultaneous proximity and a longing to get away from, even destroy, that which disgusts us. Similarly, it is this combined need for proximity and repulsion that is so characteristic of sulking.

10 As Ellmann writes, Eliot's groundbreaking "Tradition and the Individual Talent" advances through a series of paradoxes whereby the poet, "must . . . be both conscious and unconscious, and though he must 'have emotions', he must also know what it means to escape them" (36).

11 Aldington's critique of a poetics of impersonality recurs in his short story entitled "Stepping Heavenward" (1932) where Jeremy Cibber appears as a thinly disguised parody of Eliot: he is an American intellectual, an Anglophile mentored by a historian whose work is much better known than his own (i.e., Pound), has a relationship with a woman whom he drives to neurasthenia, takes up a professorship at Oxford, becomes the standard by which culture is measured, and then converts to Catholicism; throughout, his work is derided as empty, his reputation as groundless. Like any good avant-gardist, Cibber "always create[s] by destruction" and equates genius with impersonality: "This, as we now know from Cibber and his followers, is the mark of true greatness – to restrain not only the outward expression of emotion but emotion itself, until nothing remains but the pure intellect and the pure spirit of contemplation" (213–214).

References

Ahmed, Sara. (2004). *The Cultural Politics of Emotion*. Edinburgh: Edinburgh University Press.

Aldington, Richard. (1934a). *All Men are Enemies*. Hamburg: The Albatross.

Aldington, Richard. (1934b). *Women Must Work*. New York: Doubleday, Doran & Company, Inc.

Aldington, Richard. (1949). "Stepping Heavenward: A Record." In *Soft Answers* (pp. 198–248). Harmondsworth: Penguin.

Aldington, Richard. (1986). *The Colonel's Daughter*. London: Hogarth Press.

Aldington, Richard. (1998). *Death of a Hero*. Ottawa: The Golden Dog Press.

Baudelaire, Charles. (2008). "The Painter of Modern Life." In *The Painter of Modern Life and Other Essays*, trans. Jonathan Mayne (pp. 1–41). London: Phaidon Press.

Darwin, Charles. (2009). *The Expression of the Emotions in Man and Animals*. London: Penguin.

Eliot, George. (1994). *Middlemarch*. London: Penguin.

Eliot, T. S. (2010). "Tradition and the Individual Talent." In *The Norton Anthology of Theory and Criticism*, ed. Vincent Leitch (pp. 955–960). New York: W. W. Norton.

Ellmann, Maud. (1987). *The Poetics of Impersonality: T.S. Eliot and Ezra Pound*. Cambridge, MA: Harvard University Press.

Gilbert, Sandra M. (1983). "Soldier's Heart: Literary Men, Literary Women, and the Great War." *Signs* 8: 422–450.

Hall, Radclyffe. (1981). *The Unlit Lamp*. London: Virago Press.

Hall, Radclyffe. (1982). *The Well of Loneliness*. London: Virago Press.

Hall, Radclyffe. (1985). *Adam's Breed*. London: Virago Press.

Heidegger, Martin. (1996). *Being and Time*, trans. Joan Stambaugh. Albany, NY: SUNY Press.

Joyce, James. (1993). *Ulysses*. New York: Vintage Books.

Kipling, Rudyard. (1996). "The White Man's Burden." In *Rudyard Kipling: The Complete Verse* (pp. 261–262). London: Kyle Cathie Ltd.

Lewis, Wyndham. (1968). *Tarr*. London: Calder and Boyars.

Loy, Mina. (2011). "The Sacred Prostitute." In *Stories and Essays of Mina Loy*, ed. Sara Crangle (pp. 188–218). Champaign, IL: Dalkey Archive Press.

McGann, Jerome. (1996). *The Poetics of Sensibility: A Revolution in Literary Style*. Oxford: Clarendon Press.

Merleau-Ponty, Maurice. (1964a [1960]). "The Child's Relation with Others," trans. William Cobb. In *The Primacy of Perception*. Evanston, IL: Northwestern University Press.

Merleau-Ponty, Maurice. (1964b [1960]). *Signs*, trans. Richard C. McCleary.

Evanston, IL: Northwestern University Press.

Merleau-Ponty, Maurice. (2002). *Phenomenology of Perception*, trans. Colin Smith. Abingdon: Routledge.

Merleau-Ponty, Maurice. (2004). *The World of Perception*, trans. Oliver Davis. Abingdon: Routledge.

Ngai, Sian. (2005). *Ugly Feelings*. Cambridge, MA: Harvard University Press.

Perloff, Marjorie. (2002). *21st-Century Modernism: The 'New' Poetics*. Oxford: Blackwell.

Steedman, Carolyn. (1998). *Strange Dislocations: Childhood and the Idea of Human Interiority*. Cambridge, MA: Harvard University Press.

Woolf, Virginia. (1972). *Between the Acts*. Harmondsworth: Penguin.

Woolf, Virginia. (1992). *To the Lighthouse*. Oxford: Oxford University Press.

Further Reading

Crangle, Sara. (2010). *Prosaic Desires: Modernist Knowledge, Boredom, Laughter, and Anticipation*. Edinburgh: Edinburgh University Press. Informed by the phenomenological tradition and the work of Emmanuel Levinas in particular, this monograph explores everyday longings – the desire to laugh or waiting – as they emerge in the literatures of Joyce, Woolf, Stein, and Beckett.

Ellmann, Maud. (1987). *The Poetics of Impersonality: T.S. Eliot and Ezra Pound*. Cambridge, MA: Harvard University Press. A canonical critical work, Ellmann's book uncovers the importance of and paradoxes at the heart of so-called "modernist impersonality."

Glendinning, Simon. (2007). *In the Name of Phenomenology*. London: Routledge. This book is an excellent overview of phenomenology and Merleau-Ponty, wherein Glendinning emphasizes the relationship between modernist literature and phenomenology.

Goldie, Peter, ed. (2010). *The Oxford Handbook of Philosophy of Emotion*. Oxford: Oxford University Press. An extensive compilation offering chapters on phenomenology and emotion, as well as a lengthy section dedicated to the relationship between affect and aesthetics.

Lewis, Michael and Tanja Staehler. (2010). *Phenomenology: An Introduction*. London: Continuum. This book is a useful discussion of the basic precepts of phenomenology and of Merleau-Ponty's antecedents and direct influences – Nietzsche, Husserl, Heidegger, and Sartre among them.

McGann, Jerome. (1996). *The Poetics of Sensibility: A Revolution in Literary Style*. Oxford: Clarendon Press. An apt interrogation of the legacy of Romantic sentimentality; here McGann argues that the rejection of so-called sentimental styles defined and constrained the high modernist canon.

20

Queer Modernism

Benjamin Kahan

What would it mean to ask, "could World War I have been fought because of homosexuality?" Such a question is startling in part because of its seeming absurdity. If answered affirmatively, however, this question would not only unthread the familiar narrative of the war beginning with the assassination of the Archduke of Austria, Franz Ferdinand, by the Black Hand, but would install sexuality at the heart of one of the most privileged sites of literary modernism.[1] Such reconsiderations through the prism of sexuality are emblematic of queer theory and enable us to see historical events and literary texts in a new light. The Eulenberg Affair (1907–1909), which involved a mass of accusations of homosexuality and accompanying libel suits among high-ranking officials and friends of Kaiser Wilhelm II, is central to such a claim. As the historian James Steakley has argued:

> French, British, and American historians have linked the events of 1907–1909 to a far-reaching shift in German policy that heightened military aggressiveness and ultimately contributed to the outbreak of World War I. Such insights were by no means unknown to earlier observers. Writing in 1933, for example, Magnus Hirschfeld argued that the outcome of the entire regrettable affair was "no more and no less than victory for the tendency that ultimately issued in the events of the World War." (235)

Steakley contends that the international embarrassment of charges of homosexuality and effeminacy led to a more bellicose posturing on Germany's part. Further, the perceived paralysis of a government in scandal, one shedding key cabinet members, might have incited anti-German forces to take advantage of Germany's weakness. Steakley's analysis exemplifies what Susan Lanser calls the flip of "the scholarly coin from the *history of sexuality* to the *sexuality of history*: from the premise that sexuality is historically constructed to the claim that history is also sexually constructed and that the large movements of societies and cultures can be read as and through

A Handbook of Modernism Studies, First Edition. Edited by Jean-Michel Rabaté.
© 2013 John Wiley & Sons, Ltd. Published 2013 by John Wiley & Sons, Ltd.

sexuality" (72). This essay strives to display both sides of Lanser's coin simultaneously, tracing the tremendous upheaval and reorganization of sexual categories and
the sexual grammars which compose the language of modernism in all its queerness.

In the first half of this essay, I map three major discourses which provide the
constitutive possibility for the emergence of queer modernism: German sexology,
French Decadent writing, and the English scandals of Oscar Wilde and Radclyffe Hall.
All of these discourses are both literary and extraliterary; they are simultaneously
rooted in national traditions and resonate with international significance. In the
second half of this essay, I move from the work of creating a genealogy of queer
modernism to outlining its formal features and defining characteristics. As a
working definition, we might say provisionally that "queer modernism" delineates
the sexually transgressive and gender deviant energies that help fuel modernism's
desire to thwart normative aesthetics, knowledges, geographies, and temporalities.

The Grammars of Queer Modernism I: Sexology

Sexology is the academic discipline which aimed to classify sexual deviance. This
new sexual science helped judges and other members of the legal establishment to
negotiate sexual deviance and to shift sex away from the sphere of religious moral
judgment. As Michel Foucault has famously argued, sexology is the discourse which,
more than any other, is responsible for the creation of the new sexual subjectivities
with which queer modernism is associated:

> The nineteenth-century homosexual became a personage, a past, a case history, and a
> childhood, in addition to being a type of life, a life form, and a morphology, with an
> indiscreet anatomy and possibly a mysterious physiology .... Homosexuality appeared
> as one of the forms of sexuality when it was transposed from the practice of sodomy
> onto a kind of interior androgyny, a hermaphrodism of the soul. The sodomite had
> been a temporary aberration; the homosexual was now a species. (43)

By dating the transformation of the meaning of the act of sodomy into an
identarian practice to Carl Westphal's sexological essay "Contrary Sexual Feeling"
(1870), Foucault implicitly gestures toward the historical simultaneity of the advent
of modernism and the invention of homosexuality. This simultaneity is not as
coincidental as it might first appear, since sexology's literary roots run deep.

While sexology is generally understood to stand at the intersection of such varied
disciplines as medicine, psychiatry, anthropology, forensics, and legal studies, many
of its earliest practitioners were themselves poets and novelists. Inspired by the
sexual frankness of Walt Whitman's modernist verse, Edward Carpenter wrote his
own Whitman-esque celebrations of same-sex love in *Towards Democracy* (1902):

> The love of men for each other – so tender, heroic, constant;
>   That has come all down the ages in every clime, in every nation ....
>   The love of women for each other – so rapt, intense, so confiding-close, so burning
> passionate .... (322)

Additionally, his sexological writings drew heavily from Whitman's example; in *The Intermediate Sex* (1908) he praises Whitman as "the inaugurator . . . of a new world of democratic ideals and literature" (Carpenter 1984, 217). Similarly, John Addington Symonds wrote both poetry and the important privately printed sexological text *A Problem in Greek Ethics* (1883). Likewise, Edward Prime-Stevenson privately printed the novel *Imre: A Memorandum* (1908) whose conclusion features two men living together, and also authored the sexological treatise *The Intersexes: A History of Simisexualism as a Problem in Social Life* (1908). Even sexologists who did not write in distinctly literary genres often drew much of their source material and case studies from literature. For example, the massively influential sexologist Krafft-Ebing coined the term "masochism" from the writings of the Austrian writer Sacher-Masoch and the word "sadism" from the Marquis de Sade. Additionally, modernist writing often featured sexologists as characters. Henry James's "The Author of *Beltraffio*" depicts John Addington Symonds's uneasy marriage and Djuna Barnes's *Nightwood* (1936) similarly features a doctor influenced by sexology.

This revolving door between literature and sexology suggests that we should understand modernist literary works as what Stephanie Foote calls, in another context, "vernacular sexology" by which she means works which contest, define, and articulate sexual subjectivity in relation to medical sexology proper.[2] André Gide's *Corydon* (1911) calls the works of "Moll, Krafft-Ebing, and Rafflovitch" unsatisfactory, "reek[ing] unbearably of the clinic" (8, 22). The text's eponymous defender of the naturalness of homosexuality instead proposes to write the history of "normal homosexuals" (23). Likewise, Ralph Werther's *Autobiography of an Androgyne* (1918) uses his life experiences to supplement, corroborate, and dispute the findings of sexologists (40).

Even outside the confines of the West, sexology provided a vocabulary for same-sex eroticism and helped to forge a geoculture of sexuality. For example, in "The story of a certain alleyway" (1924), the Japanese avant-garde writer Taruho describes the usage of the word *kurafuto-ebing-teki* (Krafft-Ebing-ish):

> I, who ordinarily went out of my way not to pay any attention to girls, and a few of my friends who were in the know, used this strange adjective as part of our secret language. We had coined it from the proper name on the blue cover of a certain book we had managed to get our hands on somewhere. For instance, we would use it as an adjective to refer to the special feeling produced by the gaze of an adolescent boy, the glimpse of a red sweater peeking out the sleeve of his jacket, or perhaps even the boy's entire appearance. Still, one other condition for its use is that we would use it in ways that did fail to take account of the circumstantial, scenic, unfortunate, or even criminal quality of what we were trying to describe. (Angles 2011, 222)

While Taruho's relish of "the special feeling produced by the gaze of an adolescent boy" might be positioned in a long history of the celebration of homoeroticism in Japanese literature, this celebratory positioning is here placed in a dialectic with a more negative Western affect, that of the "unfortunate" and "criminal quality" of the feeling.

The Grammars of Queer Modernism II: Decadence

In his essay on Baudelaire, Walter Benjamin writes, "The lesbian is the heroine of *la modernité*" (56). By making such a claim, Benjamin draws our attention to the capacious French literary tradition which locates lesbianism at its center, a tradition which encompasses at least: Laclos's *Dangerous Liaisons* (1782), Diderot's *The Nun* (1796), many works of de Sade, Gautier's *Mademoiselle de Maupin* (1835), Balzac's *The Girl with the Golden Eyes* (1835), Baudelaire's *Flowers of Evil* (1857), Verlaine's *Scenes of Sapphic Love* (1867), Zola's *Nana* (1880), Maupassant's "Paul's Mistress" (1881), Rachilde's *Monsieur Venus* (1884), Catulle Mendès's *Méphistophéla* (1890), and Pierre Louÿs's *Chansons de Bilitis* (1894). While Terry Castle nominates this tradition "a largely masculine and potboiling enterprise" (12) and Elizabeth Ladenson (1999) attributes it to a "prurient male literary imagination," I see the figure of the lesbian raising important questions about the philosophy of modernity (as the figures of the New Negro and the New Woman will come to do in later historical periods) (3).

Certainly the pornographic element of this tradition cannot be ignored since these lesbian texts' delight in sexual pleasure exemplifies the tenets of philosophical libertinism. I follow Peter Cryle and Lisa O'Connell in seeing libertinage not just as "the free operation of sexual desire against or in delicate negotiation with conventional moral, religious, and civil codes," but also encompassing "the vernacular, dissident freedoms of everyday life" (2). But why does this novelistic tradition represent lesbianism as the sexual dissidence *par excellence* rather than adultery, incest, or other transgression?

One answer to this question emerges in the Preface of *Mademoiselle de Maupin*. In this withering attack on utilitarian understandings of art, Théophile Gautier articulates an aesthetics of "art for art's sake" which will underwrite so much of Decadent literature for the remainder of the century:

> You cannot make a cotton bonnet out of metonymy and you cannot put on a comparison as you do a slipper; you cannot use an antithesis like an umbrella; you could not, more's the pity, wrap a few multicoloured rhymes round middle way of a waistcoat. (20)

That this Preface precedes a book which centrally figures lesbianism is of the utmost importance. Benjamin suggests that "the image of the lesbian" is bound up for Baudelaire in the "change in feminine habitus" in which "women were for the first time used in large numbers in the production process outside the home" (58). Taking Benjamin's hint, we might understand the lesbian as a particularly important figure for nineteenth-century French literature because she embodies all the metaphorical reproductivity associated with women, but such reproduction is "impossible," to borrow a phrase which Gautier frequently uses throughout his novel to describe lesbian sex acts. Reproduction is the binary opposite of sodomy (the statute under which lesbianism was prosecuted in France) because sodomy encompasses the full range of non-reproductive sex acts. The lesbian as a figure capable of reproduction, but embodying non-reproductivity, accentuates the non-Utilitarian basis of art for art's sake. The lesbian is an aesthetic and philosophical aspiration as much as she is a sexual figure.

Decadent writing expands and reconfigures the institution of literature to encompass same-sex desire and pleasure. This is obviously not to claim that there are no literary representations of homosexuality prior to this period of French writing. Rather, I am contending that this literary tradition locates representations of homosexuality at its center, positioning queerness at the heart of modern life. What Susan Lanser calls "alteration plots," in which characters change sex, enable an already expanded institution of literature (which contains lesbianism) to also encompass male homosexuality (79). In *Mademoiselle de Maupin*, for example, d'Albert confesses to his friend Silvio – "I am in love with a man!" (166). Because the narrator has already hinted that the "man" he is in love with is the disguised Mademoiselle de Maupin, the threat of homosexuality is diffused. This positive and inoculated representation of homosexuality is crucial to the insurrections of queer literary modernism.

The Grammars of Queer Modernism III: The Wilde and Hall Trials

The trials of Oscar Wilde caused an international sensation and have generally been understood to effect an enormous transformation in the general legibility of homosexuality. According to Ralph Werther, "Oscar Wilde" was a "household" name in America: "[e]ven every child of the village was as familiar with that name as with that of the man next door" (202). Despite his status as one of the earliest known transgender activists, Werther condemned Wilde as "deserv[ing] his fall . . . not because he was a pederast, but because he flaunted his pederasty before the world" (205). This "fall" took the form of three trials in 1895. In the first, he sued Lord Queensberry for libel, when Queensberry left his calling card, inscribing it "For Oscar Wilde, posing somdomite [sic]" (Holland, xi). Defending himself, Queensberry hired detectives and gathered damaging evidence against Wilde, causing Wilde to drop his prosecution. Wilde's friends urged him to flee to France, but he remained in England, leading to his arrest on charges of sodomy and gross indecency. In the second trial, the state prosecuted Wilde for gross indecency, but the evidence against him was inconclusive. In the third, he was found guilty of gross indecency and sentenced to two years of hard labor.

In his path-breaking *Nameless Offences* (2003), H. G. Cocks argues that we must understand Wilde's prosecution as less anomalous and transformative than previously thought. Cocks suggests that rather than understanding the relationship between the law and homosexuality as "episodic, spectacular, and sensational," we ought to see it as "sustained, unspectacular . . . , everyday[,] and familiar" (6).

In other words, Cocks turns our attention away from headline-grabbing cases of homosexual prosecution. He contends that the Labouchère amendment outlawing gross indecency (under which Wilde was prosecuted) did not change the law or policing practices dramatically, did not increase the number of arrests for homosexuality, and did not emerge in relation to a homosexual panic. For Cocks, what is new about blockbuster homosexuality cases like the Dublin Castle affair, the Cleveland Street scandal, and the Wilde trials is the "new journalism." The new journalism referred to the evening papers with which it was associated as well as the investigative reporting and interest in the private lives of public men (135–139). These new journalistic techniques enabled the publication of much more explicit and salacious detail about famous individuals than had been circulated since the early nineteenth century.

While Cocks correctly asserts that the Wilde trial did not change police practice or the enforcement of the law, he underestimates the trials' force in generating an epistemological matrix for homosexual understanding. E. M. Forster's *Maurice*, for example, describes himself as "an unspeakable of the Oscar Wilde sort" (159) and Brian Howard and Harold Acton are described by a friend as looking "like a couple of Oscar Wildes" (Green, 115). The eponymous Paul in Willa Cather's "Paul's Case" (1906) wears a Wildean carnation. The description and negation of "nameless offences" is now replaced by an articulable epistemology, one which provided an essential condition for the establishment of a visible queer modernism.

The prosecution of Radclyffe Hall's *The Well of Loneliness* (1928) for obscene libel in the summer of 1928 had the analogous effect for lesbianism as Wilde's trial had for homosexuality – it did not invent a language of lesbianism so much as crystalize an image of the lesbian. Hall's name, like Wilde's, became a byword for homosexuality: "Mrs. Arthur is a . . . is a . . . well, you know, Radclyffe" (Doan, 194). Similarly, a lesbian journalist, Evelyn Irons, describes unpleasantly getting called "Miss Radclyffe Hall, Miss" by truck drivers when she "wore a collar and tie" immediately after the novel's publication (Doan, 123). How did a novel in which the most explicit lesbian scene between two women is described as "and that night they were not divided" become so controversial and so iconic? (Hall, 313).

The answer is James Douglas. The trial began shortly after Douglas penned an editorial in the *Sunday Express* which sensationally claimed: "I would rather give a healthy boy or a healthy girl a phial of prussic acid than this novel. Poison kills the body, but moral poison kills the soul" (Doan, 1). Douglas had earlier written of James Joyce's *Ulysses* (1922) that it is "the most infamously obscene work in ancient or modern literature." He continued: "The obscenity of Rabelais is innocent compared with its leprous and scabrous horrors. All the secret sewers of vice are canalized in its flood of unimaginable thoughts, images and pornographic words" (Ladenson 2007, 98). Douglas's skill as a scandalmonger and sanctimony in relation to sexuality set him apart from the majority of his contemporaries who reviewed Hall's novel favorably. Leonard and Virginia Woolf, E. M. Forster, Lytton Strachey, and a host of other luminaries attempted to defend the book publicly without success (Hall's novel was not printed in England again until 1949) (124–125). Garnering the support of Sherwood Anderson, Theodore Dreiser, F. Scott Fitzgerald, Ernest Hemingway, and Upton Sinclair, the campaign to get Hall's novel published fared better in America, selling more than 100,000 copies there in 1929 alone (128).

The obscenity trial forged a picture of the lesbian in the image of Radclyffe Hall: "monocled, tuxedoed, hair cropped short, cigarette in hand" (Benstock, 173). At the beginning of the twentieth century, lesbianism was not as legible or as well understood as male homosexuality. In 1921, for example, when Lord Birkenhead opposed a bill that would have extended the Labouchère amendment to women (thereby criminalizing lesbianism for the first time), he asserts, "the overwhelming majority of the women of this country have never heard of this thing at all . . . . I would be bold enough to say that of every thousand women . . . 999 have never even heard a whisper of these practices" (Doan 2001, 56). In spite of Birkenhead's claims, Laura Doan has argued that since World War I, lesbianism was in the process of becoming increasingly visible. In 1920, for example, Hall sued St. George Lane Fox Pitt, a member of the Society for Psychical Research (SPR), for slandering her to two members of the SPR, alleging that he described her as "grossly immoral" (31–32). This case and several other high-profile trials, coupled with the new gender roles adopted by women during the war, suggest that lesbianism was a discreetly discussed topic before the obscenity trial of *The Well of Loneliness* (Doan, 24).

While I have been arguing that Wilde and Hall did not "out" homosexuality (discussions of homosexuality were occurring before the trials), it is also the case that these trials did not make homosexuality and lesbianism fully legible for the general populace and for queer men and women. That is, epistemological opacities and linguistic circumlocutions remained around homosexuality. For example, in the 1940s, the playwright Rodney Ackland and his partner Arthur Boys would walk down the street holding hands, hoping to shock those around them. One day Ackland boarded a bus alone and an elderly woman asked him, "And how is your poor dear blind friend" (Duff, 144). Similarly, a 1952 episode involving the military police records the illegibility of lesbianism. Spotting a woman performing oral sex on another, the officer "did not make a report because, as he admitted subsequently, 'I wouldn't know how'" (Canaday, 191). He faced the incident with shock and bewilderment. In spite and because of these opacities and knowledges, these three discourses – sexology, French Decadence, and the Wilde and Hall trials – were crucial to the aesthetics of queer modernism.

General Characteristics of Queer Modernism

Characteristic 1: Queer modernism imagines queerness to be utterly pervasive
This pervasiveness is forged in the scandalous visibility of decadence, the Wilde and Hall trials, and sexology. In his "Ode to Walt Whitman," Federico Garcia Lorca

catalogues the "[f]aggots of the world":

Fairies of North America,
Pájaros of Havana,
Jotos of Mexico,
Sarasas of Cádiz,
Apios of Seville,
Cancos of Madrid,
Floras of Alicante,
Adelaidas of Portugal.

While Lorca's series demonizes effeminate homosexuals in contrast to comradely and manly homosexuals that take Whitman as their model, his list also suggests the pervasiveness of homosexuality more generally. Similarly, Charles Henri Ford and Parker Tyler's novel *The Young and the Evil* (1933) imagines that "ninety-five percent of the world is just naturally queer" (159). Gertrude Stein's *The Making of Americans* (1925) asserts, "everything and everyone is sometime a little queer to me . . . . It does make me a little unhappy that every one sometime is a queer one to me" (482). Stein, and to a lesser extent Ford and Parker, trade on the ambiguity of the word "queer." For those who are not wise to, who are not schooled in, to borrow Eve Sedgwick's influential phrase, "the epistemology of the closet," the word "queer" would signify as merely "odd" or "unusual" rather than as a signifier of homosexual life (67).

Perhaps no figure has done more to establish the pervasiveness of sexuality than Sigmund Freud. Both Freud's vision and its many misconstruals, distortions, and perversions established sexuality as ubiquitous. In particular, Freud's theorization of the "unconscious" made it possible to place a host of non-conscious actions within a sexual frame. Moreover, Freud's frankness about sexual matters also helped to liberalize the boundaries of the speakable.

As George Chauncey's magisterial *Gay New York* (1994) has amply demonstrated, the visibility of queer life is not merely a literary or scientific phenomenon. In 1904, one New Yorker denounced "the shoals of painted, perfumed, Kohl-eyed, lisping, mincing youth that at night swarm on Broadway in the Tenderloin section, or haunt the parks and 5th avenue, ogling every man that passes" (179). The parks and streets were more difficult to regulate than commercial or residential spaces. Moreover, parks had the express purpose of aimless roaming, making them particularly apt spaces for cruising.

Even more visible than these open spaces, however, were the gay enclaves which emerged in Greenwich Village, Harlem, the Left Bank, and Weimar Berlin, to name just a few of the most famous examples. Newspapers carried accounts of Harlem's Hamilton Lodge Ball, more commonly known as "the Faggot's Ball" (257). Thousands of participants and spectators congregated for the biggest balls by the late 1920s and early 1930s. One headline from the period reads: "Fag Balls Exposed; 6,000 Crowd Huge Hall as Queer Men and Women Dance at 64th Annual

Masquerade" (310). Blair Niles's *Strange Brother* (1931), Charles Henri Ford and Parker Tyler's *The Young and Evil*, and Langston Hughes's *The Big Sea* (1940) all feature descriptions of drag balls. This was a queerness very much on display.

Characteristic 2: The queerness of queer modernism has as much to do with gender and sex as sexuality

One of the most remarkable and compelling of *Gay New York*'s claims is the degree to which Chauncey establishes that "gender status superseded homosexual interest as the basis of sexual classification in working-class culture" (87). In a telling anecdote, Chauncey recounts an Italian youth's encounter with a boxer whom he allows to anally penetrate him:

> To the boy's horror, the boxer promptly went to the gym and told everyone what he had done; the boy, humiliated, concluded he could never go there again.... The most striking aspect of the story is the confidence the boxer felt that reporting the encounter would not endanger his status among his friends, that, indeed, having sexually subordinated the boy would enhance it. If a man risked forfeiting his masculine status by being sexually passive, he could also establish it by playing the dominant role in an encounter with another man. Sexual penetration symbolized one man's power over another. (81)

As Chauncey makes clear, modernist sexual frameworks are not our own. That queerness adheres in particular gender styles as much as or more than in sexual acts is crucial to our understanding of queer modernism.

Virginia Woolf's *Orlando* (1929) exemplifies such queerness around questions of sex. While the eponymous character's sex change is often read as a fantastic event, as a translation of Vita Sackville-West's cross-dressing (on whom Orlando is modeled), or as an attempt to shroud the text's lesbian content to evade censorship, I read the change as activating what sexology might understand as a scientific and medical possibility. For example, in *Sexual Inversion* (1897), Havelock Ellis and John Addington Symonds raise the specter that women who vote are becoming increasing masculinized; they suggest that "[t]he modern movement of emancipation" is elevating "feminine criminality" and "feminine insanity" up to "the masculine standard" (177). Participating in what they perceive as the male practice of voting, women are literally stripped of sexual difference and become men. My reading runs counter to commentators like Adam Parkes, who read *Orlando* as anti-sexological and suggest that it "mocks all normative sex and gender codes, destabilizing the very grounds on which sexological as well as legal conventions were founded" (146). Orlando has been understood variously as lesbian, transgendered, androgynous, and, I would add, bisexual. I do not mean "bisexual" in the sense commonest now (an individual who is attracted to sexual objects of "both" sexes), but in the older sexological sense of "universal bisexuality" which does not see the sexes as "distinct, immutable, and opposite," but rather sees all people as "partly male and partly female" (Meyerowitz, 5, 15). For Ellis and Symonds, the act of a woman voting might activate the male part of bisexuality to effect a masculinization or even a sex change.

In Woolf's novel, the circumstances of Orlando's sexual transformation are notoriously hard to locate. Just before his change, the biographer-narrator complains that there is little "information to go upon" and that information is "lamentably incomplete" (119). What is known is that Orlando is engaged in "a most important part in the public life of his country" (119). If we are to imagine sex (in the sense of biological sexual difference) like Ellis and Symonds do, as profoundly situational and able to change in a given context (for example, through participation in the public sphere), then we might read Woolf's transformation of Orlando as a feminist transformation. Precisely at the moment that Orlando is participating "in the public life of his country," he becomes a woman, suggesting that women are more suited than men for such offices. This sexological reading might lead us to reconsider Judith Butler's famous claim in *Gender Trouble* (1990) that sex is a back-formation of gender, that gender literally creates sex. Butler revises this claim in *Bodies that Matter* (1993), suggesting that the materiality of the body places limits on the extent to which it can be constructed by gender. Ellis's sexological and Woolf's literary imaginings more closely accord with those in *Gender Trouble*; Orlando and sexology in general imagine a space where the body and sex (in the biological sense) are completely malleable.

Characteristic 3: Queer modernism is passed from hand to hand

In spite of queer modernism's visibility, the costs of detection could be very high. For this reason, many works of queer modernism were circulated as what Mark Mitchell and David Leavitt (1997) call "pages passed from hand to hand" (xvii). By this term, they mean that queer material was often circulated at great personal risk in manuscript, among a coterie of trusted friends and loved ones, or privately printed in small, often anonymous editions. As I mentioned earlier, *Imre*, *Corydon*, and *A Problem in Greek Ethics* were all privately printed. Written in 1913 and 1914, Forster's *Maurice* (1971) was only shown to trusted friends as a gesture of intimacy (Moffat, 15). Either out of timidity, fear, or shame, Forster did not want *Maurice* published in his lifetime, but agreed to let Christopher Isherwood publish it posthumously. In preparation for this eventuality, the typescript was carried by hand by a network of confidants (all "gay" men) from Cambridge to London to New York to Chicago to Los Angeles in 1952 (17). Similarly, the Egyptian-born Greek-language poet, C. P. Cavafy, distrusted the mail system and often sent his small but important corpus of poems via a friend or chain of friends. The complexity of Cavafy's "publication" system is Dickinsonian in its range – he published a small number of poems in periodicals, produced booklets and broadsides for circulation among friends, gathered poems in folders in his "bindery," and kept many poems unpublished, sometimes showing them to his friends or objects of his desire.[2] Auden privately published his *Poems* (1928) on his friend Stephen Spender's small hand-press before publishing a revised version of it in 1930 with Faber and Faber (Bozorth, 32). In 1889, Wilde left a package with Charles Hirsch at his bookstore with the understanding that the parcel would be given to a friend who would show Wilde's card to Hirsch. A young man came and picked up the package, and brought it back several days later for another man. Three exchanges took place and the anonymous and multi-authored *Teleny* (1893) (part of which is believed to be written by Wilde) was created (Mitchell and Leavitt xv–xvi).

These systems of hand delivery were designed to limit exposure. The risks of revelation, even among friends and family, are evident in Alice B. Toklas's "discovery" of her lover and partner Gertrude Stein's *Q.E.D* in 1932. This early and, at the time, unpublished work of Stein's chronicles her relationship in a love triangle with May Bookstaver. As Ulla Dydo has brilliantly argued, Toklas understood the novel and the relationship it described as a betrayal. Toklas objected in particular to Stein's use of the words "may," "May," "many," and "maybe" (a play on May B.) in "Stanzas in Meditation" (1956) and throughout much of the rest of Stein's career. She understood these signifiers to forge a lesbian language or to use language as a queer conduit to reference May (Dydo 488–525).

While the movement from hand to hand describes an important literary sociology for the dissemination of queer modernist texts, it also describes a crucial ontology of queerness. Famous homosexual figures like Wilde and Whitman provided not just a new language for homosexuality, but were imagined to disseminate queerness to their modernist "descendants." For example, the touch of George Merrill (the lover of Edward Carpenter who had been Whitman's lover) opened "a creative spring" in Forster located "just above the buttocks" (Moffat, 113). Describing the touch, Forster writes: "It was as much psychological as physical. It seemed to go straight through the small of my back into my ideas, without involving my thoughts" (113–114). This touch inspired *Maurice*. Gavin Arthur, too, links himself to Whitman through Carpenter, and Allen Ginsberg would do the same by sleeping with Arthur (Murray 2005). Similarly, the young Samuel Steward describes the prospect of going to bed with Wilde's lover Lord Alfred Douglas as "terrifying, even repulsive," but sets out to accomplish it because, he says, "I wanted to link myself to Oscar Wilde more directly than I was linked to Whitman [through the novelist and poet Hamlin Garland, who had touched me], there was no other way" (Spring, 44–45). In these examples, sexual exchange itself becomes a mode of historiography or contact with the past.

Characteristic 4: Queer modernism is in perpetual motion

The illegality of homosexuality inspires an aesthetic, if not a practice, of movement to evade the law's reach. Describing *Nightwood*'s "wayward plot," Dana Seitler writes: "Although the world of Parisian nightlife, well known in the 1930s for its lesbian milieu, is a primary locale in *Nightwood*, its characters are nonetheless perpetually dislocated as they engage in a frenzied peripatetic mode determined by Robin's sexual adventures. Robin's marriage to Felix Volkbein lands her in Vienna; her love affair with Nora Flood leads her through Paris and the United States, then on a brief European tour; and her affair with Jenny Pretherbridge takes her back to Paris and then to the United States again . . . ." (Seitler, 123, 118). As Seitler's description makes clear, movement itself becomes the plot of the novel, giving it a feeling of plotlessness. *The Young and the Evil* similarly embodies this aesthetic, one in which, as Joseph Boone (1998) puts it, "*everything* is in transit: bodies, identities, desires"

(258). Claude McKay's *Banjo: A Story without a Plot* (1929) also takes movement as its plot, featuring an itinerant cast of vagrants, migrant seamen, former prisoners, musicians, and criminals:

> They were all on the beach, and there were many others besides them – white men, brown men, black men, Finns, Poles, Italians, Slavs, Maltese, Indians, Negroids, African Negroes, West Indian Negroes – deportees from America for violation of the United States immigration laws – afraid and ashamed to go back to their own lands, all dumped down in the great Provençal port, bumming a day's work, a meal, a drink, existing from hand to mouth, anyhow any way, between box car, tramp ship, bistro, and bordel. (6)

This motley crew derives it queerness not merely from the novel's final sentences in which Banjo tells his friend to abandon women ("Don't get soft ovah any one wimmens") and to set out with him ("Wese got enough between us to beat it a long ways from here"), but also through the novel's incessant movement. As Margot Canaday argues in *The Straight State* (2009), sodomy is associated with vagrancy, unattached persons, floaters, hoboes, and others on the move because "men who were not self-governing in their sexual practices could not be self-governing in their labor" (41). She argues that the "inchoate opposition between mobility and settlement evolved into an explicit differentiation between homosexuals and heterosexuals" (15). These novels eroticize movement, forging it as an aesthetic of queerness. This is nowhere clearer than in the term "wanderlust" in which movement is literally connected to unrestrained sexuality (98–99).

Another reason for plotlessness as a formal structure of queer modernism is suggested by Charles Warren Stoddard's *For the Pleasure of His Company: A Tale of the Misty City, Thrice Told* (1903). In a meta-moment in the novel, two characters discuss what sort of novel they will write. One character asserts, "we shall be obliged to put love into it; love with a very large L" (104). Another character ventriloquizing Stoddard's position and describing the structure of his novel counters, "Why can't I tell you the story of one fellow – of myself for example; how one day I met this person, and the next day I met that person, and next week some one else comes on to the stage, and struts his little hour and departs" (104). As Christopher Looby points outs, the form of Stoddard's narrative queers the marriage plot. With Looby's observation in mind, we might understand queer modernism's characteristic plotlessness as a way out of the compulsory heterosexuality of the novel, instead replacing coupledom with openness and seriality (Stoddard's narrative is "Thrice Told") (Looby 414–436).

If the fugitive pace of queer modernism provides one strategy to avoid detection, hiding provides another modality for escaping exposure. Claustrophilia characterizes the second half of Marcel Proust's life in which he scarcely left his bedroom (Fuss 5).This stasis is explicitly thematized in his queer epic *In Search of Lost Time* (1927). The narrator describes his great-aunt Léonie who after her husband's death "declined to leave, first Combray, then her house in Combray, then her bedroom, and finally her bed" (61). Even in this confinement, Léonie is constantly in motion – engaging "in an unceasing monologue which was her sole form of activity" – and metaphorically as well as literally restless ("for 'never sleeping a wink' was her great claim") (63).

In this essay, I have sought to account for the conjunction of queerness and modernism, marking what Heather Love calls "the pervasiveness of nonnormative desires in the making of the modern" (744). Queerness is certainly not the only marker of modernity. Michael North's *Dialect of Modernism* (1994), for example, traces a genealogy of "becoming modern by acting black" (8). For white moderns, North contends, the New Negro was the very essence of the modern. Similarly, Jennifer Fleissner sees woman as the exemplum of modernity, "embody[ing] the most salient feature of a post-Darwinian, technologized modernity" (5). Love further suggests that "queer modernism" is "particularly likely to merge into modernism proper" (744). Rather than attempt to adjudicate between these signifiers of the modern (in order to privilege one over the other), this essay has focused on one such signifier – queerness – in order to draw attention to the ways in which all of these modern categories – the New Negro, the New Woman, the queer – produce what David Halperin calls new "apparatus[es] for constituting human subjectivities" (88). Whether in Forster's dedication of *Maurice* "to a happier year" or in José Garcia Villa's anticipation of his "queer songs" which "will be queerer still," queer modernism strives to forge new varieties of sexual personhood and of being (Ponce 59).

Notes

1   While literary scholars are used to reading the queerness of the poetry of Wilfred Owen and Siegfried Sassoon, the Great War itself is not often thought of as a site of homosexuality.
2   For a much fuller discussion of Cavafy's "publication" practices, see Robert Liddell.

References

Angles, Jeffrey. (2011). *Writing the Love of Boys: Origins of the Bishōnen Culture in Modernist Japanese Literature*. Minneapolis: University of Minnesota Press.

Benjamin, Walter. (2003). "The Paris of the Second Empire in Baudelaire." In *Selected Writings*, Vol. 4, ed. Howard Eiland and Michael W. Jennings, trans. Edmund Jephcott Cambridge, MA: The Belknap Press of Harvard University Press.

Benstock, Shari. (1987). *Women of the Left Bank*. Austin: University of Texas Press.

Boone, Joseph Allen. (1998). *Libidinal Currents: Sexuality and the Shaping of Modernism*. Chicago: The University of Chicago Press.

Bozorth, Richard R. (2001). *Auden's Games of Knowledge: Poetry and the Meanings of Homosexuality*. New York: Columbia University Press.

Canaday, Margot. (2009). *The Straight State: Sexuality and Citizenship in Twentieth-Century America*. Princeton, NJ: Princeton University Press.

Carpenter, Edward. (1984). *Selected Writings*. Gay Modern Classics. New York: Heretic Books.

Carpenter, Edward. (1912). *Towards Democracy*. New York: Kessinger. Castle,

Terry. (2003). *The Literature of Lesbianism: A Historical Anthology from Ariosto to Stonewall*. New York: Columbia University Press.

Chauncey, George. (1994). *Gay New York: Gender, Urban Culture, and the Making of the Gay Male World, 1890–1940*. New York: Basic Books.

Cocks, H. G. (2003). *Nameless Offences: Homosexual Desire in the Nineteenth Century*. London: I. B. Tauris.

Cryle, Peter and Lisa O'Connell. (2004). "Sex, Liberty and License in the Eighteenth Century." In *Libertine Enlightenment: Sex, Liberty and License*. New York: Palgrave.

Doan, Laura. (2001). *Fashioning Sapphism: The Origins of a Modern English Lesbian Culture*. New York: Columbia University Press.

Duff, Charles. (1995). *The Lost Summer: The Heyday of the West End Theatre*. London: Nick Hern.

Dydo, Ulla E. and William Rice. (2003). *Gertrude Stein: The Language that Rises, 1923–1934*. Evanston, IL: Northwestern University Press.

Ellis, Havelock and John Addington Symonds. (2008). *Sexual Inversion: A Critical Edition*, ed. Ivan Crozier. New York: Palgrave Macmillan.

Fleissner, Jennifer L. (2004). *Women, Compulsion, Modernity: The Moment of American Naturalism*. Chicago: The University of Chicago Press.

Foote, Stephanie. (2006). "Afterword: Ann Aldrich and Lesbian Writing in the 1950s." In Ann Aldrich, *We Walk Alone* (pp. 157–183). New York: The Feminist Press at CUNY.

Ford, Charles Henri and Parker Tyler. (1996). *The Young and the Evil*. New York: Richard Kasak.

Forster, E. M. *Maurice: A Novel*. (1993). New York: W. W. Norton.

Foucault, Michel. (1990). *The History of Sexuality, Vol. I: An Introduction*, trans. Robert Hurley. New York: Vintage Books.

Fuss, Diana. (2004). *The Sense of an Interior: Four Writers and the Rooms that Shaped Them*. New York: Routledge.

Gautier, Théophile. (2005). *Mademoiselle de Maupin*, trans. Helen Constantine. London: Penguin.

Gide, André. (1977). *Corydon*, trans. Richard Howard. New York: Octagon Books.

Green, Martin. (1977). *Children of the Sun*. London: Constable.

Hall, Radclyffe. (1990). *The Well of Loneliness*. New York: Anchor Books.

Halperin, David M. (2002). *How to Do the History of Homosexuality*. Chicago: University of Chicago Press.

Holland, Merlin. (2003). *The Real Trial of Oscar Wilde: The First Uncensored Manuscript of the Trial of Oscar Wilde vs. John Douglas (Marquess of Queensberry), 1895*. New York: Fourth Estate.

Ladenson, Elisabeth. (1999). *Proust's Lesbianism*. Ithaca, NY: Cornell University Press.

Ladenson, Elisabeth. (2007). *Dirt for Art's Sake: Books on Trial from Madame Bovary to Lolita*. Ithaca, NY: Cornell University Press.

Lanser, Susan S. (2010). "Mapping Sapphic Modernity." In *Comparatively Queer: Crossing Time, Crossing Cultures*, ed. Jarrod Hayes, Margaret Higonnet, and William Spurlin, 69–89. London: Palgrave.

Liddell, Robert. (1976). *Cavafy: A Biography*. New York: Schocken Books.

Looby, Christopher. (2009). "The Gay Novel in the United States 1900–1950." In *A Companion to the Modern American Novel 1900–1950*, ed. John T. Matthews (pp. 414–436). Oxford: Wiley-Blackwell.

Love, Heather. (2009). "Introduction: Modernism at Night." *PMLA* 124.3: 744–748.

McKay, Claude. (1929). *Banjo: A Story without a Plot*. New York: Harper and Brothers.

Meyerowitz, Joanne. (2002). *How Sex Changed: A History of Transsexuality in the United States*. Cambridge, MA: Harvard University Press.

Mitchell, Mark and David Leavitt. (1997). *Pages Passed from Hand to Hand: The Hidden Tradition of Homosexual Literature in English 1748 to 1914*. Boston, MA: Houghton Mifflin.

Moffat, Wendy. (2010). *A Great Unrecorded History: A New Life of E.M. Forster*. New York: Farrar, Straus and Giroux.

Murray, Martin. (2005). "Walt Whitman, Edward Carpenter, Gavin Arthur, and *The Circle of Sex*." *Walt Whitman Quarterly* 22.4: 194–198.

North, Michael. (1994). *The Dialect of Modernism: Race, Language, and Twentieth-Century Literature*. New York: Oxford University Press.

Parkes, Adam. (1996). *Modernism and the Theater of Censorship*. Oxford: Oxford University Press.

Ponce, Joseph. (2012). *Beyond the Nation: Diasporic Filipino Literature and Queer Reading*. New York: New York University Press.

Proust, Marcel. (1997). *Swann's Way*, trans. C. K. Scott Moncrieff. New York: Penguin.

Sedgwick, Eve Kosofsky. (1990). *Epistemology of the Closet*. Berkeley: University of California Press.

Seitler, Dana. (2008). *Atavistic Tendencies: The Culture of Science in American Modernity*. Minneapolis: University of Minnesota Press.

Spring, Justin. (2010). *Secret Historian: The Life and Times of Samuel Steward, Professor, Tattoo Artist, and Sexual Renegade*. New York: Farrar, Straus and Giroux.

Steakley, James. (1989). "Iconography of a Scandal: Political Cartoons and the Eulenburg Affair in Wilhelmine Germany." In *Hidden from History: Reclaiming the Gay and Lesbian Past*, ed. Martin B. Duberman, Martha Vicinus, and George Chauncey (pp. 233–263). New York: New American Library.

Stein, Gertrude. (1995). *The Making of Americans: Being a History of a Family's Progress*. Normal, IL: Dalkey Archive Press.

Stoddard, Charles Warren. (1987). *For the Pleasure of His Company: A Tale of the Misty City, Thrice Told*. New York: Prentice Hall.

Werther, Ralph. (2008). *Autobiography of an Androgyne*, ed. Scott Herring. New Brunswick: Rutgers University Press.

Woolf, Virginia. (1956). *Orlando: A Biography*. New York: Harvest.

21

Cultural Capital and the Revolutions of Literary Modernity, from Bourdieu to Casanova

James F. English

Over the course of his prodigious career as a sociologist of culture, Pierre Bourdieu worked up a distinct narrative of the emergence of modernism, replete with a cast of key progenitors in literature and art and illustrated with provocative readings of the modernist works through which a decisive break with the previous cultural epoch was achieved. He elaborated as well an original theory of cultural domination that relates the experimental forms, taboo subjects, and avant-garde provocations of the modernist period to the various social positions of the individuals who produced them, helped to establish their legitimacy, or acquired the capacity for their appreciative reception. And he developed a dynamic map of generational succession and reproduction in the arts, a spatiotemporal model of the ebbs and flows in cultural status since the late nineteenth century that, while largely confined to France, has lent itself to global extrapolation. His work anticipated several tendencies in literary study – centering on the institutional and economic aspects of literary reputation, promotion, and consumption – that have shaped recent scholarly projects on modernism.[1] And one might add, further, that Bourdieu was himself in important respects a modernist, sharing many of the commitments we associate with the modernist intellectual (not least, a seemingly disproportionate investment in the literary) and tending to denigrate as false, empty, or commercially oriented the "postmodernist" cultural productions of the later twentieth century.[2]

So why, then, do so few literary critics and theorists who study modernism engage in any sustained way with Bourdieu's conceptualization of their object? Other accounts of modernist culture that share the classical sociological roots of Bourdieu's approach – notably those of the Frankfurt School – have merged into the very DNA of scholarship on modernism. We can all readily rehearse the argument that art in the modern period became increasingly commoditized through the agency of a "culture industry," thereby losing its aura of originality and serving ever more

A Handbook of Modernism Studies, First Edition. Edited by Jean-Michel Rabaté.
© 2013 John Wiley & Sons, Ltd. Published 2013 by John Wiley & Sons, Ltd.

reliably as a delivery system for cheap entertainment and distraction – a means of pacifying the exploited masses. We may choose to follow Adorno (1967), situating the ("high") modernism of Schönberg, Proust, or Kafka as a locus of exceptional resistance to this process of cultural commoditization; or, contrariwise, we may seek to expose the work of modernism as a form of pseudo-resistance that indirectly participates in and even hastens the rise of a cultural fashion system promoting novelty, scandal, and shock as saleable qualities. Or, in the interest of reclaiming jazz music or Hollywood cinema as genuine art forms and of redeeming the popular audience, we might reject as invidious any such high/low, art-vs-commodity scheme. But the point is that this entire system of concepts and arguments has been absorbed into the field of scholarship, to the degree that it is difficult even to frame a discussion of culture and society in the modernist period without reference to the main Frankfurtian coordinates.

With respect to Bourdieu, the situation is quite different. Scholars of modernism have felt no need to address his work in more than glancing ways. And this disinclination does not simply reflect a disciplinary fault line separating the empirical methods of the social sciences from the textual methods that dominate literary and cultural study. One can readily deploy Bourdieu's theoretical concepts without undertaking the kinds of ethnographic fieldwork and multiple correspondence analysis from which he derived them. Indeed, his key concepts – capital, habitus, and field – are well known, and other cogs of his theoretical apparatus – doxa, *illusio*, bodily *hexis*, reflexivity, autonomy – are at least in circulation. The difficulty arises, rather, when we try to say just how these concepts knit together to provide a distinct account of modernism. Does the Bourdieuian sociology position us as partisans of Proust, or rather of popular music? Does it direct a critique at high modernism and its elite appreciators (including the authors and readers of this volume)? At the mass entertainment industry and its indiscriminate consumers? At both, or at neither? And where, in relation to modernist practices, does it locate the radical potential of culture, the potential for a revolution in the mode of cultural production, a democratization of cultural resources and cultural power?

My first aim in this essay is to provide brief answers to these questions, sketching the main lineaments of Bourdieu's sociological theory in respect to modernism and suggesting that some of the difficulty one finds in pinning down the basic contours is due to a persistent double-valence in his work which casts the modernist as alternately heroic revolutionary and unwitting agent of symbolic domination.[3] My second aim is to extend this analysis to the more recent project of Pascale Casanova, where Bourdieu's account of literary modernism is dilated both geographically and temporally to produce a model of literary history as a struggle to achieve "modernity" within a relatively autonomous "world space" of symbolic combat. In this influential *mondialisation* of Bourdieu's cultural maps, Casanova retains something of Bourdieu's own two-mindedness regarding the social functions and effects of high literary practice. As she presents it, the great power-center of literary modernity, Paris, appears one minute as the capital of a brutal world empire of symbolic domination and next minute as the guardian of authentically artistic values and the last bulwark against ever more threatening US-based forces of commerce. For Casanova as for Bourdieu, the difficult and potentially self-contradicting aim is to demystify the literary sphere, exposing its aesthetic hierarchies as euphemized forms of social domination, without however ceasing to advance the case for a separate and autonomous economy of literary prestige, a literary "bourse" capable of defending, against hostile takeover by agents of political and commercial power, the value of its own distinct form of capital.

Modernism as a Field

Although its emergence is a central concern of his writings on art and literature, modernism is not a term that actually appears very often in Bourdieu's work. The word has become trapped between two definitional frameworks which he rejects: on the one side, an aesthetic framework that grasps modernism as a set of formal or stylistic qualities inherent in certain artistic works, opposed for example to "realism" or "classicism" and involving radical dismantlement of established conventions and genres; on the other side, an historical framework that would grasp modernism as a period or epoch wherein all manner of artistic work, including the most "traditional" or "conservative," may be seen to register the arrival of new regimes, technologies, and subjectivities which are not themselves products of the art world. Neither framework – nor the choice they imply between an "internalist" and an "externalist" criticism – squares with Bourdieu's approach, which understands modernism as a particular structuring of the "field" of cultural production (1993b, 34). By field, he does not mean some kind of "vague social background," a mere "*milieu artistique* . . . of personal relations between artists and writers" such as might be imagined by scholars who study "influences" (1993b, 163). Rather, to speak of the cultural field is to invoke

> a veritable social universe where, in accordance with its particular laws, there accumu-
> lates a particular form of capital and where relations of force of a particular type are
> exerted. This universe is the place of entirely specific struggles, notably concerning the
> question of knowing who is part of the universe, who is a real [artist] and who is not.
> (163–164)

As a kind of world apart, with its own "very particular" rules ("laws"), forms of power ("capital"), situations of advantage and disadvantage ("relations of force"), and goals or stakes ("entirely specific struggles"), a field may be thought of as a game-space, an "*espace de jeu*" (Bourdieu and Wacquant 1992b, 78). The literary field (which tends to serve in Bourdieu's work as a privileged and synecdochal subfield of culture in general) is the space in which the "games" of literature take place, comprising all the various players who are engaged in the competitive scramble for specifically literary stakes and resources, and above all for *recognition as players*: as writers, critics, or literary intellectuals of consequence (Bourdieu 1993c, 72–76).

Modernism, for Bourdieu, is defined by a new structuring of this field that comes gradually to obtain in the later nineteenth century, altering the relations between players, the laws or rules of their game, and the nature of the stakes to be fought for. Indeed, as he understands it, the literary field did not really exist prior to this moment – not as a truly distinct game-space, a world apart. Previously, authors and other literary people had had to make their way on the general "field of power," where their positions and practices were substantially determined by the maneuvers of social, political, and economic forces. Artistic "success" and cultural power aligned in a relatively straightforward way with the interests of the dominant class (the bourgeoisie) and, in particular, with money: artists understood themselves as producing work primarily for the market, and they recognized that the market could not support work that was too dissonant with prevailing social and political norms. The literary field as a world apart from these bourgeois controls had to be "invented," along with a new kind of player or personage corresponding to it: the "writer in the modern sense" (Bourdieu and Loïc, 1992a, 163), that is, the writer as a confirmed outsider to the field of power, who seeks recognition *as a writer* by pursuing a trajectory counter to the established pathways both of commercial success and of favor or renown among political and social elites.

In the terms of a normative economics, an ordinary scale of success and failure, this new (modernist) field thus functions not just as a world apart but as an "inverse world," an "economic world turned upside-down" (Bourdieu 1996a, 21). The modernist game of art appears, from the businessman's standpoint, as "a game of 'loser takes all.'" The artist who succeeds in acquiring "money, honours . . . women, . . . in short, all the symbols of worldly success, success in high society and success in the world," simultaneously compromises his chances of ascending to the highest ranks of specifically artistic regard and of achieving "salvation in the hereafter," that is, an enduring place in the pantheon of great artists (21). From this principle of inversion are derived all the many paradoxes of cultural prestige, for example the fact that artists can only demonstrate their worthiness of a prominent cultural award by refusing it outright or (more typically) accepting it in such a way as to signal their detachment from and condescension toward the sort of worldly value it represents (English 2005, 187–217). "Honors dishonor," as Flaubert famously put it; and "titles degrade."[4]

We take this upside-down cultural logic for granted today, perhaps regarding it as a timeless principle of value and status in the art world. But Bourdieu meticulously reconstructs the history of its by no means inevitable emergence, arguing that it only came to dominate the field of cultural practices around the turn of the twentieth century, when a sufficiently "high degree of autonomy" had been achieved to alter the whole style of play in the games of literature and art (1996a, 61). Only once this point had been reached did those who wished to "assert themselves as fully fledged members of the world of art" begin to understand intuitively, to experience as a kind of inner compulsion, the need to "manifest their independence" from all forms of power, political, social, and economic (61). "Then and only then," writes Bourdieu, could displays of "indifference with respect to power and honors," even seemingly legitimate honors like the Nobel Prize or membership in the French Academy, be "immediately understood, and even respected, and therefore rewarded" by others on the field (61). This was the modernist tipping point, the point at which a new, more autonomous state of the field had been internalized as a new *habitus*, that is, as a set of "durably installed" attitudes, dispositions, and strategies characteristic of modernist artists and writers, guiding their artistic practice, "regulating" their aesthetic "improvisations" (Bourdieu 1977, 78). The structural conformity of this new habitus with the new state of the field would henceforth assure – at least for a time – a positive feedback loop, further entrenching the new rules of the game. The posture of habitual, unfeigned indifference or disdain toward "external powers," and the respect accorded those who took such a stance, would tend, from the early decades of the twentieth century, to "impose themselves more and more forcefully as the practical maxims of legitimate conduct" for all serious writers and artists (1996a, 61).

The logic here, characteristic of Bourdieu's entire theoretical system, is one of reciprocal emergence: the new field (modernism in its "objective" form) and the new habitus (modernism in its "embodied" form) are mutually constituted through a process which is nothing less than the game of cultural production itself. In maneuvering for position and advantage, the players are continually struggling not only to adapt themselves to the state of play but also to conserve or transform the field of forces, to enforce or modify existing rules, even to redefine the game's underlying stakes. The early or proto-modernist writers of the nineteenth century (and for Bourdieu as for Benjamin, literary *modernité* begins with Baudelaire) are not in this scheme simply trying to take from below an established position of advantage on a settled field. They seek to force open entirely new positions, exploiting unnoticed opportunities in the gaps of the relational system, inventing new and seemingly impossible "spaces" in between existing cultural formations, and in particular between the opposed camps of lofty aestheticism and grounded engagement. Thus Baudelaire, perceiving two competing stances available to the aspiring avant-garde poet in mid-nineteenth-century Paris, that of a socially detached, pure formalism and that of an ethically responsible address to matters of worldly concern, declares a pox on both houses, "set[ting] himself against both polar positions while granting to each and taking from each that by which it is most directly opposed to the other" (Bourdieu 2000, 90). In the name of "the cult of pure form," he "refuses submission to external functions and respect for . . . the moralizing precepts of the bourgeois order." But in the name of "the critical imagination [and] the complicity between poetry and life," he "rejects just as strongly the social withdrawal of the devotees of pure form" (90). He thereby takes up a "hitherto impossible position," a position "produced, one could even say invented, by Baudelaire himself" through his effort to conjoin the "profoundly opposed and socially incompatible" projects of aesthetic avant-gardism and ethical avant-gardism – and to do so "*without conciliatory concessions*" (92).

Bourdieu offers the case of Baudelaire as a model "valid for all the authors of great *symbolic revolutions*" (92). They are able to discern, on a field of "already made possibles," a "*possible to be made*," a structurally excluded or "impossible" possible, "both rejected and called for by the space which defines it" (92). Bourdieu's account of modernism grasps it as a general upheaval and restructuring of the cultural field effected through a series of just such symbolic revolutions. The inventive and uncompromising position-takers responsible for these revolutions – notably Baudelaire, Flaubert, and Mallarmé in literature and Manet in art – emerge from the Bourdieuian narrative as heroic figures, the "great heresiarchs" of literary modernity, storming in from outside the established corridors of cultural power, reconfiguring the barriers to entry, and rewriting the rules of membership (1996a, 58). Through their "impossible" acts of double-refusal (neither art for its own sake *nor* the art of social reform) and double-attachment (both aesthetics *and* politics, artistic avant-gardism *as* political intervention), they spearheaded what in *The Rules of Art* Bourdieu calls "the conquest of autonomy," overthrowing the normal relations of force and producing a literary field capable for the first time of circulating its own form of capital and producing its own measures of genius or greatness, at odds with and ungovernable by other regimes of value. Paradoxically, according to Bourdieu, this revolution of the artists and intellectuals, which enabled them to uncouple their aesthetic projects and professional trajectories from the field of power, also provided them, for the first time, with the ability to exercise real authority on that field. They could now, in certain circumstances, convert their specific capital – their high reputations in a "world apart" from money and politics – into a general form of power and influence, becoming practitioners of a new, "anti-political politics" as exemplified by Zola's decisive intervention, in 1898, in the Dreyfus affair (Bourdieu 1991, 658).

Modernism and Cultural Capital

This paradox of an anti-political politics is the point where we may begin to appreciate the bivalent character of Bourdieu's entire project. A symbolic revolution, even one that succeeds in advancing the interests of artists on the field of power, is not a political revolution. Indeed, the "great revolutionaries" of this narrative intervened strategically to deny the claims of politically motivated writers who embraced values and doctrines external to the literary field and whose work accepted as its primary tasks the instruction and betterment of "the people" and the advancement of the cause of social reform. The defeat and retreat of such writers on the literary field was a necessary stage in the conquest of autonomy. As Timothy Brennan (2010) has observed in connection with Bourdieu's close-reading of Flaubert's *Sentimental Education*, the outlandish double-moves of modernist position-taking were intended to relocate political radicalism within the aesthetic itself, to "assert an insurrectionary core to the practices of autonomous art" (283). The modernists successfully leveraged this claim to prize open new positions of dominance – at once the most artistic and the most radical on the cultural field. But in order to do so they had to reconfigure that field according to the logic of economic inversion – as a game-space whose winners enjoyed substantial symbolic fortunes (recognition among artists), and hence substantial symbolic power (the power to confer recognition on other artists), precisely by virtue of their relative failure and inefficacy on the wider field of power. Zola's *"J'accuse"* notwithstanding, the cultural field, the world of artists, critics, and intellectuals, must remain, in accordance with its own self-definition, a space for what Bourdieu calls the "dominated fraction of the dominant class" (Bourdieu 1984, 232).

We need to consider both terms in this formula of the "dominated dominant" (1992a, 81): not only the artists' *domination by* the holders of social, political, and economic capital but their *dominance of* everybody else. The "great revolutionaries" of modernism achieved a heroic inversion of the prevailing hierarchies of value and status, depriving those who held dominant positions on the field of power – nobles, politicians, industrialists, executives, tycoons – of the capacity to impose their interests and preferences on the field of art. Henceforth, the holders of primarily economic and political capital would have to be content with a secondary position in respect to art, a role as mere followers, chasing after but never catching up to the leading edges of culture, never themselves being altogether "modern" or altogether free from the stigmas of impurity, vulgarity, and backwardness. To be sure, they would continue to maintain a controlling interest in the most broadly respectable art (occupying key positions of patronage in museums and opera companies, for example) as well as to reap the money profits deriving from the expanding mass-culture market (what Bourdieu calls the field of "large-scale" production, where artistic worth is understood in terms of economic rather than symbolic capital). But the handshake of official approval and the embrace of commerce had alike become less than worthless as instruments of symbolic advancement, finding accord with genuine art only belatedly, as trailing indicators of a cultural order already determined elsewhere by others.

The very temporality of this arrangement, however, means that the most disruptively avant-garde work of the present, comprehensible only to the most astute and uncompromised artists or intellectuals, bears the aspiration to become a museum piece or "modern classic" of the future, as valuable in money terms as it is respectable among the haute-bourgeoisie. The autonomous artist's militant preference for symbolic over economic capital (and, just as militantly, for "specific" over "general" symbolic capital) is less a refusal than a deferral of worldly success. It is a matter of long-term investment strategies, the artist devoting his available time and resources to the accumulation of strictly symbolic rewards which, though non-convertible with other forms of capital at the outset, will tend to become more fungible over time. Far from being locked into a position of pure negativity, the modernist revolutionary fits into a machinery of generational succession whereby yesterday's aesthetic rebel becomes today's distinguished artist and tomorrow's consecrated genius, this movement involving a simultaneous elevation on the field of power and demotion on the most autonomous portions of the cultural field. The whole dynamic assures that new, more or less disreputable, heretical, or "impossible" positions will be made/taken by new symbolic revolutionaries, whose claim on autonomy is strengthened by their disdain for the revolutions, now in process of being assimilated, that immediately preceded them. Such cyclical assertions of artistic autonomy tend to maintain rather than disrupt the larger system of social domination. The point at which an artist has gained sufficient social standing to impose his negative or resistant truths on the field of power (if indeed he manages to achieve this level of general symbolic capital in his lifetime) is also the point at which the field of power has begun successfully to absorb and dilute the oppositional force of his position-takings: the point when James Joyce appears on the cover of *Time* magazine, say, or when authorized replicas of Duchamp's urinal-fountain are being installed on museum walls in Paris, New York, and London.

Nor is this the only way in which the Bourdieuian scheme suggests a degree of alignment between cultural capital and worldly capital subtending the logic of their mutual inversion. Their partial alignment is in fact a feature of modernism from the beginning, in that the revolutionary artistic habitus can best thrive, if not among the haute-bourgeoisie itself, among those sufficiently privileged to maintain themselves as cultural producers through a protracted (potentially lifelong) period of deferred economic rewards. The long-term investment strategy implicitly adopted by all those who produce for what Bourdieu calls the "restricted" market of other artists and intellectuals – a market which modernism created and succeeded in expanding, but which remains relatively non-remunerative – presupposes some form of rentier income, or at least some modicum of startup capital. This applies not just to the artists who produce disorientingly new works but to the critics and intellectuals who assist in the advancement and dissemination of those works by producing the discourse of their eventual legitimation. The cultural habitus, acquired through a more or less lengthy period of aesthetic education – advanced schooling, extended travel, sustained immersion in the art world, etc. – requires an outlay of money and a deferral of gratification which those truly without capital resources cannot afford. Even after the modernist "conquest of autonomy" it remains the case that the most highly skilled players on the cultural field tend to be either from cultured families or from families well endowed with more worldly forms of capital which they are in the process of converting, generationally, into a higher cultural standing.[5]

Modern culture, in short, is for Bourdieu a class culture, and one which, for all its internal revolutions, is strongly geared toward reproduction of the existing social order. The relational structure of the cultural field, with its binaries of high vs. low, refined vs. crude, difficult vs. easy, obscure vs. popular, modern vs. traditional, abstract vs. realist, and so on and so forth, replicates on an aesthetic register the relations of social class, and reinforces these over time. One's tastes in art and reading, as also in sports and hobbies and other leisure activities, are "bound through a relation of homology" to the social positions one occupies (1993a, 273). The burden of Bourdieu's most famous book, *Distinction: A Social Critique of the Judgement of Taste* (1984), is to demonstrate these homologies empirically through multiple correspondence analysis and then to render the statistical evidence in visual as well as narrative form as mappings of class origins, taste preferences, and the "space of lifestyles" in postwar France. From these maps, we can see that by mid-century a taste for modernism – a high regard for abstract painting, for example – is mainly serving as a kind of coded signal or euphemism for membership in the dominant class. To be sure, those who are most open to the virtues of abstract or avant-garde art, most able to "recognize" it as art, are not the wealthy individuals who sit atop the dominant class but rather the dominated members of that dominant class, whose endowments largely consist of cultural and educational capital. Modernism finds its adherents above all among practicing artists and university professors, and to a somewhat lesser extent among those on the lower rungs of this same cultural fraction, the "art-craftsmen" and secondary school teachers.

In this respect, Bourdieu's maps affirm the invention by modernist revolutionaries of an upside-down world, their construction of a space for a specifically "cultural aristocracy," lacking great wealth or potent social and political connections, but nonetheless possessing the lion's share of power to recognize aesthetic merit, that is, to produce and deploy cultural value beyond the bounds of merely approved good taste. But the evidence of *Distinction* also points to the right-side-up arrangement whereby the holders of worldly power are able, over time, to acquire as much of the modernist or avant-garde habitus as is useful to assert their own relative distinction and refinement. By the 1960s, when Bourdieu gathered his data, the professionals, industrialists, and private-sector executives had nearly converged, in their appreciative respect for abstraction and other modernist innovations, with the less well capitalized sectors of the cultural class. The shopkeepers, office workers, and manual laborers meanwhile remained truly disenfranchised, their overwhelming preference for traditional, pre-modernist, realist art serving as a mark of aesthetic impoverishment, a cultural stigma reinforcing their social subjugation.

I am obviously oversimplifying the ways that cultural preference can align with social position in Bourdieu's sociology of taste. A disdain for abstraction, much like a preference for mystery novels over "literary" fiction, has symbolic meaning only in relation to other preferences and in the context of a particular style of cultural play. The same tastes can appear as "manifestations of daring and freedom" or on the contrary as "a constellation typical of middlebrow taste," depending on when and how they are exercised, and above all by whom (1984, 88). It is clear as well that the specific categories and data from which Bourdieu derived his maps of postwar French culture and society are not directly applicable to the relations among social classes, lifestyles, and cultural preferences elsewhere, such as in the contemporary United Kingdom or United States, which would require their own, differently constructed empirical studies. But these complications do not weaken the general argument Bourdieu makes in *Distinction* and reiterates throughout his career: that cultural power, however autonomously it has come to circulate since the later nineteenth century, however successfully it has been seized by a dominated fraction of the dominant class, has always remained a form of power narrowly held by individuals who "participate in the dominant order" and who tend, even in their most radical aesthetic practices, to "unconsciously endorse the dominant values" (1991, 668).

Modernism in this account is a revolution achieved, both objectively (as a field) and in embodied subjective form (as a habitus). At certain moments this establishment of a separate field of specifically cultural authority can be seen to alter the political balance, enabling the artist or intellectual to convert his specific capital into a uniquely "pure" form of political power, the power to invoke the "universal" against the special interests of ruling elites. But there is much in Bourdieu's model that limits the efficacy even of such interventions as these. The model contains no definite mechanism whereby an encroachment by artists onto the field of power, or even a progressive recalibration of the whole relationship between stronger and weaker fractions of the dominant class, would result in a more general democratization of cultural power and symbolic authority, a "universalization," as Bourdieu expresses it, "of the privileged conditions of existence that make pursuit of the universal possible" (1991, 669). Such a radical democratization of culture, appears, rather, as the utopian horizon of an otherwise rather grim sociology – a belief, located beyond the more pessimistic terms of the model itself, that in struggling to establish the objective conditions and subjective dispositions necessary to support the principle of "absolute freedom" in the domain of art, the symbolic revolutionaries of modernism took heroic steps toward a freer society.

Casanova and the Space of Literary Modernity

This ambiguously utopian embrace of artistic and intellectual autonomy reappears in the work of Pascale Casanova, which again casts the symbolic revolutionaries of literary modernism as social heroes even while detailing the cruel asymmetries of the field they command and highlighting their inefficacy as agents of wider social change. Casanova's book *The World Republic of Letters*, published in France in 1999 and in English translation in 2004, sets out to expand Bourdieu's model of the symbolic market in cultural capital, presenting a sociological narrative of modern literary history on a global scale. Casanova (2004) accepts one of the main claims of Bourdieu's field theory, that it reconciles formalist and historicist modes of literary analysis, "overcoming," as she puts it, "the supposedly insuperable antinomy between internal . . . and external criticism" (4). Like Bourdieu, she grasps the literary work as a kind of position-taking or "placement strategy": its unique formal particulars appear in her model as constitutive elements of a symbolic struggle, that is, as elements which shape the field of literary battle as surely as they are shaped by it (Casanova 2005, 89). But Casanova critiques the Bourdieuian concept of field as a narrowly "national framework, limited by the borders, historical traditions and capital accumulation processes of a specific nation state" (80). Drawing rather on the concept of a "world-economy" as developed by Fernand Braudel (1992) and elaborated in the world-systems theory of Immanuel Wallerstein (1984), Casanova proposes to consider the various national fields and national markets of literary production as relational components of a larger international system or "world space" where the symbolic fortunes of individual authors and national literatures alike are determined (2004, 351).

This cultural world-system is structured by time as well as space. There is, Casanova says, "a time specific to literature," a world literary clock that is calibrated by reference to what she terms the "literary Greenwich meridian," a Europe-based standard of the literary present, the aesthetically modern or up to date. Every national literary space, along with all the individual writers within it, is positioned in the world-system according to its temporal distance from this center. To be more distant from the symbolic meridian is at once to be more deprived of literary capital and more "backward" with respect to the literary present and the "criteria of modernity" (88). The entire world literary space is thus structured by a "simple pattern of inequality" based on temporal hierarchies of development and progress and resembling in its basic form the relations of core to periphery and semi-periphery in Wallerstein's capitalist world-system (352). The cultural map is not, however, simply a transposition of the economic one, with the richest countries also the most symbolically powerful and advanced in literary terms. Casanova's literary world-system enjoys even more substantial autonomy from the system of political and economic relations than does the modern literary field in Bourdieu's account. In the world republic of letters, it is Paris that serves as capital and center of power rather than New York, London, Tokyo, or Shanghai. And Ireland, though a politically weak, imperially dominated, economically impoverished country throughout the late nineteenth and most of the twentieth century – backward and peripheral in world-economic terms – becomes during that very time period absolutely central in terms of literary modernity, having produced some of the most advanced and enduringly consecrated masters of modernist poetry (Yeats), drama (Wilde, Shaw, Beckett), and fiction (Joyce).

Casanova's insistence that Paris is the prime meridian and seat of power for determining the worldwide criteria of literary modernity has been criticized as a Gallicist exaggeration. But her account is persuasive in many respects. The argument is not simply that Paris, as an early mover in the literary game, has over time been able to accumulate more prestige than other sites of literary production. Its place as "gateway to the present" is owing to its stores of other more materially embodied kinds of literary capital as well: in particular, certain kinds of literary and linguistic expertise, and the institutional agents capable of putting that expertise to work. Paris is the capital of the literary world not because of the number of prestigious writers it has or has had, but because of "the number of cosmopolitan intermediaries – publishers, editors, critics, and especially translators" – who do their cultural work there. These "polyglots and translators" provide the links between center and periphery; they are the "brokers" of foreign exchange who make it possible for texts to pass through the literary "bourse" of Paris and enter into wider circulation as assets of literary modernity (2004, 20–21). It is virtually impossible for a writer to achieve world-recognition, that is, a reputation extending beyond her own national and linguistic field, without the intercession of these symbolic underwriters in Paris.

The gross asymmetry and violence of this world-system, in which the power to decide what counts as literature is effectively monopolized by a Paris-based "aristocracy," are generally hidden within the collective belief in the literary as such, what Bourdieu would call the literary *illusio*. There is, says Casanova, "a fiction accepted by all who take part in the game: the fable of an enchanted world, a kingdom of pure creation, a world where universality reigns through liberty and equality" (12). And yet – again following Bourdieu, who credits Mallarmé among others with the ability to play the game while also partially seeing through it – Casanova does allow for the possibility of a writer penetrating to some degree the veil of literary enchantment (1996a, 276–277). While "very few writers at the center of world literature have any idea as to its actual structure," those who are most distant from the center and "most deprived of its resources" may be granted a special, if incomplete, lucidity regarding "the forms of violence and domination that operate within it" (2004, 12).[6]

Indeed, these writers of the "suburban outskirts," possessed of the peculiar "lucidity of the dominated," supply Casanova with the hero figures of her narrative (43, 328). Positioned though they are at great disadvantage by virtue of the aesthetic remoteness of their national fields, these dominated writers "manoeuvre with extraordinary sophistication to give themselves the best chance of being perceived, of existing in literary terms" (2005, 89). Fighting their way in from the margins, Casanova's heroic "revolutionaries" – Ibsen, Kafka, Joyce, and, later, Darió, Cortázar, Garcia-Marquez, and others – manage to impose themselves on the literary aristocracy, winning consecration from the legislators of literariness and thus gaining a place at the vanguard of literary modernity despite the "ethnocentric blindness" inherent in the Parisian monopolization of universal value (2004, 23, 324–328).

On the basis of her revolutionary posture, her radical skepticism regarding the "fable" of "literature as something pure, free, and universal," and her keen partisanship in favor of the dominated, Casanova herself has been hailed as a kind of "hero" of literary sociology, and her *Republic of Letters* acclaimed as a work of "liberating impact," even as a "literary Porto Alegre" (Anderson 2004, 16). But less generous commentators, particularly in Latin America, have been struck by the extent of Casanova's own apparent investment in the Parisian monopoly, her own seeming ethnocentric blindness. They see her less as a critic of the cultural world-system than as its ideologue, a believer in its magic who cannot, for all her demystifying intentions, see the grinding machinery of economic and political power or the wreckage of colonialism through the vapors of enchantment.[7] Even as she exposes the relations of symbolic violence that structure the literary world, Casanova insists on its virtuous autonomy, its capacity to "produce a specific form of recognition that owes nothing to political fiat, interest, or prejudice" (12).

This rhetorical counter-current, running in vigorous defense of the literary system and its legislators, becomes most adamant in the later stages of Casanova's historical narrative, where she describes a recent shift "from internationalism to globalization." This shift, as she sees it, is occasioned by the advance of an American economic model within the world space of literature, and by the concomitant rise of New York, capital of the commercial axis, as the major rival to Paris, capital of the axis of autonomy. The most insidious effect of this globalization, she says, has been the production and dissemination of a new, *ersatz* world literature, a kind of high literary airport novel labeled as "world fiction" but in fact simply "aimed at an international market," bearing the seeming hallmarks of formal innovation such as "Borgesian" reflexivity, but in fact simply recycling yesterday's devices of modernist estrangement as today's marketable clichés. By successfully feeding these "popular novels that give the appearance of literariness" into the literary world-system, the publishing conglomerates, symbolically if not always materially headquartered in New York, have in effect "created a new composite measure of fictional modernity" that threatens to undermine the currency of the Parisian bourse (171–172).

Here Casanova is restating an anxiety that appears frequently in Bourdieu: that the rising power of global media "disseminators" is tending to "confuse the most autonomous producers with the most heteronomous," blurring the "border between avant-garde work and best-seller" (1991, 665). For both writers, globalization is little more than a euphemism for Americanization, which is itself a mere cover for commodification. The specter of neoliberalism appears at such moments in the form of economic capital dressed up in the clothing of art, the merely popular donning the mantle of the literary present. This dark vision of art under the "tyranny of the market" points, in the case of both thinkers, to a ring fence of high-culturalist commitment they have erected around otherwise searching critiques of culture as symbolic violence. Their aesthetic revolutionaries are thus cast in a social role of irresolvable ambiguity. In seizing a dominant position for themselves through the unequal trade in cultural prestige, the heroes of literary modernity are seen, in this framework, as also establishing the very space of freedom in which the struggle for cultural democracy must be waged.

Notes

1   Notable examples include Rainey (1999), Outka (2008), and Braddock (2012).

2   Jeremy Lane, among others, has argued that Bourdieu, in contrast to Foucault, Deleuze, Lyotard, and other "postmodernist" contemporaries, "work[ed] within the terms of a classically modernist critique," and that his theory of habitus and bodily hexis in particular "signaled his adherence to a form of (modernist) critique whose ultimate goal was to liberate the subject through the rational grasp of those material determinants which threatened its freedom" (Lane 2000, 160). On Bourdieu's choice of literature as a privileged object for sociological inquiry, see Boschetti (2006).

3   I differ here with David Gartman (2012), who has recently argued for a fundamental break between the Bourdieu of the 1970s and 1980s and the Bourdieu of the 1990s and 2000s. As Gartman sees it, in the wake of neoliberalism Bourdieu abandoned his critique of high culture as a mechanism for legitimating inequalities and turned to defending it as a mechanism for guarding intellectual autonomy. There is to be sure a shift in emphasis and a new sense of political urgency in Bourdieu's later writings and activism. But his ambivalence regarding the social implications of the symbolic revolution of modernism was evident all along. The core arguments Bourdieu develops in *The Rules of Art*, which Gartman treats as a text of the mid-1990s, can be traced back through essays on Flaubert, Zola, and Sartre published in American and British journals in the 1980s, and, as John

Speller details, several of those essays had appeared originally in French a decade before (Speller 2011).

4   From a March 1880 letter to his niece Caroline: "*Les honneurs déshonorent, Le titre dégrade, La fonction abrutit*" (Flaubert 1906, 507).

5   This process of "capital interconversion" is a focus of Bourdieu's immensely important writings on the educational system, in particular *Homo Academicus* (1988) and *The State Nobility* (1996b).

6   Here again Casanova follows Bourdieu, who observes in *Pascalian Meditations* (2000) that those who suffer the disparagement and condescension of the dominant fraction derive from their "marginal position" a "special lucidity as regards aristocratic values and the symbolic foundations of authority" (3).

7   For a judicious reading of the hostile response among Latin Americanists, and a partial defense of Casanova's perspective, see Henneken (2010).

References

Adorno, Theodor W. (1967). *Prisms*, trans. Samuel Weber and Shierry Weber. Cambridge, MA: MIT Press.

Anderson, Perry. (2004). "Union Sucrée." *London Review of Books* 26.18: 10–16.

Boschetti, Anna. (2006). "Bourdieu's Work on Literature: Contexts, Stakes and Perspectives." *Theory, Culture & Society* 23.6: 135–155.

Bourdieu, Pierre. (1984). *Distinction: A Social Critique of the Judgement of Taste*, trans. Richard Nice. Cambridge, MA: Harvard University Press.

Bourdieu, Pierre. (1988). *Homo Academicus*, trans. Peter Collier. Stanford: Stanford University Press.

Bourdieu, Pierre. (1991). "Fourth Lecture. Universal Corporatism: The Role of Intellectuals in the Modern World." *Poetics Today* 12.4: 655–669.

Bourdieu, Pierre. (1993a). "Concluding Remarks: For a Sociogenic Understanding of Intellectual Works." In *Bourdieu: Critical Perspectives*, ed. Craig Calhoun, Edward LiPuma, and Moishe Postone (pp. 263–275). Chicago: University of Chicago Press.

Bourdieu, Pierre. (1993b). *The Field of Cultural Production*, ed. Randal Johnson. London: Polity.

Bourdieu, Pierre. (1993c). *Sociology in Question*. London: Sage.

Bourdieu, Pierre. (1996a). *The Rules of Art: Genesis and Structure of the Literary Field*, trans. Susan Emanuel. Stanford: Stanford University Press.

Bourdieu, Pierre. (1996b). *The State Nobility: Elite Schools and the Field of Power*, trans. Lauretta C. Clough. Stanford: Stanford University Press.

Bourdieu, Pierre. (2000). *Pascalian Meditations*. Stanford: Stanford University Press.

Bourdieu, Pierre and Loïc J. D. Wacquant. (1992a). *An Invitation to Reflexive Sociology*. Chicago: Chicago University Press.

Bourdieu, Pierre and Loïc J. D. Wacquant. (1992b). *Réponses: pour une anthropologie réflexive*. Paris: Editions de Seuil.

Braddock, Jeremy. (2012). *Collecting as Modernist Practice*. Baltimore: Johns Hopkins University Press.

Braudel, Fernand. (1992). *The Perspective of the World*. Vol. 3 of *Civilization and Capitalism 15th–18th Century*, trans. Siân Reynolds. Berkeley: University of California Press. Originally published in French, 1979.

Brennan, Timothy. (2010). "Running and Dodging: The Rhetoric of Doubleness in Contemporary Theory." *New Literary History* 41.2: 277–229.

Casanova, Pascale. (2004) *The World Republic of Letters*, trans. M. B. DeBevoise. Cambridge, MA: Harvard University Press. Originally published in French, 1999.

Casanova, Pascale. (2005). "Literature as a World." *New Left Review* 31: 71–90.

English, James. (2005). *The Economy of Prestige: Prizes, Awards, and the Circulation of Cultural Value*. Cambridge, MA: Harvard University Press.

Flaubert, Gustave. (1906). *Lettres à sa nièce Caroline*. Paris: Bibliotèque-Charpentier,

Gartman, David. (2012). "Bourdieu and Adorno: Converging Theories of Culture." *Theory and Society* 41: 41–72.

Henneken, Jaime. (2010). "Going Mundial: What it Really Means to Desire Paris." *Modern Language Quarterly* 71.2: 129–152.

Lane, Jeremy F. (2000). *Bourdieu: A Critical Introduction*. London: Pluto Press,

Rainey, Lawrence. (1999). *Institutions of Modernism: Literary Elites and Public Culture*. New Haven, CT: Yale University Press.

Outka, Elizabeth. (2008). *Consuming Traditions: Modernity, Modernism, and the Commodified Authentic*. New York: Oxford University Press.

Speller, John R. W. (2011). "Appendix: The composition of *Les Règles de l'art*." In *Bourdieu and Literature* (pp. 34–38). Cambridge: Open Book Publishers.

Wallerstein, Immanuel. (2004). *World-Systems Analysis: An Introduction*. Durham, NC: Duke University Press,

Further Reading

Alexander, Jeffrey C. (1995). "The Reality of Reduction: The Failed Synthesis of Pierre Bourdieu." In *Fin de Siècle Social Theory* (pp. 128–217). New York: Verso.

Bourdieu, Pierre. (1986). "The Forms of Capital." In *Handbook of Theory and Research for the Sociology of Education*, ed. John G. Richardson (pp. 241–258). Westport, CT: Greenwood Press.

Bourdieu, Pierre. (1990). *The Logic of Practice*, trans. Richard Nice. Cambridge: Polity Press.

Bourdieu, Pierre. (1991). *Language and Symbolic Power*, ed. John B. Thompson. Cambridge: Polity.

Bourdieu, Pierre. (1999). *Acts of Resistance: Against the Tyranny of the Market Vol. 1*, trans. Richard Nice. New York: The New Press.

Bourdieu, Pierre. (2003). *Firing Back: Against the Tyranny of the Market Vol. 2*, trans. Loïc Wacquant. New York: Verso.

Butler, Judith. (1999). "Performativity's Social Magic." In Richard Shusterman, ed., *Bourdieu: A Critical Reader*. Oxford: Blackwell.

Casanova, Pascale. (2006). *Samuel Beckett: Anatomy of a Literary Revolution*, trans. Gregory Elliott. New York: Verso.

Felski, Rita. (2003). "Modernist Studies and Cultural Studies: Reflections on Method." *Modernism/modernity* 10.3: 501–517. DOI: 10.1353/mod.2003.0059.

Guillory, John. (1993). *Cultural Capital: The Problem of Literary Canon Formation*. Chicago: Chicago University Press.

Guillory, John. (1997). "Bourdieu's Refusal." *Modern Language Quarterly* 58.4: 367–398.

Wexler, Joyce Piell. (1997). *Who Paid For Modernism? Art, Money, and the Fiction of Conrad, Joyce, and Lawrence*. Fayetteville: University of Arkansas Press.

22

Modernism and Cognitive Disability
A Genealogy

Joseph Valente

Modernism must be counted a seminal moment in the cultural representation of cognitive disability. Indeed, it is not an overreach to hazard that the mentally challenged first become visible as full-fledged literary subjects under the modernist aegis. That is to say, although the figure of the "idiot," "imbecile," "natural," or "feeble-minded" populates a notable cross-section of the nineteenth-century canon – from Wordsworth's "The Idiot Boy" to Gaskell's "Half a Lifetime Ago" to Bronte's *Villette* to Dickens' *Little Dorritt* and *Barnaby Rudge* (McDonagh 2008) – modernism was the first literary movement or assemblage to consistently give us cognitive disability as not just an object of derision or pity, sentimentality or paternalism, high racial anxiety or *fin du monde* panic, as something more too than a convenient mirror or metaphor for broader, tangentially related social concerns, but additionally as a distinct estate or cluster of conditions that subtends a legitimate alternative perspective on and experience of the everyday. I say "not just" and "additionally" here because far from disappearing, those received stereotyping attitudes toward the mentally deficient persisted in experimental twentieth-century literature alongside an increasingly affirmative identification with them. The result is a complex double-image of cognitive disability, differentiated by type, whose innovativeness, like that of so many high modernist artifacts, resides in its staging of an agon between conservative, even reactionary impulses on one side, and progressive, even revolutionary impulses on the other. In this essay, I propose to chart the discursive background against which the modernist subject of disability could emerge from and within the shadows of literary condescension, disparagement, and instrumentalization; to chart the contours of this emergence, and in specific the contest between the received and the revisionist portrayal of the "mentally deficient" subject; and to note the anticipation of contemporary disability theory, in particular, the "social model" variant, in this agon of modernist representation.

A Handbook of Modernism Studies, First Edition. Edited by Jean-Michel Rabaté.
© 2013 John Wiley & Sons, Ltd. Published 2013 by John Wiley & Sons, Ltd.

Biopower

The image of disability in modernist literature is a highly mediated effect of the development of the regime of biopower over the course of the nineteenth century. As Foucault has exhaustively chronicled, after the liberal revolution in Europe and America the disciplinary model of training and surveillance, which "addressed man-as-body" with a focus on the individual subject, was succeeded by the regulatory model of supervision and control, which "addressed man-as-species" with a focus upon caring for the life of a national population (1997a, 242). Operating as they did along different planes of social organization, these two power grids did not "exclude one another" but were rather articulated together. "The element," according to Foucault, that "circulates between the two," binding them together, "is the norm," for "the norm can be applied to both a body one wishes to discipline and a population one wishes to regularize" (252–253). There emerges "a norm of discipline and a norm of regulation that intersect" (253). But what makes the "normalizing society" an instance of biopower at work rather than simply a "generalized disciplinary regime" is that the norms instituted on a collective basis – social, racial, or national – exercise a decisive authority over the individual body to be disciplined, the power to determine its status as "normal" or "abnormal," healthy or pathological, fit or unfit, a benign variation or an ominous deviation. *The biopolitical regularities established for the socius fashion disciplinary imperatives for the citizen.* Such biopolitical norms can only have this sort of moral agency, however, those "regularities" can only exert motivating or mandating pressure over the individuating protocols, if the society conceives or imagines itself to be a strongly organic unity, in which its members (and I use the term advisedly) do not just populate the whole, but *embody* it. Only on these terms can the conformability of the individual to a norm determined by ethno-national or species-wide regularities be understood to be a vital contribution to the maintenance of said norm and hence to the health of the society at large. Still more urgently, it was only on these lines that individual deviations from said norms could be understood as vital threats to their maintenance and hence to the health of the society at large. Only on these strongly organic lines, in short, could individual catastrophe be posed as social crisis. It is only on these terms, in sum, that biopower could, as Foucault observed, take the *endemic* (rather than the epidemic) for its object of concern and control. The purchase of a biopolitical regularity upon the performance of individuals, accordingly, was proportionate to the investment of the individuals *in* and *by* the "massifying" construct those regularities describe (243), the sense that the members are fundamentally indissociable from the social body to be thus regularized.

Although he does not speak explicitly to this logical entailment, Foucault's anatomy of the population under biopolitics is directly on point: on one occasion "a mass of living and coexisting beings who present particular biological and pathological traits" (Foucault 1997b, 71); on another, and still more precisely, "a new body, a multiple body, a body with many heads" (Foucault 1997a, 245).

In either case, a mass of living bodies or a single hydra-headed body, Foucault's formulation provides an ontology of the normalizing society that includes how just such a society must see itself, as a continuous, unified, organic whole.

The historical evidence puts this point beyond doubt. In the later nineteenth century, when the regime of biopower had achieved maturity, "the notion of society as an organism – living, reproducing, degenerating, dying – had become, in Daniel Pick's words, "a dead metaphor . . . a metaphor used literally in social criticism" (Pick 1989, 180). Baudelaire, for one, "believed that civilizations follow the same processes of growth and decay as living organisms: "it must never be forgotten that nations, those vast collective beings, are subject to the same laws as individuals" (qtd in Bade 1985, 233). Somewhat later, Max Nordau was to cast those laws in the framework of a loose physio-social Darwinism, as involving both the "individual" and "race" in a homologous struggle of adaptation. In a similar vein, James Frazer borrowed the embryonic model from Darwin to popularize the so-called "recapitulation theory" (ontogeny recapitulates phylogeny) as an anthropological proposition: social life was held to proceed "through stages similar to those through which the [human] embryo passed".[1] But it was the Lamarckian paradigm of evolutionary change, then dominant in both the medical and human sciences, that implicated the individual members indivisibly, constitutively, in the social body, converting evolutionary parallels between human organisms and the social organism into metonymic relations of causality and symbiosis. Lamarck's governing concept of use-inheritance (or the heritability of acquired traits) had the effect of "placing the individual and society on a continuum," observes Robert Nye, because traits acquired by the individual were "fixed and stored in the social organism," which for its part grew and developed through the "persistent differentiation" of its individual members.[2] The central proposition of late Victorian social theory, the heritability of acquired traits meant that the discipline or lack thereof to which man-as-body was subject – the transmission of social value at a given moment – not only contributes to but directly constitutes, over several generations, the regularities that define "man-as-species" in the register of biopower.

But precisely here we arrive at the great paradox of biopower as a discursive formation. As a matter of logic, it needed to construe the various bodies to be disciplined as fully incorporated within the larger society to be regularized, to see that larger society as a body of bodies, an organism of organisms, all existing on the same "plane of consistency" (Deleuze and Guattari 1987, 9). But this enabling conceit could not but undermine the integrity and disturb the operation of the very element that Foucault identifies as "circulating between" the disciplinary and biopolitical regimes, the norm. Inasmuch as the norm is not a transcendent Platonic form nor a mere statistical abstraction, but draws from the "regularities" alternately discerned in and enjoined upon the population of the social organism, the norm cannot assume or occupy a moral or ontological space wholly independent of the individual members of that body, the tissues of that organism, whose various endemic forms of life amalgamate the regularities thus discerned and enjoined. The norm, accordingly, represents what Slavoj Žižek likes to call an effect of its effects or, to be more exact, it is an effect of the practices it distinguishes, measures, and judges.

The consequences of this cycle of power and agency are far-reaching indeed, nothing less than a certain erosion of the "bipolarity of the normal and the pathological or abnormal" that Foucault sees as governing the medical enterprises of the nineteenth century (qtd in Nadesan 2008, 150). To the extent that any individual mode of embodiment, however configured by the prevailing norms, could be read as distinct and singularizing, as instancing a particularity let alone an idiosyncracy of disposition, address, or being-in-the-world, it would contain as an *essential* part of its structure a liability to divergence from strict regularity, hence a valence of potential abnormality or pathology. Conversely, to the extent that any individual mode of embodiment, however deviant from pertinent norms, contributed perforce to the amalgamation of broader social, racial, or national regularities, it would maintain as an essential part of its structure an at least notional purchase upon that regularity, and hence upon its ideological correlate of normativity. If one considers further that social regularities mutate autopoetically over time, in a feedback loop with the diverse particularity of their instantiation, then no state of normality or abnormality could be perfectly immune from an unforeseeable yet systemic resignification as its opposite. In this sense, the interanimation of social organism and socialized organisms drives biopower to compromise its primary mechanism, the norm, in the act of mobilizing it. The effect of this paradox on the identification of deviancy and the enforcement of the norm can be most readily apprehended in the fin-de-siècle discourse of degeneration, which Foucault (1997) himself deems to have "almost completely covered over the category of abnormality" (51).[3]

Degeneration

In universalizing perversion as a core component of sexuality, and in theorizing neurosis as an oddly normal pathology or pathological norm, Sigmund Freud laid claim to having decisively and by conscious design "ruptured the dichotomy" between normal and abnormal individuals, behaviors, and psychic states (Nadesan 2008, 99). But in fact the broad church theory of degeneration had in the decade preceding the Vienna School begun to bring this dichotomy to a most precarious pass in the very attempt to promulgate it in the sharpest, most virulent form possible.

As a diagnostic model with influence across a number of intellectual fields (medicine, anthropology, evolutionary biology, art and literary criticism, criminology, sexology, sociology, etc.), the degeneration thesis admitted a wide array of symptomatic manifestations (hysteria, evolutionary reversion or atavism, criminal propensity, idiocy, cognitive and moral imbecility, sexual promiscuity, egomania, mysticism, physiological infirmity, hyperesthesia, neurasthenia and nervous system disorder generally, aesthetic sensibility, etc.) and an equally impressive roster of possible etiologies (overwork, hyper-civilization, urban decay, alcohol abuse, industrialism, constitutional enervation, dyshygienic lifestyles and surroundings). Indeed, as Pick observes, the difficulty the degeneration thesis poses for historical analysis "stems from the plurality of its connotations" (1989, 230). Its denotation, however – from Morel who coined the syndrome to Nordau who became its popularizing doyen – remains extraordinarily constant: "a morbid deviation from an original type," the latter defined as "the normal human type".[4] Framing difference as sickness, "enfolding pathology into abnormality," the phrase morbid deviation not only "characterizes the degenerate by his distance from the norm," but casts that distance in a most sinister light (Esposito 2008, 119). And yet degeneration proved truly menacing less for its divergence *from* the species, normatively defined, than for what it does *to* the species, that is, precipitating a decline or a reversion in the most "advanced" races. This extraordinary mode of danger, at once endemic and apocalyptic, correlated with the second main point of agreement across the highly various strands of degeneration theory: it was a mode of transmission that syncretized the available alternatives – acquisition, trauma, heredity, and contagion – rather than selecting among them.

Rooted in the Lamarckianism remarked earlier, degeneration theory proposed that dysfunctional traits acquired through environmental or occupational hazard, unhealthy habits, or the trauma of modernity, or by the effects of such contingencies on already suspect constitutions, were not only heritable by subsequent generations, but could actually increase in debilitating power over time.[5] But because the degenerative infirmity would, by all accounts, eventually vitiate the procreative capacity of those afflicted, their lineage must go defunct in the end and so their malady could not in fact conduce to a nation- or species-wide devastation.[6] To sustain that dire prospect, a supplementary line of causation was indicated. Based on "the germ theory of disease," there developed a notion of degeneracy as a contagion, indeterminably physiological and social. On this dispensation, bio-philosopher Robert Esposito observes, "degenerative pathology spreads irresistibly from one body to the next . . . it is both hereditary and contagious," (121–122) and, one might add, these two vectors of communicability feed one another ceaselessly, potentially enveloping the entire race.

What is especially important about this explanatory scenario, from our perspective, is that it thoroughly depends on a fully organic vision of society in which the degenerative plight of individual citizens affects in an immediate and thoroughgoing fashion the aggregate "regularity" of the population. Indeed, this organicist conception of part to whole provides the only viable grounds for treating individual cases of a non-infectious ailment as an assured and mortal threat to civilization as such. By extension, it was this conception that gave ideological warrant not just to eugenic policies for eliminating the degeneracy to come but to schemes for segregating, removing, and confining existing specimen-carriers of the disorder – such as those authorized in the Idiots' Act of 1886 or the Mental Deficiencies Act of 1913. Yet the same organicist logic that determines particular deviants to be impartible from and thus toxic to the normative governance of the collective entails as well that he or she is an impartible factor in determining the unfolding collective "regularities" and their corollary social norms. As the sociologist Alexander Johnson argued, degenerates would inevitably shape the human evolution of the future by "lowering the average standard of manhood and womanhood" (1998, 326). On this logic, the logic of degeneration as such, the boundaries dividing the threatened from the threatening body and the threatened from the threatening mind are irrevocably breached from the start.

On one side, for a so-called degenerate to corrupt the regularities of the public constitution is also, given the nature of such regularities, to renew them on other, albeit less favored grounds. That is why Gina Ferraro Lombroso could question whether degeneration was not a component of the upward evolutionary process to which it was generally opposed and could reach the following conclusion: "The degenerates are those who fuel the sacred torch of progress; to them is given the function of evolution, of civilization . . . they assume the office of decomposing and reconstructing institutions; the uses they make of their time activate the material exchange of this highly complex organism that is human society" (Esposito 2008, 124).

On the other side, for the normative subject to align with norms being renewed on these increasingly dubious grounds is to be complicit in their ongoing devolution, hence to participate in the advance of degeneracy. It is for this reason, I would submit, that the classes of subject designated as degenerate or as peculiarly liable to degeneration metastasized notoriously in the discourse of the time. With the prospect of social norms being recontoured by the irresistible spread of degeneracy, smaller and more various differences were taken to be morbid deviations from the "healthy type" of humanity. Thus, the mark of degeneracy was extended

a) from severe cognitive deficit – idiocy, imbecility – to what Mark Jackson calls the "borderland of feeble-mindedness" (2000, 13);
b) from the criminal type identified by Lombroso to so-called "moral imbeciles," figures of sexual errancy such as homosexuals, prostitutes, the effeminate, unwed mothers, and ill-breeding wives, rather than properly antisocial malefactors;
c) from the urban residuum, understood to be environmentally stunted in both a physiological and socioeconomic sense, to urban dwellers generally, insofar as they share the same insalubrious milieu;
d) from psychic or nervous disturbance (hysteria, neurasthenia) to psychic or nervous frailty, peculiarity, or excess (emotionalism, excitability, irritability, oversensitivity, impulsiveness, hyperesthesia); and
e) from the indolent, unproductive wastrel to those fatigued from overwork.

As if to acknowledge this internal shifting of the ground, degeneracy proponents like Lombroso and Nordau created a new pathological category, the "higher degenerate," whose intellectual faculties were as unimpaired as his moral faculties were "deranged" (Nordau 1993, 18, 18). The phrase itself points up the inversely totalizing logic of the degeneration thesis: its attempt to draw a cordon sanitaire around the truly fit and well-adapted resulted in a kind of all-inclusive exclusion, a species of otherness implicating everyone. Following the logic of (social) hysteria, the more inclusive the category of degeneracy grew, the more intense the desire to eliminate every trace of the disorder became, all the more so since in coming to occupy the norm itself, degeneracy could hide, as it were, in plain sight. The more intense that desire, in turn, the more numerous the accepted indices of degeneration and the more capacious the category.

The impetus of modern art and proto-modernist literature would seem to run in direct opposition to the agenda of the degenerationists. The experimental formal and stylistic strategies of the more decadent avant-garde privilege the exception at the expense of the norm and promote distorted modes of apprehension and unaccustomed, sometimes unsavory possibilities of experience at the expense of hale respectability and regularity. More than that, drawing upon a philosophical position that extends from Aristotle to Kant, these proto-modernists used their recognizably aesthetic media and frameworks of representation to raise the exception, the marginal, and the exorbitant to the status of the universal. Whereas degeneration theory busied itself stigmatizing deviation to the point at which the norm itself was incriminated, modernist art and literature could be seen as normalizing or regularizing the deviation.

It is no wonder, then, that toward the end of the nineteenth century, prominent exponents of degeneration targeted the new aesthetic associated with modernism as among the primary symptoms of social degeneration. They did so not only to discredit such forms of expression as morbid but to reduce them to reflexes of the present social crisis and thus to *particularize* them. In *The Insanity of Genius*, J. F. Nesbitt updates the long-established belief in the kinship of madness and creativity with a neurological twist: "All the available evidence . . . points clearly to the existence of a nerve-disorder as a fundamental element of genius," and he found support for this degenerationist position in several analyses of the works of Delacroix, Degas, Burne-Jones, and Moreau as the effects of "exhausted blood," mental weakness, sick genius, and "morbid perspicacity," each condition being ascribed to the artist's modernity (Bade 1985, 225). The literary critic Frederic Harrison judged "decadence a sure sign of some organic change taking place in our moral sense" and counterposed it to the "healthy art" of "spiritual growth".[7]

But the chief degenerationist scourge of the modern arts was none other than the chief degenerationist himself, Max Nordau. Having approved the notorious pronouncement, "Genius is a disease of the nerves," Nordau structures his entire magnum opus to frame contemporary art and literature as the embodiment of all the degenerate properties afflicting the modern age. In Book One of *Degeneration*, "Fin de Siècle," he declares

> The physician . . . if he has devoted himself to the special study of nervous and mental maladies, recognizes at a glance, in the fin de siècle disposition, in the tendencies of contemporary art and poetry, in the life and conduct of the men who write mystic, symbolic and decadent work, and the attitude taken by their admirers . . . the confluence of two well-defined conditions of disease . . . degeneration (degeneracy) and hysteria. (Nordau 1993, 15)

To bear out this contention, Nordau adds to the physical stigmata widely imputed to severe forms of degeneration (facial tics, drooling, and the like) a series of mental stigmata that find their objective correlatives in the aesthetic features of modern works, the organization of artistic movements, and the emotional states aroused in their audiences.[8] Synthesthesia and symbolic "word-sequences" reflect and appeal to a nervous intoxication with sound and surface rather than an attention to ideas; the obscurity of modern texts announces a capricious inclination to connect some meaning with every word; the spectacle of modern dramatic performance answers to a thirst for "novel sensation"; the "bliss of the beautiful" experienced by contemporary aficionados confesses their excessive "emotionalism"; the characteristically modern formation of the aesthetic coterie and the related cultivation of discipleship stems from the heightened suggestability endemic to the degenerate art-mongers (Nordau 1993, 14, 19, 28, 52, 65–66). Nordau proceeds, in the Books that follow, to widen his canvas and unfold a kind of patho-history of modern arts and letters, in which he deploys renowned figures and schools to illustrate what he holds to be the principal mental stigmata of degeneration: mysticism and egomania.

But more than an exemplary symptom, or rather precisely in being an exemplary symptom, contemporary arts and letters function for Nordau to communicate (in every sense) degeneracy throughout the social body. Explicitly, Nordau views the arts as encouraging a general disregard or even disparagement of the "normal type," from which they have so diverged (19). Implicitly, they can be seen as exerting their influence, an influence made considerable by the already degenerate trajectory of Western society, to supplant the "normal type" itself, redefining the evolutionary "regularities" upon which it is based. So degeneration does not just reduce "characteristically modern art" to symptoms of "the disease of the artist and . . . the race," as George Bernard Shaw noted in his reply to Nordau, it treats cultural transmission as an all but literal homologue of viral transmission, in both operation and consequence (1908, 17).

The kulturkampf waged by the degenerationist school arguably marks the furthest reaches of its effort to annex all segments of the populace to the deteriorating condition it delineates and to fulfill thereby the organicist imperative of biopower generally. In modern art and literature this centrifugal movement of power/knowledge found the most advanced, sophisticated endeavor that could nonetheless be theorized as leading to the debility and decline of the race, an avant-garde in reverse. But there is another, complementary aspect to the discourse of degeneration, a centripetal movement that works to focus and crystallize the pathology's variegated array of pernicious features in an exemplary subject-form, the "mentally deficient." If the modernist attitude toward cognitive disability took shape partly in response to the centrifugal sweep of degeneration theory, which terminated in an attack on modern art itself, its attitude also responds to the centripetal narrowing of degeneration theory, which results in the circling of the mentally retarded as devolutionary social menace. It is to the latter movement we now turn.

Idiocy, Imbecility, Feeble-Mindedness

Over the same period that degeneration theory strove to appropriate high cultural practices to its grim narrative of social decline and racial devolution, it attempted, rather more successfully, to do much the same thing with low cognitive function, working to shift the public perception of mental retardation from individual misfortune to social malignancy. Previously, the object of private charitable care driven by humanitarian concern, mental deficiency came toward the end of the century to be viewed as, in one critic's words, "a major social problem," and in another's "an image presaging the end of the race" (Thomson 1998, 13; McDonagh 2008, 279). The prime architect of degeneration theory, Benedict Morel, promulgated the notion that idiocy and imbecility were heritable and atavistic, and once his position took hold across the scientific community, mental retardation was resolutely positioned at the hub of a wheel composed of all the other major profiles and variants of degenerative disorder.

First, understood as physiologically transmitted conditions, idiocy and imbecility figured as sites of contagion. Thus, Dr. Robert Rantoul warned, "Day by day, hour by hour, year after year, we add diseased humanity – the children begotten by the disease, idiots, imbeciles, epileptics ... all the contaminating influences go on permeating, causing more disease, converting the river into a cesspool" (Jackson 2000, 131). One of those contaminating influences of degeneracy with which mental deficiency was strongly affiliated was criminality. The great degenerationist criminologist Lombroso maintained that idiocy and criminality alike derived from cranial degeneracy and "were forged into a single chain" (Halliday 2004, 99). Lombroso's view was tributary in turn to a broadly held conviction that idiocy and imbecility represented degeneracy not just of mind and body but of the moral will – a belief used, Foucault tells us, to justify coercion as a mode of "special" education (2003, 215–219). Furthermore, idiots and imbeciles were reckoned, on this basis, to be especially prone to sexual promiscuity and aggression, which only served to exaggerate phobias concerning their power to pollute the bloodlines of the nation or race by procreation, to repopulate the species in their own devolved image.

The imputed combination of depressed intelligence, moral insensibility, criminal propensity, and ungovernable appetite made idiocy et al. a primary site of a degenerative phenomenon much feared among medical and biological experts: evolutionary recapitulation and reversion. It was widely accepted that the mentally retarded were frozen at a rudimentary stage of growth, not just in the sense of ontogenic *bildung* (though the new science of psychometrics did rank idiocy, imbecility etc. by mental age), but in terms of phylogenic advances, each individual being assumed to repeat or "recapitulate" the history of the race. John Langdon Downs, for whom Downs' syndrome is named, "hypothesized that many forms of idiocy were in fact genetic throwbacks, avatars of earlier, less evolved races" (McDonagh 2008, 270). For his part, "the idiot," as Henry Maudsley wrote, "is arrested at different stages of its development along a path common to it and the lower animals".[9] Unable to access the higher, more cerebral, more human dimensions of the brain, on this gloss, idiots, imbeciles, and the feeble-minded exemplified social unfitness, and so it is no surprise that they were regularly grouped as part of the infamous residuum, along with paupers, prostitutes, felons, alcoholics, and the permanently unemployed. Darwinism, in the form of evolutionary reversion, dovetailed with social Darwinism under the sign of degeneration. The contaminating influences complained of by Dr. Rantoul were thought to pull society *down* and *back* simultaneously, into a futurity of intellectual, moral, and economic underdevelopment that would be an analogue to humanity's primitive past. In the words of Herbert Spencer, the eminence responsible for the scientific respectability of social Darwinism, "there is no greater curse to posterity than that of bequeathing them an increasing population of imbeciles, idlers and criminals" (1874, 344–345).

We have seen how by the organicist lights of the biopower regime, in which norms derive from "regularities" cutting across entire populations, degeneration cannot but bear upon and implicate the whole. On the same logic, however, assorted manifestations of that condition dispersed across such integrated populations can bear upon and be absorbed, serially yet en toto, by a particular segment of that population. That is to say, the organic continuity between whole and part postulated by the discourses of biopower implies an organic continuity between any given part and all the other parts. So having concatenated sundry variants of the degenerative syndrome throughout the community, nation, or race, exponents of degeneration theory reversed their steps and concentrated these variants, as documented above, within a particular group, the mentally retarded, who became emblematic of its defining properties and dangers.

A dialectical reversal of this sort always carries an additional valence not accounted for in either of the movements taken separately. In this case, having been fashioned as a degenerative nexus or depot for all degenerative "types" and their attributes, mental retardation came to function as an exception, an exceptional instance of degeneration, a remnant apart. That is, mental deficiency could be and was posed as a special, more profound, more authentic species of degeneration and thus as a break from and within the very logic of organic continuity that underwrote its emblematic status in the first place. Thus stigmatized (literally assigned stigmata) as "true" degeneration, what Nordau himself posited as its most "complete" form, mental deficiency allowed the divers branches of the theory[10] – medical, evolutionary, biological, sociological, anthropological – to maintain or restore the appearance of a distance between health and pathology, normal and abnormal, that the discursive logic of degeneration inexorably outstripped. The mentally defective were therefore conscripted as manipulable figures of "extimacy" for the degenerationist regime of biopower, allowing it to fulfill its opposed imperatives of inclusion and exclusion, totalization and discrimination, simultaneously. They were so organically intimate with the social whole as to embody a virulent contagion and yet so alien, so beyond the pale, as to be responsibly treated as a subhuman other.

It was this singularly abject social profile (in the full Kristevan sense) that explains why the mentally retarded among all those tarred as unfit or undesirable could emerge as the primary objects of preemptive genocide, otherwise known as "negative" eugenics. It was this abject profile too that explains why, in Matthew Thomson's words, the "segregation of mental defectives was accepted, whereas similar proposals for the inebriate, habitual criminals, and the unemployed all failed" (1998, 1). These measures not only strove to solve the problem of "idiocy" but to salvage the coherence of degenerationist ideology. Taken together, they impose upon mental deficiency forms of genealogical/biological separation so profound as to express, or claim to express, some preceding, absolute ontological distance. In that way, the measures symbolically denied or dissimulated the motive underlying them: a phobic sense of some degenerative proximity between the cognitively de- and pro-ficient. We might call this the rage whereby degeneration theory avoids seeing its face in the mirror.

Whereas the prophets of degeneration often denounced modern art and literature as an objectification and a conductor of the disorder in its several variants – neurological, affective, moral, and even cognitive – the indictment was always levied in terms of a "higher" degeneracy and so did not involve idiocy, imbecility, or feeble-mindedness directly. A charge did arise, however, that modern, and on this occasion specifically modernist, art was responsible for impeding the extermination of mental deficiency, which by degenerative logic meant contributing to its continued spread. Roger Fry's famous first Post-Impressionism exhibit (1910–11) "drew out," William Greenslade reports, "the avatars of a still resilient degenerationist mentality: critics such as [Sir William] Richmond, T.B. Hyslop, Robert Ross, E. Wade Cook . . . " (1994, 130). Critics of this ilk linked the paintings on show with some of the usual degenerate suspects: "lunacy and gross subjectivism," "emotions of . . . pathology and abnormality," "paralytic," "epileptic," "evidence of mental and physical collapse," and even criminality ("There are a number of post-Impressionists detained at his majesty's pleasure") (130–132). But Dr. Hyslop, self-proclaimed "eugenicist of art," took another direction. He not only coupled Post-Impressionism with insanity, another familiar degenerationist tack, he numbered this modernist aesthetic among those who "hampered by soft hearted attitudes" toward the "feeble minded" those necessary "prophylactic measures designed to benefit the greatest number" (133).

On the one hand, the exponents of degeneration theory excoriated modern art and literature as high cultural specimens and carriers of the disease, exfoliations of its characteristic debilities, including cognitive debilities, shared by artists, authors, and audiences alike. On the other hand, these exponents scored the modern arts for indulging "soft hearted" sympathy and solicitude toward certain bearers of the disease, specifically mental defectives, adjudged to be injurious to the health of the larger group. That is, the modern arts incurred criticism for being the danger of degeneration writ (or painted) large and the modern arts incurred criticism for qualms about eugenically culling those who "really" embody the danger of degeneration from an otherwise viable social herd, of which the aesthetic community is evidently a part. Now, given the hyperbolic and promiscuous nature of degenerationist discourse, this sort of inconsistency should not surprise, but the discrepancy does hold particular significance because it reflects the unacknowledged fissure between the extensive and the intensive logics of degeneration, between the impetus to subsume everyone and the impetus to protect the "greatest number" against the few.

The discrepancy is still more important, however, at least from our perspective, in its translation within modernism itself. For while literary modernists, beginning with Shaw's critique of Nordau, rejected wholesale the identification of the new experimental aesthetics with degeneracy, and even rejected the degenerationist paradigm itself, they did not in all cases, beginning with Shaw, reject the eugenics agenda that had grown out of that paradigm. Partly as a result, while refuting any imputation of degeneracy to themselves or their project, certain modernists do seem to have internalized the split-level basis from which that accusation proceeded.

Thus, prominent modernist texts featured characters with pronounced cognitive disabilities whose symptoms approximate those ascribed by degeneration theorists to the modern arts. We might call these the cognitive disabilities – nervous and neurological disorders, insanity, hysteria, traumatic derangement, autistic spectrum disorder – identified with modernity, and modernism "identifies them back," figuring such conditions as the source of legitimate alternative styles of being, vision, and experience. Whatever social objection the characters so disposed might encounter in the narrative, they are not portrayed by the narrative as simply inferior to the social norm in play, but also as living critiques of that norm. The difference their condition makes is given as something other or something more than merely privative. But literary modernism additionally features characters with that singular cognitive disability, "mental deficiency," with which degeneration theory did not identify the modern arts, except as a misbegotten voice of protective sympathy. The attitude of literary modernism to this species of cognitive disability could only be called affirmative disidentification. Not only did certain modernists subscribe to the eugenics campaign that grew out of degeneration theory, as Donald Childs (2001) has documented, mental retardation appears in modernist literature as a privative state unrelieved by any positive alloy, as not just a difference inferior to the norm but for that very reason as an abnormal reinforcement of that norm.

An Exemplary Case: Joseph Conrad

Joseph Conrad maps the division between the extensive and intensive logics of degeneration theory onto the division between mental deficiency and other, more diffuse types of cognitive disability linked to degeneracy. In Stevie of *The Secret Agent* (2004), Conrad gives us modernism's greatest nominal idiot/degenerate, that is, a character whose putative idiocy stems from his foregrounded encumbrance with various popular indices of degeneration. At the same time, Stevie is as close to a moral center as this novel displays. But he can perform this function (as he can be inveigled into placing a bomb at the Greenwich Observatory) only because he is, as his master Verloc puts it, "not so much an idiot as he looked," not so mentally deficient, in other words, as the stigmata of his degeneracy would lead one to believe (2004, 137). By this device, Conrad stages the dissociation of idiocy from the sort of disability/effect he would represent and, in a sense, redeem.

Certainly Stevie's idiocy, on which the characters and the critics of *The Secret Agent* seem to concur, was never intended to represent idiocy *sensu stricto*, that is, as it was understood in Conrad's time, as Conrad knew it to be understood, or as Conrad himself understood it. With the development of the new "science" of psychometrics – a child of degeneration theory and future ally of the eugenics movement – the identity form of idiocy had acquired a relatively narrow medical definition, an intelligence quotient of roughly thirty points, corresponding to the mental age of a two-year-old and ensconced on the bottom rung of the classified intellectual handicaps (Halliwell, 11–12; Nadesan, 147). To appreciate how far a contemporaneous portrait of this cognitive estate would differ from the depiction of Stevie, we need look no further, serendipitously enough, than Conrad's own earlier story, "The Idiots" from the volume *Tales of Unrest* (Conrad 2008).

In that story of familial despair, intrigue, and murder, the four "idiots" represented have no part in the reported action other than to catalyze it as the source of their parents' marital discord and reprisal. They were regarded, quite simply, as a curse, a role that both a) accords entirely with the estimation of cognitive deviation in the degenerationist/eugenics school, and b) differed greatly from the robust energy Stevie displays. The "idiots" likewise have a merely catalytic function in the larger narrative: after an initial appearance that occasions a retailing of the family tragedy, they drop out of sight altogether. This etiolated narrative role consists entirely with the nugatory ontological status these idiots are given. Conrad conceives their condition as one of primordial vacancy, treating the four as indistinguishable one from the other and as virtually continuous with the inanimate objects of the natural landscape. The contrast with Stevie, who fairly brims with the signs of psychic interiority and the related stirrings of idiosyncrasy, seems considerably stronger than whatever pathological likeness the common label of "idiot" might indicate. Finally, in their very blankness, the idiots have a powerful material impact that is privative, that is, without substance save for a parasitic capacity to detract. To be specific, the idiots embody forces of "monstrous darkness," which constitute an "offense," a "reproach," and a "blight" in their absolute inability to assist their parents in the work of life: cultivating the family lands (2008, 37). Throughout Conrad's oeuvre, of course, labor counts as a reliable marker of human merit, and so it is significant that whatever his limitations, Stevie always labors assiduously – as bootblack, bodyguard, valet, shopkeeper, messenger – with the singular motive of contributing to his family's welfare. Obscure as "The Idiots" may be, then, it does make for a lucid mirror of disability, in which Stevie's variance from the clinical designation he bears is plain to see in all its premeditated glory.

But there is plenty of evidence in *The Secret Agent* itself that Conrad had drawn upon the colloquial, pejorative senses of the epithet "idiot," which were already current, to strip the term of its diagnostic exactitude, in a parody of those discourses, like degeneration theory, obsessed with their necessarily indefinite taxonomies of the pathological.

Extensively, idiocy and its collaterals, like imbecility, prove to be ubiquitous in Conrad's urban universe. No one is immune to this disorder, from the "imbecile bourgeoisie" to the police to the "English middle classes" to interested cells of cynical diplomats and anarchist revolutionaries, who both invoke and invite the epithet in turn. One of Conrad's letters reveals just how deliberately he pursued this rhetorical strategy. Having first singled out Stevie as "the idiot," he likens the remainder of the cast to him: "they're all imbeciles, what's more, including an Embassy Secretary, a Minister of State, and an Inspector of Police" (Conrad 2004, xii). The foundation for this broad-based or extensive deployment of the signifiers for mental defectiveness would seem to be Max Nordau's infamously popular tract *Degeneration*, which first appeared in the very year Conrad embarked on his literary career, and it has been judged by critics such as Joseph Saveson and Martin Rey to inform many if not all the characterizations in *The Secret Agent* (Ray 1984, 125–140; de Vries 1985, 122–123). Nordau posed idiocy as the most "complete" form of degeneration, but his real targets of critique were the "higher" traits exhibited across the entire cast of characters in Conrad's novel: from monomania (the professor) to mysticism (Vladimir) to nervous irritability (Yundt) to suggestibility (the patroness) to the physical stigmata of maladaptation (Winnie's mother). That the nets of degeneracy enmesh so many in the novel serves to identify this thesis with Conrad's construct of "idiocy" in the extreme promiscuity of their application, and to show how far Stevie's own disability is neither singularly aberrant nor universally shared but is representative of a wider but internally variegated condition.

Intensively, Conrad fashions Stevie himself as something other than a poster child of the narrow psychometric medical definition of idiocy or a low-functioning foil to the remaining characters, something different too than the epitome or summary instance of their various pathologies, that is, Nordau's take on idiocy as degeneration *in excelsis*. Instead, Conrad aimed to create a socially conscious "idiot" that could be plausibly affiliated with an ethically framed, politically motivated provocation, as

a) its precursor (inciting a massive "fireworks" panic in response to "tales of oppression and injustice" (Conrad 2004, 7);
b) its secret, unlikely, but not entirely unwilling or unwitting agent (at Greenwich);
c) its emblem, a figure whose dispersed consciousness not only portends his bodily dispersion during the Greenwich explosion, but epitomizes the more broadly anarchic tendencies, the cultural entropy of Conrad's world. He is a Modern subject in extremis, embodying the simultaneously interconnective and disintegrative impact of a new age.

For Stevie to fulfill this manifold symbolic office, his disability must consist not in an intellectual apparatus diminished to the point of chronic incomprehension, the traditional fate of the simpleton, but in a phenomenological circuitry (sensory, perceptual, affective, cognitive) overloaded to the point of derangement, a state of hyperesthesia or systematic overstimulation that spasmodically distorts the information to be processed by intensifying it. Where Stevie flounders is not in his powers of *ideation* but in his powers of *mediation*. No minor distinction this, it marks the border between an intellectual handicap and a neurosensory disorder. As I argue elsewhere, the latter looks a lot like what is today diagnosed as autism, and while considerations of space prevent me from mounting this case here on a symptom by symptom basis, I would submit that autism bears a social profile not unlike the degeneracy with which Conrad plainly wished to engage, both being "spectrum disorders" featuring clusters of signature traits that are not only variable over time, but internally contradictory, and illimitable in the possible combinations they can form.[11]

In any event, Conrad grounds Stevie's condition in just such a cluster of phenomenological disturbances rather than some defining cognitive deficit. He introduces Stevie by informing the reader that "notwithstanding the [vacant droop] of his lower lip," Stevie suffered from no fatal lack of raw intelligence – he had learned to read and write – but from a profound attentional deficit correlated with emotional agitation ("he was easily diverted from the straight path of duty by the attraction of stray dogs and cats ... and the drama of fallen horses") (Conrad 2004, 7). Later, as Stevie prepares to embark on the nightmarish cab ride through London, we discover that the "vacant mouth" itself evinces not a cognitive blankness or void but just the opposite: an acute sensitivity, amounting to nervous distress, at the various human "transactions" surrounding him. Confronted by the spectacle of the "maimed driver" and his abused horse, Stevie undergoes, and his lower lip registers, one of those paroxysms of overstimulation he regularly experiences at the prospect, real or imagined, of the pangs or grievances of others. The symptoms the prospect catalyzes – "futile bodily agitation," "agitation of limbs," a "stammer," and "stutter," the prostrating waves of "morbid terror and dread" – all point to a sensory-nerve disorder (122–124), while the catalysts themselves link Stevie's disability to his acute moral sensibility. His is a "convulsive sympathy" that bespeaks a concern for social justice too ardent for his limited powers of synthesis and self-possession to process, regulate, or express with a normative degree of aplomb.

At the conclusion of the cab ride, Stevie gives voice to his crowning ethico-political epiphany, "Bad world for poor people" (125). However crudely phrased, this conclusion proceeds from an act of sound moral ratiocination. The judgment has required Stevie to navigate from a particular social contradiction – how animal-like cruelty *suffered* by the working man necessitates animal abuse *inflicted* by the working man – to a structural social ill. In other words, Stevie performs the sort of analysis that is assumed into evidence as the pretext for much of the ethico-political speechifying on the part of the anarchists. The mental processes leading to this insight, however, confirm the impediments to Stevie's mediation of his own thoughts: "He would remain there, trying to express the view ... of the human and the equine in close association. But it was very difficult. 'Poor brute, poor people!'

was all he could repeat. It did not seem forcible enough and he came to a stop with an angry splutter: 'Shame!' Stevie was no master of phrases and perhaps for that reason, his thoughts lacked clearness and precision" (125–126). The passage explicitly locates Stevie's problems of apprehension and distillation in the interface of language skills rather than the terminus of intellectual capacity.

Stevie's verbal misfires might be understood as alternatively the direct expression of his embodied turbulence and a reaction against it. Other aspects of his conduct fall out along the same dialectically opposed lines. On one side, the otherwise "amiable, attractive, affectionate and . . . only a little peculiar" (114) Stevie shows a propensity for meltdowns, for fits of loquacity, for vagrancy, for sometimes murderous aggression ("In the face of anything which affected . . . his morbid dread of pain, he turned vicious," 124), and his willingness to create a panic (the office fireworks) or even perpetrate an outrage (the Greenwich Observatory) all tend to act out the commotion intrinsic to his embodied being-in-the-world and endemic to his experience thereof; on the other side, his obsessive attachments and his tenacious insistence on moral observance, order, and clarity all seem to serve as a defense against the same incurable sensory-affective perturbation.

Even as Conrad elects to depict his anarchists "idiots" in the vernacular sense, implicated in the encompassing cultural malaise they survey, he also casts his idiot as an anarchist in the vernacular sense, an emblem of the cultural entropy that degeneracy theorists like Nordau imputed to nervous exhaustion at the traumatic changes of modernity (Nordau, 37). Conrad delineates Stevie's primary symptomology – his hyperesthesia, bodily agitation, sensory disintegration, and emotional meltdown – as what we might call the subjective correlative of anarchist provocation. Stevie's sometimes violent bodily discomposure enciphers the specter of the anarchistic eruption which, in the end, violently decomposes his body. At the same time, Stevie's reactive symptomology strives to marshal his overwrought sensory and emotional energies into a force of social order and moral direction, even as his social and moral demands incite still greater turbulence, both inner and outer, lived and created. In the very form of his subjectivity, then, Stevie encapsulates that complicity of law and disorder which, more than unalloyed chaos, constitutes the truly anarchic element animating the "monstrous town" of Conrad's London. Like that larger civic body, he cannot finally separate the tumult and brutality he wars against from that he occasions or engenders; like that larger body, his desperation to assert control, physical and moral, over the agitation that threatens to unravel the fabric of his being and his lived reality proves to be continuous, as on a Moebius strip, with the fatal agitation itself.

Belying its subtitle, "A Simple Tale," the novel teems with unforeseen alliances and entanglements between adversaries, enemies, opposite numbers, etc. (diplomat/revolutionary, Inspector Heat/the professor, the police/the anarchists, criminal class/high society, Winnie/Verloc) of which Stevie is the ultimate victim, the primary figure destroyed by the symbiosis of rule and misrule that he personifies. But the most surprising ligature, and the one that summarizes the others, is the thread linking Stevie's disability and what passes for normal or at least abled in this society. Instead of the idiot figure summarizing the most dysfunctional properties of the other degenerates, he embodies and parodies the sort of organic continuity of the social tacitly presupposed by the regulatory discourses of biopower. Stevie's differences, accordingly, need not count as pathic aberrations from fixed standards of conformity, but as variations (more or less benign) or alternatives (better or worse) within an evolving set of "regularities." What is more, in a trenchant reversal, the idiot boy is not the source but the object or terminus of whatever contagion of degeneracy might be inferred from the action of the novel. His moral perspective, the only one untainted by the Nordauian bugaboos of mysticism, ego-mania, or hysteria, is eradicated by the combined operation of other, more secretly degenerate "agents."

In Stevie, then, Conrad provides not so much an anatomy of social disability as a social anatomy of disability, a treatment of disability as social construct, as opposed to organic defect, an extraordinarily advanced conception for the time. It is not too much to say that Conrad presages the "social model" of disability, formulated in the 1970s, which insists on an overlooked distinction between impairment, an organic defect of mind or body, and disability, "the disadvantage *imposed on top* of one's impairment by the contemporary social organization" (Tremaine 2012, 9) – or even, I would add, the impairment created by a socially imposed interpretation of difference. Stevie's fate hovers somewhere between these two "social" forms of disability. We must remember, however, that as politically incisive as Conrad's anticipation of the "social model" may be when it comes to the broad degenerationism we wish to critique, it does consign mental retardation, the eponymous "idiots" of his tale of unrest, to the darkness of "mere" impairment, a deficit whose natural causation licenses cultural disregard if not defamation.

Epilogue

Although the influence of degeneration theory markedly waned in the second decade of the twentieth century, that of its activist partner-in-biopower, the eugenics movement, grew stronger. So too did the literary impulse to separate out "idiocy," understood as mental defect, from other cognitive and psychic maladies or differences, particularly following the access of traumatic disorder brought on by the Great War. Rebecca West supplies a useful case in point. In *The Return of the Soldier* (1998), the traumatic amnesia of the title character, Chris, acts as a withering rejection of the materialism, elitism, and snobbery to which he had committed himself as savior of the family's imperial holdings, master of Baudry Court, and husband to the impossibly venal Kitty. The discrepant perspective his mental breakdown has provided finds powerful legitimation in the return of his saintly, lower-class ex-love, Margaret, the last person he properly remembers, who shelters him in a life of simple pleasures (gardening, punting, napping, etc.). The moral center of this novel, Margaret initially resists the call of family and psychiatry to help bring him back to "the truth," arguing that he has found a "happiness" unattainable for most. "You can't cure him," she says to the psychiatrist, ". . . make him happy I mean. All you can do is make him ordinary" (West 1998, 81). Significantly, however, the perception that Chris's newfound idyll will over time come to simulate "senile idiocy" drives Margaret to take the lead in engineering his "return" to mental normalcy even though it means his return to the Western front as well (88). The contrast is stark: a mental disability can be transvalued as a psycho-spiritual difference superior to and critical of the sociocultural status quo, unless it smacks of cognitive deficiency or mental retardation, at which point the hell of the most infernal war ever imagined is decisively preferable.[12]

The contrast in attitude toward psychic derangement and mental defectiveness, respectively, is still more striking in the case of Virginia Woolf, and a proper appreciation of this dichotomy in her work greatly eliminates a recent controversy over the tenor of her biopolitics. In his book, *Modernism and Eugenics: Woolf, Yeats, Eliot and the Culture of Degeneration*, Donald Childs has painted Woolf as subscribing to a "most negative eugenics," based on her truly infamous diary of January 15, 1915:

> On the towpath we met and had to pass a long line of imbeciles. The first was a very tall young man, just queer enough to look at twice, but no more; the second, shuffled, & looked aside; & then one realized that every one in that long line was a miserable ineffective shuffling idiotic creature, with no forehead, or no chin, & an imbecile grin, or a wild suspicious stare. It was perfectly horrible. They should certainly be killed. (2001, 13)

After a noxiously unconvincing attempt to mitigate Woolf's genocidal sentiments – with a clichéd and vacuous invocation of "the appropriate historical context" – David Bradshaw more effectively refutes Childs' eugenicist charge by pointing to the irony with which Woolf handles the racially conscious agents of biopower in *Mrs. Dalloway*: Lady Bruton, Sir William Bradshaw, even Richard Dalloway (Bradshaw 2003, 49). Bradshaw correctly emphasizes "the fundamentally playful element . . . that seems to have eluded Childs," who regularly identifies Woolf's viewpoint with those of the characters she lampoons (2003, 49). It seems to me that Bradshaw could have gone even further along these lines and enlisted Woolf's sympathetic portrayal of, and authorial transference with, the shell-shocked Septimus Smith, one of the most prominent mentally damaged characters in modernist literature. Surely her narration of his ultimately fatal torment by the London medical establishment denotes her strong disagreement with the eugenicist equation of deviance with disposability.

But a decisive caveat must be entered at this point. Although Woolf's odious diary entry does not speak to her fictional interventions in degenerationist politics generally – quite the contrary – the passage does consist with the portrayals of idiocy, imbecility, and feeble-mindedness that appear throughout her work. In "A Sketch of the Past," "the idiot boy . . . mewing slit eyed, red-rimmed," looms as a figure of "horror," "hopeless sadness," and prolonged disturbance for young Virginia (Woolf

1976, 78). Translating the experience into her fiction, Woolf stages an encounter between young Rose of *The Pargiters* and a deformed figure "gibbering nonsense," who terrifies her in the moment and haunts her dreams thereafter (Woolf 1977, 42–47). She revises the scenario in *The Years*, where the man, now "mewing" like "the idiot boy" in "Sketches," proves to be a flasher, thus affording tangible grounds for Rose's phobic reaction (Woolf 1937, 29). The "feeble-minded boy" of "Street Haunting" is the only one of the disabled figures that Woolf observes who lends no positive carnivalesque energy to the urban scene, but just negligibly "suck[s] the silver knob of his stick" (Woolf 1994, 484). Woolf does not endeavor to occupy, let alone justify, the perspective of *any* of these figures, as she so strenuously does her psychically deviate characters like Septimus, Rhoda in *The Waves*, and Cam in *To the Lighthouse*. My point is that the hateful verdict "Surely they must be killed" may well be unrepresentative of Woolf's views on mental disability, but that the verdict was directed specifically at "imbeciles," mentally deficient or retarded subjects, rather than other bearers of mental "degeneracy" does in fact cohere with Woolf's other writing, and in drawing this particular distinction, Woolf herself proves representative of a wider strain of literary modernism.

Acknowledgments

My greatest debt in this essay is to Janet Lyons, without whose insights into the social construction of mental handicaps I could not have written it. My thanks also to Maren Linnett for her truly enlightening conversation.

Notes

1   Quoted in Sandra Siegle, "Literature and Degeneration," in Chamberlin and Gilman, 202.
2   Robert Nye, "Sociology: The Irony of Progress," in Chamberlin and Gilman, 50.
3   Michel Foucault, "The Abnormals," in *Ethics: Subjectivity and Truth*, 51.
4   Max Nordau, *Degeneration*, 16; Benedict Morel quoted in Nadesan, 144.
5   Eric Carlson, "Medicine and Degeneration," in Chamberlin and Gilman, 122.
6   See for example Benedict Morel, Traite des dégénérescences physiques, intellectuelles et morales de l'espèce humaine, cited in Janet Oppenheim, *Shattered Nerves* (Oxford: Oxford University Press, 1991), 270.
7   Siegle in Chamberlain and Gilman, 209.
8   For the physical stigmata, see Henry Maudsley, *The Pathology of Mind* (New York: St. Martin's, 1979), 339.
9   Maudsley, 341; see also William Greenslade, *Degeneration, Culture and the Novel*, 69.
10 Nordau, 64; for the fears concerning the heritability of idiocy and the impact they had on public policy, see Jackson, 34, 37–38.
11 Valente 2012.
12 I am indebted to Maren Linnet for this point.

References

Bradshaw, David. (2003). *A Concise Companion to Modernism*. Oxford: Blackwell.

Chamberlain, J. and S. Gilman, eds. (1985). *Degeneration: The Dark Side of Progress*. New York: Columbia University Press.

Childs, Donald. (2001). *Modernism and Eugenics: Woolf, Yeats, Eliot and the Culture of Degeneration*. Cambridge: Cambridge University Press.

Conrad, Joseph. (2004). *The Secret Agent*, ed. John Lyons. Oxford: Oxford University Press.

Conrad, Joseph. (2008). *Tales of Unrest*. Teddington: Echo Library.

De Vries, Jetty. (1985). "Stevie and Recent Criticism." *Conradiana* 17.2.

Esposito, Roberto. (2008). *Bios*. Minneapolis: University of Minnesota Press.

Foucault, Michel. (1997a). *Society Must Be Defended*. New York: Picador.

Foucault, Michel. (1997b). *Ethics: Subjectivity and Truth*. New York: New Press.

Foucault, Michel. (2003). *Psychiatric Power*. New York: Picador.

Greenslade, William. (1994). *Degeneration, Culture and the Novel*. Cambridge: Cambridge University Press.

Halliday, Martin. (2004). *Images of Idiocy*. Aldershot: Ashgate.

Jackson, Mark. (2000). *The Borderland of Imbecility*. Manchester: Manchester University Press.

Johnson, Alexander. (1998). "Concerning a Form of Degeneracy." *The American Journal of Sociology* 4: 326.

McDonagh, Patrick. (2008). *Idiocy: A Cultural History*. Liverpool: Liverpool University Press.

Nadesan, Majia. (2008). *Governmentality, Biopower, and Everyday Life*. New York: Routledge.

Nordau, Max. (1993). *Degeneration*. Lincoln: University of Nebraska Press.

Pick, Daniel. (1989). *Faces of Degeneration*. Cambridge: Cambridge University Press.

Ray, Martin. (1984). "Conrad, Nordau and Other Degenerate." *Conradiana* 16.2.

Shaw, George Bernard Shaw. (1908). *The Sanity of Art: An Exposure of the Current Nonsense About Artists Being Degenerate*. London: New Age.

Spencer, Herbert. (1874). *The Study of Sociology*. New York: Appleton.

Thomson, Matthew. (1998). *The Problem of Mental Deficiency*. Oxford: Clarendon Press.

Tremaine, Shelley. (2012). "Foucault, Governmentality and Cultural Disability Theory: An Introduction." In *Foucault and the Government of Disability*. Ann Arbor: University of Michigan Press.

Valente, Joseph. "The Accidental Autist: Neurosensory Disorder in Conrad's The Secret Agent," given at the Mahindra Institute, Harvard University February 2012 and under submission at Modern Fiction Studies.

Woolf, Virginia. (1937). *The Years*. New York: Harcourt Brace.

Woolf, Virginia. (1976). *Moments of Being*. New York: Harvest.

Woolf, Virginia. (1977). *The Pargiters*. New York: New York Library.

West, Rebecca. (1998). *The Return of the Soldier*. New York: Penguin.

23

From Parody to the Event; from Affect to Freedom

Observations on the Feminine Sublime in Modernism

Ewa Plonowska Ziarek

It seems to me indispensable to go back through the Analytic of the Sublime from Kant's Critique of Judgment *in order to get an idea of what is at stake in modernism.*

Lyotard, "After the Sublime, the State of Aesthetics," *The Inhuman*, 135

[A]fter the fall of formal beauty, the sublime was the only aesthetic idea left to modernism.

Adorno, *Aesthetic Theory*, 197

The constellation of feminism, the sublime, and modernism is fraught with ambivalence, contradictions, and domination, if not sheer irrelevance. On the one hand, thanks to critics of modernism and literary theorists such as de Man (1960, 129–162), Derrida (1987, 122–147), Jameson (1991, 1–37), Adorno (1997, 194–198), Lyotard (1984, I), Kristeva (1982, 11–12), Freeman (1997), among others, critical revisions of the "sublime" are implicated in the key terms of modernism and modernist aesthetics: the crisis of representation; the analysis of sensibility, affect, and shock; the role of innovation and experiment; the relation between content and form; the relation between power, nature, and history; temporality and the trauma of domination; and finally the relation between art, subjugation, and the promise of freedom. As Lyotard (1991) puts it, the sublime "has belonged (for at least two centuries) to the most rigorous kind of reflection on art," although modernist art, such as Gertrude Stein's *How to Write*, though "still the sublime in the sense that Burke and Kant described," "isn't their sublime any more" (92, 93). On the other hand, however, the import of the sublime for rethinking the stakes of modernism, so strongly stressed by Lyotard and Adorno in the opening epigrams to this essay, seems to be a thing of the past in Anglo-American studies of modernism.

A Handbook of Modernism Studies, First Edition. Edited by Jean-Michel Rabaté.
© 2013 John Wiley & Sons, Ltd. Published 2013 by John Wiley & Sons, Ltd.

Indeed, there is no single mention of the sublime in the massive *The Oxford Handbook of Modernisms* or in the *Cambridge Companion to European Modernism*. These authoritative guides, backed by the prestige of their respective presses, aim in different ways to survey the "enormous" changes in the field of modernism in the past three decades, changes characterized by a shift from experimental aesthetics to a renewed interest in empirical research and the historical situatedness of multiple modernisms within global, transnational contexts, such as unequal developments of modernity and capital, publication practices, mass media, advertising, cultural markets, and other institutional frameworks of cultural production (Brooker 2011, 2–10).[1] Given this eclipse of the sublime, one task of this essay is to reflect on whether this concept still has any traction in modernist studies. And, the second one is to think through the antinomic relationship between the sublime, gender, and feminism.

The fact that the sublime has disappeared as a key concept from the lexicon of modernism and the avant-garde is itself a symptom of the transformation of the literary field. As Lyotard points out in his celebrated 1982 essay "Answering the Question: What Is Postmodernism?", there is nothing more recalcitrant to the cognitive knowledge of literature, whether this knowledge is empirical or theoretical, than the discourse of the sublime. According to Lyotard, who is most frequently credited for the resurgence of interest in the sublime in modernist studies, what is at stake in the sublime is precisely the crisis of representation and the conflict between what is presentable and what is conceivable. We have ideas that we can conceive of – quite common ideas, in fact, such as the idea of the world presupposed in studies of globalization and transnationalism, the idea of freedom presupposed in critiques of imperialism or gender and racist oppression, or the idea of humanity in the political lexicon of equality – but we fail to present empirical examples that would correspond to these ideas. The discourse of the sublime is intertwined with the failure to present the case or a referent – say a literary text or a historical example – that would correspond to cognition. According to Kant's well-known definition (1951), this failure of imagination to present an object corresponding to the ideas of reason creates a discord of the faculties, which we experience as painful, overwhelming, and even outrageous, whereas the delight of the sublime comes from an affirmation of the superiority of moral reason over any sensible or empirical presentation (107).

Rereading Lyotard's essay "Answering the Question: What Is Postmodernism?" almost thirty years after its publication is an uncanny experience of the return of the repressed. Lyotard's rethinking of the critical purchase of the sublime is directed against calls for the end of aesthetic experimentation intertwined with a demand for historical knowledge, "recognizable meaning," and the stability of the referent (1991, 74). Although the target of Lyotard's critique was primarily Habermas, many of his points are pertinent today as a diagnosis of the state of modernist studies in particular and humanities in general: Today we witness a similar devaluation of aesthetic experimentation and theoretical questioning with priority given instead to pragmatic knowledge and the historical contexts of literary production. Lyotard sums up this situation as follows: It is an attempt to replace an aesthetic judgment about literature, which operates without fixed criteria or concepts, with a determinate cognitive judgment, which subsumes literary analysis under cognitive empirical knowledge.

Yet, as Lyotard is first to point out, the legacy of the sublime, which modern art inherits, critiques, and reconfigures, is fraught with difficulties. Lyotard underscores the violent character of the Kantian sublime, which sacrifices imagination and nature to the superiority of practical reason. The superiority of will over internal and external nature enables the transcendence of "our physical impotence" (1951, 101). The first difficulty of sublime aesthetics lies therefore in the triumphalism of moral reason, which compensates for the failure of empirical representation and the vulnerability of the body. The complicity of subjective reason with the domination of nature, body, and other subjects is precisely what is at stake in Adorno's critique of the sublime in *Aesthetic Theory*. For Adorno (1997), "the overpowering grandeur" of the sublime is implicated in the dialectic of power and powerlessness; it discloses for us a pathetic spectacle of the subject, who, in the face of calamity, still considers himself superior to the force of nature (199). As Adorno writes,

> [t]hrough the triumph of the intelligible essence in the individual who stands firm spiritually against death, man puffs himself up as if in spite of everything, as the bearer of spirit, he were absolute. (1997, 198)

Indeed, this dialectic of power and powerlessness is implicitly at stake in Kant's brief remarks on the sublimity of war (1951, 102). The second difficulty in the Kantian formulation of the sublime, which modern art inherits and to a certain degree reproduces, lies in its abstraction and formalism stemming from the crisis of representation. Since the conflict of the faculties is resolved as the triumph of reason over sensible experience and presentation, sensibility does not play any active role in the contestation of the ideas of reason or the concepts of understanding, such as the concepts of gender, race, or femininity.

For feminist critics of modernism and modern aesthetics the most obvious limitation of the sublime lies in its presumed masculinity and whiteness. Virtually any writer examining the relationship between the sublime and gender points out that the sublime in the aesthetic tradition is implicitly or explicitly associated with the masculine subject. The feminine, as Mary Bittner Wiseman (1993) points out, "is figured as a function of sense, inclination, and the beautiful, where these are the other side of reason, duty, and the sublime, respectively" (170). According to Carolyn Korsmeyer (2004), the connection between heteronormativity, gender hierarchy, racism, and aesthetic pleasure in the sublime, while most obvious in Burke's and Kant's pre-critical writings, is

> so central an exemplar of modern aesthetics that we can also view it as a paradigm of ways of thinking that appear throughout the field in subtler forms, where masculinist and Eurocentric attitudes are more covert. (43)

Indeed the presupposed whiteness and masculinity of the sublime and genius is evident not only in Kant's pre-critical texts, but also in the Critique of Judgment.

In *Observations on the Feeling of the Beautiful and Sublime*, Kant (1960) excludes orientalized and racialized subjects from the feeling of the sublime and associates them either with the "grotesque" or the "trifling" (110, 112). White femininity, or "the fair sex," fares a little better because she at least is granted "*a beautiful understanding*" in contrast to the more profound masculine "*deep understanding*" (78). It is this beautiful understanding that not only excludes women from the sublime but also makes them unsuitable for or incapable of any laborious learning or art training (78–79). Since women are excluded from the "honor" (1951, 111) of the sublime and from the creativity of genius, they are limited to the "[f]eeling for expressive painting and for music," but "not so far as it manifests artistry but sensitivity" (80–81). It goes without saying that if women are incapable of perceiving the "artistry" of art since they focus merely on its sensuous aspect, they are not capable of creating great art or having sublime judgment. "Her philosophy is not to reason, but to sense" and to be charming (1960, 79). And there is nothing more antithetical to the sublime than charm or sentimentality (1951, 114). Thus, the rethinking of the modernist sublime from the feminist point of view has to approach the incompatibility, or the "differend" in Lyotard's sense of the word, between the inherited tradition of aesthetics and the feminine.

In *A Room of One's Own*, Woolf (1981) reverses Kant's diagnosis by arguing that the exclusion of femininity from the tradition of the sublime is one of the symptoms of the destruction of women's art. As the other of aesthetic grandeur, freedom, and originality, female subjectivity and art are subjected to the destructive effects of gender and class domination: madness, torture, and the violent tearing and "pull[ing] asunder" of both the artwork and the body (49, 50–51). Consequently, the complicity of the sublime with gender and racial domination not only bears witness to the contradictions between freedom and domination, spirit and materiality, and writing and silence, but also tragically exposes their violence: "[W]ho shall measure the heat and violence of the poet's heart when caught and tangled in a woman's body?" (48). Any female poet would have been

> crazed with the torture that her gift had put her to [...] any woman born with a great gift in the sixteenth century would certainly have gone crazed, shot herself, or ended her days in some lonely cottage outside the village, half witch, half wizard, feared and mocked at [...] a highly gifted girl who had tried to use her gift for poetry would have been so thwarted and hindered by other people, so tortured and pulled asunder by her own contrary instincts. (49)

Ultimately, the exclusion of femininity from genius and the sublime leads to the untimely death of women's art, which precedes its origination and haunts its history.

However, the diagnosis of the limits of the sublime and the critique of its complicity with power lead not to an abandonment of sublime aesthetics, but rather to revisions and strategic redeployments of this concept both in artistic practices and in interpretations of modernism. According to Lyotard, for example, what resists both the Kantian flight into transcendent morality and the historicist flight into empirical reality is the indeterminacy of the modern sublime, which remains on the cusp of the unpresentable. To be sure, this shift from the aesthetic judgment and the conflict of the subjective faculties to the composition of the work of art, and even to the incongruent fragmentation of culture, points to crucial differences between the Kantian and the modernist sublime. The indeterminacy of form, whether it is achieved through the play of allusion, as is the case in the work of Joyce or Proust, or through the minimalism of Beckett, Stein, or Kafka, presents the unpresentable as unpresentable and tries to make visible what cannot be made visible. Such a negative presentation changes the stakes of literary experimentation: By rejecting pre-established rules, experimental literature attempts the impossible presentation of the unpresentable, and in so doing reveals the incommensurability between reality and the concept. Consider for example Woolf's most dazzling, "wild experiments," such as stream of consciousness, interior monologue, shifts in gender identity, and the perspectival play of multiple narrative points of view in *To the Lighthouse*, *Orlando*, or *The Waves*. According to Woolf (1991), experimental art destroys ideologically discredited literary conventions, including linear plots, syntactic unity, and the coherence of literary genres:

> [I]f one were free [. . .] there would be no plot, little probability, and [. . .] the clear-cut features of the tragic, the comic, the passionate, and the lyrical were dissolved beyond the possibility of separate recognition? (33)

Although it stresses the importance of formal experimentation and indeterminacy, this shift in the modern sublime from the judging subject to the status of the work of art departs from formalism[2] since it is intertwined with the critique of power, affect, and the question of freedom.

The second mode of modernist and feminist revisions of the sublime follows the path of parody. For Adorno, the ridiculous aspect of the Kantian theory of the sublime lies precisely in the assertion of the power of rational will even in the face of danger – at least as long as the subject remains at a safe distance from the crushing force of the calamity. As he writes, the sublime superiority of reason "becomes comical. Advanced art writes the comedy of the tragic: Here the sublime and play converge" (1997, 198). The parody of the modern sublime radicalizes its negativity by undermining its positive moment: The ridicule of the triumph of reason over sensible experience and the empirical vulnerability of the body is "the movement of the sublime toward its own negation" (198). For Adorno the emphasis on the negative sublime not only exposes "the fragility of the empirical individual," which can no longer be transcended through appeal to the transcendence of rational will, but also reinterprets the subjective conflict between the faculties as a symptom of political conflict and as the subjugation of nature (198). Yet, the parodic negation of sublime grandeur not only exposes domination but also liberates possibilities of resistance. The transformation of the sublime into playful parody reveals the fact that power can become a "nonentity" (199). By contesting domination, the parody of the sublime also redefines its relationship to nature, which instead of being a source of threat becomes an emblem of liberation: "Towering mountains are eloquent not as what crushes overwhelmingly but as images of a space liberated from fetters and strictures, a liberation in which it is possible to participate" (199). For Adorno, therefore, it is through untamed nature, and not through the sovereignty of the rational will, that the sublime speaks against domination. Consequently, the critical legacy of the sublime lies in its "unassuaged negativity," resistance, and the promise of liberation, which includes the liberation of human and nonhuman nature (199).

The reversibility of the sublime into the comic opens a path toward a feminine mimicry of the sublime. Although Irigaray does not speak directly about the sublime,[3] she famously proposes mimicry as the first step toward the feminine dislocation and re-inscription of the conceptual apparatus of philosophy, aesthetics, and politics. As Irigaray (1985) writes, it is through play with mimicry that a woman can

> recover the place of her exploitation by discourse, without allowing herself to be simply reduced to it [. . .] to make visible by a playful repetition, what was supposed to remain invisible: the cover-up of a possible operation of the feminine in language. (76)

Reinterpreted in the context of Irigaray and Adorno, the playful repetition of the sublime not only reveals the collusion of the sublime with the exploitation of the feminine, which includes the subjugation of feminized sensibility and the body to the power of reason, but also the subversive operation of the feminine in modernist aesthetics. To elaborate further such a feminist revision of the modernist sublime I would like to turn now to Virginia Woolf's *Orlando*, which, with its plural modalities of the comic, also includes a parody of the sublime and its complicity with the politics of gender and imperialism. For Woolf, parody, characterized by a tension between thought and laughter, critique and play, has the critical edge of aesthetic negativity. Parodies, Woolf (1990) writes, "first [. . .] make us laugh, and then they make us think" (89). As she puts it in her 1917 essay, "Parodies," the negative effect of a parody is far more corrosive than that of direct criticism: "A good parody is rather a complex thing, for it should be amusing in itself, and should also do the work of the critic with greater daring than the critic can usually display" (1990, 89).

At first glance, the sublime, more often discussed in Woolf studies in the context of *To the Lighthouse* or *The Waves*,[4] seems hardly compatible with *Orlando*, her most playful novel, which Woolf (1953) famously describes as a "writer's holiday" (122) and "escapade" (118), unless, of course, we reread *Orlando* as Rado (2000) does, as a feminist mimicry of the sublime (138–178). Out of the diverse manifestations of aesthetic negativity in the novel – dissonance, narrative/syntactical fragmentation, metonymic excesses, gaps, interruptions – parody is the most characteristic feature of *Orlando*. As Woolf (1980) claims, one of the overarching "impulses" of *Orlando* "(& this was serious)" was "to give things their caricature value" (203). In addition to the critique of gender identity, heterosexuality, imperialism, and the genre of the historical/biographical narrative, Woolf also bestows "the caricature value" on the aesthetics and the politics of the sublime. In *Orlando* (1956), the intersection between the aesthetics and the politics of the sublime implicates the 400 years of the history of literature and the symbolic capital of the poet in the "glory" of imperial conquest, the power of the state and its gender politics. When, as a young nobleman in the sixteenth century, Orlando becomes for the first time infatuated with poetry, he merely replaces the sublime power of politics with the glory of literary fame: "For, to Orlando . . . there was a glory about a man who had written a book and had it printed, which outshone all the glories of blood and state" (82). It is only in the twentieth century, when Orlando is transformed into a published "female" author of polymorphous sexuality, that "she" herself can mock one of the most stereotypical images of the romantic sublime, associated with the storm of the ocean. In *Orlando*, the terror of the sublime, implicated in the imperial conquest of the sea, is mockingly reversed into a ripple of water made by a female foot; and the power of the English navy is reduced to nothing more than an ecstatic childish play with a toy boat:

> Orlando mistook the toy boat for her husband's brig; and the wave she had made with her toe for a mountain of water off Cape Horn; [. . .] up and up it went, and a white crest with a thousand deaths in it arched over it; and through the thousand deaths it went and disappeared – 'It's sunk!' she cried out in an agony – and then, behold, there it was again sailing along safe and sound among the ducks on the other side of the Atlantic. 'Ecstasy!' she cried [. . .] 'A toy boat, a toy boat, a toy boat' she repeated. (287)

Yet, Woolf's parody of the sublime does not lead to the aesthetics of the beautiful; on the contrary, the parody of the sublime releases the playful, untamed aspect of art, which can be mobilized against art's complicity with power. For Orlando, literature is "something useless, sudden, violent; something that costs a life; red, blue, purple; a spirit; a splash; . . . something rash, ridiculous" (287). No longer symbolized by the crushing power of the sea, the subversive force of female literary practice, playful and dangerous at the same time, is more like the whimsical flight of a wild goose, a figure which recurs frequently in the last chapter of the novel.

Since the reversal of the sublime into feminine parody undermines the subjugating power of reason and its complicity with political and gender domination, such a critique shifts emphasis from morality to the affective dimensions of the modernist sublime and, in so doing, questions the Kantian distinction between affect, associated with reason, and pathological passions pertaining to the body (1951, 112). It is through the affective dimensions of the work of art rather than empirical representation that the modernist sublime escapes the abstraction of Kantian formalism. According to Lyotard, it is Burke rather than Kant who provides richer resources to elaborate the affective force of the sublime in modernism. For the modernist sublime, delight does not point to the superiority of moral reason, but remains tinged with terror, with powerful negative emotions, which testify to an enduring threat to self-preservation under the conditions of modernity. Such an affective reformulation of the negative sublime evokes the familiar constellation of the modernist crisis of subjectivity, from Benjamin's shock and Adorno's shudder, to Freud's trauma, all of which point to the fragmentation of consciousness, the crisis of experience, and the alienating conditions of modern life.

From the feminist perspective, however, the critique of moral reason and the parodic exposure of the violent exclusion of the feminine lead to an expansion of the affective register of the sublime, which also includes the oscillation between disgust and wonder. Such an affective oscillation re-inscribes the excluded feminine within the domain of aesthetics: either as the incestuous longing for the maternal body in the case of abjection, or as the passionate erotic dimension of sexual difference in the case of wonder. According to Julia Kristeva, the terror and delight of the modern sublime overlaps with jouissance and the disgust of abjection. As Kristeva (1982) points out in *The Powers of Horror*, the abject, like the sublime, is characterized by a lack of the representable object: "The abject is edged with the sublime. It is not the same moment on the journey, but the same subject and speech bring them into being. For the sublime has no object either" (11–12). From the psychoanalytic perspective, what shows up in place of the nonsymbolizable (maternal) object is the braid of incestuous affect – fear, disgust, or revolt. The painful, terrifying pleasure of the sublime evokes incestuous jouissance, the impossible longing for the maternal body, "ejected beyond the scope of the possible, the tolerable, the thinkable" (1). Such a longing for the maternal, though illegible in the aesthetic tradition, finds its diverse figurations in modern literature, which becomes a privileged signifier of abjection: "Great modern literature," Kristeva writes, "unfolds over that terrain: Dostoevsky [. . .] Proust, [. . .] Kafka, Celine" (18). Far from presenting a unified phenomenon, writing abjection in modernism gives rise to different stylistic experimentations and variations, from Joyce's "dazzling" rhetoric (22) and Borges's "vertiginous and hallucinatory" style (23) to being "overcome by the corpse" in Arnaud's texts (25). We could add other innumerable instances to this list, for example, Lily's longing for the incestuous reunion with Mrs. Ramsay in *To the Lighthouse*, which is one of the affective dimensions of her painting.

I would like to suggest three important implications of the sublime's proximity to abjection for feminist aesthetics. The first implication is that the concepts of reason themselves are rendered pathological, marked by the cruelty of the superego. We are reminded here of Freud's claim (1960) that the superego is a gathering place for the death drive, a pure culture of death. It is precisely because of the violence of reason that the grandeur of the sublime is reversed into disgust. The second implication is that instead of the triumph of reason over affective experience, the abject never ceases to challenge the superego and to expose its weakness. And the third implication is that the weakness of the superego not only reveals the never completely severed proximity to the maternal body, the lost narcissistic support and the unbearable Thing of incestuous wanting, but also enables its inscription in language otherwise than as a symbolic object. Confronted with such crisis of the moral law and the symbolic order, the aesthetic task of modernism is not to reassert their power, but, on the contrary, to retrace "the foundations of the symbolic construct" and the "fragile limits of the speaking being" in order to transform the relation between the symbolic (paternal) and the semiotic (maternal) dimensions of subjectivity and culture (1982, 18). By reconfiguring the nonrepresentable maternal abject within literary language, modern art provides an alternative both to the psychotic collapse of language and to the paternal moral law.

Even though the dominant affective tonality of *Orlando* is the parody of the sublime, the novel also includes a brief but crucial confrontation with the abject provoked by the bodily scar – the thumb without a fingernail: "[T]he thumb on Joe's right hand was without a finger nail [. . .] The site was so repulsive that she felt faint for a moment" (1956, 321). The loss of the world and consciousness, the dissolution of internal and external boundaries, culminates in a descent into an internal pool of darkness, where the possibilities of reflection and representation dissolve into our "most violent passions" (323). Yet such darkness not only threatens the symbolic order with collapse but also reveals a rich background of sublimation leading to "art and religion" (323). Through this narcissistic crisis of subjectivity, the violent passions of abjection lead to the overcoming of self-preservation and to a receptivity to unknown otherness. Although the feeling of disgust dissolves the internal and external world into darkness and shadow, which "is always absent from the present – whence its terror, its nondescript character," such a crisis is nonetheless a crucial condition of rebirth and transformation – it has "the power to change whatever it adds itself to" (322). That is why the crisis of abjection is a prelude to the novel's redefinition of the wild playfulness of literature as receptivity to the unknown – as a secret, unpredictable, and often threatening transaction with the human and nonhuman world, history, and language.

Lyotard also associates the pain of the sublime with the "welcoming [of] the unknown," with the surprise that, despite the threat of annihilation, there is still the occurrence of the event, the "wonder" that something, rather than nothing, is happening (1991, 92). Irigaray's reflection on wonder can be considered as another step, as another choreography of the refiguring of the affective dimension of the sublime in the context of sexual difference, even though she has rarely been considered a theorist of the feminist sublime.[5] For Irigaray (1993), wonder also points to what cannot be anticipated, "*assimilated or disassimilated as known*" (75, emphasis in the original). What is original in Irigaray's retrieval of wonder from the philosophy of Descartes is her emphasis on the fact that wonder is the only passion that has no opposite. Thus, wonder occurs prior to the sublime alternation between terror and delight, the positive and the negative, pain and pleasure, that is, prior to the aesthetic considerations of the failure of imagination or the triumph of reason. As this analysis of wonder in the context of the modernist sublime suggests, the interplay of contradictory emotions is secondary and obscures the encounter with the absolutely unknown prior to the subjective judgment whether it can be presentable or unpresentable. According to Irigaray, wonder is often regarded as fear because reason cannot tolerate the surprise of the unknown and its resistance to power/knowledge.[6] Since Irigaray's notion of wonder calls for a new *poesis*, it reminds us of Adorno's argument that wonder is art's testimony to undomesticated otherness:

> The more densely people have spun a categorial web around what is other than subjective spirit, the more fundamentally they have disaccustomed themselves to the wonder of that other [...] Art hopes to correct this [...] A priori, art causes people to wonder. (1997, 126)

Unlike Adorno, however, Irigaray links the originary experience of wonder with eroticism and sexual difference, which, like poesis, evokes the unanticipated, non-appropriative encounter with the erotic other. Thus, if the monological sublime points to the failure of the appropriation of the other and the subsequent conflict between the subjective faculties, sexual difference foregrounds the disappropriation, limitation, and relational character of subjectivity, always already exposed to the sexuate other. Such disappropriation also characterizes the supposedly sexually neutral terms, like spirit or the community. As Irigaray puts it,

> the *mine* of the subject is always already marked by disappropriation. [...] Being a man or a woman already means not being the whole of the subject or of the community or of spirit, as well as not being entirely one's self. (1996, 106)

Because sexual difference marks disappropriation, the lack of closure, and the "not all" of the subject, spirit, or collectivity, and because it negates the reduction of the Other either to the narcissistic complement or to the threat of the subject, it enables openness and respect for alterity in diverse forms. In *Orlando*, Woolf takes this event of sexual disappropriation and incompleteness, analyzed by Irigaray, in a far more radical direction, by emphasizing the plurality of being and the multiplicity of sexual relations irreducible to the heterosexual/homosexual binary (1956, 220–222). When Orlando contemplates her thousand selves, she ponders the impossibility of sexual identity and self-definition: " 'Who then? [...] Thirty-six; in a motor car; a woman. Yes, but a million other things as well" (310).

Ultimately what is at stake in the modernist critique and reinvention of the sublime is the question of freedom. As Woolf puts it in her 1919 essay "Modern Novels," "the problem before the novelist at present, as we suppose it to have been in the past, is to contrive a means of being free" (1991, 34–35). Let us recall, the idea of freedom, which is the idea of Reason, is crucial in Kant's traditional formulation of the sublime. Yet, as Woolf and Irigaray, as well as Adorno and Lyotard argue, this aesthetic ideal of freedom, associated with the domination of masculine reason and genius, is implicated in the political subjugation and exclusion of otherness. That is why, in order to reclaim the idea of freedom, it has been so crucial to reconfigure the role of reason in feminist aesthetics of the sublime. Such aesthetics not only parodies the violent sublimity of the monological, disembodied moral law, but, as we have seen in Irigaray's theory of sexual difference, foregrounds the disappropriation of reason itself, its relational and sensual character. Thus the idea of freedom emerging from the modernist and feminist revisions of the sublime is intertwined with the liberation of sensibility, passions, otherness, and the sexuate plurality of being. Yet, since such an embodied freedom is fundamentally relational, how should we understand this relationality? What are its implications for the status of the work of art and aesthetic experience? I would like to propose that the relational freedom disclosed in the feminist aesthetics of the sublime is characterized by an irreducible tension between intersubjective practice, on the one hand, and the temporality of the event, on the other.

To elaborate further this dual aspect of freedom emerging from the modernist sublime, I would like to juxtapose Woolf's conception of artistic practice with Lyotard's notion of the event. In her portraits of modern female artists – Mary Carmichael in *A Room of One's Own*, Orlando in *Orlando*, or Lily in *To the Lighthouse* – Woolf strongly emphasizes the intersubjective character of literary work, which expresses on the level of form the relationship among female artist, power relations, and the supportive community of the outsiders. Consider, for instance, the figure of Mary Carmichael (one of the fictional names the narrator assumes for herself) in *A Room of One's Own*, an innovative writer with "a very wide, eager and free" sensibility, "almost" free of resentment and fear (1981, 92). Emerging from women's economic and political struggle, this freedom allows her to laugh at the peculiarities of the other sex, to ignore the admonitions and criticisms of the bishops and the deans, and to focus instead on the process of writing itself. She stretches language to its limit in order to express the "unrecorded" gestures of femininity, to uncover "almost unknown or unrecorded things," and to bring to light that which had been buried in the literary tradition: the destroyed potential of women writers (92). Mary Carmichael inscribes on the level of form the historical contradiction between the aesthetic ideal of freedom and gendered and imperialist violence, between mute suffering and, as the title of her work suggests, the joy of *Life's Adventure*. Yet, as Woolf emphatically claims, the aesthetic practice of freedom inscribes in the structure of the work not only the contradictions in the intersubjective world "of men and women" but also "our relation [. . .] to the world of reality," that is, to the ontological dimension of life and things in themselves (114).

The ontological moments of being in Woolf's prose resonate with Lyotard's work, which, of the numerous encounters with the sublime considered in this essay, most strongly links the idea of freedom with "an ontological dislocation" (1991, 101) of the event. For Lyotard, as for Woolf, the significance of the event lies not in its meaning, but in the ecstatic surprise of its happening. If we understand one of the meanings of the modernist sublime as the disjunction between the meaning and the occurrence of the event, then sublime aesthetics represents a radical departure from both the subjective discord between the faculties and the objective contextualization of historicism. Lyotard finds traces of the ontological dislocation of the event in Burke's sublime, and its most explicit formulation in Heidegger's notion of *Ereignis*.[7] As Lyotard puts it in a well-known formulation, the happening of the event " 'precedes,' so to speak, the question pertaining to *what* happens," or the meaning of the event (90, emphasis added). That is why the event happens first and foremost "as a question mark" before becoming a question that could be answered by empirical research or theoretical knowledge (90). Since the temporality of the event precedes the determination of its meaning, its occurrence manifests itself as a disruption of subjectivity, language, and the objective determinations of social relations. On the subjective level such dislocation reveals the limits of experience, on the aesthetic level – the indeterminacy of experimental form, and on the objective level – the contingency of power/knowledge. Insofar as it implies an interrelation between aesthetic and historical indeterminacy, Lyotard's concept of the event is a condition of possibility of an intersubjective practice of freedom in the spheres of art and politics. Understood as an event in its own right, the artwork cannot be approached either in terms of the form/content opposition or in terms of the formalism/historicism divide. Neither the content of the artwork, nor its form, nor its historical contexts are adequate to the dynamic, processual character of the work, which Adorno aptly describes as a "force field" (1997, 179). The unpredictability of how such a force field might work in history both calls for its historical contextualization and renders it indeterminate and inadequate.

For a feminist formulation of such an event in terms of historical indeterminacy let us return again to Woolf's *Orlando*, a text spanning the 400 years of the history of English literature, from the Renaissance to modernism. The novel not only parodies the generic expectations of subjective or objective causality, implied by biography and literary history, but repeatedly interrupts the unfolding of the narrative by the sudden recurrence of the instant. In particular, the last chapter is structured by a tension between an involuntary reverie of subjective recollections – the "tunnel vision" into the past (319) – and the shock of the "now," which is figured, in comic exaggeration, as an "explosion" (298), "thunder," or an "earthquake" (320):

> [L]ike a hammer [. . .] the clock ticked louder and louder until there was a terrific explosion right in her ear. Orlando leapt as if she had been violently struck on the head. Ten times she was struck [. . .] it was the eleventh of October. It was 1928. It was the present moment [. . .] Orlando started [. . .] and turned pale. For what more terrifying revelation can there be than that it is the present moment? (298)

As the culminating point in Woolf's meditation on the temporality of history and the historicity of literature, the sublime happening of the event – only partially disarmed by humor – strikes us violently on our heads, "as if every time the gulf of time gaped and let a second through some unknown danger might come with it" (321). The sound of the clock measuring time is ironically reversed into the dislocation of the moment, so that it is no longer the clock that strikes time, but the moment that strikes us with its unexpected force. This "terrifying revelation" that there is an occurrence is irreducible to the Joycean epiphany because it does not disclose any insight about the meaning of the event, even retrospectively. Nor is it reserved for the sublime terror of historical upheavals. On the contrary, what mark the indeterminacy of history and the discontinuity of subjective experience are very ordinary events, such as the sound of the clock, the flight of a goose, the birth of the child, or the publication of a book. Such gaps, the narrator of *Orlando* writes, are both "our undoing" (80) – the interruption of our habitual ways of doing and thinking – and the conditions of our freedom: Indeed, "[i]t is then that sedition enters the fortress and our troops rise in insurrection" (80).

As this essay makes clear, there is no single modality of the feminine sublime in modernism. Nonetheless, different critiques and strategic reconfigurations of this concept in modernist practice in criticism have one thing in common: they contest the superiority of transcendent reason, expose its complicity with power, while preserving its central idea, namely, the idea of freedom. Yet the idea of freedom is no longer an attribute of the disembodied rationality; on the contrary, it mobilizes the whole range of affective and erotic passions, from wonder to disgust and ecstasy, in order to challenge the pathological side of reason, which psychoanalysis associates with the superego. Rather than corresponding to the rational will and the activity of the isolated subject, the possibility of freedom emerges from the irreducible tension between intersubjective practice and the impersonal dislocation of the event. I began this essay with the claim that the tradition of the sublime challenges the dominance of historicism in so far as such aesthetics is associated with the crisis of empirical representation and causality. Yet this does not mean that the modernist sublime ignores history. On the contrary, it opens the possibility of rethinking the entrenched dualism between formalism and historicism in modernist studies because the idea of freedom with which it is associated shows the interrelation between the contingency of history and the aesthetic indeterminacy of experimental art.

Notes

1   The emphasis on the broadening of historical and geographical contexts is also at stake in the reassessments of the sources of European modernism, which range from the unconscious and sexuality to empire and institutions. See Pericles Lewis's "Introduction" (2011, 1–9).

2   Given the epistemological (a suitability for cognition without a concept) and intellectual (the bridge between necessity and freedom) stakes of Kantian aesthetics, Gasché rightly contests the formalist and aestheticist readings of Kant's aesthetics, which all too often confuse Kant's subjective idea of form with the form of the work of art (2003, 179).

3   For the articulation of the feminine sublime through the juxtaposition of Woolf and Irigaray, see Barbara Claire Freeman, *The Feminine Sublime* (1997, 2). Ginette Verstraete situates the parodic feminine sublime in the context of Schlegel's ironization of the sublime. Her notion of the feminine sublime subverts the opposition between male artist and female model, art and reality, the ugly and the beautiful (1998).

4   For the discussions of the diverse approaches to the revisions of the sublime in Woolf's fiction, see Daniel Darvay's "The Gothic Sublime in Virginia Woolf's To the Lighthouse" (2011); Steven Vine's "Reinventing the Sublime" (2011); Ida Klitgard's *On The Horizon: A Poetics of the Sublime in Virginia Woolf's The Waves* (2004); Kari Elise Locke's "Orlando and Incandescence: Virginia Woolf's Comic Sublime" (1992); and Laura

Doyle's "Sublime Barbarians in the Narrative of Empire: Or, Longinus at Sea in The Waves" (1996).

5   For a rethinking of the feminine sublime as passion and non-appropriative relation to the other in the context of French feminism and modern women's fiction, see the groundbreaking work of Barbara Claire Freeman (1997). See also Jean-Michel Rabaté (2002, 132–136).

6   For further interpretation of wonder, see Ziarek (2001, 161–163).

7   Peter V. Zima's "The Subject, the Beautiful and the Sublime. Adorno and Lyotard between Modernism and Postmodernism" (2007, 143–153). For Zima, Adorno's aesthetic negativity of the sublime remains still tied to the critical potential of the subject, whereas for Lyotard – with the philosophy of the event.

References

Adorno, Theodor W. (1997). *Aesthetic Theory*, trans. Robert Hullot-Kentor. Minneapolis: University Minnesota of Press.

Brooker, Peter. (2011). "Introduction." In *The Oxford Handbook of Modernisms*, ed. Peter Brooker, et al. Oxford: Oxford University Press.

Darvay, Daniel. (2011). "The Gothic Sublime in Virginia Woolf's *To the Lighthouse*." *Genre*, 44.2: 129–156.

de Man, Paul. (1960). *Aesthetic Ideology*, ed. Andrzej Warmiski. Minneapolis: University of Minnesota Press.

Derrida, Jacques. (1987). *The Truth in Painting*, trans. Geoffrey Bennington and Ian McLeod. Chicago: University of Chicago Press.

Doyle, Laura. (1996). "Sublime Barbarians in the Narrative of Empire: Or, Longinus at Sea in *The Waves*." *Modern Fiction Studies*, 42: 323–347.

Freeman, Barbara Claire. (1997). *The Feminine Sublime: Gender and Excess in Women's Fiction*. Berkley: University of California Press.

Freud, Sigmund. (1960). *The Ego and the Id* from *The Standard Edition of the Complete Psychological Works of Sigmund Freud*, trans. Joan Riviere. New York: W. W. Norton.

Gasché, Rodolphe. (2003). *The Idea of Form: Rethinking Kant's Aesthetics*. Stanford: Stanford University Press.

Irigaray, Luce. (1985). *This Sex Which Is Not One*, trans. Catherine Porter. Ithaca, NY: Cornell University Press.

Irigaray, Luce. (1993). *An Ethics of Sexual Difference*, trans. Carolyn Burke and Gillian C. Gill. Ithaca, NY: Cornell University Press.

Irigaray, Luce. (1996). *I Love to You: Sketch of a Possible Felicity in History*, trans. Alison Martin. New York: Routledge.

Jameson, Fredric. (1991). *Postmodernism, or, the Cultural Logic of Late Capitalism*. Durham, NC: Duke University Press.

Kant, Immanuel. (1951). *Critique of Judgment*, trans. J. H. Bernard. New York: Hafner Press.

Kant, Immanuel. (1960). *Observations on the Feeling of the Beautiful and Sublime*, trans. John T. Goldthwait. Berkeley: University of California Press.

Klitgard, Ida. (2004). *On The Horizon: A Poetics of the Sublime in Virginia Woolf's The Waves*. Palo Alto, CA: Academica Press.

Korsmeyer, Carolyn. (2004). *Gender and Aesthetics: An Introduction*. New York: Routledge,

Kristeva, Julia. (1982). *Powers of Horror: An Essay on Abjection*, trans. Leon S. Roudiez. New York: Columbia University Press.

Lewis, Pericles. (2011). "Introduction." In *The Cambridge Companion to European Modernism*, ed. Pericles Lewis. Cambridge: Cambridge University Press.

Locke, Kari Elise. (1992). "Orlando and Incandescence: Virginia Woolf's Comic Sublime." *Modern Fiction Studies* 38: 235–252.

Lyotard, Jean-François. (1984). *The Postmodern Condition: A Report on Knowledge*, trans. Geoffrey Bennington and Brian Massumi. Minneapolis: University of Minnesota Press.

Lyotard, Jean-François. (1988). *The Differend: Phrases in Dispute*, trans. George Van Den Abbeele. Minneapolis: University of Minnesota Press.

Lyotard, Jean-François. (1991). *The Inhuman: Reflections on Time*, trans. Geoffrey Bennington and Rachel Bowlby. Stanford: Stanford University Press.

Rabaté, Jean-Michel. (2002). *The Future of Theory*. Oxford: Blackwell.

Rado, Lisa. (2000). *The Modern Androgyne Imagination: A Failed Sublime*. Charlottesville: University of Virginia Press.

Verstraete, Ginette. (1998). *Fragments of the Feminine Sublime in Friedrich Schlegel and James Joyce*. Albany: SUNY Press.

Vine, Steven. (2011). *Reinventing the Sublime: Post-Romantic Literature and Theory*. Eastbourne: Sussex Academic Press.

Wiseman, Mary Bittner. (1993). "Beautiful Exiles." In *Aesthetics in Feminist Perspective*, ed. Hilde Hein and Carolyn Korsmeyer (pp. 169–178). Bloomington: Indiana University Press.

Woolf, Virginia. (1953). *A Writers Diary*. New York: Harcourt.

Woolf, Virginia. (1956). *Orlando: A Biography*. New York: Harcourt.

Woolf, Virginia. (1980). *The Diary of Virginia Woolf. Vol. 3: 1925–1930*, ed. Anne Oliver Bell. New York: Harcourt.

Woolf, Virginia. (1981). *A Room of One's Own*. New York: Harcourt.

Woolf, Virginia. (1990). *The Essays of Virginia Woolf*, Vol. 2, ed. Andrew McNeillie. London: Harcourt.

Woolf, Virginia. (1991). *The Essays of Virginia Woolf*, Vol. 3, ed. Andrew McNeillie. London: Harcourt.

Ziarek, Ewa. (2001). *An Ethics of Dissensus: Postmodernity, Feminism, and the Politics of Radical Democracy*. Stanford: Stanford University Press.

Zima, Peter V. (2007). "The Subject, the Beautiful and the Sublime. Adorno and Lyotard between Modernism and Postmodernism." In *Modernism*, vol. 1, ed. Astradur Eysteinsson and Vivian Liska (pp. 143–153). Amsterdam: John Benjamins.

24

Aesthetic Formalism, the Form of Artworks, and Formalist Criticism

Jonathan Loesberg

As my title indicates, the words "form" and "formalism," even when limited to the contexts of aesthetic and literary theory, can have different meanings and refer to ostensibly very different formal objects. Specifically, "formalism" can refer to an aesthetic theory about either what artworks do or what they ought to do: they are autonomous and either do as a matter of definition or ought to, as a matter of evaluation, attend to their autonomous aesthetic form. But, of course, formalism can also refer to a school of art criticism, opposed to various other schools, claiming that art criticism, at least if it wishes to focus on the specifically artistic qualities of artworks, ought to attend to the features of form that makess the object of its attention an artwork and not something else. The *Oxford English Dictionary*, it should be noted, dates the first use of the word "formalism" in an aesthetic sense to the Russian Formalists and, without offering a separate definition of the second use, under "formalist," offers the first citation that describes a type of criticism as occurring in 1967. Given the work, not only of the Russian Formalists, but of Adorno, Greenberg, and the New Critics, one can doubt that that is the earliest such usage, but one cannot doubt that the concept dates, as does the first usage, to the rise of modernism in the early twentieth century.

From this coincidence of occurrence that we will see will emerge as causal, I will make three related claims: First, since modernism took itself to be an aesthetic built on the classic Aesthetic arguments of the prior one hundred and fifty years, the original definitions of those theories, as exemplified by Kant and Hegel, will lead to necessary, though productive contradictions in modernism's self-definitions. In particular, Hegel's seemingly historical claim in his theory that it was written after the end of art and as a culmination of it, which, we will see, is a temporal rewriting of Kant's contradictory definition of art and artworks, results in modernism's sense of itself as both the essence of art and the end of art. Second, this contradictory self-definition leads, as one might expect, to contradictions within the history of what modernism is in relation to what preceded and what followed it, particularly with regard to fin-de-siècle aestheticism and then with regard to postmodernism. And these contradictions partake of the conflation of a formal definition of art with an ostensible claim about the end of art occurring with the last term in the progression, either modernism or postmodernism. Third, and this will be the aim of the prior two claims and their part-formal and part-historical analysis, formalism, both as a theory of art and as a consequent theory of criticism, also partakes of the definitional contradiction in classic aesthetics and of the consequent contradictions in the definitions in and of, and the histories in and of, modernism. The contradictions within formalism as a critical method will turn out to be both its weakness – the constant critical desire to end it or break out of it into the real or the historical – and its strength – every time it seems successfully expelled, it keeps on turning up again, like the proverbial bad penny.

To start my own definitional argument, with the appearance of an historical argument, at what will be both its beginning and, in a certain manner of speaking, its end, we will turn to Kant's famous claim that aesthetic apprehension finds natural objects beautiful when it perceives them as having purposiveness without purpose. To telescope the argument I made in *A Return to Aesthetics*, if we follow Kant carefully, it will become clear that this apprehension can only occur in its normal state when we construe a natural object's appearance as having a meaningfulness that we have no warrant for actually thinking that it has. From this perspective, we can never perceive artworks as artworks precisely in terms of purposiveness without purpose, because artworks have the intentional purpose of being beautiful and so when we apprehend them as such, we are apprehending them according to their purpose. But it is also true that when we perceive natural objects aesthetically, we perceive them in an artificial manner, so to speak, since we look at them merely as appearances rather than as objects in the world. As Kant says, we are indifferent to their existence. This situation produces a moment in Kant that is almost Derridean: "Nature, we say, is beautiful if it is also like art; and art can be called fine art only if we are conscious that it is art while yet it looks to us like nature" (1987, 174). If we do not worry, ontologically, how such a form of apprehension can come into being, we can explain how it works fairly readily. We perceive nature aesthetically, when we focus on its appearances as having their own significance, without regard to what the natural object is: this is what it means to perceive purposiveness without purpose. But this form of perception is not natural. It is the kind of perception fit for apprehending artworks, which are created with the purpose of being perceived as we would perceive a natural object when we do not attend to its purpose or concepts. An artwork, in other words, strikes us as beautiful when it creates the illusion that it is an uncaused appearance that appears to have a significance. This appearance, however, is only an illusion, the illusion that the artwork has as its purpose to give to us. This definition of the artwork, in effect, declares that it can never appear to have the form it actually has. As an object with the purpose of being beautiful, if it appeared to have that purpose, it would cease to be beautiful since it would merely be an object that we perceived according to its concepts, one of which is the purpose for which it was made. And what it does appear to be, a beautiful appearance to which we attend without regard to a concept that would hook it to its existence as an object, it pointedly is not. An artwork becomes an artwork only to the extent that it ceases to exist as an object, or at least appears to do so.

Because Kant defines beauty as a form of perception rather than a trait of objects, he thinks of it as having no more history than any other perception has.[1] It can, thus, have neither beginning nor end. Indeed, if we translate the German word *zweck* as "end," in the sense of point, rather than as purpose, as some translations do, then the sense of beauty, at least, perceives its objects as without end. But the endlessness of beauty, in Kant, occurs because no object has beauty in reality or in completeness: we endow natural objects with it and artworks only seem to have it by hiding their ends and thus their objectness with an artistic sleight of hand. In order to give art an objective status, we will find Hegel forced to declare it at an end, thus re-creating the Kantian contradictory artwork with an artwork that ceases to exist when we understand properly what it is. Although Hegel's declaration of the end of art has always seemed not self-evident, if one traces the logic that leads up to it, we can understand, not only why Hegel would have made a statement that others have found surprising, but why that logic keeps returning to haunt the art that came after the end he declared.

Hegel takes the purpose of art – it has a purpose in Hegel, though it achieves that purpose intrinsically without any separation of means and ends – to be to "reduce to unity . . . the opposition and contradiction between the abstractly self-concentrated spirit and nature – both the nature of external phenomena and that of inner subjective feeling and emotion" (1975, 56). Effectively, this unity occurs when art gives sensuous embodiment to the idea of beauty. Although Kant also has a concept of artistic embodiment,[2] one can hardly fault him for proposing that such unifications are always subjective acts. The alternative would be to declare that one understands the meaning of nature and can make that meaning appear without linguistic reference. Hegel is no more naïve than Kant about the possibility of expressing thought of any complexity entirely in terms of sensuous embodiment:

> The development of reflection in our life today has made it a need of ours, in relation both to our will and judgement, to cling to general considerations and to regulate the particular by them, with the result that universal forms, laws, duties, rights, maxims, prevail as determining reasons and are the chief regulator. But for artistic interest and production we demand in general rather a quality of life in which the universal is not present in the form of law and maxim, but which gives the impression of being one with the senses and the feelings, just as the universal and the rational is contained in the imagination by being brought into unity with a concrete sensuous appearance. (10)

Hegel here claims that art cannot give us the kind of knowledge of things we demand, and what we do demand of art we can only have in our imagination. Central to the history he gives, of course, is the idea that when our knowledge was less abstract and thus less perfect, it could be successfully embodied. But that time has passed.

When we look at his declaration of art's pastness, however, we will find it connected with the moment at which we come to an understanding of what art is:

> In all these respects art, considered in its highest vocation, is and remains for us a thing of the past. Thereby it has lost for us genuine truth and life, and has rather been transferred into our *ideas* instead of maintaining its earlier necessity in reality and occupying its higher place. What is now aroused in us by works of art is not just immediate enjoyment but our judgement also, since we subject to our intellectual consideration (i) the content of art, and (ii) the work of art's means of presentation, and the appropriateness or inappropriateness of both to one another. The *philosophy* of art is therefore a greater need in our day than it was in the days when art by itself as art yielded full satisfaction. (11)

It should be clear that Hegel does not think that artworks will cease to be produced, or that we will cease to attend to them. It is for us a thing of the past, only in its highest vocation, which was to serve all the purposes of thought and to express our understanding of truth. Hegel's description of how we now respond to art, seeking to understand its content and its means of presenting that content, we might normally call interpreting an artwork. It follows that when art served for us the role of its highest vocation, we did not interpret it, indeed we did not recognize it as an artwork. Since it was reality visible, we could not have understood it at least as we currently understand art, whose definition always entails some contrast both to the real and to the straightforward representation of the real. Art, then, is a thing of the past, at the moment we come to recognize it as art.[3] Hegel's history thus re-creates Kant's epistemological analysis: art ceases to fulfill its ends at the moment we recognize what kind of object it is.

Since beauty in Kant and, by consequence, the artworks that display it are endless and thus without history, while in Hegel, because beauty is a surpassed form of expression and the art that displays it, having reached its terminal point, is a thing of the past, it will follow that any new art form that thinks of itself as an art, and any new art theory that would accommodate that form as an historical inauguration, if they are to build on Kant's and Hegel's definitions, will have to rewrite their terms.[4] In order to be a different form of the art they described, a new form of art will reinscribe their contradictions while declaring itself both a new beginning and a new end. At least, that has been the case, as we will see, with both modernism and postmodernism. And theories of art that attempt to rewrite a history that will accommodate those claims, as it turns out, reinscribe the contradictions in their histories. Fortunately, we do not have to hazard our own definitions or redefinitions of modernism and postmodernism as we have histories offering sufficiently similar terms to work with. In the varied cases of Clement Greenberg's essays, Peter Bürger's *Theory of the Avant-Garde* and Fredric Jameson's *Postmodernism*, both the three stages of art, though the stages are differently placed and do not overlap each other well, and their interrelationships are sufficiently similar to see the identical logic working behind them. Each by itself also has problems of inclusion or exclusion that the other, by ameliorating, reproduces in a different way. Thus each, meaning to define an essence or an end point, re-creates the contradictions of the starting point in Kant and Hegel.

Because Greenberg's theory of the avant-garde in art is an espousal, so to speak, we may jump ahead of him to Bürger, whose theory means to create a history of the avant-garde as a corrective to the identically named book by Renato Poggioli[5] and thus also proposes an implicit corrective to Greenberg's similarly framed theory from within modernism. Bürger (1984) proposes as the three periods of art, first, the classical one defined by the writings of Kant and Schiller, then, aestheticism, and, finally, the avant-garde (26–27).[6] The classical period is constituted by art's declaration of its own autonomy, but an autonomy only of form, not of content. The second period, aestheticism, occurs with art's creation of a content that matches its autonomous form, hence a reflexive, formally self-contained art. The avant-garde occurs with art's taking of its own institutional status as its content, parodying the institution of art in order to break down the boundaries between art and reality. Bürger identifies this avant-garde primarily with early twentieth-century movements such as Dada and Surrealism, and artists such as Duchamp, and only awkwardly with what we might call the high modernism of Cubism and abstraction. He makes no reference at all to literary figures such as Proust, Musil, Kafka, Woolf, Joyce, or Faulkner. Since Bürger thinks of the avant-garde he describes as the essential end and unfolding of the art defined by classical aesthetics (17), its failure to achieve its end, according to him, is, if not an end to art, at least a resting place from which he has seen no movement forward. Thus the later twentieth-century work of Andy Warhol, as one example, which will become definitive of postmodernism, he calls the neo-avant-garde and, because it is a simple restaging of the original avant-garde, he declares it "devoid of sense" (61). Since postmodernism, for him, occurs after the end of his art, he could, after all, do no other.

As a way of pointing to the vulnerable point of this history, we may compare it to Clement Greenberg's manifesto for high modernism, which he also calls the avant-garde, his early essay, "Avant-Garde and Kitsch."[7] Greenberg (1986) identifies the social cause of his avant-garde (at this point he thought of himself as a Marxist, though his definition of modernist art does not change when his politics become non-Marxist left) as the breakdown of traditional social forms, among which had been aesthetic forms (6). As a result of these breakdowns, avant-garde art (which Greenberg identifies with lists of artists such as Picasso, Braque, Matisse; poets such as Pound, Stevens, and Yeats and the novelist Joyce, but pointedly not with Dada, Surrealism, or Duchamp) attempts to create a form for itself out of itself: "it has been in search of the absolute that the 'avant-garde' has arrived at 'abstract' or 'nonobjective' art – and poetry too. The avant-garde poet or artist tries in effect to imitate God by creating something valid solely on its own terms" (8). The essential identity between Greenberg's avant-garde and Bürger's aestheticism is clear enough. And some of Greenberg's listed avant-garde poets – Rimbaud, Mallarmé – certainly would, for Bürger, belong in that earlier category. But Greenberg manifestly means to describe the same twentieth-century break that Bürger does. And if he fails to make a persuasive break between nineteenth-century aestheticism and the avant-garde, it must be said that Bürger's gestures toward fitting Cubism and abstraction (or at least dripping as technique) into his theory (1984, 67) will be unlikely to persuade any students of those movements.[8] In effect, Greenberg's essay makes Bürger's history seem to make sense only by its exclusion or misinterpretation of the main trend of the art period he means to describe. And if Greenberg's definition of the avant-garde is not one everybody holds, one can easily see its correspondence with any number of theories of modernism. Indeed, his argument, as we will see, will ground the widespread mid-century formalism, of which he is a main exemplar.

Current theories of postmodernism frequently re-create Bürger's three-part history, merely throwing the stages forward. Thus, in his influential *Postmodernism, or the Cultural Logic of Late Capitalism*, Fredric Jameson (1991) essentially tracks Bürger's periods, calling them realism, modernism, and postmodernism (36). And although he defines the periods somewhat differently, the essential relationship between modernism and postmodernism reproduces Bürger's shift from aestheticism to the avant-garde: modernism tries to find new forms to track social changes (ix) while postmodernism calls into question the aestheticism of modernism by breaking down the frontier between high culture and popular culture (2). Although Jameson does not see postmodernism as having the social force Bürger gives the avant-garde, he sees its formal emptying of modernist formal invention in obviously analogous ways.[9] Unsurprisingly, Jameson follows Greenberg in identifying modernism with "abstract expressionism in painting, existentialism in philosophy, the final forms of representation in the novel" and his postmodernism is Bürger's neo-avant-garde, with a list of artists led off by Warhol (1). Unlike Bürger, he sees his postmodernism as a significant aesthetic and cultural moment and not an empty reproduction, void of sense. But, just as Greenberg frequently tried to brush aside Duchamp and Surrealism as artistic experiments of doubtful significance, in order to concentrate on the reflexive formalism of painting that made its own painterliness both its form and its subject, Jameson, recognizing the existence of an earlier art that seems to fit his later postmodernism, brushes that earlier version aside, really with no explanation. He admits that "[i]t may indeed be conceded that all the features of postmodernism I am about to enumerate can be detected, full-blown, in this or that preceding modernism (including such astonishing genealogical precursors as Gertrude Stein, Raymond Roussel, or Marcel Duchamp, who may be considered outright postmodernist, avant la lettre)," but he does not tell us why, in the light of this concession, he ought not to question his own historical location of the causes of this form of art in the late capitalism of the late twentieth century (4). Effectively, Jameson, Bürger, and Greenberg all have the problem that the modernist or avant-garde movement contained within it both a formalist aestheticism (one that can be pushed back to include late nineteenth-century forms such as Impressionism in painting and aestheticism in literature) and a questioning of that formalism through methods of pastiche and questioning of cultural barriers that seem definitive of a logical next step. Any coherent history that means to account for these two forms of art as successive stages will have to concentrate on one of these moments as definitive of modernism or the avant-garde and dismiss the other as an historical accident or a late repetition.

One might really have recourse to this explanation, especially with regard to Duchamp, who most completely predicts, for instance, Warhol. One could consider him something like an historical accident, an attempt to ask of formalism what makes the forms of artworks art, before history was ready for the question. And evidence in favor of such a response would be the fact that, although Duchamp attempted to exhibit *Fountain* in 1917, it took on the significance of a known artwork only decades later. And even then, until the 1960s, it was, for the most part, a one-off. I would like to argue, however, that the historical difficulties I have quickly surveyed, as well as the conflicting evaluations of the aesthetic significance of what I will now refer to in shorthand as "postmodernism," are predicted by the problematic definitions of art already offered by Kant and Hegel, that modernism and "postmodernism" are two sides of the same coin that, between them, create an equivalent definition of aesthetic form coupled with a denial of its existence. From there, we may proceed to a discussion of the connection of critical formalism with modernism's and "postmodernism's" formal sleights of hand.

Although not as clearly as he might have, Duchamp asked a question always implicitly posed by modernism's definition of its form as formal self-awareness. Greenberg, early on, defined modern painting in terms of its acceptance of its own formal flatness: "The history of avant-garde painting is that of a progressive surrender to the resistance of its medium; which resistance consists chiefly in that flat picture plane's denial of efforts to 'hole through' it for realistic perspectival space" (1986, 34). Greenberg means this definition of avant-garde painting in terms of formal self-awareness to correspond with an equally frequent modernist definition of aesthetic value in terms of its enhancing our awareness of perception via the reordering or elimination of realistic representation and the consequent attention to pure perception in the absence of things perceived. But the problem with the claim is that the formal features necessary for an avant-garde artwork may be reproduced without obviously reproducing the values attached to it. In a later essay, in evident awareness of the implications of Duchamp's readymades, Greenberg (1993) imagines the presentation of "a tacked up canvas" and admits that that would already be enough to be a modernist painting, though, he says, "not necessarily a successful one" (132). Greenberg's unwillingness to grant success to this stripping down of formal self-awareness to the point that the proposed object no longer offers any of the sensuous effects of artworks, and starts to look like any old object, reproduces the challenge to the institution of art that Bürger attributes to his avant-garde. One may note that it also explains how the illuminated flatness of modernist painting becomes the pastiched flatness in Jameson's famous account of Warhol's silk-screening of shoes, where that flatness opposes the Heideggerian fullness of Van Gogh's shoes (1991, 7–9). One of the reasons that one cannot create a coherent historical succession between the modern and the "postmodern" is that modernism's notion of form already carries "postmodernism's" challenge of that notion within it. Hence Duchamp's appearance was not precisely avant la lettre, because la lettre was already modernism to the letter.

And so Kant's ambiguous definition of aesthetic beauty predicts modernism's formal contradiction just as Hegel's declaration of the end of art predicts its historical situation. Kant, as we saw, declared that art re-created a natural beauty that modeled itself on an artistic beauty. As a result, an artwork was artistic in its erasure of its own existence as an object. The consequent vexations of trying to create an historical sequence from modernism to "postmodernism" follows a similar re-creation of Hegel's historical re-creation of Kant's epistemological contradiction in the apprehension of artistic beauty. Hegel declared art at an end when human beings experienced the intellectual need for an expression of knowledge that art could no longer offer. Since that need would have to occur before human beings recognized art as art – the definition of which would entail the expression of knowledge in a form of sensuous embodiment not subject to referential definition – the recognition of art would bring with it the end of art. That both modernism and "postmodernism" should be associated, at different points, also with an end to art should not surprise us, therefore.

Writing skeptically of Hegel, Adorno (1997) asserted that "Inevitably the thesis of the end of art can be heard at dialectical nodal points where a new form suddenly emerges that is directed polemically against the established form" (320). But this claim accurately generalizes Hegel's original claim. As a new form of art described itself, as in Hegel, it would also declare its own achievement, thus its own end. What Adorno thinks of as a delusion that reoccurs with modernism, Arthur Danto (1997) thinks of as an actual end in "postmodernism."[10] But, again, the logic by which modernism's concept of itself as a purified form of art must declare its own end in terms of a "postmodernism" that occurs both with it and after it follows Hegel's recognition that knowing a thing to be art requires art to have been surpassed. This situation would apply only more strongly to an art that meant to inscribe within itself its knowledge of its own artness. "Postmodernism's" declaration of itself as the end of modernist art, at least, would be part of modernism as well as its successor.

And this brings us to our second definition of formalism: a criticism of artworks that takes as its aim attention only to those of its elements that connect directly to its form as an artwork. Obviously, even the concept of such a criticism depends not only on the notion that artworks have a specific category of form, separate from other forms and categories of form, but that the artness of those works inheres specifically in that form or at least in some identifiable formal features. As we will see, formalist criticism takes its difficulties both from the aesthetic theory of form and from modernist art's attention to its own form as a matter of its content. But, to see these connections, we must first recognize that formalist criticism has some obvious differences from formalist aesthetic theory and it can never be tied merely to modernist art. With regard to a theory that defined what aesthetic form is, while such a theory would be a prerequisite to formalist criticism – without there being a form to have as its object, formalist criticism could not exist – it would not be sufficient for it. The fact that there was a form specific to artworks would not entail any critical obligation or advantage in attending only to it. Even Kant recognizes that, though our judgment of the beautiful is disinterested, we may have an interest in people's ability to take pleasure in natural beauty, for instance. And criticism could turn to that interest and still at least take as its starting point aesthetic beauty. And, of course, to the extent that artworks are meaning-bearing (and we will see this create both the demand for and a problem in formalism), one could attend only to their meaning – because one thought what an artwork meant was wise or dangerous or something else worthy of attention in the way any meaning claim might be – without any interest in whatever formal feature made it art as well as meaning-bearing. Formalism's independence from modernism is even clearer. While formalism might be necessary to deal with modernism's reflexive attention to its own form, it cannot be limited as a critical tool only to the analysis of the art of that period without ceasing to fulfill its end of being a criticism particularly directed at analyzing all art in terms of what made it art. A formalism that worked only to analyze modernist art wouldn't be an art criticism at all but a method for understanding the art of a particular historical period, whose interest, therefore, could only be the historical one of comprehending the art of a specific period. This is a perfectly valid end, obviously: nothing about formalism's ambitions for itself entails silly claims about the invalidity or lesser importance of other intellectual endeavors. It's just that it would not be a specifically art-oriented criticism and, in defining formalism, we must presume that such a criticism is at least possible (or, obviously, we could not define it). If it were possible, it would be desirable on the principle that it would provide knowledge of something and knowledge of anything is always a net gain.

Still, the goal of classic aesthetics in defining a form special to art obviously creates the possibility for formalism, and the connection between historicist criticism and its arguments against not merely formalist criticism but the possibility of defining art as an autonomous object only emphasizes the connection at some level between a formalist aesthetics and a formalist criticism.[11] And the historical connection between formalism and modernism, if not a necessary one, is hardly random. As a matter of history, of course, the first European formalism occurs in Russia in the 1920s, and only a little later the work of Roman Jakobson establishes concepts of literary language that remain important. In the United States, the connection between New Criticism and the ideas of modernist poets about their art is old news, of course. But if, as I have been arguing, the arguments made in different ways by both Kant and Hegel establish that the form of art inheres in either the nonexistence of the art object or the passing of art as a form of expression at the moment of our recognition of it as art, then formalism would be taking as its aim the accurate description of a nonexistent object, or at least an object it made obsolete by recognizing it. And if, as I have argued about modernism and "postmodernism," the theories of Kant and Hegel manifest themselves in ongoing difficulties of definition and historical periodization, difficulties that attach directly to modernism's ambition in art to create art about its own artness, to the extent that formalism arises from this project, one should not be surprised to find it sharing its difficulties. As we will see, it takes its difficulties from both the aesthetic theory of form and from modernist art's attention to its own form as a matter of its content. And one final point: one will note above that the examples of formal art criticism have become examples of literary criticism. There are other arts and other types of formalist art criticism, of course, but interpreting literature raises the question of the connection of a literary work's meaning with its being as an art object. This question is inherent in the aesthetic definition of form, but literary criticism experiences it with enhanced intensity because works of literature must mean in order to be. For all these reasons, one might say that the truth of aesthetics argues not the possibility of formalist criticism but its impossibility. And the coming to grief of aesthetic self-awareness over issues of historical periodization argues that the forms of political and historical resistance to formalism are a predictable consequence of its endeavor. In concluding this argument, I want to claim that these difficulties – the impossibility of its project and the inevitability of objections to the limits it establishes – also create its benefits as a criticism.

Adorno, whose *Aesthetic Theory* is the most deliberate discussion of aesthetics in the light of modernism, though the discussion is made difficult by the fact that it is more a series of meditative pronouncements than an argument, has a couple of statements on the issues of meaning that, taken together, outline the situation and the difficulties of formalist criticism, though that is not Adorno's intent. The first addresses the relation of meaning to form directly:

> Form is mediation in that it is the relation of parts to each other and to the whole and as the elaboration of details. With regard to form, then, the much praised naïveté in artworks turns out to be hostile to art. What may appear intuitive and naïve in artworks, their constitution as something that presents itself as self-coherent, gapless and therefore unmediated, derives from their mediatedness in themselves. It is only through this mediatedness that they become significative and their elements become signs. (1997, 144)

This argument functions as an implicit riposte to Hegel, who defines art as the sensuous embodiment of the idea of beauty. Since he insists that art expresses directly through the senses and that it eliminates all gaps between form and meaning, Hegel disallows it any element of mediation and certainly of reference via signs. Adorno refers to this idea with the term naïve, which he takes from Schiller, and which designates organically whole art, without the separations caused by consciousness. If this unmediated wholeness is hostile to art, rather than definitive of it, it could only be because meaning as well as sensuous appearance is necessary for art. And meaning necessitates signs that mean (an indivisible sensuous appearance would merely be a presentation). But art does not only mean. Although self-coherence, gaplessness, and lack of mediation derive from mediatedness, they are nevertheless the way art presents itself as art. In other words, the form of art is the appearance of unmediated expression that actually offers mediated, signified meaning. A formal criticism that aimed at describing form without getting distracted by unaesthetic meaning, then, would still find itself concerned with meaning after all.

If Adorno thinks meaning is necessary to art, he also thinks it something art tries always to do without, or at least expel:

> Meaning is only legitimate in the artwork insofar as it is objectively more than the work's own meaning . . . The unconscious labor of the artistic *ingenium* on the meaning of the work as on something substantial and enduring transcends this meaning. The advanced production of recent decades has become self-conscious of this issue, has made it thematic and translated it into the structure of artworks. It is easy to convict neodadaism of a lack of political import and dismiss it as meaningless and purposeless in every sense of the word. But to do so is to forget that its products ruthlessly demonstrate the fate of meaning without regard to themselves as artworks. Beckett's oeuvre already presupposes this experience of the destruction of meaning as self-evident, yet also pushes it beyond meaning's abstract negation in that his plays force the traditional categories of art to undergo this experience, concretely suspend them and extrapolate others out of the nothingness. (153)

Although the first passage quoted may have made Adorno sound like a naïve social realist proclaiming responsible meaning as an obligation of art, this passage makes clear that he believes meaning-bearing to be a burden art must bear, even as it struggles against it. The opening sentence is a Kantian formulation (the paragraph in which this passage appears starts with Kant's dictum that beauty has purposiveness without purpose as signifying the importance of meaninglessness to art). Just as we may have an interest in being able to experience beauty without the experience of beauty being interested, the existence of works of art may entail meanings without those meanings being what the work means. Works may have meanings, but those meanings aren't legitimate. What matters to the work of art is not the meaning but the labor to make the meaning substantial (sensuous?). And then Adorno enters a stunning series of paradoxes. modernist art (and for Adorno, modernism includes both what we generally call modern and, as well, what I have called "postmodern") has made the labor to make meaning substantial part of its structure. Thus its structure becomes meaning-bearing as it embodies, as structure, the labor to transform meaning into substance. In rebellion against this, evidently, neodada sacrifices its status as artwork in order finally to have no meaning, which is, contra political critics of it (who would include Marxist critics of postmodernism or what Bürger calls the neo-avant-garde, as devoid of sense), its point. And, of course, the having of a point, a *zweck*, makes it no longer artwork. To stress meaninglessness, it risks meaning. And Beckett completes this series of paradoxes on art's meaningful battle not to mean by taking the neodadaist abstract negation of meaning and making it part of the form of art. The examples of neodada and Beckett, compressed as they are, are literary exegeses exemplifying the historical claim about the attempt of modernist art to inscribe the labor of giving meaning substance into its structure. One might say about this passage that, in modernism, it puts form and meaning at war with each other and also makes the war the ultimate form. A formalist exegesis cannot merely describe this war. It would have to be where the battle is joined.

If, moving only slightly forward from Russian formalism, one takes Roman Jakobson as defining the basis of literary formalism as a study of literary language, that which constitutes the literariness of literature, one can see both its connection with modernism as more than one of chronology and the inauguration of the struggle of formalism with meaning, the struggle that, one might say, is the form of literary formalism. Jakobson (1987) defines a poetic function as one among other linguistic functions: "focus on the message for its own sake is the POETIC function of language" (69). He means to include within this focus not some specific feature of language (figure rather than reference, for instance), but any moment in which language draws attention to itself rather than to reference. One can immediately see the common ground between this claim that poeticness occurs with self-awareness of the poetic medium of language and the modernist project, as defined both by Bürger's aestheticism and Greenberg's avant-garde, to create an art out of awareness of its own artistic essence.

The problem with the concept is not the usual one found with it: Jakobson does not make any claim either that the poetic function occurs only in poetry or that poetry is made up exclusively of the poetic function, the claims that opponents of the concept of literary language usually seek to disprove. He argues only that there is such a feature of language and that, while it isn't the only form of language in poetry, it is the constitutive form. Rather the problem is a combination of the one that the concept of a stretched canvas considered as a painting presented to Greenberg and the problem of escaping meaning discussed above. Language doesn't even have non-referential linguistic features of which it can be aware unless it is language and thus is also meaning-bearing. And, of course, any language has linguistic features to which we might attend. Attending to the linguistic features of language is thus not a quality of language, but a description of what the receiver of the language chooses to attend to. And Jakobson effectively admits that the choice to attend to the poetic function is not one the function signals itself: "But how does poeticity manifest itself? Poeticity is present when the word is felt as a word and not a mere representation of the object being named or an outburst of emotion" (69). In the passive "is felt," Jakobson hides from himself – or at least nothing in the article from which this sentence is taken pursues the point – that as "postmodernism" always comes to question the objectness of the modernist art object, this formulation makes the poetic function of language and thus the poeticness of poetry not an aspect of the object of poetry but of our attention to it as poetry.

His response to anti-formalist objections to his arguments thus shows both why those objections occur and why they can't succeed in quite getting a foothold: "As I have already pointed out, the content of the concept of *poetry* is unstable and temporally conditioned. But the poetic function, *poeticity*, is, as the 'formalists' stressed, an element sui generis, one that cannot be mechanically reduced to other elements" (378). If the poetic function and poeticity were aspects in language and poetry rather than forms of our attention to them, an anti-formalist might well be able to trace their temporal conditioning as well. But as forms of our attention, even if they are historically caused forms, they have the autonomy Jakobson wants for them (like Kant's aesthetic judgment, they are different from other forms of attention even if their objects are not necessarily different), but the autonomy arises from anomaly: the form that formalism defines ceases to exist in the object as soon as we become aware of it as a form.

Jakobson's formalism turns its face from meaning, even as it always knows that it is there. Other formalisms attempt to define a poetic form of discourse that avoids meaning. Cleanth Brooks (1947), having defined literary language as differing from straightforward reference in being a figure unreduced to ground and thus holding multiple meanings at once, then denies that this figural discourse means at all (3–21). We cannot paraphrase a poem because it dramatizes an experience incommunicable in other ways (213). Michael Riffaterre (1978) argues straightforwardly that "poetry says one thing and means another" (1) and, it turns out, that what matters is what poetry says and not what it means since it must deny what it means, empty itself of message, and become a verbal game (13). But in each case, meaning comes back in as a necessary part of the process. In Brooks, first the language of paradox obviously does have a meaning even if it is a complex one. Even if the figures aren't reducible to straightforward reference, they still do refer or they cannot give us the unified, complex experience that is their aim. A dramatization of an experience is still a representation of an experience, and to understand the drama we will have to understand the meanings of the signs within it. And the experience will still be the meaning. In Riffaterre, in order to understand how the poem does not say what it means, we must note moments of ungrammaticality that send us to the poem's hypogrammatic meaning, but that ungrammaticality, to the extent that it informs us of how to interpret, functions as a reference, with a system and thus a grammar. In each case, the functioning of meaning as the foil against which the significant form functions entails that the turn toward that form is one that can't occur without engaging in the kind of reference it must avoid. And so the formalism again becomes a form of attention, a looking toward what language is that depends on a blindness to what it does, rather than a form of the art object.

One understands the frustration an anti-formalism has to the kind of responses to its critiques that formalists might implicitly make. Told that literary meaning, like any other meaning, has its historical causes and political implications, the formalist responds that meaning isn't what he is talking about. Told that the formal techniques to which she attends also have historical specificity and thus political implication, the next formalist responds that the techniques she points to are still autonomous as aspects of language to which we can attend. That frustration has the same source as that which frustrated the writing of the history of aestheticism, modernism, and "postmodernism." The art objects being created would not conform to a history because the aesthetic concepts to which they responded were duplicitous, having contradictory form, coming to an end as soon as they were noticed. The formalism designed to analyze these duplicitous objects will never be fully successful on its own terms because the "objects" it means to describe will never succeed in inhering in the objects it analyzes. But its failure re-creates the "object" it fails to capture. It used to be said that criticism was a form of fiction because it created the meanings it attributed to texts. But even if one can say accurate things about what texts mean, among other things, formalism is like the form it analyzes, an apprehension of an object, the definition of which – given by aesthetics and reproduced by formalism – questions the existence of the object it defines. A frustrating formalism, perhaps, but one suited to the form it analyzes.

Notes

1   Kant thinks of perception as determined by our senses and pure concepts of the understanding that structure what are presented to our senses, and thus not historically changing. One can easily imagine a theory arguing that perception takes different forms according to different historical contexts. Since the apprehension of beauty, however, does not attend to an object's concepts and is indifferent to its existence, that apprehension could hardly change as a result of any historical change surrounding the object. Thus either such a theory would imagine the apprehension of beauty as occurring at a certain historical moment and perhaps ending at another, but not as changing with history, or it would have to construct a non-Kantian aesthetics. In other words, Kant's aesthetics could accord with an historicist theory of perception, but not with an historicist theory of his analytic of aesthetic perception.

2   See "On Beauty as the Symbol of Morality," Kant 1987, 225–230.

3   Obviously, we have had a concept of art more or less like the contemporary one since at least the Renaissance. But, for Hegel, art after the Greek classical period was already subsidiary to religion. And, if we consider the aesthetics that arose in the eighteenth century as establishing our understanding of art, the concurrence of our recognition of art and Hegel's end of art becomes reasonably close.

4   An art movement or a theory that did not build on classical aesthetics would have to claim that it had invented art or theory anew so completely as to be a different order of object or thought from what came before. For the difference to be sufficiently complete, it would have to merit a different name and thus fail at its desire to be a change on the old.

5   See the foreword to Bürger, xiv–xv.

6   Bürger's avant-garde corresponds chronologically with Poggioli's and Greenberg's. Whether it is the same movement or whether Bürger intends it to be the same is a question we will deal with further on.

7   Kitsch is something like Greenberg's third period, a decline after the end of art that corresponds to the decline marked by Bürger's neo-avant-garde and, to an extent, Jameson's postmodernism (though Jameson's theory means to be more neutral). His prior period is a nameless one in which the traditional forms of society still had validity.

8   One should compare to Bürger's casual mention of drips as the introduction of chance into art, Greenberg's discussion of Pollack's deliberation in his art and, pointedly, in his drips (Greenberg 1993, 111).

9   One might add Lyotard to the list of logical possibilities in that he generally agrees with Jameson's periodization in which postmodernism follows modernism, but he gives to postmodernism the significance Bürger gives to the avant-garde of questioning the significance of modernist formal experiment by presenting the form without the significance (Lyotard 1984).

10 For the fullest version of the argument, see Danto, 1997.
11 From the perspective of aesthetics, the difference between the two is, however, vital. Nothing about trying to define what art is (an activity that presumes that one thinks art is something and thus autonomous at least in the sense that so is, say, a hammer or a nail: it is what it is and not something else) entails any position on what kinds of comment on art should take place or indeed whether criticism of any kind follows from the theory. While some theorists, Hegel, for instance, have been acute critics, others, notoriously Kant, have had virtually nothing to say about any particular artworks.

References

Adorno, Theodor W. (1997). *Aesthetic Theory*, ed. Gretel Adorno and Rolf Tiedemann, trans. Robert Hullot-Kentor. Minneapolis: University of Minnesota Press.

Brooks, Cleanth. (1947). *The Well-Wrought Urn: Studies in the Structure of Poetry*. New York: Harcourt, Brace & World.

Bürger, Peter. (1984). *Theory of the Avant-Garde*, trans. Michael Shaw. Minneapolis: University of Minnesota Press.

Danto, Arthur C. (1997). *After the End of Art: Contemporary Art and the Pale of History*. Princeton, NJ: Princeton University Press.

Greenberg, Clement. (1986). *The Collected Essays and Criticism, Volume I: Perceptions and Judgments, 1939–1944*, ed. John O'Brian. Chicago: University of Chicago Press.

Greenberg, Clement. (1993). *The Collected Essays and Criticism, Volume IV: Modernism with a Vengeance, 1957–1969*, ed. John O'Brian. Chicago: University of Chicago Press.

Hegel, G. W. F. (1975). *Aesthetics: Lectures on Fine Art*, trans. T. M. Knox. New York: Oxford University Press.

Jameson, Fredric. (1991). *Postmodernism, or, the Cultural Logic of Late Capitalism*. Durham, NC: Duke University Press.

Jakobson, Roman. (1987). *Language in Literature*, ed. Krystyna Pomorska and Stephen Rudy. Cambridge, MA: Harvard University Press.

Kant, Immanuel. (1987). *The Critique of Judgment*, trans. Werner S. Pluhar. Indianapolis, IN: Hackett.

Lyotard, Jean-François. (1984). *The Postmodern Condition: A Report on Knowledge*. Minneapolis: University of Minnesota Press.

Riffaterre, Michael. (1978). *Semiotics of Poetry*. Bloomington: Indiana University Press.

25

Rancière's Aesthetic Regime
Modernism, Politics, and the Logic of Excess

Molly Anne Rothenberg

The Logic of Excess and the Self-Different Community

Jacques Rancière's work on modernism begins, surprisingly, with an analysis of Plato's belief that each person in a well-ordered republic will have the occupations and positions proper to them.[1] The political function of the republic is to maintain the distribution of these occupations so that those who have the relevant talents and propensities (ability to make shields, ability to reason well) will devote their energies to the appropriate activities. Activities that work against the maintenance of this distribution will be forbidden. That is, Plato advocates the prohibition of activities, such as the arts, which by their very nature could suggest an order otherwise than that established by the republic. Rancière points out that there is no such thing as aesthetics proper in Plato's formulation, because the arts have no artistic function per se: their only function is to maintain the social order. This is what Rancière means when he refers to the role of art in Plato's republic as an *ethical regime*.

Rancière calls the social organization of roles and occupations a communal "distribution of the sensible" (*le partage du sensible*, sometimes translated as "distribution of the perceptible") because it presents its hierarchies and inequalities as (apparently) given, that is, a function of positive or natural properties. Some people are high-born, some people have wealth, some people are slaves, facts confirmable by the senses. All social organizations are based on a communal distribution of the boundaries of what is able to be seen, heard, and thought. Rancière refers to the necessary ordering operations of society as the "police," by which he does not mean a force of repression so much as a status quo that works to prevent the emergence of an *otherwise*, a new set of coordinates of the perceptible.

We are in the realm of politics proper, however, only when such an otherwise, some new distribution, arises. Crucial to Rancière's argument is his insight that the status quo distribution of the sensible occludes politics by means of a "justification"

A Handbook of Modernism Studies, First Edition. Edited by Jean-Michel Rabaté.
© 2013 John Wiley & Sons, Ltd. Published 2013 by John Wiley & Sons, Ltd.

based on properties assumed to be natural because they are perceptible. Nature, not men, so this justification asserts, assigns the social hierarchy, so inequalities are simply given, and there is nothing to be done about them. Some people have the natural right to speak and be obeyed. However, as Rancière points out, there is a fundamental flaw in the logic of a justification that assigns the right of speech to some and not to others. The flaw is this: because the justification is addressed to everyone, including those who are considered to be unfit to join the community of speakers, everyone is assumed to be able to understand it. In the same way that the slave is denied the status of a speaking being but nonetheless must be able to participate in the language community in order to carry out his duties, so the distribution of the social order, which perforce is unequal, depends fundamentally upon an equality of speaking beings. Everyone – no matter how positioned in the hierarchy – has to be part of the intended audience for the justification of the social order. So, justifying the community's inequality on natural grounds obscures the paradox that such inequality depends upon a foundational equality of speaking beings. Of course, for the members of a community who accept the reigning order, "inequality exists because of inequality . . . [for them] the understanding of language has no bearing on the social order" (Rancière 1999, 49). That is, the fact of the equality of speaking beings is disavowed in an account that partitions those who have access to meaningful speech from those who do not.

It follows, then, that a "wrong" is always taking place, that is, the wronging of a part of the community that does not count – "the part of no part" or those whom the justification of the status quo discounts. Yet this formulation does not quite capture Rancière's point. It is true that some part of the community is being treated unequally, but the "wrong" itself is being done to the entire community *as a community of equals*. Rancière distinguishes between this wrong and one in which the wronged party is considered as a victim, a formulation that depends upon a logic of exclusion. In his view, "victim politics" asserts positive properties or identities as the criteria for being assigned to or excluded from places in the distribution. By that logic, even after an act of inclusion occurs, the same distribution of the sensible – that is, the same reliance on "natural properties" to allot "proper" occupations and roles – remains. For Rancière, however, equality is not a property that an individual can possess. Equality is a relation: in the case of the justification of the status quo, it is a relation of equality of intelligence.[2] What is disputed in the exposure of a wrong is the status of the speaking being, not whether a being with this or that property should be included. The truly emancipatory act, therefore, would not merely include a category of people but rather re-coordinate the entire system of distribution of the sensible to make visible this underlying equality.[3]

Rancière explores the underlying equality of speaking beings, which circulates as the unacknowledged excess of the policed community, by reference to Plato's famous anxiety about writing as a threat to social order, "hobnobbing with completely inappropriate people no less than with those who understand it, and completely failing to know who it should and shouldn't talk to" (Waterfield 2002, 70). Unlike speech, in which (so Plato imagines) the speaker is able to control the reception of the meaning of his words, writing looses the tether of its author's control and circulates freely without respect for social distinctions. This promiscuous quality of writing ignores the distinctions of rank and occupation established by the well-ordered society and as such threatens its disorganization.

While Plato seeks to limit the disordering potential of language to writing, Rancière knows that all linguistic acts – spoken or written – are carriers of an irremediable excess. This excess arises not because different words may have multiple meanings (polysemy), but rather because statements include both enunciated content and the act of enunciation. Each statement has a hidden dimension, so that for every enunciated content (e.g., "I love you") there is attached an implicit "I am saying that." Consequently, every "I love you" is actually an "I am saying that I love you." Even if the content is unexceptionable or unambiguous at the level of the enunciated, a question can always arise for the hearer at the level of the enunciation: what is at issue is not simply the enunciated content but what the person is doing by saying it. For example, you say that you love me, but are you asking me to take some action, ignore a slight, seal my fate to yours, or be your lover? Supposing that we understand "love" to mean the same thing, the question of why you are telling me that you love me cannot be answered for me by reference to a definition. The "meaning" of the statement, then, is a function of the way in which the reader appropriates the content to a specific context, an appropriation made possible by the level of the enunciation. As a result, no answer to the question "what does the statement mean?" can be definitive, since the enunciated content is always embedded within an enunciation and so available for further appropriation, which no author can control.[4] Enunciative excess is irremediable.

Nonetheless, the excess can be disavowed. We can locate a "zero degree" of enunciation in which the person speaking is not considered to be saying anything, no matter what the content. In Aristotle's view, for example, a being can make sounds that do not count as speech for its auditors. In those cases, there is *no question* as to the status of the enunciation: the question of the enunciation is foreclosed because the speaker is not granted the position of meaningful speaker. This foreclosure places all of the power in the hands of the hearer. For Rancière, invocation of this zero degree is a defense designed to put enunciative excess out of play, and therefore out of reach of those whom the hierarchization of the community discounts. The ethical regime, then, may be viewed profitably as a defense against enunciative excess, a defense, moreover, that is in constant jeopardy of breaking down and so in continual need of reinforcement.

Plato links writing's potential to disrupt entrenched social positions ("hobnobbing with completely inappropriate people") to the need for a guarantor of the desired order in the social sphere ("its father"). He implies that there is some use of language, if not in writing, that could abolish enunciative excess. But because this excess is in fact always present, efforts to govern it must be perennially at work: the very distribution of roles and occupations in society means that an order is in force that has to justify itself, and such justification necessarily depends upon an appeal to the fable that "natural" or sensorily given properties (such as birth, wealth, or gender) underwrite this distribution. When those who have been discounted in the reigning order speak on the basis of their fundamental equality as speaking beings, they address not only those who wrong them but also a third party that is called into existence by means of this address as the witness to the wrong. This "third" party is both the community as currently distributed and the community (heretofore obscured by the hierarchical social distribution) of equal speaking beings: it is both the community and *not* the community at the same time. It is the community seen as excessive to itself, as self-different. This self-difference comes into view in a moment of subjectivization, when the speaker of the wrong calls into being an "I" or a "we" as a representative of the community of equals, a "we" that is "supernumerary to the count of the original distribution" (Rancière 1999, 48).

In Rancière's framework, we are in the realm of politics proper only with this emergence of the supernumerary subject of politics. This subject is "supernumerary" on account of the excess (equality) which makes each element in the community count more than once, that is, first as a given in the distribution of social roles on the basis of supposedly natural properties and then as a member of the community of equals. But this additional count does not add up to "two": the relationship of equality traverses each member of the community as its difference from itself. More than one, but not quite two, the supernumerary subject of politics is a "singular universal," by which Rancière means that the discounted member of the social order stands both for itself as an element that counts due to its properties and for the universal condition of equality. The singular universal thus is another way to describe the excess that generates the community's self-difference.[5] The community of equals is not "to come" in Derrida's sense, but is in fact materially present *always and everywhere* in the society as the necessary foundation of the community of speaking beings. Both Plato and Rancière call this omnipresent, often invisible/silent, supernumerary community of equals the *demos*, even though Plato despises the demos and Rancière extols it. Yet the demos should be understood not as this or that excluded group (such as "the rabble" or the *Lumpenproletariat*), even though these groups sometimes come into their own politically, but rather as the community of equal speaking beings on which every society necessarily is based, the community's difference from itself.

The Aesthetic Regime

Now what does the logic of excess and the community of self-difference have to do with modernism? In the first place, insofar as the traditional use of the term modernism indexes a relation to modernity, it designates a historical period in which the value of equality is recognized as a universal. Rancière's analysis indicates that such a recognition – albeit a disavowed one – has been operative since classical times. In effect, Plato's fable of the well-ordered republic, with its defensive ploy to discount the actual equality of the speaking beings in the community, is a disavowal (and therefore a tacit acknowledgment) of that equality. The modernity of "modernism" is an illusion, since the inherent equality of speaking beings exists at all times and places.

In addition, Rancière develops a history of specific relationships between art and social life that he calls "regimes" or distributions of the sensible: this history reconceives the nature of modernism. The first regime, as Plato's exile of the mimetic arts from the republic indicates, is an effort to conceptualize the arts solely with respect to their function of maintaining social order. By contrast to this "ethical regime" of art, Aristotle inaugurated a "representational regime" in which the arts are brought back from exile to the extent that they imitate the appropriate actions of men in their proper hierarchized roles. "Representational" here does not refer to the ability of a work to mirror an object but more crucially to a mirroring of the social order and an order of genres and subject matter. The two orders make a harmonious whole of articulated hierarchies: art should only represent and reinforce the "proper" distribution of the social. Aristotle attempts to limit the role of the arts to representing that social order, that is, to fabricating "a plot arranging actions that represent the activities of men" (Rancière 2000, 21). This *normative* function "defines conditions according to which imitations can be recognized as exclusively belonging to an art and assessed, within this framework, as good or bad, adequate or inadequate" (21–22). Rancière is at pains to emphasize that the representational regime is first and foremost a "regime of visibility" that "at once renders the arts autonomous and also . . . links this autonomy to a general order of occupations and ways of doing and making" (22).

In Rancière's view, both Plato and Aristotle are committed to the same social vision, even if Aristotle makes space for some kinds of art. Correlatively, the same anxiety about art is evident in both Plato and Aristotle: both attempt to manage art's power to present a new distribution of the sensible either by banishing the arts or by enforcing strict rules of decorum for them. This analysis points directly to a third relationship of *equality* inherent in but obscured by both the ethical and representative regimes. Art perennially harbors the universalizing condition of equality – which traditional literary and political discourse regard as peculiarly modern – no matter how disavowed or delimited. This "modern" moment of equality occulted in both the ethical and representational regimes eventually erupts in a third relationship between art and life, what Rancière calls the "aesthetic" regime:

> I call this regime *aesthetic* because the identification of art no longer occurs via a division within ways of doing and making, but it is based on distinguishing a sensible mode of being specific to artistic products. The word aesthetics does not refer to a theory of sensibility, taste, and pleasure for art amateurs. It strictly refers to the specific mode of being of whatever falls within the domain of art, to the mode of being of the objects of art. (22)

For Rancière, the "aesthetic regime of the art . . . is the true name for what is designated by the incoherent label 'modernity'" (24). He locates the emergence of the aesthetic regime in the late eighteenth century, when a new distribution of the sensible arises. So, the second way in which Rancière's analysis intervenes in the discourse about modernism is by locating the overt assertion of equality that emerges with this new distribution in a precise historical period at least a century earlier than canonical modernism.

But Rancière's most important critical innovation with respect to modernism is clarified when we ask what kind of equality comes to the fore in the aesthetic regime. Rancière does not mean that art from the eighteenth century to the present is committed to democracy or to any other political form. (As we will see below, the politics of aesthetics Rancière proposes is independent of political content or ideological transmission.) Neither does the aesthetic regime mark an absolute rupture with the ethical or representational regimes: more than one regime can exist at the same time. Instead, what is distinctive about the aesthetic regime is that, in departing from the decorum of the representational regime, art becomes free to present any subject matter whether or not it upholds the social order. Such a break can only take place by way of the implicit equalizing of subject matter. The issue is not whether any given subject matter resembles reality or not: the issue is whether or not anyone so ever may use any subject matter so ever in any genre so ever for any audience so ever.

This new way of periodizing art contravenes the usual platitudes about modernism's break with mimesis and the past in that the aesthetic regime also includes Romanticism, realism, naturalism, Surrealism, art for art's sake, and other movements usually considered to be antagonists to or weak precursors of modernism per se. So, in Rancière's literary history, Flaubert's *Madame Bovary*, with its absolutization of style, is one of the first examples of the realist novel's rigorous working out of the indifference of subject matter that characterizes the aesthetic regime. That is, where standard accounts of modernism – or modernity in the arts – trace "a simple line of transition or rupture between the old and the new, the representative and the non-representative or the anti-representative" in terms of a turn to anti-mimetism, Rancière rejects this focus on the "refusal of figurative representation" as a key to the aesthetic regime (24).

Instead, he considers German Romanticism, from Schiller to Hegel, to be the inaugural moment of this new regime. He explains that Schiller recognizes the *inequality* inherent in Kant's definition of aesthetic judgment, in which intuition and its conceptual determinants are contrasted, as a political division "of those who act and those who are acted upon" (44). To counter this division, Schiller's "aesthetic" state suspends "the opposition between active understanding and passive sensibility . . . breaking down – with an idea of art – an idea of society based on the opposition between those who think and decide and those who are doomed to material tasks" (44). In this way, Schiller breaks with the representational regime's normative function for art, and in so doing offers one way in which art's new freedom with respect to subject matter might have a political valence: Schiller's aesthetic state is taken up by the German Romantics as an educational program for "the material realization of unconditional freedom and pure thought in common forms of life and belief" (27).

At this juncture it becomes possible for us to see that the aesthetic regime contains a paradox as it brings about a new distribution of the sensible in the form of an innovative yet self-contradictory relationship between art and life. If art is not regarded in terms of its ethical or representational functions in society, then what is the role of art? On the one hand, art is freed from its normative social functions to be its own kind of activity: art is singular. On the other hand, art is like any other form of "doing or making" that members of a society undertake (23). The normative functions of art in the representational regime, then, disappear in two related yet contradictory moves, one which severs art from its role of representing life as "naturally" hierarchized, leaving art free to explore its own domain for its own purposes, and the other which reconnects art to life in a non-normative way, treating art as one shaping force among many:

> The aesthetic regime asserts the absolute singularity of art and, at the same time, destroys any pragmatic criterion for isolating this singularity. It simultaneously establishes the autonomy of art and the identity of its forms with the forms that life uses to shape itself. (23)

Rancière often phrases this duality in terms of a definition of art that appears to be self-contradictory: art is simultaneously art as art (not-life) and art as not-art (life).

So, the emergence of equality as a universal exposes the paradoxical self-difference of art as well as of community, galvanizing a host of artistic strategies that attempt to manage and exploit the paradox. Rancière puts it this way:

> In the aesthetic regime, artistic phenomena are identified by their adherence to a specific regime of the sensible, which is extricated from its ordinary connections and is inhabited by a heterogeneous power, the power of a form of thought that has become foreign to itself, a product identical with something not produced, knowledge transformed into non-knowledge, *logos* identical with pathos, the intention of the unintentional, etc. (23)

In a moment we will take a look at the ways that realism and modernism bear out Rancière's analysis of an art that is self-different. But for now it will be helpful to focus on the way that this "heterogeneous power" of art's self-difference contains the generative energy of the logic of excess.

Recall that the community of equal speaking beings – in which each member counts once as itself and then (indefinitely) as part of the relation of equality – is *excessive to itself*. The excess arising from the relation of equality necessary for the (policed) community to exist in the first place both makes the community what it *is* (its identity) and divides it from itself. In the aesthetic regime, art is similarly self-different. The equality of subject matter (against which both the ethical and representational regimes defend themselves) divides art from itself. On the one hand, art freed from the necessity of matching subject matter to genre becomes autonomous, distinct from life. Art, therefore, is a singular activity. On the other hand, art's freedom to take on any subject matter so ever means that there is finally no way to distinguish the shaping activity of art from other shaping activities. When I build a house, is it art? When a toilet is put on display in a museum, is it art or not? If I write down my observations of life as it occurs, is this art? These familiar questions are not answerable by reference to what we are used to calling "aesthetic criteria": they are a necessary consequence of the self-difference of art. Art is art *because* it bears an excess that both severs and links it to life.

The generative capacity of this excess is due to the ineradicable omnipresence of a fundamental equality: Rancière's most brilliant work on the arts consists of his elucidation of these efforts to resolve this paradox and the subsequent contradictions to which they themselves give rise. These efforts sometimes afford promising avenues for political thought, for example in modernist poetry and novels that make it possible to discern new distributions of the sensible – even if the authors themselves do not see their work in that light. This is the third sense in which Rancière wields the logic of excess and self-difference as a tool for understanding modernism.

Modernism and the Paradox of the Aesthetic Regime

From this perspective, modernist discourse seeks to disavow the dual relationship of art to life in two ways, both derived from the fundamental and paradoxical premise that art is an *"autonomous form of life"* – that is, distinct from life and indistinguishable from life (26, emphasis in original). So, one familiar version of modernism conceives of art as the exploration of its specific medium, a pure form of art freed from mimetic concerns. Painting investigates color and two-dimensional surfaces, music a twelve-tone system released from expressive functions, literature takes for its focus language as intransitive or not reducible to its communicative functions, and so on. Rancière points out that the "crisis of art" so frequently remarked over the past half century is the "overwhelming defeat of this simple modernist paradigm," but unfortunately art critics regard this crisis as a failure of modernism rather than as a function of the paradox at the heart of the aesthetic regime (26). The other pole of the paradox spawns a different conception of art, which Rancière calls "modernatism": it assigns to art forms the task of fulfilling "a destiny specific to modernity," such as fostering a specific mode of living freely together in a political community (27).

Rancière's analysis suggests another way of thinking about the relationships among modernism, modernatism, and postmodernism than those currently on offer. Because the aesthetic regime cannot provide any criterion by which art and life should be related or distinguished, it sustains a variety of possible art forms (including figurative representations), genres, media, temporalities, and political potentials. Modernism disavows this formal heterogeneity in order to promote a "pure" form of art's autonomy; modernatism disavows the temporal and political heterogeneity in order to maintain that art has a teleology, such as the materialization of freedom. For example, postmodernism, à la Lyotard, insists on the separation of art and life while (contradictorily) blaming modernist thought for the worst political effects of humankind. The internal contradictions of the aesthetic regime cannot be avoided. Postmodernism is "simply the name under whose guise certain artists and thinkers realized what modernism had been: a desperate attempt to establish a 'distinctive feature of art' by linking it to a simple teleology of historical evolution and rupture" (28). What we call postmodernism is the exposition of the necessary failure of this project, but the necessity is inherent in what modernism disavows, that is, the actual paradoxical conditions of the aesthetic regime.[6]

By looking into their attempts to manage the paradox of the aesthetic regime, Rancière discovers new relationships between realism and modernism. He analyzes what he calls the "descriptive excess" of realist texts to demonstrate their consonance with the aesthetic regime (2011, 39). Critics of realism complained that Balzac, Flaubert, and Zola (to name only French targets) simply piled detail on detail for no reason, spoiling the unity of the whole. From one point of view, this is mimeticism gone wild: the world doesn't have any order or meaning, a condition mirrored by the text's proliferating and meaningless details. Yet from another point of view, the text "marks the ruin of all that was in harmony with the stability of the social body . . . the loss of poetic proposition that was strictly tied to the social hierarchy" (39). That is, in this view, the text *fails* to mirror the world, undermining precisely those forces that give meaning and order. In this sense, the realist text breaks with the decorum of the representational regime. Rancière points out that the "flaw peculiar to descriptive excess basically comes down to the opposition of one *all* to a different *all*," by which he means that the "whole" harmoniously ordered social body is opposed to the "all" of everything existing on the same plane.[7]

Many modernist texts work with the paradox of the aesthetic regime along similar lines. Nabokov's "Signs and Symbols" can serve as a primer on the aesthetic regime, not simply because its subject matter – a schizophrenic child and his elderly immigrant parents – breaks with the decorum of representationality but because the text foregrounds the very question as to whether a detail is excessive. The institutionalized boy with referential mania cannot tolerate the meaninglessness of the details of everyday life and so chooses to impose order by asserting that all of nature speaks, but only of him. The alternative to managing the flux and proliferation of the world's details by means of a singular referent would be to deny that the multitudinous and impersonal flux of being has any meaning beyond its quiddity. So, the boy's parents wish that they could discover an underlying purpose or meaning in the events of their lives, but they cannot. For them, the world is brute facticity, or rather, because any given detail *might* have another meaningful dimension, a dimension that is closed to them, they experience the tantalizing possibility of meaning as a form of cruelty. The mother reviews photographs and playing cards as if they might reveal something to her, but they never do (although the puzzle-solving reader can always find a meaning in these descriptions). The ending of the story tempts the reader to elevate herself over the parents by reading meanings into quotidian detail, imposing a pattern they don't see, but that hermeneutic superiority mirrors the boy's activity and so entails the risk of madness.[8] Rancière refers to these two options as

> a double staging of mute speech: on the one hand, there is the staging of things that speak of the common world better than political utterances do, that talk more eloquently than orators, once the hieroglyphs of the common history they bear on their bodies are unravelled; on the other hand, there is the staging of mute things that are there for no reason, meaningless, and that drag awareness down into their apathy and aphasia, into a world of less than human micro-individualities that impose a different scale of magnitude from the scale of political subjects . . . thereby put[ting] into play both super-meaningfulness and sub-meaningfulness. (44)

The choice Nabokov forces on the reader is not really a choice: the reader is stuck in the opposition between two kinds of "all." But this is a strange kind of opposition, akin to the relationship between the zero and O on the telephone that the mother seeks to differentiate. The zero and the O of the telephone can be distinguished, but because they are both ciphers – that is, indicators of both a meaningless nullity and a harmonious whole – they constitute neither a simple opposition nor an identity. Like any element of this world, the circle of the zero and the O is self-different, at once super- and sub-meaningful. The equality that traverses each element – the equalization of subject matter – produces an excess that endlessly proliferates new possibilities for equivalence and differentiation.

In a similar vein, Rancière offers a reading of Woolf that has affinities with this analysis of Nabokov's story in terms of the paradox of the aesthetic regime. Woolf strives, he (2000) says, "toward a language that eliminates its contingency at the risk of brushing shoulders with the language of the mad" (59). These two possibilities are embodied in two characters in *The Waves*, Bernard "who is incapable of not giving an identity to events, things and people . . . without connecting them to another," and Rhoda, who is "incapable of pinpointing identities . . . of ever connecting one moment to the following moment" (2011, 69). Rancière describes these polarities in terms of a diagnosis that runs underneath the history of nineteenth-century literature:

> For, between Flaubert's times and those of Proust, the issue of literature has more and more become a matter of health . . . tied to that of life-threatening forces. It's a matter of knowing whether literature is in complicity with those forces or whether, on the contrary, it is the medicine that fights them. Literature as such [the aesthetic regime] was born out of the poetic reversal that put the interpretation of life in the place of the logic of actions [the representational regime]. Life, in the strong sense of the term, not as the empirical course of things but as the power that dominates individuals and communities, is thus its own object. (65–66, my brackets)

It is possible to look at this history by means of a logic of mutual opposition between art as not-life and art as life. On the one hand, words can be regarded as having the power to lead men and women astray from their natural purposes, and in that way literature would be in cahoots with disease rather than health, that is, opposed to life. On the other hand, life as contingency is meaningless, and humankind will grasp at anything that provides form and sense to its flux. In this case, literature could provide the antidote to pure sensation, pure contingency. But, as usual, Rancière rejects a simple logic of exclusion in favor of a logic of excess. Literature has an excessive relation to life. For if (healthy) literature can interpret life as meaningful, it does so by creating objects of desire, false unities (unhealthy literature), which (healthy) literature then has the task of undoing. The "pathological connections" that create a false synthesis of "an apparition on a beach, the idea of individuality and the dream of love" (a false synthesis generated by unhealthy literature) can be rectified by returning the substance of life to "the pure multiple of sensation" (presented in healthy literature (*PL* 68)). Yet pure sensation threatens the dissolution of the self. When Woolf tries to "smash the barriers of individual subjectivity and to subscribe to the hecceities of pre-individual life," she in effect sides with literature as the antidote to false synthesis but at the risk of madness (70).

A Politics of the Aesthetic Regime

Nonetheless, Rancière does not simply track the vicissitudes of the logic of excess in literature's relation to life. He also keeps an eye out for the places where a new distribution of the sensible comes into view. Because Woolf constantly has to face the internal contradictions of her theory of fiction, she is motivated to explore new ways of configuring the perceptible. Rancière finds in Woolf's work an innovation for democratic thinking:

> Her way of working on the contraction or distension of temporalities, on their contemporaneousness or their distance, or her way of situating events at a much more minute level, all of this establishes a grid that makes it possible to think through the forms of political dissensuality more effectively than the 'social epic's' various forms. There is a limit at which the forms of novelistic micrology establish a mode of individuation that comes to challenge political subjectivization. There is also, however, an entire field of play where their modes of individuation and their means of linking sequences contribute to liberating political possibilities by undoing the formatting of reality produced by state-controlled media, by undoing the relations between the visible, the sayable, and the thinkable. (2000, 65)

Viewed politically, Woolf's writing both opens and closes the potential for a redistribution of the sensible. Insofar as her writing explores ever more particular modes of subjective perception, it can fall under the domain of pure sensation which tends to confirm the status quo distribution of the sensible. At the same time, the potential for undoing that particular distribution remains in play, albeit without guaranteeing any political result. It is to this political potential of literature – the equality specific to literature and the (different) equality specific to democracy – that we now turn. Once again, we find that the logic of excess provides the engine of Rancière's thought.

He begins by specifying that *politics of literature* does not refer to literature that exhorts political action, conducts political analyses, or otherwise falls under the category of "committed literature." Rather, literature has a specific way of intervening in the distribution of the sensible, which he terms *literarity*, or the fact that words always exceed authorial intentions and have material effects. Language, therefore, endangers the extant distributions of the sensible, be they overtly "political" or "artistic":

> Man is a political animal because he is a literary animal who lets himself be diverted from his 'natural' purpose by the power of words. This *literarity* is at once the condition and the effect of the circulation of 'actual' literary locutions. However, these locutions take hold of bodies and divert them from their end or purpose insofar as they are not bodies in the sense of organisms, but quasi-bodies, blocks of speech circulating without a legitimate father to accompany them toward their authorized addressee. Therefore, they do not produce collective bodies. Instead, they introduce lines of fracture and disincorporation into imaginary collective bodies. This has always been, as is well known, the phobia of those in power and the theoreticians of good government, worried that the circulation of writing would produce 'disorder in the established system of classification'. (39–40)

"Literarity," then, should not be mistaken for the modernist critical position that literary autonomy depends upon the "material specificity" of language, that is, a language that is unmoored from its communicative functions in order to refer only to itself in an "intransitive use of language" (2011, 65). Instead, it is a version of enunciative excess, of infinite appropriability and material effects.

Rancière emphasizes repeatedly that literarity is a political force, not because it interpellates subjects by way of "imaginary identifications" (which for him also implies that ideological interpellation is a fantasy of political theorists) but because it "causes modifications in the sensory perception of what is common to the community" (2000, 40). Literature has its own particular political mode. He contrasts the political disagreement, by which the supernumerary subject of politics appears, with the literary *mésentente*:

> Literary dissensus works on changes in the scale and nature of individualities, on deconstruction of the relationships between things and meaning. In this, it differentiates itself from the work of political subjectification which configures new collectives by means of words. Political dissensus operates in the form of subjective procedures that identify the declaration by the anonymous that they are a collective, an *us*, with reconfiguration of the field of political objects and actors. Literature goes in the opposite direction . . . it dissolves the subjects of utterance in the fabric of the percepts and affects of anonymous life. (2011, 43)

Literarity causes the "quasi-bodies" to circulate, forming "uncertain communities that . . . call into question the distribution of roles, territories, and languages"

(2000, 40). Countering the traditional view of a political group as a "communal body" functioning together because they have imbibed the same ideas, this formulation stresses "'literary' disincorporation" of the bonds of a community based on "natural" hierarchies as the route to political subjectivization (40). In Rancière's account, even though literature is not part of an interpellative mechanism, or committed to exhorting people to take political action, or representing states of society that require political remediation, it is still political because its medium is "literarity," which has the ability to make visible new distributions of the sensible. Literarity serves as the *sine qua non* of politics on account of the property-less excess inherent to language that it introduces into the taken-for-granted distribution of the sensible, making possible a disruption of the police order.

Nonetheless, disincorporation, with all of its political consequences, is not an automatic consequence of literarity. "Disincorporation" refers to the way that the democratization of subject matter and the "natural" justification of social hierarchies collapse in the aesthetic regime, not to a guarantee that a political subject will emerge. In Rancière's history of literature, literarity's capacity for disincorporation, the potential leveling of subject matter and society, evoked the prospect of a dissolution of social life, a prospect that might be viewed politically in negative or positive terms. As a result, in the nineteenth century, a dream of a new form of relationship between language and world arose, one in which things would give "direct expression of a potential for being that was immanent in beings" and in this way reconstitute a "communal body" (57). This dream sets up a "galvanizing tension" within literature itself, for if the world speaks itself, if writing does not circulate as literarity, then literature cancels itself out:

> Literature has been constructed as a tension between two opposing rationalities: a logic of disincorporation and dissolution, whose result is that words no longer have any guarantee, and a hermeneutic logic that aims at establishing a new body for writing. (59)

Rancière productively traces this tension, and the literary strategies designed to resolve it, in the work of Flaubert, Balzac, Saint-Simon, Mallarmé, Rimbaud, Woolf, Pavese, and Joyce, among others. In Rancière's writings, then, modernism names a group of authors who explore this tension, a product of the logic of excess, and in so doing expose the "political stakes of writing" (59).

Notes

1 No single essay can do justice to the richness and rigor of Rancière's work. In this essay, I have tried to demonstrate the presence of a logic that informs his work on a number of different topics. Although Rancière does not use the term "logic of excess," this logic is a common thread in his thought and generates the unusual and unusually productive branching structure of his analyses. I have limited myself to showing how this logic operates in his work on the relationships among literature, aesthetics, and politics. For the English-speaking student new to Rancière's work, I recommend as a good starting

place Kristin Ross's introduction to *The Ignorant Schoolmaster: Five Lessons in Intellectual Emancipation*. See also Jean-Philippe Deranty's *Jacques Rancière: Key Concepts*; Rancière's *The Politics of Aesthetics*; his *Disagreement*; his *Politics of Literature*; and Joseph Tanke's *Jacques Rancière: An Introduction, Philosophy, Politics, Aesthetics*. These are the works referenced in this essay.

2   Rancière presents his first and most extensive discussion of the presupposition of the equality of intelligence in *The Ignorant Schoolmaster*.

3   Rancière is very close to Badiou's description of an event here.

4   I have discussed the logic of excess more extensively in *The Excessive Subject: A New Theory of Social Change*.

5   Slavoj Žižek elucidates the singular universal in Rancière by way of Hegel's "concrete universality." As long as there is an exclusionary social order, "there will always be an excessive excremental zero-value element which, while formally part of the system, has no proper place within it, and as such stands for the (repressed) universality of this system . . . in short, it is precisely those who are without their proper place within the social Whole (like the rabble) that stand for the universal dimension of the society which generates them. This is why the rabble cannot be abolished without radically transforming the entire social edifice . . . ." See his "King, Rabble, Sex, and War in Hegel," in *Žižek Now!*, ed. Jamil Khader and Molly Anne Rothenberg.

6   One of Rancière's succinct discussions of postmodernism appears in *The Politics of Aesthetics*, pp. 27–30. Tanke has a good summary of Rancière's views on the topic (pp. 94–103).

7   Although Rancière doesn't use this terminology, we could say with Lacan that this is the opposition between the fantasied totality guaranteed by the big Other and the all that contains within itself an infinity, like the Möbius strip, what Lacan calls the "not-all" or the whole that is different from itself.

8   See William Carroll's essay "Nabokov's 'Signs and Symbols'" for a discussion of the dilemma Nabokov creates for the reader.

References

Carroll, William (1974). "Nabokov's 'Signs and Symbols.'" In *A Book of Things about Vladimir Nabokov*, ed. Carl R. Proffer (pp. 203–217). Ann Arbor: Ardis.

Deranty, Philippe. (2010). *Jacques Rancière: Key Concepts*. Durham, NC: Acumen.

Khader, Jamil and Molly Anne Rothenberg, eds. (2013). *Žižek Now!* Cambridge: Polity.

Rancière, Jacques. (1999). *Disagreement*. Minneapolis: University of Minnesota Press.

Rancière, Jacques. (2000). *The Politics of Aesthetics*. New York: Continuum.

Rancière, Jacques. (2011). *Politics of Literature*. Cambridge: Polity.

Ross, Kristin. (1991). "Introduction." *The Ignorant Schoolmaster: Five Lessons in Intellectual Emancipation*. Stanford: Stanford University Press.

Rothenberg, Molly Anne. (2010). *The Excessive Subject: A New Theory of Social Change*. Cambridge: Polity

Tanke, Joseph. (2011). *Jacques Rancière: An Introduction, Philosophy, Politics, Aesthetics*. New York: Continuum.

Waterfield, Robin, trans. (2002). *Plato: Phaedrus*. Oxford: Oxford University Press.

Index